TRANSNATIONAL FUGITIVE OFFENDERS IN INTERNATIONAL LAW

EXTRADITION AND OTHER MECHANISMS

International Studies in Human Rights

VOLUME 55

The titles published in this series are listed at the end of this volume.

TRANSNATIONAL FUGITIVE OFFENDERS IN INTERNATIONAL LAW

EXTRADITION AND OTHER MECHANISMS

by

GEOFF GILBERT

Professor of Law,
Human Rights Centre,
University of Essex,
United Kingdom

MARTINUS NIJHOFF PUBLISHERS
THE HAGUE / BOSTON / LONDON

A C.I.P. Catalogue record for this book is available from the Library of Congress.

ISBN 90-411-1040-2

Published by Kluwer Law International,
P.O. Box 85889, 2508 CN The Hague, The Netherlands.

Sold and distributed in North, Central and South America
by Kluwer Law International,
675 Massachusetts Avenue, Cambridge, MA 02139, U.S.A.

In all other countries, sold and distributed
by Kluwer Law International, Distribution Centre,
P.O. Box 322, 3300 AH Dordrecht, The Netherlands.

Printed on acid-free paper

Layout and camera-ready copy:
Anne-Marie Krens, Oegstgeest, The Netherlands

Printed in the Netherlands

to
Clare, Sarah and Mary-Ann,
my wife and children,
who lived and breathed this book as much as I did

TABLE OF CONTENTS

PREFACE

Aspects of Extradition Law, 1991, from which this book is a development, could legitimately focus on extradition law as the means by which to deal with transnational fugitive offenders. Less than ten years later, however, with *ad hoc* tribunals for war criminals from the former Yugoslavia and Rwanda, with a Statute for a proposed permanent International Criminal Court due to be concluded at about the same time as this book is published, and with the Security Council telling a State to surrender two fugitives despite there being an alternative Conventional mechanism to meet the particular situation, the focus must be on the offender, not the process.

Nevertheless, extradition is still the principal means for dealing with transnational fugitive offenders. Since 1991 there have been many developments. The emergence of new States in Central and Eastern Europe and the Balkans and the former Soviet Union has raised issues of State succession, while the reincorporation of Hong Kong into the Peoples' Republic of China gave rise to a series of cases on specialty, human rights and succession. The European Union now has a much greater role in dealing with transnational fugitive offenders, having concluded supplemental extradition treaties, and its Schengen State members co-operate ever more closely. International human rights law has also had an increasing impact on extradition law. Defences specific to extradition law have also seen case law developments. The chapter on the political offence exemption has been expanded as a result of new case law, but also by the need to address more fully the question of its continued necessity with respect to extradition requests between so-called stable democracies, particularly in the European Union. Turning to those mechanisms other than extradition law, it was welcome to find the British House of Lords, amongst others, at last holding that there was a discretion to reject competence where the accused's presence in court had been obtained by irregular means. The international community, in response to gross human rights violations during armed conflicts, moved to establish war crimes tribunals, first for the former Yugoslavia and Rwanda, and then with the establishment of an International Criminal Court. Finally, refugee law has quite separately come under pressure during the 1990s, with consequences for extradition law: the leading British authority on the political offence exemption is now a case concerning someone claiming refugee status, but more importantly the European Union in its proposed Treaty of Amsterdam has sought to exclude asylum for applicants from other member States, implicitly excluding the political offence exemption as well.

Like *Aspects of Extradition Law*, this book is not exhaustive – it still does not look at re-extradition, for instance. However, no work on transnational fugitive offenders should make a claim to be comprehensive unless it encompasses all the law pertaining to this subject at an international, regional and domestic level – and there are now over 200 independent States whose legislation and case law would need to be addressed. However, all the issues relating to transnational fugitive offenders are covered. Moreover, it is the contention of this book that although the law relating to transnational fugitive offenders, particularly extradition law, is specific to each State, it is implemented in an almost uniform manner by domestic courts and great regard is had to developments in other countries' courts. Effectively, there is an international law for transnational fugitive offenders which is enforced by domestic courts.

The law is stated in accordance with the materials available as at 1 December 1997, although the initial reports of the fifth Preparatory Committee Meeting for the Establishment of an International Criminal Court, 2-12 December, have been incorporated.

ACKNOWLEDGEMENTS

This book is the result of an interest in the topic first engendered during the final year of my undergraduate studies several years ago. Many people have been involved in helping me to develop an understanding of the law relating to transnational fugitive offenders and in producing this book. The listed academics have all influenced the following pages in some way.

D. Bonner, K.R. Redden, J.N. Moore, W.E. Wells, S.A. Williams, A. Drzemczewski, F.J. Hampson, K. Boyle, N.S. Rodley, M-C. Roberge, V. Türk.

However, especial gratitude is owed to the late *Professor Richard B. Lillich* who encouraged and guided me during the final stages of my SJD. Without him, as mentor and example, anything that is worthy of recognition in this work might never have been written – international law is the less as a result of his untimely death.

On the production side, I am indebted once again to Kluwer Law International for their assistance in bringing this book to press, especially Annebeth Rosenboom.

LATEST DEVELOPMENTS

Malta, like Cyprus (see p.31), is no longer to be treated as a Designated Commonwealth Country for the purposes of the English Extradition Act 1989, but is a foreign State listed as a party to the European Convention on Extradition, 1957. (SI 1997 Nos.1759, 1761)

The Backing of Warrants (Republic of Ireland) Act 1965 does not require that the conduct of the transnational fugitive offender in the Republic should amount to an appropriately serious offence under English law, only that the offence specified in the warrant would amount to a sufficiently serious offence under English law - *R v. Secretary of State for the Home Department, ex p.Gilligan* The Times, January 20 1998, QBD. *Cf. Nielse*[1] and the Extradition Act 1989 at p.110

The European Court of Human Rights held in *Scott v Spain* (1997) 24 EHRR 391, that States must exercise special diligence in the conduct of an investigation. However, the fact that the accused had already fled from a previous crime and was requested for extradition meant that his continued detention during the present investigation was justified while the State proceeded with that special diligence.

A requesting State under the European Convention on Extradition, 1957, must specify the place where the offence is alleged to have occurred or the High Court will order the transnational fugitive offender's release on application by way of habeas corpus. The court was not prepared to assume that if Portugal was the requesting State, then the crime had occurred there; such an approach smacks of an overly bureaucratic understanding of the

---

[1] *Nielsen v Government of Denmark* [1984] AC 606, [1984] 2 WLR 737.

role of the court under the European Convention on Extradition 1957 now that it cannot investigate the existence of a *prima facie* case - *De Canha v. Portugal*, unreported, QBD, CO/0769/97, 7 July 1997.

Although the proceeds from the crime eventually ended up in a third State, the requesting State where the fraud had occurred and where the proceeds had first been received will still have jurisdiction to prosecute. The court in *Ismail*, unreported, QBD, CO/2905/96, 2 July 1997, relied on *Treac*[2] and *Somcha*[3].

The courts and the Secretary of State may refuse extradition where to send the person to the requesting State would be unjust and oppressive on the grounds of the state of their mental health - *Re Davies*, unreported, CO/433/96, 30 July 1997, and the Roisin McAliskey case, The Guardian p.1, 10 MAR 1998, and p.4, 11 MAR 1998.

There is a growing belief that the meeting in Rome in Summer 1998 will not finalise a draft Statute for the International Criminal Court and that at least one subsequent meeting will need to be held early in 1999. To facilitate the work of PrepCom 6, Adriaan Bos, Chairman of the Preparatory Committee, convened a meeting from January 19-30 1998 in Zutphen in The Netherlands which included all the heads of the various Working Groups. They produced a composite version of the amended Statute, excluding none of the various options – however, it should be noted that only genocide, war crimes and crimes against humanity are listed without questio[4] as crimes within the jurisdiction of the court. The new Article numbers (*eg.* the list of crimes is now to be found in Article 5, not Article 20) have not been adopted in the book which preserves the 1994 International Law Commission's Draft Statute's scheme of numbering. As for PrepCom 6 (March 16-April 3, 1998), debate still raged on the powers of the prosecutor, the role of the Security Council, the definition of war crimes, complementarity, and the rules of evidence and disclosure with respect to information held by States.

---

2   *Treacy v DPP* [1971] AC 537.
3   *Somchai Liangsiriprasert v Government of the USA* [1990] 2 All ER 866 (PC).
4   Although the definition of the last two is not yet agreed.

CASE LIST

1

TRANSNATIONAL FUGITIVE OFFENDERS IN CONTEXT

'A creaking steam-engine of an affair'[1]
The present extradition laws belong to *"the world of the horse and buggy and the steamship, not in the world of commercial jet air transportation and high speed telecommunications."*[2]

a. Introduction

It is trite to point out that the world is becoming smaller thanks to increased access to speedier forms of transport. It is even becoming a commonplace to hear commentators bemoan the ease with which criminals can flee the *locus delicti* and the fact that crimes today often have cross-frontier elements. These pundits then go on to criticise the processes whereby a criminal can be brought before a tribunal having jurisdictional competence to prosecute him; usually it will culminate in a charge that the extradition system hinders the effective prosecution of crime. Unfortunately, very few people, including lawyers, understand the law relating to extradition and that relating to transnational fugitive offenders in general.

Where an accused is wanted for trial in another State, then his surrender to that State should be under the system of extradition laws. Extradition arrangements between States, either on a bilateral or multilateral basis, provide a means, the normatively preferred means, by which an accused person can be transferred to face prosecution. The extradition process under

---

1   The Observer p.4, 29 APR 1979.
2   From a letter to Senator Edward Kennedy from former US Attorney-General Benjamin R Civiletti. See 126 CONG.RECORD §13233 at §13235 col.2.

these international arrangements is carried out in the domestic courts and tribunals of the requested State, either because the treaty is self-executing under that State's laws or the State has passed implementing legislation. It is this interplay of international processes effected through domestic courts, processes which incorporate guarantees of rights for the accused, that makes it possible to talk of an international law of extradition, even though it is part of domestic legal systems. This international flavour is recognised in extradition cases which draw on other jurisdictions' experiences. It is this law relating to transnational fugitive offenders that is the principal focus of this book, although alternative means of rendition or prosecution are also examined.

Two factors contribute towards making a wide ranging overview of individual State practice sufficiently comprehensive to be worthwhile. First, States tend to try and keep their international extradition agreements relatively uniform. This practice means that particular provisions are repeatedly incorporated, and not just in individual State's treaties but in all extradition treaties – international drafters use successful precedents just as much as domestic lawyers.[3] Furthermore, domestic legislation reflects treaty provisions.[4] In comparative terms, extradition laws are very similar. Since the extradition system in all States is designed to achieve the same ends, then there is no problem of dysfunctional comparison between the laws of different States. Moreover, as will be seen, some of the great distinctions of the past between the civil law and common law traditions, such as the non-extradition of nationals and the *prima facie* case requirement, are becoming the subject of compromises, such that there is a convergence of State practice.

The second reason why it is possible to be confident that a comparative study of individual State practice will be relevant to all systems is that courts hearing extradition cases frequently refer to decisions from other jurisdictions dealing with the same point. In the British case of *Cheng v Governor of Pentonville Prison*[5] Lord Simon cited with approval the Italian decision

---

3   See SHEARER, EXTRADITION IN INTERNATIONAL LAW at p.18 (1971); hereinafter, SHEARER.
4   It is actually a two-way process, with treaties being drafted with the domestic legislation in mind.
5   [1973] AC 931 *per* Lord Simon at 947 and esp. at 956 *et seq.*

of *In re Pavelic and Kwaternik*,[6] the Ghanaian case of *The State v Schumann*[7] makes reference to the Swiss judgment in *Noblot*,[8] while the Australian decision of *Riley v The Commonwealth*[9] draws on British, US and Irish authorities. In the 1996 case of *T v Immigration Officer*,[10] the House of Lords drew on US and Swiss jurisprudence There is a sense in which the municipal application of extradition laws is itself international. Thus, there is, in effect, an international law of extradition, even if it is applied by municipal courts.

Extradition must also be understood within its wider context. First, it is part of international criminal law, impinging upon it in procedural terms, at least. The precise ambit of international criminal law is unclear.[11] Even in the confined sphere of dealing with crimes committed during the conflict in the former Yugoslavia, much ink has been spilt trying to define its scope and the jurisdiction of the International Criminal Tribunal for the Former Yugoslavia.[12] The 1991 Draft Code of Crimes against the Peace and Security of Mankind[13] proved highly controversial, and in 1995 the International Law Commission could only recommend genocide, aggression, crimes against humanity and war crimes to the Drafting Committee.[14]

---

6   [1933–34] Ann.Dig.372; *Foro Italiano*, 1935, Part II, col.20.

7   39 INT'L L REP.433 (1966).

8   [1927–28] Ann.Dig.350, referred to at 447 of the *Schumann* case, *supra n*7.

9   (1985) 159 CLR 1 (H.C.).

10   *T v Immigration Officer*, [1996] 2 All ER 865.

11   Mueller recounts the the somewhat tongue-in-cheek hypothesis that there must be such a thing as international criminal law because the subject is taught by professors in law schools. See Mueller & Besharov, The Existence of International Criminal Law and Its Evolution to the Point of its Enforcement Crisis p.5, in BASSIOUNI & NANDA, 1 A TREATISE ON INTERNATIONAL CRIMINAL LAW (1973).

12   *Duško Tadić, a.k.a. 'Dule', Decision on the Defence Motion for Interlocutory Appeal on Jurisdiction before the Appeals Chamber of ICTY*, Case No.IT-94-1-AR72 (1995). See also, Meron, *The International Criminalization of Internal Atrocities*, 89 AM.J INT'L L 554 (1995).

13   [1991] 2 Yb Int'l L Comm.198, UN Doc.A/CN.4/SER.A/1991/Add.1.

14   UN Doc.A/50/10 at 70 (1995). See Rosenstock, *The Forty-seventh Session of the International Law Commission*, 90 AM.J INT'L L 106 at p.109 (1996). And see A/51/332, 1996, which defines aggression, genocide, crimes against humanity, crimes against United Nations and associated personnel and war crimes.

"In seeking to explain what constitutes international criminal law, one's first instinct is to look at the issue as one would look at municipal law, especially as, according to Article 38 of the Statute of the International Court of Justice, one of the 'sources' of international law is described as the general principles of law recognised by civilised nations. Presumably, therefore, if one were to find that a particular act was regarded as a criminal offence by all or the overwhelming majority of States, it might be presumed that such an act was contrary to the general principles of criminal law recognised by civilised nations, and therefore contrary to international law ... [The] *corpus* of international criminal law [is found] in the unwritten customary law accepted by States, the general principles of criminal law recognised by nations and the treaties which declare this or that particular line of conduct to be criminal."[15]

This particularly wide definition of international criminal law should be contrasted with that given by Bassiouni.[16]

"The very nature of all these acts and their definition in the applicable international instruments and under customary international law indicates that there are no common or specific doctrinal foundations that constitute the legal basis for including a given act in the category of international crimes.... Nevertheless, ..., there are two alternative requirements for proscribed conduct; namely, it must contain either an international or transnational element in order for it to be included in the category of international crimes. In other words, the conduct in question must either rise to the level where it constitutes an offence against the world community *delicto jus gentium* or the commission of the act must affect the interests of more than one State."

Bassiouni goes on to point out that there is presently no scheme for the international enforcement of international criminal law and that the present

---

15 Green, *International Crimes and the Legal Process*, 29 INT'L & COMP LQ 567 at pp.568-9 (1980).
16 See *The Penal Characteristics of Conventional International Criminal Law*, 15 CASE W RES.J INT'L L 27 at pp.28 *et seq*; hereinafter, *Penal Characteristics*. See also, by the same author, Introduction: A Policy-Oriented Inquiry into the Different Forms and Manifestations of 'International Terrorism' in BASSIOUNI, LEGAL RESPONSES TO INTERNATIONAL TERRORISM: US PROCEDURAL ASPECTS, at p.xv (1988); hereinafter, LEGAL RESPONSES.

system relies on the jurisdictional competence of domestic courts and the willingness of States either to prosecute or extradite. Therefore, extradition is part of the procedural framework behind the burgeoning subject of international criminal law. As such, it is part and parcel of other elements of international criminal law, most obviously some of the substantive offences, for instance, war crimes or any of the United Nations sponsored anti-terrorist conventions.

Secondly, questions of extraterritorial jurisdiction, especially universal jurisdiction, raise issues about the competence of the requesting State on the one hand and, ultimately, about the need for extradition at all if the State holding the fugitive has the right to prosecute under the guise of an extended form of jurisdictional competence. Finally, it will be seen that because of some of the procedural failings of the present extradition arrangements, considered by some to be out-of-date, that alternative, less formal means of rendition have been employed, usually to permit the prosecution of those charged with 'international crimes'.

On another level though, extradition is but a part of the picture because it is only a means of acquiring jurisdiction over an offender; other aspects of domestic criminal law and procedure need to be in place if these offenders are to punished for their wrongdoing. Rather than being seen as a mere adjunct to international criminal law, it can be seen as part of a scheme for mutual assistance between separate States in enforcing domestic criminal matters. A 1990 British House of Commons report on policing in the European Community[17] gives the following example.

"... [A] lorry travelling from Turkey to Norway will pass in and out of [member States of the European Community]. Whether it is carrying heroin or is simply overloaded or exceeding tachograph limits is a matter of concern to a variety of police forces and jurisdictions which may need to co-operate. These countries will also need to ensure that they have legislative and criminal justice systems which ensure that those who break the law cannot use frontiers as a means of escaping justice."

---

17 HOME AFFAIRS SELECT COMMITTEE, SEVENTH REPORT, PRACTICAL POLICE CO-OPERATION IN THE EUROPEAN COMMUNITY, vol.1, para.46, (2 Volumes), 20 JULY 1990, HCP 363 (1989–90); hereinafter, HCP-I or HCP-II.

Extradition is one element in those systems designed to stop fugitives using borders as a means of escaping justice. Thus, extradition has a role to play in enforcing international criminal law and in assisting States to prosecute violations of purely domestic legislation. Since, though, international criminal law is prosecuted by individual States rather than some supra-national criminal court, for the time being at least[18], these two facets are not mutually exclusive.

Away from criminal law *per se*, extradition law has another function. So far it has been seen as a scheme whereby States assist each other in criminal matters, but it is also important in protecting the fugitive's rights. Part of the problem with extradition is in trying to achieve the correct balance between allowing the free flow of fugitive criminals to States where they may be prosecuted for their crimes, and in safeguarding the fugitive from oppressive punishment or from persecution on account of his personal characteristics, beliefs or opinions. Even where the system is being properly used to effect the return of a fugitive criminal, it is still guaranteeing that fugitive's rights, because extradition is the specific means designed by States for that purpose; alternative methods, such as exclusion, deportation or abduction, lack the built-in safeguards of extradition arrangements, thereby allowing the fugitive's rights to be ignored. Extradition itself is an element in the international protection of human rights. Conversely, when returning an offender to face legitimate prosecution for his misdeeds, it is part of the law of human responsibilities.[19] Extradition law has dual international and

---

18   See the proposals for an International Criminal Court, ILC Draft Statute for an International Criminal Tribunal, 33 INT.LEG.MAT.253 (1994); revised, pp.29 *et seq.* of A/49/10 (1994), and see also A/51/22; Rosenstock, *Current Developments: The Forty-Sixth Session of the International Law Commission*, 89 AM.J INT'L L 390 (1995); Morris and Bourloyannis-Vrailas, *Current Developments: The Work of the Sixth Committee at the Fiftieth Session of The UN General Assembly*, 90 AM.J INT'L L 491 at p.496 *et seq.* (1996). See also, Warbrick, *International Criminal Courts*, 44 INT'L & COMP. LQ 466 (1995); Graefrath, *Universal Criminal Jurisdiction and an International Criminal Court*, 1 EJIL 67 (1990).

19   See BAILEY, HUMAN RIGHTS AND RESPONSIBILITIES IN BRITAIN AND IRELAND: A CHRISTIAN PERSPECTIVE, *esp.* at pp.30 *et seq.* (1988). Impunity breeds contempt for the law, particularly relevant where the fugitive offender is accused of war crimes or gross human rights violations – see, Crelinsten, *After the Fall: Prosecuting Perpetrators of Gross Human Rights Violations*, 5.1 PIOOM Newslet-

domestic facets which are relevant with respect to several areas of inter-national criminal law and procedure, and of the international protection of human rights.

Finally in this introductory section, there is one other aspect of the international-domestic split that affects the study of extradition law. When one first encounters the topic it is usually considered within the framework of domestic legislation, case law and practice. Thus, the international ele-ments are seen in a comparative context. For commentators from the common law tradition, therefore, the requirement to prove a *prima facie* case is perfectly natural, whereas the refusal by civil law States to extradite their nationals is viewed with deep suspicion; the position is reversed for those from the civil law tradition. It is hoped that this study provides a neutral view of aspects of international extradition law and not a comparative criticism of common law and civil law practices. Nevertheless, it does tend to explain its focus on the law and practice of developed States.

b. The Problem

Despite the efforts of many academic commentators over the years, there is still no universally recognised, comprehensive system of international criminal law. Whether an offence qualifies as an international crime is a matter of experience and empirical study.[20] Certain unlawful acts have an international aspect and others are so reprehensible that States recognise a right to prosecute the perpetrator wherever he may be found. However, there are no hard and fast rules that are always followed by all States, and the number of infractions given this 'international' status is very few.[21]

---

ter 4 (1993); Hampson, Impunity and Accountability, in SIEDER (ed.), IMPUNITY IN LATIN AMERICA, at p.7 (1995); and the Applicants' Memorials in *Akdivar and others v Turkey, Case No. 99/1995/605/693, Zeki Aksoy v Turkey, Case No.100/1995/606/694, Sukran Aydin v Turkey, Case No.57/1996/676/866, Mentes and others v Turkey, Case No.58/1996/677/867.*

20 See Bassiouni, *Penal Characteristics, supra* n16, at p.28.

21 See Bassiouni, *Penal Characteristics,* at pp.27-28 and the same author, INTER-NATIONAL LAW: A DRAFT INTERNATIONAL CRIMINAL CODE at pp.3-19 (1980), both *supra* n16. See also, Green, *supra* n15, at pp.573 & 575 *et seq.*

The Draft Code of Crimes Against the Peace and Security of Mankind[22] includes aggression, genocide, crimes against humanity and war crimes, providing an indicative list; the Draft Statute for an International Criminal Court is equally circumscribed.[23] Nevertheless, most crimes only give rise to domestic jurisdiction. Predominantly, criminal acts are punished by domestic courts exercising municipal legislation. Problems arise where the accused has fled the jurisdiction. In such cases, he must be returned to the State which is competent to prosecute: extradition is one method of returning fugitives.

> "Unfortunately, there is much about extradition which is not generally known to the practitioners on the one hand and to the extradition magistrates on the other, not to speak of the general public. It is a proceeding beset by various problems, both procedural and substantive."[24]

The following hypothetical case is meant to highlight most of the issues upon which extradition impinges or which affect extradition law or procedure. Although it is focused on the United Kingdom, it is relevant to most States that have general extradition arrangements as well as more specialised schemes with certain other States, usually geographic or geopolitical neighbours.

> "Sven is a Swedish national. In Dublin, in the Republic of Ireland, he is alleged to have used explosives to rob a bank. With the funds raised from the robbery, he fled to New York, USA, where he committed financial crimes having cross-frontier aspects which seriously damaged the economic interests of France. To avoid arrest, he hijacked a plane and flew to Toronto, Canada. Shooting several security guards and Turkish tourists at the airport, he boarded a plane bound for London. At Heathrow Airport he was arrested."

Admittedly, it would be unlikely for any one individual to be liable for so many crimes in so many separate States, but in any year several individuals

---

22 *Supra nn*13 and 14.
23 *Supra n*18.
24 Comment by the late Alona E Evans, presiding in an A.S.I.L. panel on *International Procedures for the Apprehension and Rendition of Fugitive Offenders*, [1980] A.S.I.L.PROC.274, 74th Annual Meeting.

could arrive in another State who between them will have committed a similar set of offences. In Sven's case several States could request his return from the United Kingdom, which would be the 'requested State'[25] in this instance. Taking the 'requesting States' one by one, the Republic of Ireland would request Sven's surrender from the United Kingdom under specialised legislation, the Backing of Warrants (Republic of Ireland) Act, 1965, which provides for a simpler form of extradition. Like many other contiguous or proximate States with close historical ties,[26] the United Kingdom and the Republic of Ireland base their simplified extradition on reciprocal legislation rather than a treaty. Other examples would be the Australian and New Zealand system[27] and the Nordic Union scheme[28]; in other cases, the system is still treaty based, although the extradition procedures are just as simplified.[29] Furthermore, going back to Sven's case, since the offence included explosives, the United Kingdom may exercise extraterritorial jurisdiction under the Criminal Jurisdiction Act 1975 and try Sven in London for the offence committed in Dublin. This power is special to the Anglo-Irish situation under the 1975 Act, but many anti-terrorist conventions contain similar provisions requiring the requested State to extradite or prosecute.

The United States would request Sven under British domestic legislation which enables the Anglo-US Extradition Treaty. Extradition is usually effected by way of bilateral treaties, most of which, unfortunately, were concluded around the turn of the century. In treaties where the extraditable

---

25　The term 'asylum State' is preferable to the more usual 'requested State', because 'asylum' suggests a more active role than the passive idea behind 'requested'. The State where the fugitive is found must take several important decisions with respect to the fugitive's surrender which involve the exercise of judicial and political discretions – extradition policies are actively put into effect by 'requested' States. Despite these misgivings, to use asylum State would be to court confusion with the concept of asylum associated with refugee law; thus, the term requested State is, with some reluctance, used throughout this book.

26　See Chapter Two, below.

27　See the Australian Extradition Act 1988, Part III.

28　Established prior to the Union, the extradition system based on reciprocal legislation is still in force between Denmark, Finland, Iceland, Norway and Sweden: see Chapter Two.

29　See, for example, the Benelux Accord of 27 June 1962 and 1974 Protocol (see SHEARER, *supra n*3, at pp.53 *et seq.*) between Belgium, Luxembourg and the Netherlands, enhanced by the Schengen Accord of 19 June 1990.

crimes are listed, their age can create problems if the offence for which the fugitive is being requested was not envisaged one hundred years ago. Drug related crimes present difficulties in this respect, although complex cross-frontier frauds, like the one set out in the example, can prove complicated as well.

Since the financial crimes have serious consequences for France, Sven may be requested by the French authorities, too. France exercises jurisdiction over offences which seriously affect the vital interests of the State.[30] Whether the protective principle of extraterritorial jurisdiction, as it is known, covers the economic interests of the State is not clear. Even if it were found that its ambit was that wide, the double criminality requirement of extradition law may mean that a request to the British authorities, who do not generally recognise the protective principle, might fail.[31]

The hijack could also be prosecuted by the USA, but since the plane landed in Canada, it too has jurisdiction. Further, under the multilateral Hague Convention for the Suppression of Unlawful Seizure of Aircraft of 1970 and the Montreal Convention for the Suppression of Unlawful Acts against the Safety of Civil Aviation,[32] the United Kingdom could also try Sven because he has been found in the United Kingdom; the United Kingdom would again be exercising extraterritorial jurisdiction, required under the Hague Convention.

Canada would request Sven for shooting the security guards under the non-treaty based Commonwealth Scheme for the Rendition of Fugitive Offenders.[33] This Scheme, promulgated in 1966 but amended in 1990, relies on legislation in the member States of the Commonwealth to put it into effect. Nevertheless, it is very much akin to a multilateral convention, although such agreements are usually only concluded among geographic and geopolitical neighbours – the ideological stances of some member States

---

30 See *In re Urios*, [1919–22] Ann.Dig.107; (1920) 47 Clunet 195; see also DON-NEDIEU DE VABRES, LES PRINCIPES MODERNES DU DROIT INTERNATIONAL PENAL pp.95 *et seq.* (1928): Art.694 *Code de Procédure Pénal*. For a detailed examination of the interplay between questions of jurisdiction and extradition law, see Chapter Three, below.

31 On the question of jurisdiction and double criminality, see Chapter Three, below.

32 10 INT.LEG.MAT.133 (1971) and 10 INT.LEG.MAT.1151 (1971), respectively.

33 Considered in depth in Chapter Two.

are even further apart than the physical distances that separate them and so the Commonwealth Scheme is somewhat special.

The Turkish government might also put in a request on the grounds that Sven killed some of its nationals. Turkey exercises a form of extraterritorial jurisdiction known as the passive personality principle, that is, it claims to be competent to prosecute where the victims of the crime are Turkish nationals.[34] Once again, the United Kingdom does not recognise this form of jurisdiction, raising the question of the interplay of extraterritorial jurisdiction and the double criminality requirement.

Finally, Sweden, too, could request Sven's return for Sweden exercises criminal jurisdiction over all of its nationals through the so-called active personality principle[35] for crimes committed anywhere in the world. Whether the United Kingdom would regard the request as well-founded, given that it only recognises such jurisdiction in the case of certain offences, is once more open to question.

Having decided on which of the claims for Sven it will recognise, the United Kingdom would then have to decide which one, if any, it was going to grant, and whether this surrender would be before or after any trial and punishment in the United Kingdom for those offences for which it can claim jurisdiction itself.

The foregoing brief analysis of the hypothetical case set out above should have brought to light some of the issues applicable to the study of extradition. Those matters and others will be the object of discussion in the following pages.

c. Policy

As has already been stated, the law relating to fugitive offenders is not a single, self-contained system; extradition law impinges upon, and is itself impinged upon by, other fields of law. Issues of jurisdiction and questions concerning other methods of rendition overlap. Moreover, the politics of international relations also plays a part in forming the theory and practice

---

34 See, *The Lotus Case*, (*France v Turkey*), (1927), PCIJ Reports, Series A, No.10.
35 *Public Prosecutor v Antoni*, 32 INT'L L REP.140 (Swed.Sup.Ct. 1960).

of dealing with fugitive offenders, especially with regard to the pertinent topic of terrorism.

Looking at the principles of extradition common to most international arrangements, the object of this book is to present a more streamlined and coherent procedure that is acceptable to States and which, at the same time, protects fugitive's human rights. This approach is premised on the assumption that extradition, in one form or another, will continue to be the recommended method of returning a fugitive to the courts of a country with jurisdiction to deal with him, and that other, less formal methods are inferior in achieving that end and in protecting the fugitive. Therefore, *the overall objective is to design an efficient extradition law to expedite the prosecution of fugitives, given certain protections which are necessary when a person is threatened with being removed from the safety of a State where he has committed no crime.* However, there are alternatives to extradition which can not be ignored and in some cases they may well be a satisfactory supplement to the extradition processes, even if not a desired one. Since extradition law is the recognised means by which fugitive offenders are to be brought before a court for prosecution, the policy of States towards the extradition of fugitive offenders is the principal focus of this book.

Primarily, that above objective necessitates a consideration of the present law and practice and the difficulties which have arisen therefrom. Generally, if one is seeking to ensure the prosecution of fugitives, then the extradition law must be made as simple as possible with very few anomalies. The only controlling feature must be that the liberty of the alleged fugitive offender should be protected until the authorities of the requested State are satisfied that he should stand trial. If procedural amendments alone could correct the failings of the present extradition law, the task would be much simpler. Unfortunately, implicit in every extradition request there is an element of foreign policy – as has been pointed out, extradition has domestic and international facets. More often than not foreign policy may be readily dismissed early in the proceedings, but occasionally it may play a considerable part in the ultimate decision. Recognising this, it is then necessary to consider whether extradition should be, or can be, the sole method of ensuring the fugitive's prosecution.

"Extradition may be the established method of rendition, but it is by no means a convenient method, or, indeed, a popular method. In a recent study of 231 instances of rendition of persons charged with international terrorist offences, it was found that only 6 out of 87 extradition requests were granted; on the other hand, 145 terrorists were expelled by 28 States."[36]

Given extradition is only possible where an international arrangement exists between the requested and requesting States, whether permanent or *ad hoc* in nature, and that many States do not have any such arrangements, then fugitives will sometimes be returned by other means. No problems arise as long as these other options are considered to be merely alternatives *in extremis* – in terms of international public order, overall efficiency and human rights, extradition must always be the primary method. However, while extradition may be the principal means of rendition, it is only one method by which States may provide mutual assistance in matters of criminal rendition. Thus, it is appropriate to study and compare the other means, which range from the manifest illegality of abduction, through collusive deportation and simple return (that is, where one State hands over a fugitive to another without recourse to any officially recognised or organised procedure), to extraterritorial jurisdiction and international criminal courts. The overriding aim should be to prosecute fugitive offenders whenever a crime has been committed and, while extradition is limited, the use of other means will continue and cannot be ignored.

d. Problems of Circumscription and Definition

'Transnational[37] fugitive offender' is open to multiple interpretations. It self-evidently includes someone who commits a crime or has been convicted of a crime in one State and is now to be found in a third State. More debateably, it could include the offender whose crime has an effect in one State, despite the fact he never left a third State. It should also be read to encompass those whose crimes are justiciable before an international criminal tribunal. As such, transnational fugitive offenders are persons whose crimes are prosecutable before a tribunal in another State from the one within which

---

36 Evans, *supra n*24 at 276. *Cf.* The remarks of Charles Gordon on the same panel (at pp.284-6) would indicate that deportation or expulsion may not be as efficient a method as Evans would suggest.

37 See Gilbert, *The 'Law' and 'Transnational Terrorism'*, 26 NETH.YB INT'L L 3 (1995).

they are presently to be found or before one established on the international plane.

No-one would deny that extradition should be placed within the scope of public international law,[38] pertaining, as it does, to both the relations of nations and the status of the individual.[39] With regard to the relations of nations, at one level the treaties and other international agreements may be seen in contractual terms, regulating the transfer of fugitive offenders. Without this 'contract', there is no obligation to extradite.[40] However, without denying the necessity of some international arrangement, there is a growing and developing view that, for certain crimes at least, the requested State's domestic court is simply carrying out its part in an international criminal legal order which requires the punishment of criminals. There is certainly no rule of customary international law that fugitives in general should be extradited or prosecuted, but several anti-terrorist conventions make this demand and academic writers are beginning to discern an obligation not to let the individual remain unpunished – a new norm of international criminal law may be developing.[41]

"The extraditing state also has the right, in the cases where extradition for whatever reason is not possible, although according to the nature of the

---

38 Most writers on private international law specifically exclude all matters of criminal law in the first few pages of their works. CHESHIRE & NORTH, PRIVATE INTERNATIONAL LAW, pp.135-37, (10th ed., 1979). *Huntington v Attrill*, [1893] AC 150.

39 LAUTERPACHT, SURVEY OF INTERNATIONAL LAW IN RELATION TO WORK OF CODIFICATION OF THE INTERNATIONAL LAW COMMISSION, paras.27-30, U.N.Doc.A/CN.4/1/ REV.1 (1949). Reproduced in LAUTERPACHT, INTERNATIONAL LAW, (being the collected papers of Hersch Lauterpacht) vol.1, p.445 (1970).

40 Anglo-American jurisprudence is to the effect that extradition can normally only occur when there is a treaty. *Eg. R v Governor of Brixton Prison, ex p. Soblen*, [1962] 3 All ER 641 at 659; *Holmes v Jennison*, 14 Pet.540 (1840) and *Valentine v US ex rel. Neidecker*, 299 US 5 at 9 (1936). Civil law states are usually not prohibited from extraditing in the absence of a formal arrangement, but there would be no obligation; see Chapter Two, below.

41 See *The Universal Jurisdiction (Austria) Case*, 28 INT'L L REP.341 at 342 (1958). See also, Bassiouni, *Penal Characteristics, supra* n16. MURPHY, PUNISHING INTERNATIONAL TERRORISTS, pp.129-35, (1985); BASSIOUNI & WISE, *AUT DEDERE, AUT JUDICARE*: THE DUTY TO EXTRADITE OR PROSECUTE IN INTERNATIONAL LAW, (1995).

offence it would be permissible, to carry out a prosecution and impose punishment, instead of such action being taken by the requesting state."

As regards the individual, the practice and procedure of extradition in the domestic courts can be seen in terms of mutual assistance by States in criminal matters; the fugitive is the object of the system. Yet, the process can also be seen as confirming the individual's freedom in the requested State. More often than not, extradition is merely a process by which fugitive offenders are returned to the requesting State, but, in rare cases, the process is a facet of international human rights, protecting individuals from unfair trials and practices. All in all, extradition is part of public international law which operates predominantly in the domestic courts.

The early commentators all saw extradition in terms of mutual assistance in criminal matters. For J.B. Moore, extradition is

> "the act by which one nation delivers up an individual, accused or convicted of an offence outside of its own territory, to another nation which demands him and which is competent to try and punish him."[42]

Even today, this view is prevalent.

> "Extradition is the return of a fugitive criminal from the country where he is found to the country where he is accused of or has been convicted of an offence. It is an arrangement designed to prevent criminals from escaping from justice by crossing national frontiers."[43]

While accepting the above definitions, a rider must be added to the effect that extradition is permeated with special protections, unknown in municipal trials and, therefore, in part, a protection for the individual. Created mainly in nineteenth century Europe, there is an ambience of that era's liberalism which, on one interpretation, was designed to protect political activism in

---

42 EXTRADITION AND INTERSTATE RENDITION, vol.1, p.3, (1891) translating BILLOT, TRAITE DE L'EXTRADITION, p.1, (1874). See also *Terlinden v Ames*, 184 US 270 (1902).

43 A REVIEW OF THE LAW AND PRACTICE OF EXTRADITION IN THE UNITED KINGDOM, para.1.1. REPORT OF AN INTERDEPARTMENTAL WORKING PARTY, MAY 1982, CRIMINAL JUSTICE DEPARTMENT, HOME OFFICE; hereinafter, 1982 REVIEW.

autocratic regimes. Thus, today the fugitive offender may plead his offence
is political or that he may suffer prejudice due to his race, nationality,
religion or political opinions. Extradition is part of public international law,
but it is a discrete system within it and it has developed many features of
its own through its implementation before domestic courts. Deportation,
similarly, operates under domestic law, but with international constraints,
while abduction violates State sovereignty but may provide domestic courts
with jurisdiction. An International Criminal Court has a more purely international character, but the politics of its creation and operation involve
balancing domestic and international interests.[44] The law on Transnational
Fugitive Offenders is worthy of study and exposition in its own right.

---

44 See the comments of Belarus in COMMENTS RECEIVED PURSUANT TO PARAGRAPH
4 OF GENERAL ASSEMBLY RESOLUTION 49/53 ON THE ESTABLISHMENT OF AN INTER-
NATIONAL CRIMINAL COURT, A/AC.244/1, AD HOC COMMITTEE ON THE ESTABLISH-
MENT OF AN INTERNATIONAL CRIMINAL COURT 3-13 April 1995.
"4. The revised draft includes a preamble, the contents of which demonstrate
that the debate about the method of establishing the court has resulted in the
choice of the best method, namely the conclusion of an international treaty.
While Belarus supports this approach on the whole, it wishes to draw attention
to the contents of the preamble, and particularly to the final provision thereof.
The preamble should naturally reflect the close interconnection between the
international criminal court and national judicial organs. But, at the same time,
the complementarity and interaction of international and national jurisdictions
should be stressed. The court has its own function, namely to conduct proceedings in respect of international crimes, and in so far as this function is
concerned it is on an equal footing with national jurisdictions."
Cf. The comments of the International Criminal Tribunal for the Former Yugoslavia.
"*(c) State sovereignty versus international justice*
8. The draft statute presents an underlying tension between State sovereignty
and the demands of international justice ('nationalism' versus 'internationalism'),
in which State sovereignty seems in several instances, to have prevailed. This
tension may also be described as a contrast between consensualism and community interests. The Draft statute, it appears, is trying to advance community
interests, *i.e.*, international criminal justice, by the method of consensualism,
i.e., trying to obtain as much consent to the machinery of criminal justice as
possible. In this respect, there is an inherent, albeit necessary, contradiction in
its logic."

e. History of Extradition

Fugitive offenders ought to be returned by extradition and the practice has a long history which has been extensively researched.[45] While the past one hundred and fifty years of practice and comment, of statute and case law is distinct and sufficient, an understanding of the historical development of extradition law provides insights into some of the present problems.

Writers agree that the first treaty dealing with extradition was concluded in 1280 BC by Rameses II of Egypt and the Hittite prince Hattushilish III.[46] This treaty applied to the surrender of 'great men', which has been taken to refer to political offenders and not common criminals; extradition treaties today, on the other hand, specifically exempt political offenders from surrender. Nor was this agreement an isolated instance, for, as Blakesley has shown,[47] extradition was in use in pre-Christian times, even if the term itself was unknown and with very few of today's procedures being incorporated – the 'diplomatic request' was usually accompanied by a threat of war if the fugitive were not to be surrendered. Shortly after the agreement between the Egyptians and the Hittites, one finds extradition taking place, if rarely, in ancient Israel, and the Hindu Code of Manu also made provision therefor.[48] Moreover, the whole tenor of these procedures indicates the system was designed to return common criminals as well as 'great men'. The Romans also practised extradition, at least up to about 100 BC.[49] Thus,

---

45 *Eg.* SHEARER, *supra n*3, pp.5-19, (1971). O'Higgins, *The History of Extradition in British Practice*, 13 IND.YB.INT'L AFF.78 (1964). Blakesley, *The Practice of Extradition from Antiquity to Modern France and the United States: A Brief History*, 4 B.C. INT'L & COMP. LJ 39 (1981). Blakesley actually considers the whole history of extradition, not just French and American, although his review does skip from pre-Christian extradition arrangements to those of mediæval times; hereinafter, Blakesley, *Antiquity*.

46 SHEARER, *supra n*3, at p.5, citing Langdon and Gardner in 6 J EGYPTIAN ARCH.179 (1920).

47 *Antiquity, supra n*45, at pp.41 *et seq.* The issue provoked much debate amongst French lawyers at the turn of the century.

48 Blakesley, *Antiquity, supra n*45, at p.47 – see for example, the Old Testament, Judges, Ch.20, vv.12,13. See also SINHA, ASYLUM AND INTERNATIONAL LAW, at p.6 (1971).

49 See SIR EDWARD CLARKE, A TREATISE UPON THE LAW OF EXTRADITION, pp.16-29 (2nd ed., 1874); see also Buser, *The Jaffe Case and the use of International*

extradition was known in ancient times, although its practice would bear little relation to the system in operation today.

For the period of the Dark Ages there is little available evidence one way or the other about the practice of extradition; nevertheless, a treaty concluded in the tenth century by the rulers at Byzantium and the Princes of Kiev did allow for it.[50]

Probably the first treaty that dealt with extradition in Europe was made in 1174 between England and Scotland. Like most extradition treaties of the pre-modern period, extradition was but one issue in a comprehensive inter-State agreement. In continental Europe, France was providing for the extradition of common criminals as early as 1376,[51] although, even before then, it had concluded a treaty with England in 1303 that allowed for the handing over of political opponents of the ruler of the requesting State. Previous writers have said that English extradition up to 1794 was generally exercised on an *ad hoc* basis, for there were very few treaties,[52] and that it was only used to return political offenders.[53] However, O'Higgins[54] has shown that many treaties contained provisions dealing with extradition during the middle ages and that all types of offender were returned, usually only if such a treaty provision existed; the Anglo-Dutch treaty of 1662,[55] whilst primarily designed to obtain a return of political enemies also allowed for the return of any other offender requested. Whilst O'Higgins' research cannot be controverted, it would be rare for a common criminal to flee abroad from the United Kingdom in the first place and it cannot be doubted that the system was in reality a means by which the State could expel those people who were not conducive to the public good. The process then in operation would bear no direct relationship to today's law and practice.

Kidnapping as an Alternative to Extradition, 14 GA.J INT'L & COMP. L 357 at p.358.

50 Schmid, *Extradition and International Judicial and Administrative Assistance in Penal Matters in East European States*, 34 LAW IN E.EUROPE 167 at p.174 (1988).

51 Blakesley, *Antiquity*, *supra* n45, at p.48.

52 CLARK, EXTRADITION, pp.18-22 (4th ed., 1923).

53 See the Anglo-French and Anglo-Dutch treaties of 1661 and 1662, respectively, referred to in Blakesley, *Antiquity*, *supra* n45, at p.49.

54 O'Higgins, *The History of Extradition in British Practice*, 13 IND.YB.INT'L AFF. 78 (1964).

55 *Supra* n53.

Nevertheless, with regard to continental European treaties, where flight across a border was easy, the position seems to have been closer to present practice, as the Franco-Savoyan treaty of 1376, referred to above, illustrates.

The present system of extradition started to evolve during the eighteenth century in Europe between contiguous States. Since the United Kingdom is an island, it was insulated from the rest of the Continent's fleeing fugitives and so did not enter into many extradition treaties at that time. By comparison, France led the way in concluding extradition treaties[56]; it was truly the founder of modern extradition practice

According to de Martens,[57] almost one hundred treaties pertaining to extradition were made during the eighteenth and early part of the nineteenth centuries. As might be imagined, these agreements were usually between contiguous States – the fugitive would not flee far from home. The ease of movement around the world available today obviously did not exist, but, as others have noted too, this was coupled with the fact that people would ordinarily remain in the community into which they were born all their lives and the arrival of a stranger would not necessarily be welcome. Even if he had committed a crime, the offender would not readily flee because of the loss of livelihood and community that accompanied his flight. Nevertheless, extradition treaties proved increasingly necessary during the eighteenth century. The rise of extradition as the appropriate means of dealing with fugitive offenders probably stems from two movements also arising in that century. The first is the rise of the nation State and the concept of co-equal sovereignty in Europe.[58] To assert independence, authority and equality in all matters, the emerging States promulgated treaties on various matters – extradition was part of this. The other movement was the development of a nascent law of human rights.[59] The emerging States tended to have

---

56 See SHEARER, *supra n*3, at pp.8-11.

57 RECUEIL DE TRAITES, 7 vols., 1791–1826; SUPPLEMENTS AU RECUEIL DES PRINCIPAUX TRAITES, 20 vols., 1802–42; hereinafter MARTENS. See SHEARER, *supra n*3, at p.8.

58 The eighteenth century actually reflects developments during the previous two to three hundred years. As the mediæval era came to an end, international law as it is known today came into being to be regulated by treaties. Extradition was part of this movement. See SHEARER, STARKE'S INTERNATIONAL LAW, pp.7-14, (1994).

59 See BEST, HUMANITY IN WARFARE, pp.31 *et seq.*, (1983). See, for example, THOMAS PAINE, THE RIGHTS OF MAN (1791).

broken away from the autocratic empires in an attempt to assert individual freedoms: extradition treaties, by providing a system that regulated the surrender of fugitives, protected those individual freedoms. Now, to say these developments all occurred at once in the law of extradition, creating the practice and procedure known today, would be ludicrous. For example, it took until 1850 for the principle of specialty to be fully worked out in the Franco-Saxon treaty of that year.[60] However, the prevailing philosophies of the eighteenth century shaped the developing extradition law under the unfolding umbrella of international law – the eighteenth century ensured that extradition would be the appropriate method of returning fugitive offenders rather than any other system. The nineteenth century's liberalism developed the detail of the process known now.

The United Kingdom's modern law began in 1794 with the Jay Treaty,[61] concluded with the United States. It included many features known in today's treaties, such as the need for a *prima facie* case and the requisition process being initiated by diplomatic communications. The mid-nineteenth century saw three treaties being concluded[62] with the USA, France and Denmark, respectively. Each of these treaties was implemented by a separate statute. None of them contained provisions dealing with political offences or the principle of specialty, (that is, that the fugitive may only be dealt with for the offences for which he was returned), which both appear in every modern day United Kingdom treaty on extradition. By comparison, France had established extradition relations with not only most of Europe, but also with many emerging States in Latin America.[63] These agreements incorporated most of the provisions seen in present-day extradition treaties.[64] The problems created by land borders meant that fleeing criminals were much more prevalent for France than for the United Kingdom before the end of the nineteenth century and so extradition treaties were essential if France was to sustain a credible system of criminal justice. As the ease of movement improved, however, the United Kingdom, too, had to make extradition

---

60 SHEARER, *supra n*3, at p.18.
61 1 B.F.S.P.784; 5 MARTENS(I) 640. For a study of early US extradition agreements, see Blakesley, *Antiquity, supra n*45.
62 USA, 1842 (The Webster-Ashburton Treaty), 30 B.F.S.P.360; 3 MARTENS(III) 456: France, 1843, 31 B.F.S.P. 194; 5 MARTENS(III) 20: Denmark, 1862, 54 B.F.S.P.27.
63 BILLOT, *supra n*42, citing the Franco-Venezuelan treaty, 1853.
64 Blakesley, *Antiquity, supra n*45, at pp.50-52.

arrangements,[65] although even now the United Kingdom only surrenders between 30 and 40 fugitive offenders per year. These were often in the form of bilateral treaties, but within the British Empire, as it then was, extradition was governed by the Imperial Fugitive Offenders Act 1881 with no treaties at all. When the Empire turned into the Commonwealth, this less formal system was retained, even though the relationship had changed into one of equal, sovereign States. Functionally, however, the Commonwealth Scheme is the same as a multilateral treaty. Modern extradition was fully in place by the turn of the century.

(i) Recent Events: – Within the past twenty years, the western industrialised States have taken steps to bring extradition law up-to-date in both specific and general terms. The rise of terrorism caused problems within extradition law because of the protection available thereunder for political offenders. To meet the problem within Western Europe, the European Convention on the Suppression of Terrorism[66] was concluded. It excludes certain offences from the ambit of the political offence exemption. Furthermore, during the 1980's European police co-operation has been greatly improved, with the increase in cross-frontier terrorism and the policy of internal open borders adopted by the European Community since 1992 both necessitating closer liaison. The Schengen Group, which is one result of this improved co-operation, tackles issues to do with extradition in particular, and with international criminal law in general. Moving outside Western Europe, the USA and the United Kingdom concluded a supplementary bilateral treaty in 1985 on very similar terms to the ECST[67] and it came into force in 1987. These tinkerings with the political offence exemption will be examined in detail below, but this is one particular area where reform is likely to continue for some time yet.

---

65 Until 1995, thirty-four of the United Kingdom's forty-three extant treaties were concluded between 1870 and 1914, although several of these are now supplanted by the European Extradition Convention 1957, ETS 24.

66 ETS 90: 15 INT.LEG.MAT.1272 (1976); hereinafter ECST. See Chapter Six, below.

67 United States-United Kingdom Supplementary Extradition Treaty signed at Washington, Cm.294, UKTS 6 (1988) and, with comments, in Appendix 1 to the US Senate EXEC.REPT 99-17, accompanying TR.DOC.99-8. It was ratified on 23 December 1986.

More generally, procedural rules are being simplified to allow for easier extradition. Within the European Union, for example, a new extradition convention has been drafted for use within The Fifteen.[68] The United States has concluded several bilateral treaties with States with which it has particular law enforcement problems[69] to try and make sure that offenders do not 'escape justice simply by crossing borders' – these treaties are designed to make it easier to procure fugitive offenders for trial. Three thousand years later the problem is still the same. So much so, that dealing with fugitive offenders cannot be understood simply in terms of extradition; thus, deportation, abduction, *ad hoc* war crimes tribunals and the International Criminal Court are all gaining increased importance in the law relating to transnational fugitive offenders.

f. Plan and Structure

This book divides into three parts. The first section deals with the primary sources of extradition law, since that is still the principal mechanism for dealing with transnational fugitive offenders: the treaties and other international arrangements and the domestic legislation as seen through the practices and procedures of various States and legal systems. From that basis flows a critical review of the necessary improvements to make extradition more effective.

Secondly, and closely connected with the former chapters, it is necessary to discuss the options open to a fugitive offender challenging extradition which are not generally available in domestic trials. This discussion starts with a consideration of human rights conventions, especially the provisions of the European Convention on Human Rights,[70] which may be raised to prevent an order to surrender. The following two chapters review the measures in domestic extradition legislation and international arrangements

---

68 OJ 1996 No.C313/11.
69 US-Colombian Treaty of 14 SEPT 1979, implemented to counter the drug trafficking from Colombia to the USA; 27 INT.LEG.MAT.492 (1988). The treaty was declared unconstitutional by the Colombian Supreme Court. US-Italian Treaty of 13 OCT 1983, implemented to deal with organised crime (TIAS 10837).
70 ETS 5 (1950).

which are special to extradition, ending with a major study of the most controversial topic in extradition law, the political offence exemption.

It is in the final section of the book that the alternative methods of dealing with transnational fugitive offenders other than extradition are considered in more detail. Alongside extradition, other means of rendition have been utilised in the past and this final section commences by examining their lawfulness and effectiveness. Connected therewith is the intractable problem of obtaining jurisdiction over war criminals; increasingly, this will involve the use of supranational tribunals and their role *vis à vis* transnational fugitive offenders. The other part of this section deals with the related topic of refugee status which is of importance for extradition requests, fugitives' rights and for alternative methods of rendition.

PART I

EXTRADITION AND TRANSNATIONAL FUGITIVE OFFENDERS

Despite strong predictions of its imminent doom, particularly in the United States where abduction has become the hot issue, extradition is still the generally accepted method of dealing with transnational fugitive offenders. The next five chapters consider extradition law at the international level, at the procedural level and against the background of the fugitive's rights, whether deriving from international human rights instruments or extradition law, including the political offence exemption.

2

MECHANISMS FOR
INTERNATIONAL EXTRADITION[1]

a. Introduction

Extradition can be defined as a process whereby States provide to each other assistance in criminal matters. To achieve this international co-operation some form of arrangement, whether formal or informal, whether general or *ad hoc*, is necessary between the States involved. The arrangement may be based on a treaty, bilateral or multilateral, or on the application with respect to the requesting State of the requested State's domestic extradition legislation. Regardless, some level of agreement must have been reached between the two States acknowledging that a fugitive might be surrendered given that certain prerequisites are met.[2]

Where there is a treaty, then one issue that arises is priority between different types of treaty. 'Ruritania' may well have an extradition agreement with 'Arcadia', but it may simultaneously have entered into a multilateral human rights agreement. The issue then arises as to whether Ruritania's human rights commitments should apply to its extradition dealings with Arcadia. These matters are considered below in Chapter 4, but there is an overlap with the matters for discussion here. Under Article 30 of the Vienna Convention on the Law of Treaties,[3] where States have ratified "successive

---

1 My gratitude is owed to the various diplomatic officers charged with providing information in the embassies and non-governmental organisations in London. Their assistance, and that of the Ministries of Justice in their sending States, was invaluable.

2 See the agreement reached between Switzerland and the U.A.E. in *App.9012/80, X v Switzerland*, 24 D+R 205 at 213. For the difficulties where no or few extradition agreements exist, see van Zyl Smit, *Re-entering the International Community: South Africa and Extradition*, 6 Crim.LF 369 (1995).

3 8 INT.LEG.MAT.679 (1969).

treaties relating to the same subject-matter", then there is an elaborate set of rules dealing with priority. However, while extradition and human rights overlap, it is stretching a point to suggest that they are the same subject-matter. Thus, priority based on which is the most recent treaty under Article 30.3 is too simplistic. Given that the United Nations Charter provides that all members shall respect human rights[4] and that in *Barcelona Traction*[5] the ICJ held that obligations *erga omnes* derive in part from "principles and rules concerning the basic rights of the human person", then it is suggested that the requested State should *prima facie* give priority to the human rights of the fugitive. However, this is not to suggest that all types of human rights are to take precedence over the interests of international criminal procedure. The right to life[6] and freedom from torture and inhuman and degrading treatment, for instance, are in a completely different category to the right to family life, as is discussed in Chapter 4. Where the right to a fair trial as interpreted by the requested State might not be wholly satisfied by the procedures in the requesting State, then it ought to be a matter of degree as to whether there are sufficient grounds for not fulfilling the requested State's obligations under the extradition treaty.

Inherent in any international extradition arrangement is the potential for reciprocity. It is explicit in a bilateral treaty where each party has agreed to surrender up fugitives to the other on the understanding that its requests will also be honoured. In *ad hoc* arrangements, designed to meet the situation where the fugitive is found in a State with which the requesting State does not possess general extradition relations, reciprocity is not a necessary element of the special agreement, but States usually extract an understanding that in similar circumstances their requests will be considered. The question is whether reciprocity is an essential requirement of extradition relations and, wherever it is so, to what degree it is to be applied.

Some extradition legislation in civil law States does expressly demand a degree of reciprocity. The law of the Germany[7], provides as follows.

---

4   See Articles 1 and 55.
5   *Barcelona Traction, Light and Power Co. Case, (Belgium v Spain)*, ICJ Rep.3 (1970).
6   See *CDS v The Netherlands* 96 INT'L L REP.383 (Dutch S.Ct, 1990).
7   Law on International Assistance in Criminal Matters, 23 DEC 1982; 24 INT.LEG.MAT.945 (1985); now reprinted as amended in the Federal Law Gazette of 27th June 1994 – further amended in s7 of the Law of 10th April 1995.

"*s1(3)* Provisions of international treaties shall supersede the provisions of this law provided they have been implemented and have become national law.

s5 Extradition shall be granted only if, on the basis of assurances given by the requesting State, it can be anticipated that the State would execute a comparable German request."

On the other hand, the Swiss Law on International Judicial Assistance in Criminal Matters[8], is slightly more liberal as regards reciprocity.

"*Art.1(1)* Unless otherwise provided in international agreements, this law shall govern all procedures of international co-operation in criminal matters, and in particular:

(a) extradition of fugitives or convicted persons ....

Art.8(1) As a rule, a request shall be granted only if the requesting State guarantees reciprocity. The Federal Office for Police Matters of the Federal Department of Justice and Police (Federal Office) may require a guarantee of reciprocity if this is deemed necessary.

(2) Reciprocity shall not be required specifically in cases of service of documents or if the execution of a request:

(a) seems advisable by reason of the type of offence or the necessity of combating certain offences;

(b) is likely to improve the situation of the fugitive or the prospects of his social rehabilitation; or

(c) serves to clarify an offence committed against a Swiss national.

(3) The Federal Council may, within the scope of this Law, guarantee to other States reciprocity."

However, despite the less strict language of the Swiss statute, the Swiss Federal Tribunal has, on occasion, examined the precise facts of the case before it in order to see whether, if those same facts were repeated, *mutatis mutandis*, with Switzerland as the requesting State, the authorities in the

---

8   20 MAR 1981, 20 INT.LEG.MAT.1339 (1981), as amended 4 OCT 1996 (supplied by the Federal Office for Police Matters, Bern) – the text is a combination of both translations. See also the Decree on International Mutual Assistance in Criminal Matters, 24 FEB 1982 as amended 9 DEC 1996 (supplied by the Federal Office for Police Matters, Bern). The Swiss statute is only invoked where there is no applicable international agreement according to Art.1(1), such an agreement being deemed to guarantee reciprocity.

present requesting State would grant extradition.[9] Even if reciprocity is to be an issue in a case, however, it should only ever be applied with respect to general extradition relations and never to specific details of extradition procedure as the Swiss Federal Tribunal seems to have done. Common law States, for instance, will extradite their nationals to civil law jurisdictions, even though the latter will not reciprocate in that specific detail, because overall the agreement will be reciprocal.[10]

Common law States, in fact, tend not to expressly demand reciprocity. It is, of course, implicit in every treaty arrangement, but it is not a matter for the courts.

> "The Acts of 1870 to 1932 do not themselves provide that an arrangement made with a foreign State under section 2 of the [Extradition Act 1870] for the surrender by the United Kingdom to that foreign State of fugitive criminals accused or convicted of criminal conduct committed within its jurisdiction must provide for reciprocity of surrender by the foreign State to the United Kingdom of persons accused or convicted of similar criminal conduct in this country. In practice, extradition treaties do provide for a substantial degree of reciprocity, but the surrender by a foreign State of a fugitive criminal from the United Kingdom who is found in the territory of that foreign State is not governed by English law at all, but solely by the law of the foreign State that is a party to the treaty. If the foreign State fails to comply with its treaty obligations as respects surrender this is a matter for the Secretary of State; it has nothing to do with the English magistrate."[11]

This attitude reflects not only the view that it is better to be rid of a person who has previously committed crimes than to insist on reciprocity, but also the reluctance of common law courts in extradition matters to investigate the legal system of the requesting State. By contrast, civil law courts are

---

9   *T v Swiss Federal Prosecutor's Office*, 72 INT'L L REP.632 at 636 (1966).
10 *Cf.* Irish decision in the *Corry* case (The Guardian p.8, 16 JAN 1997) not to extradite an Irish national to Germany because Germany would not extradite a German national in similar circumstances.
11 *In re Nielsen*, [1984] AC 606 at 617. See also, *Hempel v Attorney-General* 77 ALR 641 (1987), Australian Federal Court, General Division.

prepared so to do and will look to see if reciprocity is possible or if it has previously been exercised in similar circumstances.[12]

While still dealing with the issue of reciprocity, the Commonwealth Scheme for the Rendition of Fugitive Offenders[13] is not a treaty, although it resembles one in form. The tradition within the Commonwealth is that the members do not conclude treaties, but that agreements are binding anyway.[14] Since the Scheme is not a true multilateral convention, reciprocity is not guaranteed. The United Kingdom, for example, designates in its domestic legislation[15] every member of the Commonwealth, regardless of whether all those countries could grant rendition to the United Kingdom. The extreme example of this approach is seen in *Re Kahan*[16], where extradition to Fiji was declared possible because Fiji was still designated under the then Fugitive Offenders Act 1967 despite the fact it had left the Commonwealth; as such, it could not reciprocate. However, other members of the Commonwealth have called for the Scheme to be converted into a treaty and for reciprocity to be an essential requirement.[17] This proposition has also been suggested by Robinson,[18] who, reflecting the views of many States, sees extradition "as a system which should only operate on the basis of reciprocity." He, therefore, supports the idea of selective designation of other Commonwealth countries based on a guarantee of reciprocity from the requesting State. To follow this approach, though, would be regressive.

---

12 See *T, supra n9*, and *In re Zahabian*, 32 INT'L L REP.290 (Swiss Fed.Trib. 1963).

13 1990 version, LMM(90)32.

14 *Cf.* Anglo-Indian Extradition Treaty 1992, and see the Suppression of Terrorism (India) Order SI 1993 No.2533; and 42 INT'L & COMP. LQ 442 (1993). Cyprus has been designated a foreign State for the purposes of the European Extradition Convention 1957, *infra n38*, so as to permit extradition without the need for the *prima facie* case – s2(2) European Convention on Extradition Order 1990 (SI 1990 No.1507).

15 See s5 Extradition Act 1989.

16 [1989] 1 QB 716. Fiji had been excluded by the Commonwealth Leaders on 16 OCT 1986.

17 See THE 1982 REVIEW OF COMMONWEALTH EXTRADITION ARRANGEMENTS, pp.23 *et seq*. The Review is available from the Commonwealth Secretariat; hereinafter COMMONWEALTH REVIEW.

18 *The Commonwealth Scheme Relating to the Rendition of Fugitive Offenders: A Critical Appraisal of some Essential Elements*, 33 INT'L & COMP. LQ 614 at p.618.

"The prevailing European view is that insistence on reciprocity is a distinct disadvantage. The number of cases is increasing where extradition is in the interests of both the requesting and the requested State."[19]

"Botswana considers that the Commonwealth should adopt a positive attitude towards criminals. It is in a country's own interests to prevent them from hiding behind borders. Why should any country wish to have within its borders a suspected criminal wanted for a serious offence – he should go back to whence he came, whether or not the other country is a party to reciprocal arrangements. His return would pave the way for reciprocity to be arranged for the future. It is strongly recommended that the Meeting exclude insistence on reciprocity."[20]

Extradition should not be viewed as an arm of foreign policy. Generally speaking reciprocity should be present, but it should not be a *sine qua non*. One aim of extradition laws is to provide for mutual assistance in criminal matters and the fugitive's prosecution for his alleged crimes should override the general requirement that extradition relations should be reciprocal. Reciprocity should go to the overall arrangement, not to specific cases or matters of procedure.[21]

b. Forms of Arrangement

The majority of international extradition agreements are bilateral treaties. During the nineteenth and early twentieth centuries, as extradition law as it is known today was developing and spreading from Europe to the rest of the world, States would conclude bilateral treaties specific to the demands of those particular relations. Bilateral treaties make for a piecemeal approach to extradition practice, given that some differences will arise during each set of negotiations, but the agreement will be that best suited to the two

---

19 Dr Torsten Stein in the COMMONWEALTH REVIEW, *supra* n17, at p.25. Nevertheless, statutes in European States still call for reciprocity – see *supra* nn7 and 8.
20 The Hon. MD Mokama, *supra* n17, at p.23.
21 In some cases the overall relations turn out not to be reciprocal. In 1978 Spain broke off extradition relations with the United Kingdom because no Spanish request had ever been granted.

parties' particular situation. However, whether arrangements can be updated in line with current practice is open to doubt unless the treaty so provides, although Kontou shows how customary international law may, in certain circumstances, provide rights for the fugitive not incorporated in the treaty.[22] Undoubtedly though, bilateral treaties will continue to be the most numerous form of extradition arrangement.

The different approaches by States to international treaties in domestic law also affect extradition laws. In England and Australia, for instance the treaty on its own cannot empower a court to grant surrender. Domestic legislation has to be passed to implement the treaties. The statutes permit extradition and the treaty can only be used to fill any gaps or to improve the rights of the fugitive. In France and Switzerland extradition treaties are self-executing and provide the law for the extradition hearing with the domestic legislation filling the gaps and being a substitute mechanism when no treaty exists. In practice, there is little difference in the two approaches.

While bilateral treaties were the first method to be used to conclude extradition relations, States have since developed alternative forms of arrangement. For instance, regional conventions have proved popular. A universal extradition treaty open to all States might be thought too general to be any more effective in dealing with transnational fugitive offenders than *ad hoc* arrangements for specific cases. However, the United Nations General Assembly has produced a model treaty on extradition[23] which has formed the basis for inter-State extradition agreements.[24] Furthermore, in an effort to ensure serious offenders do not escape justice, the United Nations sponsored anti-terrorist conventions have included clauses to permit them to be used as surrogate extradition treaties where no treaty exists between the requesting and requested States. In more specific situations, States with close geographical and historical connections have reached agreements allowing for very much simplified procedures. Finally, States have occasionally provided for extradition without any international arrangement through

---

22 KONTOU, THE TERMINATION AND REVISION OF TREATIES IN THE LIGHT OF NEW CUSTOMARY INTERNATIONAL LAW, pp.72-74 (1994).

23 UNGA Res.45/116, 14 DEC 1991, 30 INT.LEG.MAT.1407 (1991); *cf.* Swart, *Refusal of Extradition and the United Nations Model Treaty on Extradition*, 23 NETH.YB INT'L L 175 (1992).

24 CLARK, THE UN CRIME PREVENTION AND CRIMINAL JUSTICE PROGRAM: FORMULATION OF STANDARDS AND EFFORTS AT THEIR IMPLEMENTATION (1994).

domestic legislation; the object is to ensure that a State does not become a safe-haven for criminals and to facilitate in a practical way the comity of nations.

The following review is designed to highlight State practice and indicate some of the major issues relating to the form of arrangement.

(i) Multilateral Arrangements – The idea of a general, universal extradition treaty has been proposed frequently in the past[25], but has, as yet, only produced the United Nations' model treaty, discussed above. The reasons are not hard to divine. As Stein has commented with respect to Europe,

> "[the] advantage of a uniform system are beyond doubt, but on the other hand the European Extradition Convention of 1957[26] reflects only the minimum standard of joint convictions ...."[27]

At a worldwide level, joint convictions are at a minimum.[28] Moreover, since the practice of extradition tends to be regional there is little need for a universal convention, especially if extradition is permitted by domestic legislation on an *ad hoc* basis with States with which the requested State has no permanent relations. The model United Nations treaties, therefore, represent a halfway house, trying to promote extradition arrangements between States without attempting to create a universally binding treaty for the entire international community. At a regional level, though, multilateral arrangements abound.

The Americas – One of the earliest regional systems was concluded in the Americas and the States of the region have been developing it ever since, now under the auspices of the Organisation of American States. International co-operation in criminal matters commenced in 1879 with the Lima Agreement, but regional extradition is taken to have started with the Montevideo Agreement of ten years later.[29] It was then developed in 1902, 1911, 1923,

---

25   SHEARER, EXTRADITION IN INTERNATIONAL LAW, p.23 (1971).
26   ETS 24.
27   COMMONWEALTH REVIEW, p.98, *supra* n17.
28   See, for example, the Report of the Committee of Experts for the Progressive Codification of International Law, L.N.Doc.C.51 M.28.1926. V.
29   See *Harvard Research in International Law: Extradition*, 29 AM.J INT'L L Supp. at pp.275 *et seq.*

1928, 1933, 1934, 1940, 1957 and finally in 1981. The 1981 Inter-American Convention on Extradition[30] is the current regional agreement, but it expressly declares in Article 33 that it shall not supersede earlier bilateral or multilateral treaties entered into by the State parties. As well as the plethora of conventions to which regard must be had, there is also regional customary law,[31] in part based on the pervasive and persistent themes found in these agreements.[32]

The Arab League – The League of Arab States has also concluded two conventions providing for extradition amongst State parties.[33] The first was signed in 1952[34] by six States and ratified or acceded to by ten.[35] A supplementary agreement was signed in Riyadh on April 4, 1983. Nineteen States have ratified it,[36] although this group does not include Egypt, a party to the 1952 Agreement, because Egypt left the Arab League following the 1978 Camp David Accords with Israel. The 1983 Agreement not only develops the themes of the 1952 Convention, it significantly extends its geographic remit. While in 1952 the agreement covered Arab States in the Middle East, Egypt and Libya, the new agreement completes the gaps in the Middle East and now takes in the Arab and Islamic States of the Sahara and Sahel regions of Africa. It is a comprehensive extradition convention which now provides for the surrender of fugitive offenders throughout a significant portion of the world.

---

30 20 INT.LEG.MAT.723 (1981). See also Council of Europe R(82)950 instructing the European Committee on Crime Problems to study whether Council of Europe member States could accede to the Inter-American Convention.

31 *The Asylum Case*, ICJ Rep.166 at 316 (1950).

32 *Nicaragua v USA*, ICJ Rep.14 at 87-88 (1986).

33 I am extremely grateful to A. Oussayfi at the League of Arab States in London for supplying me with information.

34 Available in English, 159 B.F.S.P.606. In force 28 AUG 1954.

35 Egypt, Iraq, Jordan, Lebanon, Saudi Arabia and Syria. Documents of ratification were deposited by Egypt, Jordan, Saudi Arabia, the U.A.E., Bahrain, Kuwait, Iraq, Libya, Syria and S.Yemen, as it then was.

36 In addition to the nine remaining ratifiers of the 1952 Agreement (Egypt excluded), documents of ratification have been received from Tunisia, Algeria, Djibouti, Sudan, Mauritania, North Yemen (now reunited with S.Yemen, another ratifier), Somalia, Oman, Qatar and Morocco – the State of Palestine also ratified.

Europe – The most extensive series of regional agreements, however, is found in Europe. They also orchestrate the most traffic in extradition requests. Europe for these purposes should be seen as a series of concentric and overlapping circles[37], with various extradition arrangements in force and some States belonging to more than one grouping.

The outer circle with respect to extradition would encompass the Council of Europe's European Extradition Convention of 1957.[38] It is a highly successful regional convention, forming the procedural framework for more extraditions than any other treaty. By the end of 1997, thirty-five States had ratified it.[39] It provides for extradition without proof of a *prima facie* case and gives parties the discretion to refuse to extradite their nationals; as such, it is modelled on European practice as found in earlier bilateral agreements.

More importantly, however, in terms of the usefulness in general of regional conventions, the European Extradition Convention displays some of the failings that are inherent in multilateral arrangements' where the interests of many parties have to be satisfied. For example, Article 28, paragraphs (1) and (2) declare that the Convention supersedes existing bilateral and multilateral arrangements between the parties and that subsequent such arrangements may only be seen as supplementary to the Convention, while paragraph (3) provides that a uniform law in force in relation to two or more parties shall take precedence. Indeed, the F.R.G. only ratified the Convention in 1976 after it had concluded supplementary arrangements with most of the other parties.[40] This attitude towards the Convention reflects the fact that it is the "minimum standard of joint convictions".[41]

---

37 In relation to policing Europe generally, see HOME AFFAIRS SELECT COMMITTEE, 7th REPORT, PRACTICAL POLICE CO-OPERATION IN THE EUROPEAN COMMUNITY, (2 vols), HCP 363 (1989–90); hereinafter, HCP-I or HCP-II.

38 ETS 24. See also the two additional protocols ETS 86 (1975) and ETS 98 (1978).

39 Austria, Belgium, Cyprus, Denmark, Finland, France, Federal Republic of Germany, Greece, Iceland, Ireland, Israel, Italy, Liechtenstein, Luxembourg, Malta, the Netherlands, Norway, Portugal, Spain, Sweden, Switzerland, Turkey and the United Kingdom, plus those listed *infra n* 66 (see SI 1507/1990). Israel has acceded, although not a member of the Council of Europe.

40 See COUNCIL OF EUROPE, LEGAL ASPECTS OF EXTRADITION AMONG EUROPEAN STATES, at p.67 (1970).

41 *Supra n*17.

Secondly, Article 26 permits reservations to be made in respect of any provision of the Convention. The exhortation in paragraph (2) that such reservations should be withdrawn as soon as possible has largely gone unheeded. The ability to make reservations is essential to the conclusion of most multilateral conventions, but, as Honig observed in 1956,

> "to permit numerous reservations by signatory States, may well result in multiplying disputes which at present rarely occur in the application and interpretation of bilateral treaties."[42]

Belgium indicated during the Sixties that one reason it had not ratified the Convention at that time was that due to the large number of important reservations already entered to the Convention, a signatory would end up being bound,

> "not by a general convention but by a number of agreements parallel to existing bilateral conventions."[43]

By reason of its general applicability throughout Europe, the European Extradition Convention is not always appropriate to the special needs of any State in those general relations and in its relations with another specific State. Furthermore, it represents a compromise at the lowest level and may require supplementary details. These failings are inevitable in any multilateral extradition convention.

The European Community and then, later, the European Union, has a checkered history with regard to extradition between member States.[44] Policing powers were initially outside the purview of the European Community, but an inter-State group, known as TREVI, did form during the 1970s to co-ordinate[45] on drugs, terrorism,[46] serious crime, public order and scientific matters and, finally, the implications of the removal of internal borders in 1992. TREVI was not strictly a European Community body and,

---

42 *Extradition by Multilateral Convention*, 5 INT'L & COMP. LQ 549 at p.551 (1956).
43 *Supra n*40.
44 Austria, Belgium, Denmark, Finland, France, Germany, Greece, Ireland, Italy, Luxembourg, the Netherlands, Portugal, Spain, Sweden and the United Kingdom.
45 See Chapter 3 below.
46 See Foakes, *The European Community and Terrorism*, [1983] TOP.LAW 19.

indeed, the Commission was excluded from its deliberations. However, whilst general policing issues might have been beyond the traditionally recognised remit of the European Community, transnational fugitive offenders and their rendition to face trial should undoubtedly have been within the purview of a supranational organization which allowed for freer movement of persons within member States and which, by its very nature, would provide greater opportunities for transnational economic crimes. The creation of the European Union in 1992, however, enabled crime related matters to be brought within the Third Pillar of the Maastricht Treaty[47], Justice and Home Affairs. The work of TREVI in this field came within an Article K.4 committee and a simplified extradition scheme for use within the Fifteen was promulgated in 1995.[48] Subsequently, the European Union Council drafted another treaty to supplement existing multilateral extradition arrangements that apply between the various member States.[49]

The 1995 treaty supplements the Council of Europe's 1957 European Extradition Convention by providing for a simplified scheme of extradition between member States based on the fugitive's consent and the requested State's agreement. The level of information demanded by the 1957 Convention is also dispensed with and the fugitive can renounce his entitlement to the protection of the specialty rule.[50] The 1996 treaty supplements not only the 1957 Convention, but also the Council of Europe's 1977 Convention on the Suppression of Terrorism,[51] the 1990 Schengen Agreement[52] and the Benelux Treaty.[53] Of note, it limits the scope of the political offence

---

47   31 INT.LEG.MAT.247 (1992).

48   1995 OJ C 78, 10 MAR 1995; and see also, 1996 OJ C 375. There is also the wholly procedural Agreement between the Member States of the European Community on the Simplification and Modernisation of Methods of Transmitting Extradition Requests opened for signature in San Sebastian on 26 May 1989 – see SI 1996 No 2596.

49   Convention Relating to Extradition between the Member States of the European Union, 1996 OJ C 313 – Explanatory Report, 1997 OJ C 191. See also, Mackarel and Nash, *Extradition and the European Union*, 46 INT'L & COMP.LQ 948 (1997).

50   See Chapter 5, below.

51   ETS 90: 15 INT.LEG.MAT.1272 (1976); hereinafter ECST. See Chapter Six, below.

52   30 INT.LEG.MAT.84 (1991). See also, MEIJERS, SCHENGEN, 2nd ed. 1992.

53   Treaty on Extradition and Mutual Assistance in Criminal Matters, 27 June 1962, and Protocol, 11 May 1974.

exemption,[54] the rules on the non-extradition of nationals and the exclusion of fiscal offences from the definition of extraditable crimes, it relaxes the specialty rule[55] and improves some of the procedural elements of extradition law. With respect to both the 1995 and 1996 treaty, the European Union has not attempted to draft a comprehensive multilateral extradition treaty, but has simply tagged on less onerous obligations for the requesting State to existing agreements to which member States are already party. Whilst one might applaud this time-saving technique, there is a sense of expediency triumphing over proper provision. An agreement between the Fifteen could have been honed to produce a treaty designed for their specific needs. In particular, the Fifteen have to address the question of jurisdiction over crimes against the European Community and European Union; lacking territory and other appurtenances of Statehood, the latter's own criminal jurisdiction is in doubt and there is, anyway, no trial court before which to hold a prosecution – in addition, neither treaty provides for dispute resolution by the European Court of Justice.[56] Thus, a treaty between member States of the European Union could provide, *inter alia*, for the systems needed to deal with crimes against the supranational organization.

Staying with Europe the Dutch concluded a simplified trilateral extradition agreement with Luxembourg and Belgium in 1962. The Benelux Convention on Extradition and Judicial Assistance in Penal Matters[57] came into force for the three States before any of them ratified the European Extradition Convention,[58] however it follows the general outline of that arrangement. Nevertheless, when the Netherlands ratified the European Extradition Convention in 1969 it entered a reservation rejecting Article 28(1) and (2) in relation to Belgium and Luxembourg and went further still by reserving the future right to derogate from those same provisions to accommodate any E.C. arrangement.[59] The interplay of these multilateral

---

54 See Chapter 6, below.
55 See below on fiscal offences and Chapter 5 for the other topics.
56 See Article K.3 of the Maastricht Treaty, *supra n*47. *Cf.* the proposed Article K.7 of the Amsterdam Treaty, 1997.
57 See De Shutter, *L'Entraide Judiciaire en Matière Pénale dans le Cadre du Benelux*, [1967] REV.BELGE DE DR.INT'L 102.
58 *Supra n*38.
59 See COUNCIL OF EUROPE, *supra n*40, at p.78.

arrangements reveals how extradition agreements are best concluded between as few parties as possible so as to achieve the most effective scheme.

The Benelux Accord and the European Extradition Convention were both added to and further facilitated through Articles 59 and following of the Schengen Accord of 19 June 1990.[60] The Schengen Group comprises the three Benelux States plus France, Germany, Spain, Portugal, Italy, Greece and Austria.[61] The initial agreement of 14 June 1985 of the three Benelux States, France and Germany prepared the way for open internal borders between the five before 1993; the 1990 Accord includes a new treaty negotiated in 1989 incorporating, *inter alia*, the right to 'hot pursuit'. Schengen is yet another example of a specific response to a particular situation requiring special provisions beyond the minimum as found in the European Extradition Convention.

The final European multilateral scheme that needs to be examined applies between members of the Nordic Union.[62] The extradition agreement came into force before the Union itself[63] and is based on reciprocal legislation in the five States.[64] The scheme resembles in-State rendition more than a true international agreement with §4 of the Norwegian Act, for example, permitting the surrender of political offenders, given that the offence charged is triable under Norwegian law and the fugitive is not a Norwegian national. There is a reasonable amount of traffic under the scheme with even Iceland, the most remote party, receiving one or two requests a year and sending about three to five. Given the special relationship of the parties it proved possible for them to negotiate the arrangement best suited to their needs which went beyond the basic minimum of the European Extradition Convention.

---

60 *Supra n*52. I am indebted to my Ph.D student, Virginie Lotti, for saving me hours of time in the library by giving me the latest list of signatories and ratifications.

61 As at 26 March 1995, only Italy, Greece and Austria had not ratified.

62 Denmark, Finland, Iceland, Norway and Sweden.

63 Nordic Union Treaty, 1 JULY 1962, 434 UNTS 145.

64 *Eg*. The Danish Law No.27 of 3 February 1960 as amended by Law No.251 of 6 December 1975, the Swedish Act (1959:254), the Icelandic Law No.7/1962, as amended by 44/1975 and 19/1991, and the Norwegian Act of 3 March 1961, as amended by the 1985 Extradition Act (No.71, 14 June 1985).

Finally in this section on Europe, with the collapse of the Iron Curtain in 1989–90, most of the former Soviet Bloc States joined the Council of Europe[65] and acceded to the European Extradition Convention.[66] Prior to 1989, however, the East European States relied on bilateral agreements to conduct their extradition relations[67], although so similar were they that they were at least the equal of the European Extradition Convention, subject as it is to so many reservations. It is unlikely that any of these bilateral treaties have survived the change in government, for they permit the extradition of political offenders *inter se* on the ground that such criminals are a threat to the State socialist system as a whole.[68]

In conclusion, the many levels of extradition agreements that exist in Europe overlap and reduce the universality and uniformity of the European Extradition Convention.[69] It is, however, inevitable that an agreement that is acceptable to thirty-five States should not necessarily meet the needs of some of those States with extremely close ties and that they would wish to conclude more specific relations. Despite these criticisms, though, the European Extradition Convention has proved a great success and provides for the extradition of fugitive offenders throughout Europe.

The Commonwealth – Ever since 1843 there has been a separate system for extradition throughout what is now the Commonwealth.[70] In the days of the British Empire, the scheme was established by statute passed at Westminster. Indeed, the Fugitive Offenders Act 1881 governed extradition in the Empire and then the Commonwealth until 1966.[71] The Common-

---

65   Hungary joined in November 1990.

66   Bulgaria, Croatia, the Czech Republic, Estonia, Hungary, Latvia, Lithuania, Moldova, Poland, Romania, the Slovak Republic, Slovenia were all party as at 1 January 1998.

67   Schmid, *Extradition and International Judicial and Administrative Assistance in Penal Matters in East European States*, 34 LAW IN E.EUROPE 167, *esp.* pp.169-73 (1988), and GINSBURGS, THE SOVIET UNION AND INTERNATIONAL CO-OPERATION IN LEGAL MATTERS, 1994.

68   Schmid, *supra n*67, at p.180.

69   *Supra n*38.

70   6 & 7 Vict. c.34, An Act for the Better Apprehension of Certain Offenders.

71   See, however, *State of Madras v Menon*, [1954] All Ind.R 517 (SC India), where it was held that after India became a Republic, the 1881 Act was no longer applicable. In *Re Ashman*, [1985] 2 NZLR 244 (decided 31 May 1976), the Supreme Court of New Zealand held that the 1881 Act, with its references to

wealth adopted the Scheme Relating to the Rendition of Fugitive Offenders within the Commonwealth in 1966[72] which, although similar to a multilateral convention, does not have the status of a treaty. It provides guidelines for extradition to and from Commonwealth countries and dependencies, but it is only put into effect through domestic legislation. In 1982 the entire Scheme was reviewed[73] leading to some amendments,[74] but the latest version dates from 1990.[75] Despite pressure from the New Commonwealth,[76] the Scheme has not been converted into a treaty and there is no requirement of reciprocity[77]; therefore, even if the requesting State has not brought legislation into force to implement the Scheme, the requested State should still operate its own Scheme-based statute when dealing with the request.[78]

The most notable thing, however, about the Scheme is that it applies to States across the entire globe with many different forms of government. While it was suggested above that an international multilateral convention was a practical impossibility, the Commonwealth Scheme might indicate otherwise, although the historical ties between the member States and the

---

"Her Majesty's dominions", could not apply to the independent New Zealand. On 15 July 1976, New Zealand passed the Fugitive Offenders Amendment Act 1976, reinstating in force the 1881 Act – one has to wonder at this example of expedience over reform ten years after the Commonwealth Scheme, *infra* *n*72.

72   Cmnd 3008.
73   *Supra* *n*17.
74   LMM(83)33. See also LMM(86)64.
75   LMM(90)32. All references are to the 1990 version.
76   *Eg.* Zimbabwe, Fiji, Sri Lanka, Malaysia, Trindad & Tobago and Bangladesh. See the COMMONWEALTH REVIEW, *supra* *n*17, pp.22-26. *Cf.* Dominica which sees the Commonwealth
     "as a family of nations, and one uniform Act applicable to all Commonwealth countries could render reciprocity, at least within the Commonwealth, obsolete." *NB* Fiji is not currently a member of the Commonwealth, but, because the UK does not require reciprocity, it was able to seek a fugitive under the British domestic legislation – *Kahan, supra* *n*16; Fiji legislated for the restoration of racial equality, suggesting it may soon be readmitted – The Guardian p.21, 4 JUL 1997.
77   *Supra* *n*17 at p.79. Clause 1 talks of returning fugitives to other parts of the Commonwealth without any reference to reciprocity. Clause 18(a) speaks of supplementary and alternative arrangements, 18(b) only of modifications, neither permits non-application.
78   *Cf.* Nauru constitutionally requires reciprocity.

common legal system obviously help to make it workable.[79] Whether it could be the precursor of a general international convention is open to question. Contrary arguments may be found in the promulgation of a bilateral treaty between the United Kingdom and India[80] to meet their specific needs.[81] In and of itself, there is nothing unusual in two sovereign States making arrangements for assisting each other in criminal matters. However, this treaty represents the first general extradition agreement between the United Kingdom and another Commonwealth State; before this treaty, general extradition relations have always been carried out in line with the Commonwealth Scheme for the Rendition of Fugitive Offenders by means of domestic legislation. Moreover, the Anglo-Indian treaty being bilateral, is self-evidently reciprocal unlike the Scheme and it provides the further benefit that because it has been concluded between just two parties it can cater for their specific needs in some detail. For instance, while both the Scheme and this new treaty use the eliminative test for defining extradition crimes, the treaty requires merely one year's imprisonment as a sufficient possible sentence while the Scheme's minimum is two years. Secondly, the 1990 Commonwealth Scheme only provides an exception to extradition by way of a discretionary Annex where the death penalty could be imposed in the requesting but not the requested State; the United Kingdom and India were able to agree on the inclusion of this provision as a binding part of their bilateral treaty. Where States can agree bilateral agreements, then there is scope for creating a system that meets their individual needs and which is inherently reciprocal, but multilateral agreements are designed to obviate the need for detailed negotiations with all the other parties where this would represent too great an effort for any foreseeable return – in such circumstances the aim is to promote State co-operation in criminal matters and issues

---

79 It is interesting to note that Cyprus, a civil law system, is treated as a foreign State, not a member of the Commonwealth, by the United Kingdom and extradition is conducted under the European Extradition Convention 1957 – SI 1990 No.1507, s2(2).

80 The simplified scheme between Australia and New Zealand, discussed *infra* *n*85, is inherently different from a bilateral treaty and is a result of the proximity of the two States.

81 21st September 1992. The treaty was published and presented to Parliament on December 2nd 1992. See *supra* *n*14, and Gilbert, *The Anglo-Indian Extradition Treaty*, 42 INT'L & COMP.LQ 442 (1993).

of reciprocity should not be at the forefront. The Anglo-Indian treaty fuses
well the provisions of the Commonwealth Scheme and the 1989 British
Extradition Act and overall provides a balance between efficient assistance
in criminal matters and the protection of the fugitive's rights and freedoms.

The Multilateral Anti-Terrorist Conventions – From the 1970s onwards
the United Nations sponsored a whole series of anti-terrorist conventions
aimed to prevent certain offenders finding a safe haven. As part of that
objective, they add the designated offences to any list of extraditable crimes
and act as a surrogate extradition treaty where no arrangement exists between
the requesting and requested States.[82] The number of signatories to these
conventions is usually very great and they will permit extradition to States
with which no general relations exist.[83] In the particular case of these
specialised treaties, there is no doubt that a truly worldwide arrangement
is possible, but the actual conventions provide none of the procedural detail
which is what tends to create the difficulties in drafting general multilateral
agreements.

In conclusion, there are several multilateral, regional and otherwise, arrangements in existence, which probably govern more extraditions in practice
than bilateral treaties; however, they are usually subject to reservations and
State parties frequently draw up special sub-schemes with their geographical

---

82   *Eg.* Hague Convention for the Suppression of the Unlawful Seizure of Aircraft,
     10 INT.LEG.MAT.133 (1971), Art.8: Rome Convention for the Suppression of
     Unlawful Acts Against the Safety of Maritime Navigation, 27 INT.LEG.MAT.672
     (1988), Art.11.

83   For instance, the United Kingdom provided for extradition in relation to hijack-
     ing under the Hague Convention with following extra states: see s22 Extradition
     Act 1989 and SI 1992 No.3200, as amended:- Afghanistan, Bahrain, Benin,
     Bhutan, Brazil (an extradition treaty with Brazil came into force on 13 August
     1997), Burkina Faso, Byelorussia, Cameroon, Cape Verde, Central African
     Republic, Chad, China, Comoros, Congo, Costa Rica, Dominican Republic,
     Egypt, Equatorial Guinea, Ethiopia, Gabon, Guinea, Guinea-Bissau, Honduras,
     Indonesia, Iran, Ivory Coast, Japan, Jordan, North Korea, Republic of Korea,
     Kuwait, Laos, Lebanon, Libya, Madagascar, Mali, Marshall Islands, Mauritania,
     Mongolia, Morocco, Nepal, Niger, Oman, Philippines, Qatar, Russia, Rwanda,
     Saudi Arabia, Senegal, Sudan, Suriname, Syria, Togo, Tunisia, Ukraine, U.A.E.,
     Venezuela, Vietnam, Yemen, Zaire.

neighbours. The regional, multilateral conventions provide a useful fall-back and, more importantly, an overall framework for extradition.

(ii) Simplified Schemes – Some of these have already been touched on in the previous section; the Benelux trilateral accord, the European Union Simplified Scheme and the five party Nordic Union scheme are very simple by comparison with the usual international extradition treaties. The extradition arrangements to be considered now, though, are bilateral.

Although both countries are members of the Commonwealth and could, therefore, rely on the Scheme,[84] Australia and New Zealand conduct their extradition relations on the basis of reciprocal legislation.[85] The statutes permit the arrest warrants of one State to be endorsed and executed in the other State. There is no need for a diplomatic request and the executive has no say in the matter. Extradition is conducted solely at the level of the police and courts. A remarkably similar procedure exists between Ireland and the United Kingdom.[86] In 1949 Ireland gained full independence from the United Kingdom and so the two should have concluded a bilateral treaty like any other foreign States; oddly, they continued to use legislation and procedures dating from the time when Ireland was part of the United Kingdom. Eventually, almost simultaneously, the British House of Lords[87] and the Irish Supreme Court[88] held the process to be unlawful, requiring new legislation to regularise the situation. The British Backing of Warrants (Republic of Ireland) Act 1965 and Part III of the Irish Extradition Act 1965 provided initially that the arrest warrants of the other State would be endorsed as if the crime had occurred in the requested State. There was no *prima facie* requirement since the Irish were in the process of ratifying the European Extradition Convention[89] and wanted to keep its extradition laws consistent, while such a practice also continued the pre-independence procedure. The British statute has not been substantially altered since,[90] but major changes have occurred in the Irish law. With the passing of the

---

84 *Supra n*75.
85 See, for example, the Australian Extradition Act 1988, Part III.
86 See O'Higgins, *The Irish Extradition Act,1965*, 15 INT'L & COMP. LQ 369 (1966).
87 *R v Metropolitan Police Commissioner, ex p.Hammond*, [1964] 2 All ER 772.
88 *The State (Quinn) v Ryan*, [1965] IR 70.
89 Ireland ratified on 2 MAY 1966.
90 See the Suppression of Terrorism Act 1978 and the Criminal Justice Act 1993.

Irish Extradition (European Convention on the Suppression of Terrorism) Act 1987, the political offence exemption in Ireland was severely curtailed, so the *Dáil* provided a new protection in the Extradition (Amendment) Act 1987.[91] Although not requiring *prima facie* proof, the British authorities have to produce sufficient evidence to convince the Attorney-General that the case will proceed on surrender. The contents of the law are considered below, but it is interesting at this juncture for the way it reveals that reciprocity need only go to the general extradition arrangement and need not mean that the detailed provisions thereof have to be mirrored in the two sets of laws.[92] The Anglo-Irish and the Australian-New Zealand extradition arrangements reflect the historical, geographical and legal links between each of the two sets of States. The informality, which is akin to a system of rendition within a federal State,[93] could not be repeated outside such a closely-knit community of States. Such arrangements represent a view of extradition where mutual assistance in criminal matters as between the two

---

91   See also, the Extradition (Amendment) Act 1994.

92   *Cf. T v Swiss Federal Prosecutor's Office, supra n9.*

93   See also the US inter-State system of rendition 18 USC §3182. The final example of simplified rendition is unique in extradition pràctice and will probably never be repeated. In the period from the fall of the Berlin Wall on November 9, 1989, to the reunification of the two Germanies on October 3, 1990, several members of the terrorist group, the Red Army Faction, were found in the then German Democratic Republic. According to newspaper reports at the time (The Guardian p.8, 27 SEPT 1990), they were then 'extradited' to the Federal Republic of Germany. Given that there was no extradition treaty or reciprocal legislation in force with respect to the two Germanies, this description was not technically accurate. The terrorist suspects were surrendered on the basis of their own consent and as a result of a decision of the *Stadtgericht Berlin* (Regional Court) concerning the proceedings against Susanne Albrecht. The Albrecht case held that during the transition period to full reunification, the Federal Republic was not a "foreign State" as regards the Democratic Republic. Mutual assistance could be granted according to internal legal principles rather than those which govern two separate States. This unique situation provides yet another example of the rendition arrangements that have been used by States which are much more simplified than the general treaty based agreements. (The above information was supplied by Bernd Oetter, Consul General at the embassy of the Federal Republic of Germany in London. So unusual is the arrangement that I have quoted heavily from his letter to avoid any errors. Needless to add, I am deeply indebted to him for this information).

States prevails over the protection of the fugitive's human rights which are usually spelt out carefully in bilateral and multilateral treaties.

(iii) Extradition without a General Arrangement – Occasionally, the fugitive is requested by a State with which no extradition arrangement already exists. Despite the arguments of Grotius,[94] extradition is an imperfect obligation and there is no general international duty to extradite or punish the fugitive. If there is no arrangement, then there is no duty to extradite and everything is dependent on the comity of nations.[95] Nevertheless, there are strong arguments for providing for some means of rendition even in these circumstances.

> "It is as much to our advantage that such criminals should be punished, and that we should get rid of them, as it is to that foreign State that they should be brought within the reach of its law."[96]

Civil law States, such as France and Switzerland, statutorily provide for extradition when no treaty exists; the statutes are expressly stated to be subsidiary to any treaty,[97] such that the statute can only apply in the absence of a general international arrangement.

> "Whilst Article 1 of the Law of 10 March 1927 provides that it applies to points not regulated by the treaties, such a provision cannot override the provisions of the Treaty ...."[98]

---

94 DE JURE BELLI AC PACIS, Bk II, c.21, paras.3 and 4. *Cf.* PUFENDORF, ELEMENTS, Bk III, c.3, paras.23 and 24.

95 See the Asil Nadir Case, The Guardian pp.1 and 22, 6 MAY 1993. See also the fact that Pakistan would not extradite Agha Hasan Abedi to Abu Dhabi because there was no treaty (The Guardian p.14, 15 JULY 1994), nor to the United States because there were not good relations between the two nations.

96 Royal Commission on Extradition 1878, C 2039, and PARRY, BRITISH DIGEST OF INTERNATIONAL LAW, vol.6, at pp.805-6 (1965). See also, Canada's submission to the Human Rights Committee in *Kindler v Canada*, Communication No.470/1991, 14 HRLJ 307 at para.8.2 (1993).

97 See the French Law of 10 March 1927 and Blakesley, *The Practice of Extradition from Antiquity to Modern France and the United States: a Brief History*, 4 B.C. INT'L & COMP. L REV.39 at pp.53-55; see also the Swiss agreement of 1980 – 20 INT.LEG.MAT.1339 (1981).

98 *Croissant*, 74 INT'L L REP.505 at 509 (1978).

Nonetheless, this combination of treaties and domestic legislation does not create a duty to extradite as Grotius envisaged, because it merely empowers France to act, it does not impose an obligation to act.

Common law States tended to require some more formalised arrangement between the requesting and requested States.[99] However, several States have now adopted legislation to permit *ad hoc* extradition when no arrangement already exists.[100] Usually in these circumstances, the requested State demands greater safeguards for the human rights of the fugitive.

In conclusion, it should come as no surprise that extradition arrangements are very varied as regards form. At one extreme are the multilateral regional conventions, while at the other lie the *ad hoc* arrangements designed to ensure that the fugitive does not escape justice even if there are no permanent extradition relations between the two States. As between the States negotiating the arrangement, the emphasis will always be on providing mutual assistance in criminal matters, rather than the humanitarian protection of the fugitive. Nevertheless, the very fact that States choose with which other States they will establish extradition relations guarantees the fugitive's rights to some small degree; States will only extradite where the system of justice in the requesting State meets whatever standards the requested State deems necessary.

(iv) Transfer to international criminal tribunals – The establishment of *ad hoc* tribunals for the Former Yugoslavia and Rwanda and the preparations for an International Criminal Court mean that there is now an additional mechanism for dealing with certain types of transnational fugitive offender.[101] The issues raised cut across the whole of extradition law, but transfer to the Tribunals and International Criminal Court encapsulates several, while others will be discussed in Chapter 8.

The International Criminal Tribunal for the Former Yugoslavia (ICTY)[102]

---

99 *Valentine v United States, ex rel. Neidecker*, 299 US 5 at 9.
100 *Eg*. Canada, the United Kingdom and Australia.
101 For non-legal issues, see Forsythe, *International Criminal Courts: A Political View*, 15 NQHR 5 (1997).
102 The Statute of Tribunal was presented to the Security Council in *The Report of the Secretary-General Pursuant to Paragraph 2 of Security Council Resolution 808 (1993)*, (hereinafter, Report), 32 INT.LEG.MAT.1159 (1993). The Statute

and that for Rwanda (ICTR)[103] were established by the Security Council. Following the decision in *Tadić*,[104] it is clear that the Security Council has jurisdiction to establish such bodies. Under Article 41 of Chapter VII of the UN Charter, the Security Council "may decide what measures ... are to be employed to give effect to its decisions" to maintain or restore international peace and security.

> "The Security Council has resorted to the establishment of a judicial organ in the form of an international criminal tribunal as an instrument for the exercise of its own principal function of maintenance of peace and security, *ie*, as a measure contributing to the restoration and maintenance of peace and security in the former Yugoslavia"[105]

The constitutive Statutes of ICTY and ICTR provide that an accused person shall be 'surrendered or transferred' to the Tribunal – there is no reference to 'extradition' as the means of bringing the person to trial.[106] Necessarily, the rules of extradition law are inapplicable in so far as they are not expressly incorporated within the Statutes, Rules or domestic implementing legislation, or are part of customary international law. For instance, it is legislated that trials following transfer must be fair[107] and, if it is now part

---

was adopted by the Security Council in Resolution 827 (1993) and may be found in 32 INT.LEG.MAT.1192 (1993). The Rules of Procedure and Evidence (hereinafter, Rules) are now at Revision 6 – IT/32/Rev.6.

103 UNSC Res.935 and 955 (1994), reprinted in 5 Crim.LF 695 (1994). Rules of Procedure and Evidence, ITR/3/Rev.1 (1995), entry into force 29 June 1995.

104 *Duško Tadić, a.k.a. 'Dule', Decision on the Defence Motion for Interlocutory Appeal on Jurisdiction before the Appeals Chamber of ICTY*, Case No.IT-94-1-AR72 (1995), *per* Cassese J., at paras.9-48.

105 *Tadić*, *supra* n104, para.38.

106 See Gallant, *Securing the presence of Defendants before the International Tribunal for the Former Yugoslavia: Breaking with Extradition*, 5 Crim LF 557 (1994). Rule 58 of the Rwandan and Yugoslav Rules, *supra* nn102 and 103, state that the Statutes take precedence over any legal impediment in domestic extradition law or extradition treaties. The FCO Commentary, *infra* n119, states that the United Kingdom rules are based on the Backing of Warrants (Republic of Ireland) Act 1965, *supra*.

107 See Articles 20 and 21 of the Yugoslav Statute, *supra* n102, and Articles 19 and 20 of the Rwanda Statute, *supra* n103. And see, Rwandan and Yugoslav Rule 95, *Evidence Obtained by Means Contrary to Internationally Protected*

of custom that transfer should not take place if the accused might face capital punishment,[108] the death penalty is not available.[109] On the other hand, one of the places where a person convicted before the Rwanda Tribunal can be imprisoned is a Rwandan gaol, not noted by Amnesty International[110] as fulfilling general human rights guarantees, a normal condition in modern extradition treaties – one doubts, though, whether the Tribunal would order imprisonment in a Rwandan gaol before conditions improve. In addition, however, there is no rule of specialty before the Yugoslav or Rwandan Tribunals, although given their limited competence as regards listed crimes, that omission is unlikely to be of significance.[111]

The Prosecutor shall initiate investigations, either *ex officio* or on the basis of information received from any source. To facilitate a transfer, an indictment must be issued by the Prosecutor.

> "*Article 18.4* – Upon a determination that a *prima facie* case exists, the Prosecutor shall prepare an indictment containing a concise statement of the facts and the crime or crimes with which the accused is charged under the Statute."[112]

If the judge of the Trial Chamber is satisfied that a *prima facie* case has been established, he shall confirm the indictment and issue such orders for

---

Human Rights
"No evidence shall be admissible if obtained by methods which cast substantial doubt on its reliability or if its admission is antithetical to, and would seriously damage, the integrity of the proceedings."

108 See *Fidan*, French *Conseil d'Etat*, 100 INT'L L REP.662 (1987), and *Aylor*, French *Conseil d'Etat*, 100 INT'L L REP.664 (1993), which both hold that it would be contrary to French *ordre public* to extradite someone to face the death penalty, but there would appear to be no principle of customary international law to that effect – *Viaux-Peccate*, District Court of the Hague, 74 INT'L L REP.456 at 457 (1978).

109 Article 24, Yugoslav Statute, *supra* n102; Article 23, Rwanda Statute, *supra* n103.

110 See Amnesty International, RWANDA *Human rights overlooked in mass re-patriation*, esp. p.15, AI Index AFR 47/02/97, 14 January 1997. And see, Rodley, *The Treatment of Prisoners Under International Law* (1986).

111 See Rwandan and Yugoslav Rule 50, *supra* nn102 and 103. *Cf.* Article 55, Statute of the International Criminal Court, *infra* n124

112 Yugoslav Statute, *supra* n102. Article 17.4, Rwanda Statute is identical.

the surrender or transfer of persons.[113] Thus, the trigger mechanism for each tribunal is at the initiative of the Prosecutor's office who shall "act independently as a separate organ of the International Tribunal".[114]

Although there is concurrent jurisdiction between the International Tribunal and national courts over serious violations of international humanitarian law, States are obliged to give primacy to the Tribunal for prosecutions.[115] The decision in *Tadić*[116] upholds the right of the International Tribunal to formally request the transfer of the accused at any stage in any domestic proceedings. Article 29 of the Yugoslav Statute[117] provides that States shall co-operate with the International Tribunal in the prosecution of persons accused of serious violations of international humanitarian law and that States shall comply with an order of the Trial Chamber without undue delay for the surrender or the transfer of the accused to the International Tribunal. Thus, given that the Tribunal was established under Chapter VII of the UN Charter, States are obliged to fulfil their obligations as set out in Article 29 of the Statute under Articles 48 and 49 of the Charter.[118] Where a State cannot comply[119], then it shall notify the Regis-

---

113 Article 19 Yugoslav, Article 18 Rwanda Statutes.

114 Article 16.2 Yugoslav Statute, Article 15.2 Rwanda Statute. See also Article 18, Yugoslav Statute, Article 17 Rwanda Statute.

115 Article 9, Yugoslav Statute, Article 8, Rwanda Statute. See Gallant, *supra* n106, at pp.561-62, 564-65, 569 and 586-87.

116 *Supra* n104, *per* Cassese J., at paras.49-64. *Cf.* Albright, UN. Doc.S/PV.3217 at p.16 (25 May 1993).

117 *Eg.* surrender by Croatia to the ICTY – The Guardian p.8, 29 APR 1997: *viz.* Article 28, Rwanda Statute – Belgium's surrender to the ICTR of two former Mayors, The Times 12 NOV 1996. Occasionally S-FOR will apprehend those indicted, although practice is not uniform throughout the sectors controlled by different national contingents – The Guardian pp.1 and 14, 11 JUL 1997; p.14, 12 JUL 1997; p.11, 19 DEC 1997.
See also, Rules 56-59, *supra* nn102 and 103.

118 To the extent that this represents an interference in a State's sovereignty, Article 2.7 of the Charter is inapplicable because the Tribunal was established under Chapter VII.

119 Austria, Australia, Belgium, Bosnia-Herzegovina, Croatia, Denmark, Finland, France, Germany, Hungary, Iceland, Italy, the Netherlands, New Zealand, Norway, Spain, Sweden, Switzerland, Turkey, the United States and the United Kingdom have put in place legislation to give effect to the Statutes and Rules – necessarily, by date of publication, this information may well be incomplete.

trar; if no report is forthcoming within a reasonable time, then this shall
be deemed a failure to execute and may lead the President of the Tribunal
to notify the Security Council.[120] However, were a State to refuse to comply with a request for surrender because it was already prosecuting the
accused and, indeed, went on to convict or acquit,[121] it is arguable that
either a notification to the Security Council should not take place or the
Security Council should not act upon any notification – such would reflect
the concurrent jurisdiction to prosecute in Article 9 of the Statute and the
exceptions to the *non bis in idem* rule in Article 10.[122]

> *"Article 10.2* – A person who has been tried by a national court for acts
> constituting serious violations of international humanitarian law may be
> subsequently tried by the International Tribunal only if:

For the United Kingdom, see United Nations (International Tribunal) (Former
Yugoslavia) Order 1996 (SI 1996 No 716) and United Nations (International
Tribunal) (Rwanda) Order 1996 (SI 1996 No 1296), both made under s1 United
Nations Act 1946 – a commentary by the Foreign and Commonwealth Office
to the Joint Committee on Statutory Instruments may be found in Supplement
Three to Amnesty International's, International Criminal Tribunals: Handbook
for Government Co-operation, AI Index: IOR 40/07-10/96, August 1996; and
Warbrick, *Co-operation with the International Criminal Tribunal for Yugoslavia*,
45 INT'L & COMP.LQ 947 (1996), *cf.* Fox, *The Objections to the Transfer of
Criminal Jurisdiction to the UN Tribunal*, 46 INT'L & COMP. LQ 434 (1997). For
the USA, see Kushen and Harris, *Surrender of Fugitives by the United States
to the War Crimes Tribunals for Yugoslavia and Rwanda*, 90 AM.J INT'L L 510
(1996).

120 Rule 59, *supra nn*102 and 103.

121 Possibly because it found the accused was not the person he was believed to
be – see the right of a court in the United Kingdom to refuse to transfer an
accused where it finds, *inter alia*, that he is not the person named or described
in the warrant – s6(5)(b), United Nations (International Tribunal) (Former
Yugoslavia) Order 1996 (SI 1996 No 716).

122 Sir David Hannay in the Security Council went so far as to say that Article
9 only applied in full to courts in the former Yugoslavia, while primacy would
only be asserted with regard to courts elsewhere in the situations envisaged in
Article 10.2. – *supra n*116, at p.18. *Cf. Tadić, supra n*104, *per* Cassese J., at
para.52.

(a) the act for which he or she was tried was characterized as an ordinary crime[123]; or

(b) the national court proceedings were not impartial or independent, were designed to shield the accused from international criminal responsibility, or the case was not diligently prosecuted."

The maintenance of peace and security can be achieved through a domestic trial, though ordinarily where the Tribunal requests a transfer of proceedings that should be effected. If it were the case that the domestic trial was a sham, the Security Council could impose sanctions and, if surrender does ever take place, then Article 10.2 does not preclude trial before the ICTY.

There is no doubt that the prospects for the establishment of an International Criminal Court, as proposed by the International Law Commission[124], have been advanced by the discovered need for *ad hoc* tribunals to deal with the crimes perpetrated in the former Yugoslavia and Rwanda. However, while similar to the Tribunals, the proposed International Criminal Court is different in a number of respects and raises a veritable host of issues for international criminal law, extradition law and universal jurisdiction. Unlike the Tribunals, it will not be established under Chapter VII, transfer will not be compulsory for States, rather there are issues of complementarity, and the Prosecutor, as things stand, will not be the initiator of trials. Whether the United Nations should establish a general international criminal court, rather than *ad hoc* tribunals in order to give effect to its mandate to maintain international peace and security, is open to question,[125] but that States can establish one by international convention cannot be doubted. The problem is that there is a perception that the International Criminal Court is the direct

---

123 Would an indictment listing twenty murders, rather than a breach of the laws and customs of war, be an "ordinary crime"?

124 Report of the International Law Commission on the Work of its Forty-Sixth Session, Draft Statute for an International Criminal Court, UN Doc.A/49/355 (1994); hereinafter, Statute. And see Crawford, *The ILC's Draft Statute for an International Criminal Court*, 88 AM.J INT'L L 140 (1994), *The ILC Adopts a Statute for an International Criminal Court*, 89 AM.J INT'L L 404 (1995); and, *Symposium on International Criminal Law*, vol.5:2 TRANSNAT'L L & CONTEMP. PROBS. 237 *et seq.* (1995).

125 See Warbrick, *The United Nations System: A Place for Criminal Courts?*, 5 TRANSNAT'L L & CONTEMP. PROBS.237 (1995).

descendant of the Tribunals, whereas it is, at best, something which so far bears a mere passing resemblance.

Extradition has once again been eschewed as the mechanism for procuring the accused's appearance before the Court.[126]

> "*Article 53 Transfer of an accused to the Court*
> 1. The Registrar shall transmit to any State on the territory of which the accused may be found a warrant for the arrest and transfer of an accused issued under article 28, and shall request the cooperation of that State in the arrest and transfer of the accused.
> 2. Upon receipt of a request under paragraph 1:
>   a. all States parties:
>   i in a case covered by article 21(1)(a), or
>   ii which have accepted the jurisdiction of the Court with respect to the crime in question;
>   shall, ..., take immediate steps to arrest and transfer the accused to the Court."

Like the Tribunals, therefore, the usual rules associated with extradition are inapplicable unless specifically included in the Statute[127] or they have customary status. Thus, the accused could not claim that he should not be transferred because the offence was of a political character. At PrepCom V,[128] it was preliminarily decided that there should be very few grounds upon which a State could refuse surrender, particularly not on the basis of the nationality of the transnational fugitive offender, although the fugitive should be able to challenge a request on grounds of *non bis in idem* and lack of jurisdiction.

---

126 Extradition is referred to in Articles 53 and 54 only in terms of meeting obligations to extradite or prosecute in other treaties where a person is not transferred to the International Criminal Court. At Preparatory Committee Meeting V, December 2-12 1997, it was felt that extradition should not appear in the heading to this article, since that was an inter-State mechanism – Initial Summary Reports on Meetings of the United Nations Preparatory Committee on the Establishment of an International Criminal Court, PrepCom V, by William R. Pace, December 18, 1997.

127 Specialty is included in Article 55.

128 *Supra n*126.

c. The Effects of War and State Succession

The final topic for consideration concerns, on the one hand, how extradition relations might be affected by the outbreak of war and, on the other, whether a State might succeed to the treaties of another State of which it is the political successor or of which it was a colony.

International law makes provision for the termination or suspension of a treaty if there has been a fundamental change in circumstances since its conclusion.[129] The outbreak of war between the parties to an extradition treaty could constitute such a change. The court in *LoDolce*[130] held that while enemy forces are occupying part of a State, it lost its jurisdiction over offences committed at that time. Thus, while murder and robbery were crimes for which extradition could be granted under the US-Italian treaty, the United States refused to surrender the fugitive because the crimes occurred in 1944 when Italy exercised no effective control over its own territory.

Chandler v United States[131] avoided the issue of whether war abrogated or merely suspended the US-German Extradition Treaty of 1930, but in *Argento v Horn*[132] the court was faced with the same issue in relation to the US-Italian treaty and held, having regard to the practice and statements of the two States since the end of the war, especially the 1947 Peace Treaty, that the extradition treaty had merely been suspended during the conflict. In *R v Meroni*,[133] it was held that, although not specifically referred to in the Anglo-Italian Peace Treaty of 1948, the extradition treaty between Italy and the United Kingdom was revived with respect to the Seychelles, as well, at the time, a colony of the United Kingdom. This view concerning extradition treaties would seem to be the dominant one now, although the

---

129 Article 62, Vienna Convention on the Law of Treaties, 8 INT.LEG.MAT.679 (1969).
130 *In re LoDolce*, 18 INT'L L REP.318 (UsDist.Ct 1952).
131 171 F.2d 921 (1948).
132 241 F.2d 258 at 262 (1957).
133 91 INT'L L REP.386 (Seychelles Supreme Court).

German Democratic Republic was not treated as the successor to the old Germany in relation to pre-war extradition treaties.[134]

As for State succession to extradition treaties, in the past it would have covered the situation where a new State was formed on the break-up of an empire or as part of a peace settlement. Such was the situation in *D.C. v Public Prosecutor*[135], where the Dutch Supreme Court held that the Socialist Federal Republic of Yugoslavia was the successor to the Serbo-Dutch Extradition Treaty of 1896. Holding there was no rule as to whether States did succeed and referring to statements made with respect to the Kingdom of Yugoslavia in 1923,[136] the court found that the fact that Yugoslavia had a different constitution and was not confined to the same territorial boundaries as Serbia did not matter when compared with State practice and the intentions of the parties.

In *Arnbjornsdottir-Mendler v United States*,[137] it was held that Iceland's independence from Denmark in 1918, becoming a republic in 1944 when it stopped recognising the King of Denmark, did not abrogate the 1902 treaty of extradition between the United States and Denmark. This treaty had been specifically extended at that time to Iceland and, as part of a general provision on treaties in the Icelandic declaration of independence, the Act of Union, was deemed to have continued in force after 1918. The court held that since independence "was accompanied by neither political nor geographical upheavals", there was sufficient unity for Iceland to succeed. However, with respect to new States, the starting point ought now to be the 1978 Vienna Convention on Succession of States in Respect of Treaties.[138] State succession is now a matter of concern when a former dependency, territory or colony gains its independence and, under Article 16, the new State starts with a 'clean slate'.[139] Often new States will adopt the former

---

134 See SHEARER, *supra n*25, at p.45, and Schmid, *supra n*67. On State succession and the two Germanies, see *Espionage Prosecution Case* 94 INT'L L REP.68 (1991).

135 73 INT'L L REP.38 (1972).

136 *Supra n*135, at 39-41.

137 721 F.2d 679 at 682 (1983).

138 72 AM.J INT'L L 971 (1978).

139 *Cf.* TAMMES, INTERNATIONAL PUBLIEKRECHT, Chapter on State Succession, (1966), who held that the 'clean slate' theory is "somewhat mitigated in practice to ensure continuity in the international legal order". (Cited in *D.C.*, *supra n*135).

parent State's extradition treaties, but it is not an automatic process and there is no rule of customary international law that may be prayed in aid to that effect. In *M v Federal Department of Justice and Police*,[140] the Swiss Federal Tribunal, referring to the work of the International Law Commission which eventually led to the 1978 Vienna Convention, held that having regard to practice between South Africa and Switzerland from 1956 to 1976, as in *D.C.* above, and an exchange of notes, South Africa had succeeded to the United Kingdom's extradition treaty with Switzerland.[141] The Court of Appeal of Sierra Leone in *Lansana v R*[142] found that Sierra Leone had succeeded to the Anglo-Liberian Extradition Treaty of 1894 due to a mutual exchange of letters between the two countries and Sierra Leone's domestic extradition legislation. Moreover, in *United States v Tuttle*,[143] the Court of Appeals for the Ninth Circuit held that the Bahamas succeeded to the 1931 Anglo-US Extradition Treaty, even though that treaty had been superseded by a subsequent treaty between the United Kingdom and the United States. On the other hand, when Rhodesia, as it then was, made a unilateral declaration of independence in 1965 from the United Kingdom, it did not succeed to former extradition treaties according to the Supreme Court for the Natal Provincial Division of South Africa. In *The State v Oosthuizen*,[144] the court held that South Africa had not expressly or tacitly recognised Ian Smith's Rhodesia and that it was not the same State as had concluded the extradition arrangement a few months before it unilaterally declared independence. Therefore, extradition could not be granted thereunder.

Finally on State succession, some cases arose challenging extradition to Hong Kong because of its return to the Peoples' Republic of China on 30 June 1997. In many cases, the argument was based on the human rights record of the PRC,[145] and this was despite the fact that the British government had said that human rights should not be an issue because the

---

140 75 INT'L L REP.107 (1979).

141 See also, *Chua Han Mow v Superintendent of Pudu Prison*, 87 INT'L L REP.206 (Malaysia Fed. Ct).

142 70 INT'L L REP.2 (1971).

143 966 F.2d 1316 (1992).

144 68 INT'L L REP.3 at 4-5 (1976).

145 *R v Secretary of State for the Home Department, ex parte Launder* The Times, 29 October 1996, reversed by the House of Lords, [1997] 1 WLR 839.

Chinese and British agreed a Joint Declaration in 1984[146] on the preservation of Hong Kong's way of life for fifty years after transfer. In one United States case,[147] however, the argument did not turn on human rights in the PRC, but, in part, on the fact that the extradition agreement was with Hong Kong, not with the PRC, and that the Senate cannot have intended him to be prosecuted and punished in the PRC. The Court of Appeals held that it was the Executive which had to decide political questions on the basis of the rule of non-inquiry, but pointed to the US-Hong Kong Special Administrative Region Surrender of Fugitive Offenders Agreement of 20 December 1996, currently before Senate,[148] as evidence that extradition will continue after 1 July 1997. What is certain is that Hong Kong did not bring with it all the extradition arrangements which were extended to it in British legislation while under British rule – that is why the proto-HKSAR is negotiating new agreements for after the handover.

In conclusion, extradition treaties are capable of being revived after war and new States will usually succeed to the treaties of their former parent States, although there is no rule of international law to that effect. Treaties will continue to be predominant when extradition relations are being established, but in practice a wide variety of arrangements will permit the surrender of a fugitive. The trend towards allowing extradition when no arrangement at all exists, while promoting international comity, does, though, raise concern for the protection of the fugitive's human rights.

---

146 UKTS 26 (1985).
147 *USA v Lui Kin-Hong*, unreported, 20 March 1997.
148 143 Cong.Rec.S1846 (1997).

3

PROCEDURAL ASPECTS OF EXTRADITION LAW

a. Introduction

At one level, extradition may be viewed as a mere process by which trans-national fugitive offenders are returned to face trial before a competent court. As subsequent chapters will reveal, there are substantive rules within extradition law which provide the transnational fugitive offender with fundamental guarantees of his human rights. Some of these transfer over to the other mechanisms utilised against transnational fugitive offenders, but not all. Moreover, the procedure of extradition is itself complex and little understood and it is in that context that the fugitive's substantive rights operate. One cannot understand the scope of the protection without regard to its procedural context.

Furthermore, procedural extradition must be placed within the wider perspective of mutual assistance in criminal matters of which it is but a part. The aim of this chapter is, on the one hand, to examine the procedure by which an extradition request is processed through the system in order to analyse critically its shortcomings and propose any necessary improvements and, on the other, to establish the framework in which the transnational fugitive offender's protections are put into effect.

b. Mutual Assistance in Criminal Matters

Extradition is part of a wider network of systems of co-operation in law enforcement; to focus solely on extradition law would be to ignore several other mechanisms utilised by States to ensure the prosecution of transnational fugitive offenders. Mutual legal assistance treaties are mainly used to obtain evidence from outside the jurisdiction, but mutual assistance can also be seen in broader forms of co-operation when meeting the problem of crimes or criminals that cross frontiers.[1] These broader forms exist on three levels; *micro, mezzo* and *macro*.[2] At the *micro* level, one is dealing with individual police forces working together to deal with trans-border crimes.[3] The 1990 campaign by the Provisional IRA in continental Europe led to increased and harmonious contact between the Metropolitan Police European Liaison Service and its counterparts in the Dutch, Belgian and German security services.[4] The growing threat from the trade in drugs, and the associated money laundering, has led to worldwide assistance between police forces,[5] especially in Europe where drugs liaison officers are posted throughout the European community member States. Police officers from a member State are either placed in their own country's embassies in the other member States or with its police force.[6] There is also evidence that although their remit is to deal with drugs, if a criminal is suspected of having fled to the State to which they have been posted, officers at home will contact them directly in order to establish this fact before setting extradition proceedings in motion.[7] To take the fight against drugs even further, the European Union has established the European Drug Unit in the Hague,[8] considered below with regard to *mezzo* level co-operation. There has also been talk within the European

---

1   McCLEAN, INTERNATIONAL JUDICIAL ASSISTANCE, 1992.
2   The terms, but not their content, are taken from the evidence submitted by the Centre for the Study of Public Order to HOME AFFAIRS SELECT COMMITTEE, SEVENTH REPORT, PRACTICAL POLICE CO-OPERATION IN THE EUROPEAN COMMUNITY, vol.2, pp.181 *et seq*, HCP 363 (1989–90). Hereinafter, HCP-I or HCP-II. See also, Benyon, *Policing the European Union: the Changing Basis of Co-operation on Law Enforcement*, 70 INT'L AFF. 497 (1994).
3   A direct comparison can be drawn with federal States where policing is a matter for the regional units therein. Despite the fact that England is a unitary State, it has discrete regional police forces; however, Scotland and Northern Ireland are separate legal systems within the United Kingdom – see Walker, *Internal Cross-Border Policing within the United Kingdom: the High Road or the Low Road to Effective Co-operation?*, 56 CLJ 114 (1997).
4   HCP-I at para.11, *supra* n2.
5   See The Guardian2 p.7, 10 MAR 1993 p.3; The Guardian p.3, 11 JAN 1994.
6   HCP-I, at paras.122-26, *supra* n2.
7   *Supra n2*, at para.123. The SELECT COMMITTEE recommended that generic police liaison officers be posted throughout the community, not just drugs specialists.
8   See Benyon, *supra* n2, at pp.510-11.

Union to establish a European FBI, but it is not likely at present, requiring too great a surrender of sovereignty by States.[9]

This low-level contact is more formalised at the *mezzo* stage. One example is the work of INTERPOL, the International Criminal Police Organisation, "the principal channel for practical co-operation between police forces throughout the world, ...".[10] INTERPOL is not an investigative institution, but rather an administrative organisation the objective of which is to improve the speed and efficiency of inquiries between police forces; it is a channel of communication and, as such, it is essentially a means of providing for mutual assistance in criminal matters.[11] INTERPOL has over 170 members worldwide, although eighty per cent of its telecommunications traffic is accounted for by European inquiries. It is organised into three tiers, the first of which contains an executive committee and a general assembly of all members. However, the most pertinent for the purposes of mutual assistance is the second tier, the General Secretariat based at Lyon. Staffed in part by serving police officers, the Secretariat is the part of INTERPOL that deals with requests for information and assistance from other police forces, which requests are transmitted to Lyon by the third tier, the National Central Bureaux (NCB) based in the member forces in each State. The procedures and practices of the Secretariat have been greatly improved since 1984, such that a request for information or assistance is, on average, answered within two hours.[12] The obvious use of such facilities for the speedy arrest of a fugitive offender need not be spelt out.[13] INTERPOL's red 'wanted' notices, which contain details of the arrest warrant and the

---

9   See The Guardian p.10, 8 AUG 1994, and p.12, 12 JUL 1996.

10   HCP-I, at paras.66 *et seq* and HCP-II at pp.30-37, *supra n2*. See also, BASSIOUNI, LEGAL RESPONSES TO INTERNATIONAL TERRORISM: U.S. PROCEDURAL ASPECTS, in Ch.16 by Grotenroth, (1988); hereinafter, BASSIOUNI, LEGAL RESPONSES.

11   Founded in 1946, its objectives are set out in Art.2 of its constitution.
"(a) To ensure and promote the widest possible mutual assistance between all criminal police authorities within the limits of the laws existing in the different countries and in the spirit of the 'Universal Declaration of Human Rights'."
The overlap between international criminal law and procedure and human rights law is once again clearly established.

12   *Supra n2*, at para.70. As well, INTERPOL holds computerised records on criminals and their *modus operandi*.

13   There is one case where a suspected forger was arrested in France one hour after the British NCB sent the information to INTERPOL; *supra n2*, at para.71.

offence committed, are mainly used to track down wanted fugitive offenders and arrest them prior to a formal, diplomatic extradition request. They are an institutionalised part of extradition law within Europe and the Commonwealth with respect to the provisional arrest of fugitive criminals.[14] Furthermore, the change in attitude within INTERPOL since 1984 concerning Article 3 of its constitution, which forbids its involvement in activities, *inter alia*, of a political nature, has meant that it is now prepared to facilitate inquiries into politically motivated terrorism outside the area of conflict; that is, it will carry out all of its ordinary functions with respect to IRA campaigns on mainland Europe, but not those within the United Kingdom.[15] The role of INTERPOL, therefore, in combating all forms of cross-frontier crime cannot be underestimated, and the *mezzo* level of mutual assistance is likely to be the most active, especially in relation to extradition requests.

INTERPOL's work at the *mezzo* level has now been supplemented by a variety of European responses to transnational fugitive offenders. This response was hardly surprising given that the European Union has made freedom of movement for all citizens of member States, including transnational fugitive offenders, very much easier and, given the large sums of money which it has at its disposal, it would be foolish to imagine that it would not be the object of serious major fraud.[16] Mentioned above, the European Drugs Unit is a co-ordinating body for matters related to narcotics offences – as such, it also covers money laundering which is the result of

---

14 Art.16, European Convention on Extradition, 1957, ETS 24, 359 UNTS 273: Art.4 Commonwealth Scheme for the Rendition of Fugitive Offenders as amended – LMM(90)32.

15 *Supra n*11. HCP-I, at para.75.

16 The Guardian p.7, 24 APR 1997. The member States of the European Union have concluded a Convention on the Protection of the European Communities' Financial Interests, (1995 OJ C 316; Explanatory Report, 1997 OJ C 191) which tries to harmonize the practice of domestic laws aimed at dealing with fraud on the community. Article 5 provides with regard to extradition that nationals shall be extradited and that fiscal offences shall be extradition crimes. See also, the Protocol, 1996 OJ C 313.

the drugs trade.[17] The EDU can be seen to be the forerunner of Europol.[18] The Europol Convention of 1995 provides that

"*Article 1 Establishment*
2. Europol shall liaise with a single national unit in each Member State, to be established or designated in accordance with Article 4.
Article 2 Objective
1. The objective of Europol shall be, within the framework of cooperation between the Member States pursuant to Article K.1(9) of the Treaty on European Union, to improve, by means of the measures referred to in this Convention, the effectiveness and co-operation of the competent authorities in the Member States in preventing and combating terrorism, unlawful drug trafficking and other serious forms of international crime where there are factual indications that an organized criminal structure is involved and two or more Member States are affected by the forms of crime in question in such a way as to require a common approach by the Member States owing to the scale, significance and consequences of the offences concerned.
3. Europol's competence as regards a form of crime or specific manifestations thereof shall cover both:
(1) illegal money-laundering activities in connection with these forms of crime or specific manifestations thereof;
(2) related criminal offences."[19]

---

17 The Guardian p.10, 17 FEB 1994.
18 COUNCIL ACT of 26 July 1995 drawing up the Convention based on Article K.3 of the Treaty on European Union, on the establishment of a European Police Office (Europol Convention), 1995 OJ C 316, 27/11/95
19 Initially, Europol will have a more limited role:
"*Article 2.2* In order to achieve progressively the objective mentioned in paragraph 1, Europol shall initially act to prevent and combat unlawful drug trafficking, trafficking in nuclear and radioactive substances, illegal immigrant smuggling, trade in human beings and motor vehicle crime. Within two years at the latest following the entry into force of this Convention, Europol shall also deal with crimes committed or likely to be committed in the course of terrorist activities against life, limb, personal freedom or property. The Council, acting unanimously in accordance with the procedure laid down in Title VI of the Treaty on European Union, may decide to instruct Europol to deal with such terrorist activities before that period has expired. The Council, acting unanimously in accordance with the procedure laid down in Title VI of the Treaty on European Union, may decide to instruct Europol to deal with other forms of crime listed in the Annex to this Convention or specific manifestations thereof.

Once again, the European Union has eschewed the possibility of creating a supra-national police force and is relying on liaison and co-ordination between national forces, as set out in Article 3. There is to be a flow of information between national units and Europol. Unfortunately, the inherent anti-federal nature of criminal law within the European Union has meant that member States have retained a degree of discretion in what information national units shall pass on to Europol.[20] The restrictions are based on a State's interpretation of its own national security interests or prejudicing an ongoing investigation. Given that the idea behind Europol is that it is to co-ordinate information between police forces within the European Union, it is hard to see why it was felt necessary to limit mutual assistance in this manner – it is hardly as if Europol is open to public scrutiny.

If Europol evolved from EDU, it is of the same *genus* as the Schengen Convention structures.[21] The Schengen system is more far-reaching, going beyond the remit of Europol being a kind of advanced guard within the European Union. Like Europol, Schengen has its own information system, established in Title IV of the Convention.[22] Schengen lacks even the mini-

---

> Before acting, the Council shall instruct the Management Board to prepare its decision and in particular to set out the budgetary and staffing implications for Europol."
> And see the proposed Article K.2 of the Amsterdam Treaty 1997, *infra n33*.

20   "*Article 4.5*
> Without prejudice to the exercise of the responsibilities incumbent upon Member States as set out in Article K.2 (2) of the Treaty on European Union, a national unit shall not be obliged in a particular case to supply the information and intelligence provided for ... if this would mean:
> (1) harming essential national security interests; or
> (2) jeopardizing the success of a current investigation or the safety of individuals;
> (3) involving information pertaining to organizations or specific intelligence activities in the field of State security."

21   The Schengen Convention 1990, 30 INT.LEG.MAT.84 (1991); see Chapter 2. See also, MEIJERS, SCHENGEN, 2nd ed., 1992.

22   Mahmood, *The Schengen Information System: An Inequitable Data Protection Regime*, 7 IJRL 179 (1995). Denmark, Ireland and the United Kingdom are not Schengen States and originally they had no access, therefore, to the Schengen Information System – see The Guardian pp.1 and 6, 6 SEPT 1993. However, at the Amsterdam InterGovernmental Conference, June 1997, the United Kingdom agreed that it would seek to join the SIS – The Guardian p.2, 22 JUL 1997.

mal institutional controls of Europol, the latter being the creation of the European Union under Article K of the Maastricht Treaty[23] which should, therefore, operate in conformity with the ECHR.[24] It does provide internal mechanisms for ensuring the data is not misused, but those constraints are dependent upon national legislation.[25] The Europol Information System provides for data accuracy and the related matter of expiration in Articles 13 to 25; it, too, relies on national legislation. Again, the emphasis is on mutual assistance, rather than the individual privacy of persons within the European Union. Moreover, under Article 18, Europol can forward data it holds to third States. In sum, Europol's and the Schengen Information System both evidence a policy within Europe to combat transnational fugitive offenders through the use of data transfer – it cannot be denied that the scale of transnational crime demands efficient procedures that are not inhibited by territorial frontiers. However, there is a danger in the dearth of independent, supervisory, European-wide agencies that the information systems will infringe personal privacy (and not only that of transnational fugitive offenders, but also that of innocent persons within the EU area), in order to assist those combating transnational crime.[26]

Finally, the *macro* level of mutual assistance is concerned with intergovernmental contacts, whether formal or informal.[27] It is possible to in-

---

23 31 INT.LEG.MAT. 247 (1992).
24 Article K.2 states that the functions set out in Article K.1, including Europol, shall be subject to the obligations set out in the European Convention for the Protection of Human Rights and Fundamental Freedoms.
25 See Articles 114 *et seq.*
26 The proposed Treaty of Amsterdam of 1997 does not envisage thhe ECJ having any role in relation to operational matters:
    "*New Article K.7 of the TEU*
    5. The Court of Justice shall have no jurisdiction to review the validity or proportionality of operations carried out by the police or other law enforcement agencies of a Member State or the exercise of the responsibilities incumbent upon Member States with regard to the maintenance of law and order and the safeguarding of internal security."
    Cf. The ECJ's Treaty interpretation role, *infra* n35.
27 The reach of transnational crime can be deduced by the gathering of representatives from over 140 countries under the auspices of the United Nations to discuss international measures to combat transnational fugitive offenders (The Guardian p.8, 21 NOV 1994), and the meeting called by NATO of security and espionage services from over thirty countries, ranging from the United States,

clude in this section the full extradition requests made through diplomatic channels, but they are but a small part of *macro* mutual assistance.[28] The member States of the European Union have instigated several intergovernmental mechanisms in order to better combat transnational fugitive offenders. The first such development was the establishment of the TREVI group of countries.[29] As has been seen above, TREVI was established in 1976 and was a loose forum for ministers from the then twelve European Community States to discuss at a political level co-operation in matters of law enforcement. It was not part of the European Community, it had no permanent administration and it was not directly accountable to domestic legislatures. The ministers were assisted in their discussions by four working groups, dealing with terrorism, drugs and serious crime, public order and scientific matters and, finally, the implications of the removal of internal borders within the European Community after 1992, including immigration. Beyond the E.C. member States, there were 'friends of TREVI', including Canada, Morocco, Norway, Switzerland and the USA The twice yearly meetings of TREVI decided on policies relating to the working group areas, impinging upon mutual assistance generally, including issues to do with fugitive offenders. With the Treaty on European Union,[30] matters of justice and home affairs were brought within the Third Pillar. TREVI evolved into the Article K.4 Committee,[31] within the European Union superstructure, but still in-

---

the United Kingdom and France to Uzbekistan and Albania (The Guardian p.8, 25 NOV 1996).

28   The European Union Convention Relating to Extradition between the Member States, 1996 OJ C 313, provides in Article 13, for example, for the use of encrypted faxes to send and receive extradition requests (and see, for example, s7 of the United Kingdom's Extradition Act 1989, as amended by the Criminal Justice and Public Order Act 1994); see also the Explanatory Report of 26 May 1997, 1997 OJ C 191. The European Union also concluded a Convention on Simplified Extradition to expedite mutual assistance – 1995 OJ C 78.

29   See generally paras.48-65 of HCP-I, *supra* n2. See also, Benyon, *supra* n2, pp.507 *et seq.*; Rider, The Enterprise of Crime, in RIDER AND ASHE, MONEY LAUNDERING CONTROL, 1996, pp.89-92; Den Boer, Europe and the Art of International Police Co-operation: Free-Fall or Measured Scenario, in O'KEEFE AND TWOMEY, LEGAL ISSUES OF THE MAASTRICHT TREATY, 1994.

30   *Supra* n23.

31   See Benyon, *supra* n2, at p.509, and Den Boer, *supra* n29, at pp.280 and 287-89. The change, in the eyes of some, is akin to labelling a mad axeman, the 'official mad axeman'. Under the proposed Treaty of Amsterdam 1997 (1997

dependent of supervision by the ECJ.[32] With the InterGovernmental Conference in Amsterdam in June 1997, recommendations were proposed to amend Article K.[33] They envisage a wider role for Europol and greater harmonization[34] – furthermore, under proposed new Article K.7, the ECJ would have a supervisory role with regard to developments under new Article K.6, including "the interpretation of Conventions" promulgated under new Article K.6(2)(d),[35] potentially following a reference from a national court.

On a smaller scale, the European Union has taken steps at the *macro* level with regard to drugs and money laundering.[36] The EC Council Money Laundering Directive[37] applies to the use of financial institutions to launder the proceeds of crime and is not necessarily limited to drugs related offences (Article 1). More importantly, the Directive shows that measures to combat transnational crime need not be limited to mutual assistance in criminal matters – the Directive imposes obligations on financial and credit institutions to identify clients, to monitor transactions and to train their staff appropriately (Articles 3-7 and 11.2). In 1996, the Organization for Security and Co-operation in Europe had co-organized a seminar on transnational crime and illicit drug-trafficking in the Central Asian Republics,[38] picking up on the need for inter-State co-operation with regard to extradition and mutual assistance in criminal matters, including the creation of a common database on organized crime.[39] However, it is built into the Recommena-

---

OJ C.340), that will become an Article K.8 Committee.

32 McGOLDRICK, INTERNATIONAL RELATIONS LAW OF THE EUROPEAN UNION, 1997, pp.174-80.

33 European Report, No.2210, 26 March 1997, pp.2 *et seq*. See also, Conference of the Representatives of the Governments of the Member States, Brussels, 15 May 1997, SN/2555/97 (C 40).

34 New Articles K.1, K.2 and K.6 (an enhanced version of the present Article K.3), *supra n*33.

35 *Viz*. Article K.3, Maastricht, *supra n*23.

36 See Rider, *supra n*29, and Zagaris, The Emergence of an International Anti-Money Laundering Regime: Implications for Counselling Businesses, in ATKINS, THE ALLEGED TRANSNATIONAL CRIMINAL, 1995, at pp.127-217. See also, GILMORE, INTERNATIONAL EFFORTS TO COMBAT MONEY LAUNDERING (1997).

37 Directive 91/308/EEC, 1991 OJ L166/77, 10 June 1991.

38 ODIHR, Drugs and Crime: New Challenges – Consolidated Summary, Ref.OD/48/96, 17 July 1996.

39 Annex I, Recommendations, *supra n*38.

ations that such measures shall be subject to external monitoring with regard to the "interaction of the observance of human rights and the effective administration of criminal justice ..."[40] – would that the European Union could recognize this need.

> "The absence of a clear legal direction in the development of European crime control is coupled with the lack of information about citizens' rights and duties. The variation in criminal procedures, ..., will be to the detriment of the citizen, if and when law enforcement co-operation will be intensified (*sic.*)."[41]

Still dealing with the *macro* level, the United States has concluded some informal, bilateral agreements relating to mutual legal assistance with France and Italy.[42] The 1986 French arrangement is aimed at terrorism and seeks to improve US-French co-operation through improved exchanges of information and better law enforcement contacts. As with all informal meetings between governments on the topic of mutual assistance, the subsequently enhanced relations and understanding of each others' legal systems is useful for all forms of criminal law enforcement co-operation, including extradition.

The last element at the *macro* level is the series of formal mutual legal assistance conventions.[43] The content of these conventions, as stated above, is primarily to do with the presentation of evidence from one State in the trial in the other State. Such gathering of evidence may well relate to extradition hearings and is considered below; however, they may also be seen as part of the armoury against transnational fugitive offenders, in

---

40 Recommendation 3(b)(ii), *supra n*38.

41 Den Boer, *supra n*29, at p.287, footnotes omitted.

42 See Zagaris and Simonetti, Judicial Assistance under U.S. Bilateral Treaties, at pp.219 *et seq.* (esp. pp.226-7), of BASSIOUNI, LEGAL RESPONSES, *supra n*10.

43 See Zagaris and Simonetti, *supra n*42; Cameron, *Mutual Assistance in Criminal Matters*, 38 INT'L & COMP. LQ 954 (1989); COUNCIL OF EUROPE, EXTRATERRITORIAL CRIMINAL JURISDICTION at pp.37-8 (1990); McClean, *Mutual Assistance in Criminal Matters; The Commonwealth Scheme*, 37 INT'L & COMP. LQ 177 (1988), and McCLEAN, *supra n*1. On the position in the Former Soviet Union, see GINSBURGS, THE SOVIET UNION AND INTERNATIONAL CO-OPERATION IN LEGAL MATTERS, 1994 – how far this is solely of historical relevance awaits to be seen as Russia updates its agreements in this regard with States from the former Soviet Bloc.

general. The only point to note here about the conventions themselves is the sudden realization by common law States of their usefulness. In continental Europe, the 1959 Convention on Mutual Assistance in Criminal Matters[44] has worked well for almost forty years, but the first State of the Anglo-Saxon tradition to conclude a mutual assistance treaty was the USA in 1977 with Switzerland.[45] Following on that initial success, the USA has agreed general treaties with, amongst others, Italy[46] and Mexico,[47] and a specific drug related agreement with the United Kingdom, the Cayman Islands and Canada.[48] The United Kingdom was even slower off the mark, although it has now ratified the European Convention on Mutual Assistance in Criminal Matters and is party to the Commonwealth Scheme,[49] while it, too, has drug specific treaties with about 140 other States.[50]

To conclude, mutual assistance takes place on many levels, with greater or lesser degrees of formality. Extradition is a part of it and is also assisted by it. Mutual assistance is the wider context in which procedural extradition is founded. It also, however, reveals why extradition is inadequate on its own when considering transnational fugitive offenders. Furthermore, it is of growing importance with regard to the attempt to combat transnational crime as the sovereign, Westphalian State loses its solidity and there is

---

44 ETS 30 (1959), in force 1962; Protocol, ETS 99 (1978). The Council of the European Union proposed in 1996 that as between member States of the EU, the Council of Europe Convention should be simplified through a draft Convention drawn up on the basis of Article K.3, to expedite its operation – 5978/96, 16 April 1996.

45 12 INT.LEG.MAT.916 (1973); 27 UST 2019, TIAS 8302. See also, subsequent understandings at 15 INT.LEG.MAT.283 (1976), 22 INT.LEG.MAT.1 (1983), 27 INT.LEG.MAT.480 (1988); and 33 INT.LEG.MAT.168 (1994).

46 23 INT.LEG.MAT.231 (1984).

47 27 INT.LEG.MAT.443 (1988).

48 Cameron, *supra n*43.

49 Commonwealth Scheme on Mutual Assistance in Criminal Matters, agreed at Harare 1986; see also McClean, *supra n*43. Art.1 of the Scheme contains a very wide description of forms of assistance.

50 See also, the British Criminal Justice (International Co-operation) Act 1990 and the Drug Trafficking Act 1994 – the latter has led to agreements with over 140 countries and territories as at 1 January 1997, Drug Trafficking Act 1994 (Designated Countries and Territories) Order 1996 (SI 1996 No 2880).

increasing interdependence and a diffusion of borders, at least within an integrated Europe.[51]

c. Comparative Overview

The object of this brief section is to outline the way an extradition request is processed, prior to considering in detail the nature of the hearing and the substantive matters the requesting State has to prove. Given that the general procedure is laid down in the international arrangements between States, even if in some cases the precise rules are set out in domestic statutes, then it is hardly surprising to find that there is little difference between State practice on this issue, at least with regard to general extradition relations. Certain States with close geographical ties should be expected to have specialised agreements suited to their situation; examples include the systems in operation between the Benelux States,[52] between Australia and New Zealand[53] and between the United Kingdom and Ireland.[54]

Concentrating, therefore, on the general systems in operation, the first step in any extradition request is to inform the arresting authorities in the requested State, usually the police, of the fugitive's presence. Treaties provide two means of achieving this communication: the first comprises the formal request through diplomatic channels for the issuance of a warrant for the fugitive's surrender. Such a request will be backed up by sufficient evidence to convince the government department responsible for criminal matters and a member of the judiciary that arresting the fugitive and holding an extradition hearing is appropriate.[55] Secondly, the requesting State may make an application direct to a judge for a warrant of arrest, known as a

---

51 MacCormick, *Beyond the Sovereign State*, 56 MOD.L REV.1 (1993).
52 Treaty on Extradition and Mutual Assistance in Criminal Matters, 27 June 1962, and Protocol, 11 May 1974.
53 See Part III of the Australian Extradition Act 1988.
54 The British procedure for Irish requests is somewhat simpler than the equivalent Irish legislation: compare the British Backing of Warrants (Republic of Ireland) Act 1965, as amended by the Criminal Justice Act 1993, with the Irish Extradition Act 1965, as amended by the Extradition (ECST) Act 1987 and the Extradition (Amendment) Acts 1987 and 1994.
55 See s7 Extradition Act 1989 as amended by s158 Criminal Justice and Public Order Act 1994.

provisional warrant, to be issued. In the case of a provisional warrant, the judge is usually obliged to keep the responsible government department informed of the outcome of the issuance of the warrant.[56] Where requests

---

56 See Art.12 of the French *Loi du 10 Mars 1927* (the French statute is superseded by any self-executing treaty, but it provides a useful, generalised summary of French law and practice); Arts.8-11 of the Arab League Agreement of 3rd November 1952 concerning the Extradition of Fugitive Offenders, 159 B.F.S.P.606 (a subsequent agreement was signed at Riyadh in 1983 without the participation of Egypt – so far it is unavailable in English. I am grateful to the London office of the Arab League for this information); Arts.16, 17, 27-31 and 41-51 of the Swiss Statute on International Judicial Assistance in Criminal Matters, 20 MAR 1981, 20 INT.LEG.MAT.1339 (1981), as amended 9 DEC 1996 (supplied by the Federal Office for Police Matters, Bern) – see also the Decree on International Mutual Assistance in Criminal Matters, 24 FEB 1982 as amended 9 DEC 1996 (supplied by the Federal Office for Police Matters, Bern); Art.12 of the European Convention on Extradition, *supra n*14; ss12, 15,16 and 17 of the Australian Extradition Act 1988; ss7 and 8 of the British Extradition Act 1989; and, for the USA, 18 U.S.C. 3184.

"Whenever there is a treaty or convention for extradition between the United States and any foreign government, or in cases arising under section 3181(b), any justice or judge of the United States, or any magistrate United States magistrate judge authorized so to do by a court of the United States, or any judge of a court of record of general jurisdiction of any State, may, upon complaint made under oath, charging any person found within his jurisdiction, with having committed within the jurisdiction of any such foreign government any of the crimes provided for by such treaty or convention, or provided for under section 3181(b), issue his warrant for the apprehension of the person so charged, that he may be brought before such justice, judge, or magistrate United States magistrate judge, to the end that the evidence of criminality may be heard and considered. Such complaint may be filed before and such warrant may be issued by a judge or magistrate United States magistrate judge of the United States District Court for the District of Columbia if the whereabouts within the United States of the person charged are not known or, if there is reason to believe the person will shortly enter the United States. If, on such hearing, he deems the evidence sufficient to sustain the charge under the provisions of the proper treaty or convention, or under section 3181(b), he shall certify the same, together with a copy of all the testimony taken before him, to the Secretary of State, that a warrant may issue upon the requisition of the proper authorities of such foreign government, for the surrender of such person, according to the stipulations of the treaty or convention; and he shall issue his warrant for the commitment of the person so charged to the proper jail, there to remain until such surrender shall be made."

are received from more than one State, provision may be made in the treaty,[57] but, if not, the requested State will enjoy a large degree of discretion. In *C v Federal Police Department*,[58] the Swiss Federal Tribunal took account of the gravity of the offences in both requesting States and the fact that if surrendered to Italy he could not, as an Italian national, be subsequently extradited to Belgium, whereas re-extradition to Italy from Belgium would be possible.[59]

Once arrested, it would be rare for the fugitive to be granted bail before the extradition hearing, leading to him having to spend long periods in pre-trial custody.[60] Having completed the first administrative phase, the process enters the judicial phase, the extradition hearing itself.[61] Extradition hearings do not determine the guilt or innocence of the fugitive, only his susceptibility to surrender.[62] The hearing differs between civil and common law States, the latter usually requiring proof of a *prima facie* case, although this demand is not always included today. Having finished the hearing and any appeal, the process enters its final administrative phase.

Given that the courts have agreed to the fugitive's surrender, it is left to the executive to make its own decision on the case before authorising the fugitive's surrender – the roles of the judiciary and executive are con-

---

See also, Kassim-Momodu, *Extradition of Fugitives by Nigeria*, 35 INT'L & COMP. LQ 512 at pp.518-9 (1986).

57 See Art.17, European Convention on Extradition 1957, *supra* n14.

58 100 INT'L L REP. 657.

59 *Supra* n58, at 660-61. *NB*. Given the fugitive faced the death penalty in Belgium, the court's reasoning has a hint of the academic about it.

60 The case of Roisin McAliskey highlights this matter – requested by Germany in connection with the bombing of British Army barracks in Osnabruck in 1996, Ms McAliskey was held as a Category A prisoner, the most restrictive regime, pending her extradition hearing, despite the fact she was heavily pregnant at the time. Protests were received from the Irish government, but bail was not granted – The Guardian p.6, 21 FEB 1997.

61 In civil law countries judicial involvement was a late development – in France it only became the accepted method after the Law of 10 March 1927; see SHEARER, EXTRADITION IN INTERNATIONAL LAW, 1971, at p.17. Whether the French government has come to terms with this change is open to question following the revelations in *Bozano v France*, 9 EHRR 297 (1986).

62 Arts.10-17 of *La Loi du 10 Mars 1927*; Ch.3, Section 2; Art.52 of the Swiss Law; s19 Australian Act; s9 British Act; all, *supra* n56. And see Kassim-Momodu, again *supra* n56, at pp.19-21.

sidered in more detail below. If surrender is authorised by the executive, the requesting State has a prescribed period within which to collect the fugitive; if it fails so to do, he will usually have the right to petition for his release.[63] Under the British Extradition Act 1989, s16 allows for discharge if the fugitive is still in the United Kingdom after the expiration of one month from the date of the issue of the warrant for return under s12,[64] unless an application has been made for judicial review, whereupon the relevant period runs from whenever that has been concluded or expired. In the unfortunate case of *R v Secretary of State for the Home Department, ex p. Chetta*,[65] the application for judicial review was only instituted more than a month after the s12 warrant for return had been issued, but it was still sufficient to defeat a subsequent application for discharge under s16 because the judicial review application was still live. The European Convention for the Protection of Human Rights and Fundamental Freedoms allows for deprivation of liberty under Article 5

> "in the following cases and in accordance with the procedure prescribed by law:
> f. the lawful arrest or detention of a person against whom action is being taken with a view to deportation or extradition."[66]

---

63   Arts.57 and 61 of the Swiss Law; ss22-26 Australian Act; ss12, 13 and 16 of the British Act; all *supra n*56. See also, Art.18 of the European Convention on Extradition, *supra n*14.

64   s16(2)(b) Extradition Act 1989.

65   The Times, 11 JULY 1996.

66   The full text is as follows:-
"*Article 5*
1. Everyone has the right to liberty and security of person. No one shall be deprived of his liberty save in the following cases and in accordance with a procedure prescribed by law:
(a) the lawful detention of a person after conviction by a competent court:
(b) the lawful arrest or detention of a person for non- compliance with the lawful order of a court or in order to secure the fulfilment of any obligation prescribed by law:
(c) the lawful arrest or detention of a person effected for the purpose of bringing him before the competent legal authority on reasonable suspicion of having committed an offence or when it is reasonably considered necessary to prevent his committing an offence or fleeing after having done so:

If, however, there is too long a delay between the decision to return and the actual surrender, then detention may become unlawful, although the Court has taken into consideration the fact that the delay was due to the actions of the applicant and the government's desire to fully investigate all the applicant's grounds for challenging the decision.[67] It is not a mere question of set time limits, but rather whether the respondent government has acted with due diligence.

This brief survey should provide a sufficient background to allow an understanding of the matters to be considered below and set them in their appropriate context.

d. Pre-Hearing Detention

A major problem in extradition cases concerns the time a fugitive may have to spend waiting for the extradition hearing to take place after being arrested

---

(d) the detention of a minor by lawful order for the purpose of educational supervision or his lawful detention for the purpose of bringing him before the competent legal authority:

(e) the lawful detention of persons for the prevention of the spreading of infectious diseases, of persons of unsound mind, alcoholics or drug addicts or vagrants:

(f) the lawful arrest or detention of a person to prevent his effecting an unauthorised entry into the country or of a person against whom action is being taken with a view to deportation or extradition.

2. Everyone who is arrested shall be informed promptly, in a language which he understands, of the reasons for his arrest and of any charge against him.

3. Everyone arrested or detained in accordance with the provisions of paragraph 1(c) of this Article shall be brought promptly before a judge or other officer authorised by law to exercise judicial power and shall be entitled to trial within a reasonable time or to release pending trial. Release may be conditioned by guarantees to appear for trial.

4. Everyone who is deprived of his liberty by arrest or detention shall be entitled to take proceedings by which the lawfulness of his detention shall be decided speedily by a court and his release ordered if the detention is not lawful.

5. Everyone who has been a victim of arrest or detention in contravention of the provisions of this Article shall have an enforceable right to compensation."

67 *Kolompar v Belgium*, Series A, vol.235-C, holding no violation on the facts. See also, 28 *Cahiers de Droit Européen* 216 (1992).

in the requested State. On the basis that the alleged fugitive offender has already failed to remain to face trial, but rather fled to the requested State, he is usually remanded in custody prior to the extradition hearing. Sometimes, detention can be for long periods while the requesting State gathers its evidence; the problem is worst where the fugitive is arrested on a provisional warrant before a full diplomatic request has been formulated. While the treaties do allow generous time limits in which to present evidence, it should also be noted that the primary object must be to let the hearing take place so that judicial consideration might be given to the fugitive's extraditability: only in cases of extreme abuse of process should a fugitive be released prior to the hearing if there is a real danger he might flee from the requested State before it can take place. It may well be that in cases were abuse of process is arguable, however, a fugitive could challenge a lengthy detention – in one English case, the High Court freed the fugitive offender because there had been too much delay in presenting the case against him.[68] Moreover, regional human rights conventions which all provide for freedom from unnecessary detention and arrest.[69] Focussing on the most detailed of the convention protections on this matter, Article 5 of the European Convention on Human Rights provides that while no right not to be extradited or expelled exists under the ECHR,[70] a fugitive should not be detained for an unreasonable length of time waiting for the requesting State to submit its initial requisition to the requested State. Article 5(3) states that anyone detained shall be brought "promptly" before a judge and is "entitled to a trial within a reasonable time ...". However, Article 5(3) only applies to persons detained in accordance with Article 5(1)(c), whereas it would appear that a fugitive arrested under a provisional warrant is detained in accordance

---

68 The Guardian p.2, 30 OCT 1996. Rose LJ expressly criticised the Home Secretary for not treating the case with due importance.

69 ECHR, Art.5, ETS 5, (1950); ACHR, Art.7, 9 INT.LEG.MAT.673; ACHPR, Art.6, 21 INT.LEG.MAT.58. Further, the freedom of movement guaranteed to European Community residents in Art.48 of the Treaty of Rome (1957, Cmnd 4864) is not impinged upon by arrest prior to extradition to another State – *Re the Habeas Corpus Application of Carthage Healy*, [1984] CMLR 575.

70 *App. 1983/63, X v The Netherlands*, 8 YB.ECHR 288; *App. 2143/64, X v Austria & Yugoslavia*, 7 YB.ECHR 314; *App. 3110/67 X v Germany*, 11 YB.ECHR 494. All cited in Vol.18, para.1654, HALSBURY'S LAWS OF ENGLAND, (4th ed). And see Chapter 4 below dealing with extradition and the protections in regional human rights conventions.

with Art.5(1)(f).[71] Thus, at first sight a person detained under a provisional warrant has no protection under the Convention to prevent an unnecessarily long detention. According to the British House of Lords in *Sotiriardis*,[72] though, a provisional warrant provides for

> "...the precautionary arrest of the fugitive criminal to prevent him from fleeing the country before the requisition for his surrender has been received by the Secretary of State and signified to the metropolitan magistrate.... The purpose of this provision is clear. A person arrested on a provisional warrant is *not at that stage subject to extradition at all* and may never become so."

Therefore, if the arrest is to comply with Article 5 at all, it must be within Article 5(1)(c) and also Article 5(3). In *Brogan v United Kingdom*,[73] the European Court of Human Rights held that one could take account of the context of terrorism in Northern Ireland in assessing whether a person had been brought before a court promptly for the purposes of Article 5(3). Furthermore, one justification for arrest under paragraph (1)(c) is to prevent the detainee from fleeing after committing a crime. Criteria for determining what is a reasonable time were set out in the *Neumeister* case.[74] Where there is a danger of flight, the courts ought to look to the character of the fugitive, his morals, his home, his occupation, his assets, his family ties and his links with the country in which he is being prosecuted.[75] Since an al-

---

71 *Supra n*66.
72 *Government of the F.R.G. v Sotiriardis*, [1975] AC 1 at 25C and G-H (Emphasis added).
73 Series A, Vol.145-B, at para.61.
74 *App. 1936/63*, 11 YB.ECHR 812 at 820. Most of the cases on this provision deal with complicated financial crimes which may not provide a useful analogy as to the permissible delay in extradition cases, but in *Bonnechaux v Switzerland*, 3 EHRR 259 (1979), the Commission held that the likelihood of flight out of the jurisdiction would justify prolonged pre-trial detention.
75 See also the *Ventura* case, (*App. 7438/76 v Italy*) where an alleged subversive conspirator was detained for five years. The Commission argued that this was not a breach of Art.5(3) because of, *inter alia*, the seriousness of the offences and the danger of flight – indeed the defendant did flee to Argentina in 1979. Therefore, a person requested for extradition would not be favoured by Art 5(3) since he has already a proven record of fleeing from the courts. *Ventura* is summarized by KRUGER, STOCKTAKING ON THE ECHR, (COUNCIL OF EUROPE, 1982) pp.136-8.

leged fugitive will have fled once already, the danger of further flight is increased in all extradition cases.[76] However, to date the European Convention organs have never been asked to assess the danger of flight in an extradition case, though in a 1981 application,[77] the Commission held in relation to a German national detained in Germany and charged, *inter alia*, with murder in Spain, that account should be taken of the difficulties in obtaining evidence from abroad. This situation should prove to be an appropriate analogy for a requesting government trying to obtain a provisional warrant.

In summary, an arrest under a provisional warrant should be subject to the limits imposed by Article 5(3), since the detention is in accordance with paragraph (1)(c) rather than (1)(f) if one follows the reasoning in *Sotiriardis*. Even if arrest under a provisional warrant is deemed to be in accordance with Article 5(1)(f), the Commission has held in *Lynas v Switzerland*[78] that "only the existence of extradition proceedings justifies deprivation of liberty in such a case". The Commission went on to decide, therefore, that proceedings must be conducted with "requisite diligence".[79] If Article 5(3) is inapplicable, then any dilatory requesting State may well fall foul of the *Lynas* decision.

However, while the Convention protections are welcome they are couched in such a vague way as to be ineffective to provide practical assistance to those detained under a provisional warrant. Given the advances in telecommunications and the limited amount of evidence necessary in most cases for an extradition hearing to go ahead,[80] a maximum period of detention of 21 days seems appropriate, especially when, even if released, the fugitive can be re-arrested when sufficient evidence is presented. In conclusion, it is highly unlikely that a fugitive will be granted bail prior to the hearing and there is no effective challenge available against even a very long period of detention. In the course of time, however, the fugitive will face an extradition hearing.

---

76 *Eg. R v Governor of Pentonville Prison ex p.Teja*, [1971] 2 All ER 11.
77 *App. 9604/81, X v Germany*, (1983), 5 EHRR 587 at 590.
78 *App. 7317/75*, 6 D & R 141.
79 *Supra n*78 at 167. See also, *Sanchez-Reisse v Switzerland, App. 9862/82*, (1986), 9 EHRR 71. The majority of the court followed *Lynas*, but took into account the special factors of extradition at 85.
80 For a liberal interpretation of time limits and the presentation of evidence, see *Government of Belgium v Postlethwaite*, [1988] AC 924.

e. *The Roles of the Judiciary and the Executive*

Before looking at the hearing, the respective roles of the judiciary and
executive in extradition requests needs to be examined. As noted above,
the usual procedure is for the executive to approve the issuing of an authority
to proceed, then the request for extradition is dealt with through the courts,
and, if the decision is to allow return, the executive has a final discretion
as to whether to order the fugitive's surrender. It is this final discretion that
has given rise to questions about respective roles: in one sense, its existence
has limited the scope of judicial inquiry at the hearing stage, but, more
importantly, it leaves the way open for judicial review of the executive's
exercise of the final discretion. With respect to the role of the courts during
the extradition hearing, the existence of an executive element in the final
decision on surrender has led courts to limit their own range of inquiry; in
part, extradition involves matters of foreign relations which courts have
eschewed. In the United Kingdom, there is a long tradition of leaving some
issues to the Secretary of State; in *In re Arton (No.1)*,[81] the Queen's Bench
Division held that the court only had to deal with the strictly judicial aspect
of extradition law, not its political aspects.

> "Acts of Parliament are the sole source,[82] and at the same time the strict
> limitation, of the judicial functions. We are sitting here as judges only, and
> have nothing to do with political considerations, except as they may have
> been introduced into the language of the Acts which we are called upon
> to construe."[83]

Thus, it was not justiciable before the court to argue that the request had
not been made in good faith in the interests of justice. That was a matter
for the executive, for the courts were not competent to examine it.[84] Despite

---

81 [1896] 1 QB 108.

82 [Author's note] And the treaty in so far as it was incorporated – *supra n*81,
    at 115.

83 See Lord Russell, *supra n*81, at 112. *Cf.* The higher courts have always been
    able to investigate the good faith of the requesting State in relation to Common-
    wealth cases – see Chapter 5, §*d. (iii).*, below. A similar right was given to
    the higher courts in cases involving requests from foreign States in s11
    Extradition Act 1989.

84 *Supra n*81, at 115.

this declared incompetence with regard to matters of the comity of nations, the 1870 Act did provide that the magistrate could determine whether the offence was of a political character. Furthermore, w'th regard to rendition within the Commonwealth, the higher courts have been able to review the good faith of the requesting State.

Nevertheless, a similar desire to refrain from delving into foreign affairs can be seen in the US rules of act of State[85] and of non-inquiry. In *Lui*[86], the First Circuit Court of Appeals held against the applicant.

"[The applicant] asks this court to decide that the PRC will not adhere to the Joint Declaration with the United Kingdom, in which it declared its intention to maintain Hong Kong's legal system for fifty years. All of these questions involve an evaluation of contingent political events. The Supreme Court has said that the indicia of a non-justiciable political question include: a textually demonstrable constitutional commitment of the issue to a coordinate political department; or a lack of judicially discoverable and manageable standards for resolving it; or the impossibility of deciding without an initial policy determination of a kind clearly for nonjudicial discretion; or the impossibility of a court's undertaking independent resolution without expressing lack of respect due coordinate branches of government; or an unusual need for unquestioning adherence to a political decision already made; or the potentiality of embarrassment from multifarious pronouncements by various departments on one question. *Baker v. Carr*, 369 U.S. 186, 217, 7 L. Ed. 2d 663, 82 S. Ct. 691 (1962). While not all of these ingredients are present here, several are. Moreover, unlike many 'political questions', whose resolution, absent judicial determination, must await the vagaries of the political process, here there is a statutory scheme which provides for the resolution of these questions by an identified member of the executive branch. The case for judicial resolution is thus weaker than with many such questions."

Nor will United States courts investigate the standards of justice that the fugitive might receive if surrendered unless the treaty specifically grants

---

85 See also, *United States v Noriega* 746 F.Supp.1506 at 1521-22 (1990).
86 *United States v Lui Kin-Hong* 110 F.3d 103 (1997).

such jurisdiction.[87] In *Neely v Henkel*,[88] the Supreme Court refused to enquire into the legal system of the requesting State to see if it would match the due process guarantees of the United States.[89] However, in the Anglo-U.S. Supplementary Extradition Treaty, 1986,[90] Article 3(a) provides:

> "Notwithstanding any other provision of the Supplementary Treaty, extradition shall not occur if the person sought establishes to the satisfaction of the competent judicial authority by a preponderance of the evidence that the request for extradition has in fact been made with a view to try or punish him on account of his race, religion, nationality or political opinions, or that he would, if surrendered be prejudiced at his trial or punished, detained or restricted in his liberty by reason of his race, religion, nationality or political opinions."

In *Howard*[91] and *Smyth*[92], the Courts of Appeals for the First and Ninth Circuits, respectively, held that Article 3(a) permitted the extradition court to investigate the treatment a fugitive offender would receive on return, but did not abolish the rule of non-inquiry in its entirety.

> "Considered in this context, the language of Article 3(a) must mean that a federal court in an extradition proceeding may look to the treatment that likely will be accorded the extraditee upon the charge for which extradition is sought. This inquiry need not necessarily be limited to the prosecution

---

87 For a fuller treatment of this issue, see Wilson, *Toward the Enforcement of Universal Human Rights Through Abrogation of the Rule of Non-Inquiry in Extradition*, 3 ILSA J. INT'L & COMP.L 751 (1997). Belgian courts also eschew this role – *Ryan*, 100 INT'L L REP.616 at 618-19 (Court of Appeals, Brussels).
88 180 US 109 (1901).
89 A limited retrenchment of this absolutist position was expounded upon in *Gallina v Fraser* 278 F.2d 77 at 79 (1960). See also, *Extradition of Atta, Ahmad v Wigen* 706 F.Supp 1032 (1989), 726 F.Supp 389 at 409-20 (1989), rev'd on this point 910 F.2d 1063 at 1066-67 (1990).
90 The Supplementary Treaty in its final form is to be found in Cm.294, UKTS 6 (1988) and, with comments, in Appendix 1 to the U.S. Senate EXEC.REPT 99-17, accompanying TR.DOC.99-8. It was ratified on 23 December 1986.
91 *In re Extradition of Howard* 996 F.2d 1320 (1993).
92 *In the Matter of the Requested Extradition of Smyth* 61 F.3d 711 (1995); rehearing denied, 72 F.3d 1433 (1996); see also, 795 F.Supp.973 (1992), 820 F.Supp.498 (1993), 826 F.Supp.316 (1993), 863 F.Supp.1137 (1994).

and formal term of imprisonment, but *Article 3(a) does not permit denial of extradition on the basis of an inquiry into the general political conditions extant in Northern Ireland. The history of the provision shows that it requires an individualized inquiry.*

Accordingly, in order to defeat extradition on the basis of his prospective treatment at the hands of the justice system extending beyond the duration of his formal imprisonment term, Smyth would have to demonstrate by a preponderance of the evidence that the criminal justice system in Northern Ireland likely would exact additional retribution for his crime beyond the remaining term of imprisonment, and that such additional punishment would be inflicted on account of Smyth's political or religious beliefs, and not on account of his having attempted to murder a prison guard."[93]

There is a division in the United Kingdom between the role of the extradition magistrate and the higher courts, as well.[94] In *Nielsen*[95] and subsequently in *Sinclair v DPP*[96], the House of Lords held that under the 1870 Act, the magistrate's role was confined to what was required by that statute[97] and that, therefore, the particular treaty terms were irrelevant at that stage in the proceedings. Even when considering which crimes are extraditable,[98] the treaty is to be given a wide interpretation if it is of the enumerative variety.[99] While the magistrate's role is still restricted to what the Extradition Act 1989 stipulates, the High Court on review now has a wider remit under s11 – this wider remit was prior to 1989 only available in cases of rendition within the Commonwealth under the Fugitive Offenders Act 1967. In *Schmidt*[100], the House of Lords held that whereas under the 1870 Act there was no general discretion to refuse surrender simply because to grant

---

93 *Supra n*92, at 720. Emphasis added.

94 *Viz.* The magistrate has no power to review the issue of an authority to proceed, whereas the High Court might rarely permit a successful challenge – *Rees v Secretary of State for the Home Department* [1986] 2 All ER 321 at 333.

95 *Nielsen v Government of Denmark* [1984] AC 606, [1984] 2 WLR 737.

96 [1991] 2 All ER 366 at 377-87.

97 For a similar view of Canadian legislation's restrictions (Extradition Act RSC 1985, C.E-2) on the role of the extradition judge, see *Romania v Cheng*, [1997] NSJ No.106, C.R. No.128423, 6 MAR 1997.

98 See §f(i), below.

99 *In re Arton (No.2)* [1896] 1 QB 509 at 517.

100 *Schmidt v Federal Government of Germany* [1994] 2 All ER 65, esp. at 77.

it would be unjust or oppressive,[101] under the 1989 Act there remained no inherent common law supervisory power – s11(3) provided a statutory discretion, but it was exhaustive.

> "Without prejudice to any jurisdiction of the High Court apart from this section, the court shall order the applicant's discharge if it appears to the court in relation to the offence, or each of the offences, in respect of which the applicant's return is sought, that –
> (a) by reason of the trivial nature of the offence; or
> (b) by reason of the passage of time since he is alleged to have committed it or to have become unlawfully at large, as the case may be; or
> (c) because the accusation against him is not made in good faith in the interests of justice,
> it would, having regard to all the circumstances, be unjust or oppressive to return him."

If, however, the courts are prepared to make an order for him to await the Secretary of State's decision regarding his return under s12, then what is the scope for the courts reviewing that decision if return is so ordered? The courts recognise that it is a delicate balance for the Secretary of State to observe between the United Kingdom's treaty obligations and the fugitive's liberty. According to *Launder*,[102] the decision is reviewable if

> "it is tainted with illegality, irrationality or procedural impropriety (*Council of Civil Service Unions and others v Minister for the Civil Service* [1984] 3 All ER 935)".

This interpretation was relied on by the United Kingdom authorities before the European Court of Human Rights in *Soering v United Kingdom*[103] in order to prove that an effective remedy was available for the purposes of Article 13 of the ECHR. Furthermore, in *Chetta*,[104] the Divisional Court

---

101 See *Atkinson v United States Government* [1971] AC 197; see also, *Sinclair*, *supra* n96.
102 *R v Secretary of State for the Home Department, ex p.Launder*, The Times, 29 OCT 1996 (QBD); and see [1997] 1 WLR 839 at 848, HL (reversed on other grounds on appeal to the House of Lords).
103 Series A, vol.161 (1989).
104 *Supra* n65.

ordered that the Secretary of State had to give contemporaneous reasons for the exercise of his discretion in order to facilitate any application for leave to seek judicial review. It was also proper, according to *R v Secretary of State for the Home Department and others*,[105] for the fugitive to discover whether a third State, which had originally granted extradition to the United Kingdom, had agreed to a subsequent re-extradition.

The *Conseil d'Etat* seems to have even broader powers in France. Review is normally to protect the fugitive's liberty, not to uphold the requesting State's interest in having him surrendered. However, in *L'Affaire Gouvernement Suisse*[106], the Commissaire du Gouvernement opined that, given the *Conseil d'Etat* had assumed competence to decide on a refusal to extradite,[107] it could review a withdrawal of a grant of extradition by the executive, even where the withdrawal was made "dans l'intérêt supérieur de l'Etat français".

> "Une dérogation à l'obligation d'extrader entre pays démocratiques, parties aux mêmes conventions internationales et respectueux des mêmes principes juridiques, est certes exceptionnellement possible, mais elle est une 'anomalie' qui ne peut pas être fondée que sur des motifs impérieux, assumés par les autorités *et permettant au juge national d'exercer son contrôle*. Ce n'était pas le cas en l'espèce."[108]

Most dramatically, though, the decision of the D.C. District Court in *Lobue v Christopher*[109] held that the involvement of the executive under the U.S. extradition laws was unconstitutional, as permitting executive review of a judicial decision. However, the case has been heavily criticised in other Circuits and vacated by the Court of Appeals.[110] It is aberrant and should be ignored.

---

105 Unreported, QBD, 31 JULY 1996, CO/1142/96.

106 [1995] AJDA 56. On French review procedures in general, see Fines, *Note de Jurisprudence* [1994] RDP 525.

107 *Royaume-Uni de Grand-Bretagne et d'Irlande du Nord et Gouverneur de la Colonie royale de Hong-Kong*, Leb. p.268; [1993] AJDA 848.

108 *Supra* n106, at pp.61-62; emphasis added.

109 893 F.Supp 65 (1995).

110 82 F.3d 1081 (1996).

Setting to one side *Lobue*, there is a general policy of the judiciary in various jurisdictions restricting its own competence during the hearing stage, but being prepared to review any executive discretion regarding surrender. This balancing of interests cannot be avoided. Some matters relating to extradition are peculiarly suitable only for a decision by the executive. On the other hand, the liberty of the person is best defended by the courts. It may be that the decision to permit the issue the initial authority to proceed could be transferred from the executive, but that rarely raises any matters of importance. The difficult questions relate solely to the scope for judicial inquiry into the request and into the executive's ultimate confirmation, or otherwise, of surrender. The result is a long drawn out procedure[111] which cannot, with proper regard to due process, be shortened without unduly threatening the liberty of the person.[112]

f. Extradition Crimes, Jurisdiction and Double Criminality

Although large topics in their own right, extradition crimes, jurisdiction and double criminality can only be understood fully as a whole.[113] They arise out of the elements of reciprocity in extradition law and its creation through bilateral agreements. In simple terms, the requesting State must seek the return of the fugitive for an extradition crime over which it has jurisdiction and which satisfies the requirement of double criminality.

(i) Extradition Crimes – Extradition crimes may be designated by either the enumerative or the eliminative method. If the enumerative approach is adopted, the extradition treaty and any domestic legislation list all the offences for which surrender might be granted; if the offence is not listed, then there is no extradition crime and the fugitive will not be surrendered.

---

111 Warrant approved (executive) – extradition hearing (courts) – review/appeals (courts) – decision on surrender (executive) – review of decision to surrender (courts) and remand to the executive.

112 *Cf. Hempel v Attorney-General* (1987) 77 ALR 641 at 674 *et seq.* (Australian Fed.Ct).

113 See BASSIOUNI, INTERNATIONAL EXTRADITION AND WORLD PUBLIC ORDER, at pp.314-29 (1974), and SHEARER, *supra n*61, at pp.134-49.

The number of countries using the enumerative approach is diminishing[114] as its drawbacks become increasingly evident. The usual complaint against the enumerative method is that it is very restrictive and that any offences added after the conclusion of the treaty have to be the subject of time-consuming supplementary treaties. A variant of the enumerative method provides for a wider definition of extradition crimes; it has been included in more recent treaties and it permits extradition for offences merely extraditable under the municipal laws of the requesting and requested States, as well as for the offences listed in the treaty.[115] This extended definition still produces a delay in any update of the list, for domestic legislation will usually require amendment.

The alternative eliminative approach, seen, for example, in Article 4 of the French extradition statute of 1927, usually defines extradition crimes in terms of a minimum penalty. Article 2 of the European Extradition Convention[116] lays down a one year minimum, while the Anglo-Irish system, based in part thereon, provides for a mere six month penalty if the offence is one of summary jurisdiction and no set minimum penalty at all for indictable crimes.[117] Research in the United Kingdom has shown that one result of converting to the eliminative approach is that the number of extradition crimes is greatly increased[118], which should of course prevent fugitives escaping trial because of technicalities in the treaties or domestic legislation.

---

114 Even the U.K. has adopted the eliminative method in s1 Extradition Act 1989.

115 *Eg*. the Anglo-Finnish treaty, UKTS 23 (1977), Cmnd 6741 and UKTS 53 (1977), Cmnd 6843. Before adopting a two year minimum penalty eliminative test at Harare in 1986 (LMM(86)64), the Commonwealth Scheme (Cmnd 3008) had the worst of both worlds, combining the enumerative and eliminative tests in Article 2 and Annex 1 (see *R v Governor of Pentonville Prison, ex p.Khubchandani*, (1980), 71 Cr.App.R.241).

116 *Supra n*14.

117 See s1 Backing of Warrants (Republic of Ireland) Act 1965.

118 See THE INTERDEPARTMENTAL WORKING PARTY'S REVIEW OF THE LAW AND PRACTICE OF EXTRADITION IN THE UNITED KINGDOM, (CRIMINAL JUSTICE DEP'T, HOME OFFICE, 1982). Hereinafter, 1982 REVIEW. The list of extradition crimes under the previous legislation, the Extradition Act 1870, covered a mere two pages (pp.106-107); the extra offences are found in Appendix D at pp.108-116. Then again, under the Extradition Act 1989 one can now return a fugitive who has allegedly committed that notorious international crime, purporting to act as a spiritualistic medium for reward, contrary to s1 Fraudulent Mediums Act 1951!

Despite the fact that most requests involve either dishonesty offences, offences against the person or, occasionally, narcotics offences, already covered by nearly all the enumerative tests currently employed, the eliminative method is more appropriate and much more efficient in the light of developments in international criminal law. While the eliminative test has elements open to misinterpretation through a lack of precision,[119] it is beyond question that it is the best method of delimiting extradition crimes. However, because of its much wider ambit, it must be tied closely to the principle of double criminality if reciprocity of criminalised behaviour is going to continue to be a fundamental plank of extradition practice.

(ii) Jurisdiction[120] – It might seem obvious that the requesting State must be competent to prosecute the fugitive if surrendered, but the issue of concern is really to do with whether the requested State recognises the principle of jurisdiction asserted by the requesting State. Traditionally, common law States only acknowledged territorial jurisdiction, on the basis that it would be wrong to interfere in the internal affairs of the State where the offence occurred, while civil law States operated various forms of extraterritorial jurisdiction, as well, even if rarely. Thus, a person could be prosecuted for the same offence in two different States because each asserts a different

---

119 SHEARER, *supra n*61, at pp.136-7.
120 See generally – EXTRATERRITORIAL CRIMINAL JURISDICTION, (COUNCIL OF EUROPE, 1990), hereinafter, COUNCIL OF EUROPE, 1990 (the original data on which this is based may be found in PC-R-EJ/INF Bil.); Blakesley, Jurisdictional Issues and Conflicts of Jurisdiction, at pp.131 *et seq.* of BASSIOUNI, LEGAL RESPONSES, *supra n*10 – hereinafter, Blakesley, Jurisdiction; and Hirst, *Jurisdiction over Cross-Frontier Offences*, 97 LQR 80 (1981) – hereinafter, Hirst, *Cross-Frontier Offences*. See also *Harvard Draft Convention on Jurisdiction with Respect to Crime*, 29 AM.J INT'L L Supp.439 (1935); AMERICAN LAW INSTITUTE, RESTATEMENT OF THE LAW OF FOREIGN RELATIONS OF THE UNITED STATES (3d), 1986; hereinafter, RESTATEMENT; Bowett, *Jurisdiction: Changing Patterns of Authority over Activities and Resources*, 53 BRIT.YB.INT'L L 1 (1982); Gilbert, *Crimes Sans Frontières: Jurisdictional Problems in English Law*, 63 BRIT.YB.INT'L L 415 (1992); Maier, Jurisdictional Rules in Customary International Law, at pp.64 *et seq.* of MEESSEN, EXTRA-TERRITORIAL JURISDICTION IN THEORY AND PRACTICE, 1996; Mann, *The Doctrine of Jurisdiction in International Law*, [1964-I] Hague Rec., and *The Doctrine of Jurisdiction in International Law, Twenty Years Later*, [1984-I] Hague Rec.

principle of criminal jurisdiction.[121] The first point, however, is to determine which type of criminal jurisdiction is relevant. There are three recognised forms of jurisdiction matching the three branches of government: legislative, judicial and executive. Legislative jurisdiction goes to the ability to prescribe the reach of national laws, judicial jurisdiction refers to the ability of courts to apply the fruits of legislative jurisdiction in individual cases and, finally, executive jurisdiction is the power to enforce decisions of the courts or legislature.[122] With respect to jurisdiction over crimes, legislative and judicial jurisdiction are the main topics of consideration.

Within legislative and judicial jurisdiction, there are several principles determining the scope, accepted by a greater or fewer number of States. No-one would dispute the right of a State to try a person for a crime, the elements of which take place and the effect of which is felt solely within the territory of that State; it is an example of the sovereign nature of a State. The simple territorial principle, as that might be termed, presents no problem. However, where certain elements of a crime are committed or if the result of a crime is sustained in more than one country, or if the offence occurs wholly outside the State, then so far unanswered questions of jurisdiction arise. As yet, there is no uniformly accepted understanding on how far a State might extend its criminal jurisdiction over offenders. As regards extradition law, whether the requested State will recognise the requesting State's jurisdiction is crucial to the grant of surrender. Thus, it is necessary to consider briefly the various principles of jurisdiction which go beyond simple territoriality.

(a) Qualified Territorial Jurisdiction – In such cases, some or even all of the elements of the offence occur outside the State claiming competence to prosecute.[123] The point at issue is how little of the offence need take place or have effect in the State before it can claim territorial jurisdiction. There are various tests. The widest application of the qualified territoriality principle is seen in the "doctrine of ubiquity".[124] It allows the State to assume jurisdiction over an offence and any inchoate offence connected there-

---

121 It is interesting to note that the Schengen Accords, *supra n*21, provide for a limited sense of *non bis in idem* – Articles 54-58.
122 See COUNCIL OF EUROPE 1990, pp.7 and 18, *supra n*120.
123 Hirst's article, *supra n*120, concentrates on this principle of jurisdiction.
124 COUNCIL OF EUROPE, 1990, *supra n*120, at pp.8, 9 and 24.

with, if a part of the offence or even, according to some States, if just its effects are felt in the prosecuting State.

> "It goes without saying that a wide application of the ubiquity and effects doctrines may in fact be tantamount to an extraterritorial application of criminal laws under the guise of the principle of territoriality."[125]

Thus, it can be seen right from the outset that, on the one hand, there is no neat division between territorial and extraterritorial jurisdiction, and, on the other, that a State claiming to be conservative when it comes to asserting criminal jurisdiction by only applying the territorial principle may still have very extensive powers of prosecution.

The doctrine of ubiquity is a very unsophisticated test for the instances when territorial jurisdiction might be exercised. Blakesley[126] provides a clearer analysis; in his view, territorial jurisdiction has both subjective and objective applications. Subjective territoriality equates with that part of the doctrine of ubiquity which grants jurisdiction if an element of the offence takes place in the prosecuting State. It is found in statutory form in section 7 of the New Zealand Crimes Act 1961.[127]

> "For the purposes of jurisdiction, where any act or omission forming part of an offence, or any event necessary to the completion of an offence occurs in New Zealand, the offence shall be deemed to be committed in New Zealand, whether the person charged with the offence was in New Zealand or not at the time of the act, omission or event."

The Canadian Supreme Court decision in *Libman v The Queen*[128] reveals its practical application. In that case the accused was charged with fraud. He had telephoned residents of the United States from Canada and induced them to buy worthless shares in some Costa Rican gold mines by making false statements as to their value. The victims of the fraud sent their money

---

125 COUNCIL OF EUROPE, *supra* n120, at p.24.
126 Jurisdiction, *supra* n120, at pp.154 *et seq.*
127 Cited in Hirst, *Cross-Frontier Offences*, *supra* n120, at p.101.
128 21 DLR (4th) 174, SCC, 1986. The quotation is taken from the judgment of La Forest J at 198-201. The case is very instructive because it contains a comprehensive review of English and Canadian case law on the topic of territorial jurisdiction. See also, *Melia v United States* 667 F.2d 300 (1981).

to the accused's associates in Panama and Costa Rica as directed, although it eventually was received back in Canada. Adopting a traditional analysis of the forum of the crime, the deception took place in the USA and the result of the crime was the money being received in Central America.[129] Traditionally, the fact the funds eventually came to Canada is irrelevant. Neither the elements of the offence nor its results occurred in Canada. Nevertheless, the Supreme Court held that the accused could be prosecuted in Canada.

"[The traditional analysis] ignores the fact that the fruits of the transaction were obtained in Canada as contemplated by the scheme. Their delivery here was not accidental or irrelevant. It was an integral part of the scheme. While it may not in strictness constitute part of the offence, it is ... relevant in considering whether a transaction falls outside Canadian territory. For in considering that question we must ... take into account all relevant facts that take place in Canada that may legitimately give this country an interest in prosecuting the offence. One must then consider whether there is anything in those facts which offends international comity.

....

I might summarize my approach to the limits of territoriality in this way .... [All] that is necessary to make an offence subject to the jurisdiction of our courts is that a significant portion of the activities constituting the offence took place in Canada .... [It] is sufficient that there be a 'real and substantial link' between an offence and this country, ... Just what may constitute a real and substantial link in a particular case, I need not explore .... The outer limits of the test may, however, well be coterminous with the requirements of international comity."

Stated so broadly, subjective territoriality is tantamount to a form of extraterritorial jurisdiction. More in line with the accepted scope of the territorial principle is objective territoriality, which allows a State to assume jurisdiction where the effects of the crime are sustained in that State. This form

---

129 In *R v Governor of Brixton Prison, ex p.Rush* [1969] 1 All ER 316, the requested fugitive offender had perpetrated practically the identical crime to that in *Libman*. The English Divisional Court refused extradition because English courts would not have had jurisdiction over the completed offence if references to Canada, the requesting State, were replaced by references to England.

of territoriality has received international approval. In *The Steamship Lotus*[130], Turkey claimed to have authority to prosecute the captain of the Lotus following its collision with the Turkish collier, the Boz Kourt, with the loss of eight Turkish crewmen. The case is well known for its failure to endorse the passive personality principle of jurisdiction. Moreover though, the majority of the Permanent Court of International Justice did find in Turkey's favour on the ground that since the Boz Kourt was flying the Turkish flag it was, as such, to be assimilated to Turkish territory and that, therefore, the result of the crime occurred in the jurisdiction of the State.[131] It is a classic example of the objective territorial principle. Where a boat carrying cannabis resin from Morocco, which had been destined for the United States, was forced into Canadian territorial waters, in part by adverse weather conditions, it was still held that the accused had unlawfully imported a narcotic into Canada.[132] In *United States v Noriega*,[133] the District Court held that where the activities outside the United States produce effects within the United States, then under U.S. jurisprudence applying traditional principles of international law the perpetrator can be prosecuted, given the domestic legislation was intended to have extraterritorial effect. In *United*

---

130 (*France v Turkey*), PCIJ Rep. Series A, No.10, 1927.
131 See the dissenting judgment of Lord Finlay, at p.53, *supra n*130. See also COUNCIL OF EUROPE, 1990, *supra n*120, at pp.11 *et seq.* The flag principle is part of the territorial principle, since it brings ships and aircraft within the territory of the flag state no matter where they might be. See *R v Anderson*, (1868) 11 Cox CC 198; *R v Governor of Brixton Prison, ex p.Minervini*, [1959] 1 QB 155. The military would appear to take their law with them when they go abroad – *eg. R v Page* [1953] 2 All ER 1355, noted 30 BRIT.YB.INT'L L 513 (1953) – (s41 Army Act 1955); *R v Cox* [1961] 3 All ER 1194, noted 37 BRIT.YB. INT'L L 555 (1961) – (s70(2) Army Act 1955). See also s3(1)(b) Protection of Military Remains Act 1986. Three Czech soldiers who killed their Captain when acting as part of the UNPROFOR operation were claimed to be subject to Czech law, partly because the army took its home law with it – CET, 28 MAR 1995. Similarly, when NATO forces are stationed abroad, by agreement they are subject to the military discipline of their own forces, not the jurisdiction of the host State, unless the sending State agrees – *CDS v The Netherlands* 96 INT'L L REP.383 (Dutch Supreme Court).
132 *R v Salvador, Wannamaker, Campbell and Nunes* 101 INT'L L REP.269.
133 *Supra n*85, at 1512-15.

States v Layton[134], a U.S. Congressman was murdered in Guyana in circumstances implicating the accused; killing a Congressman was a specific offence and the court held it extended to deaths occurring abroad, in part because it was intended to and did have harmful consequences in the United States, thus falling under the objective territoriality principle.[135] A similar result is found in *Atkinson v Ministère Public*,[136] where the Luxembourg Court of Appeal was prepared to allow extradition to France where cheques had passed through banks in Luxembourg and the United Kingdom, but had eventually been presented for payment *Banque National de Paris* – the effect was, thus, in France.

The problem with objective territoriality occurs in relation to inchoate offences. If the crime is planned abroad, but intended to have an effect in the State, then the objective territorial approach is designed to grant jurisdiction: in *Ryan*,[137] the Brussels Court of Appeals was prepared to hold that the English courts had jurisdiction over a conspirator who never set foot in the United Kingdom, but who supplied bomb making equipment from Continental Europe, because the effect of the bombs would be sustained in the United Kingdom. Difficulties arise where the plan never comes to fruition. In those circumstances, neither an element of the offence nor its consequences impact within the territorial jurisdiction of the State.[138] However, British courts, among the strictest and most conservative in matters of jurisdiction, operate a variant of objective territoriality,[139] but have no problem of competence, it would seem, if the intention was that the effects of the offence would be sustained within the England and Wales. The British analysis of territorial jurisdiction divides all crimes into two categories, conduct and result. In cases of conduct crimes, such as blackmail or all varieties of inchoate offence,[140] jurisdiction is asserted only if an element

---

134 509 F.Supp.212 (1981): the best example of a 'belt and braces' approach to jurisdictional competence in the U.S. system – many different principles of jurisdiction were asserted.

135 *Supra n*134, at 216.

136 100 INT'L L REP.610. (Lux., *Ch.du Conseil*)

137 *Supra n*87, at 617-19.

138 See Blakesley, Jurisdiction, *supra n*120, at p.160, citing the French Professors Merle and Vitu.

139 See Hirst, *supra n*120.

140 See *Treacy v DPP*, [1971] AC 537.

of the *actus reus* of the crime occurs within the territory of England and
Wales. Result crimes, such as murder, only fall within the jurisdiction of
the courts if the result occurs within the territory. Thus, if a person is attacked in England, but dies in Scotland, a separate jurisdiction, the assailant
cannot be tried before English courts.[141] As such, the United Kingdom's
approach is much too narrow and needs to be extended. Furthermore, if
strictly applied in practice, it could not accommodate unfulfilled, inchoate
offences where all the conduct occurred outside the United Kingdom; all
inchoate offences under this test are conduct crimes, even offences such as
conspiracy to or attempted murder, where the completed crime is a result
offence. Nevertheless, either the judges do not seem to have noticed this
loophole, or they are constructively deeming the conduct to occur in the
United Kingdom.[142] An example which might have gone further than the
traditional analysis is found in the Privy Council extradition case of *Somchai
Liangsiriprasert v Government of the USA*.[143] The fugitive was charged
with conspiracy to import heroin into the United States. Whereas illegally
importing anything is a result crime, the inchoate offence of conspiring to
do so is a conduct crime. Furthermore, the heroin was never illegally imported. It became necessary to decide whether the United Kingdom would
have had jurisdiction if the conspiracy had been to import the drugs into
the United Kingdom.

"If the inchoate crime was aimed at England with consequent injury to
English society, why should the English courts not accept jurisdiction to
try it if the authorities could lay hands on the offenders either because they
came within the jurisdiction or through extradition procedures.
If evidence was obtained that a terrorist cell operating abroad was planning
a bombing campaign in London, what sense could there be in the authorities
not acting until the cell came to England to plant the bombs, with the risk
the terrorists might slip through the net."[144]

---

141 Hirst, *supra* n120, at p.83. *Secretary of State for Trade v Markus*, [1976] AC
     35.
142 Hirst, *supra* n120, at p.89. See also, Gilbert, *supra* n120, at pp.436 *et seq.*
143 [1990] 2 All ER 866 (PC).
144 *Somchai, supra* n143, at 877-78, *per* Lord Griffiths.

While it shows that there need be no problem assuming jurisdiction over inchoate offences under the objective territoriality principle, it is actually a departure from the conduct/result distinction in English law.[145] As Lord Griffiths went on to point out.

> "The only purpose of looking for an overt act in England in the case of a conspiracy entered into abroad could be to establish the link between the conspiracy and England, or possibly to show the conspiracy was continuing. If that could be established by other evidence it defeated the preventative purpose of creating the crime of conspiracy to have to wait until some overt act was performed in pursuance of the conspiracy."[146]

The Privy Council is asserting competence to prosecute because the effect of the full result offence, if it were to have been completed, would have been felt in the United Kingdom, even though the inchoate offence charged is a conduct crime.

There have also been statutory developments in the United Kingdom.[147] Proposed changes to jurisdictional competence over cross-frontier financial crimes in the Criminal Justice Act 1993 would probably give future courts the right to prosecute for a variety of cross-frontier financial crimes: Part I of the 1993 Act is not yet in force, so the common law is, at the time of writing, the sole means of asserting jurisdiction in such cases. However, the fact that the legislation has been enacted indicates that this is a recognised problem that is here to stay and that existing law is seen as inadequate.

Section 1 of the Criminal Justice Act 1993 lists certain property related offences under the Theft Acts 1968 and 1978 and the Forgery and Counterfeiting Act 1981, as well as conspiracies and attempts to commit such offences. Under s2 of the 1993 Act, in relation to forgery, theft or obtaining by deception, amongst other offences, English courts will be given jurisdiction over offences where any relevant event occurred in England and Wales.

---

145 The reasoning bears more than a passing resemblance to the protective principle, discussed below in §(c).

146 *Supra* n143, at 878. See also, *R v Sansom, Smith, Williams and Wilkins* [1991] 2 WLR 366.

147 See Gilbert, *Who has Jurisdiction for Cross-Frontier Financial Crimes?*, [1995] WJCLI 76 at pp.85 *et seq.*

"s2(1) For the purposes of this Part, 'relevant event', in relation to any [listed] offence, means any act or omission or other event (including any result of one or more acts or omissions) proof of which is required for conviction of the offence.

(2) For the purpose of determining whether or not a particular event is a relevant event in relation to a [listed] offence, any question as to where it occurred is to be disregarded.

(3) A person may be guilty of a [listed] offence if any of the events which are relevant events in relation to the offence occurred in England and Wales."

Section 2 ranks as one of the worst pieces of Parliamentary draftsmanship. To understand it, subsection (3) should be read first: if a relevant event occurred in England and Wales, the offence will be triable once the Act is in force. Relevant events are, according to subsection (1), any conduct or result that forms part of the offence. Under subsection (2), one determines the relevant events regardless of where they occurred, thus showing that there can be more than one relevant event. For the purposes of asserting jurisdiction, only one relevant event, no matter how minor, so long as proof of it is required for the offence, must have occurred in England and Wales. For a s1 crime, therefore, English criminal jurisdiction will eventually be as extensive as that in New Zealand under s7 of the Crimes Act 1961.

Section 4 will make it even easier to assert that a relevant event 'occurred' in England and Wales.

"s4 In relation to a [listed] offence –
(a) there is an obtaining of property in England and Wales if the property is either despatched from or received at a place in England and Wales; and
(b) there is a communication in England and Wales of any information, instruction, request, demand or other matter if it is sent by any means –
(i) from a place in England or Wales to a place elsewhere; or
(ii) from a place elsewhere to a place in England and Wales."

Taking ss2 and 4 together, it should mean that English courts could, in the future, prosecute the accused for any alleged illegal activities that had an effect in England and Wales. The Criminal Justice Act 1993, once it comes into force, is tantamount to giving English courts extraterritorial jurisdiction over international financial crimes so long as at least part of the offence has had an effect in the United Kingdom.

Given that financial transactions often take place only in terms of two computers communicating in that penumbral region called cyberspace,[148] jurisdictional issues are going to become more complex and looser rules on competence are going to prove necessary. If the move to banks in outer space based on satellites takes place, too, then cross-frontier financial crimes will take on extra facets. The satellite is deemed to belong to the State of registration[149], akin to ships sailing under a flag.[150] However, it is not clear what would be the position if a bank from another State were to 'rent' part of the satellite's memory cells – could the State in which the bank is located prosecute someone accused of financial crimes? Moreover, the Outer Space Treaty in Article 6 assumes that a satellite might be registered to an international organization, such as the European Space Agency; it might also be that the European Union 'rents' memory on this satellite, raising even more questions about the jurisdictional competence of the European Union itself in criminal matters if someone seeks to take funds 'held' in the satellite. As things stand, resolution of these questions is for the future, but cross-frontier financial crime will inevitably demand greater jurisdictional competence. The approach in *Libman*[151] based on the State's interest in prosecuting the offender has many advantages.

If all the above signals a blurring of the distinction between extraterritorial and territorial offences and the adoption of general objective territoriality jurisdiction, it is to be welcomed. It reveals that States in general need competence over offences performed outside their territorial limits and that this can only be effected if wider interpretations of jurisdictional authority are accepted. If Britain, one of the strictest States, is seen to be moving in this direction, then it can only mean that there is a widespread acknowledgement of the need for improved systems of international law enforcement.

(b) The Active Personality Principle – With this topic, extraterritorial jurisdiction proper is encountered. It is sometimes known as the nationality principle. With very few exceptions, it used to be exercised solely by civil

---

148 See The Guardian p.19, 2 JUN 1997.

149 Article 8, Treaty on Principles Governing the Activities of States in the Exploration and Use of Outer Space, Including the Moon and other Celestial Bodies 1967, 610 UNTS 205.

150 *Viz. The Steamship Lotus, supra* n130.

151 *Supra* n128.

law States.[152] However, along with a few longstanding examples, such as murder and bigamy in England, the rise in so-called sex-tourism, where men go abroad in order to have sex with children, has led governments in common law jurisdictions to make this practice prosecutable on their return.[153]

European research has shown that there are wide variations in the application of this principle, with some States imposing an obligation of double criminality. The scope of the principle is clearly demonstrated by the decision in *Public Prosecutor v Antoni*.[154] The accused, a Swedish national, was involved in a road traffic accident in the Federal Republic of Germany. One of his defences when prosecuted in Sweden was that the Traffic Code had never been intended to apply outside Swedish territory. The Supreme Court held that in principle that "every crime committed by a Swedish citizen may be punished, even if committed abroad",[155] although the purview of any penal provision may be territorially limited for special reasons.[156] During the operation of UNPROFOR in the former Yugoslavia, Czech soldiers killed their Captain – the Czech authorities asserted jurisdiction, in part, on the basis of the Active Personality Principle.[157] The ambit of the active personality principle is, thus, extremely wide. Given that civil law States refuse, whether rightly or wrongly, to extradite their nationals, such breadth of competence is essential if fugitives are not to escape punishment merely by returning to their State of nationality.

(c) The Protective Principle – Also known as *compétence réelle*, all States reserve to themselves the right to prosecute persons whose crimes damage the vital interests of the State. The problems with this principle of jurisdiction concern the ambit of vital interests; does it extend to cover protecting, for example, nationals injured abroad or the economic interests of the State. It can be distinguished from qualified territorial jurisdiction in that the latter requires either that an element of the offence takes place

---

152 It was one of the grounds asserted by the U.S. District Court in *Layton, supra* n134, at 216.
153 See The Guardian p.10, 2 JULY 1996; p.6, 24 JULY 1996; p.1, 2 NOV 1996; and p.15, 26 APR 1997.
154 32 INT'L L REP.140 (Swedish Supreme Court, 1960).
155 Ch.1, Art.1, Swedish Penal Code.
156 *Supra* n154, at 146.
157 *Supra* n131.

or the effects of the offence are felt in the State, whereas protective jurisdiction can be exercised whenever the State's vital interests are damaged or challenged, even if the crime is committed outside of and its consequences have no direct effect within the State's territory. Nevertheless, there is an obvious area of overlap, as is seen in the United States case of *Layton*,[158] where the accused killed a Congressman in Guyana.

> "The alleged crimes certainly had an adverse effect upon the security or governmental functions of the nation, thereby providing the basis for jurisdiction under the protective principle. ...The charges also suggest that the alleged offences were intended to produce and did produce harmful effects within this nation, allowing a claim of jurisdiction under the 'objective' territorial principle."

Cases from several States reveal the scope of this principle. An example of activity that would constitute the pure protective principle might be where an accused disclosed a State's international espionage activities in third countries whilst he was outside that State. In the *Espionage Prosecution Case*,[159] the head of the former East German intelligence agency was prosecuted after the reunification of Germany for spying against the former FRG – amongst many other issues, the court decided that he had violated the law of the former FRG through his activities, even though they had all been carried out in what had been, at that time, a separate State and had, in fact, been lawful there. The French case of *In re Urios*[160] concerned a Spanish national who, during World War I and whilst in Spain, maintained contact with the enemies of France. He was arrested in 1919 and sentenced to twenty years imprisonment. The *Cour de Cassation* held that the conviction could be sustained because the substantive offence was not limited to French nationals or activity within the territory of France, and Article 7 of the then *Code d'Instruction Criminelle* provided that,

---

158 *Supra n*134, at 216.
159 *Case No.2 Bgs 38/91* 94 INT'L L REP.68 at 76-81 (German Federal Supreme Court).
160 [1919–22] Ann.Dig.107.

"any alien who ... is guilty outside French territory of a crime against the security of the State is liable to prosecution and sentence under French law if he is arrested in France or if the Government obtains his extradition."[161]

The French understanding of the protective principle is now codified in Article 694,§1, of the *Code de Procédure Pénal*.[162]

"Every alien who, outside the territory of the Republic, commits, either as principal or accomplice, a crime or delict against the security of the State or of counterfeiting the seal of the State or national currency in circulation, or a crime against French diplomatic or consular agents or missions is to be prosecuted and adjudged according to French law, whether he is arrested in France or the Government obtains his extradition."

English authority is not as clear, deriving from the unsatisfactory decision of *Joyce v DPP*.[163] That House of Lords case concerned the issue of whether an alien could be guilty of the crime of treason in relation to acts committed outside the realm. The precise argument upon the applicability of the protective principle in English law was somewhat confused by the fact that the accused had been resident in the United Kingdom for some years and was travelling on a British passport when he entered enemy territory. Nevertheless, Lord Jowitt LC adopted a line of reasoning similar to that employed in the French case of *Urios*[164] and held that the substantive offence was in no way limited to acts occurring in British territory, but that the individual need only be proved to owe allegiance to the Crown regardless of his nationality. The intention to operate the protective principle, if in an idiosyncratic formulation, can be gleaned from the judgment, although the case is not wholly appropriate on its facts.

The later case of *Somchai Liangsiriprasert*[165] indicates, *obiter*, that the courts will assume jurisdiction over terrorist or drugs offences that threaten the State, although the case was decided on the basis of the objective territoriality principle. It is arguable that the spirit of the language is wide

---

161 See, DONNEDIEU DE VABRES, LES PRINCIPES MODERNES DU DROIT INTERNATIONAL PENAL, at pp.95 *et seq.* (1928).
162 ENCYCLOPEDIE DALLOZ, (1985). Author's transcription.
163 [1946] AC 347 at 372.
164 *Supra* n160.
165 *Supra* n143, and accompanying text.

enough to include offences the result of which is directly felt outside the territory of the State, although it is meant to have an impact on the vital interests of that State. An example might be the murder of a government minister while abroad as part of the Provisional IRA's campaign.[166]

The United States has a more developed jurisprudence in relation to the protective principle. *Rocha v United States*[167] was a case of conspiracy to breach immigration rules by means of sham marriages. One of the charges was based on false statements made to consular officials abroad (18 USC §1546), which offence, the defendants claimed, was beyond the jurisdictional competence of the US courts. The court found that the offence was intended to have extraterritorial effect and went on to hold that a "sovereign State must be able to protect itself from those who attack its sovereignty".[168] Who can enter into a State is a matter of vital interest to the State.

More recently, Congress has passed the Omnibus Diplomatic Security and Anti-Terrorism Act, 1986. It gives the courts jurisdiction over any killing of a US national if it was intended thereby to coerce, intimidate or retaliate against a government or civilian population.[169] The objective of the legislation is to give the courts jurisdiction over purely terrorist offences.[170] As such, it falls within the protective principle on the basis that terrorism is a challenge to the State. It also reveals the need for States to adopt the protective principle, which can easily be justified in international law as a protection of a State's own interests.[171]

Finally, Israel has also adopted the protective principle when prosecuting Nazi war criminals. In *Eichmann*,[172] the District Court of Jerusalem answered the problem that the victims of the holocaust were not Israeli citizens

---

166 *Viz. Layton, supra* n134.

167 182 F.Supp 479 (1960); 288 F.2d 545 (1961).

168 *Supra* n167, at 549.

169 See 18 USC §2332(a) and (e).

170 See the difficulties the US had when seeking the extradition of the *Achille Lauro* sea-jackers who had killed a US national; McGinley, The *Achille Lauro* Affair: A Case Study in Crisis Law, Policy and Management, at pp.341-45 of BAS-SIOUNI, LEGAL RESPONSES, *supra* n10. The PLO paid an undisclosed amount by way of settlement to the dead man's family without admitting liability twelve years later in 1997 – The Guardian p.12, 13 AUG 1997.

171 See COUNCIL OF EUROPE, 1990, *supra* n120, at pp.26-7.

172 36 INT'L L REP.5 (DC Jerusalem, 1961). See also Reiss, *The Extradition of John Demjanjuk*, 20 CORNELL INT'L LJ 281 at pp.301-7 (1987).

and, indeed, that the State of Israel had not existed between 1933 and 1945. Citing Dahm's work, *Zur Problematik des Voelkerstafrechts*,[173] the court held that jurisdiction under the protective principle required a 'linking point' between the punisher and the punished; subject to rules of international law to the contrary, States may punish those persons which concern it more than they concern other States.[174] Therefore, given that the link between the Jewish people and the State of Israel was evident, Eichmann's crimes against the Jewish people gave the court jurisdiction.[175] The reasoning on the facts may be a little strained,[176] but the principles enunciated on the application of protective jurisdiction are sound: there should be a linking point, indeed a substantial one, between the State and the accused, and the offence ought to concern the prosecuting State more than any other State. Under such circumstances, the protective principle of extraterritorial jurisdiction is justifiable in international law and one of the objectives of international criminal law is upheld because the prosecuting State has most interest in bringing the accused to trial.

(d) The Passive Personality Principle – While it used to receive little support in international law,[177] it has gained in popularity in domestic judicial practice more recently. The principle purports to give extraterritorial jurisdiction to a State whenever one of its nationals, outside the territory of that State, is the victim of the offence. Unlike the US 1986 Anti-Terrorism Act, which permits the US to exercise the protective principle because the killing of the US national was intended to influence the US government, the passive personality principle would grant jurisdiction solely on the basis of the victim's nationality. It is a very broad assertion of jurisdiction which may interfere with the sovereign status of the State where the crime occurred. In both the *Lotus* case[178] and the *Cutting* case,[179] the government of the

---

173 (1956) at p.28. See para.31 of the judgment.

174 See also Mann [1964-I], *supra* n120, at pp.49-51.

175 *Supra* n172, at paras.31-36.

176 See Fawcett, *The Eichmann Case*, [1962] BRIT.YB.INT'L L 181 at pp.190-92.

177 See Harvard Research, *supra* n120.

178 *Supra* n130. The dissent of the US judge, Mr Moore, at 92 is instructive as to the traditional views of common law countries concerning the passive personality principle.

179 Mexico, 1886. See MOORE, REPORT ON EXTRATERRITORIAL CRIME AND THE CUTTING CASE, (1887).

State of which the accused was a national, France and the USA respectively, protested vigorously at the assumption of jurisdiction based on the passive personality principle. In *Romania v Cheng*,[180] the Canadian court held that it could not extradite Taiwanese nationals to Romania where the crime had occurred on the high seas, even though the victims were Romanian, although the court's interpretation of the term 'jurisdiction' was particularly narrow.

Interestingly, though, in the light of the threat of international terrorism, France adopted its own version of the principle in 1975,[181] in Art.689, §1, *Code Procédure Pénal*. In *Layton*,[182] the District Court judge was tentative about its use, accepting it only because there were other, more acceptable principles of jurisdiction available for it to stand alongside; indeed, it was the assumed lack of jurisdiction over the *Achille Lauro* sea-jackers who had murdered a US national overseas, that led to the 1986 Anti-Terrorism Act which relies on the protective principle.[183] However, while also relying on the statutory implementation of the Hostage Taking Convention 1979,[184] which provides for passive personality principle jurisdiction,[185] the court in *Yunis*[186] was prepared to recognize a general power to exercise this head of jurisdiction, at least where the State had a particularly strong interest in prosecuting. Nevertheless, the open-ended nature of the passive personality principle makes it difficult to accept it for even the purpose of

---

180 *Supra n*97, at paras.121 *et seq.*

181 See Blakesley, Jurisdiction, *supra n*120, at pp.172 *et seq.*

182 *Supra n*134, at 216.

183 18 USC 2331, 2332. "TITLE 18. CRIMES AND CRIMINAL PROCEDURE, CHAPTER 113B TERRORISM 18 USC 2332 (1997)
   (d) Limitation on prosecution. No prosecution for any offense described in this section shall be undertaken by the United States except on written certification of the Attorney General or the highest ranking subordinate of the Attorney General with responsibility for criminal prosecutions that, *in the judgment of the certifying official, such offense was intended to coerce, intimidate, or retaliate against a government or a civilian population.*" (emphasis added). *Cf. Ahmad v Wigen* 726 F.Supp 389 at 400-01 (1989). On the *Achille Lauro*, see *supra n*170.

184 18 INT.LEG.MAT.1456 (1979).

185 See *Rees, supra n*94, where the British court recognized German jurisdiction over a crime occurring in Bolivia because the victim was a German national. *NB.* the definition of hostage taking in Article 1(1) is such that the State might be able to assert protective principle jurisdiction, too.

186 *United States v Yunis* 924 F.2d 1086 at 1091 (1991).

combating terrorism, especially since jurisdiction over such crimes may be upheld on the basis of the more widely accepted protective principle.

(e) The Representational Principle[187] – The idea behind this form of extraterritorial jurisdiction is that the State exercising it is 'stepping into the shoes' of a State with a more pressing claim to prosecute. It may be as a result of a request from this latter State, possibly under the European Convention on the Transfer of Proceedings in Criminal Matters,[188] or as a result of a refusal to extradite. In the second instance, the State takes over the prosecution of the fugitive, either voluntarily or by virtue of an obligation in some multilateral, anti-terrorist convention. Clauses incorporating the principle *aut dedere, aut judicare* are now numerous[189] in an attempt to avoid impunity through States not having power to prosecute a fugitive simply because he has crossed a border and where his extradition is refused. Another example of representational jurisdiction is seen in the reciprocal legislation promulgated by the British and Irish parliaments to allow for trial of persons in either State for a series of listed offences likely to be committed as part of the conflict in Northern Ireland.[190] Given that evidence will have to be provided by the State not being given jurisdiction over the fugitive, the representational principle is a consensual assumption of the right to prosecute.

(f) Universal Jurisdiction[191] – The adoption of the principle of universality gives the court competence over any offence committed anywhere in the world. Thus, it is only in rare cases that it will be justified, some of which overlap with the representational principle. Universal jurisdiction is established by customary international law and by conventions. Since the beginnings of international law as it is known today, piracy has been recognised as a crime subject to the universality principle.[192] The four Geneva

---

187 See p.14 of COUNCIL OF EUROPE, 1990, *supra* n120.

188 ETS 73, 1972.

189 *Eg.* Arts.6 and 7 of the European Convention on the Suppression of Terrorism, 1977, ETS 90.

190 See the British Criminal Jurisdiction Act 1975, and the Irish Criminal Law (Jurisdiction) Act 1976.

191 See Randall, *Universal Jurisdiction Under International Law*, 66 TEXAS L REV.785 (1988).

192 See, Blakesley, Jurisdiction, *supra* n120, at pp.142 *et seq.* and White, *The Marshall Court and International Law: The Piracy Cases*, 83 AM.J INT'L L 727 (1989).

Conventions of 1949 and Additional Protocol I of 1977[193] provide for mandatory universal jurisdiction over grave breaches. The *Tadić*[194] judgment before the Appeals Chamber has made it clear, *obiter*, that universal jurisdiction exists for serious violations of the laws and customs of war, crimes against humanity and genocide.[195] The various United Nations sponsored, multilateral, anti-terrorist conventions[196] grant jurisdiction over a variety of transnational fugitive offenders, based simply on their presence in the State.

The growth of universal jurisdiction since the end of the Second World War is an indication of the developments in international criminal law and mutual assistance in criminal matters. Its limitless scope renders all other forms of jurisdiction superfluous, but it is rare for it to be exercised where some other principle would not also apply. For instance, in the *Eichmann* case, universal jurisdiction was asserted alongside the protective and passive personality principles.[197]

In conclusion, there is an overlap between qualified territorial jurisdiction and extraterritorial jurisdiction and between the differing principles of extraterritorial jurisdiction. That two States might recognise the authority to prosecute an offender for a crime with cross-frontier aspects on different grounds should be of no consequence. The only question concerning the requesting State's simple competence to prosecute in extradition hearings

---

193 75 UNTS 31-417 (1950); 1125 UNTS 609, 16 INT.LEG.MAT.1391 (1977). See Chapter Eight below.

194 *Duško Tadić, a.k.a. 'Dule', Decision on the Defence Motion for Interlocutory Appeal on Jurisdiction before the Appeals Chamber of ICTY,* Case No.IT-94-1-AR72 (1995), *per* Cassese J., at paras.9-48. At the subsequent trial on the merits, he was found guilty on eleven counts.

195 With respect to genocide, this must be as a result of custom – see Articles VI and VII. See, in general, Chapter Eight.

196 In *Yunis, supra* n186, the court also held it had universal jurisdiction courtesy of the Hostages Convention and the Hijacking Conventions – at 1091. Given the large number of signatories to these multilateral conventions, if a fugitive is charged with an offence established by one of them, then it is unlikely that a State would lack jurisdiction even if, generally, its courts have a strictly limited competence over crimes beyond its territory. See also Chapter Six below.

197 *Supra* n172, at paras.12 and 31 *et seq.*

is whether under its own law it has jurisdiction.[198] It may be that due to the principle of double criminality the fugitive cannot be surrendered, as will be discussed below, but there need not be identity of principles of jurisdiction for the requested state to concede competence.

(iii) Double Criminality – The essence of double criminality is that the fugitive should not be returned unless his actions could be prosecuted in either the requesting or, *mutatis mutandis*, the requested State. His activity should be criminalised in both States. With respect to most societies, this requirement poses no difficulties; every State condemns homicides and dishonesty offences. However, even within the relatively homogenous European Community there are different cultural attitudes to certain offences.

> "Simple examples are the permissive attitude towards cannabis use in the Netherlands, the greater tolerance to certain forms of pornography in Germany, the very tough stand taken by Greek courts against hooliganism .... Even in those areas where there has been considerable international consensus, such as drug trafficking, there are differences in the 'extent to which they enforce the law and the manner in which they enforce the law'."[199]

The first issue to be considered is whether the double criminality requirement has become a rule of customary international law, obligatory in all extradition arrangements and to be implied where it is not expressly included. In the Swiss case of *M v Federal Department of Justice and Police*,[200] the Federal Tribunal held that double criminality was a tacit precondition for all extradition cases, even where the treaty was not express on the matter. The Irish case of *The State (Furlong) v Kelly*[201] held that the requirement of double criminality was "fundamental to extradition". Academic commentators earlier this century were of much the same opinion. The Harvard

---

198 *Re Reyat's Application for a Writ of Habeas Corpus*, unreported, QBD, CO/1157/88, MWC, 22 March 1989.

199 HCP-I, para.96, *supra n*2.

200 75 INT'L L REP.107 (Federal Tribunal, 1979).

201 *Per* O'Dálaigh CJ in *The State (Furlong) v Kelly* [1971] IR 132 at 141.

Research in International Law from 1935 and Oppenheim's International Law from 1955[202] both make it clear that apart from some special cases,

> "... no person is to be extradited whose deed is not a crime according to the Criminal Law of the State which is asked to extradite, as well as of the State which demands extradition."

However, the 1985 Australian case of *Riley v The Commonwealth of Australia*[203] held that positive legislation or treaty provisions could expressly exclude the requirement; it was no more than a guide to interpretation to municipal law. It would seem that its omission will be rectified, but that it can be ousted by specific language.[204]

Before considering problems to do with its application, it is worth questioning whether the requirement is appropriate. If it were to be accepted that extradition is merely a method of assisting in the domestic criminal processes of the requesting State, against the laws of which the fugitive has offended, then it appears odd that the domestic criminal law of the requested State should matter. In the Canadian case of *Rajovic (No.2)*,[205] Graburn J held that he could see no reason for foreign law needing to be proved, but assumed on the basis of precedent that it ought to be. The only justification for the requirement would be where the fugitive was not a resident of the requesting State and did not know of the particular law – yet this would offer protection on the basis of ignorance of the law, which is not usually a defence. Surely, the political offence exemption and the speciality rule would prove effective to defend the fugitive.[206] However, while this view has many appealing features and while the criminal laws of States are becoming much more closely aligned, double criminality should not be rejected. As stated previously, there are still substantial differences in

---

202 Cited in *Riley v The Commonwealth of Australia*, (1985), 159 CLR 1 at 11-12. The quotation is taken from OPPENHEIM at p.701 (8th ed., 1955).

203 *Supra n202*, at 12.

204 The Convention Relating to Extradition between the Member States of the European Union, *supra n28*, provides for loose application of the principle of double criminality in relation to fiscal offences in Article 6.

205 *Re Socialist Federal Republic of Yugoslavia and Rajovic (No.2)*, (1982), 62 C.C.C.(2nd) 538. See also LA FOREST, EXTRADITION TO AND FROM CANADA, at p.108 (2nd ed., 1977).

206 See BASSIOUNI, *supra n113*, at pp.323 *et seq.*

criminological policy even between nations in Europe. Given, Bassiouni's subjective approach, below, is adopted, then double criminality will prove no problem to requesting States whilst defending fugitives from requests for crimes either abolished or having a non-custodial sentence in the requested State.[207]

As to whether the double criminality requirement has been satisfied, Bassiouni provides the following theoretical analysis.[208]

> "There are two methods of interpreting this requirement of double criminality, namely: *in concreto* (objective) and *in abstracto* (subjective). The first approach relies on the label of the offence and a strict interpretation of its legal elements. The second approach relies on the criminality of the activity regardless of its specific label and full concordance of its elements in the respective laws of the two States."

As will be seen, there is an increasing trend to adopt the *in abstracto*, subjective, interpretation. In practice, three tests for correspondence between the requesting and requested States could be applied: correspondence of names, correspondence of the elements of the offence and, less strictly, a corresponding criminalisation of the fugitive's acts or omissions. No State requires that the names of the offence in both States be identical. The traditional test, as shown by the following cases, is whether the elements of the offence charged on the warrant correspond to an offence contrary to the criminal laws of the requested State, although the test may be applied with differing degrees of strictness. In the British case of *In re Arton (No.2)*,[209] the court looked at French law to decide whether the crime was contrary to English law and French law and whether it was included in the extradition treaty. The Divisional Court held that the facts amounted to a crime in both versions of the treaty, English and French, and that this was sufficient even though they fell under different heads in the two lists of extradition crimes. The court found as a fact, as proved by an expert on French law, that the crime as comprised in English law under the Larceny

---

207 BASSIOUNI, *supra* n113, at pp.318-9. This passage seems to refute some of his views expressed at pp.323-4. See also *Riley, supra* n202, at 17.

208 See p.322 of INTERNATIONAL EXTRADITION AND WORLD PUBLIC ORDER, *supra* n113.

209 *Supra* n99, at 517.

Act 1861 had an equivalent in Article 147 of the French Penal Code. Lord Russell of Killowen CJ was correct in his approach when he used the facts of Arton's offence to see if these amounted to a crime under English law, rather than merely use the name of the offence under French law: English law has never required that extradition should only take place if the offence as alleged by the requesting State has a direct, identical equivalent in name and content in English law.

"The English and French texts of the treaty are not translations of one another. They are different versions, but versions which, on the whole, are *in substantial agreement*. We are here dealing with a crime alleged to have been committed against the law of France; and if we find, as I hold that we do, that such a crime is against the law of both countries and is, *in substance*, to be found in each version of the treaty, although under different heads, we are bound to give effect to the claim for extradition."

After that judgment, British courts, when hearing requests had required the applicant government to prove, as a fact, the existence of a crime under its own law substantially similar to an offence under English law which is made out by the conduct of the fugitive criminal in the requesting State. The position was neatly summarised in the decision of *Ex parte Budlong*.[210] Having reviewed the pertinent English case law,[211] the court concluded that the offences did not have to be identical in each State, only that they are of the same nature, have common elements or correspond in substance. The court even held that US jurisprudence on this matter was the same[212]:

"Absolute identity is not required. The essential character of the transaction is the same and made criminal by both statutes."[213]

The court in *Budlong* concluded that double criminality would be satisfied where,

---

210 *R v Governor of Pentonville Prison, ex p.Budlong*, [1980] 1 WLR 1110, esp. pp.1118-23.

211 *Ie. In re Windsor*, (1865), 6 B&S 522; *In re Bellencontre*, [1891] 2 QB 122; *In re Arton (No.2)*, supra n99; *R v Dix*, (1902), 18 TLR 231; *R v Governor of Pentonville Prison, ex p.Ecke*, [1974] CRIM.L REV.102.

212 *Supra n*210, at 1121.

213 *Wright v Henkel*, 190 US 40 at 58 (1902). *Cf.* BASSIOUNI, *supra n*113, at pp.329 *et seq.*

"(1) ...the crime for which extradition is demanded would be recognised as substantially similar in both countries; (and)
(2) ...there is a *prima facie* case that the conduct of the accused amounted to the commission of the crime according to English law."[214]

In the instant case, while burglary under §1801(b) of Title 22 of the District of Columbia Code did not require 'entry as a trespasser', unlike s9 Theft Act, 1968, the facts did make out a s9 offence and the two crimes were "substantially similar in concept" in both countries. Therefore, the fugitives were extradited. It seems that United Kingdom practice with respect to foreign States after *Arton* had been a mixture of the *in abstracto* and *in concreto* interpretations of the double criminality rule. Objectively, the elements of the offence must be substantially similar, but the accused's conduct was also relevant.

Some United States cases have also adopted this *Budlong*-esque approach. In *Caplan v Vokes*,[215] the Court of Appeals remanded an extradition request to the District Court because of an inadequate record of the extradition hearing. In part, it did not reveal whether the dual criminality requirement had been met.

"In reviewing the extradition charges in light of the dual criminality requirement, the district judge or magistrate should look to proscription by similar provisions of federal law ...."[216]

Further, in *In the Matter of the Extradition of Prushinowski*[217] the District Court compared English law with provisions of the North Carolina General Statute S14-100, to see if the different offences were 'substantially analogous':

"The court is required to determine whether the acts upon which the English charges are premised are prescribed by N.C. Gen-Stat S14-100. The offences

---

214 *Supra n*210, at 1122-23.
215 649 F.2d 1336 (1981).
216 *Supra n*215, at 1344n.16, citing *Cucuzzella v Keliikoa*, 638 F.2d 105 at 107 (1981). See also, *Oen Yin Choy v Robinson* 858 F.2d 1400 (1988) and *Peters v Egnor* 888 F.2d 713 at 719 (1989).
217 574 F.Supp 1439 at 1446 and 1447 (1983).

of the two countries must be substantially analogous, but they need not to be identical. *Branch v Raiche*, 618 F.2d at 851; *Cucuzzella v Keliikoa*, 638 F.2d at 108; *In re Sindona*, 450 F.Supp 672 (S.D.N.Y, 1978). The scope of the liability need not be coextensive and the elements of the crime do not have to perfectly match. *Freedman v United States*, 437 F.Supp 1252 at 1261 (1967)."

However, in other circumstances a stricter test has been used to see if the elements of the offence corresponded with an offence contrary to the criminal law of the requested State. The Irish case of *The State (Furlong) v Kelly*[218] provides a clear explanation of this stricter test.

"[The] position may be illustrated algebraically as follows. If the [requesting State's] offence consists of, say, four essential elements a+b+c+d, then a *corresponding* Irish offence exists only if it contains either precisely these same four essential elements or a lesser number thereof.[219] If the only Irish offence that can be pointed to has an additional essential ingredient (that is to say, if the Irish offence may be defined as a+b+c+d+e), then there is no corresponding Irish offence to satisfy the [double criminality] requirements ... for the simple reason that, *ex hypothesi*, conduct a+b+c+d falls short of being an offence under Irish law or, in plainer words, is not an offence."

With regard to requests from Commonwealth States, English courts have applied the same principles as in *Furlong*. In *Aronson*,[220] following earlier authority, such as *R v Brixton Prison Governor, ex p.Gardner*,[221] the House of Lords held that the facts constituting the fugitive's crimes were irrelevant under the Commonwealth legislation then in force. All that mattered was whether the ingredients of the Canadian offences disclosed in the Canadian warrant sent with the request for extradition disclosed offences under English law; on that basis, the House of Lords quashed the surrender order for 69

---

218 *Supra n*201, at 141.

219 *Cf. Budlong, supra n*210, where the US offence had fewer elements than its English equivalent.

220 *Government of Canada v Aronson*, [1990] AC 579. For the Nigerian understanding, see Kassim-Momodu, *Extradition of Fugitives by Nigeria*, 35 INT'L & COMP. LQ 512 at p.516.

221 [1968] 2 QB 399.

out of 77 offences, because the Canadian definitions thereof lacked ingredients that were essential to English law.[222]

While the 'correspondence of elements of the offence' test has been applied more or less strictly in different jurisdictions and cases, the pure *in abstracto*, 'correspondence of criminalised conduct' test has been applied as well, and is increasingly the accepted method of giving effect to the double criminality requirement. In *M v Federal Department of Justice and Police*,[223] the Swiss Federal Tribunal held that the concern of the double criminality requirement was that the act or omission in question was punishable in both States. British law has now adopted the European standard as set out in Article 2 of the European Extradition Convention[224] in section two of the new 1989 Extradition Act. This statutory provision adopts the reasoning of the House of Lords under the previous Extradition Act 1870 in *In re Nielsen*.[225]

> "[The] magistrate must then hear such evidence... as may be produced on behalf of the requisitioning foreign government, and by the accused if he wishes to do so; and at the conclusion of the evidence the magistrate must decide whether such evidence would, *according to the law of England*, justify the committal for trial of the accused for an offence that is described in the 1870 list (as added to or amended by subsequent Extradition Acts) provided that such offence is also included in the extraditable crimes listed in the English language version of the extradition treaty. In making this decision it is English law alone that is relevant. The requirement that he shall make it does not give him any jurisdiction to inquire into or receive evidence of the substantive criminal law of the foreign State in which the conduct was in fact committed."

---

222 *Supra n*220, at 589-90. The 1990 version of the Commonwealth Scheme (LMM(90)32) adopts the 'correspondence of criminalised conduct' test.
223 *Supra n*200.
224 *Supra n*14.
225 [1984] 2 WLR 737 at 748-9. See also *Government of the USA v McCaffery*, [1984] 1 WLR 867.

United State's law, subject to *Caplan v Vokes* and *Prushinowski*[226] above, also applies the correspondence of criminalised conduct test. In *Wright v Henkel*[227] the US Supreme Court held as follows:

"The general principle of international law is that in all cases of extradition the *act* done on account of which extradition is demanded must be considered a crime by both parties."

And later:

"It is enough if the particular variety was criminal in both jurisdictions."

There are also phrases in the leading decision of *Collins v Loisel*[228] that indicate an analogous approach.

"It is true that an offence is extraditable if the *acts* charged are criminal by the laws of both countries."

For the most part, the United States approach is an *in abstracto* (subjective) one where the conduct of the fugitive is the paramount consideration. All that is required is that the conduct of the accused is criminal in both jurisdictions, although this does lead the courts into inquiring, on occasion, whether the acts charged satisfy the essential elements of the offence as charged in the requesting State.[229]

The logic of having regard to whether the accused's acts or omissions are criminalised in the requested State, rather than seeing whether the offence with which he is charged under the criminal law of the requesting State has an equivalent in the requested State's law, is that the latter approach tends

---

226 *Supra nn*215 and 217.
227 190 US 40 at 58 and 60-61 (1902). Emphasis added.
228 259 US 309 at 311 (1922). Emphasis added. *Cf. Factor v Laubenheimer*, 290 US 276 (1933), which, however, is finally irrelevant since US courts ignore its peculiarities for the most part. See BASSIOUNI, *supra n*113, at pp.329 *et seq.*
229 BASSIOUNI, *supra n*113, at pp.329-43 esp. p.338, citing *Gallina v Fraser*, 177 F.Supp 856 (1959), *aff'd* 278 F.2d 77 (1959), *cert. den.* 364 US 851 (1960).

to become very technical and obstructive to the efficient practice of extradition. The decision in *Riley*[230] deals with this matter in some detail.

"The utility of the principle of double criminality is, however, likely to be outweighed by the impediment which it represents to the advancement of criminal justice if its content is defined in over-technical terms which would preclude extradition by reason of technical differences between legal systems, notwithstanding that the acts alleged against the accused involve serious criminality under the law of both the requesting and requested States. One can find, in the writings of some publicists and in some judgments of international and domestic courts, support for the view that the principle of double criminality requires correspondence or substantial correspondence between an entire offence under the law of the requesting State, being an alleged offence for which extradition is sought, and an entire offence under the law of the requested State. This approach is likely to result in primary emphasis being placed upon labels and correspondence of legal elements. If unqualified, it would significantly and arbitrarily frustrate the effectiveness of extradition arrangements between States with dissimilar systems of criminal law. The preferable view – and that which commands general acceptance – rejects the need for precise correspondence between labels or between constituent elements of identified legal offences under the criminal law of the requesting and requested States and defines the principle of double criminality in terms of substance rather than technical form. On this view, the requirement of double criminality is satisfied if the acts in respect of which extradition is sought are criminal under both systems even if the relevant offences have different names and elements."

Double criminality is a widely accepted standard of extradition and, properly used, it is a valuable protection for a fugitive. It means that a State cannot obtain his surrender for conduct not recognised as criminal in the requested State. However, the emphasis must be on the fugitive's acts or omissions, not on the precise requirements of the criminal laws of each State in some search for equivalence.

(iv). Double Criminality and Jurisdiction – The requirement of double criminality, if applied on the basis of a correspondence of criminalised

---

230 *Supra n*202, at 17, *per* Deane J. See also, *Hagerman v United States* (1991) 50 BCLR (2d) 169 (Canada)

conduct in the requesting and requested States, stipulates that if the case were to be presented before the courts of the requested State, *mutatis mutandis*, it could be prosecuted on the same facts. Offences where either the elements, in whole or in part, of the offence, its results or both occur beyond the territory of the requesting State can create difficulties. Such problems do not arise so much for civil law States which operate wide extraterritorial jurisdiction, nor, for that matter, for the USA now that it has adopted several of those principles, too, but rather for other common law States with merely territorial jurisdiction. For these States, for example the United Kingdom, extradition cases might fail over disputes about the scope of extraterritorial jurisdictional competence in criminal matters. A request from France for the return of a French national from the United Kingdom to face theft charges arising out of an offence committed in Italy would fail to meet the double criminality requirement but for statutory intervention specific to the active personality principle[231]; if any other head of extraterritorial jurisdiction is being asserted by the requesting State, then a successful extradition request would depend on the United Kingdom having *Joycean*[232] protective principle jurisdiction or qualified territorial jurisdiction in similar circumstances. Yet, it might be wondered why it should matter to the requested State that the accused is being sought to face prosecution in the requesting State on the basis of extraterritorial jurisdiction. The question for the requested State should turn only on whether the facts alleged would be an extradition crime if committed in the requested State; the principle of jurisdiction asserted need not be an element of double criminality. In *Schoenmakers v DPP*,[233] the fugitive had supplied drugs from The Netherlands to persons in the United States. When Australia received a request for his extradition, while the judge was prepared to hold that a conspiracy abroad to import drugs into Australia would be a prosecutable offence, for the purposes of double criminality the only question for the magistrate is whether the conduct would have been criminal if committed in Australia. Rather than substituting the requested State for the requesting State under this test, one simply moves

---

231 Section 2(3) Extradition Act 1989.
232 *Supra* n163.
233 101 INT'L L REP.174 at 179-80 (S.Ct, W.Australia).

all the criminal acts to the requested State,[234] even if one is dealing with
extraterritorial conduct aimed ultimately at the requesting State. Nevertheless,
courts do ordinarily look at the extraterritorial jurisdictional issues in assessing double criminality and, where the requested State operates only the
territoriality principle, it may prevent extradition. For instance, in *Romania
v Cheng*,[235] the judge wrongly held double criminality would only ever
be satisfied if the acts occurred in the territorial jurisdiction of the requesting
State, but was correct to refuse extradition since Romania's only claim to
jurisdictional competence was on the basis of the passive personality principle, generally rejected by States as a valid ground on which to justify
criminal competence to prosecute.[236]

English law, a good example of a system with limited extraterritorial
competence, permits courts to assume jurisdiction in cases of simple territoriality and in cases of qualified territoriality where either the conduct
constituting the crime or the result of the crime occur within Britain, depending on the nature of the offence.[237] The case of *Reyat*[238] concerned a
Canadian request for an alleged bomber; the fugitive was alleged to have
planted a bomb in a suitcase on board an aircraft bound for Japan, which
suitcase exploded killing two Japanese baggage handlers in Tokyo. The
charges alleged manslaughter as well as explosives offences. The Divisional
Court had to decide whether, if the bomb had been made and put on board
the aircraft in Britain killing two people in Japan, British courts would have
had jurisdiction. The case turned on a specific provision giving wider powers
of prosecution in homicide cases,[239] but the court was prepared to hold

---

234 In *Melia, supra* n128, at 303, the United States court held that whether the
   courts in the requesting State would have jurisdiction was not a matter for the
   extradition court.

235 *Supra* n97.

236 See the *Lotus* case, *supra* n130.

237 Hirst, *Cross-Frontier Offences, supra* n120.

238 *Supra* n198.

239 Section 9, Offences Against the Person Act 1861. Of course, the United Kingdom has extraterritorial jurisdiction over all the offences established by the
   multilateral, anti-terrorist conventions, so it would have no problem if the facts
   made out such an offence; for instance, if Reyat had been charged with en-
   dangering the safety of aircraft contrary to the principles established in the
   Convention for the Suppression of Unlawful Acts against the Safety of Civil
   Aviation, done at Montreal, 23 SEPT 1971, 10 INT.LEG.MAT.1151.

that manslaughter was a conduct crime[240] on the basis of *R v Berry*,[241] a case concerning the making of bombs not manslaughter, and that the making and planting of the bomb in England would have given English courts qualified territorial jurisdiction. That a fugitive on such a serious charge should be prosecuted is without question, but the reasoning in the judgment leaves much to be desired. The Privy Council in *Somchai*,[242] dealt with whether extraterritorial inchoate offences, deemed in jurisdictions following the English model to be conduct crimes,[243] could be prosecuted before an English court if the intended result of the crime was to occur in England. It appeared to extend the British understanding of the territorial principle of jurisdiction by holding that when considering inchoate offences where all the preparatory steps take place abroad, the courts might assume the right to prosecute if the result was to occur in England. Nevertheless, the Divisional Court in *Naghdi*[244] reasserted that where, in applying the double criminality test, the court assumes that the fugitive's acts occurred, *mutatis mutandis*, within Britain, and that those acts constitute an attempt, namely a conduct crime, but that the full offence would only be completed outside the territory of the United Kingdom, then no jurisdiction over the offence would exist under section 1(4) of the British Criminal Attempts Act 1981 and the requirement of double criminality would not be satisfied. The court did not draw any distinction between whether the full offence would have been a conduct crime or a result crime. If the full offence were a conduct crime like blackmail, then the steps constituting the attempt, deemed under the double criminality test to occur in Britain, would surely have been sufficient to give English courts jurisdiction over the full offence if it had been completed. If Part I of the Criminal Justice Act 1993, discussed above, were to be implemented, then cases like *Naghdi* would not give rise to a lack of jurisdiction.

There is now the ridiculous situation that if the inchoate elements occur outside the requesting State, but the intention was that the full offence would have effect in the requesting State, then English courts will find that the

---

240 Murder is a result crime; see *Secretary of State for Trade v Markus, supra* n141. Not cited in *Reyat*.
241 [1985] AC 246.
242 *Supra* n143.
243 Hirst, both *supra* n120, at p.87. See also Gilbert at the same reference.
244 *R v Governor of Pentonville Prison, ex p.Naghdi*, [1990] 1 All ER 257.

double criminality requirement is met, even though inchoate offences are conduct crimes and, as such, are usually only open to prosecution if some conduct would have occurred in the State asserting jurisdiction. Nevertheless, the reasoning in *Somchai* makes sense.

> "If evidence was obtained that a terrorist cell operating abroad was planning a bombing campaign in London, what sense could there be in the authorities not acting until the cell came to England to plant the bombs, with the risk the terrorists might slip through the net."[245]

On the other hand, if the position is reversed and the inchoate elements actually occurred in the requesting State, though with the intention that the full offence would impact elsewhere, then English courts could not prosecute on similar facts and so double criminality is not met.

> "A position could arise where, according to the English approach to jurisdiction to try attempts, no country would have jurisdiction to try the offence, which is hardly a satisfactory result."[246]

Fortunately, this set of affairs is limited to those countries which have adopted the English understanding of classifying crimes into two groups, conduct and result, where inchoate offences are strictly conduct crimes. It was held in *Melia*,[247] for example, that Canadian courts would even have jurisdiction to prosecute a person for conspiracy where the ultimate crime would be committed abroad and where the fugitive's only nexus with Canada was through phone calls made to other conspiriators in Canada whilst he was in the United States. Yet, the best approach for all States might be to ignore principles of jurisdiction when deciding whether double criminality is satisfied.[248] A more sensible way of including jurisdictional matters would be for the requested State to permit extradition if it recognised as accepted under international law the principle asserted by the requesting State, even if it did not apply the particular principle in its own criminal proceedings.

---

245 *Supra n*143, at 877-78.
246 *Naghdi, supra n*244, *per* Woolf LJ at 267.
247 *Supra n*128, at 303.
248 *Supra n*233 and *Melia, supra n*128, at 303.

g. Fiscal Offences

Traditionally, fiscal offences are excluded from those crimes which are extraditable either through an explicit provision[249] or by omission from the then list of extraditable offences.[250] The Norwegian government reluctantly had to end an extradition request to the United Kingdom in 1983, because tax fraud was not a ground for extradition in the Anglo-Norwegian treaty.[251] Fortunately, a later case involving Norway and the United Kingdom resulted in the fugitive being returned for tax evasion because his acts amounted to the extradition crimes of theft and deception, even if the revenue authorities were the victims.[252] This change reflects a general policy of extraditing fiscal offenders. According to one noted civil law commentator,[253]

"Most of the older conventions excluded fiscal offences but this attitude is changing and there is now a very strong and unambiguous tendency among European States to allow extradition for fiscal offences."[254]

Dr Stein pointed out that the Second Additional Protocol to the European Convention on Extradition,[255] many national extradition statutes,[256] the

---

249 See Article 5 of the 1957 European Extradition Convention, *supra* n14.
250 Although the general trend to employing an eliminative test for extradition crimes will in time remove this particular obstacle.
251 See The Guardian p.4, 6 JAN 1983.
252 *R v Chief Metropolitan Stipendiary Magistrate, ex p.Secretary of State for the Home Department*, [1989] 1 All ER 151. The US authorities are also willing to extradite fiscal offenders; see *Prushinowski v Samples*, 734 F.2d 1016 (1984).
253 Stein in THE 1982 COMMONWEALTH REVIEW OF EXTRADITION ARRANGEMENTS, at p.31, available from the Commonwealth Secretariat.
254 See the Irish case of *Byrne v Conroy*, unreported, High Court, 1995 No.351Sp., where the abuse of the EC Common Agricultural Policy by farmers in Northern Ireland who then received unwarranted Monetary Compensation Amounts was held not to be a revenue offence. The judgment consists principally of a definition of 'revenue offence' under Irish and EC law.
255 ETS 98, 1978.
256 Article 3.3, Swiss Federal Act on International Mutual Assistance in Criminal Matters, 20 MAR 1981, 20 INT.LEG.MAT.1339 (1981), as amended 4 OCT 1996 (supplied by the Federal Office for Police Matters, Bern); see also the Decree on International Mutual Assistance in Criminal Matters, 24 FEB 1982 as amended

Inter-American Convention[257] and the 1996 Convention relating to Extradition between the Member States of the European Union[258] all make provision for the extradition of fiscal offenders. The revised 1990 Commonwealth Scheme also allows for the extradition of fiscal offenders.

> *"Description of Returnable Offences.*
> 2(3). Offences described in paragraph 2 are returnable offences notwithstanding that any such offences are of a purely fiscal character, where such offences are returnable under the law of the requested part of the Commonwealth."

The problem is still raised, though, in relation to specifically fiscal cases that are not also violations of the general criminal law. In such cases, the double criminality rule would render detailed national offences, without an equivalent provision in the requested State's law, non-extraditable. Since fiscal laws are generally very particular, the double criminality rule will limit extradition to fiscal offences that amount to the normal financial crimes. The conduct of the accused must fulfil the requirements of an offence contrary to the law of the requested State, and the likelihood of this will decrease the more specific the offence is to the fiscal laws of the requesting State. Therefore, the current increasing willingness to extradite, even when the revenue authorities are involved, ought to continue, although, given no relaxation in the double criminality rule, complete extraditability of tax offenders will not be possible, except with States which have particularly close economic links. Yet for many developing States, fugitives who have broken fiscal laws may well have substantially damaged the national economy.

---

9 DEC 1996 (supplied by the Federal Office for Police Matters, Bern). The Anglo-Irish legislation since 1994 has permitted extradition for fiscal offences - s159 Criminal Justice and Public Order Act 1994 (United Kingdom) and s3 Extradition (Amendment) Act 1994 (Ireland).

257 See SHEARER, *supra n*61, at pp.61-3.

258 *Supra n*28, Article 6; and see the Explanatory Report, pp.19-20.

"In Ghana's economic situation, in common with that of some others, it was imperative that the country be able to extradite those who had offended in such a serious area of activity."[259]

Fiscal offences that on their facts could be common crimes ought always to be extraditable. More specific revenue offences should only be subject to the ordinary restrictions of the double criminality requirement.

h. The Requirement of a Prima Facie Case

Possibly the most contentious area of United Kingdom extradition law used to be the requirement that the requesting State prove a *prima facie* case against the accused. It seems to be a problem peculiar to British extradition law, for while the rest of the common law countries practice the same requirement in one form or another, the United Kingdom's proximity to the civil law jurisdictions of continental Europe meant that in the past many more requests were received from those jurisdictions where the implications and demands of this requirement were not understood. The Continental position is well explained by Stein.[260]

"The *prima facie* case is unknown in Europe. It is on occasions a source of mystery as to precisely how much evidence is required. Because European countries are compelled by law to work to a strict timetable and only have twelve days in which to get the necessary documents to the country requested, there is a special difficulty in cases involving complex economic fraud. These are cases which could take some time to document adequately. One result of *prima facie* could be that extradition is unobtainable in certain cases. Europe enjoys a state of mutual confidence in the administration of justice in other European countries and can therefore reduce the documentation involved. However, where the good faith of the country is suspect, Europe can go well beyond the requirements of *prima*

---

259 COMMONWEALTH REVIEW, *supra* n253, *per* The Hon.GEK Aikins at p.29. Supported by several other states, such as the Seychelles and Lesotho. See NS Pholo, at p.31.
"The Meeting should take account of the considerable damage which these types of crime could inflict on developing countries with shaky economies".
260 COMMONWEALTH REVIEW, *supra* n253, at pp.57-8.

facie .... Each European country has the right to further information when it feels it needs it."

Indeed, European States found the requirement in English law burdensome and a criticism of their criminal processes. The Anglo-Spanish treaty[261] lapsed because the Spanish government had not been able to secure the extradition of its fugitives from the United Kingdom, mainly due to the *prima facie* case requirement.[262] New talks concluded a fresh treaty and it provided for a less stringent evidentiary test.[263] Even the Home Office recognised that the rule does limit extraditions.

> "Something like a third of applications made to the United Kingdom under our extradition treaties fail, and the most common cause of failure is un-doubtedly the requesting State's inability to satisfy the *prima facie* case requirement."[264]

Statistics bore this out. In the five years prior to the Extradition Act 1989, 1985 to 1989 inclusive, United Kingdom courts extradited under the 1870 Act an average of fifteen persons to its European Community partners, excluding the special case of the Republic of Ireland.[265] By way of contrast, France extradited about 150 persons each year.[266] To remedy this apparent failure, the United Kingdom adopted measures to selectively exclude the requirement in relation to certain States. Subsections (4) and (8) of section 9 of the Extradition Act 1989 combine to permit surrender

---

261 69 B.F.S.P.6, C.2182. Treaty terminated 13 OCT 1978: Spain (Extradition) (Revocation) Order, 1978, S.I.1978, No.1523.

262 See The Guardian p.1, 9 NOV 1984.

263 Cmnd 9615.

264 1982 REVIEW, *supra* n118, at para.4.6.

265 See HCP-II, *supra* n2, at p.15. That average is in fact boosted by the surrender in 1987 of a block of 25 persons in connection with the Heysel Stadium riot: see *Postlethwaite, supra* n80.

266 See AKEHURST, A MODERN INTRODUCTION TO INTERNATIONAL LAW, at p.109 (6th ed. 1987). See generally, MALANCZUK, AKEHURST'S MODERN INTRODUCTION TO INTERNATIONAL LAW, at p.117 (7th ed. 1997).

without the need to prove a *prima facie* case.[267] With the coming into force of the 1989 Act, the United Kingdom thereupon ratified the European Extradition Convention[268] and relations with the other thirty-four contracting parties are now conducted on the basis of the measures in Article 12. That provision requires only that the request is accompanied by a certificate of conviction or the warrant for arrest, a statement of the offence and a copy of the necessary laws.[269] It is a major change of policy for the United Kingdom and should guarantee a freer flow of fugitives because of the simpler requirements.

---

267 Common law states are removing the need to prove a *prima facie* case in another, less controversial, area, as well. Sometimes a fugitive may not wish to be delayed in his return to the requesting state to face trial; he would prefer to be prosecuted while the evidence is still fresh. In such cases he may opt for a simplified form of surrender. There are two types of simplified procedure and a very lucid analysis of these two levels waiver of the full rules was given by MJI Hill at the 1982 Marlborough House Meeting. COMMONWEALTH REVIEW, *supra n*253, at p.49.

"[Mr Hill] suggested there were two categories of voluntary return. The first when a fugitive was arrested and taken before a magistrate on a provisional warrant and consented to being returned. The second when a fugitive waited until the formal request had been received, but on seeing the papers, recognised the futility of contesting extradition proceedings. Those in the first category were in effect waiving the entire extradition proceedings and protections afforded by the Scheme. Those in the second were waiving only the *prima facie* requirement and the opportunities for appeal and could arguably expect to receive full protection including that afforded by the specialty rule."

See also, the United Kingdom's participation in the European Union Simplified Extradition Convention, 1995, *supra n*28.

268 *Supra n*14.

269 STEIN, the COMMONWEALTH REVIEW, *supra n*253, at pp100-101. See also Art.12, European Extradition Convention, *supra n*14. While most signatories require no more than Art.12 sets out, Ireland makes more detailed demands than the basic minimum set out therein (see the German spokesman in The Irish Times p.2, 22 JUN 1990); Israel does demand a *prima facie* case to be proven, and Germany (Art.10(2) Extradition Law 23 DEC 1982, 24 INT.LEG.MAT.94 (1985)) and the Scandinavian countries reserve the right to require such proof in any particular case – 1982 REVIEW, *supra n*118, at para.4.2; see also SHEARER, *supra n*61, at pp.157-8. The Australian Extradition Act 1988 adopts the same stance.

"It must also be remembered that the extradition procedures to which this appeal relates flow from the European Convention on Extradition and are designed to facilitate the return of accused or convicted persons from one contracting State to another. The removal of the requirement that the requesting State should provide *prima facie* evidence of the alleged crime demonstrates that extradition proceedings between contracting States were intended to be simple and speedy, each State accepting that it could rely upon the genuineness and *bona fides* of a request made by another one."[270]

However, it may well be the case that the *"baby has been thrown out with the bath water"*.

The real problem is that the nature of the requirement and the reason it caused so much difficulty were never fully examined. Were the *prima facie* requirement only to be a minor quirk of English extradition law, it would not warrant further study, but one may compare the *prima facie* requirement with the civil law rule that a State's own nationals should never be extradited.[271] If the *prima facie* requirement prevents extradition from the United Kingdom, it only does so to protect the fugitive from being surrendered when there is, at that time, no case against him.

The *prima facie* rule required the magistrate to see whether, "if the evidence adduced stood alone at the trial, a reasonable jury, properly directed, could accept it and find a verdict of guilty".[272] It was quite a low standard, nowhere near proof of guilt. The Criminal Justice and Public Order Act 1994 substituted a slightly different test, that is, to

---

270 *Schmidt, supra* n100, at 76-77.
271 See Chapter Five below.
272 *Schtraks v Government of Israel*, [1964] AC 556 at 580. See also Stratford JA in *R v Jacobson and Levy*, [1931] App.D.466 at 478:
"In the absence of further evidence from the other side, the *prima facie* proof becomes conclusive proof and the party giving it discharges his onus."
This interpretation is followed in other common law jurisdictions – *Chua Han Mow v Superintendent of Pudu Prison*, 87 INT'L L REP.206 at 208-09, Malaysia, Federal Court.
See generally, CROSS AND TAPPER ON EVIDENCE, pp.156-58, (8th ed., 1995) and *R v Galbraith*, [1981] 2 All ER 1060. All the magistrate is looking for is a case to answer, not full proof of guilt.

"make a case requiring an answer by the arrested person if the proceedings were the summary trial of an information against him."[273]

That is, the claim of 'no case to answer' could not be successfully asserted. Under either definition, the requesting State merely has to produce sufficient evidence satisfying English rules of evidence,[274] that the accused has a case to answer. Other common law States apply a similar test. The previous Australian requirement of "sufficient evidence to justify trial" was explained in *Prevato*[275] in the much same language. The US test of "probable cause" was held to require that an extradition request would not be granted "upon demand or surmise, but only upon such reasonable grounds to suppose him guilty as to make it proper he should be tried".[276] As such correspondence of terminology presupposes, the *prima facie* requirement is no problem at all for other common law States. It is well understood in those States. Moreover, that it is required of Commonwealth States refutes the continental European States' contention that it is applied because of a distrust of the civil law system.

Given that the above reveals the true nature and extent of *prima facie* proof, the real reason for it causing so many difficulties may not be its supposed excessive demands, but rather some other factor. There have been several explanations as to why the requirement is so restrictive. One possible reason is that the *prima facie* test has become stricter during the past century. This suggestion may be borne out in part by empirical research of extradition data, although a full study of the test would have to have regard to all committal hearings. Before World War I, the number of extraditions was very high:

---

273 s9(4) as amended. See FORDE, THE LAW OF EXTRADITION IN THE UNITED KINGDOM, 1995, pp.67 *et seq.*

274 *R v Governor of Pentonville Prison, ex p.Kirby* [1979] 1 WLR 541.

275 (1986), 64 ALR 37.

276 Holmes CJ in *Glucksman v Henkel*, 221 US 508 at 512 (1922), cited in *Artukovic v INS*, 628 F.Supp 1370 at 1378 (1980); see *Lui, supra n86*, and *Quinn v Robinson* 783 F.2d 776 at 783 (1986). See also BASSIOUNI, *supra n113*, at pp.518-24, and *Sindona v Grant*, 619 F.2d 167 (1980).

	Extraditions	Refusals
1894:	30	4
1898:	53	8
1903:	56	4
1913:	46	1

During World War I there were no extraditions. In 1925, eleven people were extradited and three were not surrendered: this was the highest number of surrenders in any one year between the wars. Immediately after the Second World War the number of extraditions was minimal, but the Seventies saw a general increase, such that in 1980, seventeen people were extradited and there were seven refusals. The trend is continuing (Home Office data).

	Requests made to the UK	Surrenders by the UK	Requests made by the UK	Surrenders to the UK
1992	78	36	45	25
1993	100	27	33	21
1994	100	35	45	29
1995	101	31	48	14

Yet, this is still nowhere near the level at the turn of the century. It has been suggested that these figures reveal how the *prima facie* test has become stricter as magistrates courts have become more professional, but there is nothing to prove this particular point. Many other reasons exist, including the increased complexity of the cases, which then fall foul of the double criminality rule. Furthermore, judicial understanding of the requirements of *prima facie* evidence has altered little over the years. Even so, some support for this view is found in the debates on the Fugitive Offenders Bill, later enacted in 1967.

"We have had occasion to go through the authorities on the reported cases
on this matter and I am bound to say that in a number of cases – I am not
saying today, but in the old days at least – the Bow Street Magistrate committed people to be sent abroad on very thin evidence."[277]

However, the comment supports the current test rather than any return to
the alleged laxity at the turn of the century, so there seems little room for
amendment and improvement in that direction.

Another reason that requesting States fail to meet the *prima facie* requirement is that the lawyers representing them in the United Kingdom are
no longer familiar with the concept. British extradition procedures are
designed to reflect, so far as is possible, the procedure in normal committal
hearings. The traditional procedure, known as a long form committal, had
been for an accused only to be sent for trial on indictment before a jury in
a domestic prosecution after a *prima facie* case had been proven against
him. However, it was statutorily provided by s6(2) Magistrates Court Act
1980[278] that the accused could waive the long form of committal in most
cases. Research in 1984 showed that the long form committal was only used
for eight per cent of committals in inner London and for less than five per
cent in the provinces.[279] The Royal Commission on Criminal Justice,
1993,[280] found it was only used in seven per cent of cases and recommended its abolition – long form committals were abolished altogether in
ss44 and 47 Criminal Procedure and Investigations Act 1996. Therefore,
lawyers have had little recent experience previously and will in future no
longer have any experience of proving a *prima facie* case in a domestic
hearing. It may, therefore, become an arcane piece of extradition procedure
which will eventually lead to all extradition hearings mirroring those under
the European Convention on Extradition 1957.

However, one of the main reasons for *prima facie* rules proving burdensome was that cases are often extremely complex, while at the same time
governments are obliged by treaty to prepare their case within a very tight

---

277 Lord Reid on the Bill's Second Reading in the House of Lords. Cited in
   para.9.11, 1982 REVIEW, *supra* n118.
278 Continuing s1, Criminal Justice Act 1967.
279 See Lidstone's report in the Home Office Research Bulletin, published on 3
   DEC 1984.
280 Cm.2263.

schedule.[281] Given that European authorities are not used to having to
prepare sufficient evidence that swiftly, nor according to the British rules
of evidence in order to make it admissible at the hearing, it is not surprising
that this test is the cause of failure for so many requests. Yet those problems
did not necessitate abolishing the *prima facie* requirement. They could have
been met by extending the time limits available or by relaxing the rules
governing the admissibility of evidence in extradition hearings. The *prima
facie* requirement can be defended as a means of protecting the fugitive from
unjustified removal from his domicile: only where the requesting State can
show good cause for his surrender will he be extradited.

> "The justification for the requirement of a *prima facie* case today is that
> it operates as a protection for the individual. He will not be removed to
> another country which may be hundreds or thousands of miles away, with
> the inevitable disturbance to his life and employment, unless there are very
> good grounds justifying such removal. Above all, it prevents removal to
> another State of individuals who may merely be suspected of a criminal
> offence in such circumstances that the judicial authorities of the requesting
> State are under their own law justified in issuing a warrant of arrest, al-
> though insufficient evidence has been collected at the time of the issue of
> the warrant to justify a trial, which evidence may in fact never be col-
> lected."[282]

That it is partly a protection from arbitrary requests can be seen from experiences arising out of Anglo-Irish rendition. After Irish courts started to
permit the extradition of members of the Northern Irish paramilitary organisations in 1982,[283] there were repeated claims from members of the
Dáil for the government to introduce a requirement of a *prima facie* case
into the reciprocal legislation.[284] Following Irish accession to the European
Convention on the Suppression of Terrorism,[285] concern that the fugitive
might be lacking sufficient protection prompted the passing of the Extradition
(Amendment) Act 1987. This Act does not impose a *prima facie* requirement,

---

281 STEIN, *supra n*253, and accompanying text.
282 O'Higgins, *The Irish Extradition Act 1965*, 15 INT'L & COMP. LQ 369 (1966).
283 See *McGlinchey v Wren*, [1982] IR 154.
284 See The Guardian p.28, 14 DEC 1985. See also the correspondence between
     David Moloney TD and the Minister of Justice, dated 6 JUN 1985.
285 ETS 90. See the Extradition (ECST) Act 1987.

but it does allow the Irish Attorney-General to refuse to endorse a warrant if the United Kingdom authorities fail to supply sufficient supporting evidence. As one form of protection was lost, another was created.

However, regardless of the true extent of the *prima facie* case requirement's demands, of the real reasons for it creating difficulties and of its purpose, it cannot be denied that it prevented the free flow of extradition. The British government, therefore, adopted the civil law approach for its European neighbours in 1990 by ratifying the European Convention on Extradition.[286] While it might be arguable that there is no reason to provide the protection of the requirement to a German national being requested by the Federal Republic of Germany since he would not have enjoyed it if he had been arrested before fleeing, the British national requested by the Federal Republic is also denied its protection; reciprocity is also lacking because the Federal Republic will never extradite its own nationals.[287] Furthermore, as will be considered below, the effective protection of the requirement could have been retained while relaxing the particular evidential requirements that create the difficulties for civil law States in trying to meet its limited conditions.

i. Evidence and Extradition Hearings

Again, this is a problem peculiar to the common law countries. It especially affects the United Kingdom because of the number of requests it receives from civil law States. Civil law States have never required the requesting State to prove a case against the fugitive, so there was never any issue of having to satisfy the requested State's laws of evidence. The growth, though, of mutual assistance conventions,[288] with their emphasis on easing the obtaining of evidence from abroad, may breed a greater sense of understanding and trust between common law and civil law systems, such that common law States will be more open to accepting evidence collected by civil law

---

286 SI 1990 No.1507.
287 See Art.16(II), Basic Law of the F.R.G., 1949; 159 B.F.S.P. 503.
288 *Supra n*43 and accompanying text.

authorities attempting to satisfy any demand to prove a case against the fugitive.[289]

> "It seems to us that the peculiar nature of extradition proceedings of which an important part is the need to reconcile the different laws and judicial procedures of the requesting and requested States, should permit us at least to consider whether certain features of our rules governing the admission of evidence in domestic criminal proceedings might be adapted to accommodate more readily some foreign laws and practices."[290]

Within Europe, moreover, the adoption by nearly all States, including the United Kingdom and the Republic of Ireland, the two common law jurisdictions, of the procedures set out in the European Extradition Convention,[291] of which Article 12(2)(b) only requires a statement of the facts, will also make evidential conflicts a thing of the past. Nevertheless, elsewhere problems concerning evidence will still arise where the offence may have occurred hundreds or thousands of miles away in a State with a different legal system. Moreover, it will be suggested that rather than repudiating the *prima facie* requirement in its relations with the rest of Europe, the United Kingdom ought, in fact, to have relaxed its rules on the admissibility of evidence. This section will show how such an amendment might have satisfied European States and retained the fugitive's former protection.

The issue of evidence in extradition hearings raises two questions. The first concerns the form or presentation of that evidence, while the second concerns how far domestic rules on the admissibility of evidence should apply. Obviously, the two do overlap.

(i) Form[292] – The witnesses of the offence will usually be in the requesting State which could be far away. Rather than incur the cost of bringing them to the requested State for the extradition hearing, common law States accept written evidence if it is supplied in prescribed form. For the United Kingdom that means the evidence is in an affidavit, sworn by the percipient witness.

---

289 See Gully-Hart, 'How to Obtain Evidence in the Civil Law System (Continental Europe)', in ATKINS, *supra* n36, at pp.277 *et seq.*
290 1982 REVIEW, *supra* n118, para.5.6.
291 *Supra* n14.
292 See FORDE, *supra* n273, at pp.62 *et seq.*

It might be thought that such a relaxation of the general rules would be sufficient for any requesting State to be able to muster sufficient evidence to prove the fugitive has a case to answer, even within the strict time limits laid down in extradition treaties. All that is required is that evidence is given on oath or under affirmation and the documents are then "duly authenticated"[293] and, thus, admissible. However, these statutory and treaty provisions do not have regard to procedure in civil law countries. The inquisitorial system of criminal justice is not designed to receive evidence on oath or under affirmation at this stage of the investigation. Often a police officer will have acted as agent for the *juge d'instruction* and interviewed the witnesses, none of whom, nor even the police officer, may have been required to take an oath or affirm.

In a case concerning a request by Switzerland to Canada, the proceedings were eventually dropped because of the evidential requirements. The fugitive had defrauded victims throughout Europe of $125,000,000, but the Swiss only had eighty days under the treaty to trace the witnesses and produce sworn affidavits[294] from all of them. In the event, the fugitive fled from Canada to Brazil and the Swiss obtained his surrender from there on the basis of a mere summary of the case.[295] A request from the United States, another common law State, to Australia failed to satisfy the *prima facie* case test when 175 witnesses produced over 8,000 exhibits to obtain the return of a fugitive charged with commercial fraud. The evidence was held to be too "disjointed and disconnected".[296] The obstructiveness of applying standard common law rules of evidence to extradition hearings was, however, openly displayed in *Reyat*.[297] The case concerned a request from Canada to the United Kingdom; more similar extradition procedures between two States could not be imagined, so Canadian problems could not arise out of unfamiliarity with the requirements. The difficulty was that while Canada made the request, the result of the offence had occurred in Japan and the

---

293 See *Re Vito Dell'Aglio*, unreported, QBD, CO/389/95, (Transcript: Smith Bernal), 30 APRIL 1997.

294 Under the then, s16 Extradition Act, RSC 1970 c.E-21.

295 The example is given at p.5 of Canadian Revised Draft Proposals for the Amendment of Article 5 of the Commonwealth Scheme, November 1989, available from the Commonwealth Secretariat; hereinafter, Canadian Proposals.

296 Canadian Proposals, p.5, *supra n*295.

297 *Supra n*198.

witnesses, especially the forensic experts, were there. To add to the complications, though, Japanese procedures do not permit foreign officials to take evidence from persons under oath and Japanese law has no means of allowing witnesses to give evidence under oath for the purpose of a foreign hearing. In order to proceed with the case, the Canadian government had to fly 78 witnesses to Hong Kong to give evidence there to meet British-inherited evidentiary rules.[298]

Sometimes, common law courts have been prepared to relax the requirement that the witness be sworn. In *Dowse v Governor of Pentonville Prison*,[299] the House of Lords went a long way towards allowing in evidence if it was obtained in a manner having the same effect as taking an oath. In *Dowse* the applicant had been implicated by the statement of an accomplice. This statement was part of a report of proceedings in a Swedish District Court to add Dowse's name to the list of defendants. Swedish law does not permit accused persons to give evidence on oath when implicating other people. However, the accomplice's evidence had originally been given to a pre-trial review by the police, where giving false statements is a punishable offence; this fact was pointed out to him at the district court proceedings. The House of Lords accepted the accomplice's evidence, for, although no oath was administered and it would not attract a penal sanction if it were false, the accomplice's confirmation of the truthfulness of his statements to the police amounted to an affirmation. Moreover, this relaxation is in line with Canadian and US practice, which seems much more liberal in this area. In *Republic of Italy v Piperno*,[300] the Supreme Court of Canada held that as long as the witness knew the penalty for false testimony, then the deposition should be admitted. In the United States, admissibility is governed by 18 USC. §3190, in part.[301] The 1984 decision of *Zanazanian*

---

298 *Supra* n198, and Canadian Proposals, pp.4-5, *supra* n295.

299 [1983] 2 AC 464, esp. at 470-2. *Dowse* is a case under the foreign state legislation, the Extradition Acts 1870-1935, whereas *Reyat* was a decision under the stricter Commonwealth legislation, the Fugitive Offenders Act 1967. See also *R v Governor of Pentonville Prison, ex p.Singh*, [1981] 3 All ER 23.

300 [1982] 1 SCR 320.

301 Some cases suggest that if the evidence is in the correct form and authenticated by a US official, that alone determines its admissibility – *Oen Yin-Choy v Robinson* 858 F.2d 1400 (1988).

v United States[302] followed the liberal approach adopted in *Collins v Loisel*[303]:

> "[Unsworn] statements of absent witnesses may be acted upon by the committing magistrate, although they could not have been received by him under the law of the State on preliminary examination."

Even adopting these minimal liberalisations however, would not solve the general problem that written evidence has to be obtained direct from a percipient witness in a formalised setting. Given the evidentiary rules in force, it is no wonder that the *prima facie* case proved difficult to satisfy for European States. The full solution, therefore, has to take into account the rules governing admissibility as well as form.

Before turning to those issues, there is one further matter concerning the form of evidence; the lack of opportunity to cross-examine the witnesses. It was considered, *obiter*, in the early case of *Re Guerin*.[304] That judgment cited the following dissent by Coleridge J in *R v Bertrand*[305]:

> "The most careful note must often fail to convey the evidence fully in some of its most important elements – those for which the open oral examination of the witness in the presence of the prisoner, judge and jury is so justly prized. It cannot give the look or manner of the witness, his hesitation, his doubts, his variations of language, his confidence or precipitancy, his calmness or consideration; it cannot give the manner of the prisoner, when that has been important, upon the statement of anything of particular moment;..., it is in short, or it may be, the dead body of the evidence without its spirit, which is supplied when given openly and orally by the ear and eye of those who receive it."[306]

It may be thought that the 'penalty' of being sent to another State is so grave as to require the presence of those whose evidence is to be relied upon by the requesting government. Yet, that would impose severe burdens on the practice of extradition and would be a move towards trying the fugitive in

---

302 749 F.2d 624 (1984).
303 *Supra* n228.
304 (1888) 58 LJMC 42; 16 Cox CC 596.
305 (1867) 16 LTR(NS) 752.
306 *Supra* n304, at 44-5 and 602-3, respectively.

the requested State. It must always be remembered that an extradition hearing is merely a preliminary step to full trial when the evidence will be thoroughly tested.

> "Though the magistrate ought to scrutinize the depositions and see that they afforded substantial evidence of facts going to prove an offence, his Lordship knew of no authority that because they might be criticized subsequently and cross-examined too,... they ought not to be acted upon."[307]

Thus, in the United Kingdom depositions will not be rejected simply because the accused did not have an opportunity to cross-examine. The position on cross-examining in the United States and Canada is the same traditional one, despite written constitutional guarantees, including the right to a fair trial.[308] In *Bingham v Bradley*,[309] the Supreme Court of the United States held that it would defeat the purposes of the forerunner to 18 USC §3190 if the accused could demand the presence of witnesses against him. *Re USA and Smith*[310] accepts the same principle for extradition hearings in Canada. To this extent, in all jurisdictions where evidence is demanded at the extradition hearing in order to meet some standard of proof, the courts have accepted that extradition hearings cannot be perfect facsimiles of the old form committal hearings.[311]

(ii) Admissibility – The one particular rule of evidence standard to all common law countries which causes most difficulty for civil law States seeking to present evidence is the hearsay rule. The hearsay rule, in this context, excludes a statement tendered for its truth which has not been made by a

---

307 *R v Zossenheim*, (1903), 20 TLR 121 at 122.
308 See s7, Canadian Charter of Rights and the Sixth Amendment to the US Constitution provides a right to confront witnesses. *NB.* Art.6 ECHR, ETS 5, does not apply to extradition hearings according to *App. 10479/83 v United Kingdom*, 6 EHRR 373.
309 241 US 511 (1916). See also, *Oen Yin Choy v Robinson, supra n*301, at 1406-07.
310 10 CCC(3d) 540, (1984).
311 It seems that some African member states of the Commonwealth have, in fact, required the presence of witnesses in contentious extradition cases; see the COMMONWEALTH REVIEW, *supra n*253, at pp.57-59, especially the Kenyan and Ugandan delegates.

percipient witness.[312] In civil law jurisdictions, however, practically all evidence which is relevant (whatever its source) is admitted and weighed-up by the investigating magistrate.[313] Therefore, the exclusionary nature of

---

312 See *Ex p.Deprez and Fontaine* 87 INT'L L REP.311 at 319-20 (Mauritius Supreme Court).

313 1982 REVIEW, *supra n*118, at para.5.12. In the Rules of Evidence and Procedure for the International Criminal Tribunal for the Former Yugoslavia, *infra n*334, there is no bar on hearsay evidence and the Tribunal is given a broad discretion to determine its own detailed rules.

"Rule 89 General Provisions

(A) The rules of evidence set forth in this Section shall govern the proceedings before the Chambers. *The Chambers shall not be bound by national rules of evidence.*

(B) *In cases not otherwise provided for in this Section, a Chamber shall apply rules of evidence which will best favour a fair determination of the matter before it and are consonant with the spirit of the Statute and the general principles of law.*

(C) *A Chamber may admit any relevant evidence which it deems to have probative value.*

(D) A Chamber may exclude evidence if its probative value is substantially outweighed by the need to ensure a fair trial.

(E) A Chamber may request verification of the authenticity of evidence obtained out of court." (emphasis added).

In *Duško Tadić, a.k.a. 'Dule', Decision on the Defence Motion for Preliminary Ruling on Evidence before the Trial Chamber of ICTY*, Case No.IT-94-1-AR72 (1995), the transcript reveals the interplay of civil law and common law systems (p.591 line 17 – p.592 line 14). In the end the Presiding Judge ruled at p.600 as follows:

"8 As I said, as we said in our opening remarks, this is not a national system. We are

9 guided by our Rules of Procedure and Evidence that the Tribunal has developed. When

10 we have in Rule 89(A), when it provides that the Chamber shall not be bound by national

11 rules of evidence, that is intentional, that was deliberate, on the part of drafters of the

12 rules. So we consider that we look to our rules of evidence to determine whether or not

13 evidence is admissible.

14 Rules 89 of our rules of evidence, of course, is the guiding rule. 89(C) provides that a

Anglo-American laws of evidence is alien to those States with which the
United Kingdom conducts most of its extradition practice. Had the *prima
facie* rule not been abolished with respect to European requests, then a new
law would have had to have been drafted to relax the hearsay rule in
extradition cases.[314] If, as is suggested, the *prima facie* rule ought to have
been retained, it would be essential to change the rules of evidence to make
it workable. Such a proposal is in line with Australian and US practice. In
the Australian case of *Prevato*,[315] concerning an Italian request, the Federal
Court held

> "[that it] is the substance ... of the evidence which is important so that
> statements of co-accused were admissible evidence in establishing whether
> the offence was one for which extradition would be granted ..., even though
> such statements would not be admissible at a trial in New South Wales."

---

15 Chamber may admit any relevant evidence which it deems to have probative
value. We
16 consider that, based on the proffer of the Prosecutor and considering the
objections of the
17 Defence, the testimony of Miss Greve certainly is relevant and it appears
that it has
18 probative value.
19 Under Rule 89(D), the Chamber may exclude evidence if its probative value
20 substantially outweighed by the need to ensure a fair trial. So that our determination at
21 this time that the testimony is relevant, and that it appears to have probative
value, does
22 not in any way bind the Trial Chamber from excluding the testimony, should
we make
23 such a determination after hearing the testimony and hearing the context
in which it is
24 given.
25 We are very cognizant of the fact that we are judges, experienced judges.
We are not a
26 jury. We believe we can listen to this testimony that we consider to be
relevant and
27 appears to have probative value, and give it the appropriate weight that is
necessary."
314 Similar rules have been introduced to allow documentary hearsay into domestic
criminal trials – see ss23-26 Criminal Justice Act 1988.
315 *Supra n*275, headnote.

The United States primary authority is *Collins v Loisel*.[316] The Supreme
Court was prepared to accept evidence not admissible in an ordinary hearing
and received hearsay. Although the admission of written statements is more
restricted in the USA at pre-trial hearings than in committal hearings in the
United Kingdom, the general principle behind this judicial statement could
be applied to United Kingdom practice. Subsequent to *Collins v Loisel*,
various courts have reaffirmed the Supreme Courts views:

> "It is already well established that at least one level of hearsay is competent
> for extradition purposes."[317]

Yet, it is frequently the case that the evidence which the requesting State
wishes to submit is not merely a sworn statement of a witness, but rather
a report of what a witness said to a police officer or an investigating magistrate – that is, it is multiple hearsay. The Court of Appeals in *Zanazanian*
dealt with this matter, too.[318] Some of the evidence consisted of police
officers' reports describing a witness' statement. The court accepted that
the 'extra hearsay step might in certain cases result in decreased reliability',
but found the present reports 'sufficiently reliable to be deemed competent'.
The police officer's reports were based on tape recordings and contemporaneous notes of the interrogations. Thus, the evidence was admissible.

It would seem that the United States has little or no problem in accepting
hearsay evidence in proving probable cause for extradition matters. Therefore, accepting that those deciding extradition cases at first instance are
expert in extradition matters through long acquaintance and are sufficiently
competent to be able to assess the weight, merit and worth of hearsay evidence, it would seem sensible, even if the *prima facie* requirement is only
to be retained for all States outside Europe, for the United Kingdom to receive such evidence in extradition hearings. The United States position is

---

316 *Supra n*228, at 317.
317 *Zanazanian v United States, supra n*302, at 626 (1984). See also *Argento v
Horn*, 241 F.2d 258 at 263 (1957); *President of the United States, ex rel.Caputo
v Kelly*, 190 F.Supp 730 at 737 (1957); and US, *ex rel.Sakaguchi v Kaulukukui*,
520 F.2d 730 (1975).
318 *Supra n*302 at 627. See also, *Sakaguchi v Kaulukukui* 520 F.2d 726 (1975),
Emami v United States District Court for N.D. California 834 F.2d 1444 at 1451
(1987), *Lui, supra n*86, and *Oen Yin-Choy, supra n*301, at 1406.

based on the equivalent evidence being admissible in the requesting State. At first glance, this new approach seems reasonable: an extradition hearing is to accommodate the practice and procedure of both the requesting and requested States.[319] Thus, hearsay evidence, inadmissible in a committal hearing in the United Kingdom would only be received if it were admissible in the requesting State. It may seem illogical to retain the *prima facie* requirement but relax the admissibility rules, yet the *prima facie* rule provides a safeguard to a fugitive threatened with trial in another State in a sensible manner. It is the rules of evidence which merely hinder the requesting State in its attempt to show a *prima facie* case. Given that extradition is founded partly on reciprocity, allowing evidence to be admitted that could be put forward in a trial in the requesting State and leaving the magistrate to assess its value seems fair and reasonable. An approach along those lines has been taken in Annex 3 of the 1990 revision to the Commonwealth Scheme. Acknowledging that non-Commonwealth extradition is frequently granted without the need for a *prima facie* case, the Australian government suggested similar action at the 1986 Harare Law Ministers' Conference.[320] It was rejected and in 1990 superseded by Canadian proposals[321] at the 1990 Wellington meeting. Annex 3 of the Scheme, which is discretionary, permits the *prima facie* case requirement or its equivalent to be met by a record of the case received by the requested State, even if evidence in that record does not meet the rules relating to admissibility of evidence under the requested State's law. The extradition court in the requested State will assess the reliability of the evidence in the record in deciding whether a *prima facie* case requirement has been met, but admissibility of the evidence presented will be left to the full trial if the fugitive is extradited.

While the approach found in Annex 3 of the Commonwealth Scheme is appropriate to meet the difficulties raised by the hearsay rule, however, it leaves open the question as to whether evidence obtained illegally or improperly should be admitted at an extradition hearing. In *Ex p.Francis*,[322] the Divisional Court in England refused to apply the generic exclusionary rule of the English law of evidence, s78 Police and Criminal Evidence Act

---

319 1982 REVIEW, at para.5.11, *supra* n118.
320 LMM(86)64.
321 *Supra* n295, at pp.12-14.
322 *R v Governor of Belmarsh Prison, ex p.Francis* [1995] 3 All ER 634.

1984, to extradition hearings. On the other hand, in *Re Extradition of Contreras*,[323] a United States District Court refused extradition where the requesting State's case against the fugitive was based on confessions from alleged accomplices obtained by threats or torture and which the accomplices had recanted at the first opportunity.

The problems of gathering sufficient evidence which satisfied the requested State's laws of evidence in order to prove the fugitive had a case to answer was a double burden, especially to civil law States which had no domestic equivalent of either rule of law. The level of evidence needed to prove a *prima facie* case is not demanding, but it does provide the fugitive with a safeguard against arbitrary removal. If the requesting State is allowed to collect that evidence according to its own evidential rules and practices and the requested State will accept it in that form, then there is no need to abolish the *prima facie* requirement, not even for civil law States, although some basic minimum of human rights guarantees should be imposed with regard to how the evidence was obtained.

(iii) Trial in the Requested State – The final issue concerning evidence and fugitive offenders, relates to the growing number of conventions which require the State to prosecute if it does not extradite.[324] There is also an argument, advanced in Chapter Six below, that all politically or ideologically motivated offenders, whether they fall within the traditional definition of the political offence exemption or not, ought to be tried in the requested State rather than be surrendered. The problem would be that the witnesses necessary for the trial would be in the *locus delicti*. While concessions might be in order for an extradition hearing, the full vigour of common law rules of evidence would have to be applied to an 'extraterritorial' trial. Thus, special procedures would again have to be devised.[325]

---

323 800 F.Supp.1462 (1992).
324 For an example of the standard clause, see Art.7 of the Hague Convention for the Suppression of Unlawful Seizure of Aircraft, 10 INT.LEG.MAT.133 (1971). "The Contracting State in the territory of which the alleged offender is found shall, if it does not extradite him, be obliged, without exception whatsoever and whether or not the offence was committed in its territory, to submit the case to its competent authorities for the purpose of prosecution ...."
325 See the special rules needed for the ICTY, *supra nn* 313 and 334.

At a preliminary level, there appear to have been moves in this direction in Europe. Since 1976 the Metropolitan Police Special Branch, responsible for terrorist investigations in the United Kingdom, has operated a European Liaison Section, staffed by linguists, to co-ordinate Europe-wide terrorist incidents. It has contacts with equivalent police units in the other fourteen European Community States, Gibraltar, Iceland, Malta, Norway, and Switzerland.[326] For the purposes of trying a terrorist away from the *locus delicti* and gathering evidence therefor, the ELS will make all the arrangements if European police forces wish to interview British witnesses using a *Commission Rogatoire*. In 1989 this facility was used six times. In the other direction, the equivalent units in France and Spain arranged for members of the Royal Ulster Constabulary to interview French and Spanish journalists and photographers to obtain statements and exhibits for a trial in Belfast of members of the Provisional IRA.

A more formal system is contained in the burgeoning number of mutual legal assistance treaties.[327] The common law world has become aware of their benefits only in the last two decades, but if trials are going to be held of persons accused by other countries of offences outside the territory of the prosecuting State then such treaties will be indispensable. The scope for assistance in prosecuting the fugitive in the requested State is very large. The Commonwealth Scheme,[328] for instance, provides, *inter alia*, in paragraph 1(3) that assistance includes "examining witnesses, obtaining evidence, facilitating the personal appearance of witnesses, effecting a temporary transfer of persons in custody to appear as a witness and obtaining production of judicial or official records". The US-Italian mutual legal assistance treaty[329] of 1984 went further than the Commonwealth Scheme in that it allowed the issuance of an "international subpoena" to force a person to travel to the other State to give evidence if requested.[330] Measures such as these will be essential if the policy of *aut dedere, aut judicare* is to practised to its full extent.

---

326 See HCP-II, *supra n*2, at pp.43 *et seq.*, esp. p.45, paras.34, 37-39.
327 See *supra n*43, *et seq.*
328 *Supra n*14.
329 See Nadelmann, *Negotiations in Criminal Law Assistance Treaties*, 33 AM.J COMP.L 467 at pp.492 *et seq.*(1985).
330 See Zagaris and Simonetti, *supra n*42, at pp.222-3.

An alternative but similar practice exists under the extraterritorial laws in the context of the juryless courts used in relation to the conflict in Northern Ireland.[331] Under the United Kingdom's Criminal Jurisdiction Act 1975, and the Republic of Ireland's Criminal Law (Jurisdiction) Act 1976, a person can be tried for an offence committed in the other jurisdiction. The statutes make provision for taking evidence in the other jurisdiction, too. Part of this procedure allows for the accused, either in person or through a representative, to be present at the evidential hearing along with a member of the judiciary. In fact, in a 1982 case under the Republic's 1976 Act, a British judge sat in a Dublin court to hear evidence in relation to a trial being held in Belfast.[332]

Finally, there has been an interesting development in English rules of evidence that may be of assistance in permitting a witness who is abroad to give evidence in a trial in England. Section 32 of the Criminal Justice Act 1988 allows a witness abroad to give evidence by means of a live television link with the court; the result is the same as if he were there in person and answers most of the problems raised by common law rules of evidence. It could usefully be adopted by all common law States in order to assist with trials involving the need for testimony from abroad.

Before finishing this section, there is one further matter. The cases of trial away from the *locus delicti* will usually deal with politically or ideologically motivated offenders whose group or supporters will be in dispute with the requesting State. One of the major problems, however, for trials involving politically or ideologically motivated offenders is that their colleagues may be unwilling risk appearing in court to give evidence for the defence. This situation occurred in *Kakis v Government of the Republic of Cyprus*[333] where the House of Lords refused the extradition of Kakis because an alibi witness, A, also in the United Kingdom, refused to return to Cyprus for fear of ill-treatment by his political opponents. With trials

---

331 The reciprocal legislation followed on the report of the Law Enforcement Commission, Cmnd 5627.

332 See The Guardian p.3, 4 JUN 1982. The case concerned the murder of the former Speaker of Stormont, Sir Norman Stronge. See also, O'HIGGINS AND HAYES, LESSONS FROM NORTHERN IRELAND (1990); HOGAN AND WALKER, THE LAW AND POLITICAL VIOLENCE IN IRELAND (1990); AND WALKER, THE PREVENTION OF TERRORISM IN BRITISH LAW, 2nd ed. (1992).

333 [1978] 2 All ER 634.

taking place in the requested State, the pressure may be less but would still be present, and such witnesses would still have to get to the requested State in order to give evidence. Some form of personal guarantee of safe passage may be necessary if courts are to hear all relevant evidence.

When creating *ab initio* the rules of procedure and evidence for the International Criminal Tribunal for the former Yugoslavia,[334] several safeguards were built in to protect the anonymity of witnesses for fear of reprisals and, under Rule 85, both sides are entitled to call witnesses, while under Article 21 of the Statute established by the Security Council under Chapter VII of the United Nations Charter, the accused

> "shall be entitled to the following minimum guarantees, in full equality:
> (e) to examine, or have examined, the witnesses against him *and to obtain the attendance and examination of witnesses on his behalf under the same conditions as witnesses against him.*" (emphasis added).

(iv) Conclusion – This section has focussed almost exclusively on common law procedures, especially those of the United Kingdom because of the large number of extradition requests it receives from its civil law neighbours. The reason is quite simply the double requirement common law States impose of proving that the fugitive has a case to answer according to common law rules of evidence. Civil law States are generous in the rules imposed in relation to the admissibility of evidence and only require a statement of the facts of the offence, anyway, to satisfy an extradition request. Owing to the need to improve extradition relations, the United Kingdom decided to abolish the *prima facie* case requirement with respect to the other parties to the European Convention on Extradition in 1990. However, it may be that this move was misguided. The *prima facie* requirement provided the fugitive with a useful safeguard against arbitrary removal from the State; its demands were not onerous, but it ensured that the fugitive would only be surrendered

---

334 The Statute of Tribunal was presented to the Security Council in *The Report of the Secretary-General Pursuant to Paragraph 2 of Security Council Resolution 808 (1993)*, 32 INT.LEG.MAT.1159 (1993). The Statute was adopted by the Security Council in Resolution 827 (1993) and may be found in 32 INT. LEG.MAT.1192 (1993). The Rules of Procedure and Evidence (hereinafter, Rules) are now at Revision 6 – IT/32/Rev.6. On obtaining evidence from States, see *Blaskic*, IT-95-14-AR108 *bis*, 29 October 1997.

when there was a case to answer.[335] The difficulties with it arose from the fact that civil law States had to gather this limited amount of evidence in a short time in a fashion that would make it admissible under common law rules of evidence with which they were not familiar. The *prima facie* case requirement is a legitimate imposition in extradition relations: the rules of evidence, designed to protect an accused at a full trial, are inappropriate for an extradition hearing which, by treaty, has to be convened swiftly. There is little fear of evidence being fabricated if the common law rules are not applied with full force because the requesting State would still be required to meet its own rules of evidence. Thus, the solution adopted by the 1990 Commonwealth Scheme is much better, requiring the requesting case to show that there is a case against the fugitive, but allowing in the evidence thereof so long as such evidence would be admissible in the requesting State. *Prima facie* and its equivalents were never the problem, it was the hurdles placed in the way of satisfying its demands that caused the difficulties and it is those, especially the rules of evidence, which ought to have been relaxed.

j. Res Judicata and Appeals

Partly to compensate for the difficulties in producing evidence to prove the fugitive had a case to answer, the common law States permitted the requesting State to make as many applications for the surrender of the fugitive as it wished, subject to an argument of abuse of process. There is no estoppel because the proceedings are not final. Thus, a fugitive cannot plead *res judicata*. The response is uniform throughout the common law world and is useful given that it is rare for the requesting State to have a right of appeal. In the United States, the case of *Artukovic v Rison*[336] held that repeated requests could be made for a fugitive, and according to *Hooker v Klein*[337] the only constraint is that the government act fair-mindedly.

---

335 See the allegations in the *McAliskey* case, *supra* n60, about the lack of evidence the German government has against her.

336 628 F.Supp 1370 at 1375; 784 F.2d 1354 at 1356 (1986). See also, *Extradition of Atta*, *supra* n89, at 1065 (1990), where it was held that a subsequent request was the only option open to a government when the extradition magistrate refused surrender under 18 USC §3184.

337 573 F.2d 1360 at 1365-8 (1978), *cert.den.* 439 US 932.

A similar position has been taken in the Australian case of *Wiest v DPP*[338] and in the British case of *Atkinson v Government of the USA.*[339] However, it does seem a somewhat cumbersome means of challenging the first instance decision; only if the requesting State were to fail because it did not meet evidential requirements ought it to be employed. Otherwise, the requesting State should have a more conventional method of challenging an initial failure.[340]

Indeed, extradition appeals in general in common law jurisdictions are not straightforward for the accused. Rather than allowing him a full appeal on law and fact, he is only permitted to seek review, usually restricted to

---

338 (1988), 86 ALR 464.

339 [1971] AC 197.

340 See now: Britain (s10 Extradition Act 1989), Australia (s21 Extradition Act 1988) and possibly Canada (s28(1) Federal Courts Act, RSC 1970 c.10, 2nd Supp.); *cf. Minister of Indian Affairs and Northern Development v Ranville*, [1982] SCR 518, followed in the extradition case of *Re Meier and The Queen*, (1984), 6 CCC(3d) 165). The US does not permit the requesting state a right of appeal. *Cf.* §3215 of the proposed Senate Bill, S1722 of the 96th Congress which fell with that Congress. See also Senator Thurmond's Extradition Bill of 1981, §3195 of which would have provided a right of appeal for the requesting state. *In the Matter of Mackin*, 668 F.2d 122 at 128 *per* Friendly CJ (1981). In *United States v Doherty*, DC (SDNY), Slip Opinion June 25, 1985 (LEXIS), the US on behalf of the United Kingdom, sought a declaratory judgment against a refusal to extradite Doherty. The application was made under the Declaratory Judgment Act, 28 USC §§2201 *et seq*; the Act had been used by a fugitive in conjunction with *habeas corpus* in *Wacker v Bisson* 348 F.2d 602 (1965). Haight J was not bound by *Wacker* and followed the dissenting judgment that had asserted the Declaratory Judgment Act was inapplicable to extradition hearings, (*per* Rives J at 612-3). However, Haight J went on to consider, *obiter*, whether the requesting state would be able to seek review under the Act if it did apply to extradition hearings. Once again he found against the requesting state, saying reapplication for extradition to a magistrate under 18 USC §3184 was the appropriate response to a refusal to grant extradition. His reasoning is sound, for if the Act did provide an avenue for review there would be no need to amend extradition legislation as proposed in the two failed Bills discussed above. However, the result is to be regretted. On the reform legislation in general see Bassiouni, *Extradition Reform Legislation in the United States: 1981-83*, 17 AKRON L REV.495 (1984). The US-UK Supplementary Treaty (Cmnd.9915), permits appeal if the extradition court decides under Art.3 that the fugitive would suffer prejudice if returned – see *In the Matter of the Requested Extradition of James Joseph Smyth, supra* n92; *In re Extradition of Howard, supra* n91.

appealing points of law by way of an application for a writ of *habeas corpus*. There is no reason for such restrictive rules for either the requesting State or for the fugitive. Full appeal should be available to both sides.

k. Convicted Fugitives

So far it has been assumed that the transnational fugitive offenders were merely accused of a crime, but extradition is also available to obtain the return of already convicted fugitives. There is less fear of falsely disrupting the fugitive's life if he has already been convicted, so the procedures are simpler. However, one matter of concern relates to the fact that civil law States sometimes have the power to prosecute a fugitive in his absence.[341] There are two types of conviction *in absentia*: those cases where the fugitive is permitted to challenge the conviction on his return, known as a contumacious conviction, and those where he is not. In the latter situation, it is hard not to proceed as though the fugitive is convicted, whereas contumacious convictions have been treated as if they left the fugitive in the same position as if he had been merely accused.[342] While such an approach may be suitable for contumacious convictions, it is arguable that the inability to challenge the conviction *in absentia* is a violation of the fugitive's fundamental right to a fair trial and that refusal to grant surrender could be justifiable on that ground.[343] The way is left open, though, on that approach for the courts to have to review the requesting State's standards of justice.[344]

In one other case, trial *in absentia* has an equally direct application to transnational fugitive offenders. Under Rule 61 of the Rules of Procedure

---

341 See CASSESE, TERRORISM, POLITICS AND LAW, at p.43 (1988). Common law countries tend to allow trial *in absentia* only if the accused has been charged in front of a sworn jury and then absconds – The Guardian p.1, 9 JUN 1993, and p.11 16 JUN 1993.

342 See *Wiest, supra n338; R v Governor of Pentonville Prison, ex p.Zezza*, [1983] 1 AC 46.

343 The French courts refused the extradition of a US national to the United States on the ground that he would not guaranteed a retrial in Pennsylvania – International Herald Tribune p.2, 6-7 DEC 1997.

344 *Zezza, supra n342*, at 51-56.

of the Yugoslav and Rwanda Tribunals,[345] it is provided that where the Prosecutor has taken all reasonable steps to obtain the attendance of an accused, the Trial Chamber can receive the evidence against him and determine that the accused committed the crimes set out in the indictment. If the Chamber does so find, then under paragraph (D), it can

> "issue an international arrest warrant in respect of the accused which shall be transmitted to all States."

Given that the two Tribunals are set up under Chapter VII and that States are obliged to surrender those indicted, subject to only limited exceptions, but that many of the most notorious transnational fugitive offenders are protected by their own governments, then the effect of this trial *in absentia* is to effectively 'exile' the accused in his home State. If he were to travel abroad, then all States are obliged to transfer him to the relevant Tribunal for trial. As a method of limiting impunity, Rule 61 trial *in absentia* is a useful mechanism in constraining transnational fugitive offenders.

l. Conclusion

Extradition procedures, especially those in common law States, can prove to be overly burdensome. The bulk of this chapter has been spent considering the difficulties created by common law States' failure to conclude mutual legal assistance agreements until recently, their limited extraterritorial jurisdiction, their evidential requirements and their restrictive and exclusionary rules of evidence. The "creaking steam engine"[346] is much in evidence. However, the developing co-operation at all levels by States to improve the smooth running of extradition is having a recognisable effect, with the changes occurring predominantly in the common law States. Mutual legal assistance treaties have now been concluded by several common law States, age-old procedures are being reviewed and, sometimes, replaced, and generally there is a trend to make extradition easier. The balance between ad-

---

345 Yugoslav, *supra n*334; Rwanda – UNSC Res.935 and 955 (1994), reprinted in 5 Crim.LF 695 (1994). Rules of Procedure and Evidence, ITR/3/Rev.1 (1995), entry into force 29 June 1995.
346 The Observer, p.4, 29 APR 1979.

ministrative convenience and the fugitive's rights is coming down firmly in favour of the former. Given the catalogue of other protections available to a fugitive, to be considered below, over-restrictive procedural rules are an unnecessary and inappropriate addition to that list. However, the procedures must be fair to both sides and it should not be ignored that the fugitive's whole way of life will be affected by surrender to a foreign State. As common law States increasingly adopt positions in line with the more straightforward and explicit civil law procedures, it means that extradition law will be in a state of flux for many years yet as the new policies and practices are defined and applied.

EXTRADITION AND HUMAN RIGHTS

a. Introduction

Extradition law itself provides transnational fugitive offenders with several guarantees of their freedoms and rights and these are considered below. However, this chapter looks at human rights protections available from sources other than the established principles of extradition law. Since the end of the Second World War, several regional human rights conventions have been promulgated. The first was the European Convention on Human Rights and Fundamental Freedoms,[1] which was followed by the International Covenant on Civil and Political Rights,[2] the American Convention on Human Rights[3] and the African Charter on Human and Peoples' Rights.[4] It has become trite to state that none of these conventions prohibits extradition,[5] indeed

---

1   Done at Rome, Italy, 1950, ETS 5 (1950); ECHR hereinafter. See especially, DRZEMCZEWSKI, THE POSITION OF ALIENS IN RELATION TO THE ECHR: A GENERAL SURVEY. H/COLL (83)8. This is a paper presented to the Colloquy on 'Human Rights of Aliens in Europe', held at Funchal – Madeira, Portugal (17–19 October, 1983).

2   UNGA Res.2200A(XXI), UNGAOR, 21st Sess., Supp.No.16, 52 (1966); 999 UNTS 171; 6 INT.LEG.MAT.368 (1967); 61 AM.J INT'L L 870 (1967): hereinafter, ICCPR.

3   Done at San José, Costa Rica, 22 NOV 1969; hereinafter ACHR: O.A.S. Official Records, OEA/Ser.K/XVI/1.1, Doc.65, Rev.1, Corr.2 of 7 JAN 1970; 9 INT.LEG. MAT.673 (1970). See also, the less formalised American Declaration of the Rights and Duties of Man 1948; hereinafter ADRDM: 43 AM J INT'L L Supp.133 (1949).

4   Done at Banjul, The Gambia, 1981; hereinafter ACHPR: O.A.U. Doc. CAB/LEG/67/ 3/Rev.5, 21 INT.LEG.MAT.58 (1982).

5   *App. 7456/76 v Belgium*, 8 D+R 161 and *Altun v Germany, App. 10308/83,* (1983), 5 EHRR 611;(1985), 7 EHRR 154. Trechsel, on the basis of the Council of Europe's DIGEST OF STRASBOURG CASE-LAW RELATING TO THE ECHR, vol 1,

it would be strange if instruments designed to protect human rights were
to interfere directly in a process by which States assist each other in the
interests of law enforcement.[6] Nevertheless, it is not beyond the bounds
of possibility that surrendering a fugitive to another State might lead to a
violation of that person's rights. The question is therefore raised as to
whether an order for extradition might be challenged as an infringement
of the fugitive's convention rights.[7] Case law under the ECHR and ICCPR
has considered this matter in some detail. There are two possible approaches.
On the one hand, it might be argued that the rights in the convention should
be given 'extraterritorial' effect in order to judge the requesting State's
institutions and procedures, even if that State is not a party to the Convention. On the other hand, there could be a finding that the requested State
would violate its obligations under the Convention by returning the fugitive
to a place where the rights he enjoys in the requested State will not necessarily be respected. The case law adopts the second approach.[8]

Additionally, with respect to the Americas, under Article 64 of the ACHR
a member State can seek the advisory opinion of the Inter-American Court
of Human Rights and, in a decision at the request of Peru,[9] though not
directly to do with extradition, it held that it can review the human rights'
issues in any other treaty within the Americas. This jurisdiction should
extend to extradition treaties. The only limit concerns treaties where the

---

pp.117-155 (1984), suggested at that time that there were over 40 decisions
of the Commission holding that an extradition might still have Convention
repercussions; Vogler, Scope, *infra* n6. The same applies to deportation: *App.
9203/80 v Denmark*, 24 D+R 239. NB Article 4 of Protocol No.4 to the ECHR,
ETS 46 (1963), in force 2 MAY 1968, prohibits the collective expulsion of aliens.
The UK has signed but not ratified the Protocol. Protocol No.7, ETS 117 (1984),
7 EHRR 1 (1985), provides in Article 1(1) that no lawfully resident alien shall
be expelled without the right to submit evidence, to appeal or to be represented.

6   Vogler, The Scope of Extradition in the Light of the ECHR, at pp.663 *et seq.*
    of MATSCHER & PETZOLD, PROTECTING HUMAN RIGHTS: THE EUROPEAN DIMENSION
    (1988); hereinafter Vogler, Scope.

7   All of the Conventions referred to above extend their protection to all persons
    within the jurisdiction of member States: Article 1, ECHR; Article 2 ICCPR;
    Article 1 ACHR; Article 2 ACHPR.

8   See *The Soering Case*, Series A, Vol.161, paras.81-91, *esp.* para.88; *Kindler
    v Canada*, UN Human Rights Committee, 14 HRLJ 307 (1993). Both discussed
    below.

9   Advisory Opinion No.OC-1/82 of 24 SEPT 1982.

obligations affect mainly non-American States, but that would not be the case as regards bilateral treaties between American and non-American States; the obligations therein would affect each State equally – where an American State is requested to surrender a fugitive, surely it should be able to seek an advisory opinion with regard to any human rights matter arising under the extradition treaty.[10]

b. Human Rights Provisions Applicable to Extradition

Since none of the conventions prohibits extradition, it is a delicate balancing exercise to apply their provisions to an extradition request. On the one hand, *l'Institut de Droit International* has suggested that

> "In cases where there is a well-founded fear of the violation of the fundamental human rights in the territory of the requesting State, extradition may be refused, whosoever the individual whose extradition is requested and whatever the nature of the offence of which he is accused."[11]

This apparently far-reaching clause is actually so hedged around with interpretative discretion that it offers no additional protection to the fugitive than already exists in many treaties; when is a fear well-founded, which human rights are fundamental? Yet it reveals that human rights can in some circumstances override even the international enforcement of criminal justice.[12]

Weighted against such protective views, the European Court of Human Rights recognised in *Fox, Campbell and Hartley v United Kingdom*[13] "the need for a proper balance between the defence of the institutions of democracy in the common interest and the protection of individual rights". The Court took account of the "special nature of terrorist crime and the exigencies of dealing with it". Extradition may be the subject of review with

---

10 *Cf.* DAVIDSON, THE INTER-AMERICAN HUMAN RIGHTS SYSTEM, pp.243-49, esp. pp.248-49 (1997).

11 Extradition Resolution no. IV, 68-II ANN.IDI, Session de Cambridge, at pp.304-06 (1984).

12 See van den Wijngaert, *Applying the ECHR to Extradition: Opening Pandora's Box*, 39 INT'L & COMP.LQ 757 (1990).

13 Series A, Vol.182 at para.28 (1990).

respect to human rights conventions, but there is still a wide margin of appreciation for State practice.

While the various conventions are not identical, they protect similar rights and so it is likely that extradition will be seen to violate the same sorts of guarantees in the ECHR, ICCPR, ACHR and ACHPR. On that understanding, discussion of the prolific case law under the ECHR and ICCPR[14] should be relevant to interpreting the provisions of the ACHR and the ACHPR.

All the conventions protect the right to life[15] and protection from inhuman or degrading treatment.[16]

> "The Commission recalls its *jurisprudence constante* according to which no right of an alien to enter or to reside in a particular country, nor a right not to be expelled from a particular country is as such guaranteed by the Convention. It is true that the Commission has held that expulsion may in exceptional circumstances involve a violation of the Convention, for example where there is a serious fear of treatment contrary to Article 3 in the receiving State."[17]

In other cases applicants have claimed that extradition would subject them to unfair trial practices in the requesting State.[18] They also claim that expulsion, either extradition or deportation, may violate the right to a family life,[19] the right to freedom of movement and to seek asylum[20] and the

---

14   In *Glaziou v France*, CCPR/C/51/D/452/1991, 27 July 1994, the HRC held, in line with a reservation by France to Article 5.2(a) of the Optional Protocol, that it could not deal with a communication which had already been dealt with by the European Commission of Human Rights.
"La France fait une réserve à l'alinéa a) du paragraphe 2 de l'article 5 en précisant que le Comité des droits de l'homme ne sera pas compétent pour examiner une communication émanant d'un particulier si la même question est en cours d'examen ou a déjà été examinée par une autre instance internationale d'enquête ou de règlement."
Paras.6 and 7.2.
15   Article 2 ECHR; Article 6 ICCPR; Article 4 ACHR; Article 4 ACHPR.
16   Article 3 ECHR; Article 7 ICCPR; Article 5 ACHR; Article 5 ACHPR.
17   *App. 10032/82 v Sweden*, (1984), 6 EHRR 555 at 557. See also, *Kindler, supra* n8, at para.13.2.
18   Article 6 ECHR; Article 14 ICCPR; Article 8 ACHR; Article 7 ACHPR.
19   Article 8 ECHR; Arts.17 and 23 ICCPR; Article 17 ACHR; Article 18 ACHPR.

right to obtain a remedy for breach of the convention,[21] in that, for example, once outside the member States of the Council of Europe the victim will have no effective remedy under the ECHR. Before examining those rights in detail with respect to extradition, it ought to be noted that some commentators[22] would distinguish between the rights granted in respect to life and freedom from torture, inhuman and degrading treatment and those to do with fairness of trial, family life and adequate remedies. Respect for the former may well represent *ius cogens* which would prevent surrender of any fugitive under even the most watertight extradition treaty. There is, to this extent, a hierarchy of human rights protections, the violations of some guarantees being treated more seriously than others. Case law to date under the ECHR may seem to bear this view out.

One further protection, though, is necessary for a person seeking to present his case before the human rights institutions to query an extradition request. Most applications to such institutions take a long time to be heard, whereas extradition is designed to be a speedy process. Therefore, the fugitive needs a special means of presenting his case and having his surrender stopped. With respect to the ECHR, this expedited application procedure is found in Rule 36.[23]

c. Rule 36 Procedure

It may take years to deal with applications to the ECHR organs. This is a problem in all cases, but with extradition, and also deportation, it assumes an even greater significance, for the requested State usually wishes to be rid of the fugitive very quickly in order to honour its international obligations

---

20 ECHR Protocol 4, Article 3 (*nb.* in *RHK v The Netherlands* 104 INT'L L REP.412 at 414, the Dutch Supreme Court held that Article 3 of Protocol 4 only prevented the State from *permanently* expelling a national – extradition does not result in permanent expulsion); Arts.12 and 13 ICCPR; Article 22 ACHR and Article XXVII ADRDM; Article 12 ACHPR.

21 Article 13 ECHR; Article 2(3) ICCPR; Article 25 ACHR; Arts.2 & 7 ACHPR.

22 Vogler, Scope, *supra* n6, at p.668 and see Article 53 Vienna Convention on the Law of Treaties, 8 INT.LEG.MAT.679 (1969).

23 See O'Boyle *Practice and Procedure under the European Convention on Human Rights*, 20 SANTA CLARA L REV.697 at pp.706-07 (1980).

or to remove an unwelcome visitor. The ECHR does not provide for interim relief through an injunction, but Rule 36 of the Rules of Procedure provides that the Commission[24] may indicate "any interim measure the adoption of which seems desirable in the interest of the Parties or the proper conduct of the proceedings before it". It ought to be noted that Rule 36 only allows the Commission to indicate to the requested State that it wishes a stay in the domestic proceedings, it cannot compel such action. However, most States comply with the request,[25] and thus the extradition is delayed until the Commission considers the application.[26] In *Cruz Varas v Sweden,*[27] the Commission held that by deporting the applicant while his case was pending violated Article 25 and the obligation not to effectively hinder applications.[28] Under the ICCPR, the Committee "may ... inform the State of its views whether interim measures may be desirable to avoid irreparable damage to the victim of the alleged violation".[29] It can do so even before any decision on the admissibility of the communication. Furthermore, the Human Rights Committee has found an implicit obligation within the ICCPR not to hinder communications.[30]

The two extremes of attitude towards the domestic effect of human rights obligations are displayed in the following responses of the municipal courts in the Netherlands and the United Kingdom. In *Leenaert v The Netherlands,*[31] the Hague District Court went so far as to grant an interlocutory injunction in order to prevent the applicant's extradition until after the Commission had dealt with the case. This decision seems to have been the strongest response anywhere within the Council of Europe to a finding that the Convention organs were dealing with the matter in hand. Decisions of courts in the United Kingdom, however, are not as strong. The British courts

---

24 Or the President or Vice-President when it is not in session: Rule 41.
25 See DRZEMCZEWSKI, *supra n*1, at p.9. *Cf.* The Irish Supreme Court in the *Ellis* case refused to stay an order to surrender the fugitive to the United Kingdom pending a ruling from the Commission; The Guardian p.6, 15 NOV 1990.
26 DRZEMCZEWSKI, *supra n*1,points out that in deportation cases a Rule 36 request may lead to a quashing of the order to leave.
27 Series A, Vol.201 at paras.99 *et seq.* (1991).
28 Not upheld on the facts by the European Court of Human Rights.
29 Summary Record, 17 pr.25. Cited in McGOLDRICK, THE HUMAN RIGHTS COMMITTEE, p.131 (1994).
30 *Antonaccio v Uruguay*, Doc A/37/40 p.114.
31 Cited in DRZEMCZEWSKI, *supra n*1, at p.30.

had an opportunity to consider the effect of Rule 36 in an extradition case in *Ex p.Kirkwood*.[32] Their views were, however, *obiter*, because, for some unknown reason, the Commission had let the Rule 36 indication lapse a few months before the hearing.[33] Once the Rule 36 indication was removed the Home Secretary had ordered Kirkwood's extradition. Kirkwood thereupon sought judicial review of the Home Secretary's decision and a stay of the order pending the Commission's decision.

At the *ex parte* hearing, Mann J granted a stay.[34] At this point it seemed that, on the one hand, a valuable method of checking extradition for the fugitive had been added to *habeas corpus* and that, on the other, the Home Secretary's discretion was subject to review. However, at the full hearing the Home Secretary advanced two arguments.

> "[F]irst, that the judge had no jurisdiction to grant the stay ... and, second, even if [he] did have such jurisdiction, on the merits it should not have been exercised. By 'on the merits' it was understood that the court in considering whether or not to grant interim relief must pay regard to the likely fate of the ultimate application when it is heard."[35]

The jurisdiction point turned on specific domestic legislation. The merits of the matter, though, raised the *Wednesbury* principle.[36] There are two limbs to this principle; the first is the usual *ultra vires* rule that a Minister must consider all relevant factors and only relevant factors, while the second is that he "has not, moreover, reached a decision which no reasonable

---

32 *R v Secretary of State for the Home Department, ex parte Kirkwood*, [1984] 1 WLR 913 reversing an earlier decision in the same case that a stay could be granted under R.S.C. Ord.53, r3 (10)(a). *NB* A Rule 36 Indication had lapsed in this case. See below. *Cp., R v Secretary of State for Home Dep't, ex p.Shah*, CO/1983/89, March 1990.

33 See Warbrick, *Reasonableness and the Decision to Extradite*, [1984] PUB.LAW 539; see also, Price, *Human Rights, Death Row and Administrative Law Remedies*, 34 INT'L & COMP. LQ 162 at p.164 (1985).

34 The stay was granted under R.S.C. Ord.53, r3(10)(a).

35 *Supra n*32 at 916.

36 *Associated Provincial Picture Houses Ltd v Wednesbury Corporation*, [1948] 1 KB 223.

Secretary of State could have reached".[37] The Divisional Court found that the Home Secretary's decision could not be stayed.[38]

In the 1990 case of *Ex p.Brind*,[39] the British courts simply followed their previous decisions without adding anything to the jurisprudence of the issues, but in the later decision of the same year, *Ex p.Shah*,[40] Otton J held, *obiter*, that it was "arguable on both sides whether the Secretary of State has in fact a duty to consider such an application to the European Commission on Human Rights". It may at last be the case that even British courts are beginning to accept that extradition should not violate the fugitive's human rights and that a decision on this question by the ECHR organs can be of assistance and may be the fugitive's right under the Convention. Such a change of approach recognises the growing influence of the ECHR on judges in municipal courts throughout the Council of Europe. Furthermore, distinct from the cases pertaining directly to the ECHR, the House of Lords decided in *M v Home Office*[41] that it was possible to obtain an injunction against the Crown – given that that case concerned the deportation of an applicant for refugee status, the pertinence for transnational fugitive offenders is clear. However, it needs to be noted that it was a decision by an English court that the Home Secretary ignored giving rise to contempt proceedings, not a Rule 36 application before the European Commission of Human Rights.

In cases of extradition and deportation, Rule 36 will continue to be very important and it seems strange that having accepted individual petition under Article 25, the High Contracting Parties cannot agree to mandatory interim

---

37 See Gilbert and Wright, *The Means of Protecting Human Rights in the United Kingdom*, 1 Int'l J. Human Rights L 23 at pp.30 *et seq.* (1997).

38 *Supra n*32, at 915 and 919. In *The Soering Case, infra n*73, the European Court of Human Rights held that the lack of an interim injunction against the Crown did not "detract from the effectiveness of judicial review ..., since there is no suggestion that in practice a fugitive would ever be surrendered before his application to the Divisional Court ... had been determined."; para.123. *Cf. Chahal v United Kingdom*, (70/1995/576/662), November 15 1996, European Court of Human Rights. *Mutatis mutandis*, the inability to enforce a Rule 36 indication is not a violation of Article 13.

39 [1990] 1 All ER 469.

40 *Supra n*32. The Commission referred the case to the United Kingdom government upon hearing Shah's application – *App. 16401/90 v UK*.

41 [1994] 1 AC 377.

orders.[42] However, while the procedural rules are important in practice, it is the substantive provisions of the conventions which are of most interest.

d. Substantive Human Rights Limitations on Extradition

As was indicated above, extradition will usually be challenged on the grounds that the fugitive's right to life, to his physical integrity and freedom from torture or inhuman and degrading treatment, to a fair trial, to family life or, as a composite claim, to an effective convention remedy, will be violated if he were to be returned.

(i) Right to life and physical integrity – The Convention Against Torture[43] forbids States Party from "extraditing a person to another State where there are substantial grounds for believing he would be in danger of being subjected to torture". Torture does not include, however, "pain and suffering[44] arising only from, inherent in or incidental to lawful sanctions".[45] Whether the mental suffering consequent on spending time on death row would qualify as torture so as to prevent extradition is, therefore, so far unanswered.

The Human Rights Committee[46] has had to deal with the question of whether extradition to face the death penalty would render the requested State in violation of its obligations under the ICCPR. It has also dealt with the question of whether the death row phenomenon in and of itself is in

---

42 *Viz* DRZEMCZEWSKI, *supra* n1, at pp.41-42. See Lockwood, *The Model American Convention on the Prevention and Punishment of Certain Serious Forms of Violence Jeopardizing Fundamental Rights and Freedoms*, 13 RUTGERS LJ 579 at pp.588-89 (1982).

43 United Nations Convention Against Torture and Other Cruel, Inhuman or Degrading Treatment or Punishment, 1984, 23 INT.LEG.MAT.1027 (1984) & 24 INT.LEG.MAT.535 (1985) – Article 3.

44 Whether mental or physical.

45 Article 1.1.

46 See generally, Schmidt, *Universality of Human Rights and the Death Penalty – the Approach of the Human Rights Committee*, 3 ILSA J.INT'L & COMP.L 477 *esp.* pp.481 *et seq.* (1997); Cerna, *Universality of Human Rights: The Case of the Death Penalty*, 3 ILSA J.INT'L & COMP.L 465 (1997).

breach of the ICCPR.[47] In *Kindler v Canada*,[48] the author of the communication was requested by the USA for extradition with respect to a homicide for which he could be sentenced to the death penalty in Pennsylvania. The Human Rights Committee found that extradition could lead to a violation of the ICCPR if the transnational fugitive offender's rights were to be at real risk in the requesting State.[49] However, according to the majority opinion in *Kindler*, extradition to face the death penalty is not a violation of the Covenant.[50] Furthermore, the period of time spent awaiting execution will not on its own amount to a violation of Articles 7 and 10 ICCPR.[51] Nevertheless, the Human Rights Committee has found that certain elements of the death penalty and the death row phenomenon can give rise to a violation of the ICCPR.

> "On the other hand, each case must be considered on its own merits, bearing in mind the imputability of delays in the administration of justice on the State party, the specific conditions of imprisonment in the particular penitentiary and their psychological impact on the person concerned."[52]

In *Wright v Jamaica*,[53] the Committee held that

> "The Committee is of the opinion that the imposition of a sentence of death upon conclusion of a trial in which the provisions of the Covenant have not been respected constitutes, if no further appeal against the sentence is possible, a violation of Article 6 of the Covenant. As the Committee noted

---

47 The ICCPR does not treat the death penalty as a violation of the right to life. However, Article 6.2 presupposes that there will be a progressive abolition and that it shall only be imposed for the most serious crimes where it continues – the death penalty shall not be imposed for crimes committed before the accused was eighteen and shall not be carried out on pregnant women (Article 6.5).

48 *Supra n*8.

49 *Supra n*8, para.13.2.

50 *Supra n*8, para.14.6.

51 *Johnson v Jamaica*, Doc. CCPR/C/56/D/588/1994 paras.8.2 – 8.5 (1996); *Chaplin v Jamaica* Doc. CCPR/C/55/D/596/1994 (1995), para.8.1. *Cf.* Judicial Committee of the Privy Council, *Pratt and Morgan v Attorney-General of Jamaica* [1993] 4 All ER 769.

52 *Francis v Jamaica*, Doc. CCPR/C/54/D/606/1994 at para.9.1 (1995).

53 Doc. CCPR/C/55/D/459/1991 para.10.6 (1995).

in its General Comment 6(16), the provision that a sentence of death may be imposed only in accordance with the law and not contrary to the provisions of the Covenant implies that 'the procedural guarantees therein prescribed must be observed, including the right to a fair hearing by an independent tribunal, the presumption of innocence, the minimum guarantees for the defence, and the right to review of conviction and sentence by a higher tribunal.' In the present case, since the final sentence of death was passed without legal representation for Mr. Wright at the preliminary hearing, without due respect for the requirement that an accused be tried without undue delay, and without effective representation for Mr. Harvey on appeal, there has consequently also been a violation of Article 6 of the Covenant."

Finally, in *Ng v Canada*,[54] the Committee held that death by cyanide gas asphyxiation, since it may cause prolonged suffering and agony and might take up to ten minutes, violated Article 7 ICCPR. It relied on its General Comment on Article 7,[55] asserting that "when imposing capital punishment, the execution of the sentence '... must be carried out in such a way as to cause the least possible physical and mental suffering'". As such, Canada was in breach of the ICCPR for not seeking sufficient assurances from the United States that the death penalty would not be carried out if imposed at trial.

Thus, the Human Rights Committee treats each case on its facts, but is prepared to interfere in extradition cases where the death penalty might be imposed upon surrender.

Articles 2 and 3 of the ECHR have been raised *vis à vis* extradition hearings, *inter alia*, where the fugitive might face the death penalty in the requesting State.[56] Article 3 on its own is, indeed, the most usual ground on which to try and impugn an extradition request in Strasbourg. As an example of the problem under consideration, in the case of *Amekrane*,[57] the United Kingdom paid the widow of the person returned £37,500 by way

---

54   Doc. CCPR/C/49/D/469/1991 at paras.16.2 – 16.4 (1994).

55   CCPR/C/21/Add.3, para.6.

56   *NB.* Protocol No.6 to the ECHR, ETS 114 (1983), 5 EHRR 167 (1983), encourages member States to abolish the death penalty, but it is a permitted exception to the right to life in Article 2 of the ECHR.

57   *App. 5961/72*, 16 Yb.ECHR 356 (1973); see also The Times, editorial, 14 AUG 1974. DRZEMCZEWSKI, *supra* n1, pp.12-14.

of a friendly settlement without admitting liability. In that case, the person returned had been executed having been handed over from Gibraltar to the Moroccan authorities without any formal surrender proceedings being held. The case was not considered by the Commission or Court on its merits because a friendly settlement was reached; the British government could have been convinced that it had perpetrated a *prima facie* violation of Article 2 or 3 either because of the irregular nature of the surrender or because of the treatment he received in Morocco following that surrender. However, while *Amekrane* did not set any firm precedents for extradition cases, it did reveal that arguments concerning the requested State's responsibilities *vis à vis* the enjoyment of Convention guarantees in the requesting State would not necessarily be manifestly ill-founded.

Subsequently, some cases have touched on the scope of Article 3 in relation to extradition requests and have set out what level of proof is required of the fugitive if the claim is to be substantiated. According to Drzemczewski,

> "when examining the facts, the Commission must determine that there are *substantial grounds* to fear that the person might be subjected to 'torture or to inhuman or degrading treatment or punishment' contrary to Article 3 in the State to which he is being sent *and* that there are *serious grounds* for fearing that such treatment will actually be inflicted upon him."[58]

Strong evidence from the applicant is necessary, therefore, if the Commission is to accept there would be a violation if he were to be expelled.

> "Nevertheless, the Commission finds that from the letters and documents submitted it cannot be concluded that there was a *serious fear of treatment contrary to Article 3* when the applicant was deported to Yugoslavia. It follows that this part of the application is manifestly ill-founded within the meaning of Article 27(2)."[59]

---

58 *Supra n*1, at p.10.
59 *App. 10032/82 v Sweden*, (1984) 6 EHRR 555 at 557. According to the facts, the applicant was sentenced to six years imprisonment for offences against "the State and the people" in the former Yugoslavia (at 556). (Emphasis added).

Given that, *prima facie*, such evidence exists concerning the requesting State, however, it does not necessarily mean that the requested State cannot extradite the fugitive without violating the ECHR. A series of cases have considered the scope of the protection offered in Article 3 in relation to extradition requests. In *App. 9012/80, X v Switzerland*,[60] the applicant was an Indian national requested on serious fraud charges by the United Arab Emirates for trial in Dubai. The Swiss extradited him to Dubai before an application had been made to the Commission, but his representatives took the case, acting on his behalf. Since the fugitive had already been extradited, the ECHR institutions were once again left to make merely hypothetical decisions. In fact, though, the Commission rejected the application, *inter alia*, because the Swiss had extracted thirteen guarantees from Dubai concerning the treatment that the applicant would receive on surrender. The guarantees incorporated human rights provisions from the European Extradition Convention, the previous Swiss Extradition Act and the ECHR. As such, the *prima facie* evidence was rebutted. The question of whether the Commission would have acted if the thirteen requirements had not been negotiated was not answered, thus leaving the scope of Article 3 unclear in relation to extradition.

If the requested State does not extradite the fugitive before a complaint can be made, the latter always has the option to go to the Commission. *Amekrane* and *App. 9012/80* proved that the Commission did not consider the applications to be without merit, just that on the facts the Commission could do nothing in either case. However, it should be noted that in both cases the State to which the fugitive was surrendered was outside the jurisdiction of the ECHR. German experience highlights problems created when another High Contracting Party requests a fugitive's return. Within the Council of Europe, there should be no problems with respect to human rights violations when extraditing to a fellow member. The Council has even gone so far as to promulgate the European Convention on the Suppression of Terrorism[61] to make it easier to allow for the extradition among the member States of that most sensitive group of fugitives, the political offender.[62]

---

60 24 D+R 205 (in English at 213). See also DRZEMCZEWSKI, *supra* n1, at p.11.
61 Hereinafter, ECST; ETS 90 (1977).
62 As for its success, though, see Warbrick, *The ECHR and the Prevention of Terrorism*, 32 INT'L & COMP LQ 82 at p.119 (1983); Gilbert, *The "Law" and "Transnational Terrorism"*, 26 NETH.Yb.INT'L L 3 (1995).

However, certain Council of Europe States do not grant to individuals the right to petition the Commission and thus individual violations cannot be easily questioned. This used to be the case with Turkey. In *Altun v Federal Republic of Germany*,[63] where Turkey had requested Altun's return for interfering with evidence and harbouring criminals, both, in fact, non-capital offences,[64] the Commission again did not have an opportunity to decide on the merits of the Article 3 claim because the applicant committed suicide before the hearing. Yet, it is apparent from the admissibility application that even the extradition of a fugitive to another High Contracting Party might, in certain circumstances, violate Article 3.

> "Nevertheless, if there are reasons to fear that extradition, although requested exclusively for common crimes, has been sought in order to proceed against the individual, in violation of the principle of specialty, for political offences or even for just his political views, then the Commission cannot altogether set aside the possibility of a violation of Art.3 of the Convention."[65]

While the declaration is welcome, it is a little difficult to understand how requesting a fugitive in breach of the principle of specialty or the political offence exemption would, on its own, constitute torture or inhuman and degrading treatment. Article 3 is designed to guarantee that a person is not subjected to torture or inhuman and degrading treatment. With respect to extradition law, it ought to provide a safeguard against surrender where the fugitive might suffer such treatment in the requesting State. States party to the ECHR owe an obligation to all persons within their territory to protect them from violations of Article 3, even if that violation will be carried out by the requesting State. It is hard to see how a potential violation of the political offence exemption would amount to torture or inhuman and degrading treatment. Nevertheless, the statement that Article 3 would prevent

---

63   (1983), 5 EHRR 611. See also *App. 10292/83 v Spain*, 6 EHRR 146 (1984), where the applicant was to be returned to the United States.
64   *Supra n*63, at 614. And see the merits hearing, (1985), 7 EHRR 154 at 158. See also *App. 10940/86 v France* (1986), 8 EHRR 226.
65   *Supra n*63, at 613. *Cf.* Even so, the Commission was prepared to remove its Rule 36 indications on 15 July 1983.

extradition in such circumstances marks a great leap forward in the juris-prudence of the Commission and Court.[66]

The first opportunity the Commission or Court had to consider Article 3 in the course of an extradition request with respect to the death penalty in the requesting State, arose in the *Kirkwood* case.[67] The European decision on the admissibility of the application deals with the California death row phenomenon, rather than with procedure in extradition cases *per se*. Article 4 of the Anglo-US Extradition Treaty[68] provides as follows:

> "If the offence for which extradition is requested is punishable by death under the relevant law of the requesting party, but the relevant law of the requested party does not provide for the death penalty in a similar case, extradition may be refused unless the requesting party gives assurances satisfactory to the requested party that the death penalty will not be carried out."

The British Home Secretary had obtained an assurance from the Deputy Attorney-General of California that if the death penalty were imposed, then the wish of the United Kingdom that it not be carried out would be put before the Governor.[69] Kirkwood argued that regardless of this assurance he might still spend many years on death row, which was in itself inhuman and degrading.[70] The Commission's decision examined the likelihood of this coming to pass and whether it contravened the Convention. It noted the absolute bar on derogating from Article 3, but the permission in Article 2 to use the death penalty for crimes for which that penalty is prescribed by law. It held that the death row phenomenon is troublesome having regard to Article 3, but that the delays were designed to protect life and prevent arbitrariness. On that basis, since Kirkwood had not as yet even been con-victed, the Commission held that the risk of him suffering the death row phenomenon was not serious enough to constitute a violation of Article 3.[71]

---

66 Kemal Altun was posthumously granted asylum by a West Berlin Court in February 1984, The Guardian, p.6, 17 FEB 1984.
67 *App. 10479/83*, 6 EHRR 373.
68 At that time, only UKTS 16 (1977), Cmnd 6723.
69 *Supra n*67, at 374.
70 *Supra n*67, at 376-77.
71 *Supra n*67, at 385-86.

In looking at the treatment the fugitive would encounter in the requesting State, however, the Commission went beyond what a domestic court in a common law State will usually take into account; the so-called rule of non-inquiry prevents the courts of the requested State from investigating the motives or likely behaviour of the requesting State.[72] The decision also confirmed the universal applicability of Article 3 because the USA, as the requesting State, can rightly claim to provide guarantees in its Bill of Rights which are at least the equivalent of those in the ECHR. Despite this fact, the possibility of a violation in the USA was not easily discounted by the Commission.

The Court first had cause to consider the scope of Articles 2 and 3 with respect to extradition in the 1989 *Soering* case.[73] Soering was charged with murder in Virginia for which he faced the death penalty. His arguments against extradition were the same as those in *Kirkwood*; that the death row phenomenon constituted inhuman or degrading treatment. However, his case was complicated by the fact that, in the first place, he was a German national and the government of the FRG had declared itself willing to prosecute him for the crime and that, secondly, he was suffering from delusions at the time of the crime.[74] The Court unanimously upheld Soering's claim that his extradition to face an uncertain future on death row constituted inhuman or degrading treatment under Article 3. De Meyer J went further and held

---

72 *In re Arton (No 1)*, [1896] 1 QB 108 at 114. The motive and conduct of the requesting state is never questioned: the political offence exemption should look only at the offence. *Cf.* Continental practice which would always have regard the proceedings in the requesting state; Vogler, Scope, *supra* n6, at p.664. The Anglo-US Supplementary Extradition Treaty (Cm.294, UKTS 6 (1988) and, with comments, in Appendix 1 to the US Senate EXEC.REPT 99-17, accompanying TR.DOC.99-8 – ratified on 23 December 1986) permits inquiry in limited circumstances in Article 3. See *In re Extradition of Howard* 996 F.2d 1320 (1993): and, *In the Matter of the Requested Extradition of Smyth* 61 F.3d 711 (1995); rehearing denied, 72 F.3d 1433 (1996) – see also, 795 F.Supp.973 (1992), 820 F.Supp.498 (1993), 826 F.Supp.316 (1993), 863 F.Supp.1137 (1994).

73 *The Soering Case*, Series A, Vol.161. See Quigley and Shank, *Death Row Phenomenon as a Violation of Human Rights. Is it Legal to Extradite to Virginia?*, 30 VA.J INT'L L 241 (1990).

74 *Cf.* Gubbay CJ (Zim. S.Ct) held that Soering's age and mental condition were irrelevant and that everything turned on the death row phenomenon – *Catholic Commission for Justice and Peace in Zimbabwe v A-G et al.*, 14 HRLJ 323 at 333 (1993), relying on para.106 of *Soering, supra* n73.

that if the crime would not attract the death penalty in the requested State, then it was a breach of Article 2 to extradite him to a State where he might be executed. This minority opinion was not supported by any of the other judges and should not be viewed as setting any precedent. However, with the growing disapproval of the death penalty in Europe, as evidenced by Protocol 6, it cannot be doubted that De Meyer J's view will be taken up again in future cases and may in time come to be the accepted reasoning of the Court. For the time being, if the requested State has ratified Protocol 6, then the European Commission of Human Rights would

> "not exclude the possibility that the responsibility of a Contracting State could be engaged under Article 1 of Protocol No.6 if a fugitive [were to be] extradited to a State where he runs a serious risk of being condemned to death or executed."[75]

With respect to Article 3 of the ECHR, though, the Court recognised that the Convention was limited to Council of Europe member States and that it did not make any reference to extradition. Moreover, according to the Court, the risk of the violation alleged by Soering was only potential until he had faced trial in Virginia. Furthermore,

> "inherent in the whole of the Convention was a search for a fair balance between the demands of the general interest of the community and the re-quirements of the protection of the individual's human rights. As movement about the world becomes easier and crime takes on a larger international dimension, it is increasingly in the interest of all nations that suspected offenders who flee abroad should be brought to justice. Conversely, the establishment of safe-havens for fugitives would not only result in danger for the State obliged to harbour the protected person but also tend to under-mine the foundations of extradition. These considerations must also be in-cluded among the factors to be taken into account in the interpretation and application of the notions of inhuman and degrading treatment or punishment in extradition cases ...."

Nevertheless, the Court went on to find in favour of Soering.

---

75 *Aylor v France* 100 INT'L L REP.690 at 692.

"In sum, the decision by a Contracting State to extradite a fugitive may give rise to an issue under Article 3, and hence engage the responsibility of that State under the Convention, *where substantial grounds have been shown for believing that the person concerned, if extradited, faces a real risk of being subjected to torture or to inhuman or degrading treatment or punishment in the requesting country.* The establishment of such responsibility inevitably involves an assessment of conditions in the requesting country against the standards of Article 3 of the Convention. Nonetheless, there is no question of adjudicating on or establishing the responsibility of the requesting country, whether under general international law, under the Convention or otherwise. In so far as any liability under the Convention is or may be incurred, it is the liability incurred by the extraditing Contracting State by reason of its having taken action which has as a direct consequence the exposure of an individual to proscribed ill-treatment."[76]

Soering builds on the already well-established, if previously untested, principles relating to extradition and Article 3. The Court has decided that in future the requested State must have regard to potential violations of ECHR guarantees by the authorities in the requesting State, regardless of whether the latter is a party to the ECHR. In the subsequent case of *Chahal*,[77] the European Court of Human Rights held in relation to an asylum case, where the applicant feared he would be tortured for his political views if deported to India, that the United Kingdom would violate Article 3 if he were to be returned.

"80. The prohibition provided by Article 3 against ill-treatment is equally absolute in expulsion cases. Thus, *whenever substantial grounds have been shown for believing that an individual would face a real risk* of being subjected to treatment contrary to Article 3 if removed to another State, the responsibility of the Contracting State to safeguard him or her against such treatment is engaged in the event of expulsion .... In these circumstan-

---

76 *Supra n*73, paras.89 and 91; emphasis added. Nevertheless, the United Kingdom reached an agreement with the Virginian authorities, via the federal government with which the treaty has been concluded, that Soering would only be charged with non-capital offences and his extradition was then granted. The British government argued that the extent of the Court's decision was to prohibit his return to spend time on death row. The Guardian p.24, 2 AUG 1989.

77 *Supra n*38, paras.80 and 81 (emphasis added).

ces, the activities of the individual in question, however undesirable or dangerous, cannot be a material consideration. The protection afforded by Article 3 is thus wider than that provided by Articles 32 and 33 of the United Nations 1951 Convention on the Status of Refugees (see paragraph 61 above).

81. ... It should not be inferred from the Court's remarks concerning the risk of undermining the foundations of extradition, as set out in paragraph 89 of [*Soering*], that there is any room for balancing the risk of ill-treatment against the reasons for expulsion in determining whether a State's responsibility under Article 3 is engaged."

Thus, an effective application can be made to Strasbourg to prevent extradition where there are substantial grounds for believing that the transnational fugitive offender faces a real risk that he would be subject to treatment contrary to Article 3 of the ECHR if surrendered. And it is no defence for the respondent State to question the conduct and activities of the transnational fugitive offender.

However, as noted above, obtaining a judgment from the European Court of Human Rights can be a long drawn out process. While domestic courts will also draw on extradition laws that seek to protect transnational fugitive offenders, discussed in Chapter 5 below, there is now a substantial body of case law from various jurisdictions dealing with extradition requests where the domestic court takes account of the State's obligations under its international human rights commitments. Since the cases tend to mix the protections found in the extradition and human rights treaties, this discussion focusses more on the attitude of courts to the threat of the death penalty.

During the last thirty years there has been a growing trend to abolish the death penalty, although it is nowhere near eradicated. Its demise is most thorough in western Europe. This change has been reflected in extradition law. The typical clause in treaties is found in Article 11 of the European Convention on Extradition.[78]

"If the offence for which extradition is requested is punishable by death under the law of the requesting Party, and if in respect of such offence the death penalty is not provided for by the law of the requested Party or is not normally carried out, extradition may be refused unless the requesting

---

78 ETS 24 (1957).

Party gives such assurance as the requested Party considers sufficient that the death penalty will not be carried out."

In the 1978 case of *Viaux-Peccate v The State of the Netherlands*,[79] the court held that this principle was not a rule of customary international law. A year later in 1979, the Constitutional Court of Italy, in the case of *Re Cuillier, Ciamborrani and Vallon*,[80] overruled the Italian appellate court's judgment which had decided that there was a generally recognised rule of law that a person would not be extradited to face the death penalty without receiving assurances that it would not be carried out from the requesting state. The Constitutional Court based its decision on the fact that there has to be an express treaty provision to that effect if the fugitive is to be protected, although it might be argued to the contrary that such provisions are merely declaratory of customary international law in nature. In fact, extradition was refused under the Italian Constitution rather than under some nascent principle of international law because the right to life was recognised therein. In *C v Federal Police Department*,[81] the Swiss Federal Tribunal found that the international obligation imposed by an extradition treaty took precedence over the domestic extradition legislation which required assurances *vis à vis* the death penalty from the requesting State; and, furthermore, there was no superior norm of international public policy overriding the bilateral treaty's silence on death penalty issues – the Tribunal expressly referred to Article 2 of the ECHR permitting capital punishment.[82] In *SIG v Public Prosecutor*,[83] the Dutch Supreme Court was not dealing with the death penalty, but referred to potential violations of Article 3 in the requesting State, in this case, the United States. Its argument was that The Netherlands would be presumed to have entered into extradition arrangements only with States which would not violate the ECHR and that, as such, an appeal by a transnational fugitive offender based on treatment in the requesting State will not "as a general rule lead ... to a ruling that the request for extradition is inadmissible ...". Such ingenuousness is touching! In *McF*

---

79 District Court of the Hague, 74 INT'L L REP.456 at 457 (1978).
80 78 INT'L L REP.93.
81 100 INT'L L REP.657 (1987).
82 *Supra n*81, at 659-60.
83 100 INT'L L REP.408 at 410 (1985).

and GK v *The Public Prosecutor*,[84] the courts held that because the United Kingdom was a party to the ECHR and granted a right of individual petition,[85] they were not free to decide on a complaint that if extradited, the transnational fugitive offenders would be subjected to inhuman and degrading treatment contrary to Article 3 and would not receive a fair hearing contrary to Article 6.

However, more recently some courts have taken a more active stance with respect to the death penalty in the requesting state.This change of attitude flows in part from the promulgation of Protocol 6 to the ECHR.[86] In *CDS v The Netherlands*,[87] the Dutch Supreme Court held that under Articles 1 and 6 of Protocol 6 the Dutch Government was bound under the ECHR to refrain from Acts which could "result in someone within the jurisdiction being exposed to the death penalty, even if the penalty is imposed or carried out elsewhere".[88] Despite the fact that the Dutch government was also bound in international law to hand the accused over, his right not to be exposed to the death penalty arising out of the obligations under Protocol 6 took precedence.[89] In *Fidan*,[90] the French *Conseil d'Etat* had to consider the issue in relation to a request by Turkey for the fugitive for murder and attempted murder. Taking into account the sixth Protocol, the court held that given that France abolished the death penalty in 1981, it would be contrary to French *ordre public* to extradite Fidan since any guarantees given by the Turkish government under the typical treaty clause would not be binding on the independent courts. The Swiss case of *Dharmarajah*[91] concerned extradition to a State not party to the ECHR and with which Switzerland did not have an extradition arrangement. The Sri Lankan government wanted Switzerland to extradite a Tamil. Having first obtained a guarantee that the death penalty would not be imposed, the Swiss then extracted several

---

84 100 INT'L L REP.414 at 426 and 429.

85 *Cf.* The Turkish experience – *Aksoy, infra* n95.

86 Concerning the Abolition of the Death Penalty, 5 EHRR 167 (1983).

87 96 INT'L L REP.383 (1990).

88 *Supra* n87, at 387.

89 *Supra* n87, at 388.

90 100 INT'L L REP.662 (1987); Errera, [1987] PUB.LAW 286. See also, *Aylor, Conseil d'Etat*, 1993, 100 INT'L L REP.664 at 689-90.

91 See DRZEMCZEWSKI, *supra* n1, at pp.32-33. For other examples, see the Report of the 67th Conference of the International Law Association, Helsinki 1996, Committee on Extradition and Human Rights, pp.214 *et seq.*, esp. pp.229-31.

other guarantees from the Sri Lankans, including a promise to accord to Dharmarajah those rights set out in the ECHR.[92] Despite these assurances the Swiss still did not extradite him. *Dharmarajah* shows again that in appropriate circumstances extradition may be blocked if the requested State is afraid that the fugitive might have his Convention rights infringed on surrender, thus giving efficacy to the provisions of Article 3.

Finally, the discretion to refuse extradition where the fugitive would face the death penalty if surrendered is usually vested in the executive rather than the courts.[93] It should be noted that extradition will be permitted if the executive receives sufficient assurances that the death penalty will not be carried out, although the independence of the judiciary in the requesting State may make this guarantee less of a certainty than the fugitive would like. As was seen above, the courts will sometimes oversee this executive discretion.

Although it does represent an interference in the internal affairs of the requesting State, within Europe at least the freedom from the death penalty is rapidly developing into a new human right which ought to be exercised in favour of all individuals, even if the sentence is to be imposed outside the Council of Europe. This development has most recently found further expression in the 1990 Copenhagen Conference on the Human Dimension of the then Conference on Security and Co-operation in Europe, where the representatives of the OSCE States agreed in paragraph 17 to monitor the future use of capital punishment, whilst also recognising the increasing

---

92 In the end, Dharmarajah was not surrendered because the Swiss government did not accept the guarantees given by the Sri Lankan government. DRZEMCZEWSKI, *supra* n1, at p.33. See also Recommendation 950 (1982), para.9, where Council of Europe member states were exhorted not to conclude extradition treaties with states where there is a chance of unfair trial, or arbitrary judgment, or where torture is practised, unless proper guarantees are obtained – 25 Yb.ECHR (PD) 13 (1982); and see now the European Convention for the Prevention of Torture, 27 INT.LEG.MAT.1152 (1988) and 28 INT.LEG.MAT.1341 (1989).

93 The British Extradition Act 1989 is rare in giving the fugitive an express right to seek judicial review of the Home Secretary's order for return after making representations to the latter concerning, *inter alia*, the likelihood of the death penalty being imposed; see ss.12 and 13 of the 1989 Act, discussed in Chapter 3 above.

admonitions to abolish it.[94] Moreover, the discretionary protection from the death penalty offered to fugitives in extradition treaties reveals how international criminal law and the international protection of human rights can have overlapping roles.

The jurisprudence of Articles 2 and 3 would appear, therefore, to be the following: –

1 If the requesting State is a High Contracting Party to the ECHR then, *prima facie*, extradition should not be prohibited. (*Altun*[95])

2 If the requesting State is not a member of the Council of Europe, but is another "Western democracy", then refusal of extradition should be rare, although that position may be changing. (Compare *App. 10292/83 v Spain* and *Kirkwood* with *Soering*)

3 With regard to any other State, a lot would seem to depend on whether there was an obligation to extradite under an extradition treaty. If an extradition treaty has been concluded, then the fugitive should be protected by the safeguards therein. If no treaty exists, then the requesting State could well have to guarantee Convention rights to the applicant before extradition would be granted. (*Chahal* and *App. 9012/80, X v Switzerland*).

(ii) Right to a Fair Trial and Other Fundamental Freedoms[96] – The Human Rights Committee and the European Court and Commission of Human Rights have devoted less time to considering whether the fugitive's other rights would be violated if he were to be extradited. With respect to whether the requesting State will honour Article 6, the Commission considered the matter in *App. 8299/78, X & Y v Ireland*.[97] On the facts, it found that the United Kingdom would not have been at fault if it had been joined as a respondent for extraditing the applicants to Ireland to face trial in the juryless Special Criminal Court. The Special Criminal Court was held to be independent and impartial within Article 6. However, the case indicates that in

---

94 CSCE (CHD) Copenhagen Document, 11 HRLJ 232 (1990), and Buergenthal, *A new public order for Europe*, 11 HRLJ 217 (1990).
95 *Cf. Aksoy v Turkey*, 100/1995/606/694, 18 DEC 1996, where the European Court of Human Rights found that Turkey was guilty of torture – paras.63 and 64.
96 See Vogler, Scope, *supra n*6.
97 24 Yb.ECHR 132 at 174 (1981).

certain circumstances, the fact that the fugitive's rights under Article 6 would be violated in the requesting State might impose liability on the requested State. This view was upheld by the European Court of Human rights, *obiter*, in *Soering*.

"The right to a fair trial in criminal proceedings, ..., holds a prominent place in a democratic society .... The Court does not exclude that an issue might exceptionally be raised under Article 6 by an extradition decision in circumstances where the fugitive has suffered or risks suffering a *flagrant* denial of a fair trial in the requesting country."[98]

The French *Conseil d'Etat* has gone further. In the *Galdeano, Ramirez and Beiztegui* case,[99] it held that extradition will not be granted if the requesting State's judicial system does not respect fundamental rights and freedoms. In *McF and GK*,[100] the Dutch courts were prepared to entertain the idea that extradition could violate Article 6, but rejected it on the facts on the basis that the United Kingdom was also a party to the ECHR and granted a right of individual petition. This approach is much more liberal than that advocated by the European Court of Human Rights and reveals that domestic courts applying ECHR principles may be more forthright than the supranational ECHR organs.[101] Moreover, Austria and Switzerland include the procedural guarantees of the ECHR in their domestic extradition legislation, the Swiss also incorporating the guarantees of the ICCPR.[102]

(iii)   Right to Family Life – Although Article 8 of the ECHR is often pleaded by the applicant, the Commission has always held that the right

---

98   *Soering, supra n*73, at para.113. Emphasis added.

99   26 SEPT 1984, Rec.307, [1985] PUB.LAW 328.

100 *Supra n*84.

101 See DRZEMCZEWSKI, EUROPEAN HUMAN RIGHTS CONVENTION IN DOMESTIC LAW: A COMPARATIVE STUDY, (1983).

102 See Vogler, Scope, *supra n*6, at p.669, n30; Switzerland, Law on International Judicial Assistance in Criminal Matters (I.R.S.G), Article 2, 20 INT.LEG.MAT.1339 (1981), as amended 4 OCT 1996 (supplied by the Federal Office for Police Matters, Bern) – the text is a combination of both translations. See also the Decree on International Mutual Assistance in Criminal Matters, 24 FEB 1982 as amended 9 DEC 1996 (supplied by the Federal Office for Police Matters, Bern).

to a family life must give way to the more pressing demands of enforcing criminal laws.[103]

e. Article 6 and the Extradition Hearing

So far, the discussion has centred on whether the requesting State's potential violation of the ECHR would be sufficient to impose liability on the requested State so as to prevent extradition. This final section will consider the applicability of Article 6 of the ECHR to the extradition hearing in the requested State.

Article 6 of the Convention provides:

"(1) In the determination of his civil rights and public obligations or of any criminal charge against him, everyone is entitled to a fair and public hearing within a reasonable time by an independent and impartial tribunal established by law....

(2) Everyone charged with a criminal offence has the following minimum rights ....

(d) to examine or have examined witnesses against him and to obtain the attendance and examination of witnesses on his behalf under the same conditions as the witnesses against him."

In the 1976 case of *M v Federal Prosecutor*,[104] Dutch Supreme Court held that the Article 6 requirement that a person be presumed innocent until proven guilty did not apply to extradition hearings where all that was necessary was a suspicion of guilt. As stated previously, the guilt or innocence of the fugitive is irrelevant in an extradition hearing.

In *App. 10227/82 v Spain*,[105] the applicant contested the fairness of his extradition hearing under Article 6(1)'s general provisions. The Commission, declaring the application inadmissible, questioned whether an extradition hearing was a 'determination ... of a criminal charge'. The Commission's view was that 'determination' in Article 6 required a finding of guilt or innocence, not just extraditability. Thus, it seemed extradition hearings

---

103 See *Dec. 7816/77*, 9 D+R 219.
104 8 NETH.Yb.INT'L L 275 (1977); 74 INT'L L REP.293.
105 (1984), 6 EHRR 581 at 582-83.

were not open to review under Article 6(1). However, in a later case, again involving Spain, *App. 10292/83*,[106] while the Commission was not prepared to accept that extradition hearings were open to such review, it stated *obiter* that on the facts of that case no violation of Article 6 was disclosed. This approach seemed to herald a return to the vague comments of the Commission in *App. 9742/82 v Ireland*,[107] where a fugitive broke his bail to avoid extradition.

> "The Commission recognises that occasions may arise where an alleged violation of the rights and freedoms guaranteed by the Convention may excuse an applicant from compliance with the operation of the rule of law."

It was argued that this declaration tacitly accepted that an extradition hearing may violate Article 6. Now, though, the value of this *dictum* is again open to doubt, for in *App. 10479/83 v United Kingdom*,[108] the Commission once more stated Article 6 did not apply to extradition hearings because there was no final determination of guilt or innocence;[109] in so doing, the Commission ignored *App. 9742/82* which had been argued before them.[110] In *Aylor*,[111] the Commission again reiterated that its longstanding case-law was to the effect that an extradition hearing did not concern the merits of criminal charges.

To conclude, it would be odd if an extradition hearing could deliberately flout the Convention protections with impunity. There ought to be some minimum guarantees. However, the scope of Article 6 is hotly contested and the jurisprudence of the Commission is far from clear or "*constante*".

f. Conclusion

The human rights guarantees found in the conventions will take on a growing importance in extradition law. With the ever-increasing restrictions on the

---

106 (1984), 6 EHRR 146.
107 (1983), 5 EHRR 594.
108 (1984), 6 EHRR 373.
109 *Supra n*108, at 386.
110 *Supra n*108, at 378.
111 *Supra n*90, at 694-95.

political offence exemption, attention is shifting from the offence to the offender. At the same time, the balancing exercise seen in *Soering*[112] between protecting the fugitive's human rights and ensuring that criminal laws are enforced will necessarily provide States with a great deal of discretion in this field, subject only to the absolute bar on surrender if the fugitive would face torture – *Chahal*.[113]

---

112 *Supra n*73.
113 *Supra n*38.

5

RESTRICTIONS ON RETURN

a. Introduction

Extradition law is permeated with special defences peculiar to its processes. Even if the requesting State satisfies the procedural requirements necessary for surrender to be authorised, the transnational fugitive offender can still plead that his extradition would violate provisions which tend to be included in all treaties. Further, there are some generally available defences to criminal charges which can also be utilised in an extradition hearing. The object of this chapter is to consider and criticize these restrictions on return.

b. The Extradition of Nationals

Civil law States do not usually extradite their own nationals. Common law States never adopted such a restrictive general approach, although in certain specific cases a discretionary clause to that end was included in extradition arrangements. As Oppenheim's International Law[1] explains,

> "[many] States, however, such as France and Germany, have adopted the principle of never extraditing one of their own subjects to a foreign State but themselves punishing their own subjects for grave crimes committed abroad. Other States, *eg.* Great Britain have not adopted this principle, and, in the absence of treaty provisions to the contrary, make no distinction between their own subjects and other persons who are alleged to have committed extraditable crimes abroad."

---

1   Ed. LAUTERPACHT, 8th ed. 1955, at p.699.

The effect of this restriction can be quite dramatic. In *Bonnechaux v Switzerland*[2] the European Commission on Human Rights upheld the 35 month pre-trial detention of a 74 year old French national by the Swiss authorities, despite Article 5(3) of the ECHR, on the ground that if he were to be released there was a serious risk that he might flee to France from where extradition would be impossible and where there was no guarantee that he would be prosecuted for the offences committed in Switzerland.

The rationale for this policy, as explained by civil law commentators,[3] is based, first, on one's own national judges being also the natural judges of the offence, next, on a State's alleged duty to protect its own nationals and, finally, on the fear that a foreigner would be prejudiced at a trial in the *locus delicti*.[4]

In civil law jurisdictions, this restriction has been elevated to a rule of international law. The Austrian Supreme Court put it thus.

> "It may also be observed that in criminal matters there is a generally recognised rule of international law (Article 9 of the Austrian Federal Constitution) that a State's own nationals must never be extradited to another State in whose territory they have committed a criminal offence."[5]

French extradition law is similarly absolute on this matter.

> "*Il est de principe à peu près constant depuis un siècle, du moins en droit français et malgré certaines critiques doctrinales tant sur le plan international ..., qu'un Etat n'extrade pas ses nationaux. Cette règle est exprimée en termes absolus par les articles 3, alinéa 1er, et 5, alinéa 1er, de la loi du 10 mars 1927 à l'égard de tous les 'ressortissants' de la France, c'est-à-dire tous ceux dont elle assurait la représentation internationale (Français*

---

2   (1979) 3 EHRR 259, p.264, at para.64.

3   *Eg.* LAMMASCH, BELATZIS and BEDI, all cited by SHEARER, EXTRADITION IN INTERNATIONAL LAW (1971), at p.121.

4   SHEARER, *supra n*3, at pp.18-20. This fear of prejudice and discrimination in the requesting State is one that pre-dates the State and concomitant nationality – in Article II of the Treaty of Kutschuk-Kaïnardji, 1774, between the Russian and Ottoman Empires, surrender of Christians by Russia and Moslems by the Sublime Porte was the sole exception to a duty to refuse asylum to those guilty of capital crimes, disobedience or treason.

5   *Service of Summons in Criminal Proceedings (Austria) Case*, 38 INT'L L REP.133 at 134. Austria Supreme Court.

*et 'protégés'). Elle se réduit actuellement aux Français. Elle figure égale-
ment dans toutes les conventions signées par la France."*[6]

However, the protection in French law does not extend to refugees resident
in the requested State and granted protection there.[7] There is both Swiss
and German authority to the same effect as the French law on this point.
In *T v Swiss Federal Prosecutor's Office*,[8] the Swiss Federal Tribunal,
having examined the rights conferred on refugees by the Convention Relating
to the Status of Refugees 1951, held that refugees were only assimilated
to nationals to a limited extent and this did not encompass the right not to
be extradited. However, in The Netherlands, the executive has a discretion
to refuse the extradition of a non-national who has been integrated into the
Dutch community and who can be prosecuted in Dutch courts, although this
discretion is not exercisable by the extradition courts.[9] The protection afforded to true nationals, though, verges on the absolute throughout Continental Europe. However, the protection is not confined to civil law States, although they are the principal users of this restriction on return. The government of the United Kingdom, for instance, also reserves the right not to
extradite nationals; the situations are limited to those occasions where there
is no general extradition treaty with the requesting State and the latter is
seeking the fugitive's return under a multilateral, anti-terrorist convention.[10]
While the occasions when such a provision would be implemented will be

---

6   ENCYCLOPEDIE DALLOZ: PENAL III (DR-INST), paras.151 *et seq.*, (1968). On acces-
    sion to the European Convention on Extradition, 1957, the Nordic States (De-
    nmark, Finland, Iceland, Norway and Sweden) not only extended the definition
    of nationals to include those ordinarily resident, but also the nationals and
    residents of the other Nordic States; see, Karle, Some Problems Concerning
    the Application of the European Convention on Extradition, at pp.49 *et seq.*
    of LEGAL ASPECTS OF EXTRADITION, (COUNCIL OF EUROPE, 1970).
7   *Supra* n6, at para.157.
8   72 INT'L L REP.632 at 635-6 (1966).
9   *MY v Public Prosecutor*, 100 INT'L L REP.401; see also, *KM v Netherlands*, 100
    INT'L L REP.430 (Dutch Supreme Court). The Nordic States have made
    declarations with regard to Article 6 of the European Convention on Extradition
    (ETS 24, 1957) that include within the term national, nationals of other Nordic
    States and domiciled aliens, including refugees.
10 See the Extradition (Aviation Security) Order 1991, SI 1991 No.1699, Sch.3
    Pt II para.3(2)(b).

rare, its inclusion should be avoided at all costs in the future, not least because it may in fact be unconstitutional – nationals of a friendly State enjoy all the same rights as British nationals while within the protection of the Crown.[11] The refusal to extradite nationals is, in sum, an indiscriminate protection, unsuitable to the needs of mutual assistance in law enforcement.

Despite the rationales propounded by the civil law commentators noted above, it has to be questioned whether such an absolute bar to extradition, even allowing for trial in the national's own State,[12] is still appropriate. Within the European Community with its open borders policy since 1992, two member States, Greece and the Federal Republic of Germany, refuse under any circumstances to surrender their nationals.[13] Moreover, the Nordic States refuse extradition of not just their own nationals, but those of other Nordic States and domiciled aliens, too.[14] However, given that within Europe the United Kingdom had done away with the *prima facie* requirement, having ratified the European Convention on Extradition upon passage of the 1989 Extradition Act,[15] the civil law States of the European Union were effectively obliged to consider relaxing the absolute bar on the extradition of nationals.[16] The European Union Convention Relating to Extradition between Member States, 1996,[17] provides in Article 7.1 that extradition may not be refused on the ground that the "person claimed is a national of the requested Member State". However, paragraphs 2 and 3 per-

---

11 *Johnstone v Pedlar*, [1921] AC 262 *per* Viscount Finlay at 274.
12 See ENCYCLOPEDIE DALLOZ, *supra* n6, at para.152.
13 See para.92, vol I, HOME AFFAIRS SELECT COMMITTEE, SEVENTH REPORT, PRACTICAL POLICE CO-OPERATION IN THE EUROPEAN COMMUNITY, 20 JULY 1990, HCP 363 (1989–90); hereinafter, HCP. As far as the Federal Republic of Germany is concerned, the prohibition against extraditing national is part of the Constitution; see, Art.16(II), Basic Law of the FRG, 1949, (155 B.F.S.P. 503).
14 *Supra* n6.
15 SI 1990 No.1507.
16 The British Police Service's answer at p.18, HCP-II, *supra* n13, suggested that in future all persons within the European Community would be tried in their home State once European criminal laws were harmonised. There is no further evidence for such a suggestion and even given that harmonisation may be many years off, it is not a sensible approach to law enforcement; see the decision in *In re Korosi*, [1925–26] Ann.Dig.309 (Italian Court of Cassation, 1925).
17 1996 OJ C 313.

mit a five year rolling reservation allowing States to refuse extradition of their nationals. The Explanatory Report[18] makes clear several matters: first, that the Nordic members of the European Union will no longer classify domiciled aliens as nationals for the purposes of intra-EU extradition; secondly, that the protection of nationals might be achieved by those States which do not ordinarily extradite nationals, by entering a reservation that any sentence imposed by the requesting State will be served in the requested State; next, that given that some States are constitutionally prohibited from extraditing their own nationals, that they review the scope of the restriction at least once every five years; and, finally, that reservations are not indefinite and can lapse.

The civil law States' refusal to extradite their own nationals displays a distrust of other States' systems of criminal justice. The civil lawyers' criticism of the British demand that a *prima facie* case be made out before extradition ought to be granted, was that it displayed a similar distrust of other legal systems. However, the refusal to extradite nationals cannot even be justified on the ground that a person should not be removed from a State where he is free unless the requesting State has at minimum shown that he has a case to answer, an argument that can at least be proposed in favour of the *prima facie* requirement.

Fortunately, as certain crimes increasingly threaten the international community, civil law States, with respect to their extradition relations with common law States, are generally beginning to relax their strict adherence to their previous practice of never extraditing their nationals; *inter se*, there appears to be no change of policy nor any desire for such. This change with respect to common law jurisdictions, though, is still only gradual. The United States concluded an extradition treaty with Colombia on 14 September 1979 which did allow for the surrender of nationals. The problem had previously been that Colombian nationals who had imported drugs into the United States could not be extradited and had corrupted Colombian law enforcement officials to such an extent that trial in Colombia was almost impossible. However, the change in the 1979 treaty was not popular and after several

---

18   1997 OJ C 191, pp.20-21.

attempts it was declared unconstitutional by the Colombian Supreme Court.[19] Greater success has been achieved in the United States treaty with Italy of the 13 October 1983.[20] The Treaty, Article IV of which expressly states that extradition shall not be refused on grounds of nationality, is aimed to combat the co-ordinated organised crime in the two countries. More generally, Shearer's prognostication back in 1971,[21] that the repatriation of prisoners to serve their sentence in their own country would eventually convince civil law States to extradite their nationals, is at last coming true. The idea of repatriating prisoners is an old one and was included in the Franco-Basle treaty of 1781.[22] It was also implemented in the Arab League Agreement of 1952.[23] It is based on the principle that a national's own State is likely to provide the best opportunities for rehabilitation. Given that in the event of conviction the extraditee will be returned to The Netherlands to serve his sentence, the Dutch government indicated its willingness to surrender its own nationals to the United Kingdom.[24] As noted above, this is one possible approach under the European Union 1996 Convention Relating to Extradition between Member States.[25] Such a policy, if adopted generally, would result in a substantial improvement in the free-flow of fugitives to face trial and would still provide the fugitive with the best opportunity for rehabilitation and maintenance of family contacts.

---

19 See 27 INT.LEG.MAT.492 (1988). Colombia passed a new law to allow for the extradition of its nationals in 1997, but it contained a loophole that would protect many of the leaders of the drug cartels and the United States government has criticised the new law – see The Guardian p.13, 17 DEC 1997.

20 TIAS 10837.

21 *Supra n*3, at pp.125 *et seq.*

22 MARTENS, RECUEIL DE TRAITES, 2nd ed., vol iii, 376, Arts.I & II.

23 See §17, 159 B.F.S.P.606.

24 See para.92 and supplementary para.93 (p.lv), HCP-I, *supra n*13. Para.15 of the 1990 Conference on the Human Dimension of the OSCE in Copenhagen, (OSCE (CHD) Copenhagen Document, 11 HRLJ 232 (1990), and Buergenthal, *A new public order for Europe*, 11 HRLJ 217 (1990)), encourages the transfer of sentenced prisoners to their home States and, to that end, recommends States become parties to the 1983 Convention on the Transfer of Sentenced Prisoners, ETS 112. See also, Orie, 'The Problems with the Effective Use of Prisoner Transfer Treaties', in ATKINS, THE ALLEGED TRANSNATIONAL CRIMINAL, 1995, pp.59 *et seq.*

25 *Supra n*17.

Nevertheless, whether or not the principle of non-extradition of nationals is relaxed as regards common law States, there are certain inherent problems with the principle relating to some subsidiary matters. The first of these concerns the question of reciprocity in extradition law. Since extradition is usually based on a bilateral treaty between the requesting and requested States, it is natural to conclude that it ought to be reciprocal; thus, if the Federal Republic of Germany will not extradite its nationals to the United Kingdom, then the United Kingdom ought not to surrender its nationals to the Federal Republic of Germany. With the arrest of Donna Maguire in Belgium in June 1990 bringing to light the fact that a German request for her extradition was still outstanding in the Republic of Ireland, Irish commentators and politicians, though not the Department of Justice, argued that her surrender was not permitted under the European Convention on Extradition because the Federal Republic of Germany would never extradite its own nationals and, thus, the necessary element of reciprocity was missing.[26] The commentators' view was followed by the Irish Justice Minister in 1997, though, when she released Owen Corry, an Irish national, held in relation to an extradition request from Germany for his alleged involvement in the bombing of British Army barracks.[27] On the other hand, the British courts refused to reject an extradition application from Germany for a British national, Roisin McAliskey, on the grounds that the Germans would not reciprocate.[28] The Australian courts similarly refused to reject an extradition request from Israel simply because the Israeli Extradition Law 1978 prohibited the extradition of nationals, contrary to what had been agreed in the Israeli-Australian Extradition Treaty.[29]

The idea of strict reciprocity adopted in the Corry case ought strongly to be rejected, although it does make clear the gulf that separates civil law and common law States on the issue of nationals. Common law jurisdictions will usually allow extradition, even where the treaty with the civil law State gives it a discretion not to extradite its nationals, thus revealing that reciprocity in practice will not be pursued to the detriment of co-operation

---

26   See the Irish Times, p.2, 22 JUNE 1990.
27   The Guardian p.8, 16 JAN 1997.
28   *Re McAliskey*, CO/156/97, QBD, 22 JAN 1997.
29   *Hempel v Attorney-General*, 87 INT'L L REP.159. The fugitives were Israelis who were trying to argue that the Israeli statute vitiated the treaty as a whole.

in law enforcement.[30] The Corry case, above, was concerned with terrorism and the fact that he escaped prosecution because of the application of the nationality principle by a common law State without active personality jurisdiction,[31] shows the problems with reciprocity and with blanket bans on surrender.

Another, minor issue connected with the nationality principle, is the scope of active personality jurisdiction exercised by the State after it has refused extradition. According to research carried out by the European Committee on Crime Problems,[32] some States only prosecute their own nationals for crimes committed abroad if a requirement of double criminality is satisfied, either *in abstracto* or *in concreto.*[33] On that basis, nationality might give absolute protection. Given that double criminality would have been a prerequisite of any extradition, though, then there seems to be no sustainable objection to this extra demand.

The final problem, however, does raise some serious questions about the principle of not extraditing nationals. In circumstances where a request is made for a national of the requested State, the requesting State would be asserting territorial jurisdiction over the fugitive and could press charges if the fugitive were ever to enter its borders: on the basis that it will not extradite its own nationals, the requested State claims jurisdiction over the offence under the active personality principle. The fugitive may, therefore, end up being prosecuted for the same offence twice, although in two separate jurisdictions. Case law and commentators are unanimous that, subject to a treaty provision to the contrary, there is no international rule of *non bis in idem.*[34] In *E v Police Inspectorate of Basle,*[35] the Swiss Federal Tribunal (Criminal Court of Cassation) put it as follows:

---

30 *Escobedo v US,*623 F.2d 1098 at 1106 (1980); the discretion is exercised by the executive, not the courts. See also, *Hempel, supra n*29, at 164-67.

31 The court in *Hempel, supra n*29, at 166, took note of the fact that the 1978 amendment to Israeli extradition law had been accompanied by a change to the Penal Code giving Israeli courts power to hear criminal cases against Israeli nationals and residents for offences within the Schedule to the Extradition Law 5714-1954, no matter where in the world the offence occurred.

32 EXTRATERRITORIAL CRIMINAL JURISDICTION, (COUNCIL OF EUROPE, 1990), pp.10-11.

33 See Chapter Three above.

34 See, for example, Article 9 of the European Convention on Extradition 1957.

35 75 INT'L L REP.106 (1979).

"The law of nations does not recognize any rule which would prevent the criminal authorities in the two States from exercising jurisdiction over the same offence. In other words, there is no rule in such circumstances excluding concurrent jurisdiction ...."

Green points out that "since there are two different legal systems involved, the plea of double jeopardy cannot arise" and he gives the example of Germany prosecuting its nationals under its own criminal code for offences for which they have already been tried by a war crimes tribunal.[36] However, it cannot be right that a fugitive should be subjected to double jeopardy because of a rule of jurisdiction exercised by the State. The nationality principle may be inappropriate, but given that a large number of States exercise it, then there ought to be a uniform approach by States towards accepting that the principle of *aut dedere, aut judicare*[37] binds both the requesting and requested States towards the fugitive. This matter seems eminently suitable for a multilateral treaty to set a standardised policy. Indeed, the Schengen Convention 1990[38] provides in Articles 54-58 that Schengen States shall not ordinarily prosecute a person who has already been finally judged by another Contracting Party for the same offences. There is an option under Article 55 for States to make a declaration at the time of ratification that in limited circumstances, they reserve the right to prosecute someone who has already been finally judged. Those circumstances include where the offence occurred on the territory of the second State or the offence affected the security of the State or it was committed by a State official in violation of the obligations of his office. In general, though, the Schengen Convention implements *non bis in idem*.

In conclusion, the strict application of the principle of not extraditing nationals may be on the wane, but it is still pervasive in civil law jurisdic-

---

36 *International Crimes and the Legal Process*, 29 INT'L & COMP. LQ 567, citing *Lischka et al.* in The Times, 12 FEB 1980. *Cf*, *R v Roche*, (1775), 168 ER 169; *Treacy v DPP*, [1971] AC 537; and *Libman v The Queen*, 21 DLR (4th) 174 at 199-200, (1986). However, since most extradition treaties prevent extradition where the fugitive has already been tried for the offence in the requested State, this double jeopardy could not arise through extradition, only through the voluntary visit of the fugitive to the other State after being tried in the first State.
37 See Chapter Six below.
38 30 INT.LEG.MAT.84 (1991); see Appendix. See also, MEIJERS, SCHENGEN, 2nd ed. 1992.

tions. As a blanket restriction on return it cannot be supported between States which respect each other's system of criminal justice and it can lead to offenders escaping prosecution. The common law States should press for its abolition on the basis that it is not justifiable in terms of the theories of and the rationales for extradition law.

c. Military Offences

Extradition is usually refused for military offences. The question, though, is what constitutes a military offence. The broadest application of the exemption arose in the case of *In re Banegas*.[39] The Supreme Federal Court of Brazil held that a request from Bolivia should be denied on the ground that the offence charged was military in nature. The fugitive was charged with the "common crime of homicide". The case arose in the context of the armed forces, at the behest of the State authorities, putting down a revolt by executing the military and civilian personnel involved. According to Freire J, it was thus rendered a 'military offence'. On this reading, any crime committed by members of the armed forces would be a military offence; it would even permit a defence of superior orders to war crimes violations. While the instant case was also argued on the basis of the political offence exemption,[40] it is not in conformity with the modern interpretation of the military offences exception.

The more usual definition of the military offence exception is found in the French extradition statute of 1927.[41] Article 4 holds

> "*... que l'extradition est applicable aux infractions 'commises par les militaires, marins et assimilés, lorsqu'elles sont punies par la loi française comme infractions de droit commun'... L'immunité concerne les infractions de caractère purement militaire, c'est-à-dire celles qui sont prévues par le code de justice militaire.*"[42]

---

39   Supreme Federal Court of Brazil, 15 INT'L L REP.300 (1948).
40   It would also appear not to be a political offence – see Chapter Six, below.
41   *La Loi du 10 mars 1927.*
42   ENCYCLOPEDIE DALLOZ, *supra* n6, at para.209.

Recent French extradition treaties, such as the one with Algeria,[43] provide that an offence will only fall within the exception if it consists solely of a breach of military law. The European Convention on Extradition of 1957 achieves the same result by a negative definition; Article 4 only prohibits extradition if the military offence is *not* an offence under ordinary criminal law. Although the clause is not always included in treaties made by common law States, the Commonwealth Scheme for the Rendition of Fugitive Offenders contains the exception and defines it as follows.[44]

"The return of a fugitive offender will be either precluded by law, or be subject to refusal by the competent authority if the competent authority is satisfied that the offence is an offence only under military law or law relating to military obligations."

The objective is identical in all versions; to render non-extraditable only those offences which appear solely in the requesting State's military code. Merely because the fugitive would face trial before a military tribunal if surrendered does not necessarily mean that the offence charged is of a military character. Everything turns on whether the facts make out a crime under the ordinary criminal law as well as under the military code. On that understanding of the military offence exemption, deserters and those refusing to do military service, for whatever reason, ought not to be extradited.[45] The 1990 Copenhagen Conference on the Human Dimension of OSCE[46] reaffirmed the right of persons to refuse to do military service, revealing yet again the interplay of human rights and international criminal law in protecting freedom of conscience. Strictly military offences do not give rise to an obligation within the international community to assist other States in the enforcement of domestic laws. On the one hand, breaches of a State's military code are not serious enough to warrant the use of international

---

43 *27 Août 1964, Décr. 11 Août 1965.* See Art.15.
44 1966, Cmnd 3008. As amended by the Commonwealth Law Ministers Meeting, April 1990, (LMM(90)32), Art.11, 1990 amended version. All references are to the 1990 version.
45 *Cf.* The North Atlantic Treaty, 1949, provides that members of NATO will deliver up deserters to other members' armed forces. 34 UNTS 243. See also Article 5 of the Status of Forces Agreement between the Parties to the North Atlantic Treaty, 1952, 199 UNTS 67.
46 *Supra n*24, at para.18.

agreements for mutual assistance in criminal law enforcement, unless those offences are also common crimes. On the other hand, though, the exemption is designed to promote freedom of conscience by protecting those persons who oppose military service, in the same way that the political offence exemption was designed to guarantee a person's freedom of thought.

d. Triviality, Passage of Time and Bad Faith

The Commonwealth Scheme for the Rendition of Fugitive Offenders, as amended,[47] provides in Article 10(3) that,

> "The return of a fugitive offender ... will be precluded by law if the competent judicial or executive authority is satisfied that by reason of-
> (a) the trivial nature of the case, or
> (b) the accusation against the fugitive not having been made in good faith or in the interests of justice, or
> (c) the passage of time since the commission of the offence, or
> (d) any other sufficient cause,[48]
> it would, having regard to all the circumstances, be unjust or oppressive or too severe a punishment to return the fugitive...."

This provision gives the fugitive three extra specific grounds for challenging his surrender within the Commonwealth, although elements occur in other extradition arrangements. There are different justifications for each of the three. The 'passage of time' ground most obviously seeks to protect the fugitive's right to a fair trial, whereas the denial of requests made in bad faith aims not only to preserve the fugitive's fundamental rights but also to uphold the proper use of the international arrangement between the States; requests rejected on the basis triviality re-enforce the idea that extradition is not to be granted lightly, for the fugitive's life may well be seriously disrupted. All three have been utilised in past cases.

All these grounds are predicated on return being "unjust or oppressive". Subparagraphs (a), (b) and (c) (and possibly (d), too, in future) are merely

---

47 *Supra n*44.
48 Subparagraph (d) was not in the original 1966 Scheme and it is not in s11(3) of the British Extradition Act 1989. See, however, *Hagan, infra n*51.

means of proving the lack of justice or the oppression. Lord Diplock defined "unjust and oppressive" in *Kakis*[49]:

> "'Unjust', I regard, as directed primarily at the risk of prejudice to the accused in the conduct of the trial itself, 'oppressive' as directed to hardship to the accused resulting from changes in his circumstances that have occurred during the period to be taken into consideration; but there is room for overlapping and between them they would cover all cases where to return him would not be fair."

In some respects, therefore, although its underlying rationales go further than mere denial of procedural fairness, this provision might be moving towards the concept of non-extradition where fair trial would not exist in the requesting State.[50] In *R v Secretary of State for the Home Department, ex parte Hagan*,[51] the Divisional Court on judicial review of the Home Secretary's decision to surrender heard argument that because of the association of the fugitives with an unpopular religious cult in the requesting State, they would not receive a fair trial. The case was decided under the 1870 Act, which did not provide for review by the High Court of the request on the grounds set out in s11(3) of the 1989 Act. It was clear, however, that the fairness of the trial would be one of the factors to be considered before agreeing to the surrender, separate from whether there was delay, triviality or bad faith. In *Re Vito Dell'Aglio*,[52] the court was prepared to have regard to the fugitive's personal circumstances which went beyond the issues of triviality, passage of time and bad faith, suggesting that "unjust or oppressive" provide a general ground for challenging a decision to surrender discrete from the specific descriptions.

(i) Triviality – It must be noted at the outset that as it stands only offences punishable by two years detention or greater penalty are returnable under

---

49 *Kakis v Government of the Republic of Cyprus*, [1978] 2 All ER 634 at 638h.
50 See the alleged fears of the Libyans accused of the Lockerbie bombing *re* trial in Scotland – The Guardian p.20, 11 OCT 1993, p.4, 12 OCT 1993.
51 Unreported, QBD, CO/1301/93, 15 December 1993.
52 Unreported, QBD, CO/389/95, (Transcript: Smith Bernal) 30 APRIL 1997.

Article 2 of the Scheme.[53] Thus, it cannot be the charge but the facts relating to the request that render the offence too trivial. It might be argued
that theft is theft no matter what the value of the item stolen, but there are
financial considerations to be taken into account in setting in motion legal
proceedings to extradite a fugitive, possibly from half way around the world.
This underlying principle is seen more clearly in the equivalent measure
found in Article 4 of the 1981 Swiss Law on International Judicial Assistance
in Criminal Matters.

> "A request shall be rejected if the significance of the offence does not justify
> a carrying out of the proceedings."

Whether an offence is trivial is a question of fact and law.[54] From similar
cases under the 1881 Imperial Fugitive Offenders Act it would seem that
the facts of the alleged crime are all-important. Thus, in *Re Clemetson*[55]
dishonesty by an employee working in a position of trust was held not to
be trivial, although the amount stolen was not significant in itself.

(ii) Passage of Time – So far, no fugitive has succeeded in persuading either
the European Commission or Court of Human Rights that a violation of
the right in Article 6 of the ECHR to a hearing within a reasonable time
justified refusing extradition, but a comparison might properly be drawn
with this ground under the Commonwealth Scheme. It has been the subject
of review by the British House of Lords twice, in *Union of India v Narang*
and again, shortly afterwards, in *Kakis*.[56] In both *Narang* and *Kakis* the
House of Lords indicated that the delay in bringing the request must not
result from the fugitive's actions if the safeguard is to be applied.[57]

   In *Narang*, between the commission of the offence and the extradition
request, emergency powers had been assumed in India and an indefinite,

---

53 Some jurisdictions are more lax – the United Kingdom, for instance, allows
    extradition for offences carrying a penalty of at least 12 months.
54 *Fernandez v Government of Singapore*, [1971] 2 All ER 691 at 693.
55 The Times 23 NOV 1955; [1956] CRIM.L REV.50.
56 *Narang*, [1977] 2 All ER 348; *Kakis, supra n*49; see also Jones, *Passage of Time
    and the Return of Fugitive Offenders*, [1980] CRIM.L REV.29.
57 See Lord Diplock in *Kakis, supra n*49, at 638. See also *R v Governor of Penton-
    ville Prison, ex p. Teja*, [1971] 2 All ER 11.

unappealable detention order had been made against one of the fugitives. The House of Lords held that for a request to be unjust or oppressive by reason of passage of time, the relevant factors to take into account concern only those arising from the delay in hearing the case. Events which have arisen during the passage of time, though not related directly to the delay in the trial, are to be ignored.[58] Furthermore, in *Hughes v Government of Denmark and Another,*[59] the Divisional Court was not prepared to take into account the fugitive's deteriorated medical condition in the period between the offence and the extradition hearing.

> "Section 11(3)(b) of the 1989 Act is concerned with oppression arising by reason of the passage of time. That is to say, it needs to be shown that it is the passage of time that has caused the oppression. That argument, on any view, fails in this case for two reasons. The first, and most pressing, is that in truth it is not the passage of time that is complained of, but the contingent factor that the Applicant's mental state has worsened during her time in prison. Section 11(3)(b) does not in my view direct itself to that circumstance. It is concerned with a case where time has been allowed to pass to the extent that that passage of time is oppressive. No-one can say in this case that the passage of time in itself is oppressive, or that it leads to, or causes, the return of the Applicant to Denmark to be oppressive."

The *Narang* interpretation had been, however, rejected by Lords Russell and Scarman in *Kakis*[60]:

> "It is not permissible, in my judgment, to consider the passage of time divorced from the course of events which it allows to develop. For the

---

58 *Supra n56*, at 379h and 380b-d, *per* Lord Keith.

59 Unreported, CO/667/94, QBD, (Transcript: John Larking), 11 October 1994. Of course, the fugitive might be too ill to be surrendered – see the refusal by Pakistan to extradite Agha Hasan Abedi, The Guardian p.14, 15 JUL 1994.

60 *Supra n49, per* Lord Scarman at 645; also Lord Russell at 641a-b. See, as well, *Re Reyat's Application for a Writ of Habeas Corpus*, QBD, CO/1157/88, 22 MAR 1989, (MWC); *R v Governor of Brixton Prison, ex p.Osman (No.3)* [1992] 1 All ER 122 at 128-29 and 131-32; *R v Secretary of State for the Home Department, ex p.Launder*, The Times, 29 OCT 1996, where delay was rejected by the QBD.

purposes of this jurisdiction, time is not an abstraction but the necessary
cradle of events, the impact of which on the applicant has to be assessed."

This second view is to be preferred, but it must be viewed in the context
of the facts of the case. In *Narang* and *Hughes*, the detention order and the
applicant's mental condition had nothing to do with the offence for which
the fugitives were requested, whereas in *Kakis* the passage of time had led
to the disappearance of two compellable defence witnesses for any trial in
Cyprus.[61] However, a wide interpretation of *Kakis* is still correct, for Article
10(3) of the Scheme talks in terms of 'having regard to all the circumstances', not just those to do with the offence.[62]

The Brazilian Supreme Court held with respect to the English Great Train
Robber, Ronnie Biggs, that a crime for which he had been convicted over
thirty years previously could not be the subject of an extradition request
because it would be statute barred under Brazilian law.[63] In *KM v The
Netherlands*,[64] the Dutch Supreme Court did not allow the fugitive to rely
on a general reservation to the European Convention on Extradition 1957
to the effect that surrender would cause "particular hardship" where he was
arguing that he should not be surrendered to Germany in relation to a conviction from sixteen years before because he had been resident for so long that
he had become integrated into Dutch society.[65] While the argument failed,
it should be remembered that the Dutch interpretation of Article 6 of the
1957 Convention on the non-extradition of nationals includes those integrated

---

61   In *R v Secretary of State, ex p.Hill* [1997] 2 All ER 638 at 662-65, it was held
     that a delay of ten years where a relevant witness would no longer be available
     still did not render extradition unjust. In *Re Gesugrande*, unreported, QBD, CO/
     1583/95, 30 JULY 1996, on the other hand, a delay of eight years in an ac-
     cusation case was on the borderline. See also, *Re Vitale*, QBD, 145 NLJ 631
     (1995), 14 March 1995, where it was held that because it was a conviction case,
     there was no problem that lapse of time might affect the recollection of witnes-
     ses.
62   The 1966 version of the Scheme was so limited, see Article 9(3); the British
     legislation implementing the Scheme was always worded without any restriction,
     as the 1990 Scheme is. Section 11(3) of the 1989 Act is also worded in a broad
     manner.
63   The Guardian p.1, 13 NOV 1997.
64   *Supra n9*, at 432.
65   A similar argument was rejected in *Vitale, supra n61*.

into Dutch society, so the use of the general reservation would have rendered the specific declaration redundant.[66]

(iii) Bad Faith – Given that common law jurisdictions traditionally tend to operate a rule of non-inquiry into the motives of the requesting government,[67] and that the Commonwealth Scheme, Article 10(2), provides that a fugitive's return will be precluded, anyway, if it appears that he will be prosecuted, persecuted or punished on the grounds of his race, religion, nationality or political opinions,[68] the power to prevent extradition if it appears the request was made in bad faith or not in the interests of justice will rarely be exercised. It was used in 1990 to challenge a request by Hong Kong. In *Re Osman*,[69] the fugitive alleged that since the Hong Kong authorities had already investigated him some years previously and decided not to prosecute, the request in relation to the same alleged offence must have been at the behest of the Malaysian government, another Commonwealth State, which did not want to hold the trial itself because of the domestic political implications. The court held, though, that once the fugitive admitted that the Hong Kong authorities would have jurisdiction over the serious frauds alleged, the case impugning their motives must fall. In so finding, the court has adopted a very narrow view of its bad faith jurisdiction; given that every extradition request must first satisfy the requirement that the requesting State has the power to prosecute, it is a little difficult to understand how Article 10(3)(b) might ever be pleaded successfully upon

---

66 See MY, *supra n9.*
67 *In re Arton (No.1),* [1896] 1 QB 108 at 114. And see Chapter Three, §*e.*
68 See also European Convention on Extradition 1957, Article 3.
69 Unreported, QBD, CO/252/90, MWC, 20 JUNE 1990. In support of Osman's contention, Warwick Reid, the Hong Kong prosecutor responsible for bringing him to book, has since been sentenced to eight years imprisonment for accepting bribes and, moreover, documents inadmissible on grounds of public interest immunity indicate that his request was not solely motivated by the interests of justice; The Guardian p.2, 3 DEC 1990.

this interpretation. In a subsequent *Osman* judgment,[70] Kennedy LJ held, relying on Woolf LJ in a third *Osman* case,[71] that

> "in my judgment the term 'good faith' has to be given a reasonably generous interpretation so that if the proceedings were brought for a collateral purpose,[72] or with an improper motive and not for the purpose of achieving the proper administration of justice, they would not be regarded as complying with this statutory requirement. Likewise the accusations would not be made in good faith and in the interests of justice if the prosecution deliberately manipulates or misuses the process of the court to deprive the defendant of a protection to which he is entitled by law."

---

70 *R v Secretary of State for Home Affairs Ex parte Osman*, unreported, CO/2496/92, CO/2654/92, QBD, (Transcript: Martin Walsh Cherer), 20 November 1992.

71 *Osman* reached double figures in his number of applications for judicial review and *habeas corpus* – Queen's Bench Division (Crown Office List), CO/2496/92, CO/2654/92, (Martin Walsh Cherer), 30 November 1992; Queen's Bench Division (Crown Office List), CO/2496/92, CO/2654/92, (Martin Walsh Cherer), 20 November 1992; Queen's Bench Division (Crown Office List), CO/1292/92, CO/1310/92, (Marten Walsh Cherer), 22 September 1992; Queen's Bench Division (Crown Office List), [1993] CRIM LR 214, CO/1292/92, CO/1310/92, (Marten Walsh Cherer), 30 July 1992; unreported, Queen's Bench Division (Crown Office List), CO/252/90, Martin Walsh Cherer, 20 June 1990; Queen's Bench Division (Crown Office List), [1992] Crim LR 741, (Marten Walsh Cherer), 28 February 1992; Court of Appeal (Civil Division), (Association), 11 December 1991; Queen's Bench Division, [1992] 1 All ER 579, 14 November 1991; Queen's Bench Division (Crown Office List), CO/1508/91, (Marten Walsh Cherer), 7 October 1991; [1992] 1 All ER 122, [1992] 1 WLR 36, 22 May 1991; The Times 17 December 1990, C0/252/90, (Marten Walsh Cherer), 12 December 1990; Queen's Bench Division (Crown Office List), CO/252/90, (Marten Walsh Cherer), 15 November 1990; [1992] 1 All ER 108, [1991] 1 WLR 281, 93 Cr App Rep 202, 14 November 1990; Queen's Bench Division, (Laidler, The Independent 12 January 1990, Haswell), 21 December 1989; [1990] 1 All ER 999, [1990] 1 WLR 878, 91 Cr App Rep 409, 17 November 1989; The Times 24 December 1988, The Independent 5 January 1989, 133 SJ 121, 21 December 1988; [1988] 3 All ER 173, 90 Cr App Rep 313, 11 May 1988; [1989] 3 All ER 701, [1990] 1 WLR 277, 90 Cr.App.R. 281, 1988 CRIM LR 611.

72 In *Re Ramda and Boutarfa*, The Independent, 27 June 1997, the court considered but rejected a claim that if extradited to France, one of the fugitives might subsequently be sent to Algeria where he would not obtain a fair trial.

Nevertheless, given also that governments will claim that their evidence is confidential, as was the case in *Osman*, it would be next to impossible to prove bad faith *in abstracto* anyway.

A unique example of the bad faith defence can be seen in relation to a request for surrender by Hong Kong before July 1st 1997 when it became Hong Kong Special Administrative Region (HKSAR), part of the Peoples Republic of China. Overlapping with arguments concerning specialty, discussed below, the issue concerns whether a transnational fugitive offender could argue that the PRC should not be trusted to honour its commitments to preserve Hong Kong's way of life for fifty years. The House of Lords, after careful consideration, rejected the claim in *Launder*[73] that the PRC could not be trusted to uphold the standards that Hong Kong enjoyed prior to July 1st 1997, having regard to the protracted period of negotiations between the British and Chinese prior to the handover. More specifically, it held that the Secretary of State had properly considered whether it would have been unjust and oppressive to this fugitive because of the way he might be treated by the new authorities.

In conclusion, any properly used additional protections for fugitive offenders are to be welcomed. That it was thought necessary to include Article 10(3) in an extradition system operating among members of the Commonwealth who generally trust each other, and the particular experience with Hong Kong, show that it might usefully be inserted in other bilateral and multilateral arrangements.

e. Plea Bargaining

Most crime is cleared up by confessions from those involved and the police often offer leniency in the courts as a trade-off for information. It was inevitable, therefore, that this should eventually affect an extradition request. The facts of *Geisser v United States*[74] reveal the special problems of plea-bargaining in this area. The fugitive had fled Switzerland having been

---

73 *R v Home Secretary, ex p.Launder* [1997] 1 WLR 839 at 857-59, reversing the Divisional Court, *supra* n60.
74 513 F.2d 862 (1975); 414 F.Supp 49 (1976); 554 F.2d 693 (1977); 627 F.2d 745 (1980).

convicted of murder. In the United States she gave aid to the police in breaking up a drugs ring for which she was given the assurance that the US would "use its best efforts" to prevent her rendition to Switzerland. Unfortunately for the accused, the Swiss government was not party to the agreement and requested her extradition. The magistrate agreed to this request, but on an application for a writ of *habeas corpus*, District Judge Mehrtens held her constitutional rights had been infringed, for the US government had not honoured the plea-bargain.[75] The Court of Appeals vacated this decision, but told the government to try again to see if the Swiss would withdraw their request.[76] Having tried and failed, the US government again sought to quash the writ for *habeas corpus*, but the District Court and Court of Appeals held its efforts had been insufficient and set out new guidelines to be met.[77] However, in the Court of Appeals, Coleman J dissented,[78] holding that the government had an obligation under the US-Swiss Extradition Treaty which it could not negotiate away. Only in 1980, after further discussions between the two governments without obtaining the withdrawal of the Swiss request, did the Court of Appeals hold that the US government had done sufficient for extradition to be allowed, that is it had used its 'best efforts'.[79] However, the diplomatic embarrassment caused to the United States should dissuade any future plea-bargains in extradition cases. Considering Geisser had been convicted of murder, it should have been obvious that the Swiss government would not give up its extradition request, especially since the information Geisser had provided had only helped the US law enforcement authorities, not the Swiss. Moreover, as Coleman J explains,[80] the United States was obligated by its treaty with Switzerland to extradite if Switzerland fulfilled all the requirements. Domestic dealings between the police and the fugitive could not override the international duties in the treaty. It is evident that any plan to plea-bargain over extradition in future ought to involve the potential requesting State at an early stage; with the growth in cross-frontier crimes it may well be that a fugitive's information will be of assistance to more than one State and

---

75 Unreported. See 61 INT'L L REP.443 at 444.
76 513 F.2d 862 (1975).
77 414 F.Supp 49 (1976); 554 F.2d 693 (1977).
78 *Supra n*77, at 707 *et seq.*
79 647 F.2d 745 at 755 (1980).
80 *Supra n*78.

that a bargain will not be wholly inappropriate. However, if no negotiations take place with the requesting State, then the extradition should go ahead to honour the treaty, leaving the fugitive with a right to sue for failure to fulfil the plea-bargain. International agreements must be upheld in the interests of greater international co-operation in the enforcement of criminal laws.

f. Specialty[81]

The content of this principle, accepted by most States as part of the rules of extradition,[82] is that a fugitive should only be tried in the requesting State for those offences for which he was surrendered.[83] Any offence not

---

81 Also known as 'speciality'.

82 *Eg. Melia v United States*, 667 F.2d 300 (1981). Before the Irish Extradition (Amendment) Act 1987, the Anglo-Irish procedure did not include the principle of specialty, but now, under s3 of the 1987 Act, the Irish Minister of Justice is empowered to apply it as necessary (see also, s72 Irish Criminal Justice Act 1991 and the Irish SI 1994 No.221). There was no equivalent in the British legislation until 1994 – see now, s72(3) Criminal Justice Act 1993 and SI 1994 No.1952. (See generally, FORDE, THE LAW OF EXTRADITION IN THE UNITED KINGDOM, 1995, pp.90 and 124). Considering that the Anglo-Irish system has been based on the European Extradition Convention since 1965, this delayed implementation was odd, for Art.14 thereof implements the principle of special-ty. See O'Higgins, *The Irish Extradition Act 1965*, 15 INT'L & COMP. LQ 369 (1966).

For a view that the principle of specialty is not a rule of customary international law and is dependent on a specific provision to that effect in the extradition arrangements, see *In re McFadden, per* Forbes J, The Times, 13 MAR 1982. "Even if one assumed that there was here an irreconcilable conflict between a domestic statute and the principles of international law, namely the speciality rule ..., it seems to me that this court would be bound to give effect to the statute."

See also *The State (Jennings) v Furlong*, [1966] IR 183 *per* Hendry J.

83 A treaty may well prevent incarceration for a sentence imposed pre-flight and not included in the requisition for other offences with which the fugitive is only charged. Thus, in *R v Uxbridge Justices, ex p.Davies*, [1981] 1 WLR 1080, the Divisional Court released a returned fugitive who had been imprisoned for non-payment of a fine imposed before he fled to the USA, but which had not been included as a ground for requesting his return. See Art XII Anglo-US Extradition

disclosed in the request, which occurred before surrender should, thus, no longer be capable of prosecution.[84] In *R v MacDonald*,[85] for example, the fugitive was granted *habeas corpus* because following his surrender by Australia for trial in relation to narcotics offences, he was imprisoned under a robbery conviction which had not formed part of the extradition request. White J. held that domestic Canadian law had to be applied so as to respect Canada's international commitments and the comity of nations.[86] Effectively, the fugitive should receive immunity through the extradition laws. However, the principle of specialty is not centrally concerned with protecting the fugitive's rights. While it prevents a fugitive being requested for one offence and tried for another, it upholds the contractual nature of the agreement between the two States, in that the requesting State has to accept that the requested State has granted extradition for the specified offences and no others. Furthermore, the fugitive's rights are secondary to this inter-State relationship. While the fugitive can assert violations of the principle of specialty in any trial in the requesting State, the protection exists only to the extent that the requested State so insists.[87] Furthermore, if having left the requesting State after extradition, the transnational fugitive offender subsequently returns to the requesting State of his own volition, then the specialty protection will lapse.[88]

A similar concept was first used in the Franco-Luxembourg treaty of 1844,[89] but it was first formulated in terms that would be understood today in the Franco-Saxon treaty of 1850.[90] However, its precise scope is little understood. On a strict analysis, it would mean that the fugitive could only be tried for the precise offences for which he was surrendered. On one

---

Treaty in SI 1979 No.2144. See also *Spanish-German Extradition Treaty Case*, [1925–26] Ann.Dig.308 and note at 309, *esp.* Gerland.

84 The principle has no relevance to civil proceedings – see *Re Ditfort, ex p.Deputy Commissioner of Taxation*, 87 INT'L L REP.170 at 190 (Australia, Fed.Ct).

85 101 INT'L L REP.281.

86 *Supra n*85, at 288.

87 *Najohn v United States*, 785 F.2d 1420 at 1422 (1986); *CvH et al. v The Netherlands* 100 INT'L L REP.404. *Cf. MacDonald, supra n*85. On whether the fugitive can plead specialty in any trial following surrender, generally, see CHINKIN, THIRD PARTIES IN INTERNATIONAL LAW (1996), esp. pp.13-15.

88 *R v Parisien* 92 INT'L L REP.683 (Canadian Supreme Court).

89 See BILLOT, TRAITE DE L'EXTRADITION, at pp.476 *et seq*.

90 *Supra n*89, at p.552.

reading, Article 38 of the Swiss Law on International Judicial Assistance in Criminal Matters takes this stance.[91]

> "(1) A fugitive may be extradited only on condition that the requesting State: (a) shall neither prosecute nor sentence nor re-extradite him to a third State for an offence committed prior to his extradition and for which extradition was not granted."

This view, though, would mean that the courts of the requested State would interfere excessively in the criminal processes of the requesting State.[92] Further, it misconstrues the nature of the extradition hearing. The extradition court in applying an *in abstracto* analysis of the double criminality requirement looks to see if an offence would have been committed in the requested State *on the facts* alleged by the requesting State. It is the facts of the case that are all important. Both civil law and common law precedents are to the effect that specialty allows the fugitive to be prosecuted for any charge made out by the facts on which surrender was ordered.[93] Thus, a serious fraud may make out charges of deception and theft on the facts, both of which charges would be open to prosecution upon the fugitive's surrender.

The following developments taking place in extradition law with regard to specialty are aimed to relax the rule so as to allow a wider range of offences to be prosecuted. It is part of the overall trend that sees extradition as a means of improving international co-operation in law enforcement at

---

91 20 MAR 1981, 20 INT.LEG.MAT.1339 (1981), as amended 4 OCT 1996 (supplied by the Federal Office for Police Matters, Bern) – the text is a combination of both translations. See also the Decree on International Mutual Assistance in Criminal Matters, 24 FEB 1982 as amended 9 DEC 1996 (supplied by the Federal Office for Police Matters, Bern).

92 See *Najohn, supra* n87, at 1423.

93 See *Decorte v Société Anonyme Groupe d'Assurance Nedlloyd et al.* (Belgian *Cour de Cassation, 2eme*) 69 INT'L L REP.216 (1971); *In re Davidson*, (1976), 62 Cr.App.R.209; and *In re Nielsen, sub.nom. R v Chief Metropolitan Magistrate, ex p.Government of Denmark*, (1984), 79 Cr.App.R.1 at 14, *per* Robert Goff LJ. *Quaere, United States v Rauscher*, 119 US 407 (1886); see generally, Semmelman, *The Doctrine of Specialty in the Federal Courts: Making Sense of US v Rauscher*, 31 VA.J INT'L L 71 (1993).

the expense of the fugitive's traditional rights. In more recent agreements,[94] the requesting State has been permitted to charge any other extraditable offence as well with the consent of the requested State, although knowledge of the particulars at the time of the initial request may prove a bar. It should be noted that it is limited to other extraditable offences, not just any crime, and that the consent of the requested State is essential, reinforcing that specialty goes to the relationship between the parties to the treaty as much as to the protection of the fugitive. Nevertheless, another limitation on the strict understanding of specialty is seen in the power of the requesting State to take into account any other offence with the consent of the fugitive, who may have an interest in wiping the slate clean. This development places the principle of specialty firmly in the list of those provisions designed solely to protect the fugitive, given that supporting consent from the requested State is not also required. While it may be a sensible progression, it does seem to go against the spirit of the principle of specialty which is to treat it as part of the bargain between the States, as well.[95]

Finally, specialty was raised frequently in cases involving requests by the government in Hong Kong before the handover to the PRC on July 1st 1997. The argument was that specialty would be violated because the transnational fugitive offender would effectively be extradited to a third State, that is, the PRC, on July 1st 1997. For a variety of reasons, the specialty

---

94 See Article 15 of the Commonwealth Scheme, 1990, *supra n*44; the European Union Convention Relating to Extradition between the Member States, 1996 OJ C 313, provides in Article 10 that other offences shall be prosecutable if they either will result in no loss of liberty or the fugitive waives his rights – see also the Explanatory Report of 26 May 1997, 1997 OJ C 191; and, the European Union also concluded a Convention on Simplified Extradition to expedite mutual assistance (1995 OJ C 78), Article 9 of which deals with the specialty issues surrounding simplified extradition. See also, *Najohn, supra n*87.

95 *Cf. German-Swiss Extradition Case*, (FRG, Federal Supreme Court), 61 INT'L L REP.470 (1968), in which the court held that the fugitive's previous offences could be taken into account in assessing the appropriate sentence. In *Nedlloyd, supra n*93, at 217, the court held that the accused was entitled to waive his privilege under the principle of specialty and that no reference need be made in such circumstances to the requested State – see also, Article 10 of the European Union Convention relating to Extradition between Member States, *supra n*94.

argument was ultimately found to be flawed in all cases. In *Osman (No.3)*[96] and *Lee*,[97] the Divisional Court held that specialty could only relate to the present requesting State and it was not open to the court to gaze into the future, for to act otherwise would "drive a coach and horses through the principle of comity and reciprocity". The House of Lords in *Launder*,[98] however, was able to take into account developments up to early 1997, where Hong Kong had entered into several arrangements with States that even after the transfer to the PRC, persons extradited to Hong Kong would not be surrendered to places outside the jurisdiction of Hong Kong. Two United States cases, *Lui Kin-Hong*[99] and *Oen Yin Choy*,[100] held the principle of specialty was wholly inapplicable because any transfer from the HKSAR to the PRC would not amount to re-extradition.[101] That the takeover by the PRC was feared by transnational fugitive offenders being returned to Hong Kong was understandable, but the effective block on most extraditions to the former colony would have been too disruptive of international criminal law and the comity of nations.[102]

g. Diplomatic Immunity

This defence is known in strictly domestic trials, too. The accused claims immunity from prosecution by virtue of Article 31 of the 1961 Vienna Convention on Diplomatic Relations.[103] The same argument has been raised to preclude extradition, although no conclusive decision has been reached as yet as to whether the Vienna Convention extends to extradition requests. The leading authority is *Ex parte Teja*.[104] Teja had been sought by the

---

96 *Supra n*60, at 131.
97 *R v Governor of Pentonville Prison et al., ex p.Lee* [1993] 3 All ER 504 at 510-11.
98 *Supra n*73, at 859 *et seq.*
99 *United States v Lui Kin-Hong* 110 F.3d 103 (1997).
100 *Oen Yin Choy v Robinson* 858 F.2d 1400 at 1403-04 (1988).
101 The United States is one of those States which has entered into an agreement that no-one extradited to Hong Kong will be surrendered to a place outside the jurisdiction of HKSAR – *Launder, supra n*73, at 861-63.
102 See *Oen Yin Choy, supra n*100, at 1404.
103 500 UNTS 95.
104 *Supra n*57.

Indian government from the USA and Costa Rica prior to his arrest in the United Kingdom. As part of his defence, he claimed that he had been appointed economic adviser to the Costa Rican government and was about to be appointed their economic counsellor to Switzerland. One of the problems with this line of argument was that there was no Costa Rican embassy in Switzerland and the Swiss government denied any knowledge of his impending accreditation. As a fall back position, he also claimed he held the same status for the government of El Salvador. The Divisional Court rejected the claim of diplomatic immunity by strictly interpreting Article 40 of the Vienna Convention which only grants protection to diplomats in third States when they are on their way between their posting and their home State.[105] Teja was travelling on a return ticket from Geneva to London, he was not in transit from Switzerland to El Salvador. Implicitly though, if Article 40 had been satisfied then the applicant would have been granted immunity from extradition. The Divisional Court, this time rejecting the claim on procedural grounds, seems to have followed *Teja* in *R v Governor of Pentonville Prison, ex parte Osman (No.2)*,[106] implicitly recognising, however, that if diplomatic status is proven, then extradition should be refused. In *Re Marcinkus, De Strobel and Mennini*,[107] the Vatican City Court of First Instance, relying on Article 11 of the Lateran Treaty of 1929, refused a request from Italy for the surrender of the three because the case related to their work as directors of the Institute of Religious Works, "a central body of the Catholic Church", and as such they were exempt from interference by the Italian government.

It would be surprising to find that States accorded less protection from criminal prosecution to diplomats when they are being requested by another State than they do to diplomats for crimes committed within the jurisdiction of the receiving State. Furthermore, there may well be political considerations to take into account. The *Achille Lauro* affair highlights this issue.[108] Mem-

---

105 *Cf. R v Guildhall Magistrates Court, ex p.Jarrett-Thorpe*, The Times, 5 OCT 1977, *per* Lawton J.

106 The Times, 24 DEC 1988. See also, Kassim-Momodu, *Extradition of Fugitives by Nigeria*, 35 INT'L & COMP. LQ 512 at p.515.

107 100 INT'L L REP.603 at 607.

108 See McGinley, The *Achille Lauro* Case: A Study in Crisis Law Policy and Management, at pp.323 *et seq.* in BASSIOUNI, LEGAL RESPONSES TO INTERNATIONAL TERRORISM, (1988), and CASSESE, TERRORISM, POLITICS AND LAW, esp.

bers of the Palestine Liberation Front took control of the Italian ship, the
Achille Lauro, while it was in Egyptian territorial waters. After several days
sailing around the eastern Mediterranean, during which time a US national
was murdered, the Palestinians returned to Egypt. The sea-jacking seemed
to have been organised from on shore by Abul Abbas who negotiated the
end of the affair. Having arrived in Egypt, the Egyptian authorities placed
them on a plane, alleged to be on a State mission, which then set off for
Tunis. It was intercepted by US Navy planes and diverted to an air base in
Sicily. The Italian authorities then arrested the four sea-jackers and the USA
sought their extradition and that of Abul Abbas.[109] The only point of concern in relation to diplomatic immunity is the case of Abul Abbas.[110] Not
only did he remain with the Egyptian plane which the Egyptians claimed
enjoyed extra-territorial status, but the Italian government claimed he had
diplomatic immunity. He had been granted an Iraqi passport which set out
his status as a leading member of the PLO, but he was not a representative
of Iraq and nor was he accredited to Italy. At best, even granting him
diplomatic status, he fell within Article 40 and, at the time, he was not
travelling between his posting and his home State. Nevertheless, the Italians
allowed him to leave for the then Yugoslavia on the ground that diplomats
could not be questioned or extradited. The decision was blatantly political,
made in order to preserve good relations with the Arab world; the cynicism
is evident from the fact that at the trial of the sea-jackers he was tried *in
absentia* and 'sentenced' to life imprisonment. The only conclusion to be
reached from this decision, is that States do recognise diplomatic immunity
from extradition requests, it is just that so far there has been no case where
it has properly been applied.

---

at pp.95-96, (1989). *Cf. United States v Noriega* 746 F.Supp 1506 (1990); 808
F.Supp 791 (1992); 117 F.3d 1206 (1997).

109 See The Guardian for October 8 to 22 1985.

110 CASSESE, *supra* n108, at p.43.

6

THE POLITICAL OFFENCE EXEMPTION

"He that would make his own liberty secure must guard even his enemy from oppression; for if he violates his duty he establishes a precedent that will reach to himself."[1]

"Why not ask yourself, Miss Feletti, what sort of democracy requires the services of dogs such as these? I'll tell you. Bourgeois democracy which wears a thin skin of human rights to keep out the cold, but when things hot up, when the rotten plots of the ruling class fail to silence our demands, when they have put half the population on the dole queue and squeezed the other half dry with wage cuts to keep themselves in profit, when they have run out of promises and you reformists have failed to keep the masses in order for them; well then they shed their skins and dump you, ..., and set their wildest dogs loose on us all."[2]

a. Introduction

As one commentator has put it, the political offence exemption is the "hot issue" of extradition law.[3] Whether this conclusion is justified when judicial

---

1   From the Complete Writings of Thomas Paine, vol.2, at p.588 – P. Foner, ed., 1945. Cited in *United States v Alvarez-Machain*, 504 US 655 at 688 (1995), 112 S.Ct 2188 (1995), 119 L.Ed 2d 441 at 467 (1995).

2   Dario Fo, *Accidental Death of an Anarchist*, trans. Richards and Hanna, Methuen, 1980.

3   Evans, *International Procedures for the Apprehension and Rendition of Fugitive Offenders*, [1980] A.S.I.L.PROC.244, (74th Annual Meeting).

practice is reviewed, rather than the writings of academics, will be considered below, but it cannot be denied that it is the most interesting issue.

One of the principal reasons given for the exemption in the nineteenth century was that it would permit the requested State to remain aloof from the internal affairs of the requesting State. However, whilst hiding behind the court's decision that the offence was of a political character, the requested State in fact has always passed judgment on the requesting State,[4] cast aspersions on the impartiality of its judiciary and effectively sided with the fugitive. In June 1978, for example, former President Mobutu of the former Zaire criticised Belgium for granting asylum to some of his political adversaries, "considering this act as an effective support to those willing to overthrow him and hence, as a hostile act".[5] The exemption is very controversial and its application in a particular case may have serious diplomatic consequences.

According to Stein,[6] the objective of the exemption is twofold, although this may not be clear from the wording of the provision in treaties or domestic legislation.

> "[It] mixes inseparably the humanitarian concern for the fugitive on the one hand and on the other the politically motivated unwillingness of the requested State to get involved in the international (*sic.*) political affairs of the requesting State."[7]

It may be that this conceptual confusion is part of the reason for the problems raised by the operation of the exemption. However, in attempting to

---

4   While requested State and requesting State bear their ordinary meanings, a third term, State of dispute, should be understood as the State against which the fugitive, for ideological or political reasons, is in conflict. This may or may not be the requesting State.

5   VAN DEN WIJNGAERT, THE POLITICAL OFFENCE EXEMPTION TO EXTRADITION: THE DELICATE PROBLEM OF BALANCING THE RIGHTS OF THE INDIVIDUAL AND INTERNATIONAL PUBLIC ORDER, p.204, *n*1071 (1980); hereinafter, WIJNGAERT. See also, *Ryan*, 100 INT'L L REP.616, NOTE at 622 (Belgian Court of Appeal of Brussels).

6   *DIE AUSLIEFERUNGSAUSNAHME BEI POLITISCHEN DELIKTEN* (1983); English summary, pp.377-81.

7   *Supra n*6, at p.377; it should probably read "internal political affairs". See also p.380.

analyze the exemption within a legal framework, and then circumscribe it within some justifiable confines, it may be that all that is effectively achieved is to provide the courts with a legal cloak behind which they may hide their political decisions. Given that the courts will still deal with political offenders much as they wish, though, then some sort of analysis of the exemption is essential in order to provide for more informed criticisms of the decisions and to provide the judges with appropriate guidelines for the future.

As will be seen below, the exemption is pleaded by a wide variety of fugitives, but it comes to the fore most controversially in requests for alleged terrorists.[8] Of course, 'terrorists' come in many guises and their actions may prove more or less reprehensible depending upon the court before which they appear. Indeed, the judges' decisions often seem to owe more to foreign policy than to legal reasoning.[9] In the past, political offence decisions have been based upon whether the fugitive was from the former Soviet bloc,[10] whether the requesting State was an ally,[11] support for the fugitive or his group in the requested State,[12] even economic interests.[13] 'Terrorists' are hard cases within the exemption, and hard cases make bad law. Terrorism is unlikely to disappear in the near future, however, so cases where the limits of the exemption are tested will continue to arise.

Yet, as was stated above, to see the exemption as only applying to 'terrorists' would be seriously misleading. Some of the other categories of offender who claim to be within the scope of the exemption are closely related to terrorists, but, even then, many other factors apply to such cases so as to render them distinct. The closest 'ally' of the terrorist must be those

---

8   *Eg.* The Abu Daoud Affair. Carbonneau, *The Provisional Arrest and Subsequent Release of Abu Daoud by French Authorities*, 17 VA.J INT'L L 495 (1977); Riggle, *L'Affaire Abu Daoud: Some Problems of Extraditing an International Terrorist*, 12 INT'L LAWYER 333 (1978); [1977] 1 GAZ.PALAIS 105.

9   See the French government's release of two Iranians wanted by Switzerland, according to the French Prime Minister's office, for "reasons connected to [French] national interests." – The Guardian p.8, 1 JAN 1994.

10 *R v Governor of Brixton Prison, ex parte Kolczynski et al,* [1955] 1 QB 540.

11 *Cheng v Pentonville Prison Governor,* [1973] AC 931.

12 *Eg.* The Provisional IRA in the Republic of Ireland during the 1970s. See LODGE, TERRORISM A CHALLENGE TO THE STATE, Ch.6, *esp.* at pp.151-52 (1981); hereinafter, LODGE.

13 Abu Daoud affair, *supra* n8. *Cf. L'Affaire Gouvernement Suisse, Req.no. 156490,* [1995] AJDA 56 at 60, (20 JAN 1995).

engaged in an armed conflict of some description. However, in such a case international humanitarian law may apply as well, adding a further dimension to the decision beyond that for the simple terrorist.[14] Also related is the refugee seeking protection from persecution, rather than prosecution. Moreover, into which of those categories listed above a fugitive is deemed to fall may, in the end, depend only on where and when the crime took place. There is a tremendous degree of discretion.

More removed from terrorists, war criminals have pleaded the defence in the past, too,[15] bringing yet another facet to the exemption. As civilians are more and more subjected to the direct hostilities of armies, it becomes more likely that requests for the extradition of fugitive war criminals will be made once those hostilities cease, again testing the limits of the exemption's protection. To that extent, the creation of the *ad hoc* international tribunals for the former Yugoslavia[16] and Rwanda[17] and the proposal to create an International Criminal Court[18] would suggest that States wish, in

---

14 Even if the minimum threshhold of violence required by Protocol II to the Geneva Conventions, 1125 UNTS 609 (1979), 16 INT.LEG.MAT1442-49 (1977), has not been reached, there is an argument that special rules should still govern situations of serious tension beyond mere terrorism: see KALSHOVEN, CONSTRAINTS ON THE WAGING OF WAR, 1987, pp.137-39; Gasser, *A Measure of Humanity in Internal Disturbances and Tensions: Proposal for a Code of Conduct*, 262 INT'L REV.RED CROSS 38 at pp.51-53.

15 See Chapter Eight, below.

16 The Statute of Tribunal was presented to the Security Council in *The Report of the Secretary-General Pursuant to Paragraph 2 of Security Council Resolution 808 (1993)*, (hereinafter, Report), 32 INT.LEG.MAT1159 (1993). The Statute was adopted by the Security Council in Resolution 827 (1993) and may be found in 32 INT.LEG.MAT1192 (1993). The Rules of Procedure and Evidence (hereinafter, Rules) are now at Revision 6 – IT/32/Rev.6.

17 UNSC Res.935 and 955 (1994), reprinted in 5 CRIM.LF 695 (1994). Rules of Procedure and Evidence, ITR/3/Rev.1 (1995), entry into force 29 June 1995.

18 Report of the International Law Commission on the Work of its Forty-Sixth Session, Draft Statute for an International Criminal Court, UN Doc.A/49/355 (1994); hereinafter, Statute. The ILC Draft is being developed in Preparatory Committee Meetings at the United Nations during 1996-98, prior to a diplomatic conference of plenipotentiaries in mid 1998 in Rome. See Crawford, *The ILC's Draft Statute for an International Criminal Court*, 88 AM.J INT'L L 140 (1994), *The ILC Adopts a Statute for an International Criminal Court*, 89 AM.J INT'L L 404 (1995); and, *Symposium on International Criminal Law*, vol.5:2 TRANSNAT'L L & CONTEMP. PROBS. 237 *et seq.* (1995).

part, to avoid alleged war criminals relying on the political offence exemption during extradition hearings, since all three eschew extradition as the method of surrender and, thus, the political offence exemption, too.[19]

Finally, a very disparate group has, on occasion, pleaded the exemption; their offences have a political flavour only because the government of the requesting State has taken an interest in the individual's affairs, or those of his group, distinct from the crime on which the extradition request is based.[20] In such cases, while the individual's crime is purely common, the offender or his group have acquired public notoriety and incurred government disfavour and so seek protection.

Since the political offence exemption is usually drafted in very vague terms in legislation and treaties, and since no authoritative or comprehensive definition has yet emerged, it is inevitable that difficult cases will continue to arise. The very term 'political offence' should have forewarned the nineteenth century drafters of the impending conflicts and disputes, because for every *ten* people there will always be at least *ten* different interpretations of 'politics'. Therefore, this chapter is premised to some extent on the suggestion that the exemption has been extended too far and that it has been stretched to include too many categories of fugitive. As such, it is currently too wide[21] and it needs to be circumscribed or, possibly, even abolished.

To understand the best way to meet the problems raised by the exemption, specific criticisms of certain national laws and a more general criticism of the political offence exemption will be discussed. A variety of solutions are proposed to make the exemption more applicable to present-day needs. Finally, regard will be had to methods by which States might be encouraged to ensure that the fugitive is brought to justice. First, though, the origins of the exemption need to be set in context – only by understanding the development of the exemption can one truly appreciate the original intentions behind its inclusion in extradition treaties and so see how far it is still relevant and how far it should still be bound by its own roots.

---

19 A claim that the crime was political might still be pleaded at the trial before the Tribunal or proposed Court, but the receptiveness of the judges to such claims is far from guaranteed.

20 *Eg. Sindona v Grant* 619 F.2d 167 (1980); *R v Pentonville Prison Governor, ex parte Budlong and Kember*, [1980] 1 WLR 1110; *T v Swiss Federal Prosecutor's Office*, 72 INT'L L REP.632.

21 See WIJNGAERT, *supra n5*, at p.204.

b. History

The origins of the political offence exemption help to explain the difficulties and conflicts that arise in its application today. The doctrine first entered international extradition law in 1834 in the Franco-Belgian treaty of that year.[22] It had been inspired by the changing mood in Europe following the French Revolution of 1789 and the new independence of Belgium from the Kingdom of the Netherlands. Within a very short time, the clause was incorporated in the extradition laws of the civil law and common law countries. The perceptions of the nineteenth century law-makers were founded in the political and diplomatic climate of that period. Europe was in turmoil, striving towards democracy and self-determination for national groups, as can be seen in the revolutions of 1848 and the emergence of Italy and Germany as nation-States. On the other hand, the United Kingdom, as an island, stood aloof from this Continental upheaval, seemingly a haven of liberality for European revolutionaries such as Kossuth, Garibaldi and Mazzini.[23]

> "[During] the nineteenth century those who used violence to challenge despotic regimes often occupied the high moral ground, and were welcomed in foreign countries as true patriots and democrats."[24]

It is against this background that the political offence exemption must be understood. Europe was moving away from autocratic empires, often with violent consequences.[25] However, it was those committed to establishing

---

22 22 B.F.S.P.223.

23 Karl Marx was also based in the United Kingdom. When the police investigated him, they placed an officer in hiding in a room where Marx was to hold a meeting – the officer's report adjudged him to be no threat because the meeting had been held in German! (I believe I am indebted to Lady Hazel Fox of the British Institute of International and Comparative Law for this anecdote).

24 *Per* Lord Mustill in *T, infra* n80, at 867.

25 See OPPENHEIM, INTERNATIONAL LAW (1905, 1st ed.) Vol.1, p.325; PORTER, THE REFUGEE QUESTION IN MIDVICTORIAN POLITICS (1979). See also *Quinn v Wren*, [1985] ILRM 410 (Supreme Court) where Finlay CJ held the accused, a member of the Irish National Liberation Army (INLA), could be extradited to the UK. The political offence defence was rejected partly because, although the crime had been committed on behalf of the INLA, that organisation wished to impose by force an all-Ireland workers republic, contrary to the Irish Constitution which

liberal-democratic governments who were protected. To try and apply the doctrine to the late twentieth century, especially to the issue of transnational terrorism, results in the confusion and injustice so prevalent. The exemption was aimed to protect people fighting for liberal democracy, yet the same language is still applied today to persons intent on destroying liberal democracy. It is evident, therefore, that the exemption may be in need of reassessment and it may need to be redrafted, in so far as this is possible. To paraphrase Jefferson,[26] extradition law cannot be made to wear the same clothes it wore in its infancy. As Wijngaert explains.

"[A] certain discrepancy has developed between the rule as it is enunciated and its practical application, which in many cases, may provide the impression of a real or apparent arbitrariness in the decision-making. Therefore, the question should be examined as to whether the political offence should not be explicitly re-evaluated and whether the various tendencies which presently have developed in an implicit manner should not be collected into a global and coherent legal framework. Such questions can only be answered on the basis of an analysis of the sense and function of the political offence exception on the contemporary situation."[27]

From the initial premise that political offenders were not to be extradited, an extensive jurisprudence has now developed, concentrating on the fugitive's acts and motive to varying degrees.

Interestingly, at the same time as the exemption was being formalised to protect persons striving for liberal democracy in Europe, another political

---

provided the *ultima ratio* of the defence in the first place.

"This Court cannot, it seems to me, interpret an Act of the *Oireachtas* as having the intention to grant immunity to a person charged with an offence, the admitted purpose of which is to further or facilitate the overthrow by violence of the Constitution and of the organs of State established thereby."

(Finlay C.J. at 419) *NB* The INLA was not fighting for a liberal democracy. *Cf.* Pyle, *infra* n254.

26 From a letter to a friend: "I am not an advocate for frequent changes in laws ... [but] we might as well require a man to wear still the coat which fitted him when a boy as civilised society to remain ever under the regimen of their barbarous ancestors". The inscription can be seen on the walls of the Jefferson Memorial in Washington DC.

27 WIJNGAERT, *supra* n5, at p.202.

philosophy was also undergoing development, anarchism.[28] Anarchism, in its simplest form, rejects the authority of not just the government, but of the State itself. The early anarchists, such as Godwin and Proudhon, were non-violent, but following Bakunin's association with the 'crooked, dubious adventurer', Nechaev, there arose the doctrine of 'propaganda by the deed'.

> "From 1870 on there was always to be a section of the anarchist movement ready to commit acts of terrorism, if not for their own sake, at least to symbolize a total revolt against society. Criminals and brigands were often able to claim that they were carrying out anarchist principles and that their crimes served to expose the hypocrisy and greed of the order they were attacking."[29]

Despite the eventual political failure of the anarchist movement in the twentieth century, it exerted an important influence on the development of the political offence exemption which may still be felt today. Violent so-called anarchists were responsible for many crimes towards the end of the nineteenth century, including the murder of Czar Alexander II in 1881.[30] Moreover, apart from judges declaring anarchists to be outside the protection of the exemption because they were the enemy of all governments,[31] some extradition treaties were amended to include the so-called *attentat* clause. This clause simply and solely excludes attacks on the Head of State from the exemption.[32] Today, most terrorists are labelled anarchistic by the media

---

28   JOLL, THE ANARCHISTS (2nd ed., 1979); GUERIN, ANARCHISM (1970). See PROUD-HON, LA REVOLUTION SOCIALE DEMONTREE PAR LE COUP D'ETAT DU DEUX DECEMBRE.
29   JOLL, *supra* n28, at pp.78-79. See *In re Meunier*, [1894] 2 QB 415; *Re Fedorenko (No.1)*, 17 CCC 268 (1910); *Malatesta*, a decision of the Swiss Federal Tribunal (cited in Green, *Hijacking, Extradition and Asylum*, 22 CHITTY'S LJ 135 at p.140, 1974), where the court deemed all anarchists to be thieves and brigands.
30   See OPPENHEIM, *supra* n25, at pp.393-95.
31   See *Meunier, supra* n29, at 419.
32   See SHEARER, EXTRADITION IN INTERNATIONAL LAW, at p.185, (1971). The corollary must be that otherwise such crimes would be within the protection of the exemption.

and by some courts[33] and commentators in a simplistic attempt to avoid arguments over whether their crimes are of a political character or not.

> "It is often hard to distinguish what is anarchist and what is not, especially when the aims of a terrorist group are not clear and when the actual attack on existing society seems more important than its consequences. This is certainly true of some terrorist groups of the 1980s, such as that founded in West Germany by Andreas Baader and Ulrike Meinhof, who ... revived the fear aroused by the anarchists of the 1890s and have consequently been regarded as themselves anarchists, *a label which they disclaim.*"[34]

Anarchism is now almost a buzz-word[35] and, as such, useless in attempting to clarify the ambit of the political offence exemption. Nevertheless, anarchism was an important factor in the development of the political offence exemption along with the birth of liberal-democracies in Europe. Taken together, the influence of anarchism and the traditions of the democratic nation State, it is no wonder that it is so difficult to ascertain the true meaning and purpose of the political offence exemption and its ambit at the end of the twentieth century.

---

33 See *Eain v Wilkes, infra* n117, at 521-22. The court recognized that Eain was not anarchist-inspired, but because the so-called anarchists of the late nineteenth century had engaged in acts which killed civilians, this was sufficient to exclude Eain's crimes which had also killed civilians – anarchists were excluded from the political offence exemption because they were deemed the enemy of all governments, not because the identity of their victims.

34 JOLL, *supra* n28, at p.265. Emphasis added. See also, *Della-Savia v Ministère Public de la Confédération*, 72 INT'L L REP.618 at 625-26 (Swiss Fed.Trib. 1969).

35 JOLL, *supra* n28, at p.266
"Although terrorist actions may cause shock and distress, they are nevertheless a less effective way of challenging the values of existing society than the continuous critique of our social goals and values offered by the philosophical anarchists."
See also Carbonneau, *The Political Offence Exemption to Extradition and Transnational Terrorists: Old Doctrine Reformulated and New Norms Created*, 1 ASILS INT'L LJ 1 at pp.30-31 (1977).

c. The Theory of the Present Law

There are two questions that need to be addressed before looking at the
various national approaches. First, whether it is a rule of international law
that political offenders should not be extradited and, if so, does the rule give
rights to the surrendered fugitive in the requesting State; and, secondly, how
is the present law on political offences to be classified and categorised.

The first question assumes that the fugitive is a political offender; the
issue of whether political offenders can be extradited can always be avoided
by merely defining the scope of the exemption so as to exclude the particular
fugitive. Nevertheless, the status of the exemption in international law has
created practical difficulties on occasion.

Irish courts, for instance, held that the violence in Northern Ireland in
the 1970s was political and that the non-extradition of politically motivated
fugitives was a principle of international law. Further, by virtue of Article
29(3) of the Irish Constitution,[36] which obliges Irish courts to recognize
generally recognised principles of international law, the issue took on a constitutional significance as well. The resulting failure by the British authorities
to obtain the surrender of alleged terrorists led to the establishment of the
Law Enforcement Commission, with members drawn from both jurisdictions,
to discuss how to prosecute those offenders involved in the conflict in Northern Ireland who escaped to Ireland. Once more, however, the Irish judges
on the Commission reiterated the above view[37] and refused to countenance
a change in extradition policy.

Nevertheless, most commentators and cases suggest that the political
offence question is a matter of State practice and not a general principle
of international law.[38] In the *Steiner*[39] case, for example, the Court Martial
in Sudan before which the accused appeared, having been extradited from
Uganda as a mercenary, held that while it may be a principle of the comity
of nations, it was not a rule of international law that political offenders
should never be extradited. Furthermore, the exemption can always be ex-

---

36 On which, see O'REILLY AND REDMOND, CASES AND MATERIALS ON THE IRISH
    CONSTITUTION, pp.281 *et seq.* (1980).
37 Cmnd 5627 (1974).
38 *Cf. The State (Duggan) v Tapley*, [1952] IR 62. See also, LILLICH, THE HUMAN
    RIGHTS OF ALIENS IN CONTEMPORARY INTERNATIONAL LAW, p.36 (1984).
39 *In the Trial of F.E.Steiner*, 74 INT'L L REP.478 (1971).

pressly or tacitly excluded by legislation or international arrangement. The extradition treaties concluded by States in the former Soviet bloc, *inter se*, in the late Sixties and Seventies, for instance, did not contain any protection for political offenders.[40] Thus, it is difficult to sustain the argument that it is a rule of customary international law.

However, given that most extradition arrangements do contain this safeguard for the fugitive, is it possible for him to resurrect it at the trial in the requesting State following his surrender, despite having pleaded it in vain at the extradition hearing in the first place[41]? The issue was considered in *The Spanish-German Extradition Treaty Case*.[42] The court held that it was not possible to review whether the extradition court in the requested State had erred in granting surrender if it turned out at the full trial that the offence was indeed of a political character.

"For there is no generally recognised rule of International Law to the effect that every extradition takes place under the implied assumption of the non-political character of the alleged offence .... [The extradition] treaty does not confer rights upon the extradited persons as such; it regulates solely the duties of the two States in matters of extradition. It grants them the right not to extradite political offenders; it does not impose upon them the duty not to extradite them."

At first glance, the reasoning is superficially sound. However, as Gerland pointed out,[43] the accused who has been extradited is entitled to the protection of the principle of specialty and it would be open to him to argue that his extradition was for the common crime of murder, not for a political crime, although that may be extending the usual scope of application of the specialty principle. Nevertheless, despite Gerland's arguments, recent authority is against the fugitive. The *Steiner* case,[44] above, held that it was not

---

40 See Schmid, *Extradition and International Judicial and Administrative Assistance in Penal Matters in East European States*, 34 LAW IN E.EUROPE 167 at p.180. See the Soviet-G.D.R. treaty of 19 SEPT 1979, *Ved.SSSR* 1980 No.35/712, cited in Schmid at pp.171-72.

41 See generally, CHINKIN, THIRD PARTIES IN INTERNATIONAL LAW, 1993.

42 [1925–26] Ann.Dig.308 at 308-09, First Senate in Criminal Matters of the German *Reichsgericht*.

43 Summarised at 309, *supra n*42.

44 *Supra n*39.

appropriate for the court in the requesting State to query the validity of the fugitive's surrender from the requested State. The German Federal Constitutional Court in the *Baader-Meinhof* case[45] adopted the same position and went on to hold that extradition treaties create rights for States alone, unless there is an express provision in the fugitive's favour.[46] Thus, it would seem the balance of authority is against the exemption being a rule of international law and against it conferring effective rights directly on the fugitive.

The second preliminary matter concerns the categories of political offence. No statute or treaty has so far tried to define what constitutes a political offence. Academics have attempted to delimit its boundaries,[47] but the words of Viscount Radcliffe still ring very true.

> "What then is an offence of a political character? The courts, I am afraid, have been asking this question at intervals ever since it was first posed judicially in 1890 ... and no definition has yet emerged or by now is ever likely to."[48]

Given that no absolute working definition is possible, the concept has been categorised, especially in continental Europe. A political offence may be classified as pure or relative, and a relative offence may be a *délit complexe* or a *délit connexe*.

(i) Pure Offences – A pure political offence is one "directed solely against the political order".[49] The French case of *Re Giovanni Gatti* is accepted as giving the definitive interpretation.

> "In brief, what distinguishes the political crime from the common crime is the fact that the former only affects the political organization of the State,

---

45 74 INT'L L REP.493 (1977).

46 *Supra* n45, at pp.496-97.

47 See, for example, DEFENSOR-SANTIAGO, POLITICAL OFFENCES IN INTERNATIONAL LAW, at p.321 (1977). Garcia-Mora, *The Nature of Political Offences: A Knotty Problem of Extradition Law*, 48 VA.L REV.1226 (1962).

48 *Schtraks v Government of Israel*, [1964] AC 556 at 589. See also, *T*, *infra* n80, at 899.

49 SHEARER, *supra* n32, at p.181.

the proper rights of the State, while the latter exclusively affects rights other than those of the State."[50]

It can be seen in such offences as treason,[51] sedition or espionage. Within traditional Anglo-American extradition jurisprudence, pure political offences have played little part, for they were not included in the list of extraditable offences. However, the change to using the eliminative method of defining extradition crimes will mean that in future common law judges will have to have regard to this species of political offence, too.

The only question mark in relation to pure political offences concerns espionage – the undignified chaos of *Ex parte Soblen*,[52] examined below, where a spy was deported to the 'requesting State' for fear that espionage might be regarded by the courts as a pure political offence under extradition law, is an example of the lack of clarity surrounding the scope of the exemption. In one British case, however, a judge at first instance held that acts of espionage are not political in character at all,[53] and this probably represents the current view.[54] It is yet another example of the increased cohesiveness among States within western industrialised society, as well.

(ii) Délit Complexe – This category of relative political offence covers acts which are "directed at both the political order and private rights".[55] It is this category which has presented in most detail the question of how to balance political against mere criminal activity.[56] In form, the extradition request would be for a common crime, such as murder, whereas in fact, the offence may be political with regard to the object sought and the motive

---

50 [1947] Ann.Dig.145.
51 Traitors having been the object of the first extradition treaties (see Chapter One, §e.), occasionally they are still surrendered. Suret Guseynov, former prime minister of Azerbaijan, was extradited from Russia to face charges of treason and armed rebellion – The Guardian p.18, 28 MAR 1997.
52 *R v Government of Brixton Prison, ex parte Soblen*, [1962] 3 All ER 641.
53 *R v Government of Pentonville Prison, ex parte Rebott*, [1978] L.S.Gaz.R.43; cf. *Bourke v Attorney General*, [1972] IR 36.
54 See also, *Espionage Prosecution Case* 94 INT'L L REP.68 at 74-75.
55 SHEARER, *supra* n32, at p.181.
56 Glaser, *The Conceptions of Political Delict*, 8 IND.YB.INT'L AFF.16 at pp.18-31 (1959). Glaser leaves the important question of how to weigh the various factors in the balance unanswered.

of the fugitive. As will be seen below, the most important factor is generally the remoteness of the crime from the ultimate political goal.

(iii) Délit Connexe – This variety of relative political offence is accepted in the USA,[57] Latin America[58] and in Europe.[59] It is

> "in itself not an act directed against the political order, but which is closely connected with another act which is so directed."[60]

The theft of guns in order to prepare for an armed rebellion and robbing a bank in order to provide funds for subversive political activities,[61] are the usual examples of *délits connexes*. Their very remoteness from the ultimate objective will make it very difficult to prove they are of a political character under most of the national tests, unless offences connected with a political offence are expressly brought within the protection by treaty or statute.

(iv) Politically Motivated Offences – With both varieties of relative offence, the courts are faced with a dilemma in trying to decide if the case at bar is political.

> "Which of the two elements is more grave? Is it the political or the common? What constitutes the greatest peril to society, and consequently the greatest interest to repression, the political or the non-political element? If the political right and interest are the more conspicuous, the offence is political. Otherwise it is not political."[62]

Nevertheless, commentators and courts in almost all jurisdictions have declared that mere political motive alone is insufficient to characterize a

---

57   *In re Ezeta*, 62 F.972 (1894) N.D. Cal.
58   See *In re Don Oscar Mariaca Pando*, [1925–26] Ann.Dig.310.
59   See Article 3.1 European Convention on Extradition, ETS 24 (1957).
60   SHEARER, *supra n*32, at pp.181-82.
61   *Cf. Ferrandi v Governor of Brixton Prison*, DC/205/81, (MWC), QBD, 22 JUNE 1981; *Re Kexel and Tillman's application for habeas corpus*, (CO/962/83, CO/963/83) LEXIS, 10 APR 1984, QBD.
62   ORTOLAN, vol.1, ELEMENTS DE DROIT PENAL, p.311 (1875), cited in DEFENSOR-SANTIAGO, *supra n*47, at p.76.

common crime as political.[63] At present, it is the act not the actor that predominates in establishing the nature of the offence,[64] and that is the near unanimous view to come out of Stein's extensive 1983 research.[65] While a political motive is essential it is not conclusive. In *Schtraks v Government of Israel*,[66] the House of Lords held that the true nature of offences of a political character would be lost sight of if the transnational fugitive offender merely had to show a political motive in order to satisfy the test. Both the Canadian Federal Court[67] and a United States Court of Appeals[68] have similarly expressly decided that mere motivation is insufficient. In civil law jurisdictions the same view has been expressed. German cases on terrorist fugitives have held that the motive is not determinative on its own and has to be viewed alongside the nature of the legal interest attacked when determining the political character of the offence.[69]

d. National Approaches

The theory discussed above has been interpreted in the United Kingdom, the United States, France, Switzerland and Ireland.[70] Such a categorisation of national approaches is normal, although, the separation of the United Kingdom and United States tests is not usual in such analyses. Although

---

63 The judgment of Walsh J in *Finucane v McMahon* [1990] IR 165, seemed to hold that the fugitive's political motivation was sufficient in the context of the Northern Irish conflict to render his offences political in character.

64 WIJNGAERT, *supra n5*, at p.203.

65 *Supra n6*, at p.379.

66 *Supra n48, per* Viscount Radcliffe at 591.

67 *Re State of Wisconsin and Armstrong*, 10 CCC (2d) 271, *per* Sweet DJ (1973).

68 *Escobedo v US*, 623 F.2d 1098 at 1104 (1980). *Extradition of Atta, Ahmad v Wigen*, 910 F.2d 1063 at 1066 (1990); see also, 706 F.Supp 1032 (1989), 726 F.Supp 389 (1989).

69 See *Baader-Meinhof Group Terrorist Case*, *supra n45*, at 498, and the *Yugoslav Terrorism Case (No.2)*, 74 INT'L L L REP.515 (1978).

70 Garcia-Mora, *supra n47*; SHEARER, *supra n32*; Carbonneau, *The Political Offence Exception to Extradition and Transnational Terrorists: Old Doctrine Reformulated and New Norms Created*, *supra n35*; WIJNGAERT, *supra n5*; DEFENSOR-SANTIAGO, *supra n47*; Connolly *Ireland and the Political Offence Exception to Extradition*, 12 J L & SOC.153 (1985).

stemming from the same case,[71] it is evident that the exemption does not the have equal scope in both of those jurisdictions today. In the five country-studies discussed below, the aim is to review the development of the law on offences of a political character within each jurisdiction and evaluate the usefulness of each national approach in meeting the current challenges to international public order from transnational crime. Thereafter, it will be possible to review the problems associated with the operation of the political offence exemption and the potential solutions that go beyond the analyses current in State practice. Comparing the existing national approaches with these other potential solutions, a composite response can be proposed that is best suited to developing (rather than creating anew) the jurisprudence of the political offence exemption.

(i) The United Kingdom Approach – The United Kingdom's traditional political offence exemption was found, in its most basic form, in very similar terms in s3(1) Extradition Act, 1870, s4(1)(a) Fugitive Offenders Act 1967 and in s2(2)(a) Backing of Warrants (Republic of Ireland) Act 1965. The 1870 Act described it as follows.

> "*s3(1)* A fugitive criminal shall not be surrendered if the offence in respect of which his surrender is demanded is one of a political character, or if he prove to the satisfaction of the police magistrate or the court before whom he is brought on habeas corpus or to the Secretary of State, that the re-quisition for his surrender has in fact been made with a view to try or punish him for an offence of a political character."

The Extradition Act 1989 adopts a different position, partly in line with the European Extradition Convention of 1957,[72] and uses only the first limb of the old formulation.

> "*s6(1)* A person shall not be returned ..., if it appears to an appropriate authority -
> (a) that the offence of which the person is accused or was convicted is an offence of a political character."

---

71 *In re Castioni*, [1891] 1 QB 149.
72 *Supra* n59.

The United Kingdom interpretation of the exemption developed from *In re Castioni*.[73] The test laid down by that case was that the offence had to be "incidental to and form part of political disturbances", that is, it was committed "in the course of" and "in furtherance of the political disturbance".[74] Apart from a small 'hiccup' to incorporate fugitives fleeing from the former Eastern bloc,[75] the basis of the test remained for the most part unchanged for almost a century. *Schtraks*[76] makes it clear that the political

---

73 *Supra n*71.

74 *Supra n*71, at 156 and 165-66. See also Woodcock, *Political Offences and Extradition: A Conceptual Deviation in the English Courts*, [1980] 1 TOP.LAW 22. See also Young, *The Political Offence Exception in the Extradition Law of the United Kingdom: A Redundant Concept*, 4 LEG.STUD.211 (1984).

75 *Kolczynski, supra n*10. See below.

76 See *Schtraks, supra n*48. See also the extended protection in s6(1)(c)&(d) of the Extradition Act 1989 whereby a fugitive shall not be returned if he would be prosecuted, prejudiced at trial or punished on account of his race, religion, nationality or political opinions. See also THE INTERDEPARTMENTAL WORKING PARTY'S 1982 REVIEW OF THE LAW AND PRACTICE OF EXTRADITION IN THE UNITED KINGDOM; hereinafter, 1982 REVIEW. The 1982 REVIEW OF THE SCHEME RELATING TO THE RENDITION OF FUGITIVE OFFENDERS WITHIN THE COMMONWEALTH 1966, made it optional to exclude murder and offences prescribed by multilateral convention (COMMONWEALTH SECRETARIAT, Doc.LMM (83) 33). See now, the 1990 version of the Scheme, LMM(90)32.
"ANNEX I
DISCRETION AS TO DEFINITION OF POLITICAL OFFENCES
1. It may be provided by a law in any part of the Commonwealth that certain acts shall not be held to be offences of a political character including -
(a) an offence against the life or person of a Head of State or a member of his immediate family or any related offence.
(b) an offence against the life or person of a Head of Government, or of a Minister of a Government, or any related offence ....
(c) murder, or any related offence ....
(d) an act declared to constitute an offence under a multilateral international convention whose purpose is to prevent or repress a specific category of offences and which imposes on the parties thereto an obligation either to extradite or to prosecute the person sought.
2. Any part of the Commonwealth may restrict the application of any of the provisions made under paragraph 1 to a request from a part of the Commonwealth which has made similar provisions in its laws."

disturbance in question must be a valid attempt to change the government
or its approach.[77]

> "The crime must be incidental to and form part of a political upheaval, com-
> mitted by the fugitive offender as part of an organised political party conten-
> ding for power with the established government .... The individual has to
> be at odds with the State."[78]

Furthermore, the act must be proximate to the final goal of the organization
contending for power with the government.

> "I would accept ... that the relevant state of mind is not restricted to the
> intent necessary to constitute the offence with which he is charged, for in
> the case of none of the extradition crimes can this properly be described
> as being political. The relevant mental element must involve some less
> immediate object which the accused sought to achieve by doing the physical
> act. It is unnecessary for the purposes of the present appeal, and would,
> in my view, be unwise, to attempt to define how remote that object might
> be. If the accused robbed a bank to obtain funds to support a political party,
> the object would ... clearly be too remote to constitute a political offence.
> But if the accused had killed a dictator in the hope of changing the
> government of the country, his object would be sufficiently immediate to
> justify the epithet 'political'."[79]

The case of *T v Secretary of State for the Home Department*,[80] a case concerning an application for refugee status but raising the same issues,[81] has

---

77 *Per* Lord Reid, *supra n*48, at 582-84.

78 *R v Governor of Pentonville Prison, ex parte Kakis*, 122 SOL.JO. 96 (1978), *per*
    Lord Widgery CJ. See also *Re Kexel and Tillman*, and *Ferrandi v Governor
    of Brixton Prison and Government of Italy, supra n*61.

79 *Cheng, supra n*11, *per* Lord Diplock at 945. On the facts, the killing of Chiang
    Kai Shek's son in the early 1970s might well have been too remote, but Cheng
    was not returned on that basis. See also *Watin v Ministère Public Fédéral*, 72
    INT'L L REP.614 (Swiss Fed.Trib. 1964).

80 [1996] 2 All ER 865.

81 1951 Convention Relating to the Status of Refugees, Article 1F(b), 189 UNTS
    50.
    "The provisions of this Convention shall not apply to any person with respect
    to whom there are serious reasons for considering that ... he has committed

refined the test yet further. There, the applicant, as a member of FIS, an organization seeking to overthrow the Algerian government, had been involved in the planning of a bomb attack on Algiers Airport, as a result of which ten people had been killed, and in a raid on a military depot in which one person had been killed. The majority of the House of Lords held that in determining whether there is a sufficiently close and direct link between the crime and the organization's goal, one had to have regard to the means used and to the target of the offence, whether, on the one hand it was a military or government target or, on the other, whether it was a civilian target,

"and in either event whether it was likely to involve the indiscriminate killing or injuring of members of the public."[82]

As such, proximity under the English test incorporates an element of proportionality.

The requirement that the offence be proximate to the ultimate goal of the fugitive's cause, is common throughout State practice in extradition today. For instance, it is part of the reasoning of Dutch courts, too. In *Folkerts v Public Prosecutor*,[83] the Dutch Supreme Court held that for the offences in question to have a political character, they ought reasonably to be expected, separately or combined, to yield a result "directly related to the ultimate goal". In *McF v Public Prosecutor*,[84] it held that the offences in question were too remote from the transnational fugitive offender's ultimate goal of the unification of Ireland. The Australian Federal Court has expressed the same view in *Prevato v Governor Metropolitan Remand Centre*,[85] stating that "the action which constitutes the offence must be committed in the direct prosecution of the [group's] campaign". In Canada,

---

a serious non-political crime ...."
And see the 1967 Protocol, 606 UNTS 267.

82 *Supra* n80, at 899. Lord Lloyd, in part, built on the provisions of the European Convention on the Suppression of Terrorism, ETS 90 (1977), 15 INT.LEG.MAT 1272 (1976).

83 74 INT'L L REP.498 at 501 (1978).

84 100 INT'L L REP.414 at 425 (1986).

85 (1986), 64 ALR 37.

the case of *Re Gil and the Minister of Employment and Immigration*[86] held
that injuring the commercial interests of supporters of the opposed regime
could have no objectively rational prospect of forcing that regime to fall
or change its policies.

Such an analysis of the scope of the exemption as is seen in English
case law is rooted in the immediate acts of the fugitive offender, rather than
in his mere political or ideological motivation which is insufficient in and
of itself. The test places the emphasis on the offence, not the offender. Thus,
the late nineteenth century anarchist groups were deemed to be outside the
scope of the test from the beginning.[87] Moreover, the exemption was established for those wishing to create democratic nations in the liberal-
democratic mould, not to protect those revolutionaries who wished to establish States where British[88] ideals of justice would not be cherished.
Therefore, modern-day terrorists who attempt to overthrow Western European
States are held to be outside the ambit of the exemption, in part because
they tend to want a change from the liberal-democratic tradition.[89] The
simple test of *Castioni* is overladen with the prejudices and perceptions of
nineteenth century Britain – judges today still view the exemption through
the eyes of its Victorian creators.[90] This is implicit in the decision in the
case of *Cheng*,[91] where the majority of Lords agreed to surrender the
fugitive to help combat world terrorism. Lord Simon's dissenting speech
shows that Cheng's offence was, for all intents and purposes, within the

---

86 (1994) 119 DLR (4th) 497 at 515-16.
87 The Royal Commission on Extradition (1866) thought that anarchists would
    not be regarded as political offenders under what was to be s3(1) Extradition
    Act 1870. See SHEARER, *supra n*32, at p.171, n.4. See *Kexel and Tillman* and
    *Ferrandi, supra n*61.
88 *NB.* Nowadays, the test is premised on whether the fugitive finds favour with
    'Western' political systems.
89 See *Kexel and Tillman* and *Ferrandi, supra n*61. Kexel and Tillman were neo-
    fascists from the Federal Republic of Germany and Ferrandi was an Italian who
    belonged to the Milan section of *Brigate Communiste*. Kexel and Tillman were
    returned to the Federal Republic of Germany with no further appeal. They were
    sentenced on 15 March 1985 in Frankfurt for attempted murder and bank raids
    along with three other neo-Nazis (The Guardian p.6, 16 MAR 1985). Kexel
    committed suicide following the sentencing, The Guardian p.6, 19 MAR 1985.
90 *Per* Lord Reid in *Schtraks, supra n*48, at 583.
91 *Supra n*11, *per* Lord Salmon's judgment at 961-63, *esp.*962.

classical political test of *Castioni*, yet the protection of the exemption was not granted to him. The majority, especially Lord Salmon, took account of the change in circumstances since *Castioni* and decided that this humanitarian provision could never have been intended to apply to the terrorism of the 1970s and beyond.[92]

In conclusion, therefore, the courts have interpreted the seemingly very simple test by reference to the precise mischief at which the 1870 Act was originally aimed. The result has been effectively to exclude terrorists from the scope of the test. While the outcome is acceptable, it would be more appropriate to amend the test to meet the needs of international public order openly.

> "But this [excluding terrorism] will be for governments in international conclave: there is no advantage in marginal and anomalous judicial erosion of traditional immunities."[93]

To a certain extent, Lord Simon's desire has come true. An increasingly prevalent trend, not limited to the United Kingdom's approach to interpreting the range of the political offence exemption, is for governments to restrict the ambit of its protection by treaties and domestic legislation. The government of the United Kingdom implemented the European Convention on the Suppression of Terrorism,[94] to be considered below, through the Suppression of Terrorism Act 1978.[95]

---

92 In this conclusion they are supported by Warbrick – [1980] PUB.LAW 113 at pp.118-22. The decision would be more coherent if it had been decided on the basis that Cheng would receive a fair trial in the United States, rather than that the political offence must be political *vis à vis* the requesting State. See Lord Simon's dissenting speech, *esp.* at 956 *et seq.* (*supra* n11). Nevertheless, STEIN, *supra* n6, found that the "*vis à vis*" test was commonly used by courts in several different countries – see p.379.

93 *Supra* n11, at 960 *per* Lord Simon.

94 *Supra* n82. And see Gilbert, *The 'Law' and 'Transnational Terrorism'*, 26 NETH.YB.INT'L L 3 (1996).

95 See Barratt, *The European Convention on the Suppression of Terrorism Act 1978*, [1980] 1 TOP.LAW 1 at p.1. *NB* The Genocide Act 1969 had already declared genocide not to be an offence of a political character.

"The purpose of the ECST, which was drafted under the auspices of the Council of Europe, is to assist in the suppression of terrorism by strengthening extradition procedures and mutual assistance arrangements between European States, in order to ensure that perpetrators of such acts do not escape prosecution and punishment. The intended result is that it should be impossible for terrorists to find a safe refuge in Europe."

Although a major reform of the United Kingdom's law on extradition and political offenders, the statute has had limited impact,[96] partly because the Convention is only open to signature by Council of Europe member States.[97] Further, it is difficult to envisage any crime in the normal course of events that would have been deemed political in character under the law as it was before the United Kingdom ratified the ECST that will now be outside the protection of the United Kingdom's statutorily amended political offence exemption.

This policy of limiting the scope of the political offence exemption in English law by entering into regional or bilateral arrangements with other politically homogenous States has continued. At the regional level, the members of the Commonwealth amended the 1966 Scheme Relating to the Rendition of Fugitive Offenders within the Commonwealth[98] at the law ministers meeting in Colombo, Sri Lanka in 1983.[99] Where both members of the Commonwealth are parties to an international convention designating a particular crime non-political,[100] then it will not be treated as having a

---

96   *Cf. Re Kexel and Tillman, supra n*61, where several of the charges were deemed to be non-political under the Suppression of Terrorism Act 1978.
    "It is submitted on behalf of the applicants that all the offences are of a political character within the meaning of the Act of 1870, but it is conceded that charges 12-18 (explosives offences under Sch.1, paras.12 & 13, 1978 Act) cannot be so regarded by reason of the provisions of the Suppression of Terrorism Act 1978."

97   Art.11 ECST, *supra n*82.

98   Cmnd.3008.

99   See the 1982 REVIEW OF COMMONWEALTH EXTRADITION ARRANGEMENTS, *supra n*76. The scheme was revised and adopted in Colombo as Doc.LMM(83)33; see now the 1990 version of the Scheme agreed at Wellington, New Zealand, LMM(90)32.

100 *Eg.* Convention on the Prevention and Punishment of the Crime of Genocide, 1948, Art.VII, 78 UNTS 277 (1951): Convention on Suppression and Punishment of the Crime of Apartheid 1973, Art. XI(2), 13 INT.LEG.MAT50 (1974).

political character under the Scheme.[101] Furthermore, parties to the Scheme may refuse to recognize as political in character an attack on the life of the Head of State, the Head of Government or any minister of the government, or, indeed, any murder. Finally, following the growth of multilateral conventions aimed at stamping out particular criminal activity, for example, hijacking,[102] member States of the Commonwealth have a discretion to treat these crimes as non-political, too.[103]

The more specific restrictions are to be found in the 1986 Anglo-US Supplementary Extradition Treaty[104] and the Anglo-Indian Extradition Treaty.[105] The details of these treaties will be considered below, but they follow the approach of the ECST and the amended Commonwealth Scheme by excluding certain crimes from the ambit of the exemption. The combined effect of the three former restrictive agreements may well be to abolish the political offence *vis à vis* all the countries with which the United Kingdom conducts regular extradition relations.

Another limitation on the traditional United Kingdom approach has been effected by omission; the second limb of section 3(1) Extradition Act 1870 is not reproduced in section 6 of the 1989 Extradition Act. It had granted protection to a fugitive who could prove

"that the requisition for his surrender has in fact been made with a view to try to punish him for an offence of a political character."

Under the 1989 Act the fugitive would have to rely instead on a finding that there is a 'reasonable chance' or a 'serious possibility'[106] that he would suffer prejudice or persecution on account of his race, religion, nationality

---

101 Art.10(1)(b), 1990 Scheme, LMM(90)32.
102 *Eg.* Convention for the Suppression of the Unlawful seizure of Aircraft, done at the Hague, 16 DEC 1970, 10 INT.LEG.MAT133 (1971).
103 Annex 1 of the revised Scheme, *supra n*99.
104 The Supplementary Treaty in its final form is to be found in Cm.294, UKTS 6 (1988) and, with comments, in Appendix 1 to the US Senate EXEC.REPT 99-17, accompanying TR.DOC.99-8. It was ratified on 23 December 1986.
105 21st September 1992, SI 1993 No.2533. The treaty was published and presented to Parliament on December 2nd 1992. See Gilbert, *The Anglo-Indian Extradition Treaty*, 42 INT'L & COMP.LQ 442 (1993).
106 *Fernandez v Government of Singapore*, [1971] 1 WLR 987 at 994 *per* Lord Diplock.

or political opinions. There seems little difference in practical terms between the two means of restricting extradition.

In conclusion, the only certain fact that can be stated about the political offence exemption in English law is that it has gone through a period of legislative change in form, if not necessarily in substance.

(ii) The United States Approach – The United States has no equivalent in any statute to the United Kingdom legislative formulation of the exemption, but similar provisions are found in US extradition treaties. Since these treaties are deemed to be self-executing they are the equivalent of statutes under United States law.[107] However, because it is a treaty-based approach there tends to be some variation on the theme. For example, the US-Israeli treaty of 1962[108] is very similar to s3(1) of the 1870 Act and states that extradition shall not be granted in the following circumstances:

> "*Art.VI(4)*. When the offence is regarded by the requested party as one of a political character or if the person sought proves that the request for his extradition has, in fact, been made with a view to trying or punishing him for an offence of a political character."

In the alternative though, the US-Mexican treaty of 1978[109] is much more succinct. Article 5(1) simply states:

> "Extradition shall not be granted when the offence for which it is requested is political or of a political character."

The treaty with Costa Rica[110] provides in Article 4 that extradition shall not be granted where the offence is a political offence or one connected with a political offence. The treaty with Jamaica,[111] whilst excluding offences of a political character as usual, also provides that extradition shall not be granted

---

107 Self-executing treaties are law in the US by virtue of Art.VI of the US Constitution: *Whitney v Robertson*, 124 US 190 (1888).
108 2 INT.LEG.MAT186 (1963).
109 17 INT.LEG.MAT1058 (1978).
110 TR.DOC.98-17, in force 11 October 1991.
111 TR.DOC.98-18, in force 7 July 1991.

"if it is established that extradition is requested for *political purposes*."[112]

As such, the scope of inquiry of the court could be much broader than just the character of the offence.

Despite the differences in wording in the treaties, however, the courts have concentrated on the overall theme and purpose of the exemption rather than indulging in distinguishing the particular phraseology of treaty provisions.

The United States first considered the scope of the political offence exemption in *In re Ezeta*.[113] The court in that case purported to follow the English case of *Castioni*. Unfortunately, having regard to the facts of *Ezeta*, the final decision does not fit within the *Castioni* test and is much more in line with the Mill definition which had been roundly rejected in the English case.[114] Subsequent decisions have confirmed the *Ezeta* interpretation, that if the crime is committed 'in the course of' *or* 'in furtherance of a political disturbance', then it will be of a political character.[115] As the bench in *Castioni* feared, this approach has meant that any crime committed during the course of a political disturbance, as long as some tenuous

---

112 Article III(2)(a) – emphasis added. See below.

113 *Supra n57.*

114 *Ezeta* involved, *inter alia*, bank robbery to pay troops, a *délit connexe* – *supra n57*, at 996-1003.

"The testimony shows that they were all committed during the progress of actual hostilities between the contending forces, wherein Gen. Ezeta and his companions were seeking to maintain the authority of the then existing government against the active operations of a revolutionary uprising. With the merits of this strife I have nothing to do. My duty will have been performed when I shall have determined the character of the crimes or offenses charged against these defendants, with respect to that conflict. During its progress, crimes may have been committed by the contending forces of the most atrocious and inhuman character, and still the perpetrators of such crimes escape punishment as fugitives beyond the reach of extradition. I have no authority, in this examination, to determine what acts are within the rules of civilized warfare, and what are not. War, at best, is barbarous, and hence it is said that 'the law is silent during war'." (at 996).

115 *Eg. Artukovic*, 140 F.Supp 245 (1956), 247 F.2d 198 (1957), 355 US 393 (1958), 170 F.Supp 383 (1959): *cf.* Artukovic was extradited in February 1986, 784 F.2d 1354 (1986). *Jimenez v Aristeguieta*, 311 F.2d 547 (1962), *cert.den.* 375 US 48 (1963). *In re Doherty*, 599 F.Supp 270 (1984).

connection can be proved with the ultimate object of the fugitive's group, may be deemed political.[116]

The preliminary and essential hurdle for the fugitive is the existence of a political disturbance.[117] Once that is shown, then the fugitive need only show that his crime was to do with that disturbance as part of his group's attempt to effect political change. On that understanding, the United States interpretation of the exemption is, in some ways, much the strictest, for the fugitive has no prospect of success unless a political disturbance is proven. Thus, in *Sindona v Grant*,[118] the fugitive alleged that the Italian government's request for his surrender for financial crimes was a cover to deal with him in relation to a political and financial scandal involving high ranking members of the Italian government; the US extradition court, though, held that since there was no disturbance the offences could not be political.[119] Moreover, the court in *Locatelli*[120] held that it was not competent to investigate the motives of the requesting government in seeking to prosecute the fugitive offender; it was an issue for the Secretary of State.[121] A comparison should be drawn with the approach in the British case of *Kolczynski*,[122] where the Divisional Court took account of the nature of the Polish political system as it was in 1955. However, once the US courts find that that political disturbance exists, then the remaining stages of the United States test are interpreted very liberally.

---

116 Compare the *Ezeta* case, *supra n57*, with Lord Diplock's view in *Cheng, supra n79*. See also Lubet and Czaczkes, *The Role of the American Judiciary in the Extradition of Political Terrorists*, 71 J CRIM.L & CRIMINOLOGY 193 at pp.203-06 (1980); *Cf. Ornelas v Ruiz*, 161 US 502 at 512.

117 In *Quinn v Robinson*, 783 F.2d 776 (1986), the Court of Appeals agreed to the extradition of Quinn for murder because it found there was no uprising in mainland Britain: whilst welcome, the decision is not as progressive as *Eain v Wilkes*, 641 F.2d 504 (1981), *cert.den.* 454 US 894 (1981), and *Extradition of Atta, supra n68*. See also *Report Recommending the Reform of the Law of International Extradition*, by the Committee on Immigration and Nationality Law, [1986] A.B.A. of C.N.Y., THE RECORD, 587 at pp.592-93.

118 *Supra n20*.

119 Having been extradited, Sindona died of poisoning in an Italian gaol.

120 *In the Matter of the Extradition of Locatelli*, 468 F.Supp 568 at 574-75 (1979).

121 See also *Extradition of Atta, supra n68*, at 1066-67, rev'g in part 726 F.Supp 389 at 409-20 (1989).

122 *Supra n10*.

When the United States analysis has been applied to the problem of terrorist violence, anomalous results have occurred. Until 1986 no member of the Provisional Irish Republican Army (IRA) had ever been returned following a request from the United Kingdom government.[123] The courts held that there was a political disturbance in Northern Ireland and any crime committed for the objectives of the IRA was a political offence and, thus, non-extraditable.[124] However, the problem of terrorist crimes was addressed by the Court of Appeals for the Seventh Circuit in the *Eain* case.[125] *Eain* concerned an act of indiscriminate bombing in Tiberias, Israel, by a member of the Palestine Liberation Organisation (PLO). The court held there needed to be a direct political effect from the crime if it were to fall within the exemption.[126] This view, requiring proximity between the offence and the organisation's ultimate goal, is a logical development of the analysis of political offences given by the US Supreme Court in *Ornelas v Ruiz*.[127] In *Ornelas*, the court held that in assessing the political character of the offence it was appropriate to consider the nature of the foray, the mode of

---

123 *McMullen*, 74 AM.J INT'L L 433 (1980); *Mackin*, 668 F.2d 122 (1981); *cf. Quinn*, *supra* n117. Quinn was requested for the murder of a Police Constable in London where the court held no political disturbance, the *sine qua non* of the political offence exemption test under US law, was taking place. See also *Doherty*, *supra* n115. Cases post-1986 may reflect a change in policy towards the crimes committed by those claiming to have acted on behalf of the IRA, or they may be evidence that the Anglo-US Supplementary Treaty, *supra* n104, has proved effective in restricting the scope of the political offence exemption in US jurisprudence. See, for example, *McMullen v United States* 769 F.Supp 1278 (1991), 953 F.2d 761 (1992), 989 F.2d 603 (1993); *United States v Smyth* 795 F.Supp 973 (1992), 976 F.2d 1535 (1992); 820 F.Supp 498 (1992), 826 F.Supp 316 (1993), 863 F.Supp 1137 (1994), 61 F.3d 711 (1995), 72 F.3d 1433 (1996).

124 Quinn was originally deemed extraditable by Federal Magistrate Steele Langford (The Guardian p.1, 30 SEPT 1982) because Quinn had not satisfactorily established his membership of the IRA. This was despite a conviction by a Dublin court for being a member of that organisation. Quinn won his appeal before District Judge Aguilar, but the United Kingdom government appealed and the Court of Appeals (Ninth) held him extraditable for murder, *supra* n117. He was extradited on 21st October 1986; The Guardian p.1, 22 OCT 1986.

125 *Supra* n117.

126 *Supra* n117, at 520-21.

127 161 US 502 at 511 (1912).

attack and the person of the victims. Further, in *Artukovic v Rison*,[128] decided after *Eain*, it was held that there needed to be a "rational nexus" between the crimes charged and the prevailing disturbance. In *Extradition of
Atta*,[129] the Court of Appeals held that

> "an attack on a commercial bus carrying civilian passengers on a regular
> route is not a political offence."

The focus of these judgments, therefore, is on the surrounding circumstances
and on the status of those harmed. It is hoped that if the Supreme Court
ever considers such a case that the *Eain* proximity test will be approved.

As it stands, the United States approach is both too wide and too narrow.[130] Its narrowness is seen in its absolute requirement that there be a
'political uprising'.[131] This must be more than a mere campaign of terror,
for in London in the 1970s the IRA waged many series of bombings, yet
the Court of Appeals in *Quinn* held there was no political uprising on
mainland Britain.[132] The width of the US approach is in the fact that once
such a political uprising does exist, then crimes to do with the ultimate goal
of the fugitive's group will usually be within the exemption. The United
States interpretation has only caused problems with respect to requests for
members of the IRA, and these cases may be explained as discrete anomalies,
but the potential is there, although no longer for IRA requests following the
Anglo-US Supplementary Extradition Treaty.[133] The treaty follows the approach of the ECST[134] and excludes certain crimes from the ambit of the
political offence exemption.[135]

Yet, there is evidence of a more general change in the offing. While the
attempts to amend the political offence exemption through legislation during

---

128 628 F.Supp 1370 at 1376 (1986); 784 F.2d 1354 (1986).
129 *Supra n*68, at 1066.
130 THE RECORD, *supra n*117, at pp.592-93.
131 *Supra nn*20 and 120.
132 *Supra n*117, at 813.
133 *Supra n*104.
134 *Supra n*82.
135 *United States v Lui Kin-Hong* 110 F.3d 103 (1997).

the Reagan years ultimately fizzled out,[136] there are some hints in case law that proximity to the ultimate goal of those creating the political disturbance and proportionality with respect to that goal will be relevant factors in determining the character of the offence. The first example of a new analysis is found in two cases[137] where the judges considered wider issues than merely seeing whether a political uprising occurred.

"In going beyond the narrow question of whether an offence was incidental to a disturbance, *Doherty* and *Eain*[138] suggested the following factors for consideration

· the civilian or military status of the victim of violence.[139]

· whether the crime charged is an atrocity, war crime or an act in violation of international law and inconsistent with international standards of civilized conduct.[140]

· that the person committing the violence belongs to an organisation with a well-defined organisation, discipline and command structure, as opposed to every fanatical group or individual with loosely defined political objectives.[141]

· and that the conduct be committed in the place where the political change was to be effected.[142,143]

---

136 A plethora of Bills in Congress were aimed at restricting the exemption – see Currin, *Extradition Reform and the Statutory Definition of Political Offences*, 24 VA.J INT'L L 419 (1984). Between 1981 and 1984, both the House of Representatives and the Senate considered several bills which either transferred the political offence question to the executive from the courts, or excluded certain offences from the protection of the exemption, or gave courts guidelines on how to apply the test. Some of these provisions are considered below, even though general legislative change came to nothing.

137 See also, *Extradition of Atta, supra n68.*

138 *Supra nn*115 and 117, respectively.

139 *Doherty,* at 275; *Eain,* at 521-23. See also *Atta, supra n68,* at 1066.

140 *Doherty* at 274. And see *Atta, supra n68,* 706 F.Supp 1032 at 1042 (1989), 726 F.Supp 389 at 402-08 (1989), aff'd 910 F.2d 1063 at 1066 (1990).

141 *Doherty,* at 276.

142 *Doherty,* at 275.

143 THE RECORD, *supra n*117, at pp.592-93. In *Extradition of Atta, supra n68,* the Second Circuit seems to have used such criteria in its determination that the fugitive's offence was non-political; it expressly noted that it was an attack on a commercial bus killing a civilian.

While, apart from the second and the fourth, these criteria are probably not
acceptable because they are vague and because many of those terrorist
attacks condemned by politicians worldwide would be within their ambit,
it does reveal that the exemption may be evolving at last in the United States
into something more suited to present-day needs. The uprising may be the
starting point to a decision on whether the offence is of a political character,
but it should not predominate as much as it has done in the past. Even in
Quinn,[144] which rejected the *Eain* analysis, the court took a policy decision
to exclude terrorist offences from the ambit of the exemption. The exemption
was designed to protect

> "[those] engaged in internal or domestic struggles over the form or com-
> position of their own government, including, of course, struggles to displace
> an occupying power. It was not designed to protect international political
> coercion or blackmail, or the exportation of violence and strife to other
> locations – even to the homeland of an oppressor nation."[145]

The US approach, though, has at present little to offer the international
community in terms of resolving the continuing difficulties inherent in the
political offence exemption.

(iii) The French Approach[146] – The definitive interpretation of the classical
French approach was given in *Re Giovanni Gatti.*[147]

> "Political offences are those which injure the political organism, which are
> directed against the constitution of the Government and against sovereignty
> .... The offence does not derive its political character from the motive of
> the offender, but from the nature of the rights it injures. The reasons on
> which non-extradition is based do not take account of mere motives for

---

144 *Supra n*117, at 808.
145 *Supra n*117, at 807. The Ninth Circuit seems to have decided that the British
    government had already withdrawn from N.Ireland. Otherwise, its conception
    that carrying out a bombing campaign in London is somehow '*exporting*' terror-
    ism from N.Ireland does not really make a lot of sense.
146 See generally, Baclet-Hainque, *Le Conseil d'Etat et l'Extradition en Matière
    Politique*, [1991] RDDP 197.
147 [1947] Ann.Dig.145 (Case No.70) at 145-46.

the purpose of attributing to a common crime the character of a political offence."

This interpretation of the exemption is very strict, only conferring protection on those offenders whose crimes would affect the State alone and in no way harm individuals – espionage, sedition or *lèse majesté* would fall within the test, but not murder of the head of State with the aim of securing power. Such a test does not give rise to the excesses of the United States inter-pretation,[148] but is unworkable and unreasonable in other ways. No relative political offender[149] would ever be exempted from extradition. In fact, the *Gatti* test was an anomaly, contradicting *In re Colman*,[150] and it has frequently been ignored.[151] In cases concerning alleged Red Brigade Ter-rorists, *Piperno* and *Pace*,[152] the court has moved towards the Swiss ap-proach of determining whether the political or common element of the crime predominated. Indeed in a case involving Basque separatists, long protected in France against Spanish requests, the *Conseil d'Etat* rejected the fugitive's contention that armed attacks and the murder of a policeman in Spain were political offences, and stated that even if they were their very gravity de-

---

148 *Eg. Artukovic, supra* n115.

149 *Ie.* where a common crime is perpetrated for political ends *viz. Castioni, supra* n71. See Garcia-Mora, *supra* n47, at pp.1239 *et seq.*

150 [1947] Ann.Dig.139.

151 *Eg. In re Rodriguez,* [1953] 2 Gaz.Palais 113; *In re Hennin,* [1967] *La Semaine Juridique* 15274; *In re Inacio do Palma,* [1967] *La Semaine Juridique* 15386. See Carbonneau, *supra* n35, at pp.19-22.

152 *Chambre d'Accusation de Paris,* 1979. See also the court's decision in the Klaus Croissant case:- Carbonneau, *Extradition and Transnational Terrorism: A Comment on the Recent Extradition of Klaus Croissant from France to West Germany,* 12 INT'L LAWYER 813 (1979). Croissant was arrested as a Stasi spy following Germany's reunification – The Guardian p.8, 15 SEPT 1992. Compare the decisions in Abu Daoud, *supra* n8, and the *Conseil d'Etat's* decision *vis à vis* the French government's release of two Iranian's whom the courts had ordered to be surrendered to Switzerland, *Affaire Gouvernement Suisse, supra* n13. See also Carbonneau, *The Political Offence Exception as applied in French cases dealing with the Extradition of Terrorists: The Quest for an Appropriate Doctrinal Analysis Revisited,* [1983] MICH.YB.INT'L LEG.STUD.209.

prived them of a political character.[153] Thus, in practice French courts exempt both pure and relative political offenders, and increasingly they are following the Swiss approach.

(iv) The Swiss Approach – The Swiss approach is the most developed analysis of those so far considered and receives wide acceptance from academic writers. The political motivation test, or the predominance test, as it is known, balances the political and common elements of the crime.[154] Only if the political element dominates is the fugitive non-extraditable. The method of balancing was explained in *In re Nappi*.[155]

> "[The] political character of an offence is predominant only if the offence is in direct relation to the end sought. In order that such a relation may exist, this offence must be a really efficacious method of achieving the end, or constitute an integral part of acts leading thereto, or represent an incident in a general political movement in which the parties have recourse to such methods."

Thus, the United Kingdom concept of proximity to the ultimate goal is mirrored in the Swiss test. If the crime is too remote, then the political element will not predominate. While a political disturbance is not required, it is implicit in the test, otherwise the act may not achieve the goal.[156] In practice therefore, the Swiss and United Kingdom approaches, thus far, achieve the same end.

However, the Swiss test is further refined by incorporating an independent test of proportionality. When considering the common element, the

---

153 See 26 SEPT 1984, Rec.307, [1985] PUB.LAW 328. The case note reviews the extradition hearing in the *Conseil d'Etat* of three Basque separatists, Galdeano, Ramirez and Beiztegui.
154 The Swiss test is to be found in Article 3 of the Law on International Judicial Assistance in Criminal Matters, 20 MAR 1981, 20 INT.LEG.MAT1339 (1981), as amended 4 OCT 1996 (supplied by the Federal Office for Police Matters, Bern). See also, THE RECORD, *supra* n117, at pp.598-99.
155 19 INT'L L REP.375 at 376 (1952). *Cf.* Lord Diplock in *Cheng supra* n11.
156 *Eg. In re Kaphengst*, [1929–30] Ann.Dig.282 (Case No.188). Like *Kolczynski*, *supra* n10, the Swiss test can accommodate crimes where there is no political uprising, but the offence is still of a political character – see *In re Kavic, Bjelanovic and Arsenijevic* 19 INT'L L REP.371.

violence or damage involved is weighed against the ultimate goal of the fugitive and his group. If the crime is violent then the common element will outweigh the political motive unless such violence is the only means of achieving the end. *In re Pavan*[157] provides a clear exposition of the principle.

> "Homicide, assassination and murder, is one of the most heinous crimes. It can only be justified where *no other method* exists of protecting the final rights or humanity."

In *Ktir v Ministère Public Fédéral*,[158] a fugitive murderer was returned to France where he had killed a fellow member of the FLN who was allegedly betraying the movement.

> "Although ... he acted for political, not personal reasons, it does not, however, follow that the act had a predominantly political character. For this to be the case it is necessary that the murder be the *sole means of safeguarding the more important interests of the FLN* and of attaining the political aim of that organization."[159]

Ktir should be contrasted with *Watin*,[160] another case arising out of the struggle surrounding Algerian independence. Here, the fugitive had been sentenced to death *in absentia* for an attempt on the life of the French head of State, General de Gaulle. The court held that the test for whether assassination was the "sole means" was a subjective one. Moreover, assassination may seem to be the last resort of the fugitive's group "where the person aimed at practically embodies the political system of the State so that it might be thought that his disappearance will entail a change in that system". In such circumstances, as in the instant case, the requirements of proportionality and of proximity will be satisfied. However, the test is a strict one. The interests at stake should be sufficiently important to excuse, if not to

---

157 [1927–28] Ann.Dig.347 at 349.
158 34 INT'L L REP.143 (1961).
159 *Supra* n158, at 144 (emphasis added). *Cf.* DEFENSOR-SANTIAGO, *supra* n47, at p.159.
160 *Watin v Ministère Public Fédéral, supra* n79, at 617.

justify, the infringement of private legal rights.[161] As one Irish judge has said, following a similar approach:

> "Modern terrorist violence ... is often the antithesis of what could be regarded as political."[162]

The 1996 English case of T,[163] whilst referring to the means used, incorporated that in the remoteness test. The difference from the Swiss test is that under the Swiss interpretation, even if the crime is proximate to the ultimate goal of the transnational fugitive offender's organization, the means used might still be disproportionate and, thus, not political in character. If the roles of the requesting and requested States had been reversed in *Castioni*, the Swiss probably would have extradited the fugitive to the United Kingdom because the murder of the official was described by one of Castioni's accomplices as unnecessary.[164] An equivalent to the Swiss proportionality test was suggested by the Royal Commission on Extradition (1878), but not adopted.[165] Whether T[166] would make any difference to the result in *Castioni* is unclear, because it makes the nature of the crime part and parcel of the proximity test under the English interpretation.

This added requirement in the Swiss test – that the means used must not be excessive – outlaws most terrorist crimes. It would be very difficult to prove that indiscriminate attacks on civilians, or even sporadic attacks on security forces without a co-ordinated campaign, would ever be sufficiently proximate to, and the sole means of attaining, the ultimate goal, like T. However, an attack on the government itself would still have to be proportionate under the Swiss test. The Swiss test, therefore, is the most refined of all five approaches when dealing with the traditional stereotype political offender.

---

161 *Ktir, supra n*158, at 145.
162 *McGlinchey v Wren*, [1982] IR 154 at 159.
163 *Supra n*80, at 899.
164 *Supra n*71, at 154.
165 C 2039; PARRY, vol.6, BRITISH DIGEST 805, 1965.
166 *Supra n*80.

(v) The Irish Approach[167] – As has just been stated, the Irish courts have incorporated the requirement of proximity and the Swiss proportionality test into their interpretation of the political offence exemption. In *McGlinchey v Wren*[168] and in *Shannon v Fanning*,[169] the Supreme Court granted extradition because the offences were not proximate to the ultimate goal and because they were not proportionate.[170] The High Court in *Ellis v*

---

167 See generally, Campbell, *Extradition to Northern Ireland: Prospects and Problems*, 52 MOD.L REV.585 (1989); Gilbert, *The Irish Interpretation of the Political Offence Exemption*, 41 INT'L & COMP.LQ 66 (1992); Delaney and Hogan, *Anglo-Irish Extradition Viewed from an Irish Perspective*, [1993] PUB.LAW 93; Walker, *Constitutional Governance and Special Powers Against Terrorism: Lessons from the United Kingdom's Prevention of Terrorism Acts*, 37 COLUM.J TRANSNAT'L L 1 (1997). Parts of this section are taken from my 1992 article in the *International and Comparative Law Quarterly*.

168 *Supra* n162.

169 [1984] IR 548.

170 These two elements tend to be considered together. In *Shannon, supra* n169, McCarthy J opined as follows at 598:
"The argument made on [Shannon's] behalf involves the proposition that, *however revolting the circumstances of a particular crime may be*, if the ultimate aim of the criminal, *however remote it be from the crime*, be truly political, then it is a political offence. I reject such a proposition; on the same basis it could be argued that the murder of a young woman shot down on the public street may be categorised as a political offence because her murder might deter her father, a Belfast magistrate, from carrying out his duties as such. The mind rebels against such a view." (emphasis added)
He also laid down some general guidelines with regard to proximity and proportionality (at 597-98):
"In my opinion, without seeking to delimit the circumstances there are to be considered, the objective determination of whether or not an offence charged is a political offence or an offence connected with a political offence within the meaning of the Act should primarily rest upon an assessment of three factors:
1. The true motivation of the individual or individuals committing the offence. I do not share the view that, in order to assess motive, the individual charged must admit his involvement in the crime.
2. The true nature of the offence itself.
3. The identity of the victim or victims.
In assessing all or any of these factors, the proximity of each to the alleged political aim is critically important and is capable of objective assessment." (emphasis added)

O'Dea (No.2)[171] held that

> "the offences set forth in the two warrants ... cannot be regarded as political
> offences ... as they contemplate and involve indiscriminate violence and
> can be correctly characterised as terrorism."[172]

However, Irish courts have added a further refinement. The Irish courts have
grasped the issue of extradition and democracy, although the jurisprudence
would seem to be in a state of flux – to that extent, more detailed analysis
of the reasoning in these cases is necessary. In *Quinn v Wren*[173] the Irish
Supreme Court handed down a judgment which looked not only at the
circumstances of the crime, but also at the crime in its context as part of
the INLA's campaign. As Finlay CJ explained:

> "The plaintiff states that he committed the offence charged for the purposes
> of the INLA, the aims and objectives of which are the establishment of a
> 32 county workers' republic by force of arms. The achievement of that
> objective necessarily and inevitably involves the destruction and setting aside
> of the Constitution by means expressly or impliedly prohibited by it: see
> Articles 15.6 and 39. To interpret the words 'political offence' contained
> in s50 of the Act of 1965 so as to grant immunity or protection to a person
> charged with an offence directly intended to further that objective would
> be to give to the section a patently unconstitutional construction. This Court
> cannot, it seems to me, interpret an Act of the *Oireachtas* as having the
> intention to grant immunity from extradition to a person charged with an
> offence the admitted purpose of which is to further or facilitate the over-

---

171 [1991] ILRM 346 at 362 (HC & SC). Hamilton P went on to hold that Ellis' crimes
were also non-political because they fell within the category of excluded offences under the Extradition (ECST) Act 1987. Ellis did not plead the political
offence exemption in the Supreme Court.

172 In *Clarke v McMahon* [1990] IR 228, the transnational fugitive offender withdrew his claim that his offences were political probably, according to the
judgment of Finlay CJ, with which Walsh J concurred, because the nature of
the attack on a member of the Ulster Defence Regiment was indiscriminate,
with injuries occurring to innocent men, women and children during its commission.

173 [1985] ILRM 410. Quinn had been carrying out frauds in order to raise funds
to purchase arms for the INLA – a *délit connexe*.

throw by violence of the Constitution and of the organs of State established thereby."[174]

The decision was a novel interpretation of the political offence exemption. Even if an offence were found not to violate any of the strictures of *Mc-Glinchey* and *Shannon*,[175] the fugitive could still be found to be extra-ditable if the aims of his parent organisation threatened the Irish Constitution or State. The reasoning also leaves a little to be desired, for it does not automatically follow that because the fugitive is in dispute with the requested State that the offence for which he is requested is not political *vis à vis* the requesting State. *Quinn*, however, was followed by *Russell v Fanning*,[176] a case involving a long time member of the IRA; there was much discussion in the High Court and on appeal concerning the scope of the new limitation. At first instance, the case came before O'Hanlon J, shortly after the Supreme Court's judgment in *Quinn* had been handed down. In his original affidavit Russell averred that

> "the Irish Republican Army has as its primary objectives the ending of British rule in Northern Ireland and the reintegration of the national territory, if necessary by force of arms."[177]

Russell was charged in Belfast with, *inter alia*, the attempted murder of a member of the RUC and with the murder of a prison warder during the Maze Prison mass breakout of September 1983.[178] He denied involvement in any of the offences in the warrant, but O'Hanlon J in the High Court decided the political offence issue as if the allegations were true.[179] With respect to the two major crimes mentioned above, O'Hanlon J held the offences to be *prima facie* political in character, neither too remote nor dispropor-

---

174 *Quinn, supra* n173, at 419. See also *McDonald v Bord na gCon*, [1965] IR 217.
175 See *supra* nn162 and 169.
176 [1986] ILRM 401 (H.C.); see also 5 Irish L.T.1 (1987); [1988] ILRM 333 (S.C.).
177 *Supra* n176, at 405 (H.C.).
178 The Times, 26 SEPT 1983, p.1. The charges relating to the break-out were dropped just before his surrender: see The Guardian, 18 AUG 1988, p.3.
179 To do otherwise would have either removed the protection of the exemption from any fugitive protesting his innocence or required the requesting State to prove the accused's guilt at the extradition hearing.

tionate[180]: the murder of the RUC officer was part of the IRA's campaign to make continued British rule in N.Ireland untenable, and the escape from the Maze was to enable Russell to carry on his part in that campaign. However, despite this *prima facie* finding, O'Hanlon J then went on to grant extradition, refusing protection under s50 because the IRA aimed to reintegrate N.Ireland into the Republic by force of arms if necessary, contrary to Article 6 of the Irish Constitution.[181] According to O'Hanlon J, following *Quinn v Wren*, even if the offences charged were political *vis à vis* the requesting State,[182] extradition may still be granted if the fugitive's organization wishes to subvert the Irish Constitution.

In the Supreme Court, the majority decision was given by Finlay CJ.[183] The political offence issue turned on whether the aims and objectives of the IRA, like those of the INLA, necessarily threatened the Constitution. Whereas the INLA wished to create a 32 county workers' republic, contrary to the State structure envisaged in the 1937 Constitution, the IRA wished to reintegrate N.Ireland into the national territory. Articles 2 and 3 of the Irish Constitution express the same desired end, although the IRA is prepared to use force of arms.[184] In addition, Russell had subsequently submitted a further affidavit stating that once N.Ireland was reintegrated he would thereafter live under the democratic processes of the Constitution.[185] Finlay CJ drew on Article 6 to equate the IRA with the INLA, as had O'Hanlon J at first instance. He then stated that since the Extradition Act 1965 had been passed after the coming into force of the Constitution,

---

180 *Supra* n176 at 407-09 (H.C.).

181 *Supra* n176, at 410 (H.C.).

182 *Cf. Cheng, supra* n11.

183 Henchy and Griffin JJ concurring.

184 See also, *Sloan v Culligan*, [1992] 1 IR 223 (HC & SC). The IRA's constitution is discussed at 242-43 by Lynch J.

185 Finlay CJ rejected the view that the fugitive could pick and choose which parts of his parent organisation's policies to adopt. Russell had relied on membership of the IRA to support his argument that his offences were political and could not now be heard to limit his allegiance to better his claim in the light of the decision in *Quinn*. The High Court in *Sloan, supra* n184, at 243 (approved by Finlay CJ at 262-63) held that the fugitive's 'stereotype renunciation' was ineffective. However, in *Magee v O'Dea*, [1994] 1 IR 500, Flood J dealt with this issue very superficially.

"[the] meaning of political offence within the provisions of s50 ... cannot therefore be construed as granting immunity from extradition to a person charged with an offence the purpose of which is to subvert the Constitution or usurp the functions of the organs of State established by the Constitution."[186]

The question for the court to decide, therefore, was whether on the basis of the affidavits it could be said that Russell could be imbued with the objectives of the IRA, which in turn could be held to be either subversive or usurpative. As regards the objectives of the IRA, Finlay CJ held as follows:

"For a person or group of persons, however, to take over or seek to take over the carrying out of a policy of reintegration decided upon by himself or themselves without the authority of the organs of State established by the Constitution is to subvert the Constitution and to usurp the function of Government."[187]

On this reasoning, *Russell* goes further than *Quinn*, for in the earlier case it could be readily seen that the INLA's ultimate goal would undermine the 1937 Constitution. The objective of the IRA, however, did not contradict any specific Article; it simply adopted a different policy to the one chosen by the Irish Government, in that it accepted the use of arms to unify Ireland.

For a while after *Russell* it seemed that the question of the scope of the political offence exemption had been settled, even if the reasoning of the Supreme Court left something to be desired.[188] However, in *Finucane v McMahon*[189] the courts again had to grapple with whether a member of the IRA could be granted immunity from extradition under s50 of the Extradition Act 1965. In the High Court,[190] Finucane claimed in his af-

---

186 *Supra n*176, at 338 (SC).

187 *Supra n*176, at 339 (SC).

188 *Russell, supra n*176, was a 3:2 majority in the Supreme Court and it must be admitted that the reasoning of Hederman and McCarthy JJ, dissenting, was more convincing. Hederman J argued, at 346-47, that the reintegration of N.Ireland was a constitutional imperative and that the courts could not prevent people outside the Republic from advocating methods of reunification contrary to the policies of the *Oireachtas*.

189 [1990] IR 165.

190 *Supra n*189, at 169.

fidavit that the request for his surrender related to political offences or offences connected with a political offence. Further, he stated that at no time did he intend to subvert the Constitution or to usurp the functions of the organs of the State. Hamilton P., however, held that since the IRA was a proscribed organisation under the Unlawful Organisations (Suppression) Order of 1939,[191] it must be committed to undermining the organs of the State. Furthermore, agreeing with Finlay CJ in *Russell*,[192] Hamilton P went on to hold that an accused could not pick and choose which parts of the IRA's agenda he wished to accept.[193] As such, his case was four-square with *Russell* and so his offence could not be political in character.

However, in the Supreme Court Walsh J, while acknowledging that *Quinn* had been correctly reasoned and decided,[194] reversed *Russell*. While one must agree with Walsh J's argument, that violence does not *per se* make an offence non-political[195] under traditional reasoning, he failed to consider in any detail arguments concerning proximity and proportionality established in Irish extradition jurisprudence since *McGlinchey* and *Shannon*. Nevertheless, the tenor of Walsh J's judgment, which represented the decision of the court,[196] was that the activities of the IRA, but not the INLA, could qualify as political offences, unless excluded as terrorism at common law or by statute. The IRA did not threaten to usurp the Irish constitution.[197]

---

191 SI 162/1939.

192 *Supra* n176.

193 If one claims political status on the basis of membership of an organization, one should not be able to disavow parts of its aims in order to improve one's cause before the courts of the requested State – if the transnational fugitive offender had been requested from The Netherlands, for instance, no affidavit regarding usurpation of the Irish Constitution would have been sworn.

194 *Finucane, supra* n189, at 209.

195 *Supra* n189, *per* Walsh J at 213.

196 *Cf.* Finlay CJ and Griffin J held that *Russell v Fanning* was correctly decided; nevertheless, for the sake of unanimity, they both agreed with the conclusion of Walsh J whose judgment expressly rejected the decision in *Russell*. The intention of Finlay CJ and Griffin J in agreeing with the majority was to promote certainty in this area of extradition law, but, with the greatest respect, one is left wondering how openly disagreeing with Walsh J's opinion of *Russell*, yet still agreeing with his overruling of that decision, can add anything but confusion.

197 Indeed, reunification could be seen as a Constitutional imperative.

If such were the final conclusion on this aspect of extradition jurisprudence, then the requirement of constitutionality in relation to the political
offence exemption would be extremely restricted and would not merit attention outside the Anglo-Irish context. Fortunately, the Irish High Court
in *Sloan v Culligan*[198] has qualified the absolute protection of *Finucane*
in such a way that a more general element to determining the political
character of an offence might still be divined in the Irish approach. Lynch
J took evidence on the objectives of the IRA as set out in the IRA constitution
or training manual which he held "brushed aside" the Constitution and the
institutions of State,[199] thus upholding the *ratio* of *Finucane* while effectively resurrecting *Russell*: the IRA are seen to be threatening the Constitution
rather than merely usurping the function of government. Lynch J further
rejected the fugitive's "stereotype renunciation" of any of the IRA's objectives
beyond reintegrating the Six Counties. However, rather than simply apply
the rule as set out in *Quinn* and deem the fugitive to be outside the scope
of the exemption, Lynch J went on to consider whether the crimes charged
would further those unconstitutional aims. On the facts, it was found that
Sloan's crimes did not threaten the Constitution and could, thus, be judged
on their own merits as to whether they would qualify as political in character.[200]

This compromise of examining the facts of the offence to see if there
is a present threat to the Constitution and the institutions of the State has
much to commend it. Moreover, it provides the theoretical basis for an
additional requirement to be demanded of all fugitives claiming their offence
is political in character. The rationale of *Finucane*, as interpreted by
Sloan[201] and *Magee*,[202] is that a crime which not only violated the law

---

198 *Supra n*184. The Supreme Court upheld the reasoning of Lynch J on this point.
199 *Supra n*184, at 242-43.
200 In *Magee v O'Dea, supra n*185, Flood J, dealing with the killing in England
of an army sergeant by a member of the INLA, claimed that he was following
the rationale of *Finucane*, but only superficially considered whether the crime
charged did, in fact, subvert the Constitution (at 508, where Flood J simply
relies on an affidavit that the murder in Derby had no latent aim of subverting
the Constitution). On the facts, he held that the crime was not excluded from
the scope of the political offence exemption.
201 *Supra n*184.
202 *Supra n*185.

of the requesting State, but also posed a threat to the requested State, should be outside the scope of the political offence exemption. Such an understanding of the restrictions on offences of a political character harks back to the decision in *In re Meunier*.[203] Usually *Meunier* is taken to hold that anarchists are excluded from the scope of the exemption, on the ground that anarchism is the enemy of all governments. As such, it is cited by commentators who argue that terrorists who attack liberal democratic States should be outside the scope of the political offence exemption,[204] on the basis that terrorism is the modern day anarchism. However, this betrays a superficial understanding of terrorism and of Cave J's judgment in *Meunier*. In *Meunier* the fugitive was returned to France because he threatened England, the requested State, just as much as the requesting State. The true *ratio* of *Meunier* is that a fugitive will not be protected where he is in dispute with the requested State as well as the requesting State. On this analysis *Quinn* and *Sloan* merely apply the principles of *Meunier* to a more specific situation – where the transnational fugitive offender is the enemy of both the United Kingdom and Ireland. Thus, an adequate academic underpinning to the *Quinn-Sloan* doctrine is available which renders it suitable for all political offence cases. Where the fugitive would be just as much a threat to the requested State on the basis of the offences committed, then there is no reason to refuse extradition. As such, as between States of the liberal-democratic tradition, one could argue that any fugitive who threatened that tradition ought not to enjoy the protection offered by the political offence exemption. While it may not be as readily acceptable a test as the proportionality requirement, since it relates to the 'national interest' element of the political offence exemption rather than its humanitarian aspects,[205] it is an additional refinement that is adopted in practice by courts, even if it is not usually expressly spelt out other than in these Irish cases.[206] Evidence for its wider acceptance as a general principle, though, is found

---

203 *Supra n*29.

204 Carbonneau, *supra n*35.

205 See STEIN, *supra n*6.

206 In Eastern Europe before the collapse of the Iron Curtain in 1989–90, legal commentators argued that there was no need for the political offence exemption *inter se* because an "attack on the political and economic foundations of another socialist state must therefore be understood as an attack on one's own [socialist] State." Schmid, *supra n*40, at p.180.

in an unreported French case.[207] The court held that a request from Italy should be granted because an offence would not be deemed political where the object of the accused is to destroy the democratic order and overthrow the economic and social order of a liberal-democratic country which was a party to the ECHR. This French case is also supporting evidence for Stein's analysis of the dual objectives of the exemption: that it is designed to protect both the fugitive and the national interests of the requested State.[208]

(vi) Conclusion on the Basis of the Present Law – The political offence exemption reveals the conflict between the need for international public order and the protection of human rights, including the rights of the victim as well as the terrorist.[209] The restrictions found in the Swiss and Irish approaches show the interplay of those two factors. As Wijngaert puts it:[210]

"... [The] political offence exception has appeared overly broad because it is ... applicable to very serious crimes, which, although committed for political reasons, are so dangerous to international public order that extradition should not be excluded, simply because of their being politically motivated. On the other hand, the political offence exception has proved too narrow because it does not directly protect common offenders who, if extradited would risk an unfair trial [because of their political views], in the requesting State."

Not one of the current range of tests is wholly satisfactory. Yet, if the current system is to be retained, then, generally, it is the Swiss test that ought to be adopted. It is this test that all forms of politically motivated offence should satisfy if they are to be within the exemption. This proposal is not to say, though, that the Swiss approach is perfect. To use it is merely to

---

207 A summary of the *Cour d'Appel's* decision can be found in *J.C.P. Douai*, 1985 II 20353, 29 NOV 1983.

208 *Supra n*6.

209 *Fox, Campbell and Hartley v United Kingdom*, Series A, vol.182, European Court of Human Rights. See Warbrick *The European Convention on Human Rights and the Prevention of Terrorism*, 32 INT'L & COMP. LQ 82 (1983); hereinafter, Warbrick. See also, Stein, How Much Humanity Do Terrorists Deserve?, in DELISSEN AND TANJA, HUMANITARIAN LAW OF ARMED CONFLICT: CHALLENGES AHEAD, 1991, pp.567 *et seq.*

210 *Supra n*5, at p.197.

continue applying nineteenth century standards, drafted to combat the problems of that era in Europe, to twentieth century circumstances. Moreover, the Swiss interpretation is open to abuse, since it is possible to extradite a fugitive in circumstances where his trial would be prejudiced and partial in the requesting State – the political offence exemption has nothing to say about the treatment the transnational fugitive offender might suffer if extradited. Yet, within the constraints of the current approach to the political offender exemption, and there seems to be no general trend to renounce it, the Swiss is still by far the best way of applying the nineteenth century formulation to present events. Many recent attempts to modify the exemption, as will be seen below, have all proved less acceptable and less effective. The Swiss predominance and proportionality test is a general one which, by applying both remoteness and proportionality, would promote international public order while still protecting political activism. The danger of a fugitive being returned to face persecution or prejudice could be avoided by expressly including a defence to extradition based on the treatment he would likely receive on being surrendered.

– ◄► –

Having considered the main national approaches to applying the exemption, it is necessary to consider further what extra measures are needed, if any, and whether those steps already taken on a piecemeal basis have proved to be really effective. Proper consideration of the proposed amendments requires a review of the various problems which today cloud the issue of the political offence exemption.

e. The Issues Facing the Political Offence Exemption

The fugitive raising the political offence defence may have committed the extradition crime in a variety of settings, ranging from a war to the offices of an international bank. This diversity of backgrounds is, indeed, one of the main problems with the exemption – that it is raised in so many different situations that it loses all semblance of coherence, precision or clarity. Taking as a starting point the events of the nineteenth century out of which the political offence exemption grew, it may be possible against that background to assess whether fugitives raising the defence today should be protected, using the purposive *mischief rule* as the primary canon of interpretation. On the other hand, the whole premise of this approach may be flawed because times have changed so much that the ambit of the exemption, if defined by its nineteenth century origins, may be too far removed from the types of case to which it is presently applied. In that case, its ambit may have to be completely redefined for present needs in order to secure and promote international public order. To cut it off from its roots, though, would be to lose all criteria by which to judge the crimes with respect to which it is presently pleaded. The ultimate answer may lie in having regard to the historical approach to political offences, but in recognizing that a purposive approach requires continuous reassessment.

(i) Armed Conflict – The revolutionaries attempting to overthrow autocratic European regimes were the first group to be protected by the political offence exemption. Their successors who fight guerrilla campaigns do not necessarily receive such support today.[211] Moreover, it must always be borne in mind that in many instances, the activities of nationalist and self-determinist groups will also be dealt with under the rules of armed conflict as well as the law of extradition, for their actions will fall within the Geneva Conventions and 1977 Protocols.[212] The dividing line between violent acts a few days before the general uprising and similar acts in the uprising itself, is all important, and was discussed by Lord Reid in *Schtraks*.[213]

> "They [States] have condemned as criminal isolated terrorist activities, such as ambushes of troops or the use of booby-traps against them, when those activities would be regarded as legitimate forms of warfare if carried out on a wider scale by a guerrilla army."[214]

---

211 *Cf.* Article 7 of the 1974 Resolution on the Definition of Aggression, UNGA Res.3314 (XXIX); 69 AM.J INT'L L 480 (1975), which holds that nothing in the Resolution shall be taken as prejudicing the right of peoples to struggle for self-determination, freedom and independence and to seek and receive support.

212 75 UNTS 31-417 (1950) and 1125 UNTS 3-699 (1979), 16 INT.LEG.MAT1391-449 (1977), respectively.

213 *Supra n*48, at 583. And see generally Warbrick, *supra n*209, pp.86-89.

214 Warbrick, *supra n*209, at p.89. See also Paust, *Law in Guerrilla Conflict: Myths, Norms and Human Rights*, 3 ISRAELI YB.H.R.39 (1973).

There is no doubt following the First Additional Protocol to the Geneva Conventions,[215] that wars of national liberation from colonial and racially discriminatory governments should be within the category of international armed conflict.[216] The Second Additional Protocol includes nationalist groups seeking a change of government.[217] It applies to:

> "*Article 1.1* [All] armed conflicts which take place in the territory of a High Contracting Party between its armed forces and dissident armed forces or other organised groups which, under responsible command, exercise such control over a part of its territory to enable them to carry out sustained and concerted military operations and to implement this Protocol."[218]

If such a situation exists, then the rules of armed conflict ought to apply. The law of armed conflicts legitimates the use of force against the government authorities, although it condemns the use of terror (by either party) on the civilian population.[219]

---

215 Art.1(4), *supra n*212.
216 Warbrick, *supra n*209, at p.86. See also Fleiner-Gerster and Meyer, *New Developments in Humanitarian Law: A Challenge to the Concept of Sovereignty*, 34 INT'L & COMP. LQ 267 at pp.274-77 (1985); Murray, *The Geneva Protocols and Conflict in Southern Africa*, 33 INT'L & COMP. LQ 462 (1984); DELISSEN AND TANJA, *supra n*209, at pp.81-206.
217 Second Additional Protocol to the Geneva Conventions, *supra n*14, Art.1. See also Warbrick, *supra n*209, pp.87 *et seq.*, DELISSEN AND TANJA, *supra n*209, at pp.209-66, and Gasser, *supra n*14.
218 Article 1.2 states that the Protocol shall not apply to:
"situations of internal disturbances and tensions, such as riots, isolated and sporadic acts of violence and other acts of a similar nature, as not being armed conflicts."
219 See, for example, Protocol I, Article 51, *supra n*212. See also, Warbrick, *supra n*209, p.88 *esp. n*24; MURPHY, PUNISHING INTERNATIONAL TERRORISTS, pp.5 and 11, *esp. n*16, (1985); Currin, *supra n*136, at p.450; DELISSEN AND TANJA, *supra n*209, at p.225. And see Chapter Eight on War Criminals below.

"Surely an act which would be properly punishable even in the context of a declared war or in the heat of open military conflict cannot and should not receive recognition under the [political offence exemption]."[220]

In *Extradition of Atta*, the District Court applied the Geneva Conventions and Protocols to the claim that the attack on a civilian bus on the West Bank was of a political character.[221] It proceeded on the basis that the fugitive offender had to show his crimes did not violate the Conventions or Protocols before they could *prima facie* qualify as political. The court was prepared to consider that the fugitive, as a member of the Abu Nidal Organization, was fighting a war of self-determination and that, as such, Protocol I might be applicable. Given that Article 48 calls on parties to distinguish at all times between combatants and civilians and that civilians and civilian objects shall not be the object of attack,[222] the fugitive did not meet the test. The distinction as to whether a conflict should be treated as international or non-international for the purposes of characterizing the standard for whether the offence is of a political character is open to question – most civil wars will not fall within Article 1.4 of Protocol I,[223] which means that the law relating to civilian targets will be that found in Protocol II, which is much weaker. Furthermore, parts of the 1949 Geneva Conventions and Protocol I are now customary international law applicable in non-international armed conflicts,[224] so the distinction is otiose. Subject to that caveat, the *Atta* test is helpful.

---

220 *Doherty, supra* n115, at 274. There are many unlawful acts under the international law of armed conflict which are not heinously violent (*eg.* misuse of a flag of truce where some people are killed) which might still qualify as political – the quotation needs to be interpreted as if the request is for a remote and disproportionate crime.

221 *Supra* n68, at 726 F.Supp at 405-08. The Court of Appeals did not discuss the question, but nor did it criticize the approach. *In re Marzook*, 924 F.Supp 565 (1996).

222 See Articles 51 and 52. *NB.* Article 13 of Protocol II makes a similar demand.

223 International armed conflicts include wars of self-determination against colonial domination, alien occupation or racist regimes.

224 See *Duško Tadić, a.k.a. 'Dule', Decision on the Defence Motion for Interlocutory Appeal on Jurisdiction before the Appeals Chamber of ICTY,* Case No.IT-94-1-AR72 (1995), *per* Cassese J.

"Offences that transcend the Law of Armed Conflict are beyond the limited scope of the political offences the Treaty excludes as bases for extradition."[225]

The remaining question is whether, once the conflict has finished, those charged with war crimes ought to be extradited.

(ii) War Criminals – War criminals, to be considered in detail in Chapter Eight below, have raised the political offence exemption when they have appeared before extradition courts. That it should be applied to war criminals may seem to be stretching the point to absurdity, since it is generally accepted that the action has to be extreme before it is treated as a 'war crime'.[226]

"Not every violation of the rules of warfare is a war crime ...."[227]
The International Law Commission's Report of 1950, Part III of which sets out the so-called Nuremberg Principles, attempted a definition of war crimes and crimes against humanity under Principle VI (b) and (c).[228] As will be argued in Chapter Eight below, the term 'war crime' should be limited to acts

---

225 *Supra n*68, at 408.
226 The Geneva Conventions and Protocols speak of *grave* breaches.
227 SHEARER, STARKES' INTERNATIONAL LAW, 11th ed. 1994, at p.502.
228 U.N.G.A.O.R, V Supp.12 (A/1316) 11-14, (1950).
   "(b) War Crimes: namely, violations of the laws and customs of war. Such violations shall include, but shall not be limited to, murder, ill-treatment or deportation to slave labour or for any other purpose of civilian population of or in occupied territory, murder or ill-treatment of prisoners of war or persons on the seas, killing of hostages, plunder of public or private property, wanton destruction of cities, towns or villages or devastation not justified by military necessity:
   (c) Crimes against Humanity: namely, murder, extermination, enslavement, deportation, and other inhumane acts committed against any civilian population, before or during the war, or persecutions on political, racial or religious grounds in execution of or in connection with any crime within the jurisdiction of the Tribunal, whether or not in violation of the domestic law of the country where perpetrated."

"condemned by the common conscience of mankind, by reason of their brutality, inhumanity, or wanton disregard of rights of property unrelated to
reasonable military necessity."[229]

It is difficult to see how 'ill-treatment', 'deportation to slave-labour', 'persecution' or 'devastation not justified by military necessity' as set out in
Principle VI(b), could ever amount to an offence of a political character,
that is one which is incidental to and in furtherance of a political disturbance
and which is proportionate. The only possible justification for refusing extradition would be to protect the fugitive from persecution in the requesting
State. Such abominable crimes should not otherwise be left unpunished; indeed, if the alleged war criminal is not extradited, then it will be argued
in Chapter Eight that he ought to be tried in the requested State or before
an international criminal tribunal,[230] such as the *ad hoc* tribunals for the
former Yugoslavia and Rwanda or the proposed permanent International
Criminal Court. Nevertheless, war criminals have raised the exemption as
a defence in an extradition hearing and it has, on occasion, been accepted.[231]

(iii) Terrorism[232] – Probably the greatest controversy relating to the ambit

---

229 SHEARER, *supra n*227, at p.502.
230 Geneva Conventions I-IV and Protocol I, *supra n*212: I – Arts.49 & 50; II –
Arts.50 & 51; III – Arts.129 & 130; IV – Arts.146 & 147; Protocol I – Arts.86-
89.
231 See the *Artukovic* cases, *supra n*115. *Cf.* MURPHY, *supra n*219, at p.65, and
Extradition of Atta, *supra n*68, at 726 F.Supp 389 at 405 (1989). *NB Artukovic*
was extradited thirty years later in 1986 – *Artukovic v Rison, supra n*128.
232 A general reading list on terrorism could double the length of this book. With
that in mind, the following are those items which the author found helpful and
which he had time to look at.
Volume 19 ISRAELI YB.HR (1989); CASSESE, TERRORISM, POLITICS AND LAW (1989);
FREY AND MORRIS, VIOLENCE, TERRORISM AND JUSTICE (1991); Sofaer, *Terrorism
and the Law*, 64 FOR.AFF.901 (1986); Laqueur, *Reflections on Terrorism*, 64
FOR.AFF.86 (1986); GEORGE, WESTERN STATE TERRORISM (1991); VERCHER, TER-
RORISM IN EUROPE (1992); Freestone, 'The Principle of Co-operation: Terrorism'
in LOWE AND WARBRICK, THE UNITED NATIONS AND THE PRINCIPLES OF INTER-
NATIONAL LAW (1994); Pike, '"Terrorism" and the Political Offence Exception'
in ATKINS, THE ALLEGED TRANSNATIONAL CRIMINAL (1995); HIGGINS AND FLORY,
TERRORISM AND INTERNATIONAL LAW (1997); Gilbert, *supra n*94 (from which

of the political offence exemption concerns transnational terrorism, although the issue goes much wider than extradition law. There is, indeed, no law as yet dealing with 'terrorism', rather certain crimes are labelled as 'terroristic'. Bassiouni has made it clear that the underlying problem is a failure at the international level to reach a working definition of terrorism.[233]

"There is, however, no internationally agreed upon methodology for the identification and appraisal of what is commonly referred to as 'terrorism' .... There is no international consensus as to the appropriate reactive strategies of States and the international community, their values, goals and outcomes. All of this makes it difficult to identify what is sought to be prevented and controlled, why and how. As a result, the pervasive and indiscriminate use of the often politically convenient label of 'terrorism' continues to mislead this field of inquiry."

Bassiouni's own definition of terrorism describes it as

"an ideologically-motivated strategy of internationally proscribed violence designed to inspire terror within a particular segment of society in order to achieve a power-outcome or to propagandize a claim or grievance irrespective of whether its perpetrators are acting for or on behalf of themselves or on behalf of a State."[234]

Despite the difficulties in achieving an agreed definition, a minimal one would provide that terrorism includes violent crimes committed with the intention of intimidating some government or group within a State.[235] From

---

some of the following text is taken).

233 Bassiouni, A Policy-Oriented Inquiry into the Different Forms and Manifestations of 'International Terrorism', at pp.xvi in BASSIOUNI, LEGAL RESPONSES TO INTERNATIONAL TERRORISM: US PROCEDURAL ASPECTS (1988); hereinafter, Inquiry and LEGAL RESPONSES, respectively. See also Sofaer, cited in Cassese, *infra* n256, at p.589, where he suggests that the law relating to terrorism is flawed and perverse.

234 *Supra* n233, at p.xxiii. *NB* This chapter will not deal in great detail with State-sponsored terrorism.

235 See VERCHER, *supra* n232; Freestone, *supra* n232, at p.138; Green, *infra* n241, esp. at pp.573 *et seq.*; Bassiouni, *The Penal Characteristics of Conventional International Criminal Law*, 15 CASE W.RES.J INT'L L 27 (1983), and Inquiry, *supra* n233, esp. at p.xxiii, (1988).

this foundation, a tentative distinction can be drawn between State-sponsored terrorism and other forms of terrorism. Bassiouni[236] differentiates on the following grounds.

"Individual and small group terror-violence may occur in the contexts of 'wars of national liberation' and internal political conflicts which may or may not be deemed conflicts of a non-international character within the meaning of the [Geneva Conventions 1949 or the 1977 Protocols, thereto].

State conducted or State-sponsored terror-violence may occur in the contexts of wars of international or non-international character, military occupation, in support of individual and small group terror-violence, and in the maintenance of political regimes by means of serious violations of internationally protected fundamental human rights."

The 1991 version of the Draft Code of Crimes Against the Peace and Security of Mankind[237] dealt with terrorism in two provisions, although the latest draft has not included terrorism in its list of crimes because, in part, the vagueness of the concept militates against its criminalization. Nevertheless, the 1991 Draft Code can be used for the guidance it provides as to international thinking on the meaning of terrorism.

"*Article 24* – An individual who as an agent or representative of a State commits or orders the commission of any of the following acts:
– undertaking, organizing, assisting, financing, encouraging or tolerating acts against another State directed at persons or property and of such a nature as to create a state of terror in the minds of public figures, groups of persons or the general public shall, on conviction thereof, be sentenced [to ...[238]].

See also, Articles 17 and 24 of the former Draft Articles on the Draft Code of Crimes Against the Peace and Security of Mankind, 30 INT.LEG.MAT1554 at pp.1584-93 (1991) – Bassiouni (ed)., COMMENTARIES (1993); McCormack & Simpson, *An Appraisal of the Substantive Provisions*, 5 CRIM.L FORUM 1 (1994). In the 1996 version of the Draft Code (A/51/332), these provisions are missing.

236 Inquiry, *supra* n233, in LEGAL RESPONSES, at p. xxv.

237 *Supra* n235. The latest draft may be found at A/51/332, (1996). It defines aggression, genocide, crimes against humanity, crimes against United Nations and associated personnel and war crimes – 'terrorism' is no longer included.

238 See the debates in the 46th Session of the ILC (UNGAOR, 49th Session, Supplement No.10, A/49/10, at para.103) on the need to determine penalties.

Article 17 – 1. An individual who as leader or organiser commits or orders the commission of an act of intervention in the internal or external affairs of a State shall, on conviction thereof, be sentenced [to ...].

2. Intervention in the internal or external affairs of a State consists of fomenting [armed] subversive or terrorist activities or by organizing, assisting or financing such activities, or supplying arms for the purpose of such activities, thereby [seriously] undermining the free exercise by that State of its sovereign rights."

The essence of Article 24 was that it provided for an unspecified penalty for individuals who carried out terrorist acts on behalf of a State. Article 17 was more layered – it only applied to leaders and organisers; they had to be involved in intervention in the internal or external affairs of another State; and, such intervention consisted of being involved in fomenting subversive or terrorist activities for the purpose of undermining the free exercise by that State of its sovereign rights.[239] Thus, the ordinary individual terrorist, as opposed to leader or organiser, acting on behalf of a group[240] rather than the State, would not have been readily caught by the Draft Code. The Code was, therefore, too narrow and, thus, inappropriate for the purposes of the international community and of this study. On the other hand, Bassiouni's definition is sufficiently wide not to omit incidentally any possible interpretation of terrorism. The only caveat is that international criminal law has so far concentrated on crimes by individuals rather than on Bassiouni's inter-State aspects of State-sponsored terrorism, such as international armed conflicts; such is the preserve of international humanitarian law. Therefore, terrorism is to be taken to include all acts of terror-violence intended to intimidate a State or group within a State.

One reason for this lack of an agreed definition of terrorism has been the tension within the United Nations between the developed world, which wanted to promote resolutions condemning terrorism, and the developing States, which demanded an exception for those seeking self-determination. Green argues that the United Nations more often indulges in polemics about

---

239 *Cf.* Article 17 might also include the leader of one State who supports the acts of a terrorist group in another State, but that is more related to Article 24.
240 *Eg.* Baader-Meinhof or the Red Brigades.

the background to terrorist acts, rather than condemning the particular out-rage.[241] This conflict of ideas is evident in the following General Assembly Resolution which refers to terrorism both as acts of violence by individuals (para.5) and as the behaviour of colonial, racist and alien regimes (para.4).

"The General Assembly
1. *Expresses deep concern* over increasing acts of violence which endanger or take innocent human lives or jeopardize fundamental freedoms;
2. *Urges* States to devote their immediate attention to finding just and peace-ful solutions to the underlying causes which give rise to such acts of viol-ence;
3. *Reaffirms* the inalienable right of self-determination and independence of all peoples under colonial and racist regimes and other forms of alien domination and upholds the legitimacy of their struggle, in particular the struggle of national liberation movements, in accordance with the purposes and principles of the Charter and the relevant resolutions of the organs of the United Nations;
4. *Condemns* the continuation of repressive and terrorist acts by colonial, racist and alien regimes in denying peoples their legitimate right to self-determination and independence and other human rights and fundamental freedoms;
5. *Invites* States to become parties to the existing international conventions which relate to various aspects of the problem of international terror-ism."[242]

More recent General Assembly resolutions condemn terrorism as a violation of human rights.[243] However, this adds to the confusion, for Article 1 of the International Covenant on Civil and Political Rights gives 'peoples' the right to self-determination,[244] while an internationally accepted definition

---

241 Green, *International Crimes and the Legal Process*, 29 INT'L & COMP. LQ 567 at p.582.
242 UNGA Res.3034 (XXVII), 1972. See also, UNGA Res.31/102, 1976; UNGA Res.32/147, 1977; UNGA Res.34/145, 1979; UNGA Res.36/109, 1981; UNGA Res.38/130, 1983; UNGA Res.61/40, 1985; UNGA Res.44/29, 1989; UNGA Res.46/51, 1991; *cf.* UNGA Res.48/122, 1993.
243 UNGA Res.48/122 (1993).
244 UNGA Res.2200A (XXI) (1966); 999 UNTS 171; 6 INT.LEG.MAT 368 (1967); 61 AM.J INT'L L 870 (1967). *Western Sahara Case, Advisory Opinion*, 1975 ICJ Rep.12 *Cf.* HIGGINS, PROBLEMS AND PROCESS: INTERNATIONAL LAW AND HOW

of terrorism (and how it is to be distinguished from acts perpetrated by those seeking self-determination) is still awaited. Thus, one is left balancing the right to self-determination against other human rights that terrorist acts might violate, such as the right to life.[245]

To date, the international community has appeared inconsistent in dealing with legal responses to terrorism. Judge Sofaer, formerly of the US State Department, has gone further.

> "The law applicable to terrorism is not merely flawed, it is perverse. The rules and declarations seemingly designed to curb terrorism have regularly included provisions that demonstrate the absence of international agreement on the propriety of regulating terrorist activity. On some issues the law leaves political violence unregulated. On other issues the law is ambivalent, providing a basis for conflicting argument as to its purpose. At its worst the law has, in important ways, actually served to legitimise international terror, and to protect terrorists from punishment as criminals."[246]

It should be noted, though, that certain reports from the United Nations have made it clear that there must be limits to the activities of any group, no matter how noble its ultimate aim.

> "Even when the use of force is legally and morally justified, there are some means, as in every form of human conflict, which must not be used."[247]

WE USE IT (1994); Henkin, THE INTERNATIONAL BILL OF RIGHTS, Ch.4 (1981); Gros Espiell, The Right to Self-Determination: Implementation of UN Resolutions, UN Doc.E/CN.4/Sub.2/390 (1980); Shaw, THE TITLE TO TERRITORY IN AFRICA, (1986); Epps, *The New Dynamics of Self-Determination*, 3 ILSA J.INT'L & COMP.L 433, esp. pp.435-36 (1997); Kirgis, *The Degrees of Self-Determination in the United Nations Era*, 88 AM.J INT'L L 304 at p.306 (1994). In conclusion, an argument may be made that UNGA Res.48/122 (1993) refers to 'human rights', while Article 1 ICCPR is a right of 'peoples', but in this context the distinction is fine.

245 Rodley, 'Can armed opposition groups violate human rights?' in MAHONEY AND MAHONEY, HUMAN RIGHTS IN THE 21ST CENTURY: A GLOBAL CHALLENGE, 1993, at pp.297 *et seq.*

246 See Cassese, *infra n256*, at p.589.

247 Secretary-General's Report on Terrorism, 27 U.N.G.A.O.R. A/C6/418 (1972). See also, Report of the *Ad Hoc* Committee on International Terrorism, 28 U.N.G.A.O.R. Supp.No.28 (A/2098) paras.22-26 (1973).

Therefore, while there would seem to be no doubt that some forms of 'terrorism' should be outside the ambit of the political offence exemption, the difficulty is in deciding which precise forms.[248]

It needs to be recognized, moreover, that any analysis of the exemption must take account of Sofaer's implicit assumption about its purpose and scope.

"If civilised society is to defend itself against terrorist violence, some offences must fall outside the scope of the exception, even though they are politically motivated."

Sofaer's allusion to 'civilised society' raises, in a very crude manner, a so far unmentioned facet of the debate on terrorism and the political offence, that is, that western industrialised society has borne the brunt of urban terrorism in the last twenty years. For instance, in 1984 there were 597 international terrorist incidents worldwide. Of those 597 incidents, 230 or more were recorded in Western Europe.[249] It is natural, therefore, that countries in Western Europe should be at the forefront of the fight to bring 'fugitive terrorists', as they are categorised by western industrialised society, to justice.[250] The birthplace of the political offence exemption now finds that

---

248 See the judgment of Walsh J in *Finucane, supra* n189.

249 These and any of the following statistics are taken from PATTERNS OF INTERNATIONAL TERRORISM, published by the US Department of State. For further statistics, see MURPHY, *supra* n219, Ch.5.

Of course, it all depends on your definition of terrorism as to who has suffered most: the activities of the South African-backed MNR in Mozambique, when Pretoria was seeking to preserve its *apartheid* regime by destabilizing front-line States, would rival, in terms of sheer quantity and brutality, the incidents in Europe.

250 See remarks on *Castioni, supra* n164; ECST, *supra* n82; *Croissant, supra* n152; *Piperno and Pace, supra* n152; *Cheng, supra* n11; *Tuite*, The Guardian p.2, 14 JULY 1982 & p.2, 3 MAY 1983; *McGlinchey v Wren, supra* n162; *Quinn,* [1985] IR 322; See also *Re State of Wisconsin and Armstrong,* [1972] 3 OR 229, 10 CCC (2d) 271, [1972] FC 1228 (CA). On a different plane, s507 Security and Development Act, PL 99-83 (99th Congress, 1st Session) encouraged international co-operation against terrorism among those, "democratic and open societies of the world, which are most plagued by terrorism". It suggested a treaty which would define terrorism and, *inter alia*, provide for "uniform laws on asylum and extradition".

it has to redraw the boundaries of the test to protect itself – the homogeneity and cohesiveness of western industrialised society's leaders leads to a desire to preserve the *status quo*.[251] Any new definition of the ambit of the exemption is likely to favour the State rather than the individual, at least as regards western industrialised society. Realistically, it must be conceded that within western industrialised society the idea of terroristic offences being regarded as political in character is not acceptable. In fact, the exemption may be redundant *in toto* in western industrialised society.

> "The State of refuge has the sole discretion of recognising or rejecting the relator's contention that his alleged conduct falls within the scope of the political offence exemption to extradition, but it does so in accordance with its own self-serving standards."[252]

In these times, it is increasingly apparent that the exemption as operated by courts in Western Europe and North America is being exercised mainly in the national interest of the liberal-democratic State and not necessarily for the protection of the fundamental rights of each individual.[253] 'Terrorism' threatens the State and so it is classified as outside the ambit of the protection. Some would suggest, though, to give the other side of the argument, that terrorism is defined as anything which threatens the *status quo* in western industrialised society, not necessarily the State but rather the liberal-democratic form of government of the day:[254] and yet, it may be right

---

251 One wonders whether the autocratic despots of nineteenth century Europe would smile quietly to themselves if they could see the way the liberal-democratic safe-havens of their era now rail against countries such as Libya, Iran and Syria.

252 Bassiouni, *supra n*257, at p.224. And see the discussion on possible responses below.

253 *State of Japan v Mitsuyo and Takao Kono*, 59 INT'L L REP.472 at 474-75 (1968). *NB*. In *Brogan v United Kingdom*, Series A, Vol.145-B, at para.61, the Court held that it could take account of the context of terrorism in Northern Ireland in assessing implementation of the rights in question. See also the G7 anti-terrorism programme, The Guardian p.13, 29 JUN 1996.

254 *Cf.* Pyle, 'The Political Offense Exception', at p.185 of BASSIOUNI, LEGAL RESPONSES, *supra n*233, where he argues that the "moral right of self-determination recognised in the American Declaration of Independence was not a right to establish a 'democracy' or 'a republic'. It was a right to institute any form of government which 'shall seem most likely to effect their Safety and Happiness'." Pyle's arguments are somewhat naive given the involvement of

that the protection of the exemption should not be extended to persons who wish to replace governments which protect human rights and fundamental freedoms and in which there is a free electoral process by which policies might be challenged. There is no simple answer to the question of how to balance rights, in the same way that there is no agreed definition of terrorism.

In practice, terrorism is still just a blanket term for many violent acts and, as such, is too imprecise to aid a critical analysis of the scope of the political offence exemption. It adds little to the jurisprudence of extradition law to suggest that terrorism should not be regarded as political in character, because there is no agreement, in the first place, as to what constitutes terrorism.[255] Consensus at an international level is still some distance ahead.[256]

> "These problems highlight the dependence of law upon the political order in which it operates, for successful definition must be based upon agreement as to the nature of the phenomenon to be described, and at an international level there is widespread disagreement as to the circumstances in which it is lawful to use violence for political ends."[257]

---

the USA in the overthrow of regimes of which it does not approve; *viz.* Chile in 1973. See also, HONDERICH, THREE ESSAYS ON POLITICAL VIOLENCE, (1976), esp. at pp.92-96. RAWLS, A THEORY OF JUSTICE, (1972), pp.75 et seq., and POLITICAL LIBERALISM, (1993), pp.133 et seq.

255 Having undertaken an admirable and critical review of the English understanding of the political offence exemption and the proportionality test, in line with much of the analysis suggested in this author's earlier work *Aspects of Extradition Law* (1991), Lord Mustill in a minority opinion in *T, supra n*80, lamely argues in less than one page that the political offence exemption should be premised on whether the crime constituted an act of 'terrorism' – at 885g-86e.

256 Cassese, *The International Community's 'Legal' Response to Terrorism*, 38 INT'L & COMP. LQ 589 at pp.605-06 (1989).

257 *Cf.* LODGE, *supra n*12, at p.195. See also IBRAHIM ABU-LUGHAD, UNCONVENTIONAL VIOLENCE AND INTERNATIONAL POLITICS, cited in LODGE, Ch.8, *n*3; MURPHY, *supra n*219, at p.4; Bassiouni, *Ideologically motivated offences and the political offence exception in extradition – a proposed juridical standard for an unruly problem*, 19 DE PAUL L REV.217 (1969) at pp.222-23; Lockwood, *The Model American Convention on the Prevention and Punishment of Certain Forms of Violence Jeopardizing Fundamental Rights and Freedoms*, 13 RUTGERS LJ 579 (1982); Lillich, *infra n*387.

Terrorism is not a legal concept that can be examined in such a way that it is possible to define those instances when it is within and those when it is outside the political offence exemption. It is truly a 'hot issue'. Nevertheless, one US judge has tried to provide a set of criteria by which to decide whether a violent, politically-oriented crime falls within the exemption.

> "The court must assess the nature of the act, the context in which it is committed, the status of the party committing the act, the nature of the organisation on whose behalf it is committed, and the particularised circumstances of the place where the act takes place."[258]

Does such an analysis provide a solution to the problem of applying the political offence exemption to terrorism? Is it possible to categorise, classify and distinguish different types of terrorist? Terrorist groups, on this understanding, may be classified as 'pure terrorists' (bad) and 'self determinists' (good). This obvious distinction between those terrorist groups with nationalist or self-determinist aims[259] and those groups indulging in terror to destabilise through the intimidation of the general public[260] would then restore to States all the discretion open to them before entering into any international anti-terrorist obligations. It has to be accepted, though, that an approach of this nature would still be fraught with the difficulty of making political distinctions between fugitives who may have committed very similar crimes.

> "What [nationalist terrorist groups] and other, less structured terrorist groups have in common is far more significant in applying the political offence exemption than the ways in which they may differ. All these groups exhibit a willingness to engage in the indiscriminate killing of people to achieve political ends."[261]

---

258 *Per* Sprizzo DJ in *Doherty, supra* n115. McCarthy J in *Shannon v Fanning, supra* n169, provided a similar set of guidelines at 597-98.

259 See LODGE, *supra* n12, Ch.6.

260 *Eg.* Baader-Meinhof in the former West Germany.

261 Prepared statement of Judge Sofaer, Legal Adviser, US State Department at the Senate Hearing on the Anglo-US Supplementary Extradition Treaty, S.HRG 99-703 re TR.DOC.99-8, 1 August 1985, at p.263.

To conclude, in some cases, for a variety of reasons, including even economics and history,[262] the exemption has been cast so wide as to give rise to controversy. It may be that the majority of fugitives who have indulged in terroristic crimes are extradited, but the publicity given to those cases where the minority are protected has led to governmental activity on an unprecedented (and possibly, unnecessary) scale and has given rise to fugitives being returned by means other than extradition in order to evade the exemption.

> "Extradition may be the established method of rendition, but it is by no means a convenient method or, indeed, a popular method. In a recent study of 231 instances of rendition of persons charged with international terrorist offences, it was found that only 6 out of 87 extradition requests were granted; on the other hand, 145 terrorists were expelled by 28 States."[263]

Terrorism is undoubtedly the biggest problem facing the exemption, but, nevertheless, it is not the only one.

(iv) Asylum Seekers – Difficulties arise for the traditional test when no political uprising exists, but the requested fugitive committed a crime in trying to seek asylum. The asylum issue also arises where the system of justice in the requesting State is not beyond criticism. Asylum and extradition have to be distinguished, though.[264]

> "The issue of extradition is decided on the basis of the treaty binding the two States or, in the absence of a treaty, on their customary reciprocal relations. The issue of asylum is considered a question of internal law, for it is deemed an immigration matter which is beyond the scope of the extradition question which may arise under international law."[265]

---

262 France seems to be the most flagrant offender: Abu Daoud, *supra* n8, was probably freed partly due to French economic interests in the Arab World and until recently the French government would defend its liberal asylum policy on the basis of its nineteenth century practice. See *In re Holder and Kerkhow*, cited by Carbonneau *supra* n35, at p.22. See also the different attitude by the French *Conseil d'Etat* in *Aff. Gouvernement Suisse*, *supra* n13.

263 Evans, *supra* n3, at p.276.

264 *Viz. T*, *supra* n80.

265 Bassiouni, *supra* n257, at p.234.

However, alongside the standard political offence case there developed a need to deal with political refugees who, in escaping from the State of dispute, committed a crime.[266] This separate line of cases, which rejected extradition "if only for reasons of humanity",[267] has created confusion amongst commentators trying to fit the decisions within the original incidence test. The problem, as Wijngaert points out,[268] is that simultaneously the exemption needs to be narrowed, but also broadened. One subsidiary benefit of some of the proposed amendments to the exemption, though, is that the asylum issue would be integrated into the political offence test, which should reduce the scope for confusion.

> "The very greatness of the danger illustrates the continuing positive function of political asylum. Free political competition on an international level is a weapon, however small, in the fight against the coming universal barbarity. This may also be the reason why, after each new deluge, which seemingly swept away political asylum, it staged a comeback. A necessary institution in a deeply divided world, political asylum sets limits – imperfect, broken, movable, but nevertheless tangible limits – to any regime's power."[269]

Political asylum is considered below in Chapter Nine, but it is yet another issue that needs to be addressed by the present political offence exemption. Its importance cannot be overestimated, for no-one questions that it should be part of the requirements of any reformulated test – indeed, there are some who would limit the exemption only to cases where asylum should be offered. As things stand, Stein's research showed that if the court decides the fugitive needs asylum, then the offence will always be deemed political[270]

The explicit inclusion of this requirement, furthermore, would be a salutary move for it should curb the excesses of the operation of the exemption. For example, in deciding matters of asylum, the UNHCR set out the following test.

---

266 *Eg. Kolczynski, supra n*10, *The Hungarian Deserter (Austria) Case*, 28 INT'L L REP.343, and *Kavic, Bjelanovic and Arsenijevic, supra n*156.

267 *Kolczynski, supra n*10, at 551 *per* Lord Goddard CJ.

268 *Supra n*5, at pp.197-98.

269 KIRCHHEIMER, POLITICAL JUSTICE: THE USE OF LEGAL PROCEDURE FOR POLITICAL ENDS, p.388, (1961). And see WIJNGAERT, *supra n*5, at p.204, *n*107.

270 *Supra n*6, at p.379.

"The political element of the offence should also outweigh its common-law character. This would not be the case if the acts committed are grossly out of proportion to the alleged objective. The political nature of the offence is more difficult to accept if it involves acts of an atrocious nature."[271]

The express adoption of asylum principles when assessing the political character of an offence, on the above test, recognises the Swiss proportionality requirement and the humanitarian issues surrounding the granting of political refuge. Indeed, the leading House of Lords case on the political offence exemption, which incorporated proportionality, was not to do with an extradition request, but an application for refugee status from a member of FIS from Algeria.[272] If asylum matters are now incorporated with some thought, it may well assist the operation of the political offence exemption, generally, in the future.

(v) Politically Motivated Requests – The final group of fugitives who have attempted to raise the political offence exemption is not simple to pin down. They allege that although their crime may be totally apolitical and that although their trial would be completely impartial, they should still not be extradited because the government of the requesting State has an underlying interest, usually covert, in seeking their return.

One particular sub-group consists of those who committed their crimes as officials of the former government of the State. The usual example of a transnational fugitive offender seeking protection under the political offence exemption is that of the failed revolutionary now being requested by the State – however, sometimes revolutions succeed, whereupon it might be the former Head of State who is the object of an extradition request. The crime, as such, for which extradition is requested could well have been a measure taken to attempt to ensure the continuance of the former government and 'legal' under that regime's laws. Nevertheless, certain acts will be treated as criminal regardless of the laws in force at the time according to the

---

271 United Nations High Commissioner for Refugees, HANDBOOK ON PROCEDURES AND CRITERIA FOR DETERMINING REFUGEE STATUS, para.152 (1979); hereinafter HANDBOOK.

272 *T, supra* n80. See also, *Re Gil and the Minister of Employment and Immigration* 119 DLR (4th) 497 (1994).

International Military Tribunal at Nuremberg, if the perpetrator must have known that what he did was wrong[273]:

> "[It] is to be observed that the maxim *nullem crimen sine lege* is not a limitation of sovereignty, but is in general a principle of justice. To assert that it is unjust to punish those who in defiance of treaties and assurances have attacked neighbouring States without warning is obviously untrue, for in such circumstances the attacker must know that he is doing wrong, and so far from it being unjust to punish him, it would be unjust if his wrong were allowed to go unpunished. ... The [IMT] proposes, therefore, to deal quite generally with the question of War Crimes .... Prisoners of war were ill-treated and tortured and murdered, not only in defiance of the well-established rules of international law, but in complete disregard of the elementary dictates of humanity"

In the *Border Guards Prosecution Case*,[274] the German Federal Supreme Court held that while the guards at the Berlin Wall had been mandated by the laws of the former German Democratic Republic to operate a shoot to kill policy against those attempting to cross into the then West Berlin, this was no defence to a charge of unlawful homicide post-unification.

> "A defence which was accepted as such at the material time may be considered irrelevant on the ground that it violates a superior rule of law, only if it represents a manifestly gross violation of fundamental concepts of justice and humanity. The violation must be so serious that it infringes those legal principles concerning human worth and dignity which are common to all people .... The conflict between the law as enacted and the requirements of justice must be so intolerable that such a law must yield to the requirements of justice, since it is an improper law (*Radbruch*, SJZ, 1946, 105 at 107). Such a formulation was used after the end of the Nazi tyranny in an attempt to categorize the most serious breaches of the law. Transposing that test to the present case is not easy, because the killing of people at the Berlin Wall cannot be equated with the mass murder committed by the Nazis. Nevertheless, the understanding gained at that time is still valid. When appraising acts committed on the orders of the State, it must be asked

---

273 See the IMT's Judgment in 41 AM.J INT'L L 172 at pp.217 and 225 (1947).
274 100 INT'L L REP.364 at 380.

whether the State has exceeded the outer limit set for it by general principles everywhere."

The fact that the fugitive was a State official should not affect the applicability of the political offence exemption. The District Court in *Suarez-Mason*[275] argued that the political offence exemption should be restricted to rebels, but this approach has not received widespread acceptance. In *Artukovic*,[276] one sees a decision which cannot be justified, not because the fugitive was Minister of the Interior of the Axis-controlled Croat government, but because of the nature of his crimes.[277] Furthermore, inasmuch as the former government official is the analogue of the former rebel, the first-mentioned is no more likely to be prejudiced at his trial than the latter, for in neither case can the central government stand apart.[278] In *Jimenez v Aristeguieta*,[279] the former President of Venezuela was requested on, *inter alia*, corruption charges from the United States. There was no political element to any of the crimes other than the former office of the fugitive and the exemption was denied to him.[280] *Suarez-Mason*[281] considered the fugitive's claim of a political character to his crimes in the alternative, but, following *Quinn v Robinson*,[282] found the homicides and kidnappings during Argentina's 'Dirty War' to have no rational nexus with any uprising and, thus, not to be incidental thereto and, so, outside the exemption. Finally, even where extradition is granted by the courts, the executive still retain the ultimate discretion[283]

---

275 *In the Matter of the Extradition of Suarez-Mason* 694 F.Supp 676 at 704-05 (1988).

276 *Supra n*115.

277 See *Artukovic v Rison, supra n*128.

278 See *Schtraks, supra n*48, at 591-92, and GRIFFITH, *infra n*480, at pp.292 and 343.

279 311 F.2d 547 (1962).

280 Jimenez's assertion of the political offence exemption was rejected because there was no political uprising, a pre-condition under the US test, at the time of the corrupt payments – *supra n*279, at 560.

281 *Supra n*275, at 705-07.

282 *Supra n*117.

283 See *Armah v Government of Ghana* [1968] AC 192, and the government's refusal in The Times p.11, 26 JAN 1967. See also, *Affaire Gouvernement Suisse, supra n*13.

Beyond former government officials, no general approach can be taken towards those who are the object of a politically motivated request, for they do not form a coherent group. Each case must be viewed on its facts. One of the best examples of such a situation is the *Sindona* case.[284] Sindona was requested by the Italian government to answer charges of, *inter alia*, embezzlement. There was never any claim that the financial crimes with which he was charged were intrinsically political or committed for a political purpose. Nor was there any uprising in Italy at that time. However, Sindona alleged that Italy had requested his extradition to question him about high-level corruption and the amorphous P2 Freemason Lodge. In this particular case, the United States' courts rejected the political offence defence.[285] This decision was followed in the very similar case of *Koskotas v Roche*.[286] As *Locatelli*[287] made clear, US courts will not generally inquire into the motives of the requesting State.[288]

The British case of *Kolczynski*,[289] as well as falling within the asylum seekers category, would qualify as a case where the requesting State, Poland, had underlying motives for the request which were not evident in the warrant. Another example is *Budlong and Kember*.[290] In this case the United States authorities requested the return of the accused for burglary. The fugitives claimed the offence was political because they were trying to discover files kept by the US government on the Church of Scientology of which they were members. The British courts rejected the contention that such allegations would be sufficient to categorise the offence as one of a political

---

284 *Sindona v Grant*, 461 F.Supp 199 (1978); 619 F.2d 167 (1980).

285 Sindona died of poisoning in an Italian gaol – what a coincidence: *supra* n119.

286 931 F.2d 169 (1991) – a request by Greece in relation to embezzlement, but related to PASOK, the Greek party of government at the time.

287 *Supra* n120.

288 *Cf.* Article 3 of the Anglo-US Supplementary Treaty, *supra* n104, and see *Smyth*, *supra* n123. See also, Article III(2)(a) of the US-Jamaica Treaty, *supra* n111, "Extradition shall also not be granted if:

(a) it is established that extradition is requested for political purposes."

289 *Supra* n10.

290 *Supra* n20.

character. This case has an even stronger political character than *Sindona* on its facts, but the courts were still unwilling to extend the exemption.[291]

The fugitive in *T v Swiss Federal Prosecutor*[292] unsuccessfully claimed that the former West German government was seeking his surrender because he was shipping cobalt to Eastern Europe, forbidden for political reasons in the Federal Republic. Again, in *Korosi*,[293] the Italian Court of Cassation rejected the fugitive's claim that the Czech government was only seeking his return because he was a Hungarian national and there was national antagonism between Czechoslovakia and Hungary. However, in *Astudillo-Calleja*[294] the French *Conseil d'Etat* was prepared to hold that the Spanish government was seeking the return of the fugitive for underlying political reasons.

> *"Il est évidemment très délicat de se livrer à une recherche des intentions du Gouvernement espagnol dans cette affaire. Une telle recherche est néanmoins indispensable puisqu'il s'agit de veiller au respect de la disposition 'la plus importante' de la loi de 1927 .... Si l'on se replace dans le climat de l'année 1973, on peut douter que les autorités espagnoles se soient intéressées au cas de M.Astudillo-Calleja au seul motif qu'il avait commis des vols .... Et il faut avoir une grande confiance dans la règle de droit pour penser qu'une fois l'extradition accordée, les autorités espagnoles alors en fonction se seraient bornées à poursuivre M.Astudillo-Calleja uniquement pour les vols qu'il avait commis. Le but politique est sous-jacent à la demande d'extradition."*

However, the approach of *Astudillo-Calleja* was rejected in *Urdiain Cirizar*.[295] The political motivation of the requesting State will not be a ground for the courts to refuse extradition.[296]

---

291 Later examples of politically motivated requests to the United Kingdom include Peru seeking the surrender of an apologist for *Sendero Luminoso* (The Guardian p.8, 20 MAR 1993), and a German request for Kani Yilmaz, a member of the Kurdish PKK, allegedly for arson, but, in practice, because of his political affiliations – The Guardian p.11, 11 MAY 1995.

292 *Supra n*20.

293 [1925-26] Ann.Dig.309.

294 [1977] DALLOZ (J) 695 at 699 *per* M.Genevois, *Commissaire du Gouvernement*.

295 [1992]:1 AJDA 82, 20 JAN 1992.

296 See Julien-Laferrière, [1992]:1 AJDA 83 at 84.

All the cases reveal a situation where fugitives attempt to gain the protection of the exemption for fear of ulterior motives on the part of the requesting State. As such, it is very unlikely that such claims will ever succeed within the politically cohesive western industrialised society; *Astudillo-Calleja* stood alone and has been rejected. As long as the government will stand aloof from the trial,[297] then it ought not to be possible for a court to refuse extradition, although the executive of the requested State might exercise its discretion in such cases.

(vi) Summary – As has been shown, the political offence exemption is raised to protect the transnational fugitive offender in a wide variety of circumstances. Its breadth may be its very downfall, in that it has been sought to use it so widely that no precise or credible interpretation of its scope can now be made. It has outgrown its origins in such a way as to lose its coherence. In fact, it may now be redundant, events having overtaken its value when dealing with transnational fugitive offenders. However, there is no serious doubt that there exists no common intention to abolish it, indeed it is suggested that it ought always to be treated as an essential element of any extradition law. Thus, if it is to be retained in extradition legislation, it is necessary to circumscribe it, adapt it or suspend its operation as best suits the occasion, balancing the protection of human rights with the need to preserve international public order.

f. Responses

A variety of solutions have been proposed to meet the problems facing the political offence exemption at the end of the twentieth century. The aim of this section is to review such suggestions critically and adopt so much of them as will prove useful. The problems facing the exemption range so widely that no one response will meet all situations.

There are two ways that progress might be achieved. The first involves retaining the framework of the present structure and amending the scope of the exemption. The second approach is more radical and would take the

---

297 See Viscount Radcliffe's opinion in *Schtraks, supra* n48, at 591-92. *Schtraks* itself is a similar sort of case.

trial of politically motivated offenders away from the courts of the requesting State.

$$- I -$$

(i) Abolition and Western Industrialised Society – While not accepting the case for a total abolition of the exemption, it has been suggested that a partial or regional restriction might be acceptable within western industrialised society. This view reflects not only the fact that western industrialised society has borne the brunt of terrorist action, but also the fact that the West regards its adherence to liberal-democratic principles, including the right to a fair trial, and to treaties such as the European Convention on Human Rights as obviating the need for political violence to effect change.[298]

> *"Une dérogation à l'obligation d'extrader entre pays démocratiques, parties aux même conventions internationales et respectueux des mêmes principes juridiques, est certes exceptionnellement possible, mais elle est une 'anomalie' qui ne peut être fondée que sur des motifs impérieux, assumés par les autorités et permettant au juge national d'exercer son contrôle."*

However, it should be noted that any regional response may well alienate those States excluded from joining, encouraging more safe havens for terrorists, and, further, it may appear reactionary, detracting from its efforts to combat terrorism.

Nevertheless, Sofaer in support of the Anglo-US Supplementary Extradition Treaty[299] asserted that

> "the rationale for this new Supplementary Treaty is simple: with respect to violent crimes, the political offence has no place in extradition treaties between stable democracies, in which the political system is available to redress legitimate grievances and the judicial process provides fair treatment. While this particular agreement relates to the United Kingdom, [the govern-

---

298 Consider the reasoning of the *Conseil d'Etat* in *Affaire Gouvernement Suisse*, *supra* n13, at 61-62.

299 *Supra* n104.

ment] fully intends to negotiate – and is in the process of negotiating – similar agreements with other nations that meet these criteria."[300]

While the reasoning is superficially sound, there are problems concerning what constitutes a "stable democracy", what would happen if there was a change in the political system within a "stable democracy" with which a treaty had been concluded and how "violent crimes" should be defined.[301] Democracy is very much in the eye of the beholder.[302] For most people it denotes some form of electoral process where members of the society have a vote that has a bearing on the formation of the legislative assembly. According to Raphael,[303] while the etymological roots of 'democracy' would indicate that it requires rule by the people,

> "[pure] democracy, a system in which all citizens may join in taking governmental decisions, is rare. ... In most democratic States, however, democracy has meant representative government. ... Decision on concrete issues is left to the body of elected representatives, the Legislature, or to a smaller group, the Government or 'Executive', acting with the consent of the Legislature. So what we have in practice is oligarchy, government by a few, but an oligarchy elected by the people as a whole and responsible to the people as a whole, responsible in the sense that it can be turned out at the next election and replaced by a different group of rulers.[304],[305]

---

300 See the HEARING, *supra* n261, at p.265. See also Epps, Abolishing the Political Offense Exception, at pp.203 *et seq.* in BASSIOUNI, LEGAL RESPONSES, *supra* n233. *Cf.* STEIN, *supra* n6, at p.377.

301 Contrast, Lubet, *International Criminal Law and the 'Ice Nine' Error: A Discourse on the Fallacy of Universal Solutions*, 28 VA.J INT'L L 963 (1988), with Paust, *'Such a Narrow Approach' Indeed*, 29 VA.J INT'L L 413 (1989).

302 See BEETHAM, DEMOCRATIC AUDIT OF THE UK: KEY PRINCIPLES AND INDICES OF DEMOCRACY (1993), at p.6; hereinafter, BEETHAM. And see HONDERICH, *supra* n254, at pp.92-96; Wolff, Beyond Tolerance, in WOLFF, BARRINGTON MOORE JR., MARCUSE, A CRITIQUE OF PURE TOLERANCE (1965), at pp.3 *et seq.*, and SINGER, DEMOCRACY AND DISOBEDIENCE (1973): all three works provide a more radical view of liberal democracy.

303 RAPHAEL, PROBLEMS OF POLITICAL PHILOSOPHY, at pp.146 *et seq.*, (1976). See also BEETHAM, *supra* n302, at p.7.

304 See also, BEETHAM, *supra* n302, at p.8.
"[Democracy] does not mean whatever the people may decide at any given moment; rather it describes a set of rules and procedures for securing their

Sofaer's conception of democracy, while incorporating this minimum, goes much further and is concerned more with the democratic aims of a society. Since Plato, liberty and equality have been recognised as the distinctive aims of a democratic society.[306] The French Revolution added the concept of fraternity, but that has become more associated with utopian socialism, rather than liberal democracy.[307] While liberty, in the sense of judicial guarantees of basic rights, is self-evidently part of Sofaer's view of a democracy, the relevance of equality needs to be explained. Democracy as an electoral process must contain an element of equality in that each person's vote ought to carry the same weight[308] and there must also be equality of liberty, but Rawls[309] has taken the essential inter-connectedness of democracy and equality further. From the premise that justice is the "first virtue of social institutions"[310] and that "laws and institutions, no matter how efficient and well-arranged, must be reformed or abolished if they are unjust" and that "[therefore], in a just society the liberties of equal citizenship are taken as settled ....",[311] Rawls goes on to argue that 'democratic equality' is a necessary and constituent element.

> "Assuming the framework of institutions required by equal liberty and fair equality of opportunity,[312] the higher expectations of those better situated are just if and only if they work as part of a scheme which improves the expectations of the least advantaged members of society."[313]

---

control over decision making or decision makers on an ongoing basis. To put the point most sharply, a people might agree to surrender power to a dictator, but that agreement would not make dictatorship democratic. It could only be described as a democratically arrived at decision to abolish or curtail democracy."

305 RAPHAEL, *supra n*303, at p.147.
306 RAPHAEL, *supra n*303, at p.143.
307 RAPHAEL, *supra n*303, at pp.145-46.
308 See BEETHAM, *supra n*302, at p.7.
309 RAWLS 1972, *supra n*254, esp. at pp.75 *et seq.*
310 RAWLS 1972, *supra n*254, at p.3.
311 RAWLS 1972, *supra n*254, at pp.3-4.
312 That is, liberal equality – see RAWLS 1972, *supra n*254, at pp.73-75.
313 RAWLS 1972, *supra n*254, at p.75.

Taking democratic equality and the difference principle together, Rawls proposed that the only just way for society to progress would be if any enhancement in the lot of the better-off was matched or improved upon by comparison with those worse-off.[314] Rawlsian analysis of a just society, and, it is argued, a democratic State, maximises the conditions of all and, thereby, enhances its stability. Thus, discrimination against a particular group in society might raise questions about the essential democratic quality of the State. Moreover, given that discrimination against a particular group in society often leads to the escalation of violence and conditions prone to engender terrorism, the relationship of stable democracy, political violence and the political offence exemption is central to this examination of the possible development of the exemption.

Rawls developed further arguments of a more applied nature in his 1993 book, *Political Liberalism*.[315] This new work has particular relevance to a study of the essential elements of stable democracies.

> "We saw at the outset that political liberalism tries to answer the question: how is it possible that there can be a stable and just society whose free and equal citizens are deeply divided by conflicting and even incommensurable religious, philosophical and moral doctrines? .... [This] stage of the exposition ... considers how the well-ordered democratic society of justice as fairness may establish and preserve unity and stability given the reasonable pluralism characteristic of it."[316]

The terrorist violence that Sofaer wished to exclude from the political offence exemption is frequently the result of pluralistic societies failing to meet the desires of its minority populations – for instance, the Basques in Spain and the nationalist community in Northern Ireland. It may be that those desires, or the means used to demonstrate dissatisfaction with the *status quo*, are unreasonable, but in so far as the State fails to respond to grievances caused by perceived injustice amongst groups within its society,[317] it fosters instability which may eventually boil over into terrorism. The stable democracy

---

314 *Supra n*254, at p.78.
315 Hereinafter, RAWLS 1993.
316 RAWLS 1993, *supra n*254, at pp.133-34.
317 See RAWLS 1993, *supra n*254, at p.137.

should seek to meet legitimate grievances rather than repress those who are aggrieved.

> "When there is a plurality of reasonable doctrines, it is unreasonable or worse to want to use the sanctions of State power to correct, or to punish, those who disagree with us."[318]
> "Democratic government is based not only upon common citizenship, but upon a recognition of the diversity with which different groups of citizens may choose to express it. Both common citizenship and its diversity may be better realised by some form of 'power sharing' or division of power, whether within government or between its different levels, than by simple majoritarianism."[319]

According to Rawls, whether a democracy can sustain stability depends on two factors.

> "[The] first is whether people who grow up under just institutions (as the political conception defines them) acquire a normally sufficient sense of justice so that they generally comply with those institutions. The second ... is whether in the view of the general facts that characterize a democracy's public political culture, and in particular the fact of reasonable pluralism, the political conception can be the focus of an overlapping consensus."[320]

Even where one group's views become dominant, there must still be protection for minorities.[321] Only in those circumstances can one speak of a stable democracy.[322]

> "[We] must frame the institutions of the basic structure so that intractable conflicts are unlikely to arise; we must also accept the need for clear and simple principles, the general form and content of which we hope can be publicly understood."[323]

---

318 RAWLS 1993, *supra* n254, at p.138.
319 BEETHAM, *supra* n302, at p.11.
320 RAWLS 1993, *supra* n254, at p.141; see also, pp.142-43.
321 See BEETHAM AND BOYLE, WHAT IS DEMOCRACY: EIGHTY QUESTIONS AND ANSWERS, Q.62 (1994).
322 RAWLS 1993, *supra* n254, at p.148.
323 RAWLS 1993, *supra* n254, at p.156.

Beetham puts forward criteria by which to assess the democratic credentials of a society. It is on the basis of such factors that one could judge whether the political offence exemption could be excluded in relation to a particular State, recognising, of course, that 'democracy' is not an absolute matter but is dependent on how far those factors have been achieved in practice.

> "The important question is to assess how far the criteria are achieved by whatever mechanisms the individual country has historically chosen to adopt."[324]

In conclusion, before the political offence exemption is abrogated, the so-called stable democracy must satisfy the requirements of a democracy espoused above. Given, however, that the nature of democracy and its relationship to human rights has now been adequately examined, then it is necessary to consider how far violence is still legitimate within a democracy. Liberal democracies generally allow individuals to advocate violence as part of freedom of speech: it is only when the violence is realised that the behaviour is criminalized.[325]

> "If an act is justifiably made illegal, this justification is not sufficient to prohibit speech advocating such an act, even though the speech could have that as its consequence. However, this will only be true when the speaker advocating such action intends to reject or to modify an end the law is serving, or challenges the law as an adequate means to such an end, and the effect of his message is persuasive and not provocative."

However, the focus of this paper is not on the advocacy of violence, but on those who actually perpetrate violence in a liberal democracy – indeed, most modern extradition treaties allow the requested State to refuse the surrender of a fugitive if he would face persecution or punishment on the ground of his political opinion.

The argument, as proposed, is that if a State is a true liberal democracy, then violence is otiose. On the other hand, some commentators have suggested that even where the democratic principles expounded upon above

---

324 BEETHAM, *supra n*302, at p.13.
325 Leader, *Free Speech and the Advocacy of Illegal Action in Law and Political Theory*, 82 COLUMBIA L REV.412 at p.428 (1982).

are respected, that there are still inadequacies in the system that discriminate against citizens who are, thus, entitled to use violence to achieve equality. Others, not going quite so far, argue that not all actual violence is contrary to democratic ideals. The latter group accept the principle that violence should not be necessary in a liberal democracy, while the former group of commentators consider that democracies do not necessarily obviate the need for violence to meet the needs of all citizens.

"There are so many legal precautions against violence, and our upbringing is directed towards so weakening our tendencies towards violence, that we are instinctively inclined to think that any act of violence is a manifestation of a return to barbarism. Peace has always been considered the greatest of blessings and the essential condition of all material progress, and it is for this reason that industrial societies have so often been contrasted favourably with the military ones. This last point of view explains why, almost uninterruptedly since the eighteenth century, economists have been in favour of strong central authorities, and have troubled little about political liberties."[326]

"The second question raised at the beginning of this essay was that of how political violence stands to the arguments for democracy. More particularly, how do the *ends* presupposed in these arguments stand in relation to political violence? We may approach the question by remembering that while democratic systems do make for some realization of the specified ends, they do not always do so. Historically speaking, democratic systems have not always advanced progress towards the ends of freedom and equality. They have sometimes impeded that progress. This has had to do, in part, with permanent minorities, non-accredited groups in pluralist systems, and the failure of democratic governments to respond to the intensity of distress, as distinct from its extent. It is an obvious fact that democracy has not always served progress toward the ends for Blacks in America and Catholics in the province of Ulster. This has been a question of some of the forms of freedom and some of the forms of equality."[327]

---

326 SOREL, REFLECTIONS ON VIOLENCE, (trans. Hulme and Roth, 1950) at p.202. See also, WOLFF, THE RULE OF LAW, (1971) at pp.54-55.

327 HONDERICH, *supra n*254, at p.108.

Adherents of such a philosophy would reject outright Sofaer's thesis[328] on the need to restrict the scope of the political offence exemption to non-violent offences when the requesting State is a stable democracy. For them, stable democracies do not offer such guarantees of citizens' rights that violent struggle can be dispensed with. However, without going that far, it is possible to argue that even within democracies violence can on occasions be justified.[329]

Therefore, there may be occasions when violence is justified even in a liberal democracy and where the political offence exemption might be available for violent crimes committed against the State. Rawls would allow civil disobedience in order to achieve justice within society.[330] However, according to Rawls, such disobedience is to be non-violent and it is only justified where there is a shared conception of justice in the society. With so many constraints, especially the requirement that the society already possess a shared conception of justice, it is hard to imagine that Rawls' analysis would ever apply to a real situation.[331] Honderich, on the other hand, holds that there is a moral justification for some form of *democratic violence*.[332]

> "It can be said for some political violence that it serves the ends of freedom, or equality, or both. One may argue for, although not necessarily justify, such violence as serving the ends which are also the ends of the practice of democracy, a practice which by definition is non-violent. Thus the fundamental arguments for the practice of democracy may also be used in defence of some political violence. ... The proposition that violence does as a matter of fact promote progress toward freedom and equality in some circumstances can hardly be questioned."[333]

Honderich goes on to distinguish between coercion of force and coercion of persuasion. The latter allows for reflection and judgement by the target of the violent act. He admits that the distinction might be hard to draw in

---

328 *Supra n261*.
329 See Paust, *An Introduction to and Commentary on Terrorism and the Law*, 19 CONN.L REV.697 at pp.705-06 and 741-43 (1987).
330 RAWLS 1972, *supra n254*, at p.364.
331 Rawls, of course, recognises this.
332 HONDERICH, *supra n254*, at p.109.
333 HONDERICH, *supra n254*, at pp.109-10. See also Article 7 of the 1974 Resolution on Aggression, *supra n211*.

practice, but is essential if one is to permit democratic violence. However, one of his examples highlights the confusion: a bomb attack in Northern Ireland does not force the British government to change its policy towards the minority population, it can reach a reasoned decision, but it might force the shopkeeper whose premises are bombed to move his business. While the government's response is separate from the victim's suffering, the inter-relatedness of the two events would militate against treating the bombing as democratic violence. Two of Honderich's other criteria are that the violence be used to provide approximately equal influence in society and that the end result of the violence is a fuller realization of democratic ends.[334] However, Honderich's analysis lacks any element of proportionality and is, thus, inadequate.[335] Before the violence be accorded democratic status, then the ultimate end of improving on the democracy within the society must justify the type of violence – murder, for instance, should only be justified in the most extreme circumstances, circumstances unlikely ever to arise in a stable democracy.[336]

Wolff, for his part, meets the objection that the violence be proportionate, but criticises the requirement on the ground that, in his eyes, it is based on the false premise that government's have legitimate authority.

"When is it permissible to resort to violence in politics? If 'violence' is taken to mean an *unjustified* use of force, then the answer to the question is obviously *never*. If the use of force were permissible, it would not, by definition, be violence, and if it were violent, it would not, by definition, be permissible. If 'violence' is taken in the strict sense to mean 'an il-legitimate or unauthorized use of force', then every political act, whether by private parties or by agents of the State, is violent, for there is no such thing as legitimate authority. If 'violence' is construed in the restricted sense as 'bodily interference or the direct infliction of physical harm', then the obvious but correct rule is to resort to violence when less harmful or costly means fail, providing always that the balance of good and evil produced is superior to that promised by any available alternative. ... These answers

---

334 Honderich's fourth characteristic, that the violence be not directed towards the "destruction of the democratic system", *supra n254*, at p.114, would seem to add nothing to the idea that the violence effect greater democratization of society.

335 Apart from one line at the very end of the book, *supra n254*, at p.116.

336 *Viz. Pavan, supra n157.*

are all trivial, but that is precisely my point. Once the concept of violence is seen to rest on the unfounded distinction between legitimate and il-legitimate political authority, the question of the appropriateness of violence simply dissolves.... We would all agree, I think, that under a dictatorship men have the right to defy the State or even to attack its representatives when their interests are denied and their needs ignored – the only rule that binds them is the general caution against doing more harm than they ac-complish good. My purpose here is simply to argue that a modern industrial democracy, whatever merits it may have, is in this regard no different from a dictatorship. No special authority attaches to the laws of a representative, majoritarian State; it is only superstition and the myth of legitimacy that invests the judge, the policeman, [the Legal Adviser to the US State De-partment], or the official with an exclusive right to the exercise of certain kinds of force."[337]

Wolff's anarchist views[338] would reject the very system on which extra-dition is premised, the international community of sovereign States; no State can be superior to the individual in his eyes. However, it can be extrapolated from his arguments that where a democracy is failing to meet its own ends, violence is permissible given that it is proportionate to the ultimate goals of democracy itself; thus, violent action ought not to be absolutely outlawed *vis à vis* stable democracies. Moreover, if one moves from theories of demo-cratic societies to actual practice in the so-called stable democracies of the West, then there is a wider gap between what citizens should expect of the State and their experience of discrimination and imbalance of power and influence.[339] Political theory would allow violent action, therefore, in limited circumstances where the State was not fulfilling its democratic credentials and the action was proportionate to that level of failure. While there is no doubt that if arrested for the violent activity in the State where it was perpetrated, the offender would have no defence that the crime was motivated by a desire for greater democracy. Modern extradition, however, is premised on States not surrendering fugitive offenders who have carried out political crimes. Sofaer's analysis[340] is an attempt to restrict this prin-

---

337 WOLFF, *supra n*326, at pp.62-63, 64, with this author's additional comment as regards Sofaer's ideas on stable democracies.
338 *Supra n*326, at pp.60-61.
339 See SINGER, *supra n*302, especially at pp.134-35.
340 *Supra n*261.

ciple where the requesting State is a stable democracy, but, on its own, that fact would not be an adequate justification for the restriction from the point of view of political theorists, even for non-radical commentators. From the point of view of the lawyer, the traditional discretion of the political offence exemption may, therefore, be supportable and preferable to a blanket ban: most crimes would be outside the political offence exemption, but the courts of the requested State would retain a discretion where the act was designed to further the democratic ideals considered above, was proportionate and was not too remote from the ultimate goals of democratic societies.

In addition to this analysis of the limits of violence and democracy founded in political science, comparison might also be made with the legal analysis surrounding when it is justified to derogate from human rights norms because of a state of emergency – such represents the legal understanding of the limits of a State's right to curb violent activity in a democracy by generally restricting citizens' rights, the corollary of constraints on violent protest in democracies. The international human rights agreements recognize that in certain extreme conditions a State may derogate from its obligations.[341] As such, it is derogating from its democratic status. The circumstances would include situations where violent protest had reached a certain level of intensity. Thus, there is a close inter-relationship between democracy, especially *stable* democracies, violent protest and derogations from human rights norms.

In summary, violence is not wholly without its purpose even in so-called stable democracies. The justification for the limitation seen in the various extradition treaties, therefore, is not made out. On the other hand, if the requesting State fulfils the test of democracy set out above, then it may be that limiting the political offence exemption along the lines considered is yet acceptable.

Nonetheless, questions as to the quality of the democracy in specific States are unlikely to hinder or deter judges or politicians seeking to combat terrorism. The French *Cour d'Appel* at Douai,[342] as mentioned above, was prepared to grant extradition to Italy on the ground that an offence should not be deemed political where the object of the transnational fugitive of-

---

341 Higgins, *Derogations under Human Rights Treaties*, 48 BRIT. YB INT'L L 281 (1976-77).

342 *Supra n207.*

fender was to destroy the democratic order and overthrow the economic and social order of a liberal-democratic country which was a party to the ECHR. In fact, the exemption has been so constrained in recent years in, for example, the ECST, that its outright abolition might be possible within western industrialised society. The European Union's 1996 Convention relating to Extradition between Member States,[343] provides in its preamble that extradition should operate rapidly and efficiently because the governments of the member States are all democracies and comply with the obligations laid down in the ECHR. To that end, Article 5 establishes that:

> "1. For the purposes of applying this Convention, no offence may be regarded by the requested Member State as a political offence, as an offence connected with a political offence or an offence inspired by political motives."

Paragraph 4 provides that reservations to the ECST[344] shall not apply to extradition between member States. However, a member State may limit the ambit of Article 5 of the 1996 EU treaty to the violent crimes listed in Articles 1 and 2 of the ECST, rather than apply the blanket disqualification. In addition, paragraph 3 preserves the right under the 1957 European Extradition Convention and the ECST to refuse extradition if the fugitive might be persecuted or punished on account of his race, religion, nationality or political opinion. This Convention, however, is by far the closest to an outright ban on the exemption.

Furthermore, Wijngaert[345] has suggested that the trial in the Netherlands of the South Moluccans, responsible for a 'trainjacking' and the occupation of a school in Bovensmilde, was completely fair and impartial, despite the element of terrorism: given that abolition would be predicated on the fugitive political offender receiving a fair trial in the requesting State instead, then it should be possible on the basis of the Bovensmilde incident for the Netherlands to abolish the political offence exemption. On the other hand, although fair trial is part of the ethos of the political offence exemption, the exemption goes much further and may well have become part of the 'folklaw' of the political tradition of western democracies.

---

343 OJ 96 C 313/02 of 27 September 1996.
344 *Supra n82.*
345 *Supra n5*, p.203 and *n1066.*

"Yet while abolition has proceeded so far, it may be politically difficult to achieve complete abolition. The reaction to the Suppression of Terrorism Convention both within the United Kingdom and abroad suggests that the political offence exception still has symbolic significance. Its historical function has not been forgotten and any proposal for abolition may be seen widely as an attack on the institution of political asylum. Even if domestic opposition were overcome, it is unlikely that many other countries would be prepared to remove the exception completely from extradition arrangements, and United Kingdom governments may be loath to abolish it unilaterally."[346]

Indeed, Green,[347] contrary to the popular view, has gone so far as to argue that while it may be unlikely, there should be no reason why a State may not recognize a fugitive from a politically sympathetic State as a political offender.[348] If even regional abolition is practically impossible, then all that will probably happen in the near future is that the process of excluding certain offences from the exemption will continue.

(ii) Exclusion of Offences – Exclusion of offences is by far the most popular approach to dealing with the present day difficulties of applying the political offence exemption.

"Practically every proposed or enacted legislation in the world which purports to prevent and control individual 'terrorism' is in the nature of repressive penal and administrative measures."[349]

However, the approach is almost as old as the political offence exemption, with the *attentat* clause being first incorporated into Belgian extradition law in 1856[350]; indeed, it is still found in some extradition treaties today.[351]

---

346 Young, *supra* n74 at p.221.
347 *Hijacking, Extradition and Asylum*, 22 CHITTY'S LJ 135 at p.136.
348 *Viz. Watin*, *supra* n79. See also the refusal by Belgian courts to extradite Basques to Spain and the Spanish reaction thereto – The Guardian p.11, 7 FEB 1996; p.14, 10 FEB 1996; p.18, 14 FEB 1996; p.12, 22 FEB 1996; p.15, 6 MAR 1996.
349 Bassiouni, Inquiry, *supra* n233, at p.xxvii.
350 See SHEARER, *supra* n32, at p.185.

With time, though, a wide variety of methods for implementing this response have developed. On the other hand, there may be times when either the executive or the courts would wish to protect a perpetrator of such an offence through use of the political offence exemption. A residuary discretion is still desired, probably because of the already-mentioned historico-legal 'folk-law' that surrounds the exemption.

> "A blanket exclusion of crimes involving homicide and grievous assault is one solution to the problem of condoning terrorism, but at the same time it may include such an over-inclusive definition that it creates a near-automatic duty to extradite anyone who has used violent means to either advance his cause or resist violent State action."[352]

As will be seen, all the international arrangements or statutes, however, have drawn back from excluding the exemption without leaving an alternative means of protecting the fugitive. The usual method is to include the ubiquitous non-persecution clause.

Different amending provisions in these instruments have used negative and positive definitions of the political offence.[353] The negative approach lists those offences which are to be deemed non-political, whereas the positive approach seeks to guide the courts as to those factors which distinguish violent common crimes from political offences. Sofaer provides the theory behind the negative approach.

> "While *Castioni*, narrowly construed, may have made sense when it was decided, it makes no sense today to deny extradition to a nation such as Switzerland – with a democratic system of politics and a fair system of justice – of a man who wilfully attempts to impose his will on the people through murder ... Some offences must fall outside the scope of the exception, even though they are politically motivated."[354]

---

351 See Art.4.1, 1952 Arab League Agreement, 159 B.F.S.P.606; Art.4.2(a), US-Costa Rican Treaty, *supra* n110; and, 1990 COMMONWEALTH SCHEME, LMM(90)32, Annex 1, para.1(a).

352 Currin, *supra* n136, at p.451.

353 *Viz.* Art.4.4 1952 Arab League Agreement, *supra* n351. See also Currin, *supra* n136.

354 HEARING, *supra* n261, at pp.257-58.

Some instruments, such as the ECST, use both approaches in combination, so any attempt to separate out discussion of the two approaches would be doomed to failure. However, the difference needs to be borne in mind when considering the theory of 'defining' the political offence exemption.

(a) European Convention on the Suppression of Terrorism[355] – The ECST, which was concluded in 1977, seeks to render non-political a specified list of offences of the type used by violent terrorists.[356] Thus, fugitives who have committed a listed offence are supposed to be excluded from the protection offered by the political offence exemption. Although it has been described as "essentially an extradition agreement",[357] it lacks a clause permitting it to be used as a surrogate extradition treaty where a formal one does not exist. Until 1990 the United Kingdom was in the peculiar position of having designated Turkey as a convention country while it had no extradition relations with Turkey. The limit of the ECST in those circumstances is the obligation found in Articles 6 and 7 to prosecute those fugitives it does not, or can not, extradite.[358]

The ECST does not guarantee extradition, for the normal requirements have to be met, such as the principle of speciality. Moreover, under Article 5 a State can refuse extradition if it believes the fugitive has been requested,

> "for the purpose of prosecuting or punishing a person on account of his race, religion, nationality or political opinion, or that the person's position may be prejudiced for any of these reasons."

What is remarkable is that such a provision as this was still recognised as being necessary among States where the European Convention on Human Rights is supposed to apply.[359] If Article 5 is applied, though, then the

---

355 *Supra n82*. See Müller-Rappard, The European Response to International Terrorism, at pp.385 *et seq.*, in BASSIOUNI, LEGAL RESPONSES, *supra n233*, and Gilbert, *supra n94*, at pp.14-20.

356 Arts.1 and 2. *NB* The COMMONWEALTH REVIEW, 1982, and views of DR STEIN at p.52.

357 Carbonneau, *supra n35*, at p.40.

358 Whether Arts.6 and 7 can be used when no request for extradition can be made, is open to question.

359 *Cf. Ireland v United Kingdom* Series A, vol.25, and *Aydin v Turkey*, (57/1996/676/866), European Court of Human Rights, 25 September 1997, paras.83-86.

requested State must prosecute the fugitive itself.[360] Given that Article 5 was thought to be necessary in the first place, it is regrettable that it is only a reservation on the duty to extradite and does not provide the individual with a right to appeal if he feels that he would be persecuted on return to the requesting State.[361] Since the ECST is a product of the Council of Europe, it would have been possible to provide a right of appeal through individual petition to the organs of the ECHR. If it was thought necessary to include Article 5, then the drafters should have taken its underlying principles to their logical conclusion, instead of the indirect challenge through the ECHR itself.[362]

As a model for an international worldwide convention against terrorism, the ECST would appear suitable at first sight. It abolishes the political offence exemption for various offences and forces parties either to extradite or prosecute. However, it still requires a State to find that the offence is within the list covered by the Convention and it took a long time for even a majority of member States of the Council of Europe to ratify it, although the position has improved. There are still doubts, though, about extraditing all terrorists, even within Europe.[363]

"The attempt at co-operation against terrorism by the ECST is already being branded as a failure.[364] It does not seem to have been possible to convince all States that the guarantees of the Convention on Human Rights are so secure that suspected terrorists offenders might not be put in unjustifiable jeopardy if they were extradited."[365]

---

360 Arts.6 and 7. It is interesting to consider whether any member of the Council of Europe is likely to find that a fellow member will act unfairly.

361 See WIJNGAERT, *supra n*5, at p.200.

362 *Cf. Altun v Germany, App. 10308/83*, (1983), 5 EHRR 611; (1985), 7 EHRR 154.

363 See Warbrick, *supra n*209, at p.119.

364 See Kelly, Problems of Establishing a European Judicial Area, AS/POL/COLL/TERR (32)8, p.3. Cited in Warbrick, *supra n*209, at *n*203.

365 See Nagel, A Socio-Legal View on the Suppression of Terrorism, AS/POL/COLL/ TERR(32)19. Cited in Warbrick, *supra n*209, at *n*204. And see Gilbert, *supra n*94.

Indeed, this lack of faith was perceived during the drafting.[366] This perception is reinforced by Article 13.

> '(1) Any State may, at the time of signature or when depositing its instrument of ratification, acceptance or approval, declare that it reserves the right to refuse extradition in respect of any offence mentioned in Article 1 which it considers to be a political offence, an offence connected with a political offence or an offence inspired by political motives, provided that it undertakes to take into due consideration, when evaluating the character of the offence, any particularly serious aspects of the offence, including:
> (a) that it created a collective danger to the life, physical integrity or liberty of persons; or
> (b) that it affected persons foreign to the motives behind it; or
> (c) that cruel or vicious means have been used in the commission of the offence.'

What was instituted in Article 1 can effectively be nullified by Article 13. The Irish Extradition (European Convention on the Suppression of Terrorism) Act 1987 used to incorporate elements of Article 13, but in a way that left the court with a discretion as to how to apply those principles. Section 4 of the 1987 Act would exclude from the political offence exemption a serious offence threatening the life, physical integrity or liberty of persons, or threatening property creating a collective danger for persons,[367] only after

> '... [taking] into due consideration any particularly serious aspects of the offence, including – [the matters mentioned in paragraphs (a), (b) and (c) of Art.13(1)]'

How these factors were to be applied was not made clear in the Irish legislation; it seems to be a difficult balancing exercise to try and assess the 'merit' of killing a member of the army or police in Northern Ireland, for

---

366 Some of the text in the remainder of this section is taken from the author's own article, *supra* n94.

367 Section 4(2)(a). Section 1(1) defines serious offences as those carrying a penalty of five years imprisonment under Irish law.

instance, against the fact that cruel or vicious means were used.[368] In
Magee v O'Dea,[369] Flood J found that the crimes for which the transnational fugitive offender was requested were within s3 Extradition (ECST)
Act 1987, but that since they had not presented a "collective danger to the
life, physical integrity or liberty of persons", they could still be deemed
political in character having regard to the discretion preserved to the judiciary
under s4. Partly as a result of this decision, the Irish Extradition (Amendment) Act 1994 was passed. The general discretion under s4 of the 1987
Act is repealed and the list of offences that cannot be political in character
is extended.[370]

Nevertheless, if Article 13 is to have a part to play in the implementation
of the ECST, then the original Irish model was the least destructive to the
Convention's aims. The Italian government, on the other hand, declared that
it would not extradite fugitive offenders for a 'political offence, an offence
connected with a political offence or an offence inspired by political

---

368 McCarthy J had tried, prior to the enactment in 1987 of this concept of
proximity, to provide some common law principles by which to assess just how
proximate the fugitive's offence must be in order to distinguish common crimes
from political offences: see *Shannon v Fanning, supra n*169, at 597-98 (emphasis
added).
"In my opinion, without seeking to delimit the circumstances there are to be
considered, the objective determination of whether or not an offence charged
is a political offence or an offence connected with a political offence within
the meaning of the Act should primarily rest upon an assessment of three
factors:
1. The true motivation of the individual or individuals committing the offence.
I do not share the view that, in order to assess motive, the individual charged
must admit his involvement in the crime.
2. The true nature of the offence itself.
3. The identity of the victim or victims.
*In assessing all or any of these factors, the proximity of each to the alleged
political aim is critically important and is capable of objective assessment.*"
See also, O'Higgins CJ in *McGlinchey v Wren, supra n*162, who held that
"it should not be deduced that if the victim were someone other than a civilian
who was killed or injured as a result of violent criminal conduct chosen in
pursuance of a political aim,..., the offence would necessarily be classified as
a political offence or an offence connected with a political offence."
369 *Supra n*185.
370 See s2 Extradition (Amendment) Act 1994.

motives', which seems to defeat the purpose of Article 1[371]: Article 1 lists offences which are to be deemed non-political, but Italy's reservation effectively sabotages the fundamental purpose of the ECST. By including Article 13, it is as if the drafters wanted to preserve pre-existing discretion while simultaneously allowing the governments ratifying the ECST to say that they were fighting terrorism. Subsequently, the member States of the European Community drafted the Agreement Concerning the Application of the European Convention on the Suppression of Terrorism among the Member States of the European Communities, the so-called Dublin Convention.[372] In Article 3, the text of the Dublin Convention provided that a State party to the ECST which had made a reservation under Article 13 thereof could only rely on it within prescribed limits and must submit any case where surrender was refused to its own authorities for prosecution – *aut dedere, aut judicare*. In 1996, the European Union Convention Relating to Extradition between the Member States,[373] tightened up this position, providing that the political offence exemption should be abolished as regards extradition between member States[374] and obviating all reservations under Article 13 of the ECST.

---

371 See Green, *supra n*241, at p.582. See also, Trb.1985 No.66 pp.3-5: Sweden and Cyprus entered reservations under Article 13 allowing them to refuse extradition if the offence was considered to be political. Switzerland and Norway made reservations that they would refuse extradition if the offence was deemed political, connected with a political offence or inspired by political motives, taking into account, however, any particularly serious aspects of the offence, including (a) that it created a collective danger to the life, physical integrity or liberty of persons, (b) that it affected persons foreign to the motives behind it, or (c) that cruel or vicious means had been used in the commission of the offence. The Netherlands and Iceland reserved the right to refuse extradition simply if the offence was deemed political, connected with a political offence or inspired by political motives. (I am grateful to the Editorial Board of the Netherlands Yearbook of International Law for providing me with this information produced by the Dutch government).

372 19 INT.LEG.MAT325 (1980). As at July 1995, only four States had ratified the Dublin Convention and, thus, it was not in force – I am once again grateful to the Editorial Board of the Yearbook for providing me with this information.

373 *Supra n*343.

374 While allowing parties to limit this to offences found in Articles 1 and 2 of the ECST.

The Dublin Convention, nevertheless, highlighted an aspect of the ECST, and of other multilateral anti-terrorist conventions, that is frequently overlooked and which counterbalances some of the earlier criticisms, for trial is always possible in the requested State. It has to be remembered that it is the 'European Convention on the *Suppression of Terrorism*', not the 'European Convention to *Abolish the Political Offence Exemption*': simply because a State, relying on an Article 13 reservation, still refuses extradition for an Article 1 crime on the ground that it is political in character does not vitiate the ECST's effectiveness *in toto* – if extradition is refused, for whatever reason, then the requested State is obliged to present the fugitive for prosecution before its own courts under Articles 6 and 7. It is possible that the requested States's prosecuting authorities will find that there is no case to answer, but non-extradition does not mean that the fugitive obtains effective immunity through sanctuary in the requested State. On the other hand however, Articles 6 and 7 are patently an inferior route to prosecution – *aut dedere, aut judicare* is not a balancing of equally valid and alternative means of prosecution,[375] extradition is the preferred method of disposal,[376] partly because the requesting State will have the most interest in prosecution[377] (though too great an interest, possibly, in the eyes of the requested State). Nevertheless, in assessing the effectiveness of the ECST and other multilateral anti-terrorist treaties, the possibility of trial in the requested State should not be ignored and, indeed, such a provision may have been incorporated precisely to provide States with the discretion to refuse extradition – the idea of giving priority to trial in the requested State is considered below.

There is no doubt that the political offence exemption has entered the 'historico-legal folklaw' of western European democracies; thus, any restriction on its scope would not be easily achieved and would never be absolute. On the one hand, the ECST, having regard in particular to Articles 5 and 13, and despite Articles 6 and 7, seems to be no more than a forceful example of political posturing. On the other hand, it may be that the State parties always saw it as a mere gesture, on the basis that any treaty would

---

375 Bassiouni, *supra* n235.
376 Both Articles 6 and 7 talk of referring a case to the requested State's prosecuting authorities after an extradition request has been received and rejected.
377 And it is administratively more convenient to prosecute where the offence occurred, especially for common law States bound by the hearsay rule in evidence – see Chapter Three, above.

be but part, and even an incidental part, of a system of meeting the threat of terrorism. States perceived that anti-terrorist treaties could never defeat terrorism – that would require political measures and, as such, States needed to reserve to themselves sufficient discretion. To that end, a mechanism allowing State parties to apply or disregard the political offence exemption as and when they so wished and to prosecute the fugitive when extradition was refused would be as effective in practice as abolishing the exemption outright. Thus, it should have been anticipated that States would not set out to bind themselves absolutely by any treaty. States, therefore, had two goals in tension with one another when drafting the ECST: fighting terrorism whilst preserving State discretion. The ECST is, thus, clumsy and inelegant, even incoherent, from an academic legal viewpoint, but justifiable and understandable if seen within the context of a socio-legal viewpoint. Indeed, any analysis of transnational terrorism and fugitive offenders based simply on treaty provisions alone is prone to this limited vision of State aims and objectives. The provisions have to be seen in the context of their application and of other measures designed to achieve similar ends.

(b) The Anglo-Indian Extradition Treaty – Modelled on the ECST, the Anglo-Indian Treaty is notable for one particular clause. The principal measure is Article 5. As with most anti-terrorism provisions, it seeks to exclude certain listed crimes from the ambit of the political offence exemption. The list includes the U.N. conventions mentioned under Article 6[378] as well as a broader range of other crimes that a terrorist might be supposed likely to commit. This anti-terrorist focus is express in Article 5(2)(o):

> "any other offence related to terrorism which at the time of the request is, under the law of the Requested Party, not to be regarded as an offence of a political character."

---

378 Hague Convention of 1970 on Hijacking, 10 INT.LEG.MAT133 (1971); the Montreal Convention of 1971 on Unlawful Acts Against the Safety of Aircraft, 10 INT.LEG.MAT1151 (1971); the New York Convention on Offences Against Internationally Protected Persons, 13 INT.LEG.MAT42 (1974); and, the 1980 Hostages Convention, 18 INT.LEG.MAT1456 (1979).

There is no equivalent provision in the agreement most akin to this Anglo-Indian treaty, the Anglo-US Supplementary Extradition Treaty.[379] The use of the undefined phrase 'offence related to terrorism' is unwelcome, but the limit that it must already be outside the ambit of the political offence exemption under domestic law makes it acceptable. It would be worrying if a catch-all term like 'terrorism' were to be used generally to restrict the scope of one of the best established freedoms in international extradition law. Contrary to Lubet's view,[380] extradition law should not be limited to a narrow approach designed to produce a single result, namely "law enforcement".[381] There is too much latitude granted to judges when imprecise terms are used in legal agreements.[382] Furthermore, the equivalent treaty signed with the United States has run into difficulty where the US courts found that it was concluded with the objective of extraditing persons previously protected by the political offence exemption.[383] There is nothing to suggest British courts would adopt a similar line, but it is unlikely that any offence expressly excluded in Article 5 would have been deemed political in character anyway, given the remoteness test imposed in *Schtraks v Government of Israel*[384] and *Cheng v Governor of Pentonville Prison*.[385] The benefits of Article 5 are further limited by Article 9(1)(a) and (b), which allows a court to refuse extradition where it believes that the fugitive would be discriminated in criminal proceedings in the requesting state on the basis

---

379 *Supra n*104.

380 *Supra n*301, at pp.984 and 963-65 (1988).

381 Paust, *supra n*301.

382 See, Green, *New Trends in International Criminal Law*, 11 ISRAELI YB.H.R.9 at p.24 (1981); see also, the Permanent Court of International Justice's opinion in the *Consistency of Certain Danzig Legislative Decrees with the Constitution of the Free City*, (1935) PCIJ Ser.A/B no.65 at pp.52-53.

"Instead of applying a penal law equally clear to both the judge and the party accused, ..., there is the possibility under the new decrees that a man may find himself placed on trial and punished for an act which the law did not enable him to know was an offence, because its criminality depends entirely on the appreciation of the situation by the ... judge. Accordingly, a system in which the criminal character of an act and the penalty attached to it will be known to the judge alone replaces a system in which this knowledge was equally open to both the judge and the accused."

383 *McMullen v US*, 953 F.2d 761 (1992); *cf. supra n*123.

384 *Supra n*48.

385 *Supra n*11, esp. at 945.

of his "race, religion, nationality or political opinions". Moreover, the Anglo-Indian treaty has to be read in the light of the decision in *Chahal v United Kingdom*,[386] where the European Court of Human Rights held that the United Kingdom would be in breach of its obligations under Article 3 of the ECHR if it were to deport a Sikh to India with respect to whom there were substantial grounds for believing that he would face a real risk of being subjected to torture or inhuman and degrading treatment at the hands of the Indian authorities.

In summary, the growing trend is for extradition agreements to exclude expressly violent offences from the scope of the political offence exemption, but the use of vague phrases like 'terrorism' is unacceptable.

(c) The Model American Convention – The Standing Committee on World Order Under Law of the American Bar Association, receiving its impetus from the ECST, drafted the Model American Convention on the Prevention and Punishment of Certain Serious Forms of Violence Jeopardizing Fundamental Rights and Freedoms.[387] It was designed for the Organisation of American States and, as such, is yet another regional attempt to limit the political offence exemption.

The original list of offences to which the Convention applied was more limited than the ECST, only including offences that were prescribed by a United Nations treaty, such as the Hague Convention for the Suppression of Unlawful Seizure of Aircraft.[388] However, the later version changed tack and included genocide, torture and nuclear sabotage, at the time, all new offences to the United States.[389]

However, whereas the ECST abolishes the political offence exemption in Articles 1 and 2, the Model American Convention does not "tackle the issue head-on". Rather, Article 3 States that extradition shall be,

---

386 (70/1995/576/662), 15 November 1996.

387 An article of the same name has been written by Bert B.Lockwood Jr, *supra* *n*257. After that article was published the ABA produced an updated version of the Model Convention. It can be found in Lillich, *Model American Convention*, 77 AM.J INT'L L 662 (1983).

388 *Supra n*102.

389 Compare Lockwood at pp.581-84 with Lillich at p.663: *supra nn*257 and 387, respectively. *Cf.* I.L.A. Draft Convention on International Terrorism, reproduced in MURPHY, *supra n*219, at pp.57-61.

"subject to the *procedural* conditions provided for by the law of the requested State."

The phrase is extremely vague and of uncertain import. Lockwood believed
that it excluded any reference to the political offence exemption,[390] unless
it is raised in the context of subsequent Convention provisions. Accepting
that, it is unclear what other protections peculiar to extradition hearings,
such as specialty, are excluded by the "procedural" limitation. It would have
been much better to "tackle the issue head-on".

As with the ECST, States may refuse extradition where they believe the
fugitive would be prosecuted or punished on account of his race, religion,
nationality or political opinion, or would be prejudiced for any of those
reasons.[391] However, the most constructive part of the Convention flows
from the consequences of exercising this discretion. Article 8 requires the
requested State to prosecute a fugitive offender wherever extradition is
refused. Such a clause is common to all such anti-terrorism conventions.
The operation, though, is predicated in all other conventions on the action
of the requested State alone, which may act for any of a variety of reasons
without any right for the fugitive to contest the matter. The Model American
Convention provides that the requested State may refer an extradition request
to the Inter-American Court of Human Rights by way of an advisory opinion
if it is uncertain whether extradition would violate the Model American
Convention, especially Article 5. There is still no right for the fugitive to
question a grant of extradition by this method, but at least the possibility
of a referral could be put to the extradition court. As such, it is an excellent
innovation and one that could well be incorporated into the ECST, with a
right of individual appeal included, as well. An equivalent to the advisory
opinion would be for either the requested State or the fugitive to be allowed
to apply to the European Court of Human Rights to obtain an indication
of any necessary interim measure, with an expedited hearing for the human
rights issue in the case to follow.[392] Other than the Article 9 advisory
opinion, however, the Model American Convention does not bring a solution

---

390 *Supra n257*, at p.585.
391 Art.5, Model American Convention: discussed by Lockwood, *supra n257*, at
     pp.586-87 and Lillich, *supra n387*, at p.664.
392 *Cf.* Art.11 of the Model American Convention.

to the knotty problem of political offences any closer, and, indeed, it is no nearer adoption by the O.A.S., despite the thoroughly researched drafting.

If success cannot be achieved within the O.A.S. or within the even more homogeneous Council of Europe, then there seems little hope for a universal United Nations convention which would abolish the political offence exemption for 'terrorist' offences. Furthermore, multilateral conventions such as these, only fit into the existing system and try to make a special case for alleged terrorists. Excluding offences merely pushes the balance in favour of international public order over human rights and, as such, has proved to be generally unacceptable.

(d) United States Statutes and Treaties – During the 1980s, a series of Bills[393] were introduced before both Houses of Congress in an attempt to tighten up the United States' domestic interpretation of the political offence exemption. To that extent, the bills are of limited interest, but the approaches adopted do help to elucidate the difficulties in excluding terrorists from the political offence exemption. The earliest Bill, S.1772 (1980), would have made the determination of the political offence question an executive, rather than a judicial one. The merits of this approach are discussed below in the conclusion, but the US Congress rejected it. Since the forum for determination could not be changed, the question for determination had to be. The later Bills, again, generally adopted the approach of excluding offences from the scope of the exemption. Bill HR 3347, on the other hand, as well as excluding offences, also attempted to provide positive guidelines as to the factors to be considered when determining whether any offence ought to be deemed political.

---

393 See S.1772 c32 (1980); H.R.5227 (1981); S.1940 (1982); H.R.6046 (1982); S.220 (1983); H.R.2643 (1983); H.R.3447 (1983). Since under the current law (18 USC §3184) the political offence exemption is dealt with in the bilateral treaties, the US has made the test an executive matter in some recent treaties: US-Mexico, TIAS 9656; US-Netherlands, TIAS 10733. For a critical assessment of these amendments, proposed or realised, see: Sternberg & Skelding, *State Department Determinations of Political Offences: Death Knell for the Political Offence Exception in Extradition Law*, 15 CASE W RES.J INT'L L 137 (1983); Hannay, *Legislative Reform of US Extradition Statutes: Plugging the Terrorist Loophole*, 13 DENV.J INT'L L & POL'Y 53 (1983); Bassiouni, *Extradition Reform Legislation in the United States: 1981-83*, 17 AKRON L REV.495 *esp.* at pp.546-553, (1984); Currin, *Extradition Reform and the Statutory Definition of Political Offences*, 24 VA.J INT'L L 419 (1984).

"(a) the status (whether civilian, governmental or military) of any victims
of the alleged offence;
(b) the relationship of the alleged offender to a political organization;
(c) the existence of a civil uprising, rebellion, widespread civil unrest or
insurrection within the State requesting extradition;
(d) the motive of the alleged offender for the conduct alleged to constitute
the offence;
(e) the nexus of such alleged conduct to the goals of a political organization;
(f) the seriousness of the offence."

The appropriateness of some of these criteria may be questioned, such as
the status of the victim, however, the positive approach is to be welcomed
since it would provide the courts with discretion, without leaving the way
open to abuse. Nevertheless, there are criticisms of the positive approach
of H.R.3347. As Murphy points out,

"[although H.R.3347] did not, strictly speaking, attempt to define a political
offence, it did set forth a variety of criteria that courts would have been
required to consider in determining whether an alleged criminal act was
a political offence. The bill simply listed these criteria however, it did not
specify precisely how the courts are to apply them in their deliberations,
nor what weight is to be given to each of the criteria."[394]

The analysis is accurate, yet Murphy's conclusion that "the attempt should
be abandoned" ought not to be accepted. Like all the other Bills, however,
HR 3347 failed to make it onto the statute book.

When it became apparent that Congress would not pass such general
legislation which would apply to requests from any country, the US State
Department decided to draft similar specific treaty provisions with "stable
democracies".[395] The first, and so far only, one of these was with the
United Kingdom.[396] In its original format, the Supplementary Treaty[397]

---

394 *Supra n*219, at p.67.
395 See HEARING, *supra n*261, *per* Sofaer at p.265. See also THE RECORD *supra*
    *n*117, at p.587 where it was suggested that such treaties were going to be
    negotiated with all allies of the US, not just stable democracies.
396 *Supra n*104. See Hannay, The Legislative Approach to the Political Offence
    Exception, at pp.115 *et seq*., in BASSIOUNI, LEGAL RESPONSES, *supra n*233; Paust
    and Lubet, both *supra n*301; Bassiouni, *The "Political Offense Exception"*

excluded certain violent offences and left any discretion not to extradite solely in the hands of the executive.[398] During its passage through Congressional Committee, the treaty was amended to include the standard provision allowing the court to refuse extradition where it believed the fugitive would be prosecuted, punished or prejudiced due to his "race, religion, nationality or political opinions".[399] Moreover in this case, the Chairman of the Senate Foreign Relations Committee indicated that the provision would even allow the court to inquire into the fairness of the judicial system in the requesting State.[400] In practice, this has proved to be an overstatement of the case. The courts have held that while they can investigate the requesting State's legal processes, it must be specific to the particular transnational fugitive offender. The Supplementary Treaty seeks to provide a compromise by

"placing most violent crimes beyond the political offense exception's reach but adding certain novel safeguards for the protection of potential extraditees."[401]

Article 3(a) allows the courts to look at the likely treatment the extraditee will face if surrendered. It does not permit an inquiry, however, into "the general political conditions extant in Northern Ireland".[402] Nevertheless, it needs to be noted that the protection of transnational fugitive offenders by the requested State was still felt to be essential as between such close allies as the United States and the United Kingdom.

Revisited, 15 DENV.J INT'L L & POL.255 (1987); Blakesley, *Review Essay: Executive Branch Attempts to Eviscerate the Separation of Powers*, 2 UTAH L REV.451 (1987), and *The Evisceration of the Political Offense Exception to Extradition*, 15 DENV.J INT'L L & POL.109 (1987); and, Lubet, *Taking the Terror out of Political Terrorism*, 19 CONN.L REV.863 (1987), and *Extradition Unbound*, 24 TEX.INT'L LJ 47 (1989). See also, Leich, 80 AM.J INT'L L 338 (1986) and MURPHY, *supra n*219, at pp.98-99 on US-Turkey Treaty on Extradition and Mutual Assistance in Criminal Matters, Art.22(2)(a), TIAS 9891.

397 See USTR.DOC.99-8. See Sofaer, THE HEARING, *supra n*261, at pp.247 *et seq.*
398 THE HEARING, *supra n*261, at p.5.
399 *Supra n*104, Art.3.
400 *Supra n*104, SENATE EXEC. REPT.99-17, *per* Mr Lugar, at p.5.
401 *In re Extradition of Howard* 996 F.2d 1320 at 1324 (1993).
402 *Smyth*, 61 F.3d 711 at 720 (1995); see generally, *supra n*123.

It would seem, therefore, that any attempt to limit the scope of the political offence exemption through a list of excluded offences is doomed to only partial success right from the outset.

(e) Specific United Nations Treaties – On the other hand, the entire approach considered so far may be wrong, for the regional and bilateral treaties and US Bills already discussed, started by deciding that the political offence exemption should be limited and then listed the offences that should no longer be protected. The reaction to protect the full ambit of discretion under the exemption should have been foreseen. The proper approach may be to suggest that, under the auspices of the United Nations, certain offences have already been designated universal crimes by conventions that have been ratified by a goodly number of the States in the world. For some time now, there has been a piecemeal approach of 'internationalising' various serious offences through multilateral conventions sponsored by the United Nations. A possible restriction on the political offence exemption would be to exclude these crimes from the ambit of its protection. For these offences, it would appear there should be no protection from the exemption: States have agreed, in theory, that these crimes must be punished no matter where the fugitive turns up. The right response might be, therefore, to forget regional or specific attempts to exclude offences from the political offence exemption, but rather to obtain agreement that the political offence exemption is redundant with regard to these convention offences. Since many States have taken steps to combat these offences, regardless of where the crime took place, it may be possible to argue that they are crimes *jure gentium* and, as such, it should be expressly stated in each convention that the political offence exemption can have no place with respect to such crimes.[403] It is not that the exemption is being redefined, it is merely recognising that States have already decided that these offences must be punished in every case – the exemption sometimes prevents surrender of a transnational fugitive offender and is, thus, contrary to this internationally accepted objective. In the United States treaties with Jamaica and Costa Rica,[404] there are provisions excluding from the political offence exemption those offences which are proscribed by a convention which imposes an obligation to extradite or prosecute.

---

403 *NB* See the reasoning in Lockwood at pp.582 *et seq.*, *supra n257*, and in Lillich at p.663, *supra n387*.

404 *Supra nn*111 and 110, respectively.

The range of international crimes promulgated through conventions alone since the 1960s is wide,[405] and if other sources of international law, such as custom, the writings of eminent jurists and pending conventions, are included, then the list is extremely comprehensive, going beyond merely terrorist related crimes.[406] Confining this survey to those international crimes intended to deal with terrorism, the offences are nearly all proscribed by an existing convention. The spate of major hijackings in the 1960s and 1970s produced the Tokyo Convention[407] and, more importantly, the Hague and Montreal Conventions,[408] culminating in the Bonn Declaration of 1978.[409] A change of tactics by the terrorists gave rise to the UN Conventions on the Prevention and Punishment of Crimes Against Internationally Protected

---

405 See Green, *supra n*241, at pp.573-76.

406 Bassiouni, *supra n*235, at pp.28-29 (1983).

407 The Tokyo Convention of 1963 on Offences and Certain Other Acts Committed on Board Aircraft, UKTS 126 (1969); Cmnd 4230.

408 See Convention for the Suppression of the Unlawful Seizure of Aircraft, done at the Hague, 16 December 1970, *supra n*102, and the Convention for the Suppression of Unlawful Acts Against the Safety of Civil Aviation, done at Montreal, 23 September 1971, 10 INT.LEG.MAT1151 (1971). See also McMahon, *Air Hijacking: Extradition as a Deterrent*, 58 GEORGETOWN LJ 1135 (1970); Green, *supra n*29; Shubber, *Aircraft Hijacking under the Hague Convention of 1970 – A New Regime*, 22 INT'L & COMP. LQ 687 (1973); Shubber, *Is Hijacking of Aircraft Piracy in International Law?*, 43 BRIT.YB.INT'L L 204 (1968); ALEXANDER & SOCHOR, AERIAL PIRACY AND AVIATION SECURITY (1990).

409 78 Dep't of State Bull.No.2018 (Sept 1978) at p.4; 17 INT.LEG.MAT1285 (1978). Statement of the Seven, Canada, France, Federal Republic of Germany, Italy, Japan, United Kingdom and United States. See Schwenk, *The Bonn Declaration on Hijacking*, 4 ANN.AIR & SP.L 307 (1979); Busuttil, *The Bonn Declaration on International Terrorism: A Non-Binding International Agreement on Aircraft Hijacking*, 31 INT'L & COMP. LQ 474 (1982); Chamberlain, *Collective Suspension of Air Services with States which Harbour Hijackers*, 32 INT'L & COMP. LQ 616 (1983). The Bonn Declaration was implemented against the Karmal government of Afghanistan through the Montebello Declaration, 81 Dep't of State Bull.No. 2053 (Aug 1981) at p.16; 20 INT.LEG.MAT956 (1981). See Busuttil at p.474 *n*5. The threat of its imposition forced South Africa to prosecute mercenaries who had attempted to overthrow the Seychelles government – Busuttil. Pressure from the Bonn Seven and the ICAO forced Sri Lanka to, first of all, pass anti-hijacking legislation and, subsequently, prosecute one of its nationals who extorted money through a hijack – *Ekanayake v Attorney-General*, 87 INT'L L REP.296.

Persons including Diplomatic Agents[410] and on The Taking of Hostages.[411] The final convention drafted in reaction to terrorist activity is the Convention for the Suppression of Unlawful Acts Against the Safety of Maritime Navigation, which was drawn up in response to the *Achille Lauro Affair*.[412] Although not specifically limited to individual terrorism, the UN and European Torture Conventions[413] also share features with the above measures and can be viewed as part of the same scheme for providing mutual assistance in the prosecution of international crimes.

The specialised treaties seek to combat these particular crimes by extending the criminal jurisdiction of the signatory States to encompass all offenders (regardless of their nationality, the nationality of their victims and the location of the offence), by making extradition more easily available and by requiring prosecution in the requested State whenever extradition is not granted.[414] However, they do not at present declare the proscribed

---

410 The New York Convention, 13 INT.LEG.MAT42 (1974): see *R v Donyadideh* 101 INT'L L REP.259. See also Convention to Prevent and Punish the Acts of Terrorism Taking the Form of Crimes Against Persons and Related Extortion that are of International Significance, O.A.S. Doc.AC/88.1, 10 INT.LEG.MAT255 (1971).

411 The Hostages Convention, 18 INT.LEG.MAT1456 (1979).

412 The Rome Convention, I.M.O.Doc SUA/CON/15, 10 March 1988, 27 INT.LEG. MAT668 (1988). RONZITTI, MARITIME TERRORISM AND INTERNATIONAL LAW, *esp.* Treves on the Rome Convention at pp.69 *et seq.* See also, CASSESE, TERRORISM, POLITICS AND LAW (1989). An example of a pre-emptive convention is found in the Convention on the Physical Protection of Nuclear Materials, Cmnd 8112 – see Bettauer, 74 AM.J INT'L L 205 (1980).

413 U.N. Convention Against Torture and Other Cruel, Inhuman or Degrading Treatment or Punishment, 7 EHRR 325 (1985). See also RODLEY, THE TREATMENT OF PRISONERS UNDER INTERNATIONAL LAW (1986) and Clark, *Human Rights and the U.N. Committee on Crime Prevention and Control*, 506 ANN.AMER.ACAD.-POL. & SOC.SCI.68 (1989). European Convention for the Prevention of Torture, 27 INT.LEG.MAT1152 (1988), and see 28 INT.LEG.MAT1341 (1989); CSCE/CHD Copenhagen Document, June 1990, para.16, 11 HRLJ 232 (1990), and Buergenthal, *A new public order for Europe*, 11 HRLJ 217 (1990).

414 For example, looking at the Hague, Montreal, New York and the Hostages Conventions, the following matters are dealt with by the listed articles.

	Jurisdiction	Extraditable Offence
Hague	4	8.1
Montreal	5	8.1
New York	3	8.1
Hostages	5	10.1 and 9

offence to be non-political; it is open to the requested State to find that a hijacking, for example, is a political offence. Furthermore, like all multilateral treaties, they suffer from a failure on the part of States to ratify, from having no enforcement mechanism to deal with the situation where a State-party fails to meet its obligations and from being a compromise representing a minimum level of agreement.[415]

The Hague Convention has achieved limited success and an initiative in 1990 by IATA to pool information about persons who threaten the safety of aircraft may make it even more effective. States have passed domestic laws implementing its provisions and hijackers have been extradited or prosecuted in the requested State. Offending States have even been forced through diplomatic pressure to assume their responsibilities to combat this threat to civil aviation.[416] In some cases, though, implicit acceptance of the hijacker's actions is provided where the requested State, having sentenced the fugitive, then goes on to treat him as a refugee when he is released.[417] Even worse, certain cases have resulted in hijackers being set free.[418] Nevertheless,

---

	Surrogate Extradition Treaty	Extradite or Prosecute
Hague	8.2	7
Montreal	8.2	7
New York	8.2	7
Hostages	10.2	8

415 See, in part, Cassese, *supra n*256, pp.593-96. Cassese is probably wrong in interpreting the Rome Convention, *supra n*412, as excluding the political offence exemption; Article 11 merely adds the offences in the Maritime Convention to any list of extraditable offences.

416 *Eg.* The ICAO forced Sri Lanka to prosecute one of its nationals who extorted money by hijacking and to pass anti-hijacking legislation *Ekanayake, supra n*409.

417 *Antonin L v F.R.G.*, 80 INT'L L REP.673 (1979). Or imposes a lenient sentence – The Guardian p.12, 6 NOV 1997, concerning sentences by a United Kingdom court on Iraqis fleeing Saddam Hussein.

418 *Eg.* The Guardian p.4, 21 DEC 1982; East Germans fleeing from the Soviet Union to Turkey violently hijacked an aeroplane. The Turks acquitted them because their motive was a desire to gain freedom. The Norwegian Supreme Court blocked the extradition of a Palestinian to Germany to face trial in connection with the hijacking of a Lufthansa airliner – The Guardian p.10, 13 JAN 1995.

"[at] least with respect to persons involved in hijacking of United States registered aircraft,[419] the data indicate rather widespread prosecution and conviction, and the imposition of severe penalties."[420]

However, even with regard to the Hague and Montreal Conventions, prosecution cannot be guaranteed and, where the requested State fails to fulfil its

---

419 *Author's note.* The US Federal Aviation Authority keep this information, whereas few other organisations bother.
420 MURPHY, *supra n*219, at p.109. See Table 5.1 at pp.110-12. The information from Table 5.2 is set out here.
"*International Rendition of Hijackers, 1977-81* (Rendition encompasses all methods of surrendering a fugitive from one State to another)
(*a*) *Extraditions* (the handing over of the fugitive to a State following a request by that State)
1977: USSR's request to Sweden refused, but Swedes sentenced hijacker to four years imprisonment.
1978: The disposition of Bulgaria's request to Yugoslavia is unknown.
1979: The Netherlands extradited the fugitive hijacker to Spain.
(*b*) *Deportations* (the removal of a person from the State with, in principle, no regard to that person's ultimate destination)

Year	Fight From	Apprehended	Deported To	No. of Persons
1977	USA	Ireland	USA	1 a
1977	Japan	Japan	USA	1 a
1977	Chile	Peru	Cuba	4 b
1979	Lebanon	Kuwait	Lebanon	1 c
1979	USA	Mexico	USA	1 a

(Notes:- a = 'plane registered in USA; b = 'plane registered in Chile; c = 'plane registered in Lebanon).
(*c*) *Exclusions* (the individual involved is not allowed in law to enter the State and is sent back to the State from which he arrived)

Year	Excluded From	Returned To	No. of Persons
1977	England	USA	1
1977	Finland	USSR	2
1978	Switzerland	USA	1
1979	India	Bangladesh	1
1979	Cyprus	Libya	1
1980	Cuba	USA	2
1981	Cyprus	Yugoslavia	3

(*d*) *Expulsions* (the fugitive has entered the territory, but is then sent back to the source State)
In 1979 the Costa Ricans expelled to Panama the hijacker of a flight emanating from Nicaragua."

obligations, there is little the requesting State can do. The Lockerbie Affair[421] highlights the limits of international co-operation with respect to transnational fugitive offenders. A Pan-Am flight exploded over the Scottish village of Lockerbie. Eventually, the United States and United Kingdom alleged that two Libyans had planted the bomb and asked Libya, a party to the Montreal Convention,[422] to extradite them. Libya refused and offered to prosecute the two under the *aut dedere, aut judicare* provision of the Convention.[423] The requesting States then took the issue to the Security Council. The Security Council ordered Libya to surrender the two and, on the basis of the Security Council resolution, the ICJ held at its preliminary hearing that it was not competent to intervene.[424] Despite the Security Council resolution and sanctions, Libya had still not surrendered the two in late 1997, although it had offered to let them be tried according to Scottish law in some neutral, third country.[425] Depending on how the ICJ rules on the case on the merits, it may be that trial in a third State is the only effective means of ensuring that two alleged transnational fugitive offenders are prosecuted. The failure by the United States and United Kingdom to ensure the prosecution of two people charged with a crime which was sufficiently infamous to come before the Security Council, bodes ill for a proposed International Criminal Court where domestic trials still take primacy.

---

421 *Case Concerning Questions of Interpretation and Application of the 1971 Montreal Convention Arising from the Aerial Incident at Lockerbie, Libyan Arab Jamahiriya v United Kingdom and the USA*, 1992 ICJ Rep. p.3 at paras.39 *et seq.*, 31 INT.LEG.MAT662 (1992); Beveridge, *The Lockerbie Affair*, 41 INT'L & COMP.LQ 907 at pp.916-19 (1992). *Cf.* Alvarez, *Judging the Security Council*, 90 AM.J INT'L L 1 (1996). A resolution under Chapter VI would not necessarily be unchallengeable.

422 *Supra n*408.

423 *Supra n*414.

424 See Gowlland-Debbas, *Security Council Enforcement Action and Issues of State Responsibility* 43 INT'L & COMP.LQ 55 (1994). The case on the merits was heard in October 1997 – see The Guardian p.13, 14 OCT 1997.

425 See The Guardian p.15, 18 OCT 1997. Two United Nations experts declared that the two Libyans would receive a fair trial in Scotland and should be surrendered thereto – The Guardian p.7, 23 DEC 1997.

The other Conventions have so far yielded few convictions,[426] but that may merely be a matter of time. Such a modest record of success may not on its own conclusively suggest that the proposal ought to be accepted that the political offence exemption could be abolished *vis à vis* these offences. Yet, taken along with the large number of signatories to each of the conventions, from all over the world and by all systems of government, it may be sufficient to indicate that the international community as a whole already recognises that these types of offender should not be able to avoid prosecution no matter where they are apprehended and that, thus, the political offence exemption is effectively redundant as regards these particular offence.[427] The proper response to such a finding should be that existing multilateral, U.N. sponsored conventions ought to be outside the political offence exemption, and that this exclusion should be achieved either by another multilateral convention to that effect,[428] or by obtaining the agreement of the present signatories to insert exclusion clauses into each such convention – any other method might result in many States denouncing the convention. As for future conventions of this nature, two plans are possible. First, that any exclusion of the political offence would only come into force once 60 or more countries had become parties. Alternatively, and probably preferably, the conventions should include a clause to achieve that end, but a party would have to expressly adopt it upon either signature, ratification or at some later date, as the case may be.

On the other hand though, it should be noted that Bassiouni has sounded a pessimistic note with regard to the exclusion of even these offences.

> "These measures needlessly create new categories of crime or increase the penalties for existing ones. The temptation to legislate these problems out of existence will prove futile."[429]

---

426 *Cf. Donyadideh, supra n*410, a conviction for offences created with respect to the New York Convention, *supra n*410. See also, MURPHY, *supra n*219, at pp.116-22.

427 See John Norton Moore, The Need for an International Convention, at pp.437 *et seq.* in BASSIOUNI, LEGAL RESPONSES, *supra n*233.

428 *Viz.* 1990 Commonwealth Scheme, LMM(90)32, Art.10(1)(b).

429 Inquiry, *supra n*233, p.xxvii.

This view is overly negative, although there is no strong evidence to refute Bassiouni's contention and his underlying analysis may well be proven correct. In the short to medium term, however, the U.N. Convention crimes could be accepted as non-political. Apart from this limited field of multilateral convention offences, though, exclusion of offences does not seem viable. Even here offences are not being excluded, but rather, as an international practice of universal jurisdiction with respect to certain international crimes becomes more accepted and widespread, the political offence exemption is being expressly recognised as redundant. Nevertheless, it is clear that the regional and bilateral approaches of the ECST, the Anglo-Indian Treaty, the Model American Convention, the Anglo-US Supplementary Treaty and the early, 'negative' US Bills are not a fully effective or acceptable solution. Despite its faults, the positive definition formula, seen especially in HR Bill 3347, offered a more appropriate response to the difficulties of curtailing the excesses of the operation of the political offence exemption. It allowed for judicial discretion: it may not have been precise, but with this guidance it may have been possible to trust the judges to apply the political offence exemption. Blanket exclusion clauses are too restrictive and are not accepted or implemented: the positive approach was better, so far as it went. What may be better again, though, is to adopt the more general Swiss approach.

(iii) The Swiss Approach Reprised – At least one set of US academics has suggested that the time of the Swiss proximity and proportionality tests, the predominance theory, has come.[430] That courts in several European States seem to be adopting the proximity and proportionality tests can not be doubted. In *Folkerts v Public Prosecutor*,[431] the Dutch Supreme Court ordered the extradition of a member of the Red Army Faction to the then F.R.G. The court held that the ultimate goal of the RAF being the destruction of the political, economic and military power of the F.R.G., crimes committed towards that end might be political. However, the political offence exemption would only extend to those fugitive offenders whose crimes "would yield any result directly related to the ultimate goal ...". The Dutch Supreme Court was also prepared to extradite two members of the IRA to the United Kingdom for explosive offences which were also too distant from the ultimate

---

430 THE RECORD, *supra* n117, at p.597.
431 *Supra* n83, at 501.

goal.[432] The proximity test has also been applied by British courts in the cases of *Cheng* and *Ferrandi*.[433]

With respect to proportionality, France, long a safe-haven for members of the Basque group, ETA, now willingly extradites them to Spain. The turning point was the *Conseil d'Etat's* decision in the case of *Lujambio Galdeano, Garcia Ramirez and Martinez Beiztegui*,[434] which decided that even if their offences had been committed as part of the Basque people's claim for independence, their very gravity deprived them of any political character.[435] As discussed above, the Irish Supreme Court has also taken a similar line. Here the turning point was *McGlinchey v Wren*.[436] In that case, O'Higgins CJ redefined the parameters of the exemption to include elements of proportionality and proximity with respect to the ultimate goal of the Provisional IRA and the INLA: that is, British withdrawal from Northern Ireland. The court made it clear that earlier Irish authorities on political offences were no longer binding. Previous cases on the political offence,

> "have in many respects been rendered obsolete by the fact that modern terrorist violence, whether undertaken by military or paramilitary organisations or by individuals, is often the antithesis of what could be regarded as political."[437]

O'Higgins CJ also disparaged the United States approach of depending so heavily on the existence of a political uprising, for he indicated there should be no automatic assumption that a terrorist offence is political merely because there is "widespread violence by organised paramilitary groups in Northern Ireland". He concluded by remarking that violent offences

> "done by, or at the behest of, self-ordained arbiters is the very antithesis of the ordinances of Christianity and civilisation and the basic requirements of political activity."[438]

---

432 See *McF, supra n*84.
433 *Cheng, supra n*11, and *Ferrandi, supra n*61.
434 *Supra n*153. See also, *Douai, supra n*207.
435 *Supra n*153, at p.329.
436 *Supra n*162. See also, *Shannon v Fanning, supra n*169, *Quinn v Wren, supra n*173, *Russell v Fanning, supra n*176 and *Ellis v O'Dea, supra n*171.
437 *Supra n*162, at 159 *per* O'Higgins CJ.
438 *Supra n*162, at 160.

In *Ellis*,[439] Hamilton P held that the offences charged could not "be regarded as political offences or offences connected with a political offence as they contemplate and involve indiscriminate violence and can be correctly characterised as terrorism". Dutch courts have adopted the proportionality test, too. The District Court of The Hague has held that the ultimate political goal must be in proportion to the harm inflicted as a result of the offences.[440] Even the English courts, which for long relied solely on proximity, have now in the case of *T*[441] incorporated elements of proportionality into the proximity test: this does not go far enough, but it is a step in the right direction – proportionality, if the Swiss approach is to be adopted, needs to be seen to be separate and discrete, an independent ground with respect to which the political character of an offence can be determined.

As was suggested above, the Swiss approach is the best of the current methods of applying the political offence exemption. It can test any and every politically motivated offence. It requires that the offence is sufficiently proximate to the ultimate goal of the fugitive offender and his organisation. This remoteness test rules out most terrorist crimes in the politically complex western industrialised societies, which is the aim, anyway, of most of the treaties and statutes so far considered and rejected as failures. Moreover, it preserves judicial discretion while demanding the much more stringent final, universal hurdle that the offence be proportionate to the goal: authority already exists to suggest that homicide, no matter what crime it results from, will rarely be proportionate.[442] Finally, the test is simple, unlike the positive guidelines of H.R.3347, and it does not create more difficulties than it solves.[443]

An additional benefit from adopting the Swiss test, though, would be that the political offence exemption would then coincide with part of the

---

439 *Supra* n171.
440 See the summaries of the judgments in 74 INT'L L REP.504.
441 *Supra* n80.
442 *In re Pavan*, [1927–28] Ann.Dig.347 at 349.

"Homicide, assassination and murder, is one of the most heinous crimes. It can only be justified where *no other method* exists of protecting the final rights or humanity."

See also *T*, *supra* n80.
443 Bassiouni, Inquiry, *supra* n233, at p.xxvii.

test for granting refugee status.[444] The Convention Relating to the Status
of Refugees, 1951, states that an alien may be refused refugee status if[445]

> "he has committed a serious non-political crime outside the country of
> refuge prior to his admission to that country as a refugee."

In determining whether the alien has committed such a crime, courts and
tribunals in many countries have regard to the UNHCR Handbook on Procedures and Criteria for Determining Refugee Status.[446] Paragraph 152 of
the Handbook provides guidelines for deciding whether an offence is non-
political.

> "In determining whether an offence is 'non-political' or is, on the contrary,
> a 'political' crime, regard should be given in the first place to its nature
> and purpose, *ie.* whether it has been committed out of genuine political
> motives and not merely for personal reasons or gain. There should also be
> a close and direct causal link between the crime committed and its alleged
> political purpose and object. The political element of the offence should
> also outweigh its common-law character. This would not be the case if the
> acts committed are grossly out of proportion to the alleged objective. The
> political nature of the offence is also more difficult to accept if it involves
> acts of an atrocious nature."[447]

If immigration tribunals and courts can apply such standards, then surely
an extradition court could use them when trying to assess whether the fugitive is a political offender.

Admittedly, leaving it all to the judges may give rise to the same problems now being faced, but the attempts to exclude specific offences have
all required the inclusion of the standard non-persecution clause anyway
to protect a fugitive from prejudice on the basis of race, nationality, political

---

444 The English case of *T, supra n*80, concerned whether the applicant should be
granted refugee status, not extradition.
445 189 UNTS 150 (1951), Art.1F(b); see also, the 1967 Protocol, 606 UNTS 267.
Refugee issues are dealt with in detail in Chapter Nine.
446 Published in 1979. See THE RECORD, *supra n*117, at p.601, *T, supra n*80, and
R v Secretary of State for Home Affairs, ex p Norman, Santis and Bugdaycay,
[1986] 1 All ER 458.
447 See *T, supra n*80, at 898, and THE RECORD, *supra n*117, at p.602.

opinion or religion, if surrendered. Any judge willing to refuse extradition under the Swiss test would probably protect a fugitive under the non-persecution clause, although the two tests are not identical. Furthermore, it is likely that there will still be incorrect decisions by judges applying the Swiss test, releasing fugitives who ought to be extradited. Nevertheless, that would happen with any of the other tests, too. The only difference is that the Swiss approach places a much greater discretion in the hands of the judge, but not so much greater as to cast any doubt upon the wisdom of adopting the Swiss test. The Swiss test is general and it does rely on the judge's discretion, yet, compared with either the exclusion of listed offences or a series of guidelines which cannot be effectively applied with consistency in practice, the advantages of the Swiss approach are its simplicity and universal applicability.

On the other hand, however, having regard to the homogeneity of late twentieth century western industrialised society, the Swiss test does have its limits. It imposes "the common and popular ideals and values of one nation State upon another".[448] It is a subjective test, in that it is value ridden with the views and judgments of the requested State. To provide sufficient protection for the fugitive, therefore, the Swiss approach must be tempered with the usual protection from persecution clause: a full harmonisation with asylum is necessary. Extradition law should have regard to the act and the actor.[449] Indeed, this step has already been taken by the Austrian Extradition Act.[450]

"... In one case a fugitive from Hungary who committed homicide in the course of his flight was granted political asylum upon his arrival in Austria. Extradition to Hungary was refused for various reasons, among them the danger from persecution. However, the alleged offender was tried in Austria because the crime did not qualify as a political offence, since the seriousness of the act outweighed the political motive of the flight."[451]

---

448 Bassiouni, *supra* n257, at p.245. See also *Quinn v Robinson, supra* n117.

449 *Cf.* WIJNGAERT, *supra* n5, at p.203.

450 See MURPHY, *supra* n219, at pp.55-56. MURPHY'S information was taken from PALMER, THE AUSTRIAN LAW ON EXTRADITION AND MUTUAL ASSISTANCE IN CRIMINAL MATTERS (1983).

451 MURPHY, *supra* n219, at p.56.

To conclude on the exclusion of offences, whether by a negative or positive approach, and the Swiss Predominance Test, it seems that the easiest and most effective way to render the present political offence exemption fit for the times is to combine the proportionality test with a requirement that the fugitive should face no danger of persecution if surrendered. This fusion was the conclusion reached at the end of the review of the various national approaches earlier in this chapter. If the exemption is to be retained in a substantially similar format, then the modified Swiss approach is the appropriate basis. A clause such as follows could be inserted into any extradition arrangement in future.

> "A Fugitive shall not be surrendered
> (a) if it appears to the appropriate authority upon reviewing such evidence as is adduced by both sides, that the offence is of a political character, or, if returned, the fugitive will be tried or punished for an offence of a political character, unless the common element of the offence under the ordinary law predominates; or
> (b) if the fugitive offender prove to the satisfaction of any court before whom he is brought on review, or to the executive authority,
> (i) that the request has in fact been made with a view to try or punish him on account of his race, religion, nationality or political opinions; or
> (ii) that he might, if surrendered, be prejudiced at his trial or punished, detained or restricted in his personal liberty by reason of his race, religion, nationality or political opinions."

– ◄► –

The remaining responses considered below attempt to solve the present problems by either a particular, discrete amendment, such as has already been suggested for specific United Nations treaties, or by a completely new approach distinct from the current test.

(iv) Fair Trial – Rather than use the fair trial requirement as a mere supplement to the present test, as was just suggested, some commentators have

proposed that extradition be predicated entirely on the presence or absence of due process and fair trial in the requesting State.[452]

"... A possible improvement could result from a shifting in emphasis of the criteria determining the extraditability from the *act* to the *actor*: instead of taking the nature of the act (political or common) as the decisive criterion, the treatment of the actor in the requesting State would be the criterion to determine his liability to extradition."

Fair trial is a vague concept and, on its own, is limited to those cases where there is a trial only of the issue for which the fugitive was extradited. It should be applied alongside a further test that would refuse a request for extradition where the fugitive would be persecuted on his return. Persecution in these matters would be on the grounds of race, religion, nationality, membership of a particular social group or political opinion,[453] and would extend further than the current political offence exemption.

"There can be no doubt that the humanitarian element of the exception has to be not only maintained, but broadened. Accordingly, one clause in extradition treaties should provide that extradition shall not be granted if the requested State has substantial grounds for believing that the fugitive, if returned, would risk being punished or prosecuted on account of his race, religion, nationality or political opinion, or that his position might be prejudiced for any of these reasons. The same rule should apply if there are substantial grounds for believing that the criminal proceedings in the requesting State were not or will not be in conformity with the minimum procedural guarantees binding under international law, or that the punishment or the circumstances of its execution would have to be considered as inhuman or degrading."[454]

---

452 WIJNGAERT, *supra n5*, at p.203. See also, Keith, *Asylum or Accessory: The Non-Surrender of Political Offenders by Canada*, 31 U.TORONTO FAC.L REV.93 (1973). Bassiouni, *supra n257*.

453 Taken from Articles 1 and 33 (*non-refoulement*), 1951 Convention Relating to the Status of Refugees, *supra n445*.

454 STEIN, *supra n6*, at p.380. See also, Stein, How much humanity do terrorists deserve?, in DELISSEN AND TANJA, *supra n209*, pp.567 *et seq.*, esp. at pp.574-80.

While a due process clause is not yet ubiquitous in domestic extradition laws and international arrangements, a freedom from persecution clause is almost an automatic inclusion in extradition treaties now.[455] So much so, that the Judicial Division of the Dutch Council of State has held that

> "[a] decision granting extradition for serious offences and rejecting a plea based on Article 3(2) of the European Convention on Extradition, cannot be accompanied by a decision prohibiting the person sought, as a refugee, from being returned to the country requesting his extradition, having regard to Article [1F(b)] of the ... Convention on the Status of Refugees."[456]

According to *Folkerts*, if extradition has been granted, then it must imply that the courts of the requested State have found that no persecution will take place in the requesting State and that the fugitive's application for refugee status would not be granted. Moreover, in *McF*[457] the Dutch Supreme Court held that because the United Kingdom, the requesting State, was a party to the ECHR and had granted a right of individual petition, it was not at liberty to decide that the fugitives' rights under Articles 3 and 6 might be violated. In *Smyth*[458] and *Howard*,[459] United States courts, though acknowledging that ordinarily in the United States extradition process there is no power to inquire into treatment the transnational fugitive offender might face on surrender, held that the Anglo-US Supplementary Extradition Treaty permitted investigation of the treatment the particular transnational fugitive offender would face. On the facts in each case, the transnational fugitive offender's assertion of potential persecution was rejected.[460]

Other jurisdictions, though, have been prepared to refuse extradition, even where the requesting State was a party to the ECHR. In *Finucane*,[461]

---

455 *Eg.* Article 5, ECST, *supra n*82; Article 3, Anglo-US Supplementary Treaty, *supra* n104; Article 3, European Convention on Extradition 1957, *supra n*59.
456 *Folkerts v State Secretary of Justice*, 74 INT'L L REP.472 at 474 (1978).
457 *Supra n*84, at 426.
458 *Supra n*123.
459 *Supra n*401.
460 *Howard*, *supra n*401, at 1332-33; *Smyth*, 61 F.3d 711 at 719-20 (1995). And see, Letcher, *Comparative Application of the Non-Discrimination Clause in the US-UK Supplementary Extradition Treaty*, 5 TRANSNAT'L L & CONTEMP.PROBS 493, esp. at pp.515-23 (1995).
461 *Supra n*189.

the Irish Supreme Court unanimously refused a British request for the fugitive's surrender on account of well documented fears of the treatment he might receive in Northern Irish gaols; the actual decision was based on Article 40 of the Irish Constitution, but it applied the same principles as underlie the standard persecution clause. Thus, a clause prohibiting extradition where the fugitive would be persecuted and where procedural fairness would not be accorded to him in the requesting State ought to be part of all extradition treaties.

Even so, there are problems. Both stem from the same root cause. The first is that while the requested State may be perfectly satisfied that extradition is required, the fugitive may well have serious doubts about the impartiality of the requesting State. In reality, the very act giving rise to the request for extradition may have been founded in distrust of and antagonism towards the requesting State. More pertinently, within western industrialised society it is hard to conceive of one State refusing extradition to a friendly neighbouring State,[462] partly because of the 'club' mentality of Western Europe, North America and Australia. In fact, the European Court of Human Rights has already held in *Fox, Campbell and Hartley v United Kingdom*[463] that there is a "need for a proper balance between the defence of the institutions of democracy in the common interest and the protection of individual rights".[464]

Indeed, a further problem arises from adopting the fair trial test, in that it antagonises those States outside the 'club' who feel as though their legal systems are being judged by the western industrialised States, so preventing essential international co-operation. However, given the ECHR, ICCPR, ACHR and ACHPR safeguard everyone's rights, including those of the fugitive,[465]

---

462 *In re Arton*, [1896] 1 QB 108 at 115; *Government of Greece v Governor of Brixton Prison*, [1971] AC 250; *Atkinson v USA Government*, [1969] 3 All ER 1317. *Cf. Finucane*, but the facts were extreme.

463 Series A, Vol.182 at para.28 (1990).

464 See also Schermers' dissent in the European Commission of Human Rights in *Bozano v France*, Series A, Vol.111, who commented that amongst States recognizing the same standards of justice, the guarantees found in the extradition process may have to be balanced against the need to fight transnational crime.

465 Warbrick, *supra* n209, at p.90. *Cf.* p.93.
"The other reason why the characterization of terrorist acts as breaches of human rights is important is because it is sometimes claimed that a kind of *tu quoque* principle operates, that an individual renders himself susceptible to losing his

it may be possible to set out the minimum levels of 'non-persecution' or 'fair trial' required before extradition can be granted by reference to their pertinent provisions. Article 6 of the ECHR, for example, lays down several requirements[466] if a trial is to be fair with respect to prompt, public hearings, time to prepare a defence, the provision of legal representation and the right to cross-examine all witnesses. However, all these rights are secondary to the implied right of access to the courts for a fair trial.[467] If a fugitive's access, especially a terrorist's access, to the courts is limited on grounds of national security, then the whole concept of extradition based on fair trial is redundant. Using the IRA as an example, could it be said that trial in 'Diplock Courts',[468] that is trial without a jury, guaranteed "rights that are practical and effective".[469] By establishing special courts, the whole understanding of 'fair trial' is altered. Surely, access must still be to the ordinary courts[470] if extradition is to depend on the fairness of the trial in the requested State.[471]

The second point follows on, in that it may not be possible for *any* trial in the State of dispute to be independent and impartial, either in the actual hearing or the sentence. The appearance of fairness, rather than substantive fairness, is all that may be achieved. A political offender, either by the horror

---

human rights if he interferes with the human rights of others .... It is at least a possible line of argument that the terrorist may, by his conduct, bring upon himself a diminution of his rights."
See also, *Brogan, supra n253*.

466 Warbrick, *supra n209*, at pp.101-118.

467 Warbrick, *supra n209*, at p.114.

468 Commission to Consider Legal Procedures to deal with Terrorist Activities in Northern Ireland. Cmnd 5185.

469 *Artico*, Series A, vol.37, at para.33. Cited in Warbrick at p.114, *supra n154*. However, in *App. 8299/78, X and Y v Ireland*, 24 YB.ECHR 132 at 174 (1981), the Commission held that Dublin's Special Criminal Court, also juryless, met the requirements of Art.6. The Court in *Soering*, Series A, Vol.161, para.113, held that in exceptional circumstances a finding of a flagrant denial of procedural fairness in the courts of the requesting State might to prevent extradition.

470 Warbrick, *supra n209*, at p.113.

471 With regard to the IRA, Sprizzo DJ in *Doherty, supra n115*, at 276, held that Diplock courts and justice in Northern Ireland generally were fair and impartial. *Cf. Smyth, supra n123*, where the Court of Appeals, 61 F.3d 711 at 720 (1995), implied that the Diplock system gave rise to generally discriminatory effects on Catholics and suspected Republican sympathizers.

of his act or by aiming his act at the State itself,[472] will not be treated as an ordinary criminal and may well be punished for his political motive. Therefore, 'fair trial' is both an unwieldy concept to use and is also seriously flawed in its application. For both these reasons, it may be difficult to obtain worldwide support for its introduction as the sole guarantee of the fugitive's liberty and political freedom.

In addition, merely to adjudicate requests for extradition on the fair trial provisions of Article 6, or its equivalent in other regional human rights conventions, would be insufficient. The full protection of the ECHR or other regional human rights conventions would have to be imposed.[473] Extradition should be based on non-persecution in the requesting State: there is no point in returning a fugitive to face a fair trial if the State's behaviour before or after trial contravenes the basic requirements of fundamental human rights. Procedures to combat violent political offenders should never go so far as to include the abrogation of human rights. Terrorism should never be a sufficient ground for permitting derogation from human rights guarantees relating to the physical integrity of the person and to the fairness of judicial procedures.[474]

In conclusion, whether extradition be based on the fairness of a trial or on non-persecution, the test suffers from its reliance on the requested State's concept of procedural fairness. Further, a refusal to extradite results in a much more forthright and overt condemnation of the requesting State.

> "This well-intentioned suggestion suffers from the obvious drawback that it is premised entirely upon Western and democratic notions of due process and other procedural safeguards afforded to individuals accused of crime .... [The] suggestion also obliges States to evaluate the judicial processes of another State. The political offence exception was intended to avoid such a situation. Different States have markedly different perceptions of what

---

472 See GRIFFITH, *infra* n480.

473 In *Smyth, supra* n123, the courts were prepared to take into account the treatment Smyth would face in prison and after his release. See also, Warbrick, *supra* n209, at p.99.

474 Derogation clauses in human rights conventions forbid any limitation on the right to life, on freedom from torture or cruel, inhuman and degrading treatment and on the non-retroactivity of criminal law. See for example, Article 4 ICCPR and Article 15 ECHR.

constitutes a fair trial and consequently would arrive at varying perceptions of other States' judicial processes."[475]

There is no point introducing an extradition procedure that will be as little accepted as the current one if it is sought to combat the present problems facing the political offence exemption. 'Fair trial' and 'non-persecution' are inadequate criteria on which to found a new test on their own: they may usefully complement the Swiss proportionality test discussed above, though.

(v) Summary – So far, the proposals have all attempted to return the fugitive to the requesting State. Only the modified Swiss approach and the minimal development for existing U.N. multilateral conventions seem to have any chance of improving on the present position to any significant degree. In fact, it seems apparent from the above discussion that any system that *always* requires the return of the fugitive to the State of dispute may not be acceptable to all States on all occasions.[476] Deciding the cases of fugitives on the basis of the political character or otherwise of the offence or the fairness of the trial on surrender, allows for widely divergent views, the only result of which is that the fugitive escapes prosecution. Moreover, the political offence exemption of extradition law has become, in some cases, part of the foreign policy of States.[477] Given that extradition will be refused on occasions whatever test is used, any overall solution, therefore, should have the capacity to deal with the situation where surrender is not granted, even if the streamlining amendments proposed above, which would produce a more coherent application of the exemption, were to be adopted. The new rule, which would supplement the Swiss proportionality test and the amendments to the U.N. anti-terrorist conventions, must not rely exclusively on surrender in order to deal with fugitive offenders. Nor must it rely on the character of the offence alone.

---

475 Carbonneau, *supra n*35, at pp.38-39. Carbonneau falls into the same trap by using one buzz-word, 'due process', to describe another, 'fair trial'.
476 *Viz.* The standoff between Libya and the United Kingdom and United States – *supra n*421.
477 Compare *Croissant, supra n*152, with *Abu Daoud, supra n*8, and *Affaire Gouvernement Suisse, supra n*13, respectively. In this respect there is a return to mediæval practice: SHEARER, *supra n*32, pp.5-7 and O'Higgins, *The History of Extradition in British Practice*, 13 IND.YB.INT'L AFF.78 (1964).

"So it appears to me that the motive and purpose of the accused committing the offence must be relevant and may be decisive."[478]

The new test, if it is to be acceptable to all States, must fully take into account the motivation of the fugitive. Even anarchists and revolutionary terrorists, along with all other types of political offender, should come within the new rule, otherwise the anomalous distinctions and abuses would reappear from the current system. The reasoning behind this wide application is that if extradition is currently refused because States do not believe the fugitive will be unprejudiced in the State of dispute, it must be because, regardless of the probity of the judicial system, the State of dispute cannot act in a disinterested fashion when the State itself has been threatened.[479] Political offenders are frequently punished for their political motive, especially if they are labelled terrorists, as well as for the crime itself. An attack on the State, for any reason, has to be punished to prevent recurrence. Thus, the proposal to abolish the political offence exemption in order to replace it with a 'fair trial' requirement is self-defeating – on this analysis, a trial might be procedurally fair in the requesting State, but the fact that the transnational fugitive offender intended to challenge the authority of that State by the criminal activity for which he is now requested, means that there is substantive prejudice.

"Neither impartiality nor independence necessarily involves neutrality. Judges are part of the machinery of authority within the State and as such cannot avoid the making of political decisions .... [The judges'] principal function is to support the institutions of government as established by law .... The confusion arises when it is pretended that judges are somehow neutral between those who challenge existing institutions and those who control those institutions."[480]

---

478 *Schtraks, supra n*48, *per* Lord Reid at 583.
479 See Nelson Mandela's comment with respect to the United Kingdom's and the United States's insistence that the two Libyans alleged to have committed the Lockerbie bombing be tried in Scotland, that it would not be correct for the State to act as "complainant, prosecutor and judge" (Commonwealth Heads of Government Meeting, Edinburgh, 25 October 1997) – see The Guardian p.1, 27 OCT 1997; see also, The Guardian p.17, 30 OCT 1997; p.13, 4 NOV 1997.
480 GRIFFITH, THE POLITICS OF THE JUDICIARY, at pp.292 and 343 (1997).

However, this lack of neutrality does not mean that political offenders should be set free in the requested State. Two options are open when a fugitive claims he acted with a political motive. First, there could be trial by an international criminal court or, secondly, the requested State could prosecute.[481]

– II –

(vi) International Criminal Court – This is not a new idea, at all.[482] Two reasons can be given for the establishment of an international criminal tribunal, staffed by judges from various countries with a variety of political backgrounds to deal with terrorists. First, it could try the fugitive only for the common element of the crime and punishment would not be based on the political prejudices inherent in any single State's judiciary. It is doubtful whether the fugitive would regard any such tribunal as any less biased, but the requested State would be placed in a very awkward position if it refused to give him up for prosecution. Moreover, it would diminish the western monopolisation of this area of the law and, therefore, improve the prospects for a truly international response to the problem in general of the political offender and, in particular, of the terrorist.

Secondly, it might well have led to the harmonisation of international criminal law with respect to ideologically or politically motivated offenders.

---

481 Bassiouni, *supra n*257, at pp.257-59 ; and BASSIOUNI & WISE, *AUT DEDERE, AUT JUDICARE*: THE DUTY TO EXTRADITE OR PROSECUTE IN INTERNATIONAL LAW, (1995).

482 *The Proposals of M Laval to the League of Nations for the establishment of an International Permanent Tribunal in criminal matters,* 21 Transactions of the Grotius Society 77, (1921); Hudson, *The Proposed International Criminal Court,* 32 AM.J INT'L L 549, (1938); Pella, Memorandum on the Establishment of an International Criminal Court, U.N. Doc.A/AC 48/3, 17 JULY 1951; Draft Statute for an International Criminal Jurisdiction, 9 U.N.G.A.O.R.Supp.12 (A/2645), paras.23-26 (1954); Bridge, *The Case for on International Court of Criminal Justice and the formulation of International Criminal Law,* 13 INT'L & COMP. LQ 1255 (1964); WOETZEL, REPORT ON THE FIRST AND SECOND INTERNATIONAL CONFERENCES, (1973); FERENCZ, AN INTERNATIONAL CRIMINAL COURT, 2 vols. (1980). The US Congress called on the President in 1986 to look into the possibility of an international court to deal with terrorists – §1201 PL No.99-399, Omnibus Diplomatic Security and Antiterrorism Act, 1986.

One of the major problems with the current system is the divergence in the reasoning of the domestic courts.[483] The politically motivated fugitive should be treated in the same fashion regardless of location.

However, in 1991, in *Aspects of Extradition Law*,[484] I opined that there was little prospect of such a 'court in the clouds' being created, except for trials of war criminals. Thus, when the International Law Commission produced its draft Statute for an International Criminal Court in 1994,[485] I was afraid, having regard to Article 20(e), that I might have had to eat my words:

> "*Article 20 Crimes within the jurisdiction of the Court*
> The Court has jurisdiction in accordance with this Statute with respect to the following crimes:
> (a) the crime of genocide;
> (b) the crime of aggression;
> (c) serious violations of the laws and customs applicable in armed conflict;
> (d) crimes against humanity;
> (e) crimes, established under or pursuant to the treaty provisions listed in the Annex,[486] which, having regard to the conduct alleged, constitute exceptionally serious crimes of international concern."

The Annex, *inter alia*, listed most of the United Nations multilateral, anti-terrorism conventions. It was left, however, to the Preparatory Committee

---

483 *Eg.* Compare the Swiss and United States tests, above. And they are both within western industrialised society.

484 At pp.156-57.

485 Report of the International Law Commission on the Work of its Forty-Sixth Session, Draft Statute for an International Criminal Court, UN Doc.A/49/355 (1994); hereinafter, Statute. And see Crawford, *The ILC's Draft Statute for an International Criminal Court*, 88 AM.J INT'L L 140 (1994), *The ILC Adopts a Statute for an International Criminal Court*, 89 AM.J INT'L L 404 (1995); and, *Symposium on International Criminal Law*, vol.5:2 TRANSNAT'L L & CONTEMP. PROBS. 237 *et seq.* (1995).

486 The Annex listed grave breaches of the Geneva Conventions and Protocol I (presumably already covered in para.(c)), as well as:
"2. The unlawful seizure of aircraft as defined by Article 1 of the Hague Convention for the Suppression of Unlawful Seizure of Aircraft of 16 December 1970.

Meetings (PrepComs) to take these proposals further.[487] Nothing is certain, but treaty crimes, as proposed in the ILC's 1994 Annex, are unlikely to be in the final Statute. At PrepCom III in February 1997, attention focused on war crimes, genocide, aggression and crimes against humanity – the treaty crimes were quietly ignored and dropped off the agenda. Similarly, the 1991 version of the Draft Code of Crimes Against the Peace and Security of Man-

---

3. The crimes defined by Article 1 of the Montreal Convention for the Suppression of Unlawful Acts against the Safety of Civil Aviation of 23 September 1971.

4. Apartheid and related crimes as defined by Article II of the International Convention on the Suppression and Punishment of the Crime of Apartheid of 30 November 1973.

5. The crimes defined by Article 2 of the Convention on the Prevention and Punishment of Crimes against Internationally Protected Persons, including Diplomatic Agents of 14 December 1973.

6. Hostage-taking and related crimes as defined by Article 1 of the International Convention against the Taking of Hostages of 17 December 1979.

7. The crime of torture made punishable pursuant to Article 4 of the Convention against Torture and Other Cruel, Inhuman or Degrading Treatment or Punishment of 10 December 1984.

8. The crimes defined by Article 3 of the Convention for the Suppression of Unlawful Acts against the Safety of Maritime Navigation of 10 March 1988 and by Article 2 of the Protocol for the Suppression of Unlawful Acts against the Safety of Fixed Platforms Located on the Continental Shelf of 10 March 1988.

9. Crimes involving illicit traffic in narcotic drugs and psychotropic substances as envisaged by Article 3 (1) of the United Nations Convention against Illicit Traffic in Narcotic Drugs and Psychotropic Substances of 20 December 1988 which, having regard to Article 2 of the Convention, are crimes with an international dimension."

It is all but certain that the crimes in the Annex will not make it to any final Statute, although a crime of "terrorism" was proposed at PrepCom III, 11-21 February 1997 – A/AC.249/1997/WG.1/CRP.4.

487 The International Law Commission is simultaneously drawing up the Draft Code on Crimes Against the Peace and Security of Mankind (A/51/332, 1996). It defines aggression, genocide, crimes against humanity, crimes against United Nations and associated personnel and war crimes. There are differences between those definitions, those applied in universal jurisdiction and those being contemplated in the PrepComs. As such, it is of little help and its work could usefully be subsumed by the PrepComs so at least two sources of international criminal law do not contradict each other.

kind[488] included terrorism in its list of crimes, while by 1996 it was limited, possibly to the point were it is rendered redundant, to the same crimes as are to be found in the draft Statute for the International Criminal Court.[489] Moreover, unlike war crimes, genocide, aggression and crimes against humanity, the anti-terrorist treaty crimes are more domestic in character, although possessing transnational elements – it would be better for them not to be within the ambit of the International Criminal Court, despite the fact that some States find it difficult in practice to prosecute certain offenders, such as leaders of drug cartels.

The one logical exception to the general position that the International Criminal Court should be reserved for crimes during conflicts and crimes against humanity, would be for it to have jurisdiction with respect to those responsible for violations of the Convention on the Safety of United Nations and Associated Personnel[490] because of the international character of the victims[491]; furthermore, the offences under the United Nations personnel convention will generally occur during conflicts, like the other surviving Article 20 crimes. In the light, therefore, of the exclusion from the Statute during the PrepComs of the United Nations multilateral, anti-terrorism con-

---

488 *Supra n235.*

489 *Supra n487.*

490 34 INT.LEG.MAT482 (1995). The International Law Commission in its Draft Code of Crimes, *supra n487*, lists the following offence:

"*Article 19 Crimes against United Nations and associated personnel*

1.The following crimes constitute crimes against the peace and security of mankind when committed intentionally and in a systematic manner or on a large scale against United Nations and associated personnel involved in a United Nations operation with a view to preventing or impeding that operation from fulfilling its mandate:

(a) murder, kidnapping or other attack upon the person or liberty of any such personnel;

(b) violent attack upon the official premises, the private accommodation or the means of transportation of any such personnel likely to endanger his or her person or liberty.

2.This article shall not apply to a United Nations operation authorized by the Security Council as an enforcement action under chapter VII of the Charter of the United Nations in which any of the personnel are engaged as combatants against organized armed forces and to which the law of international armed conflict applies."

491 More international than ordinary diplomats, for instance.

vention crimes, discussion of the International Criminal Court will take place in Chapter Eight, alongside consideration of the other means used to bring to justice those committing offences principally during conflicts.

On the other hand, a regional, supra-national criminal court is not beyond the bounds of possibility and may be effective. Given the cross-frontier terrorist campaigns in mainland Europe, especially those of the IRA, where crimes are committed in several States and arrests subsequently occur in several States too, a supra-national court to hear all the charges, regardless of where they arose, has much to offer.[492] In May 1989, the European Parliament adopted the Zagari Report which, *inter alia*, suggested the establishment of a European court to deal with terrorist cases.[493] Nevertheless, realistically even such a regional court is a long way off and it would suffer from one major drawback, in that it might tend to make terrorists appear to be a special case outside the ambit of ordinary domestic courts and law.

(vii) Aut Dedere, Aut Judicare[494] – If an international criminal tribunal will not meet the need when extradition is refused to the State of dispute or the requesting State (if not the same),[495] then the Grotian proposition

---

492 See The Times p.14, 20 JUNE 1990.

493 The Scottish Police Federation supported such a court "to obviate present difficulties concerning extradition". See p.54, vol.2, HOME AFFAIRS SELECT COMMITTEE, SEVENTH REPORT, PRACTICAL POLICE CO-OPERATION IN THE EUROPEAN COMMUNITY, HCP 363 (1989–90).

494 See BASSIOUNI AND WISE, *supra* n481.

495 *Eg. Cheng v Governor of Pentonville Prison, supra* n11. Can it be said that the United States was disinterested in attempts to overthrow the Chiang Kai-Shek regime in Taiwan at the end of the 1960s at the height of the Vietnam War? It may be that although politically motivated, a fugitive who killed another politically dedicated person for purely political reasons at the other end of the ideological spectrum, could be returned if the requesting State stood aloof from the dispute. *Eg.* It was reported in 1985 that a left-wing terrorist group had killed a right-wing newspaper publisher in Greece. In such circumstances it is possible that the trial in Greece would be as neutral as any normal murder case, but this cannot be certain. (The Guardian p.8, 22 FEB 1985). This position would be in line with Viscount Radcliffe's views in *Schtraks v Government of Israel, supra* n48, 591-92.

"There may, for instance, be all sorts of contending political organisations or forces in a country, and members of them may commit all sorts of infractions

that the requested State must prosecute seems the best response. The concept already exists in all the United Nations multilateral conventions[496] and it is included in the Draft Code of Crimes Against the Peace and Security of Mankind.[497]

> "*Article 9 – Obligation to extradite or prosecute*
> Without prejudice to the jurisdiction of an international criminal court, the State Party in the territory of which an individual alleged to have committed a crime set out in article 17, 18, 19 or 20 is found shall extradite or prosecute that individual."

According to Bassiouni, the obligation may apply to all international crimes however prescribed.[498] Murphy argues that this general rule is not the case, that the duty to prosecute or extradite only arises where it is explicit in the aforementioned conventions.[499] However, as well as Bassiouni, the International Law Association, in a draft convention on international terrorism set out in Murphy's, *Punishing International Terrorists*, has also indicated that there may be a general duty to extradite or prosecute.

---

of the criminal law in the belief that by doing so they will further their political ends: but, if the central government stands apart and is concerned only to enforce the criminal law that has been violated by these contestants, I see no reason why fugitives should be protected by this country from its jurisdiction on the ground that they are political offenders."
However, even here it may be better to refuse extradition and try the offender in the requested State lest in future this exception be abused.

496 *Supra* n414. See also LILLICH, THE HUMAN RIGHTS OF ALIENS IN CONTEMPORARY INTERNATIONAL LAW (1984) at p.122 where he quotes Judge Baxter, *Treaties and Custom*, 129 RECUEIL DES COURS 25 at 57 (1970-I), Hague Academy of International Law. See also Starke, *Treaties as a Source of International Law*, 23 BRIT.YB.INT'L L 341 (1946); Lillich and Paxman, *State Responsibility for Injuries to Aliens Occasioned by Terrorist Activities*, 26 AM.U.L REV.217 at pp.276-307 (1977).

497 *Supra* n487.

498 Bassiouni, *supra* n235, at pp.28-31 and 34 *et seq*. See Judge Baxter in LILLICH, *supra* n496.

499 MURPHY, *supra* n219, at p.62.

"*Article 7*

States must try or extradite (*aut dedere, aut judicare*) persons accused of
acts of international terrorism. No State may refuse to try or extradite a
person accused of an act of international terrorism, war crime, common
crime which would be a war crime but for the absence of a legal status
of belligerency, or a crime against humanity, on the basis of a disagreement
as to which of these legal categories properly applies to the situation."

Nevertheless, while extradition itself is premised on the basis of some formal
agreement and, that in the absence of a treaty, it is only a moral obligation
arising out of the comity of nations, then the better view is that the principle
aut dedere, aut judicare still only applies, at present, when expressly formulated in multilateral conventions on international criminal law. It may be
that the provision in a particular treaty has become declaratory of customary
international law[500] with regard to the relevant crime, but there is no
generic duty in international law, at least so far, of *aut dedere, aut judicare*.

Regardless, of the precise scope of the duty, a much more important
question is to determine how to apply the duty. Is it co-existent or disjunctive[501]? If it is disjunctive, then the primary response must be to extradite and, where that is not carried out, only then would the supplementary
duty to prosecute arise. This disjunctive approach would seem to be the
approach envisaged in relation to the United Nations multilateral conventions.
There is still a preference for the crime to be dealt with where it occurred.[502]

However, it would probably be more useful in combating the problems
of the political offence exemption if a co-existent analysis of the principle
aut dedere, aut judicare were adopted. This would allow the requested State
to choose from the outset whether to extradite or prosecute – it would be
a proper alternative, an independent response to dealing with politically
motivated fugitives.[503] Instead of it being a last resort if extradition fails,

---

500 See *North Sea Continental Shelf Cases* (FRG v Denmark and The Netherlands),
    1969 ICJ Rep. p.3, at paras.70 *et seq.*
501 See Bassiouni, *supra n235*, at p.36.
502 See Lockwood, *supra n257*, and Lillich, *supra n387*.
503 Or even generally – see Cuba's refusal to extradite Robert Vesco to the United
    States because it would be immoral; nevertheless, Cuba investigated Vesco's
    alleged crimes to see if he should be prosecuted there – The Guardian p.12,
    20 JUN 1995.

trial in the requested State would be elevated to a more pro-active status in international criminal law. At present, extradition, or some variant thereof, is seen as almost the only way of bringing fugitive offenders to justice. If it is accepted that the principal aim must be to prosecute the fugitive and that international public order requires international co-operation and mutual assistance, then a more positive acceptance of trial in the requested State is necessary. Along with all the other responses to the problems facing the exemption, *aut dedere, aut judicare* is growing in importance – it might further the objective of prosecuting fugitive offenders if the duty were treated as co-existent rather than disjunctive and if it were to be accepted that with respect to all politically motivated offenders there should be a genuine choice between extradition and prosecution in the requested State. Such an understanding of the obligations imposed in providing mutual assistance to other States would allow a politically motivated offender to be prosecuted before an impartial tribunal.

Yet problems exist with this procedure, too. The first concerns the assumption of criminal jurisdiction[504] generally by the requested State over all offences committed anywhere in the world by anyone, given that they acted with a political or ideological motive. Full consideration of jurisdiction over criminals has been dealt with in Chapter Three, but it will be remembered that there are generally held to be five main grounds for exercising competence over an accused person. It is self-evident that if a State is to have comprehensive jurisdiction over any politically or ideologically motivated offender who is found in its territory, then only the universality principle will be sufficient. The other bases of jurisdiction, territoriality, active and passive personality and the protective principle, all founder on their inapplicability to States not involved in the political or ideological dispute in question. Such bases of jurisdiction rest on a connection with the crime, one of the very things that trial in the requested State intends to avoid. The only ground on which the requested State could effectively exercise jurisdiction is the universality principle.[505] The universality principle allows a State to assume jurisdiction over all crimes regardless of the nationality of

---

504 See Chapter Three above.
505 See generally, Randall, *Universal Jurisdiction Under International Law*, 66 TEXAS L REV.785 (1988).

the offender and the *locus delicti*. Universal jurisdiction may arise through treaty or custom.

> "An international crime is such an act universally recognised as criminal, which is considered a grave matter of international concern and for some valid reason cannot be left within the exclusive jurisdiction of the State that would have control over it under normal circumstances."[506]

English jurisprudence, for instance, happens to be extremely strict in these matters and restricts this principle to cases of piracy,[507] the slave trade, war crimes and where the multilateral anti-terrorism treaties impose it.[508] Other States are more liberal in their use of universal jurisdiction. There would, however, seem to be little theoretical problem in expressly extending it through an international agreement to cover all ideologically and politically motivated offenders. This approach to dealing with politically motivated offenders has already been adopted by the Austrian authorities in two cases involving fugitives from the former Eastern bloc. In *The Universal Jurisdiction (Austria) Case*,[509] the Supreme Court of Austria held that it could assume jurisdiction in a representational capacity.

> "The extraditing State also has the right, in the cases where extradition for whatever reason is not possible, although according to the nature of the offence it would be permissible, to carry out a prosecution and impose punishment, instead of such action being taken by the requesting State."

The Hungarian Deserter (Austria) Case[510] involved the shooting of a border guard by a Hungarian soldier deserting to the West. Again, the Austrian Supreme Court exercised jurisdiction over the fugitive, extradition having

---

506 *Re List*, Case No.215, United States Military Tribunal at Nuremberg, 8 U.N.LRTWC 1 at 47 (1948); 15 Ann.Dig.632 at 636 (1948).

507 White, *The Marshall Court and International Law: The Piracy Cases*, 83 AM.J INT'L L 727 (1989).

508 *Supra* n414. See also MURPHY, *supra* n219, at pp.132-33. *Cf.* COUNCIL OF EUROPE, EXTRATERRITORIAL CRIMINAL JURISDICTION, which refers to jurisdiction under the multilateral treaties as representative; this seems to be at most a subset of universal jurisdiction.

509 28 INT'L L REP.341 at 342 (1958).

510 28 INT'L L REP.343 (1959).

been refused partly because he would be in danger of life and liberty if surrendered after having fled for political reasons.

If trial in the requested State is to be a full alternative to extradition, then, on present law, a new United Nations multilateral convention will have to provide for universal jurisdiction expressly – a co-existent analysis of the duty to extradite or prosecute does not exist in practice, so international legislation is needed. Terrorism *per se* is not a universal crime as yet, the multilateral and regional conventions merely outlaw aspects of terrorism. Otherwise, there would be no need to include a universal jurisdiction clause in each new convention; those clauses are not declaratory of some principle of customary international law that holds that politically or ideologically motivated offenders are subject to prosecution in whichever State they are apprehended. However, on a purely *quid pro quo* basis, if extradition is to be refused to the State of dispute in a case involving a politically or ideologically motivated offender, then trial ought to take place in the requested State. To the extent that the fugitive has 'chosen' the requested State, he has voluntarily submitted himself to its jurisdiction, rather than that of the State of the dispute.

Furthermore, a start has been already made in several countries. Section 45 of the Australian Extradition Act 1988 allows the courts to assume jurisdiction over Australian citizens whose extradition fails or is prohibited. Of course, this is an example of the active personality principle rather than universality, but it is based on the same need for offenders to be prosecuted no matter where they are found. The Italians practise true universality under Article 10(2) of the Penal Code. If extradition is refused the fugitive may be tried in Italy as long as the crime bears a minimum sentence of three years imprisonment. Furthermore, Greek law gives its domestic courts jurisdiction over anyone who had been requested for extradition, apparently with no limits.[511] A more limited step was taken by the British and Irish governments in relation to the Northern Irish troubles. It is still a secondary alternative to extradition and it is limited to a list of scheduled offences. The British Criminal Jurisdiction Act 1975 and the Irish Criminal Law (Jurisdiction) Act 1976 allow courts in one country to try offenders for specified crimes committed in the other. The listed offences are those generally attributable to terrorism. The Acts prevent terrorists escaping liability through

---

511 The Guardian p.11, 13 SEPT 1990.

the political offence exemption – since Irish courts felt unable during the 1970s to grant extradition for members of the IRA because of the exemption, the Acts allow for prosecution in the requested State.[512] In practice, the British authorities use it rarely, although it may be more effective in punishing those involved in the Northern Irish conflict than seeking extradition, which can take a long time and can prove fruitless in the end.[513]

However, there are problems with exercising universal jurisdiction. In the past, for instance, States have been unwilling to prosecute other States' political offenders and this disinclination may still cause problems.[514] Nonetheless, the above noted developments in Australia and throughout Europe may indicate a general change of approach. The United Kingdom prosecuted Tanzanian hijackers in 1983.[515] Further, the present unwillingness is probably one of the results, rather than causes, of the current preference for extradition. If prosecution in the requested State is seen as a co-existent duty, as Bassiouni explains,[516] the position may change.

Another hurdle, but one which is only apparent and not real, involves the question of whether the assumption of universal jurisdiction interferes with the requesting State's domestic jurisdiction. The unilateral assumption of universal jurisdiction could be deemed an unfriendly act under the General Assembly's Declaration on the Principles of International Law Concerning Friendly Relations and Co-operation among States in Accordance with the Charter of the United Nations,[517] in particular, the sixth principle, that of the sovereign equality of States. The proposed multilateral convention providing for trial in the requested State as an alternative to extradition is, therefore, essential.[518] As stated above, as the position stands, without such

---

512 See the conviction of Gerard Tuite, The Guardian p.2, 14 JULY 1982 and p.2, 3 MAY 1983.

513 See the *Finucane* case, *supra* n189.

514 See EVANS & MURPHY, LEGAL ASPECTS OF INTERNATIONAL TERRORISM (1978), Ch.9, by Evans, *esp.* pp.503-05.

515 *R v Moussa Membar et al.* [1983] CRIM.L REV.618. See also the trial of Iraqi hijackers fleeing Saddam Hussein's regime – The Guardian pp.1 and 2, 28 AUG 1996; p.4, 1 NOV 1997.

516 *Supra* n235.

517 Annex to UNGA Res.2625 (XXV), 24 October 1970.

518 On the customary status of the Declaration, see the *Case Concerning Military and Paramilitary Activities in and against Nicaragua*, (Nicaragua v United States), 1986 ICJ Rep. p.14, *esp.* at paras.188-205 and 228.

a convention, which would have to receive wide international support, there can be no progress beyond what already exists; that is, the possibility of trial in the requested State only as a last resort in a limited number of specified cases. To go beyond that minimal understanding of *aut dedere, aut judicare*, there would need to be a new, widely accepted convention, concluded under the auspices of the United Nations.

Other problems still exist,[519] especially with regard to the procedural rules necessary to implement the suggested approach. Evidence of a crime committed in the requesting State will be hard to obtain in the requested State, the fugitive, in particular, having a very much more difficult job, even though many treaties now provide for mutual assistance in criminal matters. Matters of evidence, however, create a further and more intractable problem. The common law system of justice and rules of evidence provide that in trials of serious crimes, the jury must hear the evidence from witnesses in person. Rarely will written evidence be accepted because it is impossible to cross-examine a document. In civil law countries, the lack of witnesses at trial is less of a problem, because an "investigating magistrate" can travel to the *locus delicti* to receive evidence, but it would be impracticable for a British judge and jury to follow the same course of action. Abolishing jury trials for political offenders would be contrary to the constraints of fairness and would invoke the criticism levelled at Diplock Courts in Northern Ireland, so either the witnesses must be brought to the requested State or the use of written evidence after cross-examination by lawyers in the *locus delicti* must be permitted. It may well be that a solution will have to be found soon, even if this general power to assume universal jurisdiction is not adopted, for many existing treaties now provide for prosecution in the requested State if extradition is refused.

In conclusion, even if a very broad power to try a fugitive offender in the requested State existed alongside all the other responses to the problems of the political offence exemption, there would still be safe havens. However, it should prevent politically motivated offenders, usually terrorists, from finding protection in western industrialised society. Even where a State is unwilling to return the fugitive, for whatever reason, international public order can still be upheld by trial in the requested State and the fugitive's human rights will not be prejudiced. Undoubtedly, extradition will continue

---

519 See, for example, SHEARER, *supra n*32, pp.68-72.

to be the favoured method of dealing with fugitive's, but a positively received duty to prosecute whenever surrender is denied will greatly enhance the effectiveness of international criminal law in this field.

Moreover, a further benefit may be derived from an enhanced duty to prosecute. Currently there is no State responsibility norm with respect to how States deal with fugitive offenders.

> "Extradition is the prerogative of the State in which the fugitive is found."[520]

If a State were to be in breach of such a new norm, then a claim could be made on behalf of those individuals injured by an attack by the State of which they are citizens.[521] If a duty were imposed on State to prosecute[522] all those not extradited because of an alleged political motive, then a sanction would be available in the form of money damages or other satisfaction from an arbitration claim if the requested State did not fulfil its obligations. Lillich and Paxman,[523] citing several other commentators, accept that the obligation to extradite or prosecute all politically motivated offenders remains essentially *de lege ferenda*. However, they go on to suggest that test cases should be brought against recalcitrant governments.[524] Murphy, for his part, initially dissented from this view.[525] He used to think that the defendant State would probably not agree to go to arbitration and that United States pressure might adversely affect international relations. Cassese is even less optimistic, arguing that States in breach of such a norm are hardly likely to be deterred by the usual peace time sanctions[526] – to a certain extent, the experience with Libya over the failure to hand over

---

520 Lillich & Paxman, *supra n*496, at p.300.

521 *Eg. Galvan Case* (*Mexico v United States*), (1927) Opinions 408, 4 R.INT'L ARB.AWARDS 273 (1927).

522 See Bassiouni, *supra n*235, and the same author's Inquiry, *supra n*233, at p.xlv.

523 *Supra n*496, at pp.304-05.

524 *Supra n*496, at pp.312-13.

525 See EVANS & MURPHY, *supra n*514, Ch.12 *esp.* pp.568-70 and MURPHY, LEGAL ASPECTS OF INTERNATIONAL TERRORISM: SUMMARY REPORT OF AN INTERNATIONAL CONFERENCE, pp.20-26. (Studies in Transnational Legal Policy No.19, ASIL 1978); hereinafter, ASIL SUMMARY REPORT. *Cf.* MURPHY, *supra n*219, at pp.134-35.

526 *Supra n*256, at p.593.

those accused of the Lockerbie bombing, despite United Nations sanctions,[527] has borne out these doubts. Nevertheless, despite such misgivings, an initiative was in part undertaken in relation to hijacking by the Bonn Declaration of 1978.[528] This joint approach, adopted by Canada, France, Italy, the then Federal Republic of Germany, Japan, the United Kingdom and the USA, takes effect if hijackers are not extradited or prosecuted and it prevents flights to and from the offending State. It was applied to Afghanistan and the threat of it forced South Africa to try the mercenaries who attempted to overthrow the Seychelles government.[529] Furthermore, within Europe, the European Convention on Human Rights may require States to take action to prevent interference with Convention rights by individuals, thus necessitating effective measures to combat, *inter alia*, threats to life and inhuman and degrading treatment perpetrated by politically motivated offenders.[530] A failure either to surrender or to prosecute violent terrorists might be a breach of Articles 2 and 3 of the ECHR, and it is likely that similar obligations would arise under the ACHR and the ACHPR.

g. Conclusion

Various responses have been proposed to render the political offence exemption fit for the times. Some would have more success than others. The main obstacle will always be obtaining international agreement to amend and restrict the exemption: its liberality is deep-rooted in historico-legal 'folklaw'. However, it is suggested that the three most profitable paths to follow would include, first, adopting the Swiss Predominance and Proportionality Test, coupled with a protection from persecution clause, to deal with the fugitive offender claiming the political offence defence. The Swiss general analysis of the exemption can be applied to any case and can be seen as a continuation of existing policy. To supplement this first step, it is likely that the widely accepted United Nations multilateral conventions on international crimes could be each amended to make it explicit that the political offence

---

527 See The Guardian p.16, 26 SEPT 1997.
528 *Supra n*409.
529 Busuttil, *supra n*409.
530 See Article 1, ECHR, Warbrick, *supra n*209, pp.97-99 and *Airey v Ireland*, Series A, vol.32, para.24.

exemption is redundant with regard to their specified offences. Making explicit what is already the case, may well aid a more general outlawing of crimes of excessive violence. Finally, the nascent obligation to extradite or prosecute must be nurtured so that it is available for all politically or ideologically motivated offenders as an alternative to extradition. With all the above in force, international public order will be maintained, fugitives will not escape justice, but human rights will not be infringed either. The other responses considered above will also be continued, but it is suggested that the most effective way forward is to adopt the three policies outlined here. In the long term, the best way forward may be to replace the exemption with trial in the requested State whenever a political dimension exists to the offence for which the fugitive is requested, but this would be too radical a step at present.

Before concluding, two other issues must be considered. The first concerns whether the exemption, however defined, should remain a judicial matter or whether it should be a matter for the executive alone. At present, the appropriate executive authority is left with a discretion not to extradite when the courts have ordered the fugitive's surrender. The position is thus, for example, in the United Kingdom,[531] the United States,[532] Switzerland, Australia and France, although following the decision of the *Conseil d'Etat* in *Affaire Gouvernement Suisse*,[533] the French executive cannot refuse extradition to another liberal democracy once the courts have ordained it except in the most anomalous of cases. The argument in favour of reallocating the decision making process is twofold. First, the executive has better access to information on political and diplomatic matters and, secondly, it is in a better position to negotiate with the requesting State concerning the fugitive's treatment on return.[534] These arguments, though, might still be satisfied by a final discretion, rather than absolute control. The executive may be in the best position to gather all the relevant information, but it must also be seen to keep its distance from 'judging' the

---

531 One example of its exercise is in the *Kotronis* case, *Government of Greece v Governor of Brixton Prison*, [1971] AC 250.

532 USC.§3186. The power is rarely exercised: Bassiouni, *International Extradition, a Summary of Contemporary American Procedure and a Proposed Formula*, 15 WAYNE L REV.733 at p.757 (1969).

533 *Supra* n13, at 61-62.

534 *Viz. Soering, supra* n469.

motivation behind the requesting State's application for the surrender of the accused.[535] Stein, though, advocates that the political offence exemption as it is known at present ought to be abolished, and that it be replaced by a freedom from persecution clause and, more radically, that the requested State should have the power to refuse extradition where it would be contrary to its own national interests.[536] He combines humanitarian concern for the fugitive's safety if surrendered with foreign policy considerations. Such an overt condemnation of the requesting State would not be appropriate for the courts and extradition would have to become the sole preserve of the executive. While such a proposal may seem unlikely to gain acceptance in the near future, it is worth noting that Article 1(a) of the Swiss extradition law adopts this approach,[537] but only as part of the wider Swiss understanding of the political offence exemption recommended above. For the time being, however, Stein's foreign policy test is only a supplement to the traditional operation of the political offence exemption, even in Switzerland.

The second argument for handing the decision over to the executive is much more cynical. The present judicial participation in the decision, it is alleged, merely serves to add an air of impartiality and objectivity that may not be deserved; the *Abu Daoud* and *Gouvernement Suisse* cases most obviously reveal this hidden agenda.[538] However, to adopt such an attitude would, in fact, be a case of "smiting one's nose to spite one's face" and would remove the last vestiges of protection that do exist.

"Judicial determination has always been found preferable to *ad hoc* political judgments responsive to passing political circumstances."[539]

---

535 For an interesting interpretation of this issue, see MURPHY, *supra n*219, at p.69.
536 *Supra n*6, at p.380.
537 Swiss Law on International Judicial Assistance in Criminal Matters, 20 March 1981, 20 INT.LEG.MAT1339 (1981), as amended 4 October 1996 (supplied by the Federal Office for Police Matters, Bern) – the text is a combination of both translations.
538 *Supra nn*8 and 13.
539 Anglo-US Supplementary Treaty, S.HRG.99-703 re TR.DOC 99-8, 1 AUG 1985, *per* Bassiouni at p.302.

The justification for retaining judicial discretion is that otherwise extradition of fugitives would become a matter of foreign policy to the detriment of human rights.

> "Thus, the national interest will become almost the exclusive consideration, disregarding any concern for the effect of the decision to grant or deny extradition on the maintenance and preservation of world public order and without regard for the individual's human rights or concern for his prosecution or punishment."[540]

Indeed, one aim of terrorism, in particular, is to create an oppressive, reactionary State leading to an alienated population who will increasingly rebel. The above suggestion to make the decision an executive one, like the earlier idea of trying to place politically motivated offenders outside the exemption, will create more problems than it solves, in part, because, by taking the decision out of the realm of the courts, it treats terrorists as distinct from ordinary criminals. Further, it aids their claim that they are engaged in a 'war' and that they are not merely violent common criminals. Most importantly and finally, it infringes human rights. The extradition system as a whole will be discredited because of the repressive measures directed at politically motivated fugitives.

> "Being aware of the danger ... a [repressive] law poses of undermining or even destroying democracy on the grounds of defending it, [the Court] affirms that the Contracting States may not, in the name of the struggle against ... terrorism, adopt whatever measures they deem appropriate."[541]

The final issue to be considered, concerns whether there are political measures that could be taken to coerce States who harbour politically motivated offenders without prosecuting them. It has already been suggested

---

540 Bassiouni, *supra n*257, at p.232. See also *US v Gonzalas*, 217 F.Supp 717 (1963), which highlights how State terrorism could be encouraged by executive control according to Sternberg and Skelding, *supra n*393, at pp.154-55 (1983). Robinson has suggested that extradition should be seen as an element of foreign policy. *The Commonwealth Scheme Relating to the Rendition of Fugitive Offenders: A Critical Appraisal of some Essential Elements*, 33 INT'L & COMP. LQ 614, *esp.* at pp.617 *et seq.*

541 *Klass*, Series A, vol.28, para.49.

that monetary compensation could be sought through arbitration if a State were to be in breach of a responsibility norm through harbouring politically motivated fugitive offenders. Even Murphy, who originally disapproved of such actions, has come round to believe that it may now be necessary.[542] Nevertheless, Murphy's original views[543] with regard to the other measures of self-help, such as armed force, economic sanctions and diplomatic protest, should still be abided by. Armed force, as in the United States raid on Libya, should only be employed *in extremis*, since its long-term effectiveness is very doubtful. The Libyan raid itself was disproportionate and a violation of international law.[544] Economic sanctions, such as those imposed on Libya as a result of not handing over the alleged Lockerbie bombers,[545] have little effect, especially after it is noted that the terrorist-harbouring States, for example, do little trade with western industrialised society. The only area where this might prove more successful is in putting pressure on countries in South America to hand over war criminals, for these States are heavily dependent on the United States. As for diplomatic protest, as Murphy commented in 1978,

"[this] is likely to be the most effective measure of self-help that can be employed to induce recalcitrant States to join co-operative efforts to prevent and suppress international terrorism."[546]

To sum up, the political offence exemption is very much the 'hot issue'.[547] So hot, indeed, that many responses to its problems have been devised. Most of these responses have been *ad hoc* and, thus, lack coherence and long-term acceptability. The proposals set out at the beginning of this *Conclusion* present the best way forward with regard to dealing with individual fugitives as they come before the courts, for the time being. However, a global solu-

---

542 *Supra* n219, at pp.134-35.
543 See ASIL SUMMARY REPORT, *supra* n525, at pp.20-26.
544 Even though it is now clear that Libya, along with the former East Germany, was behind the bomb attack on the Berlin nightclub in 1986 which was the spark for the United States raid – The Guardian p.14, 19 NOV 1997.
545 See *supra* n527.
546 MURPHY, *supra* n525, at p.26. See also Cassese, *supra* n256, at p.607.
547 More so in the rest of the world than in the United States, where abduction from another State has primacy – so much for the sovereign equality of States.

tion to the problems that create politically motivated offenders, of whatever type, is beyond the ability of any statute, treaty or this commentator.

> "[The] international community ... must summon the necessary political will to delve into the reasons why the frustrations of the dispossessed are vented in this manner. A glib condemnation of terrorism alone, without a scientific and impartial study of its origins will not ... eradicate the pheno-menon."[548]

---

548 The Ghanaian representative, Mr Ghebo, to the U.N. Security Council, cited in Cassese, *supra n*256, at p.608.

PART II

ALTERNATIVE MECHANISMS FOR DEALING
WITH TRANSNATIONAL FUGITIVE OFFENDERS

The remaining chapters of this book will deal with matters inextricably inter-twined with and overlapping with formal extradition laws. Chapter seven will consider irregular methods of rendition. On occasions States have either ignored extradition treaties or used alternative means where no extradition treaty existed. With the growth of *ad hoc* extradition procedures in domestic extradition legislation, there should be less need for States either to abduct fugitives from other States or to connive with the requested State to use deportation to obtain the fugitive's return instead. Nevertheless, at present there is evidence to suggest that methods of rendition other than extradition are frequently used in the so-called problem cases.

The next chapter concentrates on war criminals. This group of fugitive offenders is seen as being in gross violation of international norms of human behaviour such that the whole panoply of international criminal law has been utilised against them. They have been tried before international courts and made subject to universal jurisdiction, as well as being kidnapped and de-ported. It is necessary to look at the treatment of war criminals within the law on extradition and, to do this properly and comprehensively, regard must also be had to the wider methods which have been used to deal with them. Therefore, they will be considered only after all other forms of obtaining jurisdiction have been reviewed.

Finally, the concept of refugee status with respect to extradition will be examined. Increasingly, extradition and refugee status will develop into op-posite sides of the same coin as humanitarian matters influence decisions on whether to surrender a fugitive.

7

IRREGULAR FORMS OF RENDITION

*a. Active De Facto Extradition and the Fugitive's Rights in the Requesting
State*

With faster and cheaper means of travel, it is becoming increasingly easier
for criminals to flee from the country where the crime was committed and
seek refuge in another State. Generally, as has been discussed in Part I of
this book, the country where the crime was committed will request the return
of the fugitive from the requested State under the terms of a bilateral extradition treaty. This treaty, as previously explained, will lay down the procedure to be followed on such a request and will provide certain extra defences
for the fugitive not available to him in a domestic trial.

Occasionally, however, extradition may be impossible or too slow. For
instance, there may not be a bilateral treaty between the requesting and requested States or, even if there is, the crime may not be extraditable or the
fugitive may have a defence or, finally, the length of the extradition proceedings may give the fugitive time to flee again.[1] In such cases, if the requesting State has a strong enough interest in prosecuting the fugitive, it
may try to acquire his appearance before its courts by alternative means.
These means are usually either abduction or collusive deportation. In the
case of the former, the requesting State actively utilises *de facto* or irregular
methods, while in the latter case it is more passive as the requested State
takes the measures to avoid the strict regime of extradition law. Where the
requesting State abducts the fugitive from the requested State, the rights
of both the fugitive and the requested State may have been violated, giving
rise to separate rights of action.

---

1   *Eg. R v Governor of Pentonville Prison, ex p.Teja*, [1971] 2 All ER 11.

(i) Introduction – The *Savarkar Arbitration* case[2] involved an Indian fugitive being extradited from England to India under the then Fugitive Offenders Act 1881 who jumped ship and swam ashore in Marseilles. Believing that he was a member of the crew, a French policeman arrested him and handed him over to the British police officer who was accompanying him back to India. Subsequently, the French authorities discovered the true situation and sought reparation for the alleged violation of territorial sovereignty by way of the return of Savarkar. The Permanent Court of Arbitration held that on the facts it had been an honest mistake by all concerned and that the British officers had acted in good faith. However, implicit in the judgment is the view that if the fugitive's return had been obtained by force or subterfuge, then it would have been possible for France to demand his return because of the violation of sovereignty.[3] No mention was made of an independent right for the fugitive to challenge this irregular surrender.

McNair[4] reports the *Lawler* incident in 1860, where a prisoner on Gibraltar escaped to Spain. He was recaptured by a British warder and taken back to Gibraltar; at no time was Spanish permission obtained for any of these actions. British Law Officers at the time thought that if Spain had requested reparation for the violation of territorial sovereignty, then the British Government would have had to have restored the *status quo ante*, including, possibly, the return of the prisoner to Spanish territory.[5] Again, though, no mention was made of any violation of the individual's rights.[6]

The leading abduction case must be that of Adolf Eichmann.[7] Eichmann was taken from Argentina to Israel in 1960. The abduction patently violated Argentinean sovereignty. If the abduction was by Israeli agents, then State

---

2   Scott, Hague Court Reports p.275 (1911).

3   *Supra n*2, at p.279.

4   INTERNATIONAL LAW OPINIONS, vol.1, p.78 (1956).

5   Specific restitution, envisaged in *Savarkar* and *Lawler*, was applied as a sanction in the *Temple Case (Cambodia v Thailand)*, [1962] ICJ Rep p.6. The case concerned stolen religious artefacts, however.

6   *Cf. Bozano, infra* n176.

7   The Eichmann trial in Israel is to be found at 36 INT' L REP5.5 (1961). For a discussion of the kidnap see Lasok, *The Eichmann Case*, 23 MOD.L REV.507 (1960); Cardozo, *When Extradition Fails is Abduction the Solution*, 55 AM.J INT'L L 127 (1960). See also the Vanunu Affair, The Times, p.3, 12 OCT 1986; p.2, 13 OCT 1986; p.1, 21 OCT 1986; p.14, 26 OCT 1986; p.20, 10 NOV 1986; p.1, 23 DEC 1986; p.7, 6 MAR 1987.

responsibility arose for that infringement. If, as Israel maintained throughout, it was by private individuals, then no State responsibility arose. However, even if State responsibility does arise, it may be possible for it to be settled either by the offending State surrendering the kidnappers to the offended State for trial[8] or by financial compensation. Furthermore, from the point of view of the sanctity of the extradition process, Argentina could also have claimed the return of Eichmann.[9] It did not.

The parties eventually agreed to defer to the approval of the trial by the United Nations Security Council[10] and treated the matter as closed.[11] That settled the matter as far as Argentina was concerned, but could Eichmann use the abduction as a defence before the Israeli court on the basis that his human rights had been violated? At the trial for his war crimes committed in Poland in World War II, he alleged that the court had no jurisdiction because, in taking him, Israel had violated the fundamental international rights of Argentina. The court held Eichmann had no *locus standi* to raise this point and that, regardless, under Anglo-American precedent at that time, the manner in which a person comes before a court is irrelevant to the trial. He further argued that the abduction violated his asylum in Argentina. The court summarily refuted this contention by stating that the grant of asylum is at the discretion of the State of refuge and that Argentina had never granted it.[12]

The result, that regardless of the method by which the fugitive is brought before the court, his trial will be valid, seems prejudicial to good international relations and world public order. To that end, there is good reason to adopt the Harvard Draft Convention on Extradition[13] on this point.

"*Art 16: Apprehension in Violation of International Law.* In exercising jurisdiction under this convention, no State shall prosecute or punish any person

---

88 See *Kear v Hilton*, 699 F.2d 181 (1983).

9 Preuss, *Kidnapping of Fugitives from Justice on Foreign Territory*, 29 AM.J INT'L L 502 (1935). See also the *Vincenti Affair*, vol.1, HACKWORTH'S DIGEST OF INTERNATIONAL LAW at p.624 (1920).

10 Resolution of 24th June 1960, 15 UNSCOR SPECIAL SUPP. (JAN-DEC 1960) Doc.S/ 4349.

11 *Attorney-General of the Government of Israel v Adolf Eichmann*, *supra n7*, at 59 (Dist.Ct.Jerusalem).

12 *Supra n7*, at 56-76 and 306-98 (S.Ct.Israel).

13 29 AM.J INT'L L (SUPP.) 623 (1935).

who has been brought within its territory or a place subject to its authority by recourse to measures in violation of international law or international convention, without first obtaining the consent of the State or States whose rights have been violated by such measures."

Even under this provision, the Eichmann trial would have been valid, for Argentina consented to the trial. However, it would have forced Israel to seek permission. As it was, Israel merely relied on Anglo-American precedent which ignores international public order, violations of the fugitive's human rights and State sovereignty.

(ii) The Common Law Tradition – Modern authority on active *de facto* extradition, especially international abduction, comes from the USA. An abduction to the United States may be in breach of the US Bill of Rights as well as international law. The former is only specifically relevant to the USA, but in other countries the same rights may well be guaranteed by a regional human rights convention, such as the European Convention on Human Rights[14] or the American Convention on Human Rights or the African Charter on Human and Peoples Rights.[15]

The United States takes the view that if the fugitive is before a court that has jurisdiction over his alleged offence, then the manner in which he arrived there is irrelevant except, apparently, in one very specialised case. The usual position is laid down in a doctrine known as the *Ker-Frisbie* rule. This rule is based on two decisions of the US Supreme Court, *Ker v Illinois*[16] and *Frisbie v Collins*.[17] In the former case, Ker was living in Peru. An indictment was issued against him by a grand jury in Illinois for larceny and embezzlement. The President invoked the then current extradition treaty between the United States and Peru and issued a warrant to a Pinkerton agent to take custody of Ker and return him. Unfortunately, by the time the Pinkerton agent reached Lima, Chilean forces had taken control of the town. An expeditious extradition was impossible, so the Pinkerton agent abducted Ker and took him back to the USA. In the USA, an Illinois court convicted him. He appealed to the Supreme Court contending that his right to asylum in

---

14   *Infra n*108.
15   See, generally, Chapter Four: ACHR, 9 INT.LEG.MAT.673; ACHPR, 21 INT.LEG.MAT.58.
16   119 US 436 (1886).
17   342 US 519 (1952).

Peru had been violated, that the US-Peruvian extradition treaty[18] had been ignored and that the 'due process' clause of the Fourteenth Amendment to the Constitution had been infringed, such that the Illinois court had no jurisdiction over him. Miller J, for the Court, held that Ker had no right to asylum; that could only be granted at the discretion of the Peruvian government. Moreover, the extradition treaty between the two States did not guarantee the fugitive asylum.[19] As regards the 'due process' argument, the Fourteenth Amendment was satisfied if the procedural rules for arrest and trials were met.[20] As to whether forcible abduction *per se* vitiated the court's right to hear cases, this was held to be within the province of the State courts and so the Supreme Court was incompetent to review it. The Court, therefore, decided not to pass judgment on that point.[21]

Surely, the violation of another sovereign State's territory is such a gross infringement of international law that, for the preservation of good relations between States, an abducted fugitive ought not to be tried, at least not without the express permission of the violated State. A valid analogy can be made with the principle of specialty in extradition treaties which prevents trial of offences for which the fugitive was not surrendered.[22] In the instant case, it was held relevant that Peru lodged no protest over the infringement of its territorial sovereignty by the United States government's Pinkerton agent – it might be suggested, however, that Peru was probably more concerned with a similar, but much larger, infringement by the Chilean army. The Supreme Court acknowledged, though, that Peru could request the extradition of the Pinkerton agent for kidnapping and that Ker could sue him for assault and false imprisonment.

---

18 61 B.F.S.P.1302 (1870).

19 *Supra n*16, at 442.

20 *Supra n*16, at 440. The *Frisbie* case, *supra n*17, involved no points of international law because the abduction occurred between two States of the USA. Nevertheless, it confirmed that US courts will not have regard to the manner in which the fugitive is brought before the courts.

21 *Supra n*16, at 444. Whether there was, in fact, a violation of international law in this case was doubted by Morgenstern in *Jurisdiction in Seizures Effected in Violation of International Law*, 29 BRIT.YB.INT'L L 265 at p.269 (1952).

22 *United States v Rauscher*, 119 US 407 (1886); Semmelman, *The Doctrine of Specialty in the Federal Courts: Making Sense of US v Rauscher*, 31 VA.J INT'L L 71 (1993). Fairman, *Ker v Illinois Revisited* 47 AM.J INT'L L 678 (1953).

However, a rider had to be attached to those principles following the *Jaffe* incident.[23] Jaffe was kidnapped from Canada by two private citizens of the United States for failure to answer his bail in Florida. In *Kear v Hilton*,[24] the US courts extradited his kidnappers back to Canada to face trial for abduction, in line with the remedies set out in *Ker*. In *Jaffe v Miller*,[25] the High Court of Justice of Ontario, on the other hand, held that Florida State officials involved in planning Jaffe's kidnap from Canada could claim State immunity when sued by Jaffe for the damage he suffered as a consequence of that conspiracy. Whether State immunity should be available for such a gross violation of State sovereignty culminating in a criminal act is open to question. *Jaffe v Boyles*[26] reasserted the position that the extradition treaty sets out the obligations of the State parties alone; it gave rise to no private right of action for Jaffe. However, in *Jaffe v Smith* the Court of Appeals held, *obiter*, that a fugitive might be able to object to his trial if he can prove governmental involvement in the abduction amounting to a violation of the extradition treaty.[27]

> "Absent governmental action, either through a direct violation of the treaty or through circumvention of the treaty, a fugitive has no basis upon which to challenge his/her return to the prosecuting jurisdiction .... Jaffe's removal from Canada can constitute a treaty violation only if governmental actors were involved, that is if the government conducted or condoned his removal by means other than those outlined in the [extradition] Treaty."

While it was always acknowledged that an official kidnapping would be a violation of territorial sovereignty giving rise to State responsibility, *Jaffe v Smith* may well have been conferring a new right on the fugitive.

The *Jaffe* line of decisions left unresolved several matters to do with the abduction of transnational fugitive offenders. It would, in fact, be more

---

23 *Kear v Hilton, supra n8; Jaffe v Boyles*, 616 F.Supp 1371 (1985); *Jaffe v Smith*, 825 F.2d 304 (1987); Buser, *The Jaffe Case and the Use of International Kidnapping as an Alternative to Extradition*, 14 GA.J INT'L & COMP.L 357 (1984); *Jaffe v Miller*, (1991) 73 DLR (4th) 420.
24 *Supra n8.*
25 *Supra n23*, (1991) at 424-25.
26 *Supra n23.*
27 *Supra n23*, at 307-08.

accurate to state that *Jaffe v Smith* was affirming a view previously asserted in *United States v Toscanino*,[28] but which had been severely criticised in subsequent cases, such that *Jaffe v Smith* was something of a 'Lazarine revivification by proxy'. In *Toscanino*, the Court of Appeals for the Second Circuit had considered whether abduction was a breach of international law and whether such breach should divest the courts of jurisdictional competence. Unlike *Ker-Frisbie*[29] and, for that matter, *Jaffe v Smith*, *Toscanino* had gone beyond whether the violation of the procedures in the extradition treaty ought to vitiate jurisdiction and considered whether the violation of international law *per se* was sufficient to divest the courts of competence. Although now again left languishing as one of those many cases that might be applicable in extreme circumstances following subsequent Supreme Court authority which is considered below, *Toscanino*, and for that matter *Jaffe v Smith*, raised issues that need to be considered if a true analysis of international abduction is to be made in full – both cases raise issues which are unaddressed by simply ignoring the means by which the accused's presence in court is obtained.

Toscanino concerned an Italian national living in Uruguay, from where he was exporting narcotics into the United States. Toscanino alleged that he was kidnapped by Uruguayan police in the pay of the United States government, driven to the border with Brazil and there handed over to the police of that country, also in the pay of the USA. The Brazilian police were alleged to have held him for seventeen days, during which time he was, according to his own evidence, tortured and interrogated incessantly. He also claimed that a member of the United States Department of Justice, Bureau of Narcotic and Dangerous Drugs, was present. Finally, he told the court that he was drugged and place on board a plane to the USA. He was convicted there and appealed to the District Court which affirmed the lower court's authority to try the case under the *Ker-Frisbie* rule. He then made a further appeal to the Court of Appeals for the Second Circuit. That court based its decision on the facts as set out above, but directed a hearing be held to ascertain the extent of United States involvement in the case. At that subsequent hearing, Toscanino failed to prove the presence of any members of the Bureau of

---

28 500 F.2d 267 (1974); not cited in *Jaffe v Smith*.
29 See also *United States v Crews* 455 US 467 (1980); *Stone v Powell*, 428 US 465 (1976); and *Gerstein v Pugh* 420 US 103 (1975).

Narcotic and Dangerous Drugs or any directions by them to the Uruguayan or Brazilian police.[30]

The Court of Appeals' judgment referred to the fact that the due process clause has been greatly expanded since the *Ker-Frisbie* rule was first promulgated,[31] such that the rule could no longer be binding.[32]

> "Accordingly, we view due process as now requiring a court to divest itself or jurisdiction over the person of a defendant where it has been acquired as the result of the government's deliberate, unnecessary and unreasonable invasion of the accused's constitutional rights."[33]

The court felt it relevant that the method of acquiring Toscanino was unnecessary, for extradition was possible under the United States-Uruguay treaty.[34]

Regardless of the constitutional issues, which only apply directly to abductions by or on behalf of the United States government, the court also reviewed breaches of two treaties, to which both the USA and Uruguay were parties, which guaranteed their territorial sovereignty.[35] The court rejected the contention that abduction in open defiance of an operational and applicable extradition treaty would render the courts incompetent to try the case. This opinion was subsequently confirmed by *United States v Cordero*,[36] in which the court specifically held that extradition treaties are for the sole benefit of the signatory States, although that has to be understood in the light of the judgment in *Jaffe v Smith*.[37] However, the court in *Toscanino* referred instead to the United Nations Charter[38] and the Charter of the Organisation of American States.[39] Both treaties contain clauses recognising the territorial sovereignty of the other parties and while the latter

---

30 *United States v Toscanino*, 398 F.Supp 916 (1975).
31 *Eg. Mapp v Ohio*, 367 US 643 (1961); *Miranda v Arizona*, 384 US 436 (1966); *United States v Archer*, 486 F.2d 670, 674-75 (1973).
32 *Cf.* Cases cited *supra n29*.
33 *Supra n28*, at 275.
34 *Supra n28*, at 276.
35 *Supra n28*, at 276-79.
36 668 F.2d 32 (1981).
37 *Supra n23*.
38 Signed at San Francisco, June 26th 1945. UKTS 67 (1946) Cmd 7015.
39 119 UNTS 3.

is only relevant on the American continent, the former applies to most countries throughout the world. Therefore, following the precedent laid down in *Cook v United States*,[40] the Court of Appeals in *Toscanino* decided that if the abduction violated a treaty obligation, the Courts were not competent to hear the case. If abductions are not going to be outlawed upon an extradition treaty being ignored, as Article 16 of the Harvard Draft Convention on Extradition[41] would require, the *Toscanino* ruling with respect to Article 2(4) of the United Nations Charter would present a serious obstacle to this manifestly illegal practice. That abductions breach this provision is apparent from the Eichmann resolution given by the Security Council.[42] In Europe, the breach of the Charter of the Organisation of American States can be equated with a violation of the Statute of the Council of Europe,[43] while Article 3 of the Charter of the Organisation of African Unity is similar effect.[44]

Unfortunately, *Toscarino*, although it is still good law, to has been consistently distinguished since it was decided and not one case expressly affirms it. It has been restricted to its precise facts as alleged. The Second Circuit itself avoided the ruling in *United States, ex rel.Lujan v Gengler*.[45] With two of the judges from the *Toscanino* case sitting on the bench in *Lujan*, the Court of Appeals distinguished its former decision on two grounds. First, that there was no torture, terror or custodial interrogation, and, secondly, because in order for the treaty violation to oust the court's jurisdiction, the offended State or States must have made a complaint; the accused did not allege this in the instant case.[46] This view severely limited the *ratio* of *Toscanino* with respect to its analysis of treaty violations and it would have been preferable for the court in *Lujan* to have required the requested

---

40 288 US 102 at 121-22 (1933).

41 *Supra* n13.

42 *Supra* n10.

43 ETS 1 (1949).

44 2 INT.LEG.MAT.766 (1963).

45 510 F.2d 62 (1975); see also *United States v Lira*, 515 F.2d 68 (1975), (*cf.* the opinion of Oakes CJ and Sarosdy, Case Note, 54 TEX L REV.1439 (1976)); *In the Matter of the Extradition of Atta, Ahmad v Wigen* 706 F.Supp 1032 (1989), 726 F.Supp 389 at 409-20 (1989), rev'd on this point 910 F.2d 1063 at 1066-67 (1990); and *United States v Orsini*, 424 F.Supp 229 (1976), *aff'd* 559 F.2d 1206 (1977).

46 *Supra* n45, at 68.

State's express consent to the trial of the abductee in the USA, rather than mere silence from the offended State. However, this presumption in favour of the prosecuting State, merely reflects the view that treaties and customary international law are matters for States not individuals.[47]

Outside the Second Circuit *Toscanino* fared even worse. The Fifth Circuit rejected it outright,[48] while the other Circuits have reserved their opinion.[49] The case of *United States v Noriega*[50] arose out of the United States' military action in Panama in December 1989, which resulted in Noriega's surrender to United States troops on 3 January 1990. In the Court of Appeals, the court decided, *inter alia*,[51] that the fact that he had been brought back following a military invasion of Panama during which significant numbers of Panamanian civilians were injured and lost property did not mean that

> "the manner in which he was brought before the district court was so unconscionable as to constitute a violation of substantive due process [and, that in the alternative,] the district court should exercise its supervisory power to decline jurisdiction."[52]

The court followed the *Ker-Frisbie*[53] doctrine, declined to follow *Toscanino*[54] on the ground that the injuries were to third parties, not the accused, and held the District Court to have been competent. It would seem, therefore, that bearing in mind the circumstances of Noriega's 'arrest', treatment of the fugitive by United States officials would have to be outrageous

---

47   *Cordero, supra n*36, and *United States v Williams*, 617 F.2d 1063 (1980). *Cf.* *Ker, supra n*16, at 444.

48   *United States v Herrera*, 504 F.2d 859 (1974).

49   *United States v Lovato*, 520 F.2d 1270 at 1271 (1975, CA9); *United States v Valot*, 625 F.2d 308 (1980); *Darby, Yamanis & Calise*, 744 F.2d 1508 (1984, CA11). In *Darby* the court questioned the whole basis of *Toscanino*, without rejecting it though, quoting from *Gerstein v Pugh, supra n*29, at 119, where the Supreme Court
     "refused to retreat from the established rules that illegal arrest or detention does not void a subsequent conviction."

50   746 F.Supp 1506 (1990); 808 F.Supp 791 (1992); 117 F.3d 1206 (1997).

51   Apart from some evidential issues, Noriega also challenged his conviction on the basis of head of State immunity – rejected, *supra n*50, at 1212 (1997).

52   *Supra n*50, at 1214; see generally, 1213-15 (1997).

53   *Supra nn*16 and 17.

54   *Supra n*28.

if it is to be "so unconscionable as to constitute a violation of substantive due process" and any discretion to decline jurisdiction would be contemplated. In *Matta-Ballesteros v Henman*,[55] the Seventh Circuit declined to follow *Toscanino* because the Supreme Court had twice reaffirmed the *Ker-Frisbie* rule since the *Toscanino* judgment; however, this reasoning missed the point that the Supreme Court, unlike the Second Circuit Court of Appeals, had still to consider whether abduction from a foreign State should vitiate jurisdiction because of the violation of international law occasioned in apprehending the fugitive. Nevertheless, unless there are "grossly cruel and unusual barbarities", then *Toscanino* is not going to be followed.[56]

---

55 895 F.2d 255; 896 F.2d 255 (1990).
56 *Lovato, supra n*49, at 1271. Even where prison conditions are disgusting and degrading, this will not suffice; *Cordero, supra n*36.
    The due process and other constitutional issues raise one other relevant question, that is to what extent and on whom does the US Bill of Rights confer protection outside the USA. Within the USA, aliens and citizens enjoy similar protection [*Graham v Richardson* 403 US 365 (1971); *Foley v Connelie*, 435 US 291, (1978)]. It has been argued by Stephan [*Constitutional Limits on International Rendition of Criminal Suspects*, 20 VA.J INT'L L 777, (1980)], however, that outside the USA the constitutional protections only extend to United States' citizens, permanent resident aliens and foreign nationals possessing 'substantial' ties with the United States. Apart from the difficulty in assessing who possesses 'substantial' ties, the test is open to abuse; information obtained in violation of the Constitution from someone not protected would be inadmissible if the infringement took place in the USA, whereas, for example, it would be good evidence if obtained a mile beyond the Mexican border. Furthermore, Stephan's argument ignores the fact that United States officials only obtain any of the powers they do have through the Constitution. If they are using Constitutional powers, surely Constitutional obligations as set out in the Bill of Rights ought to apply, too. As Saltzburg [*The Reach of the Bill of Rights Beyond the Terra Firma of the United States*, 20 VA.J INT'L L 741 (1980)] explains.
    "The government of the United States has only the powers entrusted to it by the Constitution. Whenever and wherever it acts it relies on the Constitution as the source of its powers. Whenever it acts, it must, therefore, accept the limits on its powers imposed by the same Constitution that provides the affirmative grant of power [*Kinsella v United States, ex rel Singleton*, 361 US 234 (1960); *Mitchell v Harmony*, 54 US (13 HOW.) 115 (1852); *Stockwell v United States*, 405 F.2d 738 at 751, Browning J dissenting, *cert.den* 395 US 960 (1969)]. Thus, the Bill of Rights controls the activities of the United States law enforcement officers wherever they occur."

In the related cases of *United States of America v Humberto Al-varez-Machain*[57] and *United States of America v Rene Martin Verdugo-Ur-quidez*,[58] the Supreme Court reasserted the *Ker-Frisbie* doctrine. Both Machain and Verdugo had been abducted from Mexico in relation to an investigation into the torture and murder of a United States DEA official and had been brought to the USA. There was an extradition treaty in force between the US and Mexico.[59] The Court of Appeals for the Ninth Circuit held that if the Mexican Government had protested about the kidnapping of each man, then jurisdiction was vitiated and the appropriate reparation was repatriation of the two accuseds to Mexico. An accused might successfully plead a breach of an international extradition agreement where the violated State made a protest. Such a stance by the Court of Appeals reflected the fact that State sovereignty had been breached by the taking of a person from within a State where he has committed no offence and the proper remedy was to restore the *status quo ante*, incidentally correcting the infringement of abductee's human rights – it also recognises that extradition is the accepted method of international rendition and that the use of an alternative where extradition is available ignores the procedural guarantees it provides.

However, the United States Supreme Court in June 1992 reversed the Court of Appeals' decisions in *Machain* and *Verdugo* by a six to three majority,[60] Rehnquist CJ giving the prevailing judgment of the Court. The Supreme Court held that the decision in *Ker* governed the jurisdiction of trial courts – if the accused is before the court, then the means by which his presence was acquired is irrelevant to the standing of those proceedings. It is almost as if extradition laws and treaties are a subset of the *Ker* rule. The majority's reasoning, however, lacks persuasiveness. Rehnquist CJ starts by rejecting any claim that the US-Mexican treaty expressly prohibits forcible

---

See also Pregent, *Presidential Authority to Displace Customary International Law*, 129 MIL.L REV.77 (1990), and Evans, *International Kidnapping in a Violent World: where the United States Ought to Draw the Line*, 137 MIL.L REV.187 (1992) .

57 946 F.2d 1466 (1991). See also, 745 F.Supp.599 (1990).
58 939 F.2d 1341 (1991).
59 Given that both men were Mexican nationals, though, there was no real possibility that Mexico would extradite them to the USA if a request had been made.
60 *United States v Alvarez-Machain*, 504 US 655 (1995).

abduction, as though two States negotiating an international agreement would make provision for the possible violation by one of the parties of the territorial sovereignty of the other, contrary to customary international law and antithetic to the very instrument under discussion. The judgment even refers to the 1906 *Martinez* incident,[61] ignoring the fact that both *Ker* and *Martinez* were cases of private individuals abducting fugitives, rather than federal agents as in *Machain*.[62] Nevertheless, in line with *Machain*, the Court of Appeals in *Noriega* held that the fact that there was a US-Panama Extradition Treaty did not mean that the presence of the fugitive before a United States court through means other than extradition rendered the court incompetent.[63]

Furthermore, the majority in *Machain* went on to reject the idea that customary international law might give rise to an implied provision in the extradition treaty vitiating jurisdiction where the fugitive had been kidnapped by State officials from another sovereign State.

"In a broad sense, most international agreements have the common purpose of safeguarding the sovereignty of signatory nations, in that they seek to further peaceful relations between nations. This, however, does not mean that the violation of any principle of international law constitutes a violation of this particular treaty."[64]

In fact, the Supreme Court ducked the issue and held that the return of a fugitive who had been abducted and where the violated State protested, as Mexico had done, was a matter not for the courts, but rather the Executive which had instigated and perpetrated the breach of international law in the first place.

The dissenting opinion of Stevens J[65] in *Machain*[66] is instructive and shows that while the individual case may have been lost, the arguments in favour of international abduction are not legally watertight, nor, for that matter, practically sound. The dissent adopts the common-sense position that where two States have concluded an international agreement for the

---

61 *Supra n*60, at n.11 at 666.
62 See dissent at 682 and n.30 of the judgment at 685; *supra n*60.
63 *Supra n*50, at 1212-13 (1997).
64 *Supra n*60, at n.14 of the judgment at 668.
65 Joined by Blackmun and O'Connor JJ.
66 *Supra n*60, at 670.

return of fugitive offenders, then no such person should return to face trial by the unilateral action of one party. An extradition treaty must be exclusive, otherwise the inter-State procedural and the fugitive's human rights guarantees are "little more than verbiage".[67] Stevens J went on to show that it was the accepted view of leading international law commentators that if the violated State protested, then the proceedings to prosecute the abductee ought not to take place.[68] The crimes with which Machain was charged were serious and deserving of punishment, but that did not justify United States officials snatching him from Mexico.

"It is ironic that the United States has attempted to justify its unilateral action based on the kidnapping, torture, and murder of a federal agent by authorizing the kidnapping of respondent, for which the American law enforcement agents who participated have now been charged by Mexico. This goes to my earlier point that extradition treaties promote harmonious relations by providing for the orderly surrender of a person by one State to another, and without such treaties, resort to force often followed."[69]

One immediate consequence of the *Machain* decision was that Mexico withdrew its co-operation with the United States to counter drug trafficking until the latter agreed to revise the relevant legal instruments.[70] However, it is the dissent by Brandeis J in *Olmstead v United States*[71] that best generally describes why human rights are better protected if, *inter alia*, extradition treaties are utilised rather than kidnap.

---

67 *Supra n60*, at 673.
68 See LAUTERPACHT, OPPENHEIM'S INTERNATIONAL LAW, vol.1, at p.295 (8th ed.; 1955). Henkin, *A Decent Respect to the Opinions of Mankind*, 25 JOHN MARSHALL LJ 215 at p.231 (1992). Abbell, The Need for US Legislation to Curb State-Sponsored Kidnapping, in ATKINS, THE ALLEGED TRANSNATIONAL CRIMINAL (1995), at pp.87-93; *cf.* Woltring and Greig, State-Sponsored Kidnapping of Fugitives: An Alternative to Extradition, at pp.115-25. AMERICAN LAW INSTITUTE, RESTATEMENT OF THE LAW OF FOREIGN RELATIONS OF THE UNITED STATES §432 and Comment c. (3d, 1986).
69 *Supra n60*, at n.12 at 675.
70 See The Guardian p.8, 17 JUN 1992, and p.11, 19 JUN 1992. Ironically, on remand to the trial court in California, the case against Machain failed for lack of evidence.
71 277 US 438 at 485 (1928), cited in *Machain, supra n60*, at n.33 at 687.

"In a government of laws, existence of the government will be imperilled if it fails to observe the law scrupulously. Our Government is the potent, the omnipresent teacher. For good or for ill, it teaches the whole people by its example. Crime is contagious. If the Government becomes a law-breaker, it breeds contempt for law; it invites every man to become a law unto himself; it invites anarchy. To declare that in the administration of the criminal law the end justifies the means – to declare that the Government may commit crimes in order to secure the conviction of a private criminal – would bring terrible retribution. Against that pernicious doctrine this Court should resolutely set its face."

On another tack, however, academics have also questioned whether it is appropriate for United States judges to inquire into the foreign policy of the United States; their comments are equally relevant to cases in any country. Foreign policy, it is suggested, is a question for the executive, not the judiciary: judges may well harm international relations by their decisions. In as much as abduction can be viewed as foreign policy, however, it must harm international relations and so disapproval by any branch of government is to be welcomed. This same argument can be used in support of the discredited theory that violations of Article 2(4) of the United Nations Charter *per se* ought to vitiate proceedings. The courts should not hear the case and thereby implicitly condone a breach of such a fundamental treaty entered into by the governments of most States in the world. Nevertheless, although one of many issues in the case, international abduction was sanctioned in *United States v Noriega*.[72] A clearer example of actions challenging Article 2(4) of the United Nations Charter it would be harder to find. In the first District Court hearing, Noriega tried to rely on Article 2(4) of the Charter, but it was held that individuals in court could only rely on international treaties if the affected State complained or if the treaty was self-executing – neither avenue was available to Noriega.[73]

In conclusion on the United States law, however, the majority's decision in *Machain* may, despite *Noriega* which can be explained away as *sui gene-*

---

72 *Supra n*50.

73 *Supra n*50, at 1532-34 (1990). He did not continue with this argument in subsequent hearings.

ris and as 'tidying up' earlier problems,[74] hasten the demise of State-sponsored kidnaps of alleged international criminals, for it has brought to the fore this attempt to authorize the "manifestly illegal".[75]

In the past, the United Kingdom,[76] like the United States, was treated as considering the mode by which the fugitive arrived before the court as irrelevant, as well. The authorities cited in support of this argument were *Ex p.Susannah Scott*[77] and *Ex p.Elliott*.[78] Scott was wanted for perjury and was 'arrested' by an English police officer in Brussels and returned to England. In England she was brought before Tenterden LCJ. He considered that the question the court had to answer was whether a person charged with a crime in the United Kingdom was amenable to the jurisdiction of the courts regardless of the circumstances under which she was apprehended. He decided the court could not inquire into the manner in which the fugitive was brought to the United Kingdom. Yet his Lordship's reasoning completely disregards whether there was a breach of international law at all. He is concerned solely with any infringements of the domestic law of the United Kingdom and Belgium.

> "If the act complained of were done against the law of a foreign country, that country might have vindicated its own law. If it gave her a right of action, she may sue upon it."[79]

Thus, the case cannot be authority for the proposition that a breach of international law will not divest English courts of jurisdiction, since this matter was not considered.

---

74 The invasion of Panama was in 1989 – the Court of Appeals was only seized of the matter in 1997.
75 The US Department of Justice held that *Machain* should not be seen as a green light for international kidnapping of fugitives. Moreover, the Inter-American Juridical Committee gave a legal opinion holding that the kidnap was a serious violation of public international law – 32 INT.LEG.MAT.277 (1993).
76 See O'Higgins, *Unlawful Seizure and Irregular Extradition*, 36 BRIT.YB.INT'L L 279 (1960).
77 109 ER 166 (1829).
78 [1949] 1 All ER 373.
79 *Supra n77*, at 167.

In *R v O/C Depot Battalion, RASC, Colchester, ex p. Elliot*,[80] the defendant was a deserter from the army. He had been 'arrested' in Antwerp by British and Belgian police and held in custody there for two days. He was returned to England via an army base in West Germany, whereupon he applied for *habeas corpus*. Goddard LCJ held it was no answer to the apparent lawfulness of his detention for the defendant to allege that he was arrested abroad contrary to the laws of that State. The Lord Chief Justice was of the opinion that an action might lie against the arresting officers, but that the courts could still try the fugitive.

Yet again, the question of whether an 'arrest'[81] by a British policeman in a foreign country in breach of that State's sovereignty and, therefore, in violation of international law would oust the competence of the court was not considered. Unlike *Ex p.Scott*, this 'arrest' was carried out with the aid of Belgian police, but since he was then taken to England in complete disregard of the processes of extradition law, the treaty obligations must have been ignored or even violated. With all due respect to the judges involved, the decisions evince inadequate and incomplete reasoning with regard to all the questions raised.

Before 1993, only one case had ever considered whether a breach of international law would vitiate jurisdiction, and, even then, it was only *obiter*. *R v Garrett ex p.Sharf et al.*[82] involved the arrest of four Russians on board a Danish ship which had been brought into an English harbour to search for contraband. The Russians were charged under Reg.45(b), Defence of the Realm Regulations Consolidated 1916, with having knowingly made false declarations in order to obtain passports. The passports were issued by the Russian consulate in London and the four were on their way to Denmark to catch a ship to the USA. Following their arrest, no complaint was received from either the Russian or Danish governments. At their trial at Bow Street Police Court, the four alleged the magistrate had no jurisdiction because their arrest took place on the high seas and that the English police authorities lacked jurisdiction outside territorial waters. On appeal by way of case stated, Viscount Reading CJ rejected their argument by saying

---

80 *Supra n*78.

81 Outside the territorial jurisdiction of England and Wales, a British policeman has no authority at all. Thus, any detention overseas cannot be a lawful arrest. However, see the discussion on hot pursuit below.

82 (1917), 86 LJ(KB) 894; [1917] 2 KB 99.

the arrest actually took place in Kirkwall harbour. However, he went on to say, *obiter*, that an arrest on the high seas would raise a question requiring careful consideration.[83] Furthermore, he averted to the issue again at the end of his judgment, where he said it may be possible for some defendants to raise the issue without the intervention of the State whose international rights had been violated – in this case, Denmark. However, because, Viscount Reading had held the arrest took place in the United Kingdom, the instant case had not give rise to such a problem.[84]

In conclusion, none of the early English cases had ever dealt head-on with the question of jurisdiction in relation to a violation of international law. The *obiter dictum* of Viscount Reading CJ is all that existed and, since it preceded *Ex p.Elliott*, one could not say with certainty that it would be followed if the problem ever presented itself again. However, from the beginning of the 1980s, the English courts had considered the possibility of refusing jurisdiction, not because of any violation of international law, but to prevent abuse of their own process.[85] In *R v Bow Street Magistrates, ex p.Mackeson*,[86] the Court of Appeal had to decide whether to divest itself of jurisdiction where the accused had been returned by way of deportation rather than extradition.[87] He had been arrested in, as it then was, Rhodesia, with which the United Kingdom had no extradition relations. However, he was eventually deported by the officials of the newly independent Zimbabwe, to which the Fugitive Offenders Act 1881[88] and related legislation did apply. It was alleged that British police officers instigated and played a large

---

83 *Supra n*82, at 898.
84 *Supra n*82, at 900.
85 See Warbrick, *Irregular Extradition*, [1983] PUB.LAW 269, and Kodwo Bentil, *When Extradition Masquerades as Deportation*, 127 SOL.JO.604 (1983). *Cf. DPP v Sang*, [1980] AC 402.
86 (1981), 75 Cr.App.R 24. See also *United States v Lira*, 515 F.2d 68 (1975), where the fugitive was expelled from Chile because extradition was impossible since he was a Chilean national.
87 The principle would apply to an abduction case, too. See *Ex p.Elliott, supra n*78.
88 The Rhodesian government was not party to the 1966 SCHEME RELATING TO THE RENDITION OF FUGITIVE OFFENDERS WITHIN THE COMMONWEALTH, Cmnd 3008, so the old imperial statute of 1881 was probably still applicable. See Lord Lane CJ, *supra n*86, at 33. If no extradition arrangement is in force, then the *Mackeson* argument is irrelevant.

part in obtaining Mackeson's deportation. The question which arose, therefore, was whether jurisdiction should not be accepted because the appropriate extradition law had been deliberately avoided. Lord Lane CJ, having regard to cases from New Zealand[89] and Australia,[90] decided to exercise the court's discretion and declined jurisdiction.

"[The Court] rejected any suggestion that [extradition] could be put in motion by any constable who thought he knew the law of a foreign country, and thought it desirable that a person whom he thought he suspected of having offended against that law should be surrendered to that country to be punished."[91]

After *Mackeson* it seemed that where extradition was deliberately avoided, or even possibly where it was not used when available, then the courts would be willing to exercise their discretion not to hear the case. This optimistic view was soon dispelled in relation to the latter scenario in *Healy*.[92] Here the defendant, while on bail, went to the United States using a false passport. He was arrested in Los Angeles and was served with a deportation order. At the hearing before the Immigration Tribunal two British police officers gave evidence of the charges the defendant would face on return to the United Kingdom. Following the initial hearing, the two policemen returned to the United Kingdom and, after several further hearings, the defendant was deported from the United States and arrived back in London. After being indicted, he applied for judicial review. The Divisional Court distinguished *Mackeson* on the basis that the British police in *Healy* did not influence the US inquiries in any improper way. It was perfectly permissible to provide immigration authorities with information about how the accused entered the country and his previous crimes in the United Kingdom, whereas the police in *Mackeson* had suggested deportation and actively urged on the proceedings according to the evidence. There was no such collusion in *Healy*.[93]

---

89 *R v Hartley*, [1978] 2 NZLR 199.
90 *Brown v Lizars*, (1905), 2 CLR 837.
91 *Ex p.Mackeson*, *supra* n86, at 33, citing *Hartley*, *supra* n89 at 216-17 where the NZ judge was citing Griffith CJ in *Brown v Lizars*, *supra* n90, at 852.
92 *R v Guildford Magistrates Court, ex p.Healy*, [1983] 1 WLR 108.
93 *Supra* n92, at 113, *per* Griffiths LJ.

Following *Healy*, therefore, where extradition had been deliberately avoided at the instigation of British authorities, the courts could exercise their discretion, but not otherwise. This interpretation of *Mackeson* and *Healy* was reconsidered in *Driver*,[94] which dealt with the return of the accused from Turkey. No-one denied that British and Turkish authorities had worked together to return Driver to the United Kingdom. It was held, though, that *Mackeson* was, in fact, inapplicable because no extradition treaty existed with Turkey at the time, and that police activity had been more on a par with *Healy* than *Mackeson*.[95] However, although unable to overrule *Mackeson* under the principles of *stare decisis*,[96] the Divisional Court's *obiter dicta* in *Driver* undermined *Mackeson's* authority. Referring at length to English, Scottish and United States case law, Stephen Brown LJ decided that there was, in fact, no discretion to refuse jurisdiction if the defendant is before the court simply on the grounds of the means used to produce him there. *Mackeson* and *Healy*, which both spoke of this discretion, had accordingly been decided *per incuriam* if *Driver* was correct.[97] The Lord Justice held that the New Zealand case of *Hartley*[98] was in error in its interpretation of *Elliott*.[99] *Driver* held that there was, in fact, no discretion for a court to deny itself competence on the basis of the means used to bring the accused before the court in Anglo-American jurisprudence.[100] This view, however, ignored the English decision of *Ex p.Sharf* and *Toscanino*[101] from the United States, neither of which were cited in *Driver*.

The current English law, however, has been laid down by the House of Lords in *Bennett v Horseferry Road Magistrates' Court*.[102] The accused's claim was that he had been kidnapped in South Africa and, as a result of collusion between the South African authorities and the English police, forcibly returned to England without recourse to lawful extradition

---

94 *R v Plymouth Magistrates Court et al., ex p.Driver*, [1985] 2 All ER 681.
95 *Supra n*94, implicit in the judgment of Stephen Brown LJ at 690-91.
96 *Supra n*94, at 697-98, citing *R v Greater Manchester Coroner, ex p.Tal*, [1984] 3 All ER 240.
97 *Driver, supra n*94, at 698.
98 *Supra n*89.
99 *Supra n*78.
100 *Supra n*94, at pp.695-97.
101 *Supra n*28. The US authorities cited in *Driver* were at least thirty years old.
102 [1994] 1 AC 42, [1993] 3 All ER 138.

procedures.[103] The House of Lords held that the English High C(
authority to inquire as to the means adopted to bring the fugitive b(
reversing *Driver*[104] – disregard of extradition procedures, however, is a
prerequisite to the court staying the prosecution as an abuse of process and
ordering the fugitive's release.

> "If the court is to have the power to interfere with the prosecution in the
> present circumstances it must be because the judiciary accept a responsibility
> for the maintenance of the rule of law that embraces a willingness to oversee
> executive action and to refuse to countenance behaviour that threatens either
> basic human rights or the rule of law. My Lords, I have no doubt that the
> judiciary should accept this responsibility in the field of criminal law."[105]

Furthermore, not only does abduction breach international law according
to the House of Lords, it is a violation of the human rights of the fugitive,
sufficient to vitiate the jurisdiction of the courts in such circumstances.[106]
Thus, the two strands of argument previously proposed in the Divisional
Court for justifying the exercise of a discretion to deny competence have
both been accepted by the House of Lords. The fact that the fugitive was
under the sovereign protection of another State, therefore, provides certain
basic guarantees which ought to be respected by all other States according
to English law.[107]

---

103 *R v Commissioner for the Police of the Metropolis, ex parte Bennett*, QBD, 1
November 1994, unreported, per Rose LJ.

104 *Supra n*94.

105 *Bennett, supra n*102, at 61H and 150, respectively.

106 The limit on *Bennett, supra n*102, is that it prevents the trial, but not the issuing
of a warrant for the fugitive's arrest once back in the United Kingdom – *R v
Commissioner of Police for the Metropolis, ex parte Bennett, supra n*103.

107 *Bennett* would seem to be limited to challenging a criminal trial before English
courts. Where a fugitive from Germany was lured to the United Kingdom from
Ireland, a German extradition request having already been denied there, it was
held that *Bennett* could be distinguished; it did not protect someone being sought
by a third country through extradition proceedings in the English courts –
Schmidt v Federal Government of Germany [1994] 2 All ER 65, esp. at 77; see
also, *Atta, supra n*45; and see Walker, *Internal Cross-Border Policing Within
the United Kingdom: the High Road or the Low Road to Effective Co-operation*,
56 CLJ 114 at pp.120-21 (1997).

The other option open to an accused, is to apply for relief under the European Convention on Human Rights.[108] Article 3 is as follows:

> "No-one shall be subjected to torture or to inhuman and degrading treatment or punishment."

Disregarding the torture element, forcible abduction succeeded by enforced transit to a foreign country might qualify as inhuman or degrading treatment. In the alternative, if the Strasbourg organs find that this general provision has not been infringed, one can turn to the more specific terms of Article 5:

> "(1) Everyone has the right to liberty and security of the person. No-one shall be deprived of his liberty save in the following cases and in accordance with a procedure prescribed by law: ....
> (c) the lawful arrest or detention of a person effected for the purpose of bringing him before the competent legal authority on reasonable suspicion of having committed an offence or when it is reasonably considered necessary to prevent his committing an offence or fleeing after having done so."

Abduction is so obviously illegal[109] that it fails the requirement of paragraph (1) that the arrest be in accordance with a legally prescribed procedure. Moreover, it does not meet the rule set out in sub-paragraph (c) that the arrest be lawful. If an arrest is effected by a British police officer in another country, he lacks any form of authority outside the territorial limits of the United Kingdom. An arrest by a police officer of the requested State may be *prima facie* lawful, but if effected for the purpose of assisting in the fugitive's kidnap or deportation to the prosecuting State on orders from that State's authorities, it will be unlawful as regards the Convention. The thorny problem of the requested State turning a blind eye to the activities of its police officer still remains; however, having regard merely to the wording of the Article 5(1)(f), an arrest made with a view to a subsequent extradition is expressly held to be lawful and, thus, since abduction and collusive deportation clandestinely avoid extradition, an arrest for either purpose must,

---

108 European Convention for the Protection of Human Rights and Fundamental Freedoms, ETS 5 (1950); hereinafter, ECHR.
109 SHEARER, EXTRADITION IN INTERNATIONAL LAW, at p.75 (1971).

by definition, be unlawful. Therefore, if a fugitive is convicted after having been abducted by or on behalf of the United Kingdom authorities, he could try to seek redress in the form of his release and compensation before the European Court of Human Rights. Even if remedies are available under the ECHR, though, it must still be recognised that these do not reflect the violation of general international law, but infringements of the Convention itself.

Other common law countries have equally been grappling with the issue of whether jurisdiction should be waived where the accused was brought before the court by irregular means. For many years, excepting New Zealand,[110] the prevailing view was that jurisdiction would not be rejected because of the means by which the accused was brought before the court. The Canadian case of *Re Hartnett and Hudson and The Queen*[111] was permissive. However, having regard to the change in approach wrought by the passing of the 1982 Canadian Charter of Rights and Freedoms as part of the Constitution Act, as evidenced by decisions such as *R v Jewitt*,[112] it may be that pre-1982 law would now be suspect on this matter. The South African cases of *Abrahams v Minister of Justice* and *The State v Heymann and Dinzaka*[113] also permitted the prosecution to proceed, despite the fact the accused were returned to South Africa by irregular means. Nevertheless, in *The State v Ebrahim*,[114] the South African Supreme Court, relying on Roman Law, Roman-Dutch Law of the 16th-18th centuries and *Toscanino*,[115] held that under both types of legal system illegal rendition should render the courts incompetent and that *Toscanino* reflected the proper rule. Furthermore, in *Beahan v State*,[116] the Zimbabwe Supreme Court decided that if a transnational fugitive offender were to be brought back to the State in violation of the sovereignty of another State, then the court should decline jurisdiction.

---

110 *Hartley, supra n*89.

111 (1973), 14 CCC (2nd) 169 (Ont.H.C.J.); see also, *Miyanda v The Attorney-General*, (1992) 88 INT'L L REP.263 (Zambian S.Ct).

112 (1983), 5 CCC (3rd) 234 (BCCA); see also Peiris, *Legal Protection of Human Rights: the Contemporary Canadian Experience*, [1985] LEG.STUD.261 at p.276.

113 *Abrahams*, [1963] So.Afr.L Rep.542, cited in [1963] ANN.SURV.SO.AFR.L 38; *Heymann and Dinzaka*, [1966] 4 So.Afr.L Rep.599.

114 31 INT.LEG.MAT.888 (1992)

115 *Supra n*28.

116 103 INT'L L REP.203 (Zimbabwe S.Ct, 1991).

"In my opinion it is essential that in order to promote confidence in and respect for the administration of justice and preserve the judicial process from contamination, a court should decline to compel an accused person to undergo a trial in circumstances where his appearance before it has been facilitated by an act of abduction undertaken by the prosecuting State. There is an inherent objection to such a course both on grounds of public policy pertaining to international ethical norms and because it imperils and corrodes the peaceful coexistence and mutual respect of sovereign nations. For abduction is illegal under international law .... A contrary view would amount to a declaration that the end justifies the means, thereby encouraging States to become law-breakers in order to secure the conviction of a private individual."[117]

Where the mode of surrender resulted in a breach of the fugitive's fundamental rights, then it was held that the court would have a discretion to decline jurisdiction.[118]

(iii) The Civil Law Tradition – The usefulness to States of irregular rendition is so great on occasions that it is not surprising to find that courts in civil law States also refuse to divest themselves of jurisdiction. In the Belgian case of *Geldof v Meulemeister and Steffen*,[119] the *Cour de Cassation* held that the balance must be in favour of prosecuting an alleged criminal. The French *Cour de Cassation* in *Re Argoud*[120] decided that French courts would only be deprived of jurisdiction if the State from which the accused was taken objected and sought his return. This position was reiterated in *Barbie*.[121] The means by which the accused is brought before the court are irrelevant.[122] Finally, the Italian courts did not refuse to try the case of the *Achille Lauro* seajackers,[123] even though their presence there was

---

117 *Per* Gubbay CJ, *supra* n116, at 214.
118 *Supra* n116, at 216-17.
119 31 INT'L L REP.385 (*Cr de Cass.*), cited in SHEARER, *supra* n109, at p.74. See also, *RHK v The Netherlands*, 100 INT'L L REP.412 (Dutch S.Ct).
120 45 INT'L L REP.90 (1964).
121 78 INT'L L REP.125 (*Cr de Cass.*, 1983).
122 *Supra* n121, at 131. *NB* There was no valid Franco-Bolivian extradition treaty.
123 See McGinley, The *Achille Lauro* Case: A Case Study in Crisis Law, Policy and Management at p.323 of BASSIOUNI, LEGAL RESPONSES TO INTERNATIONAL TERRORISM (1988).

due to the illegal actions of the United States in forcing the 'plane in which they were travelling to land in Italian territory.[124] On the other hand, *Ebrahim*[125] was argued on the basis of *Toscanino*, and also Roman law and Roman-Dutch law.

(iv) Conclusion – On present authority, a fugitive who is brought before criminal courts in breach of international law may still be tried, but there is a growing trend to give courts a discretion to refuse jurisdiction, most forcefully expressed by Gubbay CJ in *Beahan*.[126] The fact that there is a valid extradition treaty that would have been applicable in the instant case is increasingly relevant as to whether the courts will decide to discontinue the proceedings where it has been ignored. The traditional approach of ignoring the means by which the fugitive appeared before the courts was harmful to both international public order and human rights. The *Eichmann* abduction led to a United Nations Security Council debate. In a 1982 kidnap from Bolivia by the Italian government, a neo-fascist responsible for the 1980 Bologna Railway Station bombing, Pierluigi Pagliai, was fatally wounded and died without recovering from the coma in a Rome Hospital.[127] This happened even with the help of the requested State, Bolivia. As far as is known to this writer, the processes of extradition have yet to kill anyone.[128] Nevertheless, it is only the United States where the courts still cling to the traditional approach; elsewhere, it is recognised that the State must be seen to be abiding by the law.

The problem remains, though, that extradition cannot meet all situations where rendition is required. To date, deportation and expulsion have proved much more popular.[129] However since no-one acknowledges their lawful use, the practice is inherently informal and lacks guidelines to protect the individual. What is unacceptable is for States to obtain jurisdiction by means

---

124 *Supra* n123, at p.353. See also, CASSESE, TERRORISM, POLITICS AND LAW, at pp.101 *et seq.* (1989).

125 *Supra* n114.

126 *Supra* n116.

127 The Guardian p.1, 6 NOV 1982.

128 There is an extant, valid extradition treaty between Bolivia and Italy, concluded in 1901.

129 See Evans, *International Procedures for the Apprehension and Rendition of Fugitive Offenders*, [1980] A.S.I.L PROC.274.

of abduction. Since deportation of fugitive offenders will never be abolished in full, a regulated system must be devised to operate alongside formal and *ad hoc* extradition procedures. However, abduction violates both international public order and the individual's most basic human rights.

> "Abduction is such a manifestly extra-legal act, and in practice so hazardous and uncertain, that it is unworthy of consideration as an alternative method to extradition in securing custody of the offender."[130]

Its manifest illegality ought not to be approved, implicitly at least, by the judiciary accepting jurisdiction to try the fugitive. Abduction denies the fugitive's rights and ignores the proper and negotiated mechanism for obtaining the surrender of criminals who have fled the jurisdiction. Thankfully, abduction is rarely used[131] and is increasingly condemned by the courts before which the transnational fugitive offender is brought for prosecution.

b.   Passive De Facto Extradition and the Fugitive's Rights in the Requested State

So far, only the protection afforded to a fugitive who has been returned to the requesting State without use of the processes of extradition has been considered. However, can a fugitive do anything whilst still in the State where he sought refuge to guarantee himself a safe haven or at least to obtain the safeguards contained in extradition laws?

It is obvious that no State would actively encourage a violation of its sovereignty by letting other States abduct fugitives at will. Indeed, the United Kingdom, which, as was seen above, used to accept jurisdiction over fugitives no matter how they come before its courts until the 1990s, was strongly critical of Nigeria, another member of the Commonwealth, when the latter State tried to kidnap Umaru Dikko, one its own nationals, from London.

---

130 SHEARER, *supra* n109, at p.75.
131 *Cf.* At time of writing, the trial is about to start of Ilich Ramírez Sánchez, *a.k.a.* Carlos or The Jackal, who was 'kidnapped' by the French secret service in August 1994 with the connivance of Sudan where he was living at the time – see The Guardian *The Week* pp.1 and 2, 8 NOV 1997.

Relations between the two countries were severely strained.[132] On the other hand, no State wishes to keep another State's criminals within its borders, even if extradition is not possible in the circumstances. Several more or less formal mechanisms are open to the requested State to assist in the return of a fugitive offender to the requesting State as an alternative to the extradition process.

The first of these methods is 'hot pursuit',[133] which is undergoing a revival in Europe. It is not a new concept,[134] allowing, as it does, for the police authorities of one State to cross into a neighbouring State in order to effect the arrest of a fugitive in flight. Its popularity in Europe is due to the policy of internal open borders within the European Union from 1993. The then TREVI Programme of Action,[135] agreed at its June 1990 Dublin meeting, talked of bilateral or multilateral arrangements to permit police forces to cross land frontiers in pursuit of flagrant violators of the law and when following the authors of serious offences. Moreover, the Schengen Accord of June 1990[136] allows the various police agencies of the States parties to cross land frontiers in hot pursuit, although it has to be acknowledged that it is still a contentious issue. Once the pursuit is completed and the fugitives have been 'arrested' by the pursuing police force in any of the Schengen States, there are two possible options: first, it might be that the police officers from out-of-State could simply take the fugitive back to their own jurisdiction or, secondly, having arrested him, they may have to hand him over to the authorities of the State where he was apprehended. In the latter case, the fugitive would then be the subject of an extradition request, somewhat defeating the objectives behind hot pursuit. On the other hand, if the pursuing police could take the fugitive back with them, then

---

132 For a fuller history of the Dikko Affair, see The Times p.1, JULY 6 1984; p.2, 9 JULY 1984; and p.2, 10 JULY 1984.

133 See Bewley, *Hot Pursuit*, 105 POLICE REV. p.18, 19 May 1995; Gilmore, *Hot Pursuit: The case of R v Mills and Others*, 44 INT'L & COMP.LQ 949 (1995).

134 See the Franco-Basle Treaty of 1781, MARTENS, RECUEILS DE TRAITES, vol.2, at p.188 – cited in SHEARER, *supra* n109, at p.10 n2. See also, the Anglo-Scottish "hot trods" in agreements signed in 1563 and 1640 – cited in Walker, *supra* n107, at p.118 n24.

135 Now carried on by the responsible Article K.4 Committee under the Maastricht Agreement.

136 30 INT.LEG.MAT.84 (1991), Articles 39 *et seq*. See also, MEIJERS, SCHENGEN, 2nd ed. 1992.

it would be more accurate to talk of 'diffused borders' than of hot pursuit, for the authority of the police forces is effectively extended beyond the territorial border. Regardless of the correct terminology, it would certainly be more effective for the pursuing police to be able to take the fugitive back with them; there is no point making frontiers less of a hindrance to law enforcement in one aspect, only to then impose the need for extradition. Subject to appropriate safeguards in the bilateral or multilateral arrangements, the requested State granting a right of hot pursuit should permit the pursuing police force to apprehend and return with the fugitive, even though ordinarily a fugitive should only be surrendered to another State by means of extradition.

The second form of assistance that the requested State can offer is to exclude the fugitive before he enters its territory, thereby denying him the opportunity to avail himself of the protections and procedural delays that extradition affords. Whereas hot pursuit will be a lawful mechanism for both the requesting and the requested States, because it will have been established by treaty or other formal arrangement, exclusion is legally questionable if its purpose is to avoid the processes of extradition. While States have the right to refuse entry to any non-national,[137] especially ones who may be undesirable criminals, excluding a fleeing fugitive is tantamount to sending him back to the *locus delicti* without using extradition. Nevertheless, exclusion is widely used. Statistics of the former West German Border Police show that in 1986–88 approximately 90,000 people were at least temporarily detained trying to enter or leave the F.R.G., seventy per cent of them for serious offences, such as drugs offences or crimes against the State.[138] At a formalised level, since 1986 the United States has, through its Alien Border Control Committee, attempted to devise procedures to prevent known terrorists from entering its territory.[139] In the United Kingdom, the Immigration Rules[140] allow for refusal of leave to enter to anyone convicted

---

137 *Quaere* refugees. See Chapter Nine below.

138 See pp.58 and 189 of HOUSE OF LORDS SELECT COMMITTEE ON THE E.C., 22nd REPORT, 1992: BORDER CONTROL OF PEOPLE, HL 90 (1988–89). See *Note Verbale* from United Kingdom Permanent Representative to the Council of Europe, Appendix VI, DH (89) 1.

139 See Mock, The I.N.S. Response to Terrorist Threats, at pp.231 *et seq.* of BASSIOUNI, LEGAL RESPONSES, *supra* n123.

140 Immigration Rules (HCP395, 23 May 1994), para.320(18).

anywhere of an offence that would constitute an extradition crime.[141] With the coming in 1993 of an internal open borders policy within the European Union, even greater emphasis was placed on exclusion at the external frontiers.

> "The [European] Commission proposes that around the external borders of the Community there should be erected – by agreement between member States – a *cordon sanitaire* to keep out drug traffickers, terrorists and other criminals, refugees together with unwanted immigrants. Greatly increased co-operation between police and judicial authorities, shared intelligence and stricter internal controls would offset the consequences of permitting these undesirables – if they have breached the perimeter fence – to circulate freely around Europe."[142]

More informally, police forces will sometimes notify the immigration authorities of the State to which a fugitive is heading in order that he might be excluded. There will be no international agreement to be brought into play as considered above, but rather *de facto* extradition will be effected at the low level of the individual police officer and immigration officer. In a 1990 British murder case, local police tipped off the New York immigration authorities that a suspect was expected to arrive there imminently. He was denied leave to enter the USA and, technically, he had to be sent back to his point of departure; in point of fact, British police flew to New York to escort him back.[143] On the ground that he had never entered the United States, there was no question of him having any of the safeguards associated with extradition; it was as if he was still in British territory when 'arrested' at New York airport.

Finally, and even more questionably, if the fugitive has already entered the requested State, then rather than use the proper procedure of extradition, the authorities in the requested State might assist in returning the fugitive

---

141 That is, it would be punishable by a term of imprisonment of 12 months or more if it had been committed in the United Kingdom.

142 Para.21, HOME AFFAIRS SELECT COMMITTEE REPORT ON PRACTICAL POLICE CO-OPERATION IN THE EUROPEAN COMMUNITY, vol.1, HCP 363 (1990); hereinafter, HCP-I or HCP-II.

143 See The Guardian p.2, 1 SEPT 1990, concerning the murder in Leeds of Frank Harris.

by deporting him.[144] While abduction will be treated as a violation of sovereignty by requested States, collusive deportation will actively involve the government of the requested State. In such a situation, can the fugitive look to the courts of the requested State for protection?

The law in this area is in a state of flux. Some decisions favour the fugitive, while others merely look to see if the deportation or expulsion is technically lawful, regardless of the underlying motive of the requested State to avoid its extradition procedures. Within the latter category, one of the most absolute cases is *Sitaram*.[145] The Burmese High Court held that the courts would not inquire into the desirability of using deportation instead of extradition and that the executive did not have to give any reasons for its actions.

Probably, the leading common law authority is *R v Brixton Prison (Governor), ex p.Soblen*.[146] The facts of the case were as follows. Soblen was a naturalised citizen of the United States who had been convicted of espionage for passing secrets to the former USSR. Pending appeal to the Supreme Court, he was released on bail. When his appeal was dismissed, he fled to Israel. There was no extradition treaty between the United States and Israel at that time, but the Israelis put him on a specially chartered aeroplane to Athens.[147] It was alleged that the United States Chief Marshal was on board, although, since the latter was outside the USA, he obviously lacked any authority. At Athens, Soblen was put on board an El Al flight bound for the USA via London. The British Home Office had been warned of his impending arrival and had drawn up a refusal of leave to enter the United Kingdom. However, with the 'sole intention' of obtaining entry to the United Kingdom, Soblen inflicted knife wounds on himself necessitating hospitalisation in England. Two days after arrival, he was served with a refusal of

---

144 See the summary deportation of Enrique Gorriarán, one of latin America's most notorious guerrilla leaders from Mexico to Argentina – The Guardian p.19, 20 JUN 1997.

145 *Sitaram v Superintendent Rangoon Central Jail*, 28 INT'L L REP.313 (1957).

146 [1962] 3 All ER 641. See O'Higgins, *Disguised Extradition – The Soblen Case*, 27 MOD.L REV.521 (1964); Thornberry, *Dr Soblen and the Alien Law of the United Kingdom*, 12 INT'L & COMP. LQ 414 (1963); Evans, *Reflections on the Political Offence in International Practice*, 57 AM.J INT'L L 1 (1963). For the detailed facts of the case see The Times, JUNE-SEPT 1962.

147 For the Israeli government view of its actions in the Soblen affair, see the Ministerial Report, 2 INT.LEG.MAT.419 (1963).

leave to land under Article 1(1) of the Aliens Order, 1953. El Al was also ordered to take him on his interrupted journey to the United States. He applied *ex parte* for a writ of *habeas corpus* which issued; simultaneously he was served with a detention notice under Article 8(3) of the Aliens Order, 1953. The writ of *habeas corpus* was discharged and an appeal to the Court of Appeal was dismissed. El Al was again ordered to take him, but they refused to comply; by this time opinion in Israel had changed and the government of the day was pressured into denouncing Soblen's proposed removal to the USA which it had initiated.

A deportation notice was served on *Soblen* under Article 20(2)(b) of the 1953 Order. The Home Secretary stated at the time that it was his intention that Soblen be placed on a vessel going to the USA. Soblen reapplied for *habeas corpus* on four grounds:

(i) the Aliens Order, 1953, was invalid because there was no war or emergency when it was made, such that the Aliens Restriction Act 1914 was inoperative in 1953;

(ii) the deportation order was invalid because it purported to be made in respect of an alien who had previously been refused leave to land. The two orders could not co-exist;

(iii) further, the deportation order was invalid because the deportee had not had the chance to make representations to the Home Secretary before it was made; and

(iv) finally, the deportation order was being used for an *ultra vires* object by the Home Secretary, in that Soblen was being returned to the United States to serve a prison sentence for an offence for which extradition could not be granted, namely espionage. This final ground alleged 'disguised extradition'.

It is of note that the Home Secretary claimed crown privilege in relation to certain correspondence between himself and the United States government.[148]

The Divisional Court dismissed this reapplication, so he again appealed to the Court of Appeal. For the purposes of *de facto* extradition only the

---

148 *Supra n*146, at 641-43 (Headnote).

fourth point is of importance.[149] Can a deportation order be challenged
with any hope of success where the process is being used in substitution
for or to avoid extradition? The Court of Appeal relied heavily on the decision in *R v Secretary of State for Home Affairs, ex p.Duke of Chateau
Thierry*.[150] The Duke was a French national of military age who had been
living in England for several years. A deportation order was made against

---

149 However, for the sake of completeness, the first three will be dealt with briefly.
  (i) Soblen's first argument was rejected because the 1914 Act had been amended
  in 1919 and the powers thereunder could be invoked irrespective of whether
  there was a war or emergency. [s1, Aliens Restriction (Amendment) Act 1919.
  See Lord Denning MR, *supra n*146, at 658 C-E]. Deportation is now dealt with
  in the Immigration Act, 1971, which is unrestricted as to circumstances of application.
  (ii) The second ground is irrelevant today, for the rules on deportation are now
  contained in the Immigration Rules made under the Immigration Act, 1971.
  On the 1953 rules, Lord Denning and Donovan LJ, with whom Pearson LJ concurred, [*supra n*146, at 658 E-F, 663 A-B and 669 H, respectively] held that
  where the order to take a person refused leave to land on his journey is ignored
  by a carrier, then a deportation order could be made. The powers under Articles
  8 and 20 were cumulative and complementary, not mutually exclusive. Under
  the present rules, [HCP395; and see Chapter Nine, below] Soblen may have fared
  a little better, for within the provisions on deportation [Paras.362 *et seq.*,
  especially Para.380] express reference is made to the Convention and Protocol
  Relating to the Status of Refugees [189 UNTS 137 at p.150 and 606 UNTS 267,
  respectively; Paras.327-52 of the Immigration Rules deal with asylum applicants
  – Para.348 deals with their special rights of appeal]. The Convention and
  Protocol prohibit states returning people to where they will face persecution,
  inter alia, for their political views.
  (iii) As for the assertion that the fugitive has the right to make representations
  to the Home Secretary before a deportation order is made, it was rejected on
  grounds of convenience, although the fact the denial of the alleged right violated
  a general common law principle, was recognised. The Court of Appeal relied
  on the 1920 decision of *R v Leman Street Police Station Inspector, ex p.Venicoff*,
  [1929] 3 KB 72. That case was held to be good law, for Parliament had re-
  enacted the rules in 1953 in exactly the same terms, obviously assuming it was
  still applicable. Lord Denning MR also considered relevant the fact that many
  deportees could make representations to the Chief Magistrate at Bow Street
  and thought that there may be a right to do so after the order is made, but before
  execution. The present position is set out in *Chahal v United Kingdom*, European
  Court of Human Rights, (70/1995/576/662) 15 November 1996.
150 [1917] 1 KB 552 and 922 (CA).

him under s1(1) Aliens Restriction Act 1914 and Article 12, Aliens Restriction (Consolidation) Order 1916. The order did not state where he was to go after being deported from the United Kingdom,[151] but the Attorney-General, on behalf of the Home Secretary, admitted that it was intended to use the said order to return him to France for military service. The Divisional Court made absolute a *rule nisi* for a writ of *certiorari*, holding the Home Secretary had no power under the legislation then in force to specify any particular destination, even impliedly. The Divisional Court held deportation could not be used to effect an extradition.[152]

The Home Secretary in *Chateau Thierry* appealed and the Court of Appeal reversed the lower court's decision. First, it held that if a deportation order is valid on its face the court will not go behind it to see the purpose to which it is being put.

> "The order on the face of it, however, is only an order that the respondent be deported, and if that be a valid order it cannot be quashed."[153]

An order could only be quashed if the deportee was not an alien.[154]

Finally, the court held there was nothing wrong in using deportation to effect the return of military absentees. Indeed, there was in existence a treaty whereby the English and French governments agreed to return nationals of military age to their respective countries.[155] However, such persons were deserters under French law; they were, thus, fugitive offenders and should have been dealt with under the then 1870 Extradition Act. It is a well settled principle that the Crown does not have a prerogative power to send persons who have committed an offence in a foreign State back to the *locus delicti*.[156]

---

151 *Supra* n150, at 923.

152 Under the Immigration Act 1971, once a deportation order is made under s5 thereof, the Home Secretary can nominate either a country of which he is a national or citizen, or any country or territory to which there is reason to believe he will be admitted. Sch.3(1), 1971 Act.

153 *Supra* n150, at 932 *per* Pickford LJ.

154 *Cf. R v Superintendent of Chiswick Police Station, ex parte Sacksteder*, [1918] 1 KB 578 at 586.

155 111 B.F.S.P.251.

156 *Barton v Commonwealth of Australia*, (1974) 131 CLR 477 at 484 *per* Barwick CJ.

"For some time the law was doubtful, but later it became recognised that the Crown could not surrender an alleged criminal even if it wished to do so, unless the surrender was authorised by legislation."[157]

The power is statutory only and, with respect to France, it was to be found at the time of *Chateau-Thierry* in the Extradition Act 1870. For the 1870 Act to have applied, there needed to be an 'arrangement'. The 1917 Agreement would have fulfilled this requirement, but there was no Order in Council implementing it, as required. Therefore, the Duke could have argued that the Crown was bypassing the pertinent extradition procedures which should have been the sole basis for the power it was exercising. It should not be asserted on the one hand, that the only method of returning fugitive offenders is by way of the processes of extradition, if, on the other hand, the relevant statute is then to be disregarded while the Government use deportation to effect the same purpose.[158] The Duke could have alleged the Crown was acting *ultra vires* in using deportation in order to extradite. In *Ex p.Sacksteder*,[159] Pickford LJ, stated the following.

"But I am certainly not inclined to say that in no case can the court go behind an order which on the face of it is valid, ordering detention or custody. If the purpose behind it is such as to show that the order is not a genuine or *bona fide* order, it seems to me the Court can go behind it."

Therefore, it has been recognised that although a deportation order may appear valid, it may in fact be a sham, a disguise to effect an extradition, and that in such a case the court may quash it.

In *Soblen* itself, the defendant was alleging that the Home Secretary was using the deportation processes to extradite him when this would otherwise be impossible – espionage was not a listed extradition crime for the purposes of the then law. Under present English law, if Soblen was to be deported on the ground his presence was not conducive to the public good as being not in the interests of national security or of the relations between the United Kingdom and any other country (here, the USA), or for other reasons of a

---

157 McNAIR, INTERNATIONAL LAW OPINIONS, vol.2, at p.41 (1956); cited by Lord Denning MR, *supra* n146, at 659.
158 *Cf.* Thornberry, *supra* n146, at pp.463-64.
159 *Supra* n154, at 586-87.

political nature, he could question the order through a non-statutory advisory procedure.[160] However, the opinion of the three advisers is not binding on the Home Secretary and Lord Denning MR, in the *Hosenball* case, held they did not even have to abide by the rules of natural justice.[161] Thus, Soblen would still probably have more chance of success alleging that the order was *ultra vires* as a means of challenging the use of deportation powers to effect extradition.

As for Soblen's contention that the deportation order was *ultra vires*, having been issued for the ulterior motive of a 'disguised extradition' to the United States for a non-extraditable, political offence, their Lordships followed *Chateau Thierry*. They held that if a deportation order is good on its face, it will not be questioned without further evidence. On the other hand, if the Home Secretary was deporting Soblen for an unlawful purpose, Lord Denning MR did say the court would investigate.[162] The Court of Appeal found that Soblen had not proved the Home Secretary's *mala fides*. However, it is contended that on the evidence their Lordships refer to themselves, there is sufficient evidence to show that the Home Secretary had always intended to help in the transit of Soblen from Israel to the USA. Whether Soblen's presence in the United Kingdom was conducive to the public good or not, the Home Secretary was going to send him on his way

---

160 See HCP395, Para.374.
161 *R v Secretary of State for Home Affairs, ex parte Hosenball*, [1977] 2 All ER 542.
162 *Supra* n146. The problem, however, would be in proving the Home Secretary's *mala fides*. The Court of Appeal laid down two different tests as to the amount of evidence that ought to be adduced and, with regard to this question, it must be remembered that the Home Secretary can claim crown privilege, making it very difficult for the deportee to prove bad faith. Lord Denning MR called for sufficient evidence upon "which it could reasonably be supposed that the Home Secretary was using the power of deportation for an ulterior purpose" [at 661F]. If this amount is brought before the court, then the Home Secretary will be required to give an answer if he wants to preserve the order. Donovan LJ, realising that crown privilege will usually be claimed for government documents, provided a test relating to what needed to be shown without such evidence. Under his test, the deportee needs to raise a *prima facie* case or "sow such substantial and disquieting doubts in the mind of the court about the *bona fides* of the order he is challenging, that the court will consider that some answer is called for" [at 664H]. All three members of the court found that Soblen failed to discharge the burden.

to the USA through a *de facto* extradition, in much the same way that Israel had unofficially assisted in his departure.[163] Lord Denning's *dictum* indicates that it is technically possible in English law to challenge a disguised extradition, but there was an evident unwillingness on the part of the courts to tread into the arena of international politics.[164]

In the event, Dr Soblen committed suicide on the morning of his intended deportation.[165] It is one of the saddest and unworthiest events in the United Kingdom's participation in international assistance in criminal matters.[166] It also reaffirms the importance of using the appropriate procedures agreed between States to effect a desired result. The words of a Member of Parliament commenting on the Home Secretary's defence of his actions in the *Soblen* case sum up the problems in taking part in collusive deportation either to avoid, expedite or ignore the processes of extradition.

> "When the [Home Secretary] said that his defence was what had been said by the Court of Appeal, it would have been more convincing if he himself had not suppressed the evidence on which the Court of Appeal came to its decision ... [in the course of the incident]. I could not help feeling that

---

163 See *United States v Salzmann*, 417 F.Supp 1139 at 1159 (1975).
164 See Thornberry and O'Higgins, both *supra* n146.
165 The Times, 12 SEPT 1962, p.8, col.6.
166 Since *Soblen*, the United Kingdom has avoided such a spectacular *de facto* extradition. *R v Governor of Pentonville Prison, ex parte Cheng*, [1973] AC 931, involved another fugitive bound for the United States who injured himself in order to enter the UK. The government rejected deporting Cheng and chose to extradite him because of fears of repeating *Soblen*. However, the *Hosenball* case, *supra* n161, is one example of disguised extradition being attempted and there is the slightly ridiculous case of Vladimir Leontev. Leontev, a Russian émigré living in France, appeared before a British court on a driving charge. During the hearing he collapsed, but doctors decided he was feigning. The French police requested his return to interview him about the robbery of £25,000, a sum he just so happened to have on him when arrested in England. While still 'unconscious', he was deported to face questioning in France. Because of the slightly ridiculous circumstances surrounding Leontev's departure, it was not noticed that the power to deport was being used to effect a *de facto* extradition. See The Times p.3, 13 DEC 1985.

the Rt.Hon.Gentlemen was lucky that he was the man he is, for anybody else in his shoes would have felt bitterly ashamed of himself."[167]

Regardless of its irregularity, States throughout the world have used deportation in order to effect a *de facto* extradition. The Dutch Supreme Court in 1963 held in the *Wallace* case[168] that a foreign national might be deported if convicted of a criminal offence, even though he might face prosecution in the State of which he was a national. However, it was prepared to countenance the possibility that in some cases the deportation order might be illegal. Similarly ambivalent is the decision in *CvH v The Netherlands*.[169] Here The Netherlands withdrew an extradition request because of problems with the principle of specialty for fugitives wanted from France, in the expectation that the French authorities would then deport them to The Netherlands. The District Court of the Hague held that there was no legal duty on the Dutch authorities to prevent France from expelling the fugitives to The Netherlands.

Japan performed a remarkably similar 'service' to *Soblen* for the Republic of China in 1971. In *State of Japan v Mitsuyo Kono and Takao Kono*,[170] the Tokyo High Court deported the respondents' husband and father, Liu Wen Chen, to Taiwan following an informal request for his return. His wife and son sued the State on the basis that if extradition had been used, as was appropriate, the political offence exemption would have been available as a defence to him. The court held that deportation could properly be used, if permitted, and the processes of extradition avoided thereby.

Notwithstanding the above authorities, there seems to be a trend for courts to query more forcefully attempts to achieve *de facto* extradition by deporting the fugitive offender. The Superior Administrative Court of Münster in the *Residence Prohibition Order case (No.2)*[171] refused to order the fugitive's expulsion because he would not be guaranteed the rights inherent in extradition. The Court of Appeals in *Doherty v United States*

---

167 Paget MP, 28 NOV 1962, 662 H.C.DEB.445-6. Cited in Thornberry, *supra* n146, at p.465 n91.
168 *Wallace v The State of Netherlands*, [1963] Ned.Jur. No.509, cited in SHEARER, *supra* n109, at p.82.
169 100 INT'L L REP.404 at 407.
170 59 INT'L L REP.472 (1971).
171 61 INT'L L REP.433 (1968).

Department of Justice, INS[172] overturned the Attorney-General's decision
to designate the country to which Doherty should be deported because it
believed the decision to have been influenced by foreign policy considerations.[173] The Federal Court of Australia also dealt with the issue in
Schlieske.[174] Extradition to the former FRG having twice failed, the
Australian government sought to deport Schlieske. While accepting that it
was permissible to deport a person who would face criminal charges in the
country to which he was being sent, the court went on to hold that deportation for the sole purpose of bringing a person to justice in a foreign State
was outside the purposes of the relevant statute: disguised extradition was
not permissible.

> "The relevant principle is that the power to deport a prohibited non-citizen,
> while wide and unqualified by any statutory provision, must be exercised
> for the purposes of the Migration Act, that is to say, in aid of the sovereign
> right of this country to determine who shall be permitted to enter it and
> who should be excluded therefrom .... [It] is plainly extraneous to the
> decision to deport a person, and to deport that person to a particular country,
> that the person is wanted by the government of that country upon criminal
> charges. It is not one of the purposes of the Migration Act to aid foreign
> powers to bring fugitives to justice. There is a distinct head of constitutional
> authority – namely the external affairs power – and a distinct mechanism
> – the extradition legislation – under which that object may be pursued."

The Austrian Law on Extradition and Mutual Assistance in Criminal Matters
goes so far as to prohibit the use of deportation as an alternative to extradition.[175] The most forthright judicial statement against disguised extradition, however, is to be found, not in the decision of some municipal court,
but in the judgment of the European Court of Human Rights in *Bozano v
France*.[176] The Italian government's extradition request for Bozano had

---

172 908 F.2d 1108 at 1121 (1990).
173 Reversed on other grounds – *INS v Doherty* 502 US 314 (1992).
174 *Schlieske v Minister for Immigration and Ethnic Affairs*, (1988), 84 ALR 719
   at 729.
175 See MURPHY, PUNISHING INTERNATIONAL TERRORISTS, p.88 (1985).
176 Series A, vol.111, 9 EHRR 297 (1986). The decision is also binding on English
   practice, casting doubt on the possibility of any repeat of *Soblen, supra* n146.
   See also *Chahal, supra* n149.

been rejected by the French courts on the ground of *ordre public*; such a finding was binding on the French government. However, since extradition was impossible, the French authorities agreed to deport him to Switzerland from where his extradition to Italy would present no problem. Having been sent to Italy by these means, he applied to the European Court of Human Rights, partly on the basis that his rights under Article 5(1)(f) had been violated. The Court held that actions to deport must be lawful having regard to domestic law if Article 5(1)(f) is to be satisfied.[177] Moreover, the arbitrariness of deportation, lacking as it does, the safeguards and proper procedures of extradition, also renders it contrary to the European Convention on Human Rights. Finally, the Court held that disguised extradition, *per se*, was unlawful under Article 5(1)(f), because it meant that the fugitive was not detained "with a view to deportation".[178] Thus, within the Council of Europe it now seems to be the case that if the fugitive is deported for the sole purpose of effecting a *de facto* extradition, then such deportation will violate Article 5(1)(f). The Court has effectively held that *de facto* extradition is not a lawful use of the powers of deportation. It remains to be seen whether the governments of the member States will, in practice, abide by this ruling.

c. Conclusion

So far it has been seen that there are no universally applied controls on *de facto* extraditions, whether in the requested State or on return to the requesting State. As an alternative to extradition, abduction must be rejected, but it is very unlikely that States will ever completely cease to use deportation, despite *Bozano*, even if *ad hoc* extradition develops in future years. Opinion seems to be divided as to whether deportation is something that should be officially rejected or whether a regulated system of expulsion, providing quasi-extradition safeguards, should be imposed.

As Bassiouni has noted, the law enforcement authorities will flout the law to obtain jurisdiction in some instances.

---

177 *Supra* n176, paras.53-58.
178 *Supra* n176, para.60.

"This creates, of course, serious problems for the integrity of the legal process, even though it may be a manifestation of the frustration of law enforcement authorities with their inability to make the extradition system work with the speed and satisfaction they desire."[179]

Indeed, the number of instances may be increasing.[180]

Thus, extradition on its own is insufficient and inadequate. As was argued by Judge Schermers, dissenting in the Commission's the decision in *Bozano*,[181] the extradition process may sometimes be too formal. Among States recognising the same standards of justice, it may be that the aim should be to ensure that the fugitive is returned to face trial or serve his sentence, even if the traditional extradition procedures are not followed. Rather than react with indignation as successive fugitives are subjected to informal rendition procedures, it would be better to develop rules of practice for returning fugitives by means other than extradition. They should only be available *in extremis* and never where the extradition merely means reasonable delay, not escape for the fugitive. To back up this procedure, the fugitive should be able to use any inappropriate use of this less formal system as a defence at the trial. Any other method of rendition not sanctioned by these new rules would automatically divest the court of jurisdiction. Evans and Murphy suggested the following approach in 1978.

"A multilateral convention should establish a common standard regarding the use of exclusion and expulsion for purposes of international rendition with procedural safeguards for the interests of the offender as well as those of the States involved."[182]

However, two points should be noted. First, the very popularity of other methods of rendition is due to their current informality. If a multilateral convention were to regularise informal rendition, the new procedures could well still detract from the system of extradition laws and yet they might now

---

179 BASSIOUNI, INTERNATIONAL EXTRADITION: UNITED STATES LAW AND PRACTICE, vol.V, sec.3-5. Cited in MURPHY, *supra* n175, at p.72.
180 MURPHY, *supra* n175, at p.93.
181 *Supra* n176, at pp.326-27.
182 EVANS & MURPHY, LEGAL ASPECTS OF INTERNATIONAL TERRORISM, pp.508-09 (1978).

be circumvented themselves because they would have lost their most appealing feature, their informality. Secondly, Gordon[183] has produced evidence that deportation and expulsion are not that much more speedy or effective than extradition, anyway, countering the popular belief to the contrary[184]; however, conclusive proof one way or the other is difficult to obtain.

In conclusion, changes must be made in the field of informal rendition, but the direction of the changes is unclear. Further, there is an inertia among States to regulate an informal system designed to expedite State interests at the expense of the transnational fugitive's protections.

---

183 *Supra n*129, at pp.284-86.
184 See Evans, *supra n*129.

8

TRANSNATIONAL FUGITIVE OFFENDERS AND ARMED CONFLICTS[1]

'War criminals', *lato sensu*, are *sui generis*. Their crimes are so heinous that all means, some more lawful than others, have been used to ensure that they are prosecuted. This chapter reviews current practice and policy, and makes recommendations for future developments in the law pertaining to transnational fugitive offenders and the law of armed conflicts.[2]

It is almost forty years since the end of World War II, yet reports in newspapers even now regularly tell of requests for the return of war criminals from that era.[3] However, a uniform approach towards alleged war criminals, from past and current conflicts, is still lacking, although there is an increasingly discernible international policy of prosecuting war criminals whenever possible, to the extent that *ad hoc* tribunals for the former Yugoslavia and Rwanda were established by the Security Council and the proposed

---

1   This chapter does not cover the extradition of prisoners of war: see *United States v Noriega* 746 F.Supp 1506 at 1525-29 (1990), 808 F.Supp 791 (1992). See also, Meyer, *The Astiz Affair*, 32 INT'L & COMP. LQ 948 (1983).
    Nor will it deal with the possibility of civil actions brought by victims in third States where they have found refuge – *viz. Kadic v Karadzic*, 70 F.3d 232 (1995); noted in 90 AM.J INT'L L 658 (1996).

2   It will be argued below that crimes against humanity, which initially had to be committed as part of an armed conflict, need no longer be so associated.

3   See (i) The Observer p.8, 29 JAN 1984 and The Guardian p.6, 2 FEB 1984; p.6, 17 FEB 1984; p.6, 10 MAR 1984, concerning Walter Rauff, now resident in Chile: (ii) The Guardian p.7, 19 JAN 1983 and The Times p.10, 23 MAY 1983, concerning Canada's agreement to return Helmut Rauca: (iii) for the case of Klaus Barbie's expulsion by Bolivia to France, see The Times p.1, 6 FEB 1983 and The Guardian, Editorial, 8 FEB 1983: (iv) The Guardian p.15, 15 JUN 1995, on Eric Priebke's extradition from Argentina to Italy.
    'Return' will be used throughout this chapter to include all the various methods of rendition: extradition, transfer, abduction or expulsion/deportation.

International Criminal Court has now predominantly focussed its jurisdiction on crimes in conflicts.[4]

The first task must be to distinguish the various offences collectively known as 'war crimes' and to examine their individual scope. Once the terms are understood, it will be possible to review the United Nations' measures designed to provide no safe-haven for fugitive war criminals and to consider the national approaches towards rendition.[5] Finally, the problem of what is the best forum for trial of war criminals will be examined.

a. Distinguishing Types of War Crime

Genocide is not truly a 'war crime'. It was established by the Genocide Convention, 1948,[6] which was the first such positive move against war criminals. It made genocide, defined in Article 2, or conspiracy, incitement or attempt to commit it, an international crime. Thus, those who are involved in genocide, whether in times of peace or during a war,[7] are not to escape

---

4 Writing in 1991 in *Aspects of Extradition Law* (pp.156-57 and 224), the idea of creating another 'Nuremberg Tribunal' was at that time mere hypothesis. That it is almost certain at time of writing that there will be an International Criminal Court in place for the new millennium to deal with crimes pertaining to armed conflicts, as postulated in 1991 as the only possible basis on which to form an international criminal tribunal, suggests that following the wars in the former Yugoslavia and Rwanda, such should be the preferred route for dealing with such offenders.

5 See Garcia-Mora, *Crimes against humanity and the principle of non-extradition of political offenders*, 62 MICH.L REV.927 (1964); Green, *Political Offences, War Crimes and Extradition*, 11 INT'L & COMP. LQ 329 (1962); Green, *War Crimes, Extradition and Command Responsibility*, 14 IS.YB.H.R.17 (1984); Neumann, *Neutral States and the Extradition of War Criminals*, 45 AM.J INT'L L 495, (1951); O'Higgins, *Disguised Extradition – The Soblen Case*, 27 MOD.L REV.521 (1964); FALK, KOLKO, LIFTON, CRIMES OF WAR, (1971).

6 78 UNTS 277 (1951). The term genocide was coined by Lemkin in his 1944 book *Axis Rule in Occupied Europe*. It took 21 years for the United Kingdom to pass enabling legislation and the United States only adhered to it in 1986. See Le Blanc, *The Intent to Destroy Groups in the Genocide Convention: The Proposed US Understanding*, 78 AM.J INT'L L 369 (1984).

7 Genocide is one type of crime against humanity; see Donnewille in *Barbie, infra* n14, at 147.

punishment and are to be refused a safe haven. Unfortunately, its good intentions have not been fulfilled in practice, partly because very few fugitives are prosecuted for genocide *per se*, but rather for crimes against humanity or war crimes which do not come within the provisions of the 1948 Convention,[8] and partly because several States did not become parties to it.

The generic title 'war crimes' covered three separate offences according to Article 6 of the Charter of the International Military Tribunal at Nuremberg.[9]

"(a) Crimes against Peace: namely, planning, preparation initiation or waging a war of aggression, or a war in violation of international treaties, agreements or assurances, or participation in a common plan or conspiracy for the accomplishment of any of the foregoing:

(b) War Crimes: namely, violations of the laws and customs of war. Such violations shall include, but shall not be limited to, murder, ill-treatment or deportation to slave labour or for any other purpose of civilian population of or in occupied territory, murder or ill-treatment of prisoners of war or persons on the seas, killing of hostages, plunder of public or private property, wanton destruction of cities, towns or villages or devastation not justified by military necessity:

(c) Crimes against Humanity: namely, murder, extermination, enslavement, deportation, and other inhumane acts committed against any civilian population, before or during the war, or persecutions on political, racial or religious grounds in execution of or in connection with any crime within the jurisdiction of the Tribunal, whether or not in violation of the domestic law of the country where perpetrated."

It is generally believed that Crimes against Peace can only be committed by high ranking members of either the military or the executive of the State

---

8   *Viz* Klaus Barbie, *infra* n14; *R and Federal Republic of Germany v Rauca*, (1983), 34 C.R.(3d) 97, 145 DLR (3d) 638 (Ont CA). *Cf. Eichmann*, 36 INT'L L REP.5. *Cf.* A German court sentenced a Serb, Nikola Jorgic, to life imprisonment for genocide for leading a death squad that murdered Bosnian Muslims and perpetrating ethnic cleansing – The Guardian p.15, 27 SEP 1997.

9   Cited in the International Military Tribunal at Nuremberg's Judgement, which may be found in vol.XXII, pp.413-14, of TRIAL OF THE MAJOR WAR CRIMINALS BEFORE THE INTERNATIONAL MILITARY TRIBUNAL (1948). See also 41 AM.J INT'L L 172 (1947).

in starting an armed conflict, an issue considered below with respect to the proposed International Criminal Court.[10] Thus, the focus of this chapter will be on war crimes, *stricto sensu*, under Article 6(b) and crimes against humanity, as defined in Article 6(c).[11] War criminals will be taken to include, though, those guilty of violations of Article 6(b) or 6(c), unless otherwise stated.

War crimes under Article 6(b) must have been committed during an armed conflict.[12] Crimes against humanity, however, are probably not constrained as to the setting. Fenrick[13] distinguished the two offences as follows:

> "(a) war crimes are offences committed by persons linked to one side to an armed conflict against neutral citizens or citizens of a belligerent on the other side, while the victims of crimes against humanity may be citizens of any country, (b) crimes against humanity must be carried out in pursuance of a policy of persecution on political, racial or religious grounds, while no such policy is required for war crimes, and (c) to be a war crime, an act must have been committed during a war or an international armed conflict."

In the *Barbie* case,[14] the distinction was of importance because of questions about the scope of the statute of limitations with respect to war crimes and crimes against humanity. Barbie was accused in the initial indictment with crimes against humanity committed against Jews and members of the French Resistance in the Lyon area. However, the Examining Magistrate of Lyon and the Lyon *Cour d'Appel* struck out the charges with respect to members

---

10   *Infra n*190. See also, Dinstein, 'The Distinctions between War Crimes and Crimes Against Peace', in DINSTEIN & TABORY, WAR CRIMES IN INTERNATIONAL LAW, 1996, at p.1; Rosenne, 'War Crimes and State Responsibility', *id.*, at p.65.

11   On crimes against humanity, see Bassiouni, *Crimes Against Humanity: The Need for a Specialized Convention*, 31 COLUM.J TRANSNAT'L L 457 (1994); CRIMES AGAINST HUMANITY IN INTERNATIONAL CRIMINAL LAW, 1992.

12   Hampson, 'Liability for War Crimes', in ROWE, THE GULF WAR 1990-91 IN INTERNATIONAL AND ENGLISH LAW, 1993, at p.241.

13   *The Prosecution of War Criminals in Canada*, 12 DALHOUSIE LJ 256 at pp.266 *et seq.* (1989).

14   *Fédération Nationale des Déportés et Internés Résistants et Patriotes et al. v Barbie*, 78 INT'L L REP.125 (1985).

of the Resistance because crimes against humanity required that the accused committed the offence as part of a policy based on persecuting the victims on account of their race or religion; as such, only the charges relating to persecution of Jews by Barbie would have qualified as crimes against humanity. On appeal, the *Cour de Cassation* reversed the earlier rulings.

> "The following acts constitute crimes against humanity ... which are not subject to statutory limitation of the right of prosecution, even if they are crimes which can also be classified as war crimes: ... inhumane acts and persecution committed in a systematic manner in the name of a State practising a policy of ideological supremacy, not only against persons by reason of their membership of a racial or religious community, but also against the opponents of that policy, whatever the form of their opposition.
>
> ....
>
> [The Court considers] however that the judgment under appeal States that the 'heinous' crimes committed systematically or collectively against persons who were members or could have been members of the Resistance were presented, by those in whose name they were perpetrated, as justified politically by the national socialist ideology. Neither the driving force which motivated the victims, nor their possible membership of the Resistance, excludes the possibility that the accused acted with the element of intent necessary for the commission of crimes against humanity."[15]

While the two offences are separate, it may be that a war crime is also a crime against humanity. Advocate-General Donnewille went even further in his submissions to the *Cour de Cassation*.[16] He was of the opinion that,

> "[to] accept a distinction between the victims would be to play the game of the perpetrator of the crime in the arbitrary discrimination which he operated in relation to the human race .... It matters little ... faced with an orchestrated and collective programme of action which denies civilisation as such, whether the victim was a member of a group, whether or not he was 'useful for the war' to his enemies, whether he espoused a particular political persuasion, or even whether he belonged to a particular race ...."

---

15 *Supra n*14, at 137 and 140.
16 *Supra n*14, at 146-47. JANACZEK, NUREMBERG JUDGMENT IN LIGHT OF INTERNATIONAL LAW, at p.97 (1949), argues that crimes against humanity were created by the Charter as the only way of punishing some Nazis for certain crimes.

Donnewille argues that crimes against humanity should be defined by reference to the fate of the victim rather than the motivation of the accused. It is possible to interpret Article 6(c) so that only "persecution" has to be motivated by reason of the victim's race, religion or political opinion and that "murder, extermination, enslavement, deportation and other inhumane acts committed against any civilian population" can be crimes against humanity without any particular motivation *vis à vis* the victims.

A more detailed and up-to-date analysis of the content of war crimes and crimes against humanity is provided in the section on international criminal tribunals, based on the various Statutes. The present brief discussion is designed solely to highlight their overlapping scope.

b. Multilateral Conventions

The United Nations has taken several steps to ensure that war criminals are eventually punished and exhorts its members to,

> "take measures to arrest such persons and extradite them to the countries where they had committed war crimes or crimes against humanity."[17]

The Genocide Convention of 1948[18] made the various crimes therein promulgated offences which ought to be tried before a tribunal in the State where they occurred· or before an international tribunal. Towards this end, genocide was to be added to the list of extraditable crimes and is designated a non-political offence.[19] Thus, as stated above, those who are involved in genocide are not to escape punishment and are to be refused a safe haven.

The four Geneva Conventions of 1949,[20] promoted under the auspices of the International Committee of the Red Cross, all make provision in simi-

---

17 General Assembly of the United Nations, 25th Session, 1970. The quotation
   is taken from WILLIAMS, INTERNATIONAL CRIMINAL LAW: CASES AND MATERIALS,
   at p.592 (3rd ed., 1978).
18 *Supra n*6, Art. VI. See also, *Case Concerning Application of the Convention
   on the Prevention and Punishment of the Crime of Genocide, (Bosnia-Herzegovina v Yugoslavia)* [1996] ICJ Rep., General List No.91, 11 July 1996.
19 *Supra n*6, Art.7; and see Art.3, too.
20 75 UNTS 31-417 (1950).

lar terms for High Contracting Parties to pass legislation giving themselves either jurisdiction over or the power to extradite to the *locus delicti*, those committing grave breaches of the Conventions.[21] The options would appear to be coextensive from the wording of those provisions. Moreover, Articles 88 and 89 of Protocol I to the Geneva Conventions[22] provide that States shall afford one another the greatest assistance and co-operation in criminal proceedings to do with grave breaches and special reference is made to extradition to the *locus delicti*. However, the conventions sponsored by the Red Cross leave the question of whether a war crime or crime against humanity could be political in character to the domestic law of the High Contracting Parties, unlike the Genocide Convention.

In 1968, the U.N. General Assembly adopted the Convention on the Non-Applicability of Statutory Limitations to War Crimes and Crimes against Humanity.[23] The aim of the Convention, evident from its title, is to prevent war criminals escaping liability merely because of lapse of time and statutory limitation periods. Once again the Convention makes provision (Article III) for the extradition of war criminals by the States party to it, and once again, few States have ratified it and not many have even signed it. In *JK v Public Prosecutor*,[24] it was held that under Dutch law that war crimes as defined in Article 6(b) of the Charter of the International Military Tribunal are not statute barred. However, in one German case, the trial under the active personality principle in Germany itself was time-barred, and the alleged war criminal's extradition to the State with territorial jurisdiction was prohibited on the ground that nationals cannot be extradited under German law.[25]

---

21 Respectively, Articles 49 (I); 50 (II); 129 (III); 146 (IV).

22 1125 UNTS 3-608 (1979); 16 INT.LEG.MAT.1391 (1977). See also Green, *Rewriting the Laws of War: the Geneva Protocols of 1977*, International Perspectives, December 1977, pp.36 *et seq.*; Schutte, 'The System of Repression of Breaches of Additional Protocol I' (pp.177-96) and van den Wijngaert, 'The Suppression of War Crimes under Additional Protocol I' (pp.197-206), in DELISSEN & TANJA, HUMANITARIAN LAW OF ARMED CONFLICT: CHALLENGES AHEAD, 1991.

23 8 INT.LEG.MAT.68 (1969); G.A.Res/2391 (XXIII) DEC 9 1968; 65 AM.J INT'L L 476 (1971), Miller; see also the equivalent Council of Europe Convention, 25 JAN 1974, 13 INT.LEG.MAT.540 (1974); ETS 82.

24 87 INT'L L REP.93 (Dutch Supreme Court, 1981). See also, *Barbie*, 100 INT'L L REP.330 at 332-33 (1988).

25 The Guardian p.11, 2 MAR 1995, concerning Wolfgang Lehnigk-Emden.

Finally, in 1973, the General Assembly of the United Nations declared the 'Principles of international co-operation in the detection, arrest, extradition and punishment of persons guilty of war crimes and crimes against humanity'[26] which exhorts signatories to combat war crimes whenever and wherever committed. Each State can try its own nationals, although trial in the *locus delicti* is preferable; to that end, extradition is once again favoured.

The United Nations is consistent in its aim that all war criminals should be prosecuted and punished and that ordinarily this should be done by the State where the offence occurred – with armed conflicts increasingly being non-international in character, it may be that this preference will be more difficult to achieve in the subsequent peace, such that unless the proposed International Criminal Court is established, the Security Council will have to continue to create *ad hoc* tribunals such as those for the former Yugoslavia and Rwanda. The United Nations is not in favour of the adoption of universal jurisdiction, although it does not reject it completely.[27] The International Committee of the Red Cross places emphasis on High Contracting Parties having jurisdiction over grave breaches in order that the fugitive war criminal should not escape prosecution, but it makes extradition to the State where the offences occurred an equally valid alternative. Against this background, State practice with regard to the extradition or other means of return of war criminals must be considered.

c. The Extradition of War Criminals

Although war criminals ought to be prosecuted in the *locus delicti*, the usual rules concerning extradition procedures still have to be met. Thus, in *In re Rukavina*[28] the Court of Appeal at Rome refused extradition to Yugoslavia where the identity of the accused was not proven. The 1959 United States' case of *Artukovic*[29] was decided partly on the basis that the Yugoslav government had failed to provide sufficient evidence that Artukovic had per-

---

26 U.N.G.A.O.R. A/RES/3074 (XXVIII) 3 December 1973.
27 *Eg.* Art.6, Genocide Convention, *supra n*6; Art.1 of the 1973 Principles, *supra n*26.
28 16 INT'L L REP.273 (1949), Court of Appeal, Rome, Italy.
29 170 F.Supp 383 (1959) DCSD Cal.

petrated the alleged war crimes. Maybe less correctly, Germany refused to extradite one of its own nationals where it could not prosecute under its statute of limitations.[30] Finally, even if the fugitive is extradited, the principle of speciality still applies to his trial in the requesting State.[31] Thus, the alleged war criminal could only be prosecuted for those crimes for which he was extradited.

However, extradition requests have also been successfully challenged on the ground that the offence was allegedly political in character. The political offence exemption, which arose during the nineteenth century, was designed to provide asylum for those who committed crimes while attempting to overthrow a government.[32] It may be thought that war is one way of overthrowing a government, but 'war crimes' are excesses, unnecessary acts of barbarism; it is generally accepted that for the purposes of international criminal law, not every breach of the laws and customs of war shall be considered a 'war crime'.[33] The International Law Commission's Report of 1950, Part III of which set out the so-called Nuremberg Principles, attempted a definition of war crimes and crimes against humanity under Principle VI(b) and (c).[34] The term 'war crime' should be limited to acts

---

30 *Supra n25.*

31 *In re Issel*, 18 INT'L L REP.331 (1950), Eastern Provincial Court, Denmark.

32 See Chapter 6, above.

33 See Fenrick, *supra n*13, at pp.264 *et seq.* Traditionally, any violation of the laws of armed conflict is a war crime, but there is a growing consensus that the measures of substantive and procedural international criminal law should be confined to dealing with those responsible for severe breaches as outlined in the Nuremberg Principles.

34 U.N.G.A.O.R., V, Supp.12 (A/1316) pp.11-14, 1950. See paragraphs 119-124.
    "*Principle VI(b) War Crimes*: – Violations of the laws or customs of war which include, ... murder, ill-treatment or deportation to slave-labour or for any other purpose of civilian population ..., murder, ill-treatment of prisoners of war, ..., killing of hostages, ..., or devastation not justified by military necessity.
    Principle VI (c) Crimes Against Humanity:- Murder, extermination, enslavement, deportation and other inhuman acts done against any civilian population, or persecutions on political, racial or religious grounds, when such acts are done or such persecutions are carried on in execution of or in connection with any crime against peace (Principle VI(a)) or any war crime."
    The Principle is closely modelled Article 6 of the Charter of the International Military Tribunal at Nuremberg; see, *supra n9.*

"condemned by the common conscience of mankind, by reason of their brutality, inhumanity, or wanton disregard of rights of property unrelated to
reasonable military necessity."[35]

Lauterpacht also believed the term should not include every violation of
the Geneva Conventions.[36]

"[War crimes should include] such offences against the law of war as are
criminal in the ordinary and accepted sense of fundamental rules of warfare
and of general principles of criminal law by reason of their heinousness,
their brutality, their ruthless disregard of the sanctity of human life and
personality, or their wanton interference with rights of property unrelated
to reasonably conceived requirements of military necessity."

It is difficult to see conceive how "ill-treatment", "deportation", "slave-
labour", "persecution" or "devastation" not justified by "military necessity",
for example, could ever amount to an offence of a political character, that
is, one which "is incidental to and in furtherance of a political disturbance".[37] Unfortunately, the United States' analysis of the political offence
exemption, for instance, which is theoretically based on *Castioni*, used to
be interpreted such that any offence to do with a political disturbance or
uprising would be of a political character, given that there was no personal
motive[38]; a state of armed conflict would constitute such a political uprising.
Other courts similarly defined a political offence in terms wide enough to
include war crimes.

The Brazilian case of *In re Kahrs*[39] concerned a Norwegian group accused by Norway of 'war crimes': the facts of the case provide no greater
detail concerning the offences, other than that the fugitives supported a
nationalist organisation and the views it propagated. The Supreme Federal
Court of Brazil refused to grant the extradition request because the offence
was of a political character or a "crime of opinion". Having regard to the

---

35 SHEARER, STARKE'S INTERNATIONAL LAW, (11th ed., 1994) at p.502.
36 *The Law of Nations and the Punishment of War Crimes*, 21 BRIT.YB.INT'L L 58
    at p.79 (1944); cited in Fenrick, *supra* n13, at p.265.
37 Hawkins J, in *In re Castioni* [1891] 1 QB 149 at 166.
38 *In re Ezeta* 62 F.972 (1894).
39 15 INT'L L REP.301 (1948), Supreme Fed.Court of Brazil. Facts are set out at
    302.

definition of war crimes set out in the Nuremberg Principles, above, it is difficult to understand how the court arrived at such a conclusion. It must be hoped that if the full facts of the case were known, the decision would be found to be correct due to an extremely wide Norwegian interpretation of war crimes that goes beyond the grave breaches of the Geneva Conventions to include offences that, in fact, restrict the freedom of speech.[40] That is the only basis on which the fugitives could be prosecuted on political grounds for a "crime of opinion" if they were surrendered.

However, such a generous view cannot be extended to the original decision in the United States case of *Artukovic*.[41] Artukovic was Minister of the Interior under the Axis controlled Croatian Government of World War II. In that position he had allegedly ordered the death of 1,293 named persons and approximately 30,000 unidentified persons. The District Court for the Southern District of California held that these were political offences because they were committed at the time of a political uprising, namely the power struggle taking place during World War II in Croatia. The Court of Appeals for the Ninth Circuit upheld the refusal to extradite to Yugoslavia, stating that the principle that war crimes were automatically non-political did not have sufficient force of law.[42] Even accepting that stance by the United States' courts, it is difficult to see how the murder of 30,000 people, in the main civilians, could be part of or incidental to a political disturbance. The Supreme Court granted *certiorari*, vacated the Court of Appeals decision and remanded the case to the District Court. As stated above, the District Court at this second attempt again decided to refuse extradition, partly because of lack of evidence. Yet, it also found that the offences alleged were of a political character. The 1959 decision in the series of *Artukovic* cases would seem to be a most disturbing misinterpretation of the exemption. Not only should war crimes be excluded from the ambit of political offences,[43]

---

40 However, it may be that during armed conflicts, the media have a responsibility not to incite violations of the laws and customs of war – see HAMPSON, IN-CITEMENT AND THE MEDIA, Papers in the Theory and Practice of Human Rights, (1993).

41 140 F.Supp 245 (1956); 247 F.2d 198 (1957); 355 US 393 (1958); 170 F.Supp 383 (1959). *NB* Artukovic was eventually extradited thirty years later:- 628 F.Supp.1370 (1985); 784 F.2d 1354 (1986).

42 247 F.2d 198 at 205 (1957).

43 See, for example, the Genocide Convention, *supra n6*.

but the offences charged here were of a type and were of such a nature as
to stretch the scope of the accepted political incidence test beyond rational
limits.[44]

Fortunately, a line of cases has held that war crimes cannot be of a political character and this view appears to be gaining precedence. *In re Spiessens*[45] concerned a request to France by Belgium for a collaborator; collaboration with the enemy is not necessarily a war crime, but if such an offence were to lack a political character, then the more heinous war crimes and crimes against humanity discussed above are obviously mere common crimes. The court held as follows:

> "Moreover, in time of war, in a country occupied by the enemy, collaboration with the latter excludes the idea of a criminal action against the political organisation of the State which characterises the political offence."[46]

Since war crimes and crimes against humanity will usually be committed during an occupation, the French interpretation would exclude them from the category of political offences[47]; the developing trend towards non-international armed conflicts will require *Spiessens* to be read more widely, but the principle remains true.

More recently, the Ghanaian Court of Appeal, following the *Castioni* test, held that war crimes were not of a political character. In *The State v Schumann*,[48] the Federal Republic of Germany requested the extradition of the accused fugitive for murder: the offences had been committed at a mental institution and a concentration camp during the Nazi regime. The court said such offences were not political since the residents of the mental institution and the Jews in the concentration camp had not been opponents of the State who were trying to replace it. Merely carrying out Nazi ideology

---

44 The Ninth Circuit has accepted it erred in the 1959 decision; see, *Quinn v Robinson*, 783 F.2d 776 at 799 (1986). The Court of Appeals for the Seventh Circuit had accepted the criticisms of *Artukovic* somewhat earlier in *Eain v Wilkes* 641 F.2d 504 at 522 (1981).

45 16 INT'L L REP.275 (1949), Court of Appeal of Nancy, France.

46 *Supra* n45, at 276. *Cf. Residence Prohibition Order Case (No.2)*, 61 INT'L L REP.433 (Superior Admin.Ct. of Münster, F.R.G., 1968).

47 See, however, the strict French interpretation of the political offence test as laid down in *Re Giovanni Gatti*, [1947] Ann.Dig.145 at 145-46.

48 39 INT'L L REP.433 (1966).

was insufficient to brand the offences as political. It is odd that while the Swiss political offence test was also relied upon in part,[49] the predominance test of *Pavan*[50] was not referred to:

"Homicide – assassination and murder – is one of the most heinous crimes. It can only be justified where no other method exists of protecting the final rights of humanity."[51]

When the death constitutes a war crime or crime against humanity, murder hardly protects the final rights of humanity.

The Swiss courts have also held that war crimes and crimes against humanity are outside the ambit of the political offence exemption. In *Kroeger v The Swiss Federal Prosecutor's Office*,[52] the fugitive was requested for a series of mass executions in Poland and the Ukraine. The victims were Jews, communists and inmates of mental institutions, with no distinction being made on grounds of gender, age or helplessness. The accused raised a variety of defences,[53] including that the crimes were political in character and that they were legitimate reprisals under the laws of war.[54] With respect to the political offence exemption, Kroeger claimed that the murders were carried out as part of Nazi ideology. The Federal Tribunal found against him on the basis that mere political motivation was insufficient to render an offence political in character.[55]

"The offence must have been committed in the course of a struggle for power in the State and must also be in appropriate proportion to the object pursued, in other words suitable to the attainment of that object. The extinction of human life, one of the most reprehensible crimes, can only appear excusable if it constitutes a last resort in the pursuit of a political objective. On the facts, ... such a situation does not come into question. The accused

---

49 *Noblot*, [1927-28] Ann.Dig.350, referred to at 447 of the *Schumann* judgment.
50 *In re Pavan*, [1927-28] Ann.Dig.347, the case preceding *Noblot* in the reports.
51 *Supra n*50, at 349.
52 72 INT'L L REP.606 (Swiss Fed.Trib., 1966).
53 Including, that the offences were statute barred and that he had acted under superior orders. The latter defence was held to be a question for the full trial in the requesting State and so it was not examined on its merits.
54 See generally, KALSHOVEN, BELLIGERENT REPRISALS (1971).
55 *Supra n*52, at 612-13.

was acting at a time when the nationalist socialist regime stood at the pinnacle of its power. He acted against helpless women, children and sick persons who could not possibly have threatened German dominion."

The claim that the offences were a legitimate reprisal against a prior Soviet violation of the laws of armed conflict also failed on the ground of proportionality. "At the very least, the reprisals must not be obviously disproportionate to the wrong suffered ....".[56] Thus, war crimes and crimes against humanity are unlikely under the Swiss interpretation ever to be deemed non-extraditable on the basis of their underlying nature. The Swiss test has due regard to the gravity of the offences charged in assessing the motivation and context of the crime.

The Argentinean Supreme Court in the 1968 case of *In re Bohne*[57] reversed a previous practice of providing safe refuge to war criminals.[58] It adopted a stance not unlike that of the Swiss court in *Kroeger*.

"Extradition will not be denied on grounds of the political or military character of the charges where we are dealing with cruel or immoral acts which clearly shock the conscience of civilised people."

The British position towards war crimes and crimes against humanity and the political offence exemption used to be somewhat ambivalent. As Shearer explains, one reason it took the United Kingdom so long to ratify the Genocide Convention[59] was because it attempted to restrict the concept of political offences and the British view of asylum.[60] However, the current view can be inferred from the decision of *Re Gross, ex parte Treasury Solicitor*.[61] The case concerned a request for evidence from someone resident in the United Kingdom under s24 of the then Extradition Act 1870, for use in the trial of four former members of the SS in the then Federal Republic of Germany. The offences had taken place in Gusen Concentration Camp between

---

56 *Supra n*52, at 612-13.
57 62 AM.J INT'L L 784 at 784 (1968) – translated from *Jurisprudencia Argentina*, 1966-V, 339 at 340-41.
58 *Viz. Eichmann, supra n*8.
59 *Supra n*6.
60 SHEARER, EXTRADITION IN INTERNATIONAL LAW, (1971), at p.186. See also the statement of the Home Secretary, The Times, 19 JULY 1962, p.14.
61 [1968] 3 All ER 804 *esp.* at 807-10.

1941 and 1942. Section 24 provided that the witness in the United Kingdom should not have to give evidence if it was for a case where there was a "criminal matter of a political character". Chapman J held that atrocities committed by the accuseds in the F.R.G. were not of a political character and that the "proceedings" or "matter" were not political even though it had been suggested that the F.R.G. had to prosecute such persons for the purposes of improving international relations after World War II.[62] Therefore, it is fair to assume that a war criminal would be extradited from the United Kingdom, the political offence exception being of no avail to the fugitive. In a similar case before the Australian High Court, *R v Wilson, ex parte Witness T*,[63] Murphy J went so far as to hold that war crimes should not be protected by the political offence exemption.

The United States position has also changed. In *Re Ryan*,[64] the accused was returned to the then West Germany for crimes committed in Poland. In the mid-1980s, a US court ordered the extradition of John Demjanjuk to Israel for offences he was alleged to have committed while a concentration camp guard: he had been resident in the United States since 1952.[65]

"The murdering of numerous civilians while a guard in a Nazi concentration camp, as part of a larger 'Final Solution' to exterminate religious or ethnic groups, is not a crime of a 'political character' and is thus not covered by the political offense exception to extradition."

---

62 *Supra n*61, at 810.
63 86 INT'L L REP.169 at 179-81.
64 360 F.Supp 270 (1973); *aff'd* 478 F.2d 1397n (1973).
65 *In re Extradition of Demjanjuk*, 612 F.Supp 544 at 571; *Demjanjuk v Petrovsky*, 776 F.2d 571 (1985); *cert.den.*106 S.Ct 1198 (1986). See Reiss, *The Extradition of John Demjanjuk: War Crimes, Universality Jurisdiction and the Political Offense Doctrine*, 20 CORNELL INT'L LJ 281 (1987); Kremnitzer, 'The Demjanjuk Case' in DINSTEIN & TABORY, *supra n*10, at p.321.
   Demjanjuk was eventually acquitted in Israel on appeal. There then followed a farcical situation while he tried to return to the United States which did not want him. On the Israeli trial and its aftermath, see The Guardian p.20, 30 JUL 1993; p.9, 31 JUL 1993; p.18, 2 AUG 1993; p.9, 5 AUG 1993; p.10, 12 AUG 1993; p.6, 19 AUG 1993; p.8, 21 AUG 1993; p.8, 20 SEP 1993; p.13, 18 NOV 1993.

In *Atta*,[66] the District Court held that the political offence exemption as interpreted in the United States had been limited as a result of "international concern over the effect of hostilities on the innocent". The transnational fugitive offender accused of war crimes must prove the acceptability of his conduct under the rules of the international law of armed conflict, including wars of self-determination.

> "*Protocol I, Article 48*: In order to ensure respect for and protection of the civilian population and civilian objects, the Parties to the conflict shall at all times distinguish between the civilian population and combatants and between civilian objects and military objectives and accordingly shall direct their operations only against military objectives."[67]

Finally, the long standing anomaly of the decision in *Artukovic* was reversed in 1986 with his extradition to Yugoslavia.[68] The court took the opportunity to lay down further guidelines as to the interpretation of the political offence exemption, as it is understood in United States jurisprudence, *vis à vis* war crimes and crimes against humanity.[69] To be a political offence, the offence charged must be "incidental to" or "part of" a political disturbance. The prevailing situation in Croatia during World War II was such a disturbance. However, the court went on to decide that there must in addition be a "rational nexus" between the offences charged and the prevailing disturbance. The focus of the reasoning should be on the context of the crimes and the status of the victims. Reliance was placed on the Supreme Court's decision in *Ornelas v Ruiz*,[70] where the offences were held not to be political in view of the character of the foray, the mode of attack, the persons killed or captured and the property taken or destroyed. The Court also had regard to the Seventh Circuit's judgment in *Eain v Wilkes*,[71] where it was held that mere motivation was insufficient. In *Artukovic v Rison*, the offences

---

66 *In the Matter of the Extradition of Atta, Ahmad v Wigen* 726 F.Supp 389 at 406 (1989); *aff'd* 910 F.2d 1063 (1990).
67 *Supra* n22; cited in *Atta, supra* n66, at 406.
68 The original 1959 decision is dealt with at *supra* n41. See now, *The Matter of the Extradition of Artukovic*, 628 F.Supp 1370 (1985); *Artukovic v Rison*, 784 F.2d 1354 (CA9, 1986).
69 *Supra* n41, at 1376.
70 161 US 502 at 511.
71 *Supra* n44, at 520.

had been committed for personal gain, racial or religious hatred and/or impermissible vengeance on disarmed enemy soldiers: they were, thus, not of a political character.

Canadian courts dealt with the matter in *R and Federal Republic of Germany v Rauca*.[72] Here, the fugitive did not even bother to attempt to claim that the offence was political, but relied on rights under the Canadian Charter of Rights and Freedoms, Constitution Act 1982; Rauca wished to be tried in Canada for his crimes.[73] The Ontario Court of Appeal refused his application for *habeas corpus* and ordered his surrender.

There is a developing customary international law to the effect that war crimes and crimes against humanity are not to be regarded as political offences. As well as these individual cases, at a regional level the 1975 Additional Protocol to the European Convention on Extradition[74] excludes war crimes and crimes against humanity from the ambit of political offences under the parent convention.

"*Article 1* – For the application of Article 3 of the Convention, political offences shall not be considered to include the following:

a) the crimes against humanity specified in the Convention on the Prevention and Punishment of the Crime of Genocide adopted on 9 December 1948 by the General Assembly of the United Nations;

b) the violations specified in Article 50 of the 1949 Geneva Convention for the Amelioration of the Conditions of the Wounded and Sick in Armed Forces in the Field, Article 51 of the 1949 Geneva Convention for the Amelioration of the Conditions of Wounded, Sick and Shipwrecked Members of Armed Forces at Sea, Article 130 of the 1949 Geneva Convention relating to the Treatment of Prisoners of War and Article 147 of the 1949 Geneva Convention relating to the Protection of Civilian Persons in Time of War;

c) any comparable violations of the laws of war having effect at the time when this Protocol enters into force and of customs of war existing at that time, which are not already provided for in the above-mentioned provisions of the Geneva Conventions."

---

72 *Supra n*8.
73 See now, Fenrick, *supra n*13, at p.294.
74 ETS 86.

In conclusion, the trend of extraditing the fugitive to Germany is encouraging. However, it must be remembered that the U.N. treaties suggest trial in the State where the crime occurred and the government of the Germany has indicated it is only prepared to prosecute its own nationals.[75] It would also be helpful if a court would categorically state that war crimes and crimes against humanity are outside the purview of the political offence exemption, obviating the need for any more piecemeal municipal legislation or regional or international multilateral treaties which depend for their effectiveness on States ratifying them.

d. Asylum, Deportation, Expulsion and Abduction

Extradition is occasionally unavailable and alternative methods of return have been used. Coupled with deportation and expulsion is the admonition that war criminals should not be granted asylum.

(i) Asylum –

> "... States shall not grant asylum to any person with respect to whom there are serious reasons for considering that he has committed a crime against peace, a war crime or a crime against humanity."[76]

Taken from the 1973 Principles, discussed above, this is an all-pervasive exhortation to refuse asylum to war criminals. When refugees were eventually forcibly returned to Rwanda from Tanzania, many were arrested as genocide suspects.[77] However, the 1973 Principles are merely a recommendation, a pious hope, not a direction to States that is binding upon them.

The 1951 Convention Relating to the Status of Refugees and its 1967 Protocol[78] provide in Article 1F(a) of the Convention that those guilty of

---

75 See correspondence between US Attorney-General, William French-Smith, and German Justice Minister, Jurgen Schmude, 4 JAN and 12 FEB 1982, and covering press release 11 JUNE 1982. Referred to by Narvey, *Trial in Canada of Nazi War Criminals: Overcoming Certain Obiter in Rauca*, 34 CR (3d) 126 (1983).

76 *Supra n26*, Art.7.

77 The Guardian p.9, 3 JAN 1997.

78 189 UNTS 137 at p.150 & 606 UNTS 267, respectively.

war crimes are not to be treated as refugees for the purpose of granting asylum. Moreover, whilst Article 33 forbids *refoulement*, which encompasses the idea of a State refusing entry as well as deporting a refugee, the prohibition is circumscribed in that the right does not extend to those guilty of a 'serious crime'. It is self-evident that war crimes and crimes against humanity would fit within this category of serious offences.[79] Article 1F(c) also excludes from the scope of refugee status those who have acted contrary to the principles of the United Nations and who cannot, therefore, claim the protection of its humanitarian measures. Thus, the Convention and Protocol rights are not available to such fugitives.[80] Coupled with the direction to extradite war criminals previously considered, and the non-political nature of such offences, it would appear that there should be no safe havens. How, though, have individual States applied these Convention measures?

The United Kingdom incorporated the Convention and Protocol into its own immigration rules.[81] However, such provisions are ineffective against fugitive war criminals who have managed to become naturalised British citizens.[82] The United States, though has passed an Act which implements the Convention and Protocol in US law and which includes all the above-mentioned Convention provisions,[83] but has a specific measure pertinent to the issue of war criminals. The United States' Immigration and Naturalisation Service has power to deport aliens who, between March 23rd

---

79 Melaku Tefera was extradited from Djibouti to Ethiopia on charges of crimes against humanity, even though he had formerly been under the protection of UNHCR – The Guardian p.11, 19 MAY 1994; p.12, 23 MAY 1994.

80 It should be borne in mind that unarmed UNHCR workers may not be in a position to exclude heavily armed "refugees" in camps – everything is dependent on the host State and the political will of the international community. See Landgren, *Safety Zones and International Protection: A Dark Grey Area*, 7 INT'L J REFUGEE L 436 (1995).

81 See generally, MACDONALD AND BLAKE, IMMIGRATION LAW AND PRACTICE, (4th ed., 1995).

82 See the ability to prosecute even naturalized citizens for homicides committed during the Nazi era, regardless of the nationality they held at that time – War Crimes Act 1991. Universal jurisdiction already existed for those committing grave breaches of the Geneva Conventions 1949 – Geneva Conventions Act 1957 and the Geneva Conventions (Amendment) Act 1995.

83 8 USC §1253(h).

1933 and May 8th 1945, were connected with Nazism.[84] Connected thereto
is a power to strip the war criminal of his US citizenship. This amendment,
brought in with the Refugee Act 1980,[85] was initially applied to Artukovic.
In *Artukovic v I.N.S.*,[86] the Court of Appeals agreed to the deportation subject to a hearing to determine whether the appellant had participated in the
Nazi persecution in Croatia;[87] it rejected a claim that 8 USC. §1251(a)(19)
was unconstitutional as being contrary to the rules of natural justice on
grounds of retroactivity. In the end, Artukovic was eventually extradited
to Yugoslavia, rather than deported. However, the United States did deport
Feodor Fedorenko to the former Soviet Union to face war crimes charges,
having first stripped him of his citizenship.

In the case of Argentina, long a safe haven for Nazis, the government
adopted a new approach in 1984. It rescinded the grant of political refugee
status and ordered the expulsion of two Bolivian generals accused, *inter
alia*, of genocide.[88] It would seem therefore, that governments throughout
the world are increasingly willing to rid themselves of war criminals. However, extradition between the two concerned States rather than deportation
would be a more suitable vehicle for dealing with such fugitives – the two
Bolivian generals went missing somewhere in South America and their trial
in Bolivia had to continue *in absentia*.

(ii) Deportation or Expulsion – Nevertheless, deportation and expulsion have
successfully been used in the past. Immediately after World War II, when
there was no *de jure* German government following the unconditional surrender, many war criminals were returned to States in occupied Europe
despite the fact that extradition treaties had lapsed during the war.[89] Gen-

---

84   8 USC §1251(a)(19). *Cf.* Gordon in Evans, *International Procedures for the
     Apprehension and Rendition of Fugitive Offenders*, [1980] A.S.I.L. PROC.274 at
     pp.284-86, on the problems of deporting war criminals.
85   PL 69-212; 94 Stat.107.
86   693 F.2d 894 (1983).
87   See the doubts expressed by the District Court in 170 F.Supp 383 (1959), on
     Artukovic. On Fedorenko, see The Guardian p.6, 21 DEC 1984. See also Avdzej,
     a former US citizen who voluntarily returned to the then F.R.G. The Guardian,
     20 OCT 1984.
88   The Guardian p.4, 18 FEB 1984.
89   See *Argento v Horn*, 241 F.2d 258 (1957); *cert.den.*355 US 818 (1957). See
     also SHEARER, *supra* n60, at pp.43-45.

erally, special arrangements were concluded between the Allied Powers and the formerly occupied States.[90] As was stated in *In re Flesche*.

> "[from] this series of declarations and agreements it was evident that it was the firm intention of all the Powers allied against Germany and her allies to ensure, in despite of all the traditional rules relating to the extradition of political criminals and of a State's own nationals, that, by a form of collaboration to be defined later, all war criminals should be delivered over to the respective allied States in which they had perpetrated their crimes."[91]

Such arrangements did not contain the usual protections of extradition treaties, such as the principle of specialty in *Flesche's* case. They were a hybrid of extradition and deportation and they were obviously necessary in the aftermath of World War II.

However, Klaus Barbie was expelled from Bolivia to France[92] in relation to crimes against humanity in the 1980s. He alleged that expulsion to France amounted to disguised extradition and that France was in violation of international law for having obtained jurisdiction in these circumstances. The *Cour de Cassation* held that

> "'all necessary measures' are to be taken by the Member States of the United Nations to ensure that war crimes, crimes against peace and crimes against humanity are punished and that those persons suspected of being responsible for such crimes are sent back 'to the countries in which their abominable deeds were done in order that they may be judged and punished according to the laws of those countries'"[93]

On the basis of the *Cour de Cassation's* reasoning, the power to deport or expel is to be treated as coextensive with extradition. Where no extradition treaty exists,[94] or where it is likely that the fugitive may flee again, then

---

90 See the St James' Palace Declaration of 13 JAN 1942 and the London Agreement of 8 AUG 1945. See also, OPPENHEIM, DISPUTES, WAR AND NEUTRALITY, at p.583,*n*2, (7th ed., 1952).

91 16 INT'L L REP.226 at 228 (1949), Special Criminal Court, Amsterdam, Holland.

92 *Supra n*14.

93 *Supra n*14, at 131.

94 For example, there is no extradition treaty between Israel and Chile for the Rauff request, *supra n*3.

deportation or expulsion may be suitable as alternatives, but it would be inappropriate to use them in a general fashion to deny rights granted by extradition treaties.[95] Even the United Nations recognises this through its exhortations to extradite fugitive war criminals rather than summarily surrendering them to the requesting State.[96] It is possible that such procedures might also violate regional human rights conventions, such as the European Convention on Human Rights following the decision in *Bozano v France*.[97]

(iii) Abduction – The attitudes to war crimes have led on at least one occasion to an offender being kidnapped, as was seen in Chapter Seven above. In 1960, Adolf Eichmann was abducted from Argentina to Israel; whether by Israeli agents or private individuals is not clear, but Israel definitely 'adopted' these acts by prosecuting Eichmann.[98] There was no extradition treaty between Argentina and Israel, but the kidnap obviously violated Argentine sovereignty and resulted in a United Nations Security Council resolution to try to solve the matter. As Shearer points out, "abduction is such a manifestly extra-legal act"[99] it should not be adopted even with respect to war criminals.[100]

(iv) Summary – Although extradition is the recommended process for returning war criminals to the *locus delicti*, expulsion especially is being used as a viable alternative. It would appear that it is now accepted that war crimes are not political offences and it is to be hoped that kidnapping will

---

95 *Eg. R v Governor of Brixton Prison, ex p.Soblen*, [1962] 3 All ER 641.
96 Although it still continues – see Central Europe Today on Canada's plans to deport former Nazis to the Czech Republic and Latvia, 20 APR 1995; see also, The Guardian p.9, 10 APR 1993.
97 See Chapter Seven; 9 EHRR 297 (1986).
98 *Attorney General of the Government of Israel v Adolf Eichmann*, *supra n8*; Cardozo, *When Extradition fails is Abduction the Solution*, 55 AM.J INT'L L 127 (1960); see Chapter Seven.
99 *Supra n60*, at p.75.
100 On the other hand, with respect to the International Criminal Tribunal for the former Yugoslavia, the failure by the authorities in Serbia, Croatia and Republika Srpska, in particular, to surrender indicted war criminals to the Hague, has seen S-FOR apprehend those wanted, although they would be authorised so to act under Chapter VII. And see, The Guardian p.10, 20 DEC 1996.

remain dormant for war criminals. Unfortunately,[101] many war criminals are still at large, enjoying immunity,[102] although it should be noted that the State where they obtain asylum may suffer sanctions as a result,[103] and they are effectively condemned to a life of internal exile as they dare not travel abroad for fear of arrest.[104]

e. Jurisdiction and War Criminals

The final question concerns the ultimate destination of such fugitives. Who has jurisdiction over war criminals? Obviously, the State where the crimes were perpetrated may claim territorial jurisdiction.[105] If territorial jurisdiction is claimed, however, then it must be shown that the State had control of that territory at the time the offences were committed, a not simple post-conflict question if new States have been created or borders have been re-drawn. Moreover, the case of *In re Lo Dolce*[106] was decided partly on the basis that at the relevant time the Italian government was not in control of its territory because it was occupied by the allied forces. As an alternative to the exercise of territorial jurisdiction, Germany has undertaken to prosecute its own nationals for war crimes wherever committed[107] and, for the

---

101 Halberstam, *What Price Peace: From Nuremberg to Bosnia to the Nobel Peace Prize*, 3 ILSA J INT'L & COMP.L 570 (1997).

102 D'Amato, *Peace vs. Accountability in Bosnia*, 88 AM.J INT'L L 500 (1994); Orentlicher, *Swapping Amnesty for Peace and the Duty to Prosecute Human Rights Crimes*, 3 ILSA J INT'L & COMP.L 713 (1997).

103 The Guardian p.14, 10 JAN 1997.

104 The Independent p.15, 27 MAR 1997.

105 See France's prosecution of Klaus Barbie, *supra* n14, and Italy's somewhat inglorious but eventually successful prosecution of Erich Priebke – The Guardian p.3, 2 AUG 1996; p.9, 5 AUG 1996; p.11, 14 AUG 1996; p.15, 16 OCT 1996; p.10, 23 JUL 1997. Belatedly, France started to prosecute its own nationals for crimes committed as part of the Vichy government – see *Touvier* 100 INT'L L REP.337 (1992, with 1994 addendum at 364), and the trial of Maurice Papon, The Guardian p.13, 24 JAN 1997.

106 18 INT'L L REP.318 (1952), District Court, Western District, New York, USA *Cf. In re Flesche*, *supra* n91, where the Allies returned a Nazi war criminal to the Netherlands for trial, even though his crime must have occurred while The Netherlands was occupied.

107 *Supra* n75.

time being, that would seem appropriate in the present circumstances. Occasionally though, neither Germany nor the State where the offence occurred will be willing or able to prosecute. In such cases, should universal jurisdiction be adopted and, in particular in the case of alleged Nazi atrocities, should Israel assume jurisdiction?

(i) Israel and Nazi War Criminals – Israel claims jurisdiction under its own 'Nazi and Nazi Collaborators (Punishment) Law of 1951' over war crimes, crimes against Jewish people and crimes against humanity.[108] It is not disputed that the Israeli government has the greatest interest in prosecuting Nazi war criminals, even though the State of Israel did not exist at the time of the crimes and the Jewish people were not the only ones to be victimized during the holocaust. Lest the war criminal would otherwise escape punishment, Israel should have jurisdiction like any other State. However, if the State where the crime occurred is willing to prosecute, then both United Nations policy and the general principle of international law that territorial jurisdiction takes primacy, would suggest that the fugitive should be surrendered to the authorities there.

Israel asserts the right to prosecute by exercise of three principles of jurisdiction; protective, passive personality and universal. The protective principle was used in *Eichmann*.[109] There are problems with this principle in Israel's case, for, at the time of the offences, the State of Israel did not exist and therefore it is questionable whether the crimes could threaten the vital interests of the State. The court in *Eichmann* argued, however, that the vital interests of the Jewish people had been threatened by the holocaust and on that ground the linking-point with Israel had been established.[110] Indeed, the language of the judgment would go so far as to permit an assertion of jurisdiction on the basis of the passive personality principle,[111] even though the victims were not Israeli nationals. Technically, the argument that the Jewish people could constitute the State-of-Israel-in-waiting, as it were, is not supported by international law, but, with respect to jurisdiction over war crimes alone, it does not seem that the issue has been contested.

---

108 See the *Eichmann* case, *supra n*8.
109 *Supra n*8. See Reiss, *supra n*65, at pp.301-07.
110 *Supra n*8, at paras.30-38.
111 See also the *Lotus Case (Turkey v France)* 1927 PCIJ Reps, Series A, No10.
    See Fenrick, *supra n*13, at pp.281-82.

If the universality principle is applicable, however, then there is no difference between Israel and any other State. On the other hand, there is a general principle of international practice[112] that before arrogating to itself such jurisdiction, the holding State ought to offer the fugitive for prosecution to the State with territorial jurisdiction. However, since many of the victims and much of the information concerning Nazi war crimes are in Israel, it may be that the rationale for this rule of practice is not as forceful. In the *Demjanjuk* extradition cases in the United States, both the District and Circuit courts supported Israel's right to prosecute the accused on the basis of the universality principle.[113] Neither court dealt in any great depth with either of the other two principles of jurisdiction asserted by Israel in *Eichmann*. The only jurisdictional question, therefore, is the appropriateness of the universality principle to war crimes and crimes against humanity.

On the other hand, it may be asked whether the trial in Israel will be neutral. This is not to allege overt bias or lack of impartiality on the part of the judiciary; indeed, Israeli trials of Nazi war criminals have been conducted with an impeccable regard to the rules of evidence – and it needs to be noted that John Demjanjuk was eventually acquitted.[114] However, it is a natural function of that branch of government that exercises legal punishment in a State to be harsher when the State or its citizens have been attacked, while the public opinion in the State coalesces to create almost a national will to find those accused guilty. An analogy may be drawn with the release of the Guildford Four and the quashing of the Maguire Seven's convictions in the United Kingdom in 1990,[115] both of which cast doubt

---

112 See Fawcett *The Eichmann Case*, 38 BRIT.YB.INT'L L 181 (1962), where he considers Poland's readiness to try Eichmann at pp.206-07.

113 612 F.Supp 544 at 555; 776 F.2d 571 at 582.

114 The effect on the collective psychology of Israel of having to release someone suspected of having committed crimes other than those for which he had been extradited equally needs to be borne in mind. In the words of an Israeli commentator (The Guardian2 pp.2 and 3, 30 JUL 1993):
"Whoever thought of turning it into a new Eichmann trial made a grievous error. There was only one Eichmann and it was enough to have that one trial of its kind conducted by the State of Israel in the name of the victims of the Holocaust."

115 Guildford Four, The Times pp.1 and 5, 19 OCT 1989; Maguire Seven, The Guardian p.20, 12 JULY 1990. See also the Patrick Ryan farrago. Ryan was arrested in Belgium in the Summer of 1988 on suspicion of being involved in

on the neutrality of the British legal system as regards Irish nationals charged with terrorist offences. There is no simple answer to the problem posed and, in the end, the balance must come down in favour of the war criminal being prosecuted for his heinous crimes. Yet, it does provide further support for the argument for trial in the *locus delicti* wherever possible. In conclusion, to prevent Nazi war criminals enjoying immunity, Israel should continue to prosecute and punish them, but this should only be where the State with territorial jurisdiction refuses to prosecute.

(ii) Nationals as War Criminals – The active personality principle of jurisdiction is pertinent to war crimes. The idea that trials of war criminals are mere victor's justice ignores the fact that members of the armed forces are regularly prosecuted by their own military courts for violations of the various laws and customs of war.[116] In the United Kingdom, s220 Army Act 1955 provides jurisdiction over crimes committed anywhere in the world by a serving member of the British military.[117] Canada convicted one of its

---

terrorist activities on behalf of the IRA. After two months in Belgian custody a request for his extradition was made by the British government. For reasons not very clearly explained, the Belgian cabinet refused his extradition and deported him to Ireland – see *Ryan*, 100 INT'L L REP.616, esp. at 622. Whilst waiting for the decision of the Irish authorities concerning his surrender, the British press and certain members of the House of Commons made allegations about Ryan's involvement in terrorist activities that might have prejudiced any future trial in Great Britain. The Irish Attorney-General refused to endorse the British arrest warrant on December 13 1988. Contrary to normal practice, however, the Attorney-General issued a sixteen page statement setting out his reasons for refusing extradition. The problem, as far as the Irish government was concerned, was that press reports and statements in the British House of Commons had prejudged Ryan's guilt (see paras.9 and 16 of the statement – I am grateful to the Irish Embassy in London for a copy). However, he did raise the possibility of a trial in Dublin under the Criminal Law (Jurisdiction) Act 1976 – in the end, the British authorities could not provide sufficient evidence for an extra-territorial trial to be instituted. See The Times, p.1, 26 NOV 1988; p.1, 29 NOV 1988; p.1, 3 DEC 1988; p.1, 5 DEC 1988; p.2, 8 DEC 1988; pp.1 & 6, 14 DEC 1988; and pp.1 & 16, 15 DEC 1988; The Guardian, p.2, 9 FEB 1989.

116 See Hampson, 'Liability for war crimes', in ROWE, *supra* n12.
117 See also *R v Page* [1953] 2 All ER 1355.

soldiers who had served in Somalia as part of the United Nations peace-keeping force for torture, a war crime and a crimes against humanity.[118]

(iii) Universal Jurisdiction[119] – Israel's claim to jurisdiction is made under the universal, the passive personality and the protective principles, since the 'vital interests of the State' are deeply concerned. Only the universality principle would apply to other States, leaving open the question whether war crimes and crimes against humanity are universal crimes. Judge Moore in the *Lotus Steamship*[120] gave a dissenting judgment that tells against the use of the universality principle.

> "But the case is fundamentally different where a country claims either that its penal laws apply to other countries and to what takes place wholly within such countries or, ..., that it may punish foreigners for alleged violations, even in their own country, of laws to which they were not subject."

However, given that war crimes and crimes against humanity are so heinous that anyone committing one would be aware of the gravity of the offence, which same fact would justify his prosecution no matter where he is found, Judge Moore's strictures are not determinative in these circumstances. War crimes and crimes against humanity, as understood in this chapter, would be known by their perpetrators to be contrary to the general principles of law common to all nations, acknowledging thereby their universal status.

> "[The] development of the law in this field seems to be moving towards a recognition of universal jurisdiction over all serious war crimes; and it would not seem unreasonable to conclude that this recognition was already complete."[121]

---

118 The Guardian p.15, 8 MAR 1994; see also, p.12, 28 APR 1994.
119 Gasser, 'Ensuring Respect for the Geneva Conventions and Protocols: The Role of Third States and the United Nations', in FOX & MEYER, EFFECTING COMPLIANCE, 1993, at p.15.
120 *Supra* n111, at 82.
121 Carnegie, *Jurisdiction over Violations of the Laws and Customs of War*, 39 BRIT.YB.INT'L L 402, at p.424 (1963). A Danish court has convicted a Bosnian Muslim of gross violence and murder for crimes committed in a camp near Mostar – The Times p.13, 23 NOV 1994. See also, *Tadić, infra* n143.

Moreover, it has been suggested that Article V, Genocide Convention 1948[122] confers universal jurisdiction on all States and that this is part of customary international law.[123] Further, the United Nations War Crimes Commission stated:

> "... the right to punish war crimes ... is possessed by any independent State whatsoever, ..."[124]

The Geneva Conventions and 1977 Additional Protocol I require High Contracting Parties to enact legislation to provide effective penal sanctions for persons committing such grave offences as are set out.[125] By way of example, the United Kingdom has implemented this requirement in the Geneva Conventions Act 1957 and the Geneva Conventions (Amendment) Act 1995.[126] In consequence of actions perpetrated during the performance of duties on behalf of the United Nations, Canada, Italy and Belgium have all had to carry out war crimes investigations of members of their armed forces.[127] Canada also prosecuted alleged war criminals from the Nazi era,

---

122 *Supra n*6. (*Cf.* Art. VI)
   "The Contracting Parties undertake to enact, in accordance with their respective Constitutions, the necessary legislation to give effect to the provisions of the present Convention and, in particular, to provide effective penalties for persons guilty of genocide or any of the other acts enumerated in Article III."

123 Carnegie, *supra n*121, at p.421. Canada investigated the case of Leon Mugesera, a former Hutu government official from Rwanda, accused of inciting genocide, relying on its power to prosecute anyone accused of crimes against humanity under its War Crimes Act – The Guardian p.8, 17 AUG 1994.

124 15 War Crimes Reports 26 (1949). Cited in HARRIS, CASES AND MATERIALS ON INTERNATIONAL LAW, (4th ed., 1991) at p.275.

125 *Supra n*20, Geneva Convention I, Arts.49 & 50; II, Arts.50 & 51; III, Arts.129 & 130; IV, Arts.146 & 147. Protocol I to the Geneva Conventions, 1977, applies the same protections for the new fields now covered – Art.85 (see *supra n*22).

126 See Rowe and Meyer, *The Geneva Conventions (Amendment) Act 1995: A Generally Minimalist Approach*, 45 INT'L & COMP.LQ 476 (1996); Hampson, *The Geneva Conventions and the Detention of Civilians and Alleged Prisoners of War*, [1991] PUB.LAW 507. For the trial of persons for crimes committed in WWII prior to the Geneva Conventions, see the War Crimes Act 1991.

127 See Canada's experience of violations committed by its troops in Somalia (The Guardian p.8, 5 April 1993, p.15, 17 January 1997, and p.21, 3 July 1997) and Bosnia-Herzegovina (The Guardian p.12, 18 January 1997), and, again in Somalia, Belgium's (The Guardian p.21, 12 April 1997, p.14, 23 June 1997

although their acquittals, especially that in the *Finta* case[128] led to a change in the Canadian law. Furthermore, the extremely broad interpretation of the defence of superior orders[129] begs the question as to how far universal crimes[130] can best be prosecuted in domestic courts which all apply different notions of the crimes and the scope of any pertinent defence.

Apparently war crimes, like piracy, are triable by a court anywhere in the world, although it would be preferable for the time being that they be tried in the State where the crime was committed.[131] This policy is the general practice[132] and only Israel seems prepared to act independently, for the obvious reasons.

(iv) An International Criminal Tribunal? – An alternative arising out of the Nuremberg Tribunal and Article 6 Genocide Convention is to establish an international court for the trial of war criminals. The idea is an old one, dating back to the fifteenth century at least. McCoubrey[133] cites the case of Peter von Hagenbach from 1474.[134] Hagenbach, as Governor of Brei-

---

and p.12, 1 July 1997) and Italy's (The Guardian p.18, 7 June 1997 and p.15, 25 June 1997). Somali faction leaders have asserted that they should receive damages from the United Nations for the behaviour of these troops – The Guardian p.14, 12 July 1997. See also, Alex de Waal, A Brutal Peace, The Guardian, Editorial, p.21, 30 October 1997.

128 (1989) 61 DLR (4th) 85 (Ont HC); (1992) 92 DLR (4th) 1 (Ont CA); [1994] SCR 701, (1994) 112 DLR (4th) 513, 88 C.C.C. 3d 417. See also, Cotler, 90 AM.J INT'L L 460 at p.475.

129 *Supra n*128, (1994) 112 DLR (4th) 513 at 604-20 (SCC).

130 See *Polyukhovich v Commonwealth of Australia* 91 INT'L L REP.1 at 104-05(1991), where the Australian High Court on a preliminary matter refused to accept that the domestic legislation was retroactive since the offences would have been proscribed in any civilized society – Polyukhovich was eventually acquitted in 1993.

131 The success rate for prosecuting alleged Nazis from WWII is not high – see The Guardian p.2, 15 DEC 1993.

132 *Eg.* The *Rauca* case where Canada refused jurisdiction which it probably had under its then War Crimes Act and Geneva Conventions Act, *supra n*8, and Narvey, *supra n*75.

133 Paper delivered at the University of Southampton, England, September 1989, at p.3. See also BASSIOUNI, *supra n*11, at p.416.

134 Also cited by SCHWARZENBERGER, vol.2, INTERNATIONAL LAW AS APPLIED BY INTERNATIONAL COURTS AND TRIBUNALS, at pp.462-66 and Fenrick, *supra n*13, at p.275.

sach, instituted a reign of terror on behalf of the Duke of Burgundy. After
the defeat of the Burgundian forces, Hagenbach was put on trial for what
would today be crimes against humanity, since, for the most part, his offences occurred before the start of the armed conflict. The tribunal was drawn
from Breisach and from other cities within the Holy Roman Empire. Such
was the state of the Empire at this time, though, that it was tantamount to
an international tribunal.[135] Hagenbach was found guilty and beheaded.
The Breisach court shows that from earliest times it has been useful to try
war criminals before a widely drawn court. Such a tribunal should remove
any fear of prejudice that a national court might suffer from. In the 1950s,
the International Law Commission was asked to consider the establishment
of a permanent international criminal tribunal. Unfortunately, nothing came
of the General Assembly's efforts at that time. Oppenheim's International
Law,[136] while noting the political practicalities of establishing such a
tribunal, has stated that "an important international judicial organ open to
all and established prior to the hostilities", is a requirement both of justice
and of the effectiveness of international law. The need for consistent
judgments and a judiciary familiar with the appropriate law leads one to
the conclusion that such an organ should be of a permanent nature. An international court would mean that all of the fugitive's war crimes, wherever
committed, could be dealt with at once,[137] obviating, at the same time,
the need for extradition or other form of return. The advantages do not need
to be spelt out. To that end, the *ad hoc* tribunals for Rwanda and the former
Yugoslavia and the proposed International Criminal Court are worthy of
some detailed consideration, although they could easily fill several volumes
on their own.

---

135 McCoubrey, at pp.3-4.
136 Vol.2, DISPUTES, WAR AND NEUTRALITY (7th ed., LAUTERPACHT, 1952) at p.586.
137 The Netherlands expressed an interest in prosecuting Klaus Barbie as well as
    France. The Guardian p.8, 8 MARCH 1984.

International Criminal Tribunals[138]: – Issues concerning transfer to such tribunals were considered in Chapter Two.[139] In this section, more substantive questions about the tribunals' own practice will be examined. The establishment of *ad hoc* tribunals for the Former Yugoslavia and Rwanda and the preparations for an International Criminal Court mean that transnational fugitive offenders accused of certain specific offences generally associated with armed conflict are now to be dealt with under the closest approximation so far to truly international criminal law, rather than through the domestic application of norms drawn up by the international community in the wake of international armed conflicts.[140]

The International Criminal Tribunal for the Former Yugoslavia (ICTY)[141] and that for Rwanda (ICTR)[142] were established by the Security Council. Following the decision in *Tadić*,[143] it is clear that the Security Council

---

138 See generally, Broms, 'The Establishment of an International Criminal Court', in DINSTEIN AND TABORY, *supra* n10, at p.183; Meron, *War Crimes in Yugoslavia and the Development of International Law*, 88 AM.J INT'L L 78 (1994), and *International Criminalization of Internal Atrocities*. 89 AM.J INT'L L 554 (1995); Green, *Low-Intensity Conflict and the Law*, 3 ILSA J INT'L & COMP.L 493 (1997).

139 Certain introductory paragraphs may be found in both Chapters.

140 For non-legal issues, see Forsythe, *International Criminal Courts: A Political View*, 15 NQHR 5 (1997).

141 The Statute of the Tribunal was presented to the Security Council in *The Report of the Secretary-General Pursuant to Paragraph 2 of Security Council Resolution 808 (1993)*, (hereinafter, Report), 32 INT.LEG.MAT.1159 (1993). The Statute was adopted by the Security Council in Resolution 827 (1993) and may be found in 32 INT.LEG.MAT.1192 (1993). The Rules of Procedure and Evidence (hereinafter, Rules) are now at Revision 6 – IT/32/Rev.6. And see Zagaris, 'War Crimes Tribunal in Former Yugoslavia' in ATKINS, THE ALLEGED TRANSNATIONAL CRIMINAL, 1995, at pp.9 *et seq*.

142 UNSC Res.935 and 955 (1994), reprinted in 5 CRIM.LF 695 (1994). Rules of Procedure and Evidence, ITR/3/Rev.1 (1995), entry into force 29 June 1995. And see Morris, *Justice in the Wake of Genocide: the Case of Rwanda*, 3 ILSA J.INT'L L 689 (1997).

143 *Duško Tadić, a.k.a. 'Dule', Decision on the Defence Motion for Interlocutory Appeal on Jurisdiction before the Appeals Chamber of ICTY*, Case No.IT-94-1-AR72 (1995), *per* Cassese J., at paras.9-48: noted by Warbrick and Rowe, 45 INT'L & COMP.LQ 691 (1996). Tadić was convicted on 7 May 1997 (IT-94-1-T) and sentenced in July to 20 years imprisonment – The Guardian p.11, 15 JUL 1997.

has jurisdiction to establish such bodies. Under Article 41 of Chapter VII of the United Nations Charter, the Security Council "may decide what measures ... are to be employed to give effect to its decisions" to maintain or restore international peace and security.

> "The Security Council has resorted to the establishment of a judicial organ in the form of an international criminal tribunal as an instrument for the exercise of its own principal function of maintenance of peace and security, *ie*, as a measure contributing to the restoration and maintenance of peace and security in the former Yugoslavia"[144]

First, the issue of the definition of crimes for the purposes of the Tribunals and for the purposes of universal jurisdiction[145] needs to be addressed. According to *In re List*[146]:

> "An international crime is ... an act universally recognised as criminal, which is considered a grave matter of international concern and for some valid reason cannot be left within the exclusive jurisdiction of the State that would have control over it under ordinary circumstances."

As such, whether it is prosecuted before an international tribunal or a domestic court on the basis of universal jurisdiction, the elements of the crime should be similar, lest a narrow definition under one system detracts from the scope of the other – given that the Tribunals' definitions are the more recent, it is those which might cause a re-interpretation of the definitions accepted for the purposes of universal jurisdiction.

The Tribunal in *Tadić*[147] was aware of its place in the overall scheme of enforcement of breaches of international criminal law[148] – it may be

---

144 *Tadić, supra* n143, para.38.
145 See generally, Randall, *Universal Jurisdiction under International Law*, 66 TEX.L REV.785 (1988).
146 Case No.215, United States Military Tribunal at Nuremberg, 15 Ann.Dig.632 at 636 (1948).
147 *Supra* n143, *per* Cassese J., at paras.79-142.
148 See para.80 *per* Cassese J., *supra* n143.

geographically and temporarily restricted,[149] but it is part of a wider picture and its deliberations will necessarily impact upon the enforcement of those crimes defined within its Statute when similar breaches, perpetrated outside the former Yugoslavia and Rwanda, are prosecuted before domestic courts. In *Eichmann*,[150] the Israeli Supreme Court used, *inter alia*, universal jurisdiction to justify the trial of *Eichmann* before Israeli courts for war crimes and crimes against humanity. However, the International Tribunals are different in nature to domestic courts asserting universal jurisdiction. Nor are these two new *ad hoc* tribunals identical to the Nuremberg Tribunal – that was established as a military tribunal by occupying forces after an international armed conflict,[151] whereas the Yugoslav and Rwanda Tribunals are the result of a Security Council Resolution under Chapter VII of the United Nations Charter. The Yugoslav Statute[152] provides for the prosecution of grave breaches of the Geneva Conventions of 1949,[153] violations

---

149 *"Article 1 Competence of the International Tribunal*
The International Tribunal shall have the power to prosecute persons responsible for serious violations of international humanitarian law committed in the territory of the former Yugoslavia since 1991 in accordance with the provisions of the present Statute."
150 36 INT'L L REP.5 (1962); see District Court at 26 and Supreme Court at 277.
151 See Randall, *supra* n145, at pp.801-03. It is not clear that the Nuremberg Tribunal was an example of universal jurisdiction – pp.804 *et seq.*
152 *Supra* n141.
153 *"Article 2 Grave breaches of the Geneva Conventions of 1949*
The International Tribunal shall have the power to prosecute persons committing or ordering to be committed grave breaches of the Geneva Conventions of 12 August 1949, namely the following acts against persons or property protected under the provisions of the relevant Geneva Convention:
(a) wilful killing;
(b) torture or inhuman treatment, including biological experiments;
(c) wilfully causing great suffering or serious injury to body or health;
(d) extensive destruction and appropriation of property, not justified by military necessity and carried out unlawfully and wantonly;
(e) compelling a prisoner of war or a civilian to serve in the forces of a hostile power;
(f) wilfully depriving a prisoner of war or a civilian of the rights of fair and regular trial;
(g) unlawful deportation or transfer or unlawful confinement of a civilian;
(h) taking civilians as hostages."

of the laws or customs of war,[154] genocide[155] and crimes against humanity.[156] The Rwanda Statute, dealing with crimes which occurred in a non-

---

154 *"Article 3 Violations of the Laws or Customs of War*
   The International Tribunal shall have the power to prosecute persons violating
   the laws or customs of war. Such violations shall include, but not be limited
   to:
   (a) employment of poisonous weapons or other weapons calculated to cause
   unnecessary suffering;
   (b) wanton destruction of cities, towns or villages, or devastation not justified
   by military necessity;
   (c) attack, or bombardment, by whatever means, of undefended towns, villages,
   dwellings, or buildings;
   (d) seizure of, destruction or wilful damage done to institutions dedicated to
   religion, charity and education, the arts and sciences, historic monuments and
   works of art and science;
   (e) plunder of public or private property."
155 *"Article 4 Genocide*
   1. The International Tribunal shall have the power to prosecute persons committing genocide as defined in paragraph 2 of this article or of committing any
   of the other acts enumerated in paragraph 3 of this article.
   2. Genocide means any of the following acts committed with intent to destroy,
   in whole or in part, a national, ethnical, racial or religious group, as such:
   (a) killing members of the group;
   (b) causing serious bodily or mental harm to members of the group;
   (c) deliberately inflicting on the group conditions of life calculated to bring about
   its physical destruction in whole or in part;
   (d) imposing measures intended to prevent births within the group;
   (e) forcibly transferring children of the group to another group.
   3. The following acts shall be punishable:
   (a) genocide;
   (b) conspiracy to commit genocide;
   (c) direct and public incitement to commit genocide;
   (d) attempt to commit genocide;
   (e) complicity in genocide."
156 *"Article 5 Crimes Against Humanity*
   The International Tribunal shall have the power to prosecute persons responsible
   for the following crimes when committed in armed conflict, whether international or internal in character, and directed against any civilian population:
   (a) murder;
   (b) extermination;
   (c) enslavement;
   (d) deportation;

international armed conflict, has slightly different jurisdictional competence[157]: genocide,[158] crimes against humanity[159] and violations of common Article 3 to the Geneva Conventions and of Additional Protocol II.[160] Mandatory universal jurisdiction[161] only applies to the grave breach

---

(e) imprisonment;
(f) torture;
(g) rape;
(h) persecutions on political, racial and religious grounds;
(i) other inhumane acts."
Cf. Paust, *Threats to Accountability after Nuremberg: Crimes Against Humanity, Leader Responsibility and National Fora*, 12 NYLS J HUM.RTS 547 at p.553 (1995).

157 Several cases are proceeding through the Arusha Tribunal – see the Independent Newsletter on the International Criminal Tribunal for Rwanda, *Ubutabera*, distributed by email in French (see also: http://persoweb.francenet.fr/~intermed).

158 Article 2 – identical to the provision for ICTY, *supra* n155.

159 "*Article 3 Crimes against humanity*
The International Tribunal for Rwanda shall have the power to prosecute persons responsible for the following crimes when committed as part of a widespread or systematic attack against any civilian population on national, political, ethnic, racial or religious grounds:
(a) Murder;
(b) Extermination;
(c) Enslavement;
(d) Deportation;
(e) Imprisonment;
(f) Torture;
(g) Rape;
(h) Persecutions on political, racial and religious grounds;
(i) Other inhumane acts."
Cf. Paust, *supra* n156, at pp.556 *et seq.*

160 "*Article 4 Violations of Article 3 common to the Geneva Conventions and of Additional Protocol II*
The International Tribunal for Rwanda shall have the power to prosecute persons committing or ordering to be committed serious violations of Article 3 common to the Geneva Conventions of 12 August 1949 for the Protection of War Victims, and of Additional Protocol II thereto of 8 June 1977. These violations shall include, but shall not be limited to:
(a) Violence to life, health and physical or mental well-being of persons, in particular murder as well as cruel treatment such as torture, mutilation or any form of corporal punishment;
(b) Collective punishments;

provisions of the 1949 Geneva Conventions and Protocol I. While customary international law could establish mandatory universal jurisdiction over certain international crimes,[162] so far universal jurisdiction, established principally by treaty, is permissive[163] for war crimes (other than grave breaches),[164] crimes against humanity and genocide.[165]

A host of issues arise as a result of this complex web of inter-related matters.[166] Does the fact that Article 2 of the Yugoslav Statute only refers to grave breaches under the 1949 Conventions indicate that the crimes enumerated in Articles 11 and 85 of Protocol I are different in nature and should be treated differently when a domestic court is asserting universal

---

(c) Taking of hostages;

(d) Acts of terrorism;

(e) Outrages upon personal dignity, in particular humiliating and degrading treatment, rape, enforced prostitution and any form of indecent assault;

(f) Pillage;

(g) The passing of sentences and the carrying out of executions without previous judgement pronounced by a regularly constituted court, affording all the judicial guarantees which are recognized as indispensable by civilized peoples;

(h) Threats to commit any of the foregoing acts."

161 High Contracting Parties are required "to search for persons alleged to have committed, ..., such grave breaches, and shall bring such persons, regardless of their nationality, before its own courts."

162 Just because custom imposes *erga omnes* obligations on States does not mean that individual criminal responsibility should attach to those whose actions place their State in breach of international law.

163 It may become mandatory if the treaty requires extradition or prosecution and extradition is refused.

164 *Eg.* Article VI(b), Nuremberg Charter, *supra n9.*

"(b) War Crimes: namely, violations of the laws and customs of war. Such violations shall include, but shall not be limited to, murder, ill-treatment or deportation to slave labour or for any other purpose of civilian population of or in occupied territory, murder or ill-treatment of prisoners of war or persons on the seas, killing of hostages, plunder of public or private property, wanton destruction of cities, towns or villages or devastation not justified by military necessity."

165 With respect to genocide, this may be as a result of custom – see Articles VI and VII, *Cf.* Article V.

166 For a prescient critique of these issues, see the unpublished Essex LL.M. dissertation (1994-95) of Marie-Claude Roberge.

jurisdiction? The Secretary-General's Report pursuant to Resolution 808 (1993) stated[167] that the International Tribunal should only apply rules of international humanitarian law which are without doubt part of customary international law; as such, the 1949 Convention grave breaches were deemed included, but not those in Protocol I. On the other hand, Sidhwa J. in *Tadić*[168] held that Protocol I would be within Article 3 of the Yugoslav Statute as a 'law or custom of war'. Moreover, while Cassese J. does not explicitly refer to Protocol I in his deliberations on Article 3 of the Yugoslav Statute, he does hold that Article 3 covers those parts of international humanitarian law which have become custom and which apply in internal armed conflicts.[169] However, the situation is not wholly clear, because the former Yugoslavia had ratified the Protocols in 1979 and it could therefore be argued that they were applicable under Article 3 as a result thereof.[170] Universal jurisdiction on grave breaches may, thus, be wider than the jurisdiction of the ICTY under Article 2.

Furthermore, one also has to consider the scope of the grave breaches provisions in the 1949 Conventions and Protocol I with respect to non-international armed conflicts. The *Tadić* decision states that Article 2 of the Yugoslav Statute is limited to international armed conflicts – however, domestic courts have prosecuted grave breaches as defined within the Geneva Conventions when the crimes occurred in non-international armed conflicts.[171] Moreover, the Agreement between the parties to the conflict in Bosnia-Herzegovina of 1 October 1992 applied the grave breach provisions of the four Geneva Conventions and Protocol I to what was arguably an internal armed conflict,[172] and the *amicus* brief submitted by the US government in *Tadić* argued that Article 2 of the Yugoslav Statute should encompass non-international armed conflicts.[173] That would suggest that

---

167 *Supra* n141, at paras.34 and 35.
168 *Supra* n143, *per* Sidhwa J., at para.118.
169 See paras.94 *et seq.*, *supra* n143.
170 See Cassese J., at para.143, *supra* n143.
171 See *Tadić*, *supra* n143, at para.83.
172 There is no question that Bosnian Muslims fighting Bosnian Serbs is a question of a non-international armed conflict, but does the presence of foreign troops and/or logistical support from other States render the whole conflict or even part of it international? See the *Case Concerning Military and Paramilitary Activities in and against Nicaragua, (Nicaragua v USA)*, [1986] ICJ Rep. p.14.
173 *Tadić*, *supra* n143, at para.83.

the grave breaches may, as a result of custom, soon apply to international and non-international armed conflicts, if they do not do so already. Thus, the Statutes for Yugoslavia and Rwanda and the *Tadić* decision have narrower conceptions of grave breaches than universal jurisdiction is ordinarily understood to embrace.

Some of the restrictiveness of Article 2 may be remedied by Article 3 of the Yugoslav Statute[174]; regard should also be had to Article 4 of the Rwanda Statute.[175] Given that the Security Council was prepared to give jurisdiction over breaches of common Article 3 to the Geneva Conventions and of parts of Protocol II to the ICTR,[176] it might further be suggested that the scope of universal jurisdiction with respect to crimes perpetrated in internal armed conflicts also extends at least this far.[177] That would seem to be more of a case of *de lege ferenda*, however. Article 3 of the Yugoslav Statute, especially as interpreted in *Tadić*, appears to offer more scope for expansion of universal jurisdiction. The phrase "laws and customs of war" comes from the 1907 Hague Convention (IV) Respecting the Laws and Customs of War on Land and the annexed Regulations, as interpreted at Nuremberg.[178] Article 2 of the Hague Rules[179] states that they are only to apply as between contracting Parties and where all the belligerents are party to the Convention. At first blush, therefore, they should be inapplicable to the non-international armed conflict in Bosnia-Herzegovina. However, it was not intended that Article 3 of the Yugoslav Statute be limited to the Hague Rules and the phrase should be read to bear a wider import.[180] Furthermore, there was little doubt that aspects of the laws and customs of war for international armed conflicts applied to non-international armed conflicts. To that extent, *Tadić*[181] is non-controversial. Where there is room for disagreement is with regard to the scope of individual criminal responsibility

---

174 *Supra n*154.

175 *Supra n*160.

176 *Supra n*160.

177 See also, Gasser, *New Draft Declaration of Minimum Humanitarian Standards*, 282 INT'L REV.RED CROSS 328 (1991).

178 Report, *supra n*141, at paras.41 *et seq.*

179 2 AM.J INT'L L (SUPP.) 90 (1908); UKTS 9 (1910), Cd 5030.

180 Report, *supra n*141, para.41, and UN Doc.S/PV.3217, 25 MAY 1993, pp.11, 15 and 19.

181 *Supra n*143, at paras.89 and 96 *et seq.*, *per* Cassese J.

for breaches of the laws and customs of war in non-international armed conflicts. Referring to the international interest in the prohibition of serious breaches of customary rules and principles on internal conflicts, various military manuals, domestic legislation in the former Yugoslavia and Belgium, and two Security Council Resolutions,[182] Cassese J. holds in paragraph 134 of his judgment that

> "[all] of these factors confirm that customary international law imposes criminal liability for serious violations of common Article 3, as supplemented by other general principles and rules on the protection of victims of internal armed conflict, and for breaching certain fundamental principles and rules regarding means and methods of combat in civil strife."

If it had been limited to parts of common Article 3 and specified provisions of Additional Protocol II, then it may have been acceptable, but as para.134 stands, it has to be doubted whether customary international law does impose individual criminal liability and, even more so, whether universal jurisdiction would reach so far. There would not appear to be the required degree of specificity to create crimes.[183]

---

182 *Tadić, supra* n143, at paras.129-33, *per* Cassese J.

183 *Nullem crimen sine lege* and *Consistency of Certain Danzig Legislative Decrees with the Constitution of the Free City* Case.
"Instead of applying a penal law equally clear to both the judge and the party accused, ..., there is the possibility under the new decrees that a man may find himself placed on trial and punished for an act which the law did not enable him to know was an offence, because its criminality depends entirely on the appreciation of the situation by the Public Prosecutor and by the judge. Accordingly, a system in which the criminal character of an act and the penalty attached to it will be known to the judge alone replaces a system in which this knowledge was equally open to both the judge and the accused."
(1935), Series A/B, No.65 at pp.52-3.
Cf. The *Border Guards Prosecution Case*, 100 INT'L L REP.364 (German Federal Supreme Court), where the court rejected a defence claim based on *nullem crimen sine lege* because the Guards should have known that the defence they relied on under the former East German law was contrary to the human rights obligations of East Germany itself and where "the act, when committed, was criminal according to the general principles of law recognized by the international community" (at 389). The court used human rights as set out in the ICCPR to strike down the defence.

Turning to crimes against humanity, there are slightly different definitions in the Yugoslav and Rwanda Statutes.[184] The Yugoslav Statute gives jurisdiction over crimes against humanity when committed in "armed conflict, whether international or internal, ... directed against any civilian population". For the Rwanda Tribunal, crimes against humanity have to be committed "as part of a widespread or systematic attack against any civilian population on national, political, ethnic, racial or religious grounds". Both are limited to crimes committed in armed conflicts, since the victims under the Rwanda Statute must be part of a *civilian* population. Custom does not limit crimes against humanity to armed conflicts.[185] It is questionable whether they ought to be "part of a widespread or systematic attack on national, political, ethnic, racial or religious grounds". The widespread or systematic character of the crimes would be unexceptional, given that those conditions are disjunctive, if one is to find that an international crime has been perpetrated which is suitable for prosecution before an international tribunal rather than a domestic court, but that is a matter of jurisdictional competence, not definition. In addition, the reference to "civilian population", rather than civilians, would suggest that implicit in the definition of crimes against humanity for the Yugoslav Tribunal is the requirement that they be widespread.[186] More worrying, custom ought not be limited to where the attack was "on national, political, ethnic, racial or religious grounds".[187] This inconsistency, both between the Statutes and with custom's understanding of crimes against humanity, detracts once again from the development of a truly international criminal law.

With regard to the ICTY and the ICTR, therefore, they are different from the existing systems based on extradition designed to bring fugitive offenders to trial, but may well have an impact thereon and on universal jurisdiction. As regards the latter, only the grave breach provisions of the 1949 Conven-

---

184 *Supra nn*156 and 159.
185 Acknowledged by Cassese J. in *Tadić, supra n*143, at paras.140-41. See also, Bassiouni, *supra n*11.
186 *Cf.* Article 51.1 Protocol I.
187 *Fédération Nationale des Déportés et Internés Résistants et Patriotes et al. v Barbie, supra n*14, at 137, 140 and 146-7 (1985); Paust, *Threats to Accountability after Nuremberg: Crimes Against Humanity, Leader Responsibility and National Fora*, 12 NYLS J HUM.RTS 547 (1995). *Cf.* Fenrick, *supra n*13, at pp.266 *et seq.*

tions have been held to be "without doubt part of customary international law". For States not party to Protocol I, this might be seen as a reason not to feel bound to act against a person accused of crimes in Article 85 thereof,[188] whereas, unless Articles 3 or 5(i) of the Yugoslav Statute provide the solution, a State party to Protocol I would have to prosecute a person accused of violating Article 85 because the ICTY would not have jurisdiction under Article 2.[189] Furthermore, the ICTY and the ICTR have jurisdiction over 'crimes' where it is debateable whether those acts when committed in non-international armed conflicts would give rise to individual criminal responsibility in customary international law. As such, a State may be obliged to surrender a person to one of the tribunals, since they were established under Chapter VII, where there is no double criminality, because custom does not impose individual criminal responsibility. The different definitions which now exist for certain international crimes leave this part of international criminal law in a state of confusion – the scope of universal jurisdiction may well be impaired by what is perceived to be a loose definition of war crime and a narrower than accepted definition of crimes against humanity, especially given the Tribunals' primacy over domestic jurisdiction. While the fact that the Tribunals' jurisdiction is *ad hoc* and is established under Chapter VII may well lead them to be treated as a special case, such that the difference in definitions is attributable to their particular purpose, setting no precedent for universal jurisdiction in domestic courts, the same could not be said for a general international criminal court which took a similar line.

There is no doubt that the prospects for the establishment of an International Criminal Court, as proposed by the International Law Commission,[190] have been advanced by the discovered need for *ad hoc* tribunals

---

188 With respect to the United Kingdom, see s6(5)(c) of United Nations (International Tribunal) (Former Yugoslavia) Order 1996, SI 1996 No 716.

189 Cassese J. studiously avoids referring to Protocol I in his judgment, *supra* n143.

190 Report of the International Law Commission on the Work of its Forty-Sixth Session, Draft Statute for an International Criminal Court, UN Doc.A/49/355 (1994); hereinafter, Statute. And see Crawford, *The ILC's Draft Statute for an International Criminal Court*, 88 AM.J INT'L L 140 (1994), *The ILC Adopts a Statute for an International Criminal Court*, 89 AM.J INT'L L 404 (1995); and, *Symposium on International Criminal Law*, vol.5:2 TRANSNAT'L L & CONTEMP. PROBS. 237 *et seq.* (1995).

to deal with the crimes perpetrated in the former Yugoslavia and Rwanda.[191] However, while similar to the Tribunals, the proposed International Criminal Court is different in a number of respects and raises a veritable host of issues for international criminal law, extradition law and universal jurisdiction. Unlike the Tribunals, it will not be established under Chapter VII, transfer will not be compulsory for States, rather there are issues of complementarity, and the Prosecutor, as things stand, will not be the initiator of trials. There are also different definitions of crimes emerging from the Preparatory Committee Meetings (PrepComs) which, so far, have been held in 1996 and 1997.[192] Whether the United Nations should establish a general international criminal court, rather than *ad hoc* tribunals in order to give effect to its mandate to maintain international peace and security, is open to question,[193] but that States can establish one by international convention cannot be doubted. The problem is that there is a perception that the International Criminal Court is the direct descendant of the Tribunals, whereas it is, at best, something which so far bears a mere passing resemblance. Turning to the crimes that will be prosecutable before the International Criminal Court, Article 20 of the ILC Draft Statute[194] was extremely terse.

"Article 20 Crimes within the jurisdiction of the Court
The Court has jurisdiction in accordance with this Statute with respect to the following crimes:
(a) the crime of genocide;
(b) the crime of aggression;
(c) serious violations of the laws and customs applicable in armed conflict;
(d) crimes against humanity;

---

191 See Corell, 'International War Crimes Inquiry and Tribunal' in ATKINS, *supra* n141, at pp.1 *et seq.*
192 More are scheduled for 1998 prior to a diplomatic conference of plenipotentiaries to be held from 15 June to 17 July 1998 in Rome: A/C.6/52/L.16, 14 November 1997.
193 See Warbrick, *The United Nations System: A Place for Criminal Courts?*, 5 TRANSNAT'L L & CONTEMP. PROBS.237 (1995).
194 *Supra* n190.

(e) crimes, established under or pursuant to the treaty provisions listed in the Annex,[195] which, having regard to the conduct alleged, constitute exceptionally serious crimes of international concern."

It has been left to the PrepComs to take these proposals further.[196] Nothing is certain, but it seems that genocide will bear the same meaning as in the 1948 Convention.[197] As for the other crimes,[198] there remain a plethora of questions. Whether aggression should be an individual crime, rather than a violation of international law by a State[199] is arguable. Nuremberg prosecuted for crimes against peace, not aggression. Given that aggression is also a breach of international law, then one could foresee the International Criminal Court and the ICJ both dealing with the same matter at an individual

---

195 The Annex lists grave breaches of the Geneva Conventions and Protocol I (presumably already covered in para.(c)), as well as the UN multilateral anti-terrorist conventions. It is all but certain that the crimes in the Annex will not make it to any final Convention, although a crime of "terrorism" was proposed at PrepCom III, 11-21 February 1997 – A/AC.249/1997/WG.1/CRP.4.

196 The International Law Commission is simultaneously drawing up the Draft Code on Crimes Against the Peace and Security of Mankind (A/51/332, 1996). It defines aggression, genocide, crimes against humanity, crimes against United Nations and associated personnel and war crimes. There are differences between those definitions, those applied in universal jurisdiction and those being contemplated in the PrepComs. As such, it is of little help and its work could usefully be subsumed by the PrepComs so at least two sources of international criminal law did not contradict each other.

197 A/AC.249/1997/WG.1/CRP.1.

198 See A/AC.249/1997/WG.1/CRP.5 (Crimes Against Humanity) and 6 (Aggression); War crimes were first debated at PrepCom III (A/AC.249/1997/WG.1/CRP.2), but, while its final definition is still not resolved at time of writing, it was considered further in a series of consultations led by the German government (A/AC.249/1997/ WG.1/CRP.8), and at PrepCom V in Working Group 1 (A/AC.249/1997/WG.1/CRP.9) The views of the ICRC may be found at:- http://www.igc.apc.org/icc.
So unlikely is it that "terrorism" from the original Article 20 will survive, that it is ignored in the rest of this discussion.

199 *NB.* Article 19.3(a) of the ILC Draft Code on State Responsibility makes aggression an international crime for States – A/CN.4/L.528/Add.2 (1996). Furthermore, Article 23.2 of the Statute requires that prosecution of an individual for aggression can only follow a determination by the Security Council that a State has committed an act of aggression. See, however, the evidence against Serbian President Milosevic – The Guardian pp.8-9, 3 FEB 1997.

and State level. The definition as it stands appears to be criminalizing for individuals the law relating to *ius ad bellum* and to be reviving, implicitly, the little lamented concept of the just war. Individuals should be liable only for violations of *ius in bello*, unless it is felt that those who planned or initiated an international armed conflict should be prosecuted specifically therefor, and then they should be prosecuted for a crime against peace, not aggression, which is an act of State – the difference may be subtle, but it recognizes the difference between the nature of responsibility in public international law and criminal responsibility of individuals in international criminal law. Moreover, given that prosecution can only occur if the Security Council has decided that a State has committed an act of aggression (Article 23.2), then the head of that State would, it is ventured, be presumed guilty by decision of the unchallengeable Security Council,[200] rather than the International Criminal Court.

The next offence to be considered is war crimes. Nothing specific can be said on the final definition of war crimes.[201] The final paper from Prep-Com III, which ran to nine sides, was based on a restrictive definition submitted by the United States,[202] which required that the crimes be committed as part of a systematic plan or policy or as part of a large-scale commission of such offences, and one submitted by New Zealand and Switzerland,[203] but which was originally drafted by the ICRC – the ICRC in its address to PrepCom III specifically rejected the United States' precondition.[204] The ICRC's original submission to PrepCom III, while making individuals

---

200 *Case Concerning Questions of Interpretation and Application of the 1971 Montreal Convention Arising from the Aerial Incident at Lockerbie, Libyan Arab Jamahiriya v United Kingdom and the USA*, 1992 ICJ Rep.3 at paras.39 *et seq.*, 31 INT.LEG.MAT.662 (1992); Beveridge, *The Lockerbie Affair*, 41 INT'L & COMP.LQ 907 at pp.916-19 (1992). *Cf.* Alvarez, *Judging the Security Council*, 90 AM.J INT'L L 1 (1996).

201 See the papers from PrepComs III and V, *supra* n198. The definition of war crimes will not be agreed until the Rome Summit.

202 A/AC.249/1997/WG.1/DP.1.

203 A/AC.249/1997/WG.1/DP.2.

204 I am deeply indebted to Marie-Claude Roberge, Legal Division of the ICRC, for supplying me with the materials for this section and for discussions on these matters during her visit to Essex in February 1997 – needless to add, the views expressed are mine alone. PrepCom V, *supra* n198, left three options open on the question of an initial threshhold for war crimes, including not having one.

criminally responsible for certain breaches of Protocols I and II which had not necessarily attracted such liability before,[205] was coherent and would provide a good working definition of war crimes for the International Criminal Court – the problem with the United States definition was that it included elements more suitable to provisions dealing with the Court's jurisdiction and ignores the advances made in *Tadić*.[206] After PrepCom V, however, it is extremely likely that the International Criminal Court would have jurisdiction over crimes committed in non-international armed conflicts.[207]

As for crimes against humanity, the definition[208] includes all the possible variations on a theme considered above in relation to the International Tribunals,[209] including needing to be part of an armed conflict. Treaty crimes, as proposed in the ILC's Annex, are unlikely to be in the final Statute. Moreover, unlike aggression, crimes against humanity, war crimes and genocide, they are more domestic in character, although possessing transnational elements – it would be better for them not to be within the ambit of the International Criminal Court, despite the fact that some States find it difficult in practice to prosecute certain offenders, such as leaders of drug cartels. The one exception may be for those responsible for violations of the Convention on the Safety of United Nations and Associated Personnel[210] because of the international character of the victims.[211]

---

205 *Allowing* under-15s to participate in hostilities (§§2(v) and 3(xii)), for example, is contrary to Article 77 of Protocol I and Article 4.3(c) of Protocol II, but does not easily lend itself to criminalization if *mens rea* is going to be insisted upon. PrepCom V improved upon the PrepCom III implementation (A/AC.249/1997/WG.1/ CRP.2, B.4(s) and C(p)) through the inclusion of "allowing children to take part in the armed forces" as an additional supplement to the initial text as another option.

206 *Supra n*143.

207 Only the Russian Federation and India were opposed.

208 A/AC.249/1997/WG.1/CRP.5.

209 See text accompanying *nn*184 – 187.

210 34 INT.LEG.MAT.482 (1995). The International Law Commission in its Draft Code of Crimes, *supra n*196, lists the following offence:
"Article 19 Crimes against United Nations and associated personnel
1.The following crimes constitute crimes against the peace and security of mankind when committed intentionally and in a systematic manner or on a large scale against United Nations and associated personnel involved in a United Nations operation with a view to preventing or impeding that operation from

If definitions have proved difficult, the relationship with the domestic jurisdiction of States through complementarity and trigger mechanisms is even more complicated[212] and there is little hope of any agreement on Articles 21-25 before the Rome Summit in 1998. It is possible, however, that the International Criminal Court may be created and then have so little work as to render it redundant. Complementarity is only mentioned in the preamble to the ILC draft, but it is known that some States wish to see it included in an Article in the final Statute.[213] It is not at all clear, however, that there is agreement as to the understanding of complementarity – on the one hand, it could mean that domestic courts should take primacy and the International Criminal Court should only step in to fill gaps in jurisdiction, while, on the other, it may mean that both the International Criminal Court and domestic systems are equal and complement each other.[214] Regardless, complementarity is linked to trigger mechanisms. Unlike the ICTY and the

---

fulfilling its mandate:
(a) murder, kidnapping or other attack upon the person or liberty of any such personnel;
(b) violent attack upon the official premises, the private accommodation or the means of transportation of any such personnel likely to endanger his or her person or liberty.
2.This article shall not apply to a United Nations operation authorized by the Security Council as an enforcement action under chapter VII of the Charter of the United Nations in which any of the personnel are engaged as combatants against organized armed forces and to which the law of international armed conflict applies."

211 More international than ordinary diplomats, for instance.
212 Discussed at PrepCom IV in August 1997, A/AC.249/1997/WG.3/CRP.1/Rev.1 and A/AC.249/1997/WG.3/CRP.2 – consolidated text at A/AC.249/1997/L.8/Rev.1. See Bassiouni, *The International Criminal Court: Observations and Issues before the 1997-98 Preparatory Committee; and Administrative and Financial Implications*, particularly pp.172-76 and 201-12.
213 Article 35 on admissibility was considered at PrepCom IV, *supra* n212, in August 1997 and the revised paragraph 2 includes a reference to the Preambular paragraph which refers to complementarity.
214 Since States will not be under a Chapter VII obligation to prosecute, then the International Criminal Court's need for co-operation in the supply of evidence will render it a 'gap-filler' – see the problems addressed by the Appeal Chamber of the ICTY in *Blaskic*, IT-95-14-AR108 *bis*, 29 October 1997, and the unwillingness of the French government to let their troops testify before even the ICTY or ICTR, Washington Post p.A22, 16 DEC 1997.

ICTR, the prosecutor does not initiate investigations,[215] there has to be a complaint by a State or a reference by the Security Council.[216] To take the latter first, the Security Council can refer a matter to the Court, acting under Chapter VII.[217] Two fears arise: the first is that this will compromise the independence of the International Criminal Court, especially since under the original draft no prosecution can be commenced where a situation is being dealt with under Chapter VII unless the Security Council decides otherwise (Article 23.3); the second fear is that the power to refer in Article 23.1 will make it harder for the Security Council to broker peace – it may be better for the Security Council to be able to refer a case to the prosecutor's office for the latter to determine whether to initiate a prosecution, a proposal that could usefully be extended to all cases, not just those under Article 23. It is this writer's view that, at most, a reference to the Court by the Security Council or a State party to the Statute should suffice to give the Court 'jurisdiction to investigate', but that in defined circumstances, the prosecutor should be able to initiate a prosecution without any reference, if only to avoid the politics of international relations interfering with the bringing to justice of persons accused of crimes as serious as those in Article 20 – jurisdiction over the alleged offender should be a matter for the Court and should

---

215 Criticised by some delegations at PrepCom IV, Working Group 3:-
"Many states agreed that the complaint mechanism as provided for in Article 25 was too narrow and needed to be expanded. These delegations argued that states may for a variety of reasons be reluctant to lodge complaints with the ICC. It was therefore necessary to expand the complaint mechanism by giving the Prosecutor the authority to initiate investigation *ex officio*. Again the ICTY and ICTR were mentioned as precedents. States in favor of this proposal explained that there were sufficient procedural safeguards in the statute to avoid the 'loose cannon' or 'a paranoid Dr. Strangelove' Prosecutor that a small number of states feared."
(Report of an independent non-governmental observer to the proceedings of the fourth session of the Preparatory Committee – not to be construed as an official record. Provided by the *Coalition for an International Criminal Court*).

216 Indeed, under Article 26.5, if the Prosecutor decides not to proceed, the Security Council or complainant State can request a review by the Presidency of the Court – see also, consolidated text from PrepCom IV, *supra* n212.

217 Indeed, the Court cannot assume jurisdiction over the crime of aggression "unless the Security Council has first determined that a State has committed the act of aggression which is the subject of the complaint". Article 23.2.

depend on the offence, not the source of the complaint.[218] That, however, is not the current position, reflecting States' unwillingness to surrender their sovereignty over criminal prosecutions, even where the crimes bear such an international character and are not peculiar to any one State's jurisdiction. At PrepCom V in December 1997, the role of the Prosecutor was one of the most contentious issues, although not part of its official agenda.[219] The government of the United Kingdom broke with the United States and other permanent members of the Security Council and accepted the recommendation of the Singaporean government that the prosecutor should be able to investigate matters within the purview of the Security Council, even those under Chapter VII. At PrepCom V, the United Kingdom confirmed its decision to oppose the provision in the draft Statute of the International Criminal Court which would require prior approval by the Security Council before the Court could proceed with investigations and trials. This provision in effect gave the Security Council veto power over the ICC. Instead the United Kingdom indicated it would support a modified formulation of the so-called "Singapore proposal" which would require a positive decision to be taken by the Council to prevent or delay or block the ICC, and then only for a limited length of time.[220] The consequence is that any of the Permanent 5 could block by means of its veto power any proposal to delay the work of the Court.

Turning to the State-oriented trigger mechanisms, with respect to genocide, a complaint has to be made by a State party to the Statute which is also a Contracting Party to the Genocide Convention 1948, whereupon the Court would have jurisdiction (Articles 25.1 and 21.1(a)). For other crimes, the position is more complex and less certain.[221] A State, again, has to bring a complaint (Article 25.2). That State must have accepted the Court's jurisdiction over the crime under Article 22. Furthermore, the State with custody of the accused and the State where the crime occurred must also

---

218 *Viz.* Article 24.
219 See The Guardian p.17, 12 DEC 1997 and the Washington Post p.A5, 12 DEC 1997.
220 Taken from the emailed Initial Summary Report, December 18, 1997, of William R. Pace, Convenor.
221 At PrepCom IV, *supra n*212, there was general agreement that there should not be this dual system. For the various recommendations for Articles 21-25, see the consolidated text, *supra n*212.

have accepted the Court's jurisdiction over the crime under Article 22 (Article 21.1(b)); in addition, if an extradition request has already been received by the State where the accused is to be found, which can in these circumstances logically only have come from the State of which the accused is a national, of which the victim is a national or which was itself the target of the crime,[222] then that State, too, must have accepted the Court's jurisdiction with respect to the crime (Article 21.2). There are two ways to interpret Article 21. The pertinent phrase is "[the] Court may exercise its jurisdiction over a person with respect to a crime ... if,": under a subjective test, the States under Article 21.1(b) and 21.2 must give their consent to the trial of this particular fugitive, for the Court is given jurisdiction over "a *person* with respect to a crime"; on the other hand, an objective test would simply require that the relevant States in paragraphs 1(b) and 2 of Article 21 had accepted the Court's jurisdiction over this type of crime under Article 22. The objective test is in line with Article 24, which requires the Court to satisfy itself of its jurisdiction, not wait upon consent from States, and Article 53.2(a)(ii). Moreover, it would equate the jurisdiction of the International Criminal Court with that of domestic courts, rather than leave the former as subsidiary, dependent for jurisdiction more often that not on a referral by the Security Council – in such circumstances, it would, in all but name, be as *ad hoc* as the ICTY and the ICTR. Given the doubts expressed above about States' willingness to surrender sovereignty, however, there has to be a presumption that it will be the subjective test that is preferred. Given the international, as opposed to transnational, character of the crimes that will probably be included in the final version of Article 20, on the other hand, there is every reason to establish an international criminal court which has the right to initiate its own prosecutions.

The International Criminal Court would not be necessary if all States prosecuted those accused of the serious crimes in Article 20 before their domestic courts. Sometimes such trials are unfair, but the International Criminal Court is not to be established to remedy that particular evil.[223] It is there to prevent impunity. However, if it is only to have jurisdiction with

---

222 Active Personality Principle, Passive Personality Principle and Protective Principle jurisdiction, respectively.

223 *Cf.* Graefrath, *Universal Criminal Jurisdiction and the International Criminal Court*, 1 EJIL 67 at pp.84 *et seq.* (1990).

State consent or upon reference by the Security Council, then one can foresee that States exercising universal jurisdiction over those crimes will continue to play a large part in the enforcement of international criminal law. The fact that the definition of crimes for the purposes of universal jurisdiction and for the Court differs, is of more consequence than the differences that existed with the definition of crimes for the Tribunals.[224] There, States were obliged, because the Tribunals were established under Chapter VII, to surrender anyone accused of a Tribunal crime and it is legitimate to view their definition as particular to the Tribunals temporal and geographic remit. Here, because of complementarity, the domestic system and that of the International Criminal Court are more likely to be seen as competitive, although not mutually exclusive.[225] One can but hope that in time the definition for the purposes of universal jurisdiction will coincide with that for the International Criminal Court, and that the PrepComs will not unduly restrict definitions of crimes that have become established in customary international law.[226]

Of course, having gone to the trouble of creating an International Criminal Court that will, in all likelihood, have jurisdiction over crimes that are international in character, in the sense that they are not merely domestic crimes with transnational elements, it is too much to expect that States will give it primacy to prosecute such offenders. If that were to be the case, however, one would avoid the charges that are usually laid against 'victor's courts' and Security Council imperialism under Chapter VII.

It will be remembered that in Chapter Six on the political offence exemption the same two solutions were suggested as alternatives to extradition; that is, universal or representational jurisdiction and an international criminal court. However, the opposite conclusion was reached which, at first sight, may seem inconsistent. Why is it more appropriate to assume universal jurisdiction over politically motivated offenders, but to establish an international criminal court for war criminals? The difference lies in the source of the

---

224 Some delegations, New Zealand, Switzerland, Argentina and Sweden, at Prep-Com III were concerned about the different definitions – daily report by International Human Rights Law Institute at DePaul University Law School and Lawyers Committee for Human Rights, supplied by email by *NGO Coalition for an ICC.*

225 Graefrath, *supra* n223, at p.82.

226 *Viz.* Paust, *supra* n187.

law violated and the status of the offender. War crimes and crimes against humanity are defined and created by international convention and they take place when ordinary rules of law are suspended.[227] Therefore, an international criminal court is suitable to try all the offences committed during the hostilities. With respect to politically motivated offenders, their offences violate domestic laws common to every nation in the world and so can suitably be tried by municipal courts in the requested State. Further, to extend to terrorists the special status that would go with trial before an international criminal court, would destroy the promoted view that such offenders are common criminals, not political fugitives.

On the other hand,

"[for] these reasons, it is unlikely that any solution short of a permanent international criminal jurisdiction can prove adequate in relation to what is a vital aspect of the enforcement of the law of war."[228]

Furthermore, in the meantime only where there is no alternative should an unconcerned State assume jurisdiction, and the preferred method of obtaining the return of an offender to a concerned State must always be extradition.

---

227 This is one inference of Art.60(5) of the Vienna Convention on the Law of Treaties, 8 INT.LEG.MAT.679 (1969).
228 OPPENHEIM, *supra n*90, at p.584. See also McDOUGAL, LASSWELL & CHEN, HUMAN RIGHTS AND WORLD PUBLIC ORDER (1980), pp.354-7; LILLICH AND NEWMAN, INTERNATIONAL HUMAN RIGHTS: PROBLEMS OF LAW AND POLICY, pp.773-804 (1979).

9

REFUGE AND RETURN

a. Introduction

No study of the law of extradition can avoid considering the allied topic of refugee status. If not extradited, the fugitive may receive asylum-protection from the requested State.[1] Furthermore, the development of the political offence exemption can be seen as a logical progression from the well established idea of offering political asylum. Indeed, some present day judges have advocated a return to refugee and asylum principles in assessing the political character of an offence.

> "The analogy of 'political' in [the context of the political offence exemption] is with 'political' in such phrases as 'political refugee', 'political asylum' or 'political prisoner'."[2]

By way of corollary, the Proposed Treaty of Amsterdam of 1997[3] provides in Section C, *Protocols annexed to the Treaty establishing the European Community*, the following protocol on Asylum for Nationals of Member States of the European Union:

> "Sole Article
> Given the level of protection of fundamental rights and freedoms by the Member States of the European Union, ... any application for asylum made

---

1 This Chapter will not look at the complex question of crimes committed by migrants – see the very detailed research by Tomaševski, Host Country Crime Problems, in SCHMID (ed.), MIGRATION AND CRIME (ISPAC, 1996), at pp.67 *et seq.*

2 *Schtraks v Government of Israel*, [1964] AC 556, *per* Viscount Radcliffe at 591.

3 1997 OJ C.340.

by a national of a Member State may be taken into consideration or declared admissible for processing by another Member State only in [certain, very limited] cases."

The necessary consequence, as pre-envisaged in Article 5.1 of the 1996 European Union Convention relating to Extradition between Member States,[4] is that no offence for which a transnational fugitive offender is requested by another member State can be regarded as political, although there are exceptions.

However, refugee status and *non-refoulement*, (that is, not placing the refugee in the position of having to return to where he will be persecuted), are distinct from extradition and must be understood in their own right before any inter-relationship can be considered. This chapter will start by examining the present day situation of refugees. It will then go on to consider the nature of 'rights' in refugee law. From this it will emerge that any study must have regard to three separate ideas, refugee status, *non-refoulement* and asylum, and that will be followed by a review of applicable international and regional instruments. The remainder of the chapter will concentrate on those refugee matters most pertinent to extradition law, refugee status and *non-refoulement*, and it will be concluded by an overview of the thorny question of whether a refugee may be extradited.

b. Refugees in Context

The news that an individual is seeking 'asylum' has become a much more common occurrence within the last century. The post-war growth in bi-polarism increased the frequency with which the governments of East and West were requested to provide a refuge.[5] The transition to democracy throughout the former Soviet Bloc might have been expected to reduce the flow of refugees from that source, but the resulting instability in parts of the region

---

4   1996 oj c.313.
5   Citizens of the Eastern bloc crossing to the West received wide coverage in the media, but West-East crossings also took place. For example, between 30,000 and 100,000 Greeks fled to Eastern Europe after the 1947-49 Greek Civil War.

merely changed the cause of flight from political persecution to war.[6] However, for over thirty years cross-border movements of peoples in Africa and South East Asia have been the main source of *de facto* refugees, anyway. Amongst their vast numbers[7] there were those seeking refuge from political persecution.[8] The growth in people seeking asylum in Europe since the mid-1980s[9] led to drastic and racist measures in once liberal States to stem the flow. Countries are assimilating their refugee laws to those of the least open States for fear that a failure to be equally as strict with similarly inhumanitarian measures would result in a flood of asylum-seekers previously turned away by neighbouring States.[10]

"In 1986 ... the Swiss Parliament modified its law on asylum in response to the substantial increases in asylum applications that country was experiencing. In addition to enacting various procedural changes, Parliament made it easier for the Federal Council to derogate from the ordinary statutory guarantees of asylum. Theretofore, such derogation was permissible only in times of armed conflict; since the 1986 law, derogation is also authorised in peacetime when there is an 'extraordinary' influx of asylum seekers."[11]

The Member States of the European Community have erected an external *cordon sanitaire*, sometimes known as the Golden Curtain, to keep out those who are not European Union citizens, to the detriment of a liberal refugee

---

6   COUNCIL OF EUROPE, PEOPLE ON THE MOVE: NEW MIGRATION FLOWS IN EUROPE, 1992.

7   According to UNHCR (http://www.unhcr.ch/) as at 1 January 1997 almost 23 million people were of concern to the High Commissioner – overall, there are 50 million people who have had to flee their homes throughout the world.

8   See *Armah v Government of Ghana*, [1968] AC 192.

9   See, for example, the imposition of carrier sanctions on airlines who bring undocumented persons who would ordinarily need visas – Feller, *Carrier Sanctions and International Law*, 1 INT'L J REFUGEE L 48 at p.65 (1989). See also, WALLACE, REFUGEES AND ASYLUM: A COMMUNITY PERSPECTIVE, 1996; Neuman, *Buffer Zones Against Refugees*, 33 VA.J INT'L L 503 (1993); Achermann & Gattiker, *Safe Third Countries: European Developments*, 7 INT'L J REFUGEE L 19 (1995), (and see also, 7 INT'L J REFUGEE L 119-27); Dunstan, *Playing Human Pinball*, 7 INT'L J REFUGEE L 606 (1995).

10   See The Schengen Convention 1990, 30 INT.LEG.MAT.84 (1991).

11   Martin, *Reforming Asylum Adjudication: On Navigating the Coast of Bohemia*, 138 U.PENN L REV.1247 at 1269 *n*67 (1990).

policy. In particular, at the Dublin meeting of the European Community in June 1990, the member States signed the new European Convention on Asylum Determination,[12] designed to prevent 'asylum shopping' and to harmonize refugee practice amongst the member States. Within that *cordon sanitaire*, the Member States of the European Union have drafted a Protocol to the proposed Treaty of Amsterdam, 1997, intended to preclude applications for asylum by citizens of other European Union States.[13] These changes have led to a fresh consideration as to whether the so-called 'right to asylum' is vested in the individual or is a matter of grace to be dispensed by the government of the requested State.[14]

c. The Rights of Asylum and Non-Refoulement

It needs to be made clear that there are three distinct concepts in use that are frequently confused; refugee status, *non-refoulement* and asylum. Asylum, in its colloquial sense, means a decision by the host State to offer an applicant for refugee status a permanent residence. Under Article 33 of the 1951 Convention Relating to the Status of Refugees,[15] States Parties are prohibited from returning a refugee to a country where his life or freedom would be threatened – this obligation is termed *non-refoulement*. Asylum is a much more serious measure in that it grants to the refugee rights ap-

---

12 Dublin Convention Determining the State Responsible for Examining Applications for Asylum Lodged in one of the Member States of the European Communities, 30 INT.LEG.MAT.425 (1991) – in force, 1997.

13 *Supra n3.*

14 Compare GROTIUS, DE JURE BELLI AC PACIS, LIBRI TRES, Bk 2, Ch.2, sec.16 (1646), with VATTEL, LE DROIT DES GENS, Bk 1, Ch.19, sec.230 (1861).

15 189 UNTS 150. And see the 1967 Protocol, 606 UNTS 267. The Protocol removed the time-bar and geographical restrictions in the Convention.

proaching those of a national.[16] The right to seek asylum[17] is set out in Article 14 of the United Nations' Universal Declaration of Human Rights.

"1. Everyone has the right to seek and enjoy in other countries asylum from persecution.
2. This right may not be invoked in the case of prosecutions genuinely arising from non-political crimes or from acts contrary to the purposes and principles of the United Nations."

The Universal Declaration, though, is not a treaty "but a mere statement of pious hope as to the standards of conduct that might one day be achieved".[18] Fortunately, the United Nations followed up this initial step in the 1951 Convention Relating to the Status of Refugees and the 1967 Protocol thereto which are true multilateral treaties imposing international obligations on the parties. No mention is made in either instrument of asylum, but the related concept of *non-refoulement* is spelt out in Article 33.

"Prohibition of Expulsion or Return ('Refoulement')
1. No Contracting State shall expel or return (*'refouler'*) a refugee in any manner whatsoever to the frontiers of territories where his life or freedom would be threatened on account of his race, religion, nationality, membership of a particular social group or political opinion.

---

16 See the Declaration on Territorial Asylum, U.N.G.A.Res.2312 (XXII), and the Draft Convention on Territorial Asylum 1977, U.N.Doc.A/CONF.78/12. Neither creates binding obligations. *Cf.* Article 34 of the 1951 Convention, *supra n*15.

17 Morgenstern, *The Right of Asylum*, 26 BRIT.YB.INT'L L 344 (1949); Green, *The Right of Asylum in International Law*, Inaugural Lecture at the University of Malaya, 1961; Evans, *Observations on the Practice of Territorial Asylum in the United States*, 56 AM.J INT'L L 148 (1962); Evans, *Reflections upon the Political Offence in International Practice*, 57 AM.J INT'L L 1 (1963); Note, *Behind the Paper Curtain: Asylum Policy versus Asylum Practice*, 7 N.Y.U.REV.L & SOC.CHANGE 107 (1978); Plender, *Recent Trends in National Immigration Control*, 35 INT'L & COMP. LQ 531 (1986); DEFENSOR-SANTIAGO, POLITICAL OFFENCES IN INTERNATIONAL LAW, (1977); GARCIA-MORA, INTERNATIONAL LAW AND ASYLUM AS A HUMAN RIGHT, (1956); MARTIN (ed.), THE NEW ASYLUM SEEKERS (1988); GOODWIN-GILL, THE REFUGEE IN INTERNATIONAL LAW, pp.117-204, (1996, 2nd ed.).

18 Green, *supra n*17, at p.17.

2. The benefit of the present provision may not, however, be claimed by
a refugee whom there are reasonable grounds for regarding as a danger to
the security of the country in which he is, or who, having been convicted
by a final judgment of a particularly serious crime, constitutes a danger
to the community of that country."

The only international documents to make reference to a possible right of
asylum, rather than a right to seek asylum, are the 1967 Declaration on Territorial Asylum and the unadopted 1977 Draft Convention on Territorial Asylum.[19] At a regional level, however, more progress has been achieved in
relation to asylum.[20] Nevertheless, both popularly and even judicially, the
right to asylum is confused with the principle of *non-refoulement*, which
does not help make for a clear analysis. For the purposes of this chapter
the right to asylum will be confined to a right to enter and remain in a State;
non-refoulement will bear its technical meaning.[21]

In the past, commentators in all fields have glibly talked about a *right*
of asylum, thereby providing advocates and their refugee clients with material to claim that entry and residence cannot be denied. Unfortunately, the
courts and tribunals have in the past disagreed with this contention, casting
doubts on whether there is a true 'right'.

Hohfeld,[22] in 1913, laid down the definitive approach on how to classify
legal capacities possessed by an individual. Of relevance to the present discussion is his definition of a right.[23] A right is to be understood in relation
to its jural correlative, a duty. A right exists if a duty is placed on another
that can be enforced by the holder of the former. To use Hohfeld's example,

"... if X has a right against Y that he shall stay off the former's land, the
correlative (and equivalent) is that Y is under a duty towards X to stay off
the place."[24]

---

19 *Supra n*16.
20 See below, Section *d*.
21 See GOODWIN-GILL, *supra n*17.
22 Hohfeld, *Some Fundamental Legal Conceptions as applied in Judicial Reasoning*, 23 YALE LJ 16 (1913).
23 Hohfeld considers eight terms: right, duty, privilege, no-right, power, disability,
immunity and liability, pairing them as jural opposites and jural correlatives
– *supra n*22, at pp.28-58.
24 *Supra n*22, at p.32.

Applying this analysis to the instant issue of asylum, it can be seen that whether a refugee has a right to enter and remain depends on the obligations, if any, of the State of refuge, that is, the State where the refugee seeks asylum, and on her[25] powers of enforcing any such obligation. Turning to such an individual trying to enter a sovereign State of which she is not a national, generally speaking she can, in practice, be refused entry, for the State is under no duty to grant admission. If allowed in, it would be as a matter of grace and the individual would be the holder of a mere revocable privilege, unenforceable against the State. This assessment accurately describes the traditional view of refugee status, indicating the confusion as to terminology and the precarious nature of refugee 'rights'.

(i) The Traditional Approach – The traditional view is that the State of refuge has a complete discretion as to whether to grant protection. Under this approach the refugee could not complain if he was a qualifying applicant, but was still returned to face persecution. This traditional view is grounded in the concept of State sovereignty. The belief was such that the State could refuse leave to enter to anyone as part of its sovereign rights.[26] As Evans[27] pointed out in 1963, "in general practice the 'right to asylum' is permissive for States".

Furthermore, in *The Asylum Case*,[28] the International Court of Justice held there was no customary rule of international law that States even had to recognize the grant of asylum by another State. The test for whether State practice has developed into a rule of customary international law has changed since *The Asylum Case*,[29] but the grant of asylum is probably still personal

---

25   In point of fact, most applicants for refugee status are women.
26   *United States, ex rel.Donnelly v Mulligan, US Marshall*, 74 F.2d 220 at 223 (1934); 76 F.2d 511 (1935).
   "Asylum necessarily means absolute immunity from the jurisdiction of another State, subject to the will of the State of asylum, and it must be borne in mind that the right of the State is sovereign and unlimited, excepting in so far as it imposes limits on itself."
   See also *Varro v The King*, [1933] SCR 36 at 40 *per* Lamont J.
27   *Reflections upon the Political Offence in International Practice, supra n*17, at p.2.
28   *Colombia v Peru*, ICJ Rep.266 at 277 (1950).
29   See now, *The Nicaragua Case*, (*Nicaragua v USA*), ICJ Rep.14 at pp.87-88 (1986).

to the granting State and the asylee, subject to the overriding rule that any third State must not violate the territorial sovereignty of the granting State.[30] However, the individual asylum seeker is given no enforceable rights; the granting of asylum is a matter for States alone.

This position was bolstered by the theory that individuals were not the subjects of international law. If only a State is subject to international law, then the 'right' in international law to asylum cannot be claimed by an individual. Even where there are conventions guaranteeing asylum, rights are not directly granted to individuals, but mutual obligations on States are established to grant such rights to individuals. Breach of such obligations gives the refugee/asylum seeker no rights, but the offending State is liable to the other States party to the convention.

The municipal case law also supports this view.[31] In *Ker v Illinois*,[32] a case concerning abduction of a fugitive from Peru to stand trial in Illinois, the following position was asserted by the US Supreme Court.

"It is idle, therefore, to claim that either by express terms or by implication, there is given to a fugitive from justice in one of these countries any right to remain and reside in the other; and if the right to asylum means anything, it must mean this. The right of the Government of Peru voluntarily to give a party in Ker's condition an asylum in the country, is quite a different thing from the right in him to demand and insist upon security in such an asylum."

This view was restated in *Chandler v United States*,[33] again in the context of 'disguised extradition'.

"... it has long been the practice of States to give asylum. But the right is that of the State voluntarily to offer asylum, not that of the fugitive to insist upon it."

---

30 See *The Eichmann Case*, 36 INT'L L REP.5 (1962) and U.N.Doc. S/4336.
31 *Re Argoud*, 45 INT'L L REP.90 at 94 (French *Cr de.Cass*, 1964).
32 119 US 436 at 432 (1886).
33 171 F.2d 921 at 935 (1948).

Courts in Israel[34] and Australia[35] have also made it plain that the right to enter a country is within the prerogative of the executive, as is any grant of asylum. In *Knauf v Shaughnessy*,[36] another United States case, the court made it clear that under the traditional view there is no 'right' to enter the State.

> "At the outset we wish to point out that an alien who seeks admission to this country may not do so under any claim of right. Admission of aliens to the United States is a *privilege* granted by the sovereign United States Government."

However, the position of the individual may be improving.

(ii) Right in the Individual – There are two interrelated problems here. First, whether an individual can be the subject of international law and, secondly, whether, even if he does possess the right, he could enforce it. A further problem concerns exactly what any such 'right to asylum' confers. Asylum, or some lesser protection such as *non-refoulement*?

The individual's position depends on which is the authoritative voice in international law at the time; the positivist or the naturalist. The positivists look to who creates international law and accordingly deem that only States can be subject thereto. The naturalists argue that it is individuals who are the subjects of international law.[37] In support of this contention they generally cite such international crimes as piracy, hijacking and genocide of which individuals are objects. Moreover, the past forty years has seen the European Convention for the Protection of Human Rights and Fundamental Freedoms[38] provide to individuals, in an ever-increasing number of countries which are parties thereto, the right to petition the Strasbourg organs with regard to State practices in violation of the said Convention. Thus, it would appear that individuals are increasingly being recognised as having rights as well as liabilities under international law. Indeed, the ECHR has

---

34 See *Eichmann, supra* n30.
35 *Schlieske v Minister for Immigration and Ethnic Affairs*, 84 ALR 719 at 729 (1988).
36 338 US 537 at 542 (1949).
37 OPPENHEIM, INTERNATIONAL LAW, p.636 (8th ed., 1955).
38 ETS 5 (1950); hereinafter, ECHR. See also the ACHR and the ACHPR, below.

been used to protect persons from being returned to face torture or inhuman or degrading treatment where the 1951 Convention has not been found to provide protection against *refoulement*.[39] *Prima facie* the first hurdle has been cleared.

Irrespective of whether the individual is in fact a subject of international law, could he enforce any right to asylum, hypothetical or actual, that he may possess? There is no equivalent of the European Court of Human Rights in this field. Unfortunately, without domestic legislation enacting these rights, or a decision that the particular treaty is self-executing, then they cannot be enforced in domestic courts. Therefore, although an individual may be guaranteed the right to asylum, he may not be able to question any breach. In Hohfeldian terms, since there is no correlative enforceable duty upon anyone or any State, the individual does not have a 'right'. The subsequent use of the word must be understood in these terms, unless otherwise stated.

Finally, States have always denied a right to 'asylum' *per se* and, at best, the refugee may have a right to seek asylum and then enjoy '*non-refoulement*'. As for seeking asylum, that is, a right of access to fair refugee status determination procedures, it is not clear how far States have impinged on this 'right' through incremental restrictions. It is true that the Executive Committee of UNHCR in its 1997 Conclusion on *Safeguarding Asylum*[40] drew attention to particular aspects of "the institution of asylum", including:

> "access, consistent with the 1951 Convention and the 1967 Protocol, of asylum-seekers to fair and effective procedures for determining status and protection needs."

On the other hand, the increasing need for people from States most likely to produce refugee flows to possess a visa to come to a western State, the imposition of carrier sanctions on airlines which bring people to western States without proper documentation and the right of interdiction on the High Seas,[41] would all suggest that any 'right' to seek asylum implicit in the 1951 Convention is extremely limited.[42]

---

39 See *Chahal v United Kingdom*, (70/1995/576/662), 15 November 1996
40 EXCOM Conc. No.82 (XLVII) 1997, para.(d)(ii).
41 See *Sale v Haitian Centers Council, Inc.* 113 S.Ct 2549 (1993).
42 There is a wealth of literature on these matters in books and articles dealing with refugee law – see generally, GOODWIN-GILL, *supra n*17.

Lasting rights to residence in the new State may not be enforceable at all, but the individual might be protected from return to the persecuting State under the principle of *non-refoulement*.[43] Goodwin-Gill goes so far as to suggest that after forty years, the principle of *non-refoulement*, at least, has arguably been accepted as general international law, applicable to anyone fleeing persecution, war, civil strife and unrest, not just refugees within the meaning of the 1951 Convention.[44] In that the persecutee wants immediate protection and the right not to be returned to a State where he might suffer persecution, *non-refoulement* may be adequate; however, for the fugitive offender fighting extradition, full asylum may be the only effective protection.

Having studied the so-called 'right' to 'asylum' in the abstract, it is appropriate to consider the international agreements governing State practice.

d. Treaty Obligations

Refugee status, *non-refoulement* and asylum are now the creatures of conventions. Article 14 of the Universal Declaration of Human Rights has already been discussed. The General Assembly empowered the United Nations High Commissioner for Refugees to provide 'international protection' and seek "'permanent solutions' to the problems of refugees".[45] The High Commissioner uses the powers in the Statute and general international law, but most important for the asylum-seeker is the Convention relating to the Status of Refugees and the 1967 Protocol to it.[46] The 1951 Convention sets out in Article 1, as amended, the accepted definition of the term 'refugee' which is still used. It is someone who

---

43 See GOODWIN-GILL, *supra* n17; according to GOODWIN-GILL, State practice suggests that the international community does not accept that there is an obligation to accord a right to asylum – at p.174.

44 *Supra* n17, at pp.170-71.

45 GOODWIN-GILL, *supra* n17, at pp.207 *et seq.* The Statute of the UNHCR is found in G.A.Res.428, 5 U.N.G.A.O.R.Supp. (No.20), 46, U.N.Doc.A/1775 (1950); reprinted in full at pp.384-89 of GOODWIN-GILL. See also LILLICH, THE HUMAN RIGHTS OF ALIENS IN CONTEMPORARY INTERNATIONAL LAW, Ch.4, (1984).

46 *Supra* n15.

"owing to a well-founded fear of being persecuted for reasons of race, religion, nationality, membership of a particular social group or political
opinion, is outside the country of his nationality and is unable or, owing
to such fear, is unwilling to avail himself of the protection of that country;
or who, not having a nationality and being outside the country of his former
habitual residence, is unable or, owing to such fear, is unwilling to return
to it."[47]

Such a person would be granted refugee status. If he satisfied Article 33,
set out above, he would be protected from being expelled or returned by
the State of refuge. Article 33 of the Convention refers to *refoulement* which
encompasses the idea of a State refusing entry as well as deporting a refugee.
The right is not absolute, though. Article 33(1) implies that a refugee could
be expelled if he could go somewhere other than the State where he would
be subject to persecution.[48] Furthermore, in the second paragraph, the State
could refuse entry if the refugee would constitute a danger to the security
of the State or, by reason of his conviction for a "particularly serious crime",
he would be a danger to the community.

In addition to the Convention and Protocol, several other international
and regional agreements can provide supplementary assistance to the person
seeking protection by means of refugee status. On the international plane,
it has been argued,[49] so far unsuccessfully, that the Fourth Geneva Convention Relative to the Protection of Civilian Persons in Time of War[50] should
prevent an asylum-seeker being returned to a war zone, even where the
armed conflict is not of an international character or the applicant cannot

---

47 The O.A.U. Convention on Refugee Problems in Africa, 1969, 1001 UNTS 45,
    adds those compelled to leave their place of habitual residence through external
    aggression, occupation, foreign domination or events seriously disturbing public
    order: Art.1(2). Probably not even the O.A.U. Convention grants refugee status
    to those fleeing famine or drought, another major cause of mass trans-border
    migration. See also, the Cartagena Declaration on Refugees, 1984, OAS/Ser.L/V/
    II.66, doc.10, rev.1, pp.190-93; at pp.444-48, GOODWIN-GILL, *supra* n17.
48 The applicant for asylum could also be refused on the ground that they could
    move to a different part of their State where they would be safe, the so-called
    internal flight alternative – see GOODWIN-GILL, *supra* n17, at pp.74-75, but note
    Gashi v Home Secretary, Appeal No.HX/75677/95 (13695), unreported, 22 July
    1996.
49 *In re Medina*, Docket A26 949 415, 7 OCT 1988 (BIA).
50 75 UNTS 287.

prove persecution under the 1951 Convention. The United States Board of Immigration Appeals held that common Article 3 of the Geneva Conventions only imposed burdens on the parties to the internal conflict, while Article 1 does not create a directly enforceable right for individuals. Nevertheless, the argument that Geneva IV should have some bearing on a decision to deport to a war zone carries weight. More directly on the international plane, the 1984 U.N. Convention Against Torture[51] provides in Article 3 that no-one shall be expelled, returned, *refouled* or extradited to a place where there are substantial grounds for believing that he would face torture.

At a regional level there have been developments in Africa and America. Having regard to the fact that approximately half the world's *de facto* refugee population is in Africa, it is unsurprising that the member States of the Organisation of African Unity have drawn up their own regional refugee convention.[52] Broader than the 1951 and 1967 arrangements, in Article II it speaks of the granting of asylum, although in terms recognising it as a permissive power of the State. Article 12(3) of the African Charter of Human And Peoples' Rights[53] also guarantees the right to seek asylum in line with domestic laws and international conventions.

The American Convention on Human Rights[54] also includes the right to seek asylum. More interestingly, though, the O.A.S. concluded two conventions in 1954 on Territorial and Diplomatic Asylum.[55] The Conventions set out obligations as regards asylum as they apply between States, not as they might affect an individual. However, Article 4 of the Territorial Convention does provide that extradition shall not be allowed if the granting State determines the offence or the motive for the request to be political.

On the other hand, in Europe there is a developing policy of restricting asylum. A protocol to the proposed Treaty of Amsterdam,[56] provides that nationals of member States of the European Union shall not succeed in any application for asylum in other EU States except in very limited circumstan-

---

51 23 INT.LEG.MAT.1027 (1984) & 24 INT.LEG.MAT.535 (1985).
52 *Supra n*47.
53 21 INT.LEG.MAT.58 (1982).
54 Art.22(7), 9 INT.LEG.MAT.673 (1970).
55 1954 Caracas Convention on Territorial Asylum, in force 29 DEC 1954; OASTS 34. 1954 Caracas Convention on Diplomatic Asylum, in force 29 DEC 1954, OASTS 34.
56 *Supra n*3.

ces. The justification is that EU States provide a very high degree of protection of fundamental rights and freedoms. While it cannot be gainsaid that
human rights are well protected in Europe, the proposed restriction on
seeking asylum would go against the universalist philosophy of the 1951
Convention Relating to the Status of Refugees, it would reimpose a geographical limitation on the 1951 Convention which has applied without such
since the 1967 Protocol[57] and it might set a dangerous precedent for other
parts of the world – such criticisms are particularly pertinent since the 1996
European Union Convention Relating to Extradition,[58] whilst abolishing
the political offence exemption still provides that extradition might be refused
where the requested State finds that the transnational fugitive offender might
be persecuted or punished on the grounds of his race, religion, nationality
or political opinion.

All in all, Europe apart, while there are instruments other than the Convention and the Protocol to provide rights to the asylum-seeker, they are
all predicated in practice on determinations with respect to Articles 1 and
33 of the former. It is to those two fundamental clauses that attention must
now be given.

e. Refugee Status and Non-Refoulement

Those conventions that do speak of asylum tend to consider it in terms of
obligations between States. The individual has no more than a right to seek
asylum and his request may be granted or denied at the whim of the State.
The person seeking to prevent his exclusion, expulsion, deportation or extradition has to rely on the right not to be subject to *refoulement* as set out
in Article 33 of the 1951 Convention. This is a lesser form of protection
because it does not prevent the State from sending a person to another State
as long as his life or freedom would not be threatened there.[59] To qualify
in law for *non-refoulement* protection, the person must satisfy the test for

---

57 The Protocol to the proposed Treaty of Amsterdam might even be construed
    as a reservation to Article 1 of the 1951 Convention, contrary to Article 42 of
    that Convention.
58 *Supra* n4.
59 The so-called safe third country principle – see *In re Musisi* [1987] 1 All ER
    940, [1987] AC 514, and GOODWIN-GILL, *supra* n17, esp. at pp.333-48.

refugee status under Article 1 of the 1951 Convention, as amended by the 1967 Protocol. The interplay of Articles 1 and 33 are of the most immediate importance to a person seeking refuge, and it will be those provisions on which the person threatened with extradition will rely.

To qualify as a refugee, the person must be outside the country of his nationality and unwilling to return there or seek its protection

"... owing to a well-founded fear of being persecuted for reasons of race, religion, nationality, membership of a particular social group or political opinion."

The reasons are all-embracing and allow the courts in the State of refuge to find a ground for accepting the person will be persecuted if it is so minded. In *R v Secretary of State for the Home Department, ex p.Jonah,*[60] Nolan J defined persecution as amounting to being subjected to injurious action and oppression. Moreover, following *Gashi,*[61] it is possible that in appropriate circumstances, violation of economic, social and cultural rights could give rise to behaviour amounting to persecution. The real difficulty lies in determining whether the applicant's fear of persecution is well-founded; the test is subjective and objective and turns on how much evidence is necessary to convince the court that the fear is well-founded. In 1979, UNHCR issued a handbook[62] to help the appropriate authorities interpret their obligations. Paragraph 42 explains Article 1's well-founded fear, in part, in the following terms.

"As regards the objective element, it is necessary to evaluate the statements made by the applicant .... In general, the applicant's fear should be considered well-founded if he can establish, to a reasonable degree, that his continued stay in his country of origin has become intolerable to him for the reasons stated in the definition, or would for the same reasons be intolerable if he returned there."

---

60 [1985] Imm.AR 7.

61 *Supra n*48.

62 HANDBOOK ON PROCEDURES AND CRITERIA FOR DETERMINING REFUGEE STATUS, 1979 (available on the internet at *http://www.unhcr.ch*). See also, PLENDER, INTRODUCTORY REPORT ON HUMAN RIGHTS OF ALIENS IN EUROPE, H/COLL (83)2, p.12.

In *I.N.S. v Cardoza-Fonseca*[63] the majority of the US Supreme Court adopted the Handbook test. It rejected standards such as 'clear probability' and 'more likely than not' and held that the well-founded fear standard

> "would indicate that so long as an objective situation is established by the evidence, it need not be shown that the situation will probably result in persecution, but it is enough that persecution is a reasonable possibility."[64]

As an example of the application of this standard, the Court cited Grahl-Madsen's example of the applicant who has fled a country where one in ten of the population is murdered or sent to a labour camp: such a person does not have a 51% probability of being persecuted, but his fear of persecution is undoubtedly well-founded.[65] Nevertheless, to be free from the possibility of deportation, the applicant must satisfy a clear probability test – the discretionary grant of asylum in line with *Cardoza-Fonseca* is premised on the 'well founded fear', but the statutory right under United States law not to be deported is based on showing a clear probability.[66]

The British House of Lords in *R v Secretary of State for the Home Department, ex parte Sivakumaran*[67] did not engage itself with deciding whether an applicant might qualify as an Article 1 refugee separate from his right not to be *refoulé* contrary to Article 33. It rejected the "reasonable and plausible" test of the High Commissioner's Handbook and held the applicant must show a "real and substantial risk of persecution", although claiming in practice the two tests would have the same effect.[68] The test

---

63 480 US 421, 94 L Ed.2d 434, 107 S.Ct 1207 (1987). See also, Anker and Blum, *New Trends in Asylum Jurisprudence: the Aftermath of the US Supreme Court Decision in I.N.S. v Cardoza-Fonseca*, 1 INT'L J REFUGEE L 67 (1989).

64 480 US at 440, citing *I.N.S. v Stevic*, 467 US 407 at 424-25 (1984).

65 THE STATUS OF REFUGEES IN INTERNATIONAL LAW at p.180 (1966).

66 *Stevic, supra* n65.

67 [1988] AC 958. The Tamil applicants were sent back to Sri Lanka where they subjected to persecution. Moreover, although they applied *in absentia* under the ECHR, alleging their removal to Sri Lanka left the United Kingdom in breach of Article 3, the Court held that a mere possibility of ill-treatment was not sufficient to constitute such a violation – *Vilvarajah v United Kingdom*, Series A, vol.215, paras.103 *et seq.* (1991).

68 *Supra* n67, at 998-1000, *per* Lord Goff.

appears to be purely objective and to set the standard very high.[69] The US understanding displays a deeper analysis of the issues surrounding a grant of refugee status and, on that particular matter, must be viewed as the better approach, although the refugee's deepest interest is in *non-refoulement* in line with the House of Lords' reasoning. The US Supreme Court's analysis of the interplay of Articles 1 and 33 is clear and sound, but given that refugee status without *non-refoulement* protection is practically worthless, Lord Bridge's assimilation of the two provisions in *Musisi*, while it may be unsophisticated, it does reflect the applicant's own objectives. Under both approaches, *non-refoulement* will only be granted where on the balance of probabilities the applicant has proved a clear danger of persecution if returned.

The only remaining question is whether the fugitive offender is protected by Article 33.

f. Extradition and Refugees

The 1951 Convention includes express provisions to exclude from the class of refugees those persons with respect to whom there are serious grounds for believing that they have committed either war crimes, *lato sensu*, a serious non-political offence or that they have been guilty of acts contrary to the purposes of the United Nations.[70] Thus, in *Georg K v Ministry of the Interior*,[71] the Austrian Administrative Court held that an Italian national previously convicted in Austria of carrying out a bombing campaign in the South Tyrol to try and reunite that province with Austria, could not be granted asylum since his actions violated Article 1F(c) of the 1951 Convention; an individual whose actions affect the relations of nations, in this case Austria and Italy, could be in breach of the United Nations Charter. *Georg K* should be contrasted with *Antonin L v F.R.G.*,[72] where it was held that an asylum application could be accepted from a person who had just been

---

69 See also, *Musisi, supra* n59, at 952-53, *Abdi v Secretary of State for the Home Department* [1996] 1 All ER 641, *R v IAT, ex p.Sandralingham* [1996] Imm.AR 97, and *Gashi, supra* n48.

70 *Supra* n15, Art.1F.

71 71 INT'L L REP.284.

72 80 INT'L L REP.673 (Sup.Admin.Ct of Bavaria, 1979).

released after serving a sentence for hijacking, a serious international crime. The court decided that the applicant had hijacked the 'plane to flee Czechoslovakia to escape persecution for his political opinions and that the hijacking had not prejudiced the relations between the F.R.G. and Czechoslovakia.[73] Regard should also be had to cases such as *Gil*[74] and *T*,[75] where it was held that those perpetrating violent and indiscriminate attacks which injured innocent civilians did not qualify for refugee status.

Moreover, under Article 33(2) even someone who qualifies as a refugee may be the object of *refoulement* to a country where he might suffer persecution if there are reasonable grounds for believing, *inter alia*, that he is a danger to the country in which he is. The fugitive offender sought through the extradition process can, therefore, easily be denied the protection of the 1951 Convention.

There is a further underlying difficulty, too, in that during the drafting of the Convention pre-1951, several States expressed the view that extradition should not be prejudiced by Article 33.[76] Not only, according to this view, should it be possible to extradite someone responsible for a serious non-political offence, but also someone suspected of a less serious charge. Against that initial view must be set the fact that all the United Nations sponsored, multilateral, anti-terrorist conventions include a clause permitting the requested State to refuse extradition where the fugitive would be prejudiced or punished on account of his race, religion, nationality or political opinion. That persons suspected of such serious crimes may still be protected from extradition on grounds derived from the 1951 Convention shows that

---

73 *Supra* n72, at 678 *et seq*. See also the case of the Swedish government indicating its willingness to grant asylum, after he serves his sentence, to a Soviet national after who hijacked a 'plane to Sweden; The Guardian p.8, 12 SEPT 1990; p.9, 7 AUG 1992. See The Guardian p.12, 6 NOV 1997, concerning lenient sentences imposed by a United Kingdom court on Iraqis who hijacked a 'plane whilst fleeing Saddam Hussein – it is unlikely that they will be returned to Iraq upon completion of those sentences, but it remains to be seen if they will be allowed to remain in the United Kingdom. See also the case of the former Stasi officer who had collaborated with international terrorists and then sought asylum in Greece – The Guardian p.8, 23 AUG 1992.

74 *Gil v Minister for Employment and Immigration* (1994) 119 DLR (4th) 497.

75 *T v Secretary of State for the Home Department* [1996] 2 All ER 865.

76 See GOODWIN-GILL, *supra* n17, at pp.147-50. See also EXCOM Conclusion No.17 (XXXI) 1980.

the issue is not at all clear-cut. Nevertheless, it should be remembered that the European Union in its protocol to the proposed Treaty of Amsterdam[77] is seeking at time of writing to make it impossible for nationals of one member State to receive asylum in another member State – despite the Annex to the earlier European Union Convention relating to Extradition between Member States[78] providing that that agreement was without prejudice to the right of asylum, the proposed protocol would have the effect of abolishing the political offence exemption for European Union nationals in other member States.

The practice of courts on this matter has also lacked consistency. The Dutch Council of State in *Folkerts v State Secretary of Justice*[79] was faced with the question of whether an application for refugee status should hinder extradition under the 1957 European Convention on Extradition. It was decided that since extradition could only be granted if the requirements of Article 3(2) of the 1957 Convention were met, which provides that a fugitive shall not be surrendered if he would face persecution or prejudice in the requesting State on account of his race, religion, nationality or political opinion, then an application for refugee status was redundant; if article 3(2) was satisfied, then either the applicant would not qualify as a refugee or he would fall within the exception set out in Article 33(2) of the 1951 Convention. Additionally, though, the court received an opinion from the representative of the United Nations High Commissioner for Refugees that owing to the serious terrorist charges alleged against the accused he would not be deemed a refugee under Article 1F of the 1951 Convention.[80]

French courts have also had to deal with the issue. In *Galdeano, Ramirez and Beiztegui*,[81] the applicants were Basque separatists being extradited to Spain who sought refugee status to prevent surrender. The *Cour de Cassation* held that Article 33 did not prevent extradition, but the *Conseil d'Etat* avoided the issue by declaring them to be outside the scope of Article 1 of the 1951 Convention by virtue of their serious, non-political crimes. The decision of the *Cour de Cassation* harked back to the views expressed by

---

77 *Supra* n3.
78 *Supra* n4, 1996.
79 74 INT'L L REP.472 (1978).
80 *Supra* n79, at 475-76.
81 26 SEPT 1984, Rec.307, noted in [1985] PUB.LAW 328.

some of the delegations in 1951.[82] Fortunately, the *Conseil d'Etat* became apprised of the matter once more in *Bereciartua-Echarri*.[83] The fugitive, a Spanish Basque, had been granted refugee status by France in 1973. His surrender was requested by Spain and the *Cour de Cassation* found that since extradition was not expressly mentioned in Article 33, then it could not be prohibited under the 1951 Convention. On appeal to the *Conseil d'Etat*, it was held that subject to matters of national security, extradition should be refused, not under Article 33 and the principle of *non-refoulement*, but on the basis of general principles of refugee law deriving from Article 1A(2) of the 1951 Convention. On such grounds, a State that recognised a fugitive offender's refugee status would be forbidden from returning him *by any means, method or mechanism whatsoever* to a State where he might face persecution. *Bereciartua-Echarri* lays down that extradition is subject to the humanitarian measures set out in the 1951 Convention, a decision consistent with the ethos of Article 33 and the principle of *non-refoulement* and which should put an end to the legalism that has surrounded a provision designed to protect the life and physical integrity of the applicant. No person should ever be extradited to a place where he might face persecution.

g. Conclusion

Refugee status and its concomitant rights can prove ephemeral in practice. There is definitely an element of foreign policy at work on occasions.[84] Nevertheless, the applicant has limited rights which may provide substantial guarantees. That those rights should prohibit extradition where there is a danger of persecution in the requesting State is the only consistent approach that can be effective, and there should be no geographical limitations on where that persecution might occur.

---

82   See GOODWIN-GILL, *supra n*17, at *n*132.
83   1 April 1988, to be published in *Recueil Lebon*.
84   See Meissner and Dietrich, at pp.57-73 of MARTIN, *supra n*17.

APPENDIX

Commonwealth Scheme for the Rendition of Fugitive Offenders as amended in 1990 - LMM(90)32.

1(1) The general provisions set out in this Scheme will govern the return of a person from one part of the Commonwealth, in which he is found, to another part thereof, in which he is accused of an offence; and in particular his return will only be precluded by law, or be subject to refusal by the competent executive authority, in the circumstances mentioned in this Scheme. (2) For the purpose of this Scheme a person liable to return as mentioned in paragraph (1) is described as a fugitive offender and each of the following areas is described as constituting a separate part of the Commonwealth, that is to say

(a) each sovereign and independent country within the Commonwealth together with any dependent territories (which expression, for the purpose aforesaid, includes protectorates and protected States) which that country designates, and
(b) each country within the Commonwealth, which, though not sovereign and independent, is not a territory designated for the purposes of the preceding sub-paragraph.

Returnable Offences

2(1) A fugitive will only be returned for a returnable offence.
(2) For the purpose of this Scheme a returnable offence is an offence however described which is punishable in the part of the Commonwealth where

the fugitive is located and the part of the Commonwealth to which return is requested by imprisonment for two years or a greater penalty.

(3) Offences described in paragraph (2) are returnable offences notwithstanding that any such offences are of a purely fiscal character, where such offences are returnable under the law of the requested part of the Commonwealth.

Warrants, other than Provisional Warrants

3(1) A fugitive offender will only be returned if a warrant for his arrest has been issued in that part of the Commonwealth to which his return is requested and either

> (a) that warrant is endorsed by a competent judicial authority in the part in which he is found (in which case, the endorsed warrant will be sufficient authority for his arrest), or

> (b) A further warrant for his arrest is issued by the competent judicial authority in the part in which he is found, not being a provisional warrant issued as mentioned in clause 4.

(2) The endorsement or issue of a warrant as mentioned in this clause may be made conditional on the competent executive authority having previously issued an order to proceed.

Provisional Warrants

4(1) Where a fugitive offender is, or is suspected of being, in or on his way to any part of the Commonwealth but no warrant has been endorsed as mentioned in clause 3(1)(a) or issued as mentioned in clause 3(1)(b), the competent judicial authority in that part of the Commonwealth may issue a provisional warrant for his arrest on such information and under such circumstances as would, in the authority's opinion, justify the issue of a warrant if the returnable offence of which the fugitive is accused had been an offence committed within the authority's jurisdiction and for the purposes of this paragraph information contained in an international notice issued by the International Criminal Police Organisation (INTERPOL) in respect of a fugitive may be considered by the authority, either alone or with other information, in deciding whether a provisional warrant should be issued for the arrest of that fugitive.

(2) A report of the issue of such a provisional warrant, together with the information in justification or a certified copy thereof, will be sent to the competent executive authority and, in a case in which that authority decides on the said information and any other information which may have become available that the fugitive should be discharged, that authority may so order.

Committal Proceedings

5(1) A fugitive offender arrested under a warrant endorsed or issued as mentioned in clause 3(1), or under a provisional warrant issued as mentioned in clause 4, will be brought, as soon as practicable, before the competent judicial authority who will hear the case in the same manner and have the same jurisdiction and powers, as nearly as may be, including power to remand and admit to bail, as if the fugitive were charged with an offence committed within that authority's jurisdiction.

(2) The competent judicial authority will receive any evidence which may be tendered to show that the return of the fugitive offender is precluded by law.

(3) Where a provisional warrant has been issued as mentioned in clause 4 but, within such reasonable time as with reference to the circumstances of the case the competent judicial authority may fix -

(a) a warrant has not been endorsed or issued as mentioned in clause 3(1), or

(b) where such endorsement or issued of a warrant has been made conditional on the issue of an order to proceed, as mentioned in clause 3(2), no such order has been issued,

the competent judicial authority will order the fugitive to be discharged.

(4) Where a warrant has been endorsed or issued as mentioned in clause 3(1) the competent judicial authority may commit the fugitive to prison to await his return if -

(a) such evidence is produced as establishes a prima facie case that he committed the offence of which he is accused, and

(b) his return is not precluded by law

But, otherwise, will order him to be discharged.

(5) Where a fugitive offender is committed to prison to await his return as mentioned in the preceding paragraph, notice of the fact will forthwith be given to the competent executive authority in that part of the Commonwealth in which he is committed.

Consent Order for Return

6(1) A fugitive offender may waive committal proceedings, and if satisfied that the fugitive offender has voluntary and with an understanding of its significance requested such waiver, the competent judicial authority may make an order by consent for the committal of the fugitive offender to prison, or for his admission to bail, to await return.

(2) The competent executive authority may thereafter order return at any time, notwithstanding the provisions of clause 7.

(3) The provisions of clause 15 shall apply in relation to a fugitive offender returned under this Clause unless waived by him.

Return or Discharge by Executive Authority

7 After the expiry of 15 days from the date of the committal of a fugitive offender the prison to await his return, as mentioned in clause 5, or, if a writ of habeas corpus or other like process is issued with reference to him, from the date of the final decision thereon of the competent judicial authority (whichever date is the later), the competent executive authority will order his return unless it appears to that authority that, in accordance with the provisions set out in this Scheme, his return is precluded by law or should be refused, in which case that authority will order his discharge.

Discharge by Judicial Authority

8(1) Where after the expiry of the period mentioned in paragraph (2) a fugitive offender has not been returned, an application to the competent judicial authority may be made by or on behalf of the fugitive for his discharge and if -

(a) reasonable notice of the application has been given to the competent executive authority, and

(b) sufficient cause for the delay is not shown, the competent judicial authority will order his discharge.

(2) The period referred to in paragraph (1) will be prescribed by law and will be one expiring either -

(a) not later than two months from the fugitive's committal to prison as mentioned in clause 5, or

(b) not later than one month from the date of the order for his return made as mentioned in clause 7.

Habeas Corpus and Review

9(1) It will be provided that an application may be made by or on behalf of a fugitive offender for a writ of habeas corpus or other like process.

(2) It will be provided that an application may be made by or on behalf of the government of the requesting part of the Commonwealth for review of the decision of the competent judicial authority in committal proceedings.

Circumstances Precluding Return

10(1) (a) The return of a fugitive offender will be precluded by law if the competent judicial or executive authority is satisfied that the offence is of a political character.

(b) Paragraph (a) shall not apply in relation to offences established under any multilateral international convention to which both the requesting and the requested parts of the Commonwealth are parties and which are declared thereby not to be regarded as political offences for the purposes of extradition.

(c) Any part of the Commonwealth may adopt the provisions set out in Annex 1.

(2) The return of a fugitive offender will be precluded by law if it appears to the competent judicial or executive authority

(a) that the request for his surrender although purporting to be made for a returnable offence was in fact made for the purpose of prosecuting or punishing the person on account of his race, religion, nationality or political opinions, or

(b) that he may be prejudiced at his trial or punished, detained or restricted in his personal liberty by reason of his race, religion, nationality or political opinions.

(3) The return of a fugitive offender, or his return before the expiry of a specified period, will be precluded by law if the competent judicial or executive authority is satisfied that by reason of -

(a) the trivial nature of the case, or

(b) the accusation against the fugitive not having been made in good faith or in the interests of justice, or

(c) the passage of time since the commission of the offence, or

(d) any other sufficient cause,

it would, having regard to all the circumstances be unjust or oppressive or too severe a punishment to return the fugitive or, as the case may be, to return him before the expiry of a period specified by that authority.

(4) The return of a fugitive offender will be precluded by law if the competent judicial or executive authority is satisfied that he has been convicted (and is neither unlawfully at large nor at large in breach of a condition of a licence to be at large), or has been acquitted, whether within or outside the Commonwealth, of the offence of which he is accused.

(5) The competent authorities for the purposes of this and the next following clause will include -

(a) any judicial authority which hears or is competent to hear such an application as is mentioned in clause 9, and

(b) the executive authority by whom any order for the fugitive's return would fail to be made.

(6) It will be sufficient compliance with any one of the paragraphs (1), (2), (3), (4) and (5) if a country decides that the competent authority for the purposes of that paragraph is exclusively the judicial authority or the executive authority.

(7) If the competent executive authority -

(a) is empowered by law to certify that the offence of which a fugitive offender is accused is an offence of a political character, and

(b) in the case of a particular fugitive offender, so certifies,

the certificate will be conclusive in the matter and binding upon the competent judicial authority for the purposes mentioned in this clause.

Offences under Military Law

11 The return of a fugitive offender will either be precluded by law, or be subject to refusal by the competent authority if the competent authority is satisfied that the offence is an offence only under military law or a law relating to military obligations.

Double-Criminality Rule

12 The return of a fugitive offender will either be precluded by law or be subject to refusal by the competent executive authority if the facts on which the request for his return is grounded do not constitute an offence under the law of the country or territory in which he is found.

Postponement of Return of Fugitive and Temporary Transfer of Prisoners to Stand Trial

13(1) Subject to the following provisions of this clause, where a fugitive offender -
    (a) has been charged with an offence triable by a court in that part of the Commonwealth in which he is found, or
    (b) is serving a sentence imposed by a court in that part of the Commonwealth,
then until such a time as he has been discharged (whether by acquittal, the expiration or remission of his sentence, or otherwise) his return will either be precluded by law or be subject for refusal by the competent executive authority as the law of the country or territory concerned may provide.
(2) Subject to the provisions of this Scheme, a prisoner serving such a sentence who is also a fugitive offender may, at the discretion of the competent executive authority of that part of the Commonwealth in which the prisoner is held, be returned temporarily to another part of the Commonwealth in which he is accused of a returnable offence to enable proceedings to be brought against the prisoner in relation to that offence on such conditions as are agreed between the respective parts of the Commonwealth.

Priority where Two or More Requests made

14 Where requests for the return of a fugitive offender to two or more parts of the Commonwealth fall to be dealt with at the same time, the competent executive authority will determine to which part he should be returned and, accordingly, may refuse the other requests; and in determining the matter that authority will consider all the circumstances of the case and in particular -

(a) the relative seriousness of the offences,
(b) the relative dates on which the requests were made, and
(c) the citizenship or other national status of the fugitive and his ordinary residence.

Speciality Rule

15(1) This clause relates to a fugitive offender who has been returned from one part of the Commonwealth to another part thereof, so long as he has not had a reasonable opportunity of leaving the second mentioned part.
(2) In the case of a fugitive offender to whom this clause relates, his detention or trial in the part of the Commonwealth to which he has been returned for any offence committed prior to his return (other than the one for which he was returned or any lesser offence proved by the facts on which that return was grounded, or, with the consent of the requested country or territory, any returnable offence) will be precluded by law.
(3) When considering a request for consent under paragraph (2) the executive authority of the requested part of the Commonwealth may call for such particulars as it may require in order that it may be satisfied that such request is otherwise consistent with the principles of this Scheme, and shall not unreasonably withhold consent; but where in the opinion of the requested part of the Commonwealth it appears that, on the facts known to the requesting part of the Commonwealth at the time of the original application for return of the fugitive offender, application should have been made in respect of such offences at that time, that fact may constitute a ground for refusal.
(4) The requesting part of the Commonwealth shall not, without the consent of the requested part, return or surrender to another country or territory a fugitive offender returned to the requesting part and sought by such other country or territory in respect of any offence committed prior to his return;

and in considering a request under this paragraph the requested part of the Commonwealth may call for the particulars referred to in paragraph (3) and shall not unreasonably withhold consent.

(5) Nothing in this clause shall prevent a court in the requesting part of the Commonwealth from taking into account at the request of the fugitive any other offence, whether returnable or not under this Scheme, for the purpose of passing sentence on a fugitive convicted of an offence for which he has been returned under this Scheme, where the fugitive desires that such other offence shall be taken into account.

Return of Escaped Prisoners

16 (1) In the case of a person who -
(a) has been convicted of a returnable offence by a court in any part of the Commonwealth and is unlawfully at large before the expiry of his sentence for that offence, and
(b) is found in some other part of the Commonwealth, the provisions set out in this Scheme, as applied for the purposes of this clause by paragraph (2), will govern his return to the part of the Commonwealth in which he was convicted.

(2) For the purposes of this clause this Scheme shall be construed, subject to any necessary adaptations or modifications, as though the person unlawfully at large were accused of the offence of which he was convicted and, in particular
(a) any reference to a fugitive offender shall be construed as including a reference to such a person as is mentioned in paragraph (1), and
(b) the reference in clause 5(4) to such evidence as establishes a prima facie case that he committed the offence of which he is accused shall be construed as a reference to such evidence as establishes that he has been convicted.

(3) The references in this clause to a person unlawfully at large shall be construed as including reference to a person at large in breach of a condition of a licence to be at large.

Ancillary Provisions

17 Each Commonwealth country or territory will take, subject to its constitution, any legislative and other steps which may be necessary or expedient in the circumstances to facilitate and effectuate -
(a) the return of a fugitive offender who is in transit in its territory for that purpose,
(b) the delivery of property found in the possession of a fugitive offender at the time of his arrest which may be material evidence of the offence at which he is accused, and
(c) the proof of warrants, certificates of conviction, depositions and other documents.

Alternative Arrangements and Modifications

18 Nothing in this Scheme shall prevent
(a) the making of arrangements between two or more parts of the Commonwealth for further or alternative provision for the return of offenders, or
(b) the application of the Scheme with modifications by any part of the Commonwealth in relation to any other part which has not brought clauses 1 to 17 fully into effect.

Supplementary Provisions

19(1) Any part of the Commonwealth may or may not adopt either or both of the supplementary provisions set out in Annex 1 but, where such a provision is adopted, any other part of the Commonwealth may in relation to the first part reserve its position as to whether it will give effect to clauses 1 to 17 or will give effect to them subject to such exceptions and modifications as appear to it to be necessary or expedient or give effect to any arrangement made under clause 18(a).
(2) Two or more parts of the Commonwealth may make arrangements under which in matters of rendition between them clause 5(4) will be replaced either by Annex 3 or by other provisions agreed by the Governments of those parts.

Annex 1: Discretion as to Definition of Political Offences

1 It may be provided by a law in any part of the Commonwealth that certain acts shall not be held to be offences of a political character including -

(a) an offence against the life or person of a Head of State or a member of his immediate family or any related offence (i.e. aiding and abetting, or counselling or procuring the commission of, or being an accessory before or after the fact to, or attempting or conspiring to commit such an offence),

(b) an offence against the life or person of a Head of Government, or of a Minister of a Government, or any related offence as aforesaid,

(c) murder, or any related offence as aforesaid

(d) an act declared to constitute an offence under a multilateral international convention whose purpose is to prevent or repress a specific category of offences and which imposes on the parties thereto an obligation either to extradite or to prosecute the person sought.

2 Any part of the Commonwealth may restrict the application of any of the provisions made under paragraph 1 to a request from a part of the Commonwealth which has made similar provisions in its laws.

Annex 2: Supplementary Provisions Discretion as Respects Return for Offences Punishable by Death

1(1) The return of a fugitive offender may be refused by the competent executive authority where it appears to that authority that, by reason that -

(a) if he was returned he would be likely to suffer the death penalty for the offence for which his return is requested, and

(b) in the country or territory in which he is found or in any part thereof that offence is not punishable by death,

it would, having regard to all the circumstances of the case and to any likelihood that if not returned he would be immune from punishment, be unjust or oppressive or too severe a punishment to return him.

(2) In determining whether a fugitive would be likely to suffer the death penalty, the executive authority shall take into account any representations which the authorities of the requesting part of the Commonwealth may make with regard to the possibility that the death penalty, if imposed, will not be carried out.

Discretion as Respects Return of Citizens etc.

2(1) The return of a fugitive offender who is a national or permanent resident
of the part of the Commonwealth in which he is found -
   (a) may be precluded by law, or
   (b) may be refused by the competent executive authority:
Provided that return will not be so refused if the fugitive is also a national
of that part of the Commonwealth to which his return is requested.
(2) For the purposes of this paragraph a fugitive shall be treated as a national
of a part of the Commonwealth if that part consists of, or includes -
   (a) a Commonwealth country of which he is a citizen, or
   (b) a country or territory his connection with which determines his
   national status,
in either case at the date of the request.

Annex 3: Alternative Provisions as to Committal Proceedings

1   Where a warrant has been endorsed or issued as mentioned in clause
    3(1) the competent judicial authority may commit the fugitive to prison
    to await his return if
    (a) the contents of the record of the case received under this Annex
    whether or not admissible in evidence, under the law of the requested
    part, and any other evidence admissible under the law of the requested
    part, are sufficient to warrant a trial of the charges for which rendition
    has been requested; and
    (b) the fugitive's return is not precluded by law, but otherwise will order
    the fugitive to be discharged.
2   The competent judicial authority will receive a record of the case
    prepared by an investigating authority in the requesting part if it is
    accompanied by
    (a) an affidavit of an officer of the investigating authority stating that
    the record of the case was prepared by or under the direction of that
    officer, and that the evidence has been preserved for use in court; and
    (b) a certificate of the Attorney General of the requesting part that in
    his opinion the record of the case discloses the existence of evidence
    under the law of the requesting part sufficient to justify a prosecution.

3 The record of the case will contain

(a) particulars of the description, identity, nationality and, to the extent available, whereabouts of the person sought;

(b) particulars of each offence or conduct in respect of which rendition is requested, specifying the date and place of commission, the legal definition of the offence and the relevant provisions in the law of the requesting part, including a certified copy of any such definition in the written law of that part;

(c) the original or a certified copy of any document of process issued in the requesting part against the person whom it seeks to have committed for rendition;

(d) a recital of the evidence acquired to support the request for rendition of the person sought;

(e) and a certified copy, reproduction or photograph of exhibits or documents evidence.

Convention Applying the Schengen Agreement of 14 June 1985 between the Governments of the States of the Benelux Economic Union, the Federal Republic of Germany and the French Republic on the Gradual Abolition of Checks at their Common Border, 1990.
(Spain, Portugal, Italy, Greece and Austria subsequently acceded)

TITLE I
Definitions
Article 1

For the purposes of this Convention:
Internal borders shall mean the common land borders of the Contracting Parties, their airports for internal flights and their sea ports for regular trans-shipment connections exclusively from or to other ports within the territories of the Contracting Parties not calling at any ports outside those territories;
External borders shall mean the Contracting Parties' land and sea borders and their airports and sea ports, provided they are not internal borders;
Internal flight shall mean any flight exclusively to or from territories of the Contracting Parties not landing within the territory of a Third State;
Third State shall mean any State other than the Contracting Parties;
Alien shall mean any person other than a national of a Member State of the European Communities;
Alien reported as a person shall mean any alien listed reported as a person not to be permitted entry not to be permitted entry in the Schengen Information System in accordance with Article 96;
Border crossing point shall mean any crossing point authorized by the competent authorities for the crossing of external borders;
Border control shall mean a check made at a border in response solely to an intention to cross that border, regardless of any other consideration.

TITLE III
Police and security

CHAPTER ONE
Police Co-operation
Article 39

1. The Contracting Parties undertake to ensure that their police authorities shall, in compliance with national legislation and within the limits of their responsibilities, assist each other for the purposes of preventing and detecting criminal offences, insofar as national law does not stipulate that the request is to be made to the legal authorities and provided the request or the implementation thereof does not involve the application of coercive measures by the requested Contracting Party. Where the requested police authorities do not have jurisdiction to implement a request, they shall forward it to the competent authorities.

2. The written information provided by the requested Contracting Party under paragraph 1 may not be used by the requesting Contracting Party as evidence of the criminal offence other than with the agreement of the relevant legal authorities of the requested Contracting Party.

3. Requests for assistance referred to in paragraph 1 and the replies to such requests may be exchanged between the central bodies responsible in each Contracting Party for international police co-operation. Where the request cannot be made in good time by the above procedure, it may be addressed by the police authorities of the requesting Contracting Party directly to the competent authorities of the requested Party, which may reply directly. In such cases, the requesting police authority shall as soon as possible inform the central body responsible in the requested Contracting Party for international police co-operation of its direct application.

4. In border regions, co-operation may be covered by arrangements between the responsible Ministers of the Contracting Parties.

5. The provisions of this Article shall not preclude more detailed present or future bilateral agreements between Contracting Parties with a common border. The Contracting Parties shall inform each other of such agreements.

Article 40

1. Police officers of one of the Contracting Parties who, within the framework of a criminal investigation, are keeping under observation in their

country, a person who is presumed to have taken part in a criminal offence to which extradition may apply, shall be authorized to continue their observation in the territory of another Contracting Party where the latter has authorized cross-border observation in response to a request for assistance which has previously been submitted. Conditions may be attached to the authorization.

On request, the observation will be entrusted to officers of the Contracting Party in whose territory it is carried out.

The request, for assistance referred to in the first subparagraph must be sent to an authority designated by each of the Contracting Parties and having jurisdiction to grant or to forward the requested authorization.

2. Where, for particularly urgent reasons, prior authorization of the other Contracting Party cannot be requested, the officers conducting the observation shall be authorized to continue beyond the border the observation of a person presumed to have committed offences listed in paragraph 7, provided that the following conditions are met:

(a) the authorities of the Contracting Party designated under paragraph 5, ln whose territory the observation is to be continued, must be notified immediately, during the observation, that the border has been crossed:

(b) A request for assistance submitted in accordance with paragraph 1 and outlining the grounds for crossing the border without prior authorization shall be submitted without delay.

Observation shall cease as soon as the Contracting Party in whose territory it is taking place so requests, following the notification referred to in (a) or the request referred to in (b) or where authorization has not been obtained five hours after the border was crossed.

3. The observation referred to in paragraphs 1 and 2 shall be carried out only under the following general conditions:

(a) The officers conducting the observation must comply with the provisions of this Article and with the law of the Contracting Party in whose territory they are operating; they must obey the instructions of the local responsible authorities.

(b) except in the situations provided for in paragraph 2, the officers shall, during the observation, carry a document certifying that authorization has been granted.

(c) The officers conducting the observation must be able at all times to provide proof that they are acting in an official capacity.

(d) The officers conducting the observation may carry their service weapons during the observation save where specifically otherwise decided by the requested party; their use shall be prohibited save in cases of legitimate self-defence.

(e) Entry into private homes and places not accessible to the public shall be prohibited.

(f) The officers conducting the observation may neither challenge nor arrest the person under observation.

(g) All operations shall be the subject of a report to the authorities of the Contracting Party in whose territory they took place; the officers conducting the observation may be required to appear in person.

(h) The authorities of the Contracting Party from which the observing officers have come shall], when requested by the authorities of the Contracting Party in whose territory the observation took place, assist the enquiry subsequent to the operation in which they took part, including legal proceedings.

4. The officers referred to in paragraphs 1 and 2 shall be:

· as regards the Kingdom of Belgium: members of the "police judiciaire près les Parquets", the "gendarmerie" and the "police communale" as well as customs officers, under the conditions laid down in appropriate bilateral agreements referred to in paragraph 6, with respect to their powers regarding illicit traffic in narcotic drugs and psychotropic substances, traffic in arms and explosives, and the illicit carriage of toxic and dangerous waste:

· as regards the Federal Republic of Germany, officers of the "Polizeien des Bundes und der Länder" as well as, with respect only to illegal traffic in narcotic drugs and psychotropic substances and arms traffic, officers of the "Zollfahndungsdienst" (customs investigation service) in their capacity as auxiliary officers of the public ministry;

· as regards the French Republic: officers and criminal police officers of the national police and national "gendarmerie" as well as customs officers, under the conditions laid down in appropriate bilateral agreements referred to in paragraph 6, with respect to their powers regarding illicit traffic in narcotic drugs and psychotropic substances, traffic in arms and explosives, and the illicit carriage of toxic and dangerous waste:

· as regards the Grand Duchy of Luxembourg: officers of the "gendarmerie" and the police as well as customs officers, under the conditions laid down in appropriate bilateral agreements referred to in paragraph

6, with respect to their powers regarding illicit traffic in narcotic drugs and psychotropic substances, traffic in arms and explosives, and the illicit carriage of toxic and dangerous waste;

- as regards the Kingdom of the Netherlands: officers of the "Rijkspolitie" and the "Gemeentepolitie" as well as, under the conditions laid down in appropriate bilateral agreements referred to in paragraph 6, with respect to their powers regarding illicit traffic in narcotic drugs and psychotropic substances, traffic in arms and explosives and the illicit carriage of toxic and dangerous waste, officers of the fiscal information and research service responsible for entry and excise duties.

5. The authority referred to in paragraphs 1 and 2 shall be:
- as regards the Kingdom of Belgium: the "Commissariat general de la Police Judiciaire";
- as regards the Federal Republic of Germany: the "Bundeskriminalamt";
- as regards the French Republic: the "Direction centrale de la Police judiciaire";
- as regards the Grand Duchy of Luxembourg: the "Procureur general d'Etat";
- as regards the Kingdom of the Netherlands: the "Landelijk Officier van Justitie" responsible for cross-border observation.

6. The Contracting Parties may, at bilateral level, extend the scope of this Article and adopt additional measures in implementation thereof.

7. The observation referred to in paragraph 2 may take place only for one of the following criminal offences:
- assassination,
- murder,
- rape,
- arson,
- counterfeiting,
- armed robbery and receiving of stolen goods,
- extortion,
- kidnapping and hostage taking,
- traffic in human beings,
- illicit traffic in narcotic drugs and psychotropic substances,
- breach of the laws on arms and explosives,
- use of explosives,
- illicit carriage of toxic and dangerous waste.

Article 41

1. Officers of one of the Contracting Parties following, in their country, an individual apprehended in the act of committing one of the offences referred to in paragraph 4 or participating in one of those offences, shall be authorised to continue pursuit in the territory of another Contracting Party without prior authorization where given the particular urgency of the situation it was not possible to notify the competent authorities of the other Contracting Party by one of the means provided for in Article 44 prior to entry into that territory or where these authorities have been unable to reach the scene in time to take over the pursuit.
The same shall apply where the person pursued has escaped from provisional custody or while serving a custodial sentence.
The pursuing officers shall, not later than when they cross the border, contact the competent authorities of the Contracting Party in whose territory the pursuit is to take place. The pursuit will cease as soon as the Contracting Party on the territory of which the pursuit is taking place so requests. At the request of the pursuing officers, the competent local authorities shall challenge the pursued person so as to establish his identity or to arrest him.

2. The pursuit shall be carried out in accordance with one of the following procedures, defined by the declaration provided for in paragraph 9:
(a) The pursuing officers shall not have the right to apprehend.
(b) If no request to cease the pursuit is made and if the competent local authorities are unable to intervene quickly enough, the pursuing officers may apprehend the person pursued until the officers of the Contracting Party in the territory of which the pursuit is taking place, who must be informed without delay, are able to establish his identity or arrest him.

3. Pursuit shall be carried out in accordance with paragraphs 1 and 2 in one of the following ways, defined by the declaration provided for in paragraph 9:
(a) in an area or during a period as from the crossing of the border, to be established in the declaration;
(b) without limit in space or time.

4. In a declaration referred to in paragraph 9, the Contracting Parties shall define the offenses referred to in paragraph 1 in accordance with one of the following procedures:
(a) The following offences:
· assassination,

· murder,
· rape,
· arson,
· counterfeiting.
· armed robbery and receiving of stolen goods,
· extortion,
· kidnapping and hostage taking,
· traffic in human beings
· illicit traffic in narcotic drugs and psychotropic substances,
· breach of the laws on arms and explosives,
· use of explosives,
· illicit carriage of toxic and dangerous waste.
· taking to flight after an accident which has resulted in death or serious injury.
(b) Extraditable offenses.

5. Pursuit shall be subject to the following general conditions:
(a) The pursuing officers must comply with the provisions of this Article and with the law of the Contracting Party in whose territory they are operating; they must obey the instructions of the competent local authorities.
(b) Pursuit shall be solely over land borders.
(c) Entry into private homes and places not accessible to the public shall be prohibited.
(d) The pursuing officers shall be easily identifiable, either by their uniform or by means of an armband or by accessories fitted to their vehicle; the use of civilian clothes combined with the use of unmarked vehicles without the aforementioned identification is prohibited; the pursuing officers must at all times be able to prove that they are acting in an official capacity.
(e) The pursuing officers may carry their service weapons; their use shall be prohibited save in cases of legitimate self-defence.
(f) Once the pursued person has been apprehended as provided for in paragraph 2(b), for the purpose of bringing him before the competent local authorities he may be subjected only to a security search; handcuffs may be used during his transfer; objects carried by the pursued person may be seized.
(g) After each operation mentioned in paragraphs 1, 2 and 3, the pursuing officers shall present themselves before the local competent authorities

of the Contracting Party in whose territory they were operating and shall give an account of their mission; at the request of those authorities, they must remain at their disposal until the circumstances of their action have been adequately elucidated; this condition shall apply even where the pursuit has not resulted in the arrest of the pursued person.

(h) The authorities of the Contracting Party from which the pursuing officers have come shall, when requested by the authorities of the Contracting Party in whose territory the pursuit took place, assist the enquiry subsequent to the operation in which they took part, including legal proceedings.

6. A person who, following the action provided for in paragraph 2, has been arrested by the competent local authorities may, whatever his nationality, be held for questioning. The relevant rules of national law shall apply by analogy.

   If the person is not a national of the Contracting Party in the territory of which he was arrested, he shall be released no later than six hours after his arrest, not including the hours between midnight and 9.00 in the morning, unless the competent local authorities have previously received a request for his provisional arrest for the purposes of extradition in any form whatever.

7. ....

8. This Article shall be without prejudice, where the Contracting Parties are concerned, to Article 27 of the Benelux Treaty of 27 June 1962 on Extradition and Mutual Assistance in Criminal Matters as amended by the Protocol of 11 May 1974.

9. On signing this Convention, each Contracting Party shall make a declaration in which it shall define, on the basis of paragraphs 2, 3 and 4 above, the procedures for implementing pursuit in its territory for each of the Contracting. Parties with which it has a common border.

   A Contracting Party may at any moment replace its declaration by another declaration, provided the latter does not restrict the scope of the former.

   Each declaration shall be made after consultations with each of the Contracting Parties concerned and with a view to obtaining equivalent arrangements on both sides of internal borders.

10. The Contracting Parties may, on a bilateral basis, extend the scope of paragraph 1 and adopt additional provisions in implementation of this Article.

Article 42

During the operations referred to in Articles 40 and 41, officers operating on the territory of another Contracting Party shall be regarded as officers of that Party with respect to offences committed against them or by them.

Article 43

1. Where, in accordance with Articles 40 and 41 of this Convention, officers of a Contracting Party are operating in the territory of another Contracting Party, the first Contracting Party shall be responsible for any damage caused by them during the course of their mission, in accordance with the law of the Contracting Party in whose territory they are operating.
2. The Contracting Party in whose territory the damage referred to in paragraph 1 is caused shall repair such damage under the conditions applicable to damage caused by its own officers.
3. The Contracting Party whose officers have caused damage to whomsoever in the territory of another Contracting Party shall reimburse in full to the latter any sums it has paid out to the victims or other entitled persons.
4. Without prejudice to the exercise of its rights vis-a-vis third parties and without prejudice to paragraph 3, each Contracting Party shall refrain, in the case provided for in paragraph 1, from requesting reimbursement of the amount of the damages it has sustained from another Contracting Party.

CHAPTER FOUR

Extradition

Article 59

1. The provisions of this Chapter are intended to supplement the European Convention of 13 September 1957 on Extradition as well as, in relations between the Contracting Parties which are members of the Benelux Economic Union, Chapter I of the Benelux Treaty on Extradition and Mutual Assistance in Criminal Matters of 27 June 1962, as amended by the Protocol of 11 May 1974, and to facilitate the implementation of these agreements.
2. Paragraph 1 shall not affect the application of the broader provisions of the bilateral agreements in force between Contracting Parties.

Article 60

In relations between two Contracting Parties, one of which is not a party to the European Convention on Extradition of 13 September 1957, the provisions of the said Convention shall apply, subject to the reservations and declarations made at the time of ratifying this Convention or, for Contracting Parties whiCh are not parties to the Convention, at the time of ratifying, approving or accepting the present Convention.

Article 61

The French Republic undertakes to extradite, at the request of one of the Contracting Parties, persons against whom proceedings are being taken for offences punishable under French law by deprivation of liberty or under a detention order for a maximum period of at least two years and under the law of the requesting Contracting Party by deprivation of liberty or under a detention order for a maximum period of at least a year.

Article 62

1. As regards interruption of prescription, only the provisions of the requesting Contracting Party shall apply.
2. An amnesty granted by the requested Contracting Party shall not prevent extradition unless the offence falls within the jurisdiction of that Contracting Party.
3. The absence of a charge or an official notice authorizing proceedings, necessary only under the legislation of the requested Contracting Party, shall not affect the obligation to extradite.

Article 63

The Contracting Parties undertake, in accordance with the Convention and the Treaty referred to in Article 89, to extradite between themselves persons being prosecuted by the legal authorities of the requesting Contracting Party for one of the offences referred to in Article 50(1), or being sought by them for the purposes of execution of a sentence or detention order imposed in respect of such an offence.

Article 64

A report included in the Schengen Information System in accordance with Article 95 shall have the same force as a request for provisional arrest under Article 16 of the European Convention on Extradition of 13 September 1957 or Article 15 of the Benelux Treaty on Extradition and Mutual Assistance in Criminal Matters of 27 June 1962, as amended by the Protocol of 11 May 1974.

Article 65

1. Without prejudice to the option to use the diplomatic channel, requests for extradition and transit shall be sent by the relevant Ministry of the requesting Contracting Party to the relevant Ministry of the requested Contracting Party.
2. The relevant Ministries shall be:
- as regards the Kingdom of Belgium: the Ministry of Justice:
- as regards the Federal Republic of Germany: the Federal Ministry of Justice and the Justice Ministers or Senators of the Federal States;
- as regards the French Republic: the Ministry of Foreign Affairs;
- as regards the Grand Duchy of Luxembourg: the Ministry of Justice;
- as regards the Kingdom of the Netherlands: the Ministry of Justice.

Article 66

1. If the extradition of a wanted person is not obviously prohibited under the laws of the requested Contracting Party, that Contracting Party may authorize extradition without formal extradition proceedings, provided that the wanted person agrees thereto in a statement made before a member of the judiciary after being examined by the latter and informed of his right to formal extradition proceedings. The wanted person may have access to a lawyer during such examination.
2. In cases of extradition under paragraph 1, a wanted person who explicitly states that he will not invoke the rule of speciality may not revoke that statement.

Council Act of 27 September 1996 drawing up the Convention relating to extradition between the Member States of the European Union Convention drawn up on the basis of Article K.3 of the Treaty of European Union, relating to extradition between the Member States of the European Union

The High Contracting Parties to this Convention, Member States of the European Union

...

Stressing that Member States have an interest in ensuring that extradition procedures operate efficiently and rapidly in so far as their systems of government are based on democratic principles and they comply with the obligations laid down by the Convention for the Protection of Human Rights and Fundamental Freedoms signed in Rome on 4 November 1950 [ECHR],

...

Taking account of the interest in concluding a Convention between the Member States of the European Union supplementing the European Convention on Extradition of 13 December 1957 and the other Conventions in force on the matter,

...

Have agreed as follows:

Article 1
General Provisions
1. The purpose of this Convention is to supplement the provisions and facilitate the application between the Member States of the European Union:
− of the [European Convention on Extradition, 1957; the European Convention on the Suppression of Terrorism, 1977; the 1990 Convention applying the Schengen Agreement of 1985; the Benelux Convention on Extradition and Judicial Assistance in Penal Matters, 1962, as amended by the 1974 Protocol].

Article 5
Political Offences
1. For the purposes of applying this Convention, no offence may be regarded by the requested Member State as a political offence, as an offence connected with a political offence or an offence inspired by political motives.

2. Each Member State may, ..., declare that it will apply paragraph 1 only in relation to:

   (a) the offences referred to in Articles 1 and 2 of the European Convention on the Suppression of Terrorism; and

   (b) offences of conspiracy or association – which correspond to the description of behaviour referred to in Article 3(4) – to commit one or more of the offences referred to in Articles 1 and 2 of the European Convention on the Suppression of Terrorism.

3. The provisions of Article 3(2) of the European Convention on Extradition and of Article 5 of the European Convention on the Suppression of Terrorism remain unaffected.

4. Reservations made pursuant to Article 13 of the European Convention on the Suppression of Terrorism shall not apply to extradition between Member States.

Article 6
Fiscal Offences

1. With regard to taxes, duties, customs and exchange, extradition shall also be granted under the terms of this Convention, the European Convention on Extradition and the Benelux Treaty in respect of offences which correspond under the law of the requested Member State to a similar offence.

2. Extradition may not be refused on the ground that the law of the requested Member State does not impose the same type of taxes or duties or does not have the same type of provisions in connection with taxes, duties, customs and exchange as the law of the requesting Member State.

Article 7
Extradition of Nationals

1. Extradition may not be refused on the ground that the person claimed is a national of the requested Member State within the meaning of Article 6 of the European Convention on Extradition.

2. [Upon ratification], any Member State may declare that it will not grant extradition of its nationals or will authorize it only under certain specified conditions.

Annex

Joint Declaration on the right of asylum

The Member States declare that this Convention is without prejudice either to the right of asylum to the extent which it is recognized by their respective constitutions or to the application by the Member States of the provisions of the Convention Relating to the Status of Refugees of 28 July 1951, as supplemented by the Convention Relating to the Status of Stateless Persons of 28 September 1954 and by the Protocol Relating to the Status of Refugees of 31 January 1967.

(*Cf.* Treaty of Amsterdam)

INDEX

International Studies in Human Rights

International Studies in Human Rights

This series is designed to shed light on current legal and political aspects of process and organization in the field of human rights.

MARTINUS NIJHOFF PUBLISHERS – THE HAGUE / BOSTON / LONDON